NEW ENGLAND

CONNECTICUT
MAINE
MASSACHUSETTS
NEW HAMPSHIRE
RHODE ISLAND
VERMONT

FODOR'S TRAVEL PUBLICATIONS

are compiled, researched, and edited by an international team of travel writers, field correspondents, and editors. The series, which now almost covers the globe, was founded by Eugene Fodor in 1936.

OFFICES
New York & London

Fodor's New England:

Editor: Audrey Liounis
Area Editors: Helen Dalzell, Alma Eshenfelder, Ira Mayer, Bob Murphy, Monique Panaggio, Paul Robbins, William G. Scheller, Jane E. Zarem
Contributing Editors: Judson Hale, Geoffrey Norman
Drawings: Sandra Lang, Michael Kaplan
Cartography: Pictograph, Jon Bauch

FODOR'S

NEW ENGLAND

1987

CONNECTICUT
MAINE
MASSACHUSETTS
NEW HAMPSHIRE
RHODE ISLAND
VERMONT

FODOR'S TRAVEL PUBLICATIONS, INC.
New York & London

ISBN 0-679-01450-0
ISBN 0-340-40053-6 (Hodder & Stoughton)
First Edition

The following Fodor's Guides are current; most are also available in a British
edition published by Hodder & Stoughton.

Country and Area Guides

Australia, New Zealand
& the South Pacific
Austria
Bahamas
Belgium & Luxembourg
Bermuda
Brazil
Canada
Canada's Maritime
Provinces
Caribbean
Central America
Eastern Europe
Egypt
Europe
France
Germany
Great Britain
Greece
Holland
Hungary
India, Nepal & Sri Lanka
Ireland
Israel
Italy
Japan
Jordan & the Holy Land
Kenya
Korea
Loire Valley
Mexico
New Zealand
North Africa
People's Republic
of China
Portugal
Province of Quebec
Scandinavia
Scotland
South America
South Pacific
Southeast Asia
Soviet Union
Spain
Sweden
Switzerland
Turkey
Yugoslavia

City Guides

Amsterdam
Beijing, Guangzhou,
Shanghai
Boston
Chicago
Dallas & Fort Worth
Florence & Venice
Greater Miami & the
Gold Coast
Hong Kong
Houston & Galveston
Lisbon
London
Los Angeles
Madrid
Mexico City &
Acapulco
Munich
New Orleans
New York City
Paris
Philadelphia
Rome
San Diego
San Francisco
Singapore
Stockholm, Copenhagen,
Oslo, Helsinki &
Reykjavik
Sydney
Tokyo
Toronto
Vienna
Washington, D.C.

U.S.A. Guides

Alaska
Arizona
Atlantic City & the
New Jersey Shore
California
Cape Cod
Chesapeake
Colorado
Far West
Florida
Hawaii
I-10: California to Florida
I-55: Chicago to
New Orleans
I-75: Michigan to Florida
I-80: San Francisco to
New York
I-95: Maine to Miami

New England
New Mexico
New York State
Pacific North Coast
South
Texas
U.S.A.
Virginia
Williamsburg, Jamestown
& Yorktown

Budget Travel

American Cities (30)
Britain
Canada
Caribbean
Europe
France
Germany
Hawaii
Italy
Japan
London
Mexico
Spain

Fun Guides

Acapulco
Bahamas
Las Vegas
London
Maui
Montreal
New Orleans
New York City
The Orlando Area
Paris
Puerto Rico
Rio
Riviera
St. Martin/Sint Maarten
San Francisco
Waikiki

Special-Interest Guides

The Bed & Breakfast Guide
Selected Hotels of Europe
Ski Resorts of North
America
Views to Dine by around
the World

MANUFACTURED IN THE UNITED STATES OF AMERICA
10 9 8 7 6 5 4 3 2

CONTENTS

CONTENTS

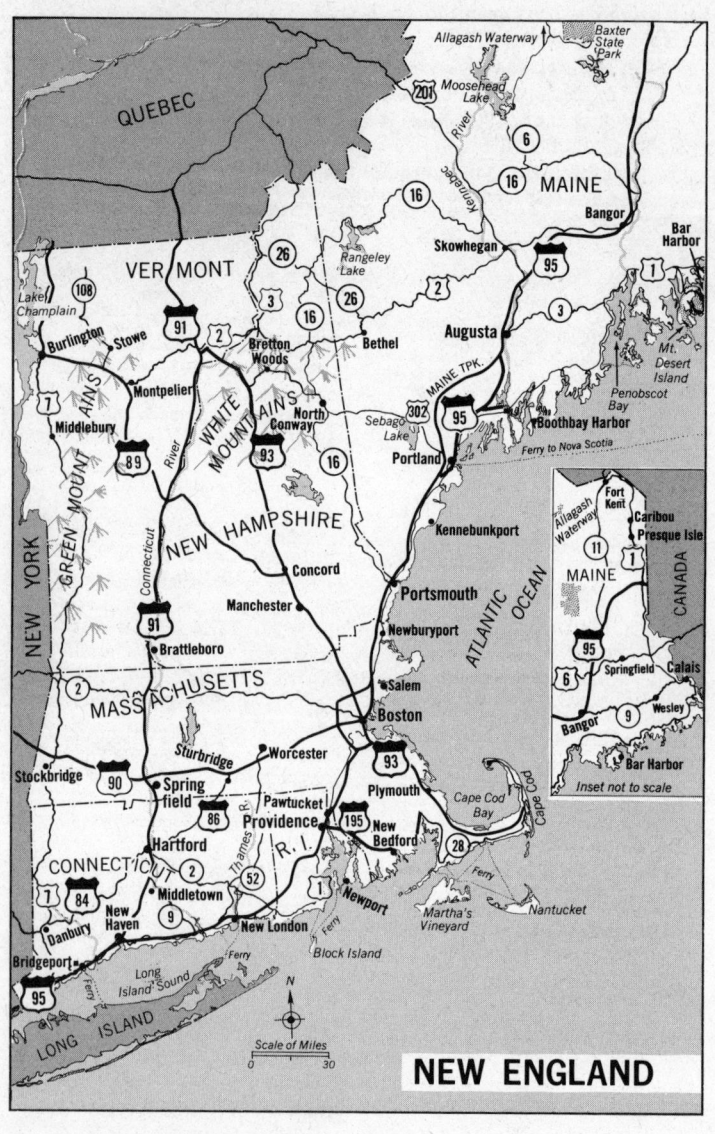

NEW ENGLAND

FOREWORD

Even to those who have never been there, New England conjures up a flood of images. New England is historical Boston, Lexington, and Concord or skiing down one of Vermont's smooth mountains. It is a splash of color on a bright fall day when the air is crisp and cool. It is also seaport towns still bustling from days of whaling, and it remains an area where towns feature a village green and white-steepled clapboard churches. To nearly everyone, New England evokes a sense of this nation's history and an on-going Norman Rockwell-style of life that doesn't seem to exist elsewhere in the United States.

Yet each of New England's six states—Maine, New Hampshire, Vermont, Massachusetts, Rhode Island, Connecticut—has such distinct appeal, different physical beauty and personality, and unique choices of cultural and sporting activities; that you may want to narrow your visit to just one or two states. Or you may choose to cover all or most of New England—a relatively small area—from Maine's forests and lakes to Rhode Island and Connecticut's beaches and seaports, from Vermont's picturesque villages to Massachusetts's educational centers. Our New England area editors have put together information on a wide range of sites and activities throughout the six New England states. Within that range they present you with selections of events and places that will be safe, worthwhile, and of good value. The descriptions they have provided are just enough for you to make your own informed choices.

All selections and comments in *Fodor's New England* are based on personal experiences. We feel that our first responsibility is to inform and protect you, the reader. Errors are bound to creep into any travel guide, however. Much can change in the New England area even while we are on press and during the succeeding 12 months or so when this edition is on sale. We sincerely welcome letters from our readers on these changes, or from those whose opinions differ from ours, and we are ready to revise our entries for next year's edition when the facts warrant it.

Send your letters to the editors at **Fodor's Travel Publications, 201 East 50th Street, New York, NY 10022.** Continental or British Commonwealth readers may prefer to write to Fodor's Travel Publications, 9–10 Market Place, London W1N 7AG, England.

FACTS AT YOUR FINGERTIPS

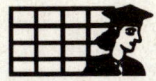 **FACTS AND FIGURES.** Of all the regions in the United States, New England is the smallest, most compact and easiest to travel in. Its six states—Connecticut, Maine, Massachusetts, New Hampshire, Rhode Island and Vermont—are also among the most hospitable, and the best geared for every type of tourism, from super deluxe to backwoods camping. Covering an area of almost 67,000 square miles, with a population of approximately 11.5 million people, New England is a unique blend of natural and man-made wonders. It is an area equally blessed with spectacular scenery and cultural wealth. As the first part of the country to have been developed by European settlers, it also boasts a sense of history that is unparalleled in the U.S.

When discussing the pertinent facts and figures for New England, it quickly becomes apparent that there is a difference in scale here compared to other parts of the country. For example, the region's largest city, Boston, has a population less than 600,000—compared to New York's 7.5 million. Distances between major points of interest are much shorter. And the changes in terrain, customs and folklore come quickly and drastically. The area is seemingly condensed— and yet the expanses of its White and Green Mountain ranges, the winding Appalachian and Heritage Trails and a never-ending supply of rivers, lakes and waterfalls give it a feeling of great expansiveness.

The coastline runs 473 miles, much of it rugged and rocky, with limited stretches suitable for swimming. Inland, which is 75 percent forest, is largely mountainous, with New Hampshire's Mt. Washington capping the region at 6,288 feet. Given this setting, it is easy to understand that the first New England fortunes were made from fishing and shipping in the 17th and 18th centuries. In the 19th century this was one of the first areas in the nation to industrialize. Today, almost every type of modern industry is represented, with computers leading the technological way and such craft-based goods as shoes and furniture representing the region's more traditional bent.

 **PLANNING YOUR TRIP.** The best way to see New England is by car. As stated, the distances between major points are relatively short (though the roads often wind their way through mountains or along coastal waters, thereby stretching out the driving time). Thruways and turnpikes abound, but the local roads are also excellently maintained. They afford a real chance to take in the countryside, to stop at antique and craft shops, to appreciate the Georgian, Greek Revival, and Federalist architecture, or to visit some outstanding small museums.

If you don't belong to an auto club, you should consider joining one before your trip. The *American Automobile Association,* 8111 Gatehouse Road, Falls Church VA 22047 and the *Amoco Motor Club,* Box 9014, Des Moines, IA 50306 offer maps, general travel information and over-the-phone directions for members. In addition, the AAA has a network of garages whose members it will summon should you require emergency service on the road.

Other sources for those embarking on motoring holidays:

Exxon Travel Club, 4550 Dacoma, Houston, TX 77092, which provides information, low-cost insurance and some legal services;

National Travel Club, 51 Atlantic Avenue, Travel Building, Floral Park NY 11001 for information, insurance and tours;

Texaco Travel Service, Box 538, Comfort, TX 78013;

For those not inclined to venture out on their own, package bus tours are available; and there is a growing number of full-service resorts springing up where a stay-put vacation can be most enjoyable. Some of each of these are described in individual state chapters; generally it is a good idea to consult a travel agent when making such arrangements. There is no fee for an agent's services, and if well-informed he or she will be familiar with the latest offerings and best prices.

Insurance. The different varieties of travel insurance cover everything from health and accident costs, to lost baggage and trip cancellation. Sometimes they can all be obtained with one blanket policy; other times they overlap with existing coverage you might have for health and/or home; still other times it is best to buy policies that are tailored to very specific needs. Insurance is available from many sources, however, and many travelers unwittingly end up with redundant coverage. Before purchasing separate travel insurance of any kind, be sure to check your regular policies carefully.

Generally, it is best to take care of your insurance needs before embarking on your trip. You'll pay more for less coverage—and have less chance to read the fine print—if you wait until the last minute and make your purchases from, say, an airport vending machine or insurance company counter. If you have a regular insurance agent, he or she is the person to consult first.

Flight insurance, which is often included in the price of the ticket when the fare is paid via American Express, Visa or certain other major credit cards, is also often included in package policies providing accident coverage as well. These policies are available from most tour operators and insurance companies. While it is a good idea to have health and accident insurance when traveling, be careful not to spend money to duplicate coverage you may already have—or to neglect some eventuality which could end up costing a small fortune.

For example, basic Blue Cross-Blue Shield policies do cover health costs incurred while traveling. They will not, however, cover the cost of emergency transportation, which can possibly add up to several thousand dollars. Emergency transportation *is* covered, in part at least, by many major medical policies such as those underwritten by Prudential, Metropolitan and New York Life. Again, we can't urge you too strongly that in order to be sure you are getting the coverage you need, check any policy carefully before buying. Another important example: most insurance issued specifically for travel does not cover pre-existing conditions, such as a heart condition.

Recently, several organizations have appeared which offer coverage designed to supplement existing health insurance and to help defray costs not covered by many standard policies, such as emergency transportation. Some of the more prominent are:

Carefree Travel Insurance, c/o ARM Coverage Inc., 120 Mineola Blvd., Box 310, Mineola, NY 11501 offers medical evacuation arranged through Europe Assistance of Paris (212–517–7911). *Carefree* coverage is available from many travel agents.

International SOS Assistance Inc, Box 11568, Philadelphia, PA 19116, has fees from $15 a person for seven days to $195 for a year (800–523–8930).

IAMAT (International Association for Medical Assistance to Travelers), 736 Center St., Lewiston, NY 14092, in the U.S.; or 188 Nicklin Rd., Guelph, Ontario N1H 7L5 in Canada.

Another frequent inconvenience to travelers is the loss of baggage. It is possible, though often a complicated affair, to insure your luggage against loss through theft or negligence. Insurance companies are reluctant to sell such coverage alone, however, since it is often a losing proposition for them. Instead, it is most often included as part of a package that would also cover accidents or health. Remuneration is often determined by weight, regardless of the value of the specific contents of the luggage. Should you lose your luggage or some other personal possession, be sure to report it to the local police immediately. Without documentation of such a report, your insurance company might be very stingy. Also, before buying baggage insurance, check your homeowners policy. Some such policies offer "off-premises theft" coverage, including the loss of luggage while traveling.

The last major area of traveler's insurance is trip cancellation coverage. This is especially important to travelers on APEX or charter flights. Should you get sick abroad, or for some other reason be unable to continue your trip, you may be stuck having to buy a new one-way fare home, plus paying for space on the charter you're not using. You can guard against this with "trip cancellation insurance," usually available from travel agents. Most of these policies will also cover last minute cancellations.

VISITORS' INFORMATION. For general information on the entire region, including a pamphlet describing tour packages by a variety of operators write to New England USA, Summer St., Boston, MA 02109. Do-it-yourself information may also be obtained from the *New England Vacation Center*, 630 Fifth Avenue, New York, NY 10020 (212–307–5780). A map of New England can be obtained from the *New England Innkeepers Association*, Box 1997, Hampton, NH 03842.

For details on the specific states in the area see the individual chapters of this guide.

TIPS FOR BRITISH TRAVELERS. *Passports.* You will need a valid passport (cost £15) and a U.S. visa (which can only be put in a passport of the 10-year kind). You can obtain the visa either through your travel agent, or directly from the *United States Embassy*, Visa and Immigration Department, Upper Grosvenor St., London W1 (tel. 01–499–5521). No vaccinations are required for entry into the U.S.

Customs. If you are 21 or over you can take into the U.S. 200 cigarettes, 50 cigars or 3 lbs. of tobacco (combination of proportionate parts permitted); 1 U.S. quart of alcohol; duty-free gifts to a value of $100. Be careful not to try to take in meat or meat products, seeds, plants, fruits, etc., and certainly no non-prescription narcotics.

Insurance. We heartily recommend that you insure yourself to cover health and motoring mishaps with *Europ Assistance*, 252 High St., Croydon CRO 1NF (01–680–1234). Their excellent service is all the more valuable when you consider the possible costs of health care in the U.S.

Tour Operators. The price battle that has raged over trans-Atlantic fares has meant that most tour operators now offer excellent budget packages to the U.S., though most are likely to include only a few days in New England. Among these you might check for more extensive tours through this region are:

Aer Lingus Holidays, 52 Poland St., London W1 (tel. 01–437–8000).

Albany Travel (Manchester)Ltd., 190 Deansgate, Manchester M3 3WD (tel. 061–833–0202).

Thomas Cook, P.O. Box 36, Thorpe Wood, Peterborough PE3 65B (tel. 0733–63200).

Saga Holidays Enbrook House, Sandgate Rd., Folkestone, Kent CT20 3SG (tel. 0303–30000).

Speedbird, Alta House, 152 King St., London W6 (tel. 01–741–8041).

Trekamerica, Ryelands House, Aynho, Banbury, Oxon OX17 3AT (tel. 0869–810080).

Air Fares. We suggest that you explore the current scene for budget flight possibilities into either Boston, which is in the heart of New England itself, or to New York, the next nearest major port of entry. Unfortunately, there is no longer any standby service on the major airlines; but do check their APEX and other reduced fares. Frankly, only business travelers who don't have to watch the price of their tickets, or those who require a definite last-minute reservation fly full-price these days—and often find themselves sitting right beside APEX passengers.

Another boon to budget travel is People Express which has very inexpensive flights direct to Newark, New Jersey, from which connecting flights are easily arranged.

Hotels. For booking in advance, you can write directly to smaller inns and bed-and-breakfasts, enclosing an international money order as a deposit. Write well ahead, however, as inns in particular often fill up as much as six months in advance for weekends during fall foliage and summer music festival seasons. Reserve at major hotels through your travel agent. For further information on accommodations, write to the *New England Innkeepers Association,* PO Box 4977, Hampton, NH 03842, in the U.S.

WHEN TO GO. New England offers a radically different environment in every season. **Summers** are the most culturally active, with major music festivals at Tanglewood in the Berkshire Mountains of Massachusetts and in the Bretton Woods of New Hampshire. Dozens of smaller music, theater and dance festivals can also be found. Hiking is excellent throughout the summer as the mountains tend to be shaded and fairly cool even during the hottest days; trails are numerous and well-marked. Summer sports include boating and swimming, while crafts-hunters can find fairs somewhere just about every week.

Fall is unquestionably the most colorful season. For those near the region, a "pilgrimage" to view New England's fall foliage is an annual event not to be missed. The season starts in early October in the more northern reaches of the area, moving southward as the month goes on; the third weekend is generally the most popular because it can be counted on as the "peak." The days will be on the warm side in the sun but still crisp feeling—excellent for walking—but at night the temperature will drop to the freezing point and below. It's a perfect time to take advantage of inns' and guest houses' glowing fires.

Winter is given over to skiers—downhill and, increasingly popular, cross-country. Each state's slopes and trails are discussed in later chapters; suffice it to say here that every level of skier can find appropriate terrain, with downhillers preferring Vermont and cross-country skiers taking to the summer hiking trails all over.

Spring brings the flowering of apple blossoms, dogwood, rhododendron, lilac and forsythia. The waterfalls are at their strongest and the earth, thawing after the winter snows, is rich and hearty.

Regardless of the time of year, New England is an antiquer's paradise; there are thousands of craftspeople with their wood, metal, glass and pottery workshops-cum-stores open for browsing or buying; and there are outstanding museums, often in the most unlikely locales!

PACKING. What to take varies greatly with the season and with the activities you plan to pursue, but do keep in mind that the further north you go the colder the nights will be—even in the dead of August, when the days might be 90 degrees or warmer. Skiers know that several layers of thin clothing are better than one heavy jacket; hikers will want insect repellent; those whose main interest is art will want comfortable walking shoes.

Generally speaking, it is always a good idea to make a checklist of what you'll need. It will save time and reduce confusion. Except for backwoods campers, you'll be able to stock up on anything you might forget or run out of, so don't weigh down your baggage with excess film or other items that are easily obtained while on the road.

New England tends to be informal (which is not to say sloppy) as far as dress, though dining rooms at some resort hotels and at finer restaurants in the major cities as well as in the mountains require men to wear jackets. If driving, full picnic supplies are good to have as there are many scenic roadside rests with tables and barbecue pits.

CLIMATE. Temperatures in New England range from lows around 16 degrees F. in January to highs around 73 degrees F. in July, although such averages can be misleading. Altitudes change frequently within the region, as does the proximity to the ocean—both factors that can seriously influence the weather. Detailed temperature charts are given for each state separately.

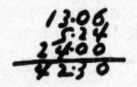

WHAT WILL IT COST? That question is difficult to answer. Price is dependent on the type of trip you are interested in making and the activities you plan to do. Staying in homey and often charming bed-and-breakfasts (more commonly known as "guest houses") will help keep the price down *and* afford an opportunity to get to know the region's natives. Such guest houses are also more common in New England than anywhere else in the U.S. Full services in major hotels will obviously cost more, though less in Manchester, New Hampshire than in Boston or New York. Attending concerts at Tanglewood can raise the cost significantly if you want a reserved seat near the stage; most people opt for sprawling out on a blanket under the stars—for much less money, more comfort and in fine earshot of the music.

We recommend that you chart out your planned activities in order to create a realistic budget. As an example, the following chart would be applicable for a couple traveling in a ski area or during the music festival season, staying at an inn (somewhere between guest house and hotel in level of accommodations— usually having a restaurant and bar, private bath and common sitting rooms, sometimes with pool or lake):

Typical Expenses for Two People

Room with continental breakfast	$60.00
Lunch at inexpensive restaurant (with tip)	20.00
Dinner at moderate restaurant or inn (with tip)	50.00
Evening drinks or coffee and dessert	6.00
Total	$136.00

Other suggestions for controlling lodging costs: if you have a car, choose accommodations a little bit away from the central attraction in the area; traveling off-season will help, too, though in New England the few weeks a year that constitute off-season tend to be when the innkeepers and such close for their own vacations. Check into the lodgings available at local YMCA's and YWCA's (write or call *YMCA of the USA,* 101 N. Wacker Dr., Chicago, Il 60606, (312) 977–0031). Consider efficiency apartments and/or cabins, or camping in either public or private campgrounds. During the summer, investigate whether the colleges and universities in the area you will be in offer dormitory rooms to visitors. A directory of some 200 such opportunities all over the U.S. is *Mort's Guide to Low-Cost Vacations and Lodgings on College Campuses, USA-Canada* ($7.00), from Mort Barish Associates Inc., Research Park, 218 Wall St. Princeton, NJ 08540.

New England also offers as much diversity for dining as it does for sleeping. In Maine, roadside stands offer excellent lobster dinners for $4–6; indeed, seafood is a primary culinary attraction throughout the region, both for quality and price. When the season is cooperative, a picnic lunch is an excellent alternative to restaurants: Vermont cheeses, locally-produced sausages and fresh fruits and vegetables abound. When deciding on a restaurant, check the menu before you sit down; consider sharing a main course and ordering an extra vegetable or appetizer; when appropriate, find out if there is a special children's menu or senior citizen's discount. Most inns will have a book with local restaurants' menus—often with other visitors' comments about them noted.

HINTS TO THE MOTORIST. Certainly New England is adequately supplied with Interstates, parkways, freeways, thruways, turnpikes, and all the other expensive devices that enable you to whiz through an area swiftly and smoothly without ever seeing it, but here if anywhere they have got to be irrelevant to your purposes as a visitor. Distances are short, the towns and cities are close to each other, and pushing for the 200–250 miles a day that you might aim for in another part of the country would simply take you out of the region entirely. Besides, some of your pleasantest sightseeing will be off the major traffic movers and along New England's secondary and back roads, which are so winding that you can't rush on them anyway and would be foolish to want to or try to. It is advisable to avoid driving on them at night; they are unlit and often poorly marked. The whole six-state region has adopted the 55-miles-per-hour speed limit recommended for fuel saving. The major highways are well designed with frequent rest stops and gas stations, and you will only occasionally encounter a desolate stretch of highway, such as those in central and upper Maine, and begin to wonder where to find the next service station.

If you are driving your own car, be sure to have it checked before you leave. As stated earlier, you should also join an auto club if you don't already belong to one. If you are renting, be sure to inspect the car and make sure that windshield wipers, lights, horn and other necessary gear work properly before taking it from the garage; drive it around the block a few times to make sure the steering and brake mechanisms are in order. In either case, see to it that the spare tire is properly inflated, that there is a jack with necessary attachments, tools for emergencies, jumper cables, an extra set of keys (even renters should have these!), road flares, a flashlight and, in winter, an ice scraper, some de-icer for the windshield and locks, and a small shovel. Many states also require that you carry evidence that you are insured in addition to the car's registration and your license.

 **TRAVELING WITH PETS.** Traveling by car with your dog or cat? Some hotels and motels will accept them, but be sure to check ahead. This matter is usually specified in the free directories the motel chains publish. If it's a first-time trip for your pet, accustom it to car travel by short trips in the neighborhood. And when you're packing, include its favorite food, bowls, and toys. Your dog may like to ride with its head out the window. Discourage this. Wind and dust particles can permanently damage its eyes. Dogs are especially susceptible to heatstroke. Don't leave your pet in a parked car on a hot day while you dawdle over lunch. Keep your pet's bowl handy for water during stops for gas; service station attendants are usually very cooperative about this. Make sure your pet exercises periodically; this is a good way for you and the kids to unwind from unbroken traveling, too.

 **HOTELS AND MOTELS. General hints.** Don't take potluck for lodgings. You'll waste a great deal of time and often won't be happy with the accommodations you finally find. In Boston you'll certainly want an advance reservation, since driving around in search of a room can be especially difficult and frustrating. But if you arrive in any of New England's more typical small cities or larger towns late in the afternoon, chances are you'll pass a local visitor's bureau on the literal or proverbial Main Street; the people there will almost always be able to find you a room somewhere, whether in a guest house, inn, hotel or motel.

The earlier in the day you begin to look the better off you'll be, though keep in mind that check-out time at most places is around 1 P.M., so many won't always know whether any rooms are available until then. If you plan to arrive after six P.M. it is best to advise the hotel (or whomever); some will ask for a guarantee by way of your credit card number. Inns and guest houses tend to be somewhat more lenient about this so long as they are notified in advance that you'll be late. If you're moving from one city to the next you can also ask at the hotel or motel where you are whether the chain to which it belongs has a branch at your next stop. If the answer is yes they will call ahead to book your room for you.

Hotels will almost always have laundry and dry cleaning service; motels frequently have laundromats. Many motels have telephones in every room, though almost all have televisions. Parking is generally free at motels but not at hotels (except for resorts, and then it is usually valet parking requiring a tip when you leave). Pools are common at both. The "services" of this nature are not the norm at inns and guest houses; what they lack in the way of such amenities they make up for in individuality, character and charm.

Among the national non-budget hotel and motel chains, the most expensive are Hilton, Marriott, and Sheraton; the middle range includes Holiday Inns, Howard Johnson's, Quality Inns, and TraveLodge; and the least expensive are usually Best Western, Ramada, and Rodeway. Of the many budget chains that have arisen in recent years, and whose rates are less than half those of the others, only two, unfortunately, operate in New England. These are: *Susse Chalet International,* Chalet Drive, Rte. 101, Wilton, NH 03086 (800–258–1980); and *Econo-Travel Motor Hotel Corp,* 6135 Park Rd., Suite 200, Charlotte, NC 28201 (800–446–6900). Write or phone for free directories to both chains. For more information on accommodations, contact the *New England Innkeepers Association,* PO Box 1997, Hampton, NH 03842 603–926–6335).

Hotel and Motel Categories

Hotels and motels in all the Fodor's guidebooks to the U.S.A. are divided into five categories, arranged by price. Our ratings are flexible and subject to change.

Limitations of space make it impossible to include every establishment. We have, therefore, listed those which we recommend as the best within each price range. In some instances, prices reflect a certain number of meals. *Full American Plan* (FAP) includes three meals daily; *Modified American Plan* (MAP) includes breakfast and dinner; *Continental Plan* (CP) offers European-style breakfast (roll or croissant and tea or coffee); *European Plan* (EP) means no meals are included in the price quoted.

Although the names of the various hotel and motel categories are standard throughout this series, the prices listed under each category may vary from area to area. This variance is meant to reflect local price standards, and take into account the fact that what might be considered a *moderate* price in a large urban area might be quite *expensive* in a rural region. In every case, however, the dollar ranges for each category are clearly stated before each listing of establishments.

Super deluxe: this category is reserved for only a few hotels. In addition to giving the visitor all the amenities discussed under the deluxe category (below), the super deluxe hotel has a special atmosphere of glamor, good taste, and dignity. It will inevitably be full of historical anecdotes, and will probably be a favored meeting spot of local society. In short, super deluxe means tops.

Deluxe: for a rough rule-of-thumb index, we suggest that the minimum facilities must include bath and shower in all rooms, valet and laundry service, suites available, a well-appointed restaurant and a bar (where local law permits), room service, TV and telephone in room, air conditioning and heating, pleasing décor, and an atmosphere of luxury, calm and elegance, ample and personalized service. In a deluxe *motel,* there may be less service rendered by employees and more by machine or automation (such as refrigerators and ice-making machines in your room), but there should be a minimum of do-it-yourself in a truly deluxe establishment.

Expensive: all rooms must have bath or shower, valet and laundry service, restaurant and bar (local law permitting), at least some room service, TV and telephone in room, attractive furnishings, heating and air conditioning. Although décor may be as good as that in deluxe establishments, hotels and motels in this category are frequently designed for commercial travelers or for families in a hurry and are somewhat impersonal in terms of service. As for *motels* in this category, valet and laundry service will probably be lacking; the units will be outstanding primarily for their convenient location and functional character, not for their attractive or comfortable qualities.

Moderate: each room should have an attached bath or shower, there should be a restaurant *or* coffee shop, TV available, telephone in room, heating and air conditioning, relatively convenient location, clean and comfortable rooms and public room. *Motels* in this category may not have attached bath or shower, may not have a restaurant or coffee shop (though one is usually nearby), and may have no public rooms.

Inexpensive: nearby bath or shower, telephone available, clean rooms are the minimum.

Baby sitter lists are always available in good hotels and motels, and cribs for the children are always on hand—sometimes at no cost, but more frequently at a cost of a few dollars.

The cost of a cot in your room, to supplement the beds, will be around $3 per night, but moving an extra single bed into a room will cost from $7 in better hotels and motels.

INNS, GUEST HOUSES, AND BED-AND-BREAK-FASTS.

Inns, guest houses, and bed-and-breakfasts have become quite popular in the United States as American travelers have increasingly taken to exploring their own country—and sought out ways to get a true taste of the region in less uniform accommodations. Nowhere has this trend manifested itself more than in New England.

Inns, which often charge as much as motels and hotels but provide far more personal service and atmosphere, are frequently booked weekends from one year to the next by a regular clientele. Some offer pools, mini-golf courses, cross-country ski trails, and other diversions; most derive a good portion of their income from restaurants catering to guests and outsiders. Meals range from communal home-style to haute cuisine. Many have bars and almost all have pleasant public rooms with fireplaces, reading material, card tables, board games, and comfortable sofas and stuffed chairs. Rooms run from a low of $25 per night for two to about $90, with some establishments offering MAP weekend deals. A reasonable average for room alone is $50–$60 for a double, though this average takes in the outer reaches of Maine and New Hampshire as well as, say, the Berkshires.

Guest houses and bed-and-breakfasts tend to be on the simpler and less expensive side. Essentially private homes with anywhere from one to a dozen extra bedrooms, most serve breakfast. During the summer music-festival and winter ski seasons it is best to book as far ahead as possible. A few sources with specific listings include *Sleep Cheap,* by Jon and Nancy Kugelman, published by McBride Publishers, 161 S. Whitney St., Hartford, CT 06105 ($6.95 plus $ .88 postage); *Guest Houses and Tourist Homes USA,* published by Tourist House Associates of America, Inc., PO Box 355-A, Greentown, PA 18426. *Bed & Breakfast Registry,* P.O. Box 8174, St. Paul, MN 55108, is a nationwide bed-and-breakfast reservation service (612–646–4238). *INNter Lodging,* P.O. Box 7044, Tacoma, WA 98407, is a cooperative in which members must make their own homes available for bed-and-breakfast for a certain period during the year but are thereby entitled to services from other members. Nightly charges are $4 to $5 per adult; breakfast is extra.

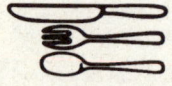

HOSTELS.

Because of the great size of the United States and the distances involved, Youth Hostels have not developed in this country the way they have in Europe and Japan. In the entire 3½ million square miles of the U.S. there are upwards of 200 Youth Hostels, and because they are, in any case, designed primarily for people who are traveling under their own power, usually hiking or bicycling, rather than by car or commercial transportation, they tend to be away from towns and cities and in rural areas, near scenic spots. In the U.S. they are most frequent and practical in compact areas like New England. Although their membership is mainly younger people, there is no age limit. Accommodations are simple, dormitories are segregated for men and women, common rooms and kitchen are shared, and everyone helps with the cleanup. Lights out 11 P.M. to 7 A.M., no alcohol or other drugs allowed. Membership fees: under 17—$10, 17 and over—$20, family—$30. Hostel rates vary; $4 to $9 per person per night is average. In season it is wise to reserve ahead; write or phone directly to the particular hostel you plan to stay in. You must be a member to use Youth Hostels; write to *American Youth Hostel Association, Inc.,* P.O. Box 37613, Washington DC 20013. A copy of the Hostel Guide and Handbook will be included in your membership. In New England, Youth Hostels number 4 in Connecticut, 6 in Maine, 13 in Massachusetts, 5 in New Hampshire, 8 in Vermont, 2 in Rhode Island.

DINING OUT.

Heavily forested, and with thin rocky soil, New England is hardly a rich agricultural area, yet even at the first Thanksgiving, in 1621, the earliest New Englanders managed to feast on corn and beans, venison, roast duck, roast goose, eels, clams, wheat bread, corn bread, leeks, watercress, wild plums, and home-made wine; and ever since, New England has enjoyed a culinary tradition that is both plain and solid on the one hand and richly satisfying on the other. The early settlers found strawberries, cranberries, blackberries, blueberries, melons, pumpkins, squash, four kinds of corn (white, blue, yellow, and red), turkeys, maple sugar, woods teeming with game, tidelands that yielded clams, oysters and scallops, and fish "at our doorstep." New England's first fortunes were made from the sea, in fishing and shipping, and seafood is still an important part of this region's diet, but it is certainly not the only pleasure of dining out here. A few possibilities, among many, are:

For seafood—lobster stew, baked stuffed haddock, and broiled Boston scrod; clams and oysters either steamed or fried; codfish balls; Block Island swordfish; crabs and scallops. And if you go in summer you may be lucky enough to get in on a beach party where clams or lobsters will either be boiled over an open fire of driftwood or will be packed with corn in seaweed and baked over hot stones. New England clam chowder is a fine and special art form all its own and one in which everyone is his own artist. Clams, pork, spices, onions, milk, butter and wine or cider are the ingredients, but the proportions and the seasoning are personal matters, and disputes over the use of tomatoes and the distinction between clams and quahogs can take on theological overtones.

To make a New England Boiled Dinner, some prefer saltpork as the center around which the vegetables are arranged, while others make it with corned beef, particularly around Boston; and baked beans are yet another area where every variation of bean, molasses, pork and baking technique has its own defenders. There is, however, a delightful recipe for the rich brown bread that always goes with baked beans that is gratifyingly clearcut as well as lyrical: one cup of sweet milk, one cup of sour; one cup of corn meal, one cup of flour; Teaspoon of soda, molasses one cup; steam for three hours, then eat it all up.

Cornbread, Indian pudding, apple pandowdy, mincemeat pie, deep dish apple or blueberry pie, and in Vermont, sharp cheeses and sweet maple syrup and sugar. Everywhere are apples and blueberries, poultry, dairy products, and potatoes. Cape Cod produces cranberries, and in southern New England cherries and peaches are grown. Although nowadays some of the finest old New England inns take pride in their sophisticated international cuisine (chicken provençal and yogurt and parsley pilaf in rural Vermont!), the region's typical cooking is still very much alive and well and still reflects that "plain style" beloved of its Puritan ancestors. But there is nothing gloomy, pinched or austere about this plain style. It is, like New England craftsmanship, a kind of simple, direct respect for the materials native to the region. In their own distinctive way, New Englanders always have eaten well. They still do.

Reservations are advisable at better restaurants, especially when there are skiers or music festivals nearby, and so as to ascertain what the dining hours are (they tend to be fairly narrow in this part of the country). Dress codes depend upon the establishment, but New Englanders generally lean toward the casual—without being unkempt. Only the more exclusive eateries require men to wear jackets. Children's menus are frequently available, senior citizen discounts more rarely.

Restaurant Categories

Restaurants located in Boston are categorized in this volume by type of cuisine: French, Chinese, etc., with restaurants of a general nature listed as American-International. Restaurants in other areas are divided into price categories as follows: *super deluxe, deluxe, expensive, moderate,* and *inexpensive.* As a general rule, expect restaurants in metropolitan areas to be higher in price.

We should also point out that limitations of space make it impossible to include every establishment. We have, therefore, included those which we consider the best within each price range.

Although the names of the various restaurant categories are standard throughout this series, the prices listed under each category may vary from area to area. This variation is meant to reflect local price standards, and take into account the fact that what might be considered a *moderate* price in a large urban area might be quite *expensive* in a rural region. In every case, however, the dollar ranges for each category are clearly stated before each listing of establishments.

Price designations are for a complete meal (appetizer or soup, entrée, and dessert), but do not include drinks, tax, or tip.

Super deluxe: This category will probably be pertinent to only one or two metropolitan areas. It indicates outstanding cuisine in a setting that is often lavishly decorated. As in all our categories, the price range does not include drinks, cover or table charges, tip, or extravagant house specialties. The restaurants in this category must have a superb wine list, excellent service, immaculate kitchens, and a large, well-trained staff.

Deluxe: Many fine restaurants around the country fall into this category. Such a restaurant will have its own well-deserved reputation for excellence, perhaps a house specialty or two for which it is famous, and an atmosphere of elegance or unique décor. It will have a good wine list, and will be considered among the best in town.

Expensive: In addition to the expected dishes, it will offer one or two house specialties, a representative wine list, cocktails (where law permits), and a general reputation for very good food and an attentive staff.

Moderate: Cocktails and/or beer where the law permits, air conditioning, when needed, clean kitchen, adequate staff, better-than-average service. Most important—good wholesome food.

Inexpensive: The bargain place in town, it is clean, even if plain. It will have air conditioning when necessary, tables (not a counter), clean kitchens and attempt to provide adequate service.

Chains: There are now several chains of restaurants, some regional, some nationwide, that offer reliable eating at budget prices. Some chains that operate in New England are: 1) *Howard Johnson's;* 2) *Holiday Inns* (some offer all-you-can-eat buffets), Connecticut, New Hampshire, Vermont; 3) *Pizza Hut,* Maine, New Hampshire, Massachusetts, Connecticut. On the whole, New England is worse served by restaurant chains than any other part of the country. The familiar designs of *McDonald's, Burger King, Kentucky Fried Chicken* and similar establishments, though, are fairly well represented.

 **TIPPING.** Tipping is supposed to be a personal way of thanking someone who has taken pleasure and pride in giving you attentive, efficient, and personal service. When you get genuinely good service, feel secure in rewarding it; but when you feel that the service you get is slovenly, indifferent or surly don't hesitate to tip accordingly. Remember that in most places the help are paid very little and depend on tips for the better part of their income. This is supposed to give them incentive to serve you well.

These days the going rate for tipping on *restaurant* service is 15% before taxes. Tipping at counters is not universal; however, most customers do leave 25¢ on anything up to a dollar and 15% on checks higher than that. There is no tipping in fast-food and take-out places. For *bellboys,* 50¢ per bag is usual. However, if you load him down with all manner of bags, cameras, coats, etc., you might consider giving quite a bit extra. For one-night stays in hotels or motels you leave nothing. If you stay longer, at the end of your stay leave the maid $1.25 to $1.50 per day, or $7 per person per week for multiple occupancy. If you are staying at an *American Plan* hostelry (meals included), $1.50 per person per day for the waitress is considered sufficient, and is left at the end of your stay. If you have been surrounded by an army of servants (one bringing relishes, another rolls, and such), add a few extra dollars and give the lump sum to the captain or *maitre d'hotel* when you leave, asking him to allocate it.

For other services in a hotel or resort, figure roughly: doorman—25¢ for taxi handling, 50¢ for help with baggage; parking attendant—50¢ to $1; bartender—15%; room service—10% to 15% of that bill; laundry or valet service—15%; pool attendant—50¢ per day; snackbar waiter at pool, beach or golf club—15% of the food and beverage bill; masseurs and masseuses—15% to 20%; golf caddies—$2 or $3 per bag, or 15% of the greens fee for an 18-hole course, or $3 on a free course; barbers—15%; shoeshine attendants—50¢ to $1; hairdressers—15%; manicurists 15%.

Transportation: Give 25¢ for any taxi fare under $1 and 15% for any above. Limousine service—25%. Car rental agencies—nothing. Bus porters are tipped

25¢ per bag, drivers nothing. On charters and package tours, conductors and drivers usually get $5 to $10 per day from the group as a whole, but be sure to ask whether this has already been figured into the package cost. On short local sightseeing runs, the driver-guide may get 50¢ per person, more if you think he has been especially helpful or personable. Airport bus drivers—nothing. Redcaps, 50¢ per suitcase. Tipping at curbside check-in is unofficial, but same as above. On the plane, no tipping.

SENIOR CITIZEN AND STUDENT DISCOUNTS. Generally, both groups can obtain discounts at many museums and other cultural institutions upon presentation of proof of age or student status. (Note that the international student ID card that is mandatory in Europe is not accepted in the U.S.) Movie houses also frequently discount admission for senior citizens, though sometimes only for daytime showings. In addition, some *Holiday Inns* give a discount to members of the NRTA (write to National Retired Teachers Association, 3200 E. Carson, Lakewood, CA 90712) and of the AARP (write to American Association of Retired Persons, Membership Division, 3200 E. Carson, Lakewood, CA 90712). Members of the AARP, the NRTA, the National Association of Retired Persons, the Catholic Golden Age of United Societies of the U.S.A., the Old Age Security Pensioners of Canada, and similar organizations benefit increasingly from a number of discounts, but the amounts, sources, and availability of these change, so it is best to check with either your organization or the hotel, motel or restaurant chain you plan to use. The *National Council of Senior Citizens,* 925 15th St. NW, Washington, DC 20005, works especially to develop low-cost travel possibilities for its members. Unfortunately, there is little uniformity in the amount of discount, the type of proof needed to obtain it (more stringent for students than for senior citizens) or when a cut rate is available.

DRINKING LAWS. Drinking laws vary from state to state, including what hours bars may operate, whether grocery stores can sell wine and beer and what type of establishments can serve alcohol on Sundays. As for drinking age, the minimum for all the New England states is 21.

BUSINESS HOURS AND LOCAL TIME. Eastern Daylight Savings Time is in effect from the last Sunday in April until the last Sunday in October.

Business hours are generally 8 or 9 A.M. to 5 P.M., but some stores, especially in the many communities used to catering to vacationers, are likely to stay open later in the evening.

SUMMER SPORTS. With 473 miles of coast, New England has 6,130 miles of now sandy, now rocky, serrated shoreline, making for a host of saltwater activities. There are many forms of *boating,* with their attendant races and regattas. There's *small-craft sailing,* too. If you're not adept at the tiller, you can take lessons, or just be a contented passenger.

Surf casting is done extensively, as is *deep-sea fishing.* Giant tuna, swordfish, white marlin, and blue marlin are plentiful, and charter boats for this type of fishing are available in Rhode Island, Massachusetts, southern Maine, and along New Hampshire's short but active seacoast.

Swimming is excellent in New England. The region has thousands of lakes, especially in Maine, and from Portland to New York there are beaches everywhere. The outer part of Cape Cod is a National Seashore. Temperature is another matter; even in August, the ocean from Cape Cod north can be numbingly cold, while Long Island Sound can be tepid and flat. The condition of the ocean varies so much with tides, currents, storms and sunshine that you'll just have to try your luck, but be sure to do so.

A number of *racetracks* draw people to see the thoroughbreds run; there are *sports* and *stock car races, tennis tournaments, horse shows,* and the classic *Yale-Harvard crew races* held in early June on the Thames River at New London, Conn.

Inland, all manner of sports abound from *boating* and *canoeing,* to *hiking* and *mountain climbing. Lake swimming, tennis,* and *golf* are outstanding in many areas, and in the northern areas, *rockhounds* can have a heyday. *Water skiing* is popular, as is *horseback riding* on numerous forest trails. Freshwater fish abound in many lakes and ponds, streams, and rivers (*fly-fishing* only is allowed on some streams), and favorite catches throughout the region are trout (lake, brook, brown, speckled, rainbow, and squaretailed), bass, perch, pike, pickerel, and land-locked salmon.

Many types of boats as well as canoes can be rented on a number of lakes and rivers, but for several-day or week-long canoe trips, it is best to bring your own. There are places, too, where you can rent water skis, and at some marinas there are water-ski towing boats for rent.

WINTER SPORTS. To many, "New England" has become almost synonymous with *skiing,* and with good reason. Facilities for both downhill and cross-country skiing are excellent, and are offered in a wide variety of areas, from virtually a few miles above Connecticut's southern border to the deep woods near Moosehead Lake in Maine. With skiing has come the resurgence of *ice-skating,* particularly on well-lighted rinks at night. *Sled dog races,* becoming very popular with spectators, are held during the first three months of the year in the northern New England states, and *ice fishing* is gaining a steadily increasing number of enthusiasts in this entire region. New England is also a center for *snowmobiling,* and marked trails abound in the region.

In the late fall, *hunting* brings many people to New England, out after deer, bobcat, moose, and bear, and there is bow-and-arrow hunting in some areas. For hunters who can take frigid, rough, lake water, there are whistlers (goldeneye) and bluebills (scaup) for the taking from late November to early December, and on Cape Cod, waterfowl, quail, pheasant, and rabbit lure many a sportsman from late October through November.

For spectators, there are also fall *football* games (Ivy League and others), a number of *race tracks* are open through December, and for the first three months of the year, there are a number of *championship events* at the better-known ski resorts and at colleges and universities. Though it is only now spreading to the rest of the country, *soccer* has been played in the colleges and prep schools of New England for forty years or more and is a leading fall sport there.

CAMPING AND HIKING. More, and improved, camping facilities are springing up each year across the country, in national parks, national forests, state parks, in private camping areas, and trailer parks, which by now have become national institutions. *Useful Addresses: National Parks Service,* P.O. Box 37127, Washington, DC 20013; *National Forest Service,* P.O. Box 2417, Washington, DC 20013. For information on state parks, see the addresses given in the *Practical Information* sections for each of the individual states.

New England is a favorite among U.S. hikers and rock climbers, boasting thousands of miles of well-marked (and some not-so-well-marked) trails. An excellent resource for hikers, or even those who just enjoy extended walks, is *Berkshire Trails for Walking and Ski Touring* by Whit Griswold, East Woods Press, 429 East Blvd., Charlotte, NC 28203; however the publisher is, at press time, out of stock with no firm plans to reprint.

The *National Campers & Hikers Assoc.,* 7172 Transit Road, Buffalo, NY 14221 (716–634–5433), is an informal organization of camping enthusiasts. Commercial camping organizations include: for organized children's camping for a few days to a whole summer contact *American Camping Assoc., Inc.,* Bradford Woods, Martinsville IN 46151 (317–342–8456) and *Kampgrounds of*

America, Inc., Box 30558, Billings MT 59114 (406–248–7444). Headquarters of the *Appalachian Mountain Club* is 5 Joy St., Boston MA 02108 (617–523–0636).

FARM VACATIONS. Farm vacations continue to gain adherents, especially among families with children. Some are quite deluxe, some extremely simple. Some are real working farms with animals and machinery, others are large and sometimes elegant country homes with housekeeping cottages attached and programs of activities. For a directory of country places which take vacationers, write to *Adventure Guides, Inc.,* 36 East 57 St., New York, NY 10022, for their book, *Farm, Ranch and Country Vacations.* The cost is $11, including shipping, or $12 if you want it sent by First Class Mail.

STATE AND NATIONAL PARKS. Probably the most famous of national parks in New England is Acadia, on Mt. Desert Island in Maine, but there are numerous parks and preserved forests throughout the Green and White Mountain ranges and the Berkshires. For complete information, contact the agencies mentioned above under *Visitors' Information* and see the individual state listings.

HINTS TO HANDICAPPED TRAVELERS. One of the newest and largest groups to enter the travel scene is the handicapped. Generally, their tours parallel those of the non-handicapped traveler, but at a more leisurely pace and with all the logistics carefully checked out in advance. Important sources of information in this field are the *Travel Information Center,* Moss Rehabilitation Hospital, 12th Street and Tabor Road, Philadelphia PA 19141, and *Easter Seal Society for Crippled Children and Adults,* Director of Education and Information Service, 2023 West Ogden Avenue, Chicago IL 60612; the books: *Travel Ability,* by Lois Reamy, published by Macmillan, Front & Brown St., Riverside, NJ 08075. This guide is also available free on loan as a recording (Book #BA 135) from *Recording for the Blind,* 725 Park Ave., 10021, (212) 517–9820. *Access to the World: A Travel Guide for the Handicapped,* by Louise Weiss, available from Facts on File, 460 Park Ave. South, New York, NY 10016.

The President's Committee on Employment of the Handicapped, Washington DC 20210, has issued a list of guidebooks for the handicapped that tells where to write for information on nearly 100 U.S. cities. The Committee also has a guide to highway rest area facilities that have been designed for access by the handicapped. And for a list of tour operators who arrange this kind of travel, write to: *Society for the Advancement of Travel for the Handicapped International Office,* 26 Court Street, Suite 1110, Brooklyn, NY 11242, (718) 858–5483.

One publication which gives valuable information about motels, hotels, and restaurants (rating them, telling about steps, table heights, door widths, etc.) and is annually revised is *The Wheelchair Traveler* by Douglass R. Annand, Ball Hill Road, Milford NH 03055. Also, *National Parks Guide for the Handicapped* is available from the U.S. Government Printing Office, Washington, DC 20402. International Air Transport Association (IATA) publishes a free pamphlet entitled *Incapacitated Passengers' Air Travel Guide,* explaining various arrangements and how to make them. Write IATA, 2000 Peel Street, Montreal, Quebec H3A 2R4.

POSTAGE. At press time rates for international mail from the United States are as follows: surface letters to Canada and Mexico are at the U.S. domestic rate of 22 cents for 1 ounce or under, 39 cents for 2 ounces or under, but these rates actually get airmail carriage to those countries. Surface letters to other foreign destinations are 37 cents for the first ounce and 57 cents for up to 2 ounces. Airmail letters to foreign destinations other than to Canada, Mexico and some Caribbean and South American countries are 44 cents per half ounce, 88¢ for 1 ounce, $1.32 for 1½ ounces, $1.76 for 2 ounces. Postcards, except for Canada and Mexico, which go airmail for 14 cents, are 25 cents for surface mail and 33 cents for airmail to any foreign destination. Standard international aerogram letters, good for any foreign destination, are 36¢, but of course nothing may be enclosed in them. Postal rates are no exception in this period of inflation, so check before you mail—in case they have gone up.

CONVERTING METRIC TO U.S. MEASUREMENTS

Multiply:	by:	to find:
Length		
millimeters (mm)	.039	inches (in)
meters (m)	3.28	feet (ft)
meters	1.09	yards (yd)
kilometers (km)	.62	miles (mi)
Area		
hectare (ha)	2.47	acres
Capacity		
liters (L)	1.06	quarts (qt)
liters	.26	gallons (gal)
liters	2.11	pints (pt)
Weight		
gram (g)	.04	ounce (oz)
kilogram (kg)	2.20	pounds (lb)
metric ton (MT)	.98	tons (t)
Power		
kilowatt (kw)	1.34	horsepower (hp)
Temperature		
degrees Celsius	9/5 (then add 32)	degrees Fahrenheit

CONVERTING U.S. TO METRIC MEASUREMENTS

Multiply:	by	to find:
Length		
inches (in)	25.40	millimeters (mm)
feet (ft)	.30	meters (m)
yards (yd)	.91	meters
miles (mi)	1.61	kilometers (km)
Area		
acres	.40	hectares (ha)
Multiply:	**by**	**to find:**
Capacity		
pints (pt)	.47	liters (L)
quarts (qt)	.95	liters
gallons (gal)	3.79	liters
Weight		
ounces (oz)	28.35	grams (g)
pounds (lb)	.45	kilograms (kg)
tons (t)	1.11	metric tons (MT)

Power
horsepower (hp)　　　　　　　　　.75　　　　　　　　kilowatts

Temperature
degrees Fahrenheit　　　5/9 (after subtracting 32)　　degrees Celsius

 **SECURITY.** New England, you'll be happy to hear, is among the safer areas of the country, particularly in the more rural regions. In Boston and other large cities, caution is *always* advised—as it is anywhere—but consider that outside the cities, many New Englanders barely even lock their front doors! Carrying travelers checks rather than cash is a good idea any time—remembering to keep a record of the checks' serial numbers. Always lock your car and don't leave valuables in sight in an automobile or ever in a hotel room. (Inns rarely even have locks on their guest-room doors.)

 **EMERGENCY TELEPHONE NUMBERS.** Calling the Operator (dial "0") will always bring assistance; the use of 911 as an emergency number is not consistent throughout the region.

 **RECOMMENDED READING. Fiction:** A superb evocation of the New England temperament is John P. Marquand's Pulitzer Prize novel, *The Late George Apley.* For the early history that is still so vividly present in New England, the historical novels of Maine's Kenneth Roberts, *Arundel, Oliver Wiswell, Rabble in Arms,* etc., are solidly researched and well written. Edith Wharton's famous *Ethan Frome* is a rather narrow view of an archetypal New England of her imagination that the visitor is highly unlikely to see except in his.

Nonfiction: Although they were written in the late 1930s, the individual state volumes of the Federal Writers Project are still surprisingly useful. The background information—history, geography, geology, flora, fauna, etc.—has not changed. The political, social and economic material is variously out of date but makes interesting comparisons with present conditions. The sightseeing material—specific sites, monuments, museums, natural beauty—is still very helpful, as are in particular the suggested walking itineraries. At your public library.

For a thorough, serious, and unvarnished look at this region as it is today, see *The New England States, People Power, and Politics in the Six New England States,* by Neal R. Pierce (W.W. Norton, 1976). For an informative and amusing look at New England and New Englanders, read Judson Hale's *Inside New England* (Harper & Row, 1982).

For specific areas, try, among others: *The Proper Bostonians,* by Cleveland Amory (Parnassus, 1984); *The Old Post Road* (Boston to New York), by Stewart H. Holbrook (McGraw-Hill, 1962); *Connecticut: A New Guide,* By William Bixby (Scribners, 1974); *The Outermost House* (Cape Cod), by Henry Beston (Ballantine, 1976). If out of print, these books can probably be found at your local library.

Those with an interest in hiking the thousands of miles of trails throughout this region should obtain a copy of the Appalachian Mountain Club trail book for the particular area in which they'll be staying. For a wider range of hikers, walkers and cross-country skiers, consult *Berkshire Trails for Walking and Ski Touring,* by Whit Griswold (East Woods Press, 1979). And an outstanding guide to the local flora and fauna is *A Sierra Club Naturalist's Guide to Southern New England,* by Neil Jorgensen (San Francisco, 1978). Antique collectors will do well to follow the advice of *The Weekend Connoisseur,* by Joan Brasin (Dolphin, 1979), which covers New England extensively.

The great photographer of New England was Samuel Chamberlain; any of his books will give you a beautiful evocation of the flavor of this region. Regional magazines published in and about New England include *Vermont Life, New Hampshire Profiles, New England Monthly,* and *Yankee.* For a closer look at the real daily life and non-tourist side of New England, when you are there read *The Maine Times* and *The New Hampshire Times,* both weekly newspapers specializing in feature articles, investigative journalism and the long-range issues and problems that confront New England as they do the entire country in a fast-changing time. The livelier side of Boston can be found in *The Boston Phoenix,* a weekly tabloid, or the slick monthly magazine, *Boston.*

THE NEW ENGLAND SCENE

INTRODUCTION

Yankee Come Home

by
JUDSON D. HALE, SR.

Born in Boston, raised on a farm in Maine, Judson Hale has been with
Yankee Magazine *and* The Old Farmer's Almanac *(both published in
Dublin, New Hampshire) since 1958—Editor of both since 1970—and
is author of* Inside New England, *a book published in 1982 by Harper
and Row and from which the following is adapted.*

A "Yankee" has been variously defined as an American, a northern
American, a New Englander, an old native of Vermont, Maine, or Cape
Cod, and an old Vermont native who eats apple pie for breakfast—with
a knife.

There is no real consensus on the word. Some define it by geography;
others maintain it is more a state of mind.

The same is often said about New England. However, in actual fact,
New England consists of everything within the geographical bound-
aries of Maine, New Hampshire, Vermont, Massachusetts, Rhode Island, and Connecticut. No more, no less. Six very proud, very
independent, and very different entities, which, together, represent a
formidable political, economic, and spiritual force in America. The

American character, as it's generally perceived, is derived historically from the people who inhabited and migrated west from these six states.

Maine's Four Faces

Maine is beautiful and Maine is ugly. I remember driving from Sedgwick to Brooksville several summers ago and stopping at the top of Caterpillar Hill. There before me was Maine the beautiful—Walker Pond in the foreground, the ocean beyond dotted with dark, pine-covered islands of all shapes and sizes, the bridge crossing Eggemoggin Reach, so familiar to yachtsmen, Deere Isle with its thin road winding down towards Stonington, and, in the far distance, the Camden hills. This is the Maine that lives in the hearts of all New Englanders as well as visitors—the Maine of artists, of poets, of the soul.

Then there is back-country Maine, "the Maine that artists do not paint, writers do not usually describe, and visitors do not talk about," wrote Charles E. Clark in *Maine, A History.* It is "the Maine where scrubby woodlands alternate with bleak, unshaded villages marked by an old general store and a Baptist Church, but also by a laundromat, a couple of gas stations, and a Dairy Joy, and where the houses may have sheet metal roofs . . . " People in back-country Maine say a house is a house, but a house with a shed is a village. This is the Maine that shows up near the bottom of annual United States per capita income listings.

A third Maine is the forested wilderness, the Maine of white-water canoeing, hunting, fishing, mosquitoes big enough to carry you away, old Maine guides, lumbering, and tall tales. In *The Jonesport Raffle,* author John Gould recalls a fishing story contest in Montana that a Maine backwoodsman decided to enter by mail. "The prize was to be a new fly rod, but he (the Mainer) said he never used a rod—he hid on the bank of the stream and clubbed the trout with a baseball bat when they came up to pick blueberries."

Still another Maine is potato Maine, hugging the New Brunswick border for over a hundred miles, an open, rolling area that everyone in the United States has heard about but fewer than several outsiders have ever been to! School starts in Aroostook County in mid-August, and that's bad news for kids. On the other hand, all the schools then close for three whole weeks in September to enable children to spend (legally) dawn-to-dusk days harvesting potatoes. Up there, that's known as a bad news–bad news story.

I once asked a little New Hampshire first grader touring the *Yankee* offices if she'd like to pick potatoes in Maine in September instead of going to school. She said, "Sure—it wouldn't last long, anyway. No one lives in Maine all year 'round. Maine's closed in the winter."

Although traditionally Down Easterners are noted for their plain and direct manner of communicating, I think Mainers are actually the most *indirect* of all New Englanders. To obtain a straight answer to a straight question in Maine is often next to impossible.

For example:

Visitor: "Can you tell me where the hotel is in this town?"

Mainer: "What hotel?" (Mainers like to answer a question *with* a question.)

Visitor: "Oh, is there more than one hotel here?"

Mainer: "Didn't know there was any."

Somewhere deep within the Maine psyche is a strong instinct to avoid being pinned down.

Frugality and Shrewdness in New Hampshire

New Hampshire and Vermont are often lumped together by outsiders, but residents of both states are aware how remarkably different each is from the other. New Hampshire is mentally oriented to small businesses and manufacturing. On the other hand, there's probably no other state in the union as rural in complexion as Vermont. New Hampshire is politically conservative. In recent years, Vermont has enacted some of the most liberal environmental legislation in the nation, including the banning of all billboards. I'm always conscious of the immediate difference one "feels" when crossing the Connecticut River from Vermont to New Hampshire or vice versa. Much of Vermont is open farmland. New Hampshire is almost completely forested. So many of Vermont's villages appear almost unreal—as if they had been created by Grandma Moses. New Hampshire's villages seem totally unconscious of whether or not they are picturesque. (Thus, many are not.)

In a cultural sense, the two states lean away from each other, too— Vermont in spite of itself, towards New York and New Yorkers; New Hampshire towards Massachusetts and southern New England.

Like Maine, New Hampshire has more than one personality. There's the prosperous, booming if somewhat faceless southern half of the state that has all but become a suburb of Boston. Then there's the northern half. Up there are towns like Pittsburg, the largest town east of the Mississippi River, with a 30-mile-long main street that rambles through a wilderness of lakes, mountains, and evergreen forests, inhabited by moose, bear, deer, loons, a few humans, and snowmobiles. Movie theaters, department stores, and hospitals are as far as twenty miles away. Many jobs are further.

"When people ask us how we like living up here in the northern New Hampshire woods," a Colebrook man told me recently, "it's like asking someone who has eaten porridge every single day of his entire life, 'How's the porridge?' "

Though frugality and shrewdness in business dealings are traits characteristic of New Englanders as a whole, I think New Hampshirites are the most frugal of all. Possibly it has something to do with the overall conservative and business orientation of the state.

A typical New Hampshire story, for instance, concerns two Berlin (remember—pronounced *Ber*lin) men discussing the hard financial times. One asks the other how in the world he has managed to feed his large family on such a low income.

"I'll tell you," is the reply, "I find out what they don't like and then I give 'em plenty of it."

Vermont's Responsibilities

Being a Vermonter carries with it some heavy responsibilities. To be precise, six of them.

(1) First of all, a Vermonter must possess a great deal of common sense. Although 100,000 adults living in Vermont today never finished high school, ignorance is not a lack of education but rather a lack of common sense.

"That Hardwick road sign back there is pointing off in the wrong direction, isn't it?"

"Sure it is, but anyone with a little common sense knows how to get to Hardwick."

(2) A Vermonter is expected to display a certain amount of dry humor. Senator George Aiken fulfilled this Vermont duty throughout his political career—as did Cal Coolidge—and the country appreciated the effort. It's somehow comforting to Americans when a Vermonter acts like "a Vermonter." We all smiled and felt good inside when Aiken advised President Lyndon Johnson to declare the Vietnam war won and pull out the troops. It would not have been as amusing or even as wise if someone from another state had said it.

(3) A Vermonter must have integrity. Its state government does. Historian Neal Peirce ranks it as one of only five states in America—and the only state in New England—that is free of political corruption. (The others: Minnesota, Wisconsin, Oregon, and Hawaii.) The old story is that there are so few nickels in Vermont that every politician knows where each one is located, making it impossible for anyone to steal one.

The closest thing to official "manipulating" of finances I've ever heard about in Vermont—and the story is actually more an example of honesty—occurred at a small country church then located outside Rutland. Because the congregation had dwindled down to almost nothing, the members decided to disband. The question of the disposal of funds in the church treasury came up during the final meeting, when the treasurer reported there was a sum of eighty dollars on hand. One of the members suggested that forty dollars of this be given to Zeke Tuttle, a church member who was ill with tuberculosis at the time.

Several months later, a member who had not attended the final meeting ran into the church treasurer in town and asked him whatever became of the money in the treasury of the now-disbanded church.

"At our last meeting, we voted to give forty dollars of the eighty we had to Zeke Tuttle because he was sick," the treasurer replied.

"What about the rest?"

"Well," said the treasurer without a hint of hesitation, "I wasn't feeling any too good myself, so I kept the rest."

(4) Vermonters, unlike Mainers, are expected to speak in a simple, direct, no-nonsense manner. Possibly it's all part of the Vermont version of honesty and integrity.

Many, many Vermont stories, like those collected in Keith Jennison's book, *"Yup . . . Nope" and Other Vermont Dialogues,* feature this sort of direct approach in conversation:

Question: "What do you suppose they'll do when old man Appleby dies?"

Answer: "Bury him."

Question: "Think it's ever going to stop snowing?"

Answer: "Always has."

Question: "Can you tell me when the next train leaves for Boston?"

Answer: "It left more'n ten years ago."

There must be a thousand more of these.

(5) A Vermonter has the responsibility to be a free and independent thinker. Independence and freedom are honored throughout New England but in Vermont they are virtually a religion. An Ethan Allen statement along that line is a popular quote: "I am as determined to preserve the independence of Vermont as Congress is that of the Union,

and rather than fail I will retire with my hardy Green Mountain boys into the caverns of the mountains and make war on all mankind."

(6) Finally, some Vermonters are expected to be willing to put in a full hard day's work for a meager day's pay. Throughout the state, but particularly in the three northern counties known as the Northeast Kingdom, there is much poverty.

Charles Morrissey describes it with brutal clarity:

"Do the touring shutterbugs who snap pictures of scenic Vermont vistas ever wonder who lives in all the trailers and all the shacky houses they don't record on films? Do they notice the sad and ugly towns they drive through to get to the pristine villages which outsiders have restored?"

Nonetheless, most residents of the Green Mountain State would agree that Vermont is "an experience" as well as a geographic area of New England, but to outsiders, who own most of the state anyway, Vermont is a place you feel homesick for even before you've left it.

Puritan Massachusetts

Massachusetts is called the Hub of the Universe. That's not a name given in jest. As a Massachusetts native, I can say that pride in the Bay State has always spilled over into what outsiders might consider to be arrogance. The Massachusetts image exported to the outside seems to consist of Harvard, Boston Brahmins, the Puritans, the Kennedys and their accent, liberalism, do-gooders, Concord/Lexington, and a sort of "we know best" attitude toward the rest of America. Not included in the exported image are the high taxes and cost of living, the interminable political corruption, racial antagonism, and the fact that besides lawyers the Massachusetts legislature is dominated by funeral directors.

The notion that a region's humor often is based on regional personality traits, much exaggerated, is borne out by Massachusetts. Its high self-esteem shines forth in all the old favorites, such as . . .

Two Massachusetts (or Boston) women went to San Francisco and ran into a particularly hot spell there. As they were stewing on Treasure Island, one said to the other, "My dear, I never expected to be so hot in San Francisco." To which her companion replied, "But, my dear, you must remember that we're 3,000 miles from the ocean."

Or, and there are many variations to this one . . .

A visitor in Boston sought to speak with A. Lawrence Lowell, then president of Harvard, who had been called to Washington by President William Howard Taft for a White House conference on education. The visitor was informed by the secretary in Lowell's outer office that "The president is in Washington seeing Mr. Taft." Tell that story to many Massachusetts residents, most Bostonians, or *any* Harvard graduate, and they won't understand why it's funny.

Massachusetts is still fueled by the Puritan ethic, probably more so than any other New England state. When the late Mary Peabody, mother of Governor Endicott Peabody and wife of the late Malcolm Peabody, Episcopal Bishop of central New York, went to St. Augustine, Florida, at age 72 to join in a civil rights demonstration and ended up in jail, she was considered by many people across America as simply a meddling, do-gooding, old coot looking for headlines. New Englanders knew better. While not everyone agreed with her actions, she was recognized as being sincere. The tradition she was exemplifying runs strong and deep in Massachusetts.

"Do your duty, do your part in life—that's what being a New Englander means to me," she later told my Dublin, New Hampshire neighbor, author Richard Meryman, when he talked with her in her Cambridge home fourteen years later. "Doing your duty, caring for things that are good and true, being a terrible prig, I suppose."

The fuel shortage had begun at the time of Meryman's *Yankee* interview. "I don't allow myself a fire if I don't have anybody here," said this frail, then-86-year-old widow lady, as she sat, covered by a shawl, the thermostat set at sixty, in her ancestral home surrounded by memorabilia of her distinguished, wealthy, and influential ancestors.

"In my mother-in-law's Bible, after she died, I found a little note she had written to herself. It said, 'Remember to be cheerful.' I think that's very important, not to complain, to say you're lonely all the time. All I say is, I'm cold all the time . . . I'm very frugal. Also, the thing to do is to save energy. So I put on layers like the Chinese. My layers of clothes."

After reading this I felt like calling John Winthrop, Cotton Mather, or any of the old-time Massachusetts Puritans and asking them to let poor old Mary Peabody off the hook. Tell her she can have a fire now. She can say she's lonely. Let her alone! But of course that wouldn't help. *She* would tell *them* how it ought to be. The Puritan tradition doesn't depend upon "permission" from anybody, past or present. For Mary Peabody, the only voice of authority was that which was deep within her—the voice of her New England Conscience.

West of the general Boston area is, naturally and logically, western Massachusetts. Because of its political isolation, growing educational institutions, and curious mixture of old-time natives and idealistic but maturing dreamers left over from the hippie generation, Ralph Nader once referred to western Massachusetts as "the most interesting part of the United States." In what's known as the Pioneer Valley, bankers are likely to grow organic vegetables, communes are running hard-nosed businesses for profit, the solar-heated Williamsburg General Store sells unsalted potato chips, and, as a food cooperative worker was heard to remark, "It's hard to find a good Swiss cheese that's politically acceptable."

Accuracy in Rhode Island

The State of Rhode Island and the Providence Plantations are the official names. Other names for it have been "The Plantation of the Otherwise-Minded" and "Rogues Island." At one time the greatest slave-trading colony in America, Rhode Island was the first civilized community anywhere that allowed freedom of religion. Of its Roger Williams psyche emphasizing freedom of conscience and action, Massachusetts Puritan Cotton Mather said, "If a man lost his religion, he might find it at this general muster of opinionists."

Little Rhody or The Ocean State is still a "general muster of opinionists" and, as such, has just naturally developed a reputation for tolerance. It has the only fishing cooperative in New England; it calmly abides various elements such as the Mafia in its little midst; of all today's native New Englanders, only Rhode Islanders will tolerate adding a can of tomato (ugh!) soup to the end of their clam chowder recipes; and probably due to its "sweatshop," nonunion costume jewelry factories, its average factory wage is almost 20% below the national average.

Of course, it's small. Only 47½ miles long and, at most, 40 miles wide. Yet it has more people than either Vermont or New Hampshire. If you live in the Rhode Island countryside you can, as they say, be in the city in seven minutes. But, like a person of small stature, Rhode Island absolutely refuses to be overlooked or ignored in any situation. Once a Rhode Islander gets started on the subject of Rhode Island, he or she can almost, but not quite, become downright belligerent.

"Do you realize Rhode Island was the *first* colony to disregard the British stamp act?" a museum curator suddenly sprung on me as we were sifting through some photographs of nineteenth-century Cranston (pronounced "Creeanston").

"We were also the *first* to officially renounce allegiance to Great Britain," the little bombardment continued, "among the *first* to adopt the Articles of Confederation, and *first* to fire a cannon at any British naval vessel."

"Really?" I responded, attempting to lift the appearance of my own interest to his earnest level. "Oh, sure," he continued, "and the *first* Baptist Church is in Providence, the *first* Jewish Synagogue in America is in Newport, the country's *first* cotton mill, started by Samuel Slater, was begun in Pawtucket in 1790, the *first* lighthouse on the American coast was built at Beavertail back in 1749 . . . " and on and on.

Concern for accuracy—particularly historical accuracy—is a trait shared by all New Englanders, but it seems most highly developed in Rhode Islanders. Their noted tolerance in other matters evidently does not extend to errors.

When we mentioned in an article that the distance from Rhode Island to New York was many miles, we heard not a word from our subscribers in New York, the second largest state for the number of *Yankee* subscriptions. From Rhode Island we received an avalanche of mail, each letter and postcard pointing out to us that the two states actually border one another—out in Long Island Sound. Many gave us a seagull analogy. "A seagull, should he choose to, might sit in the water at a certain point in Long Island Sound and have his tail in New York, his beak in Rhode Island, and his left wing in Connecticut."

In southern Massachusetts, near Webster, is a lake we once called in *Yankee* Lake Chargoggagoggmanchauggauggagoggchaubunagungamaugg. A few days after the issue was sent out, we heard from several Rhode Islanders who told us we had misspelled it. It should have been Lake Chargoggagoggmanchaugagoggchaubunagungamaugg. We noted and corrected the error in our next issue.

Connecticut Yankees

Historically, Connecticut is the most "Yankee" of all the New England states. If you are of the school that believes that the Dutch were responsible for the word "Yankee" (evolving from "John Cheese"), then it is logical to believe it was the Dutch in New York who began applying the term to their English neighbors in Connecticut.

Connecticut Yankees were principally responsible for establishing the smart, shrewd, clever, and, well, slippery reputation of Yankees everywhere. Early Connecticut peddlers, with their leaky calf weaners, wooden nutmegs, defective clocks, and cigars that would not draw, traveled from town to town around New England and eventually the entire country—always moving fast enough to be out of town before anyone realized they'd been had. It was often said, "You might as well try to hold a greased eel as a live Connecticut Yankee."

Now, when two Connecticut Yankees bargained together, that was the stuff of stories—hundreds of them. This one's typical:

While plowing his fields one spring, a Connecticut farmer's horse suddenly expired and fell lifeless in the field. The farmer left it lying there still hitched to the plow and walked several miles to the house of his neighbor who, it so happened, had tricked the farmer's wife into buying what turned out to be a fake nutmeg the year before. He found his neighbor whittling something out on his back doorstep. "Ben," he said after suitable exchanges on the weather, "I feel like swapping something today. You know that black and white horse of mine?"

"Yes," replied his neighbor as he continued to whittle, "I know him well."

"Well, then, you know he's younger than your big bay but he may not be as big and strong. How would you like to swap your bay horse for him?"

"Even?"

"Yes. Even."

"You've got a deal," said his neighbor, and they solemnly shook on it, whereupon the farmer, typically honest about his double dealings and with a pleased smile on his face said, "Well, Ben, your brand new horse is dead. He's lying out in the field. Keeled over while I was plowing with him this morning."

"All right, fine," replied his neighbor. "My big bay horse died last night before last, and his skin is hanging out in the back shed."

But there was a more positive side to the Connecticut Yankee. In time his ingenious approaches, clever ideas, original thinking, and skillful craftsmanship evolved into a virtue proudly claimed by *all* New Englanders today. In fact, it's claimed by all Americans. Usually preceded by the words "good" and "old," it's now known as Yankee Ingenuity, and it's credited with, among other things, winning World War II.

Connecticut has a valid point in claiming Yankee Ingenuity as its own. Since the United States Patent Office opened in 1790, Connecticut has averaged more patents each year per thousand of population than any other state in the Union or any other country in the world! Nutmeggers have invented everything from the submarine, anesthesia, radar speed detectors, sky hooks, and the grinder to the cotton gin, pistols with revolving cylinders, lattice-truss covered bridges, and the lollipop. And it was a Connecticut inventor, one Samuel Morey, who *steamed* down the Connecticut River in 1787, fourteen years before "Tricky Bob" Fulton did *his* steamboat thing.

Like New Hampshire, Connecticut has a split personality. There's Fairfield County with its "Gold Coast" New York bedroom towns of New Canaan, Darien, Westport, Stamford, Greenwich et al. And then there's the rest of Connecticut. From time to time, a movement begins to lop off Connecticut's Fairfield County from New England and either give it to New York or make it a state on its own. That will never happen, of course. One doesn't disown one's own brother simply because he has become, over the course of many years, rich, white, Protestant, successful, Republican, country-clubby, and in love with New York City and the train ride to and from.

The coast of Connecticut is divided, too. From New Haven on down to the New York line is general industrial ugliness occasionally relieved by fancy yacht sanctuaries. Yet many harbors from New Haven east have lobster boats and a "Down East" look. The towns in the general area around the mouths of the Connecticut and Thames Rivers— Groton, Stonington, Old Saybrook, Old Lyme, Essex—are among the most picturesque and well-to-do in all of New England. They're also *very* protective of their privacy. In Garson Kanin's *Tracy and Hepburn,* the late Spencer Tracy told a story about a Sunday dinner with Katharine Hepburn, a Connecticut native, and her family at their beach house in Old Saybrook. They were all debating the basic "rights of the common man" when the actress's father, in the middle of an impassioned speech on the subject, spotted a lone stranger walking along the beach in front of the house. In an instant, the whole family was out on the porch yelling, "Hey—this is private property! Get off the beach immediately!" When the intruder had been properly routed, Dr. Hepburn and family returned to the table and, a bit short of breath, took up the defense of the common man once again.

The very nature of the Connecticut Yankee is that of a survivor. So if the future can be called an everlasting extension of the past, Connecticut will always be Connecticut—Fairfield County and all, insurance companies and all, changes and all—forever and ever.

What other state in the Union can *ever* truthfully say that one of its existing daily newspapers reported the story of the Boston Tea Party as straight news? The *Hartford Courant* did, and shortly thereafter counted among its advertisers a Virginian named George Washington.

Coming Home to New England

Each New England state shares the characteristics of the other five to some degree. Mix Maine's tall stories and run-around manner of answering questions with New Hampshire's frugality and Vermont's common sense, integrity, and laconic, wise humor. Then add the Puritan ethic of Massachusetts with a generous dash of Rhode Island tolerance, pride, and concern for historical details. Top all that with a dose of Connecticut's shrewdness and Yankee Ingenuity and, behold, New England! For authentic additional flavoring, garnish with the ethnic influences of the French, Portuguese, Irish, Italians, Poles, and Armenians and, for good measure, throw in some fickle weather, five thousand or more legends, a ghost or two, exactly nine versions of the word ayuh (an outsider can learn the nine definitions and when to use each but can never, in a lifetime, learn the proper pronunciations), a good old-fashioned Rhode Island clambake and a smattering of clam chowder (*without tomatoes*), baked beans, codfish, lobsters, maple syrup, jonnycake, hulled corn, and apple pie.

And yet New England means something slightly different to each New Englander.

At a recent church supper in Springfield, Massachusetts, following a talk about New England I gave at an historical society there, we all started discussing what New England meant to each of us.

"New England is where neighbors help neighbors mend each other's fences, and New England is where they say what they *mean.* "

"New England is where it all began and where a feeling of continuity is still strong."

Several people chose to describe it in physical or visual terms.

"New England is the little village in the Christmas cards—and what many outsiders are surprised about is that the little village really exists!"

"New England is coming into Northeast Harbor under sail after a beautiful day in Frenchman's Bay—and picking up the buoy the first time around!"

"New England is eating homemade coffee ice cream and sitting on the cannon in front of the Old Sloop Church in Rockport, Massachusetts, watching some fife and drum corps march by in the Fourth of July parade."

A visitor from Cleveland, Ohio, at the table said, "New England—it all seems so *substantial.*"

Finally, an elderly, distinguished-looking gentleman at the head of the table said quietly, "To me, New England is coming home." We all nodded in agreement, but none of us wished to risk diminishing the statement by attempting further explanation.

However, I think we could all *feel* his meaning. "Coming home" constitutes, perhaps, an image that doesn't necessarily have anything to do with maple-shaded village greens, lobsters, Beacon Hill, Vermont's orange hills in autumn, or anything else commonly associated with our region. "Coming home" is a personal, very private image of New England.

At a certain time when I'm as old or older than the gentleman in Springfield, I know where I'll be, wherever I am. It will be very early on a calm, warm late-June morning on New Hampshire's Lake Winnipesaukee. I'll walk down to the water's edge below my camp on Sleepers Island, rest on the bench I built there years before, and sip from a mug of hot coffee. The sun will glisten through the tall pine trees behind me. In the distance, I'll hear the faint sound of an outboard motor, but the huge lake before me, lying there in its myriad of undulating reflections, will be otherwise free of human activity. Then, far down near The Witches and Forty Islands, I'll see a dark, faintly ominous-looking band of ruffled water creeping slowly toward me along the entire breadth of the lake from Meredith Bay to Moultonborough Neck. There'll be long-ago voices and laughter like distant music. A solitary leaf on the poplar tree leaning over the shore near me will flap lazily as if in preparation for the daily summertime wind—inevitably on its way as always. While I wait for it calmly in the temporary magical stillness of early morning, just as I have done a thousand times before, I'll look across the water to the hills that rise over the faraway shores and then on and on beyond for miles and miles of misty-blue mountains to the north.

THE HERITAGE TRAIL

A Special Tour of New England

by
GEOFFREY NORMAN

Geoffrey Norman is a resident of Vermont and a contributing editor of Esquire *magazine.*

If you have the time—and there is almost no upper limit on the amount of time you could spend doing it—then the best way to see New England is to follow the Heritage Trail. The trail has some of everything that New England has to offer, and what New England has to offer is both ample and varied. By driving the trail you will be giving yourself the opportunity to take things at the New England pace which can be as briskly urban as Boston during rush hour or as serene as a Vermont village on the Fourth of July.

The trail makes a rather ragged loop and it is perhaps easiest to imagine it as starting in Boston and then heading north. From Boston, the trail follows the coast of northern Massachusetts past Salem then through Gloucester, Rockport, and Ipswich on across the state line and into New Hampshire. The coast of New Hampshire is an abrupt affair consisting, it seems, almost entirely of Portsmouth. Then you are in Maine, driving its celebrated coast to such destinations as Freeport and

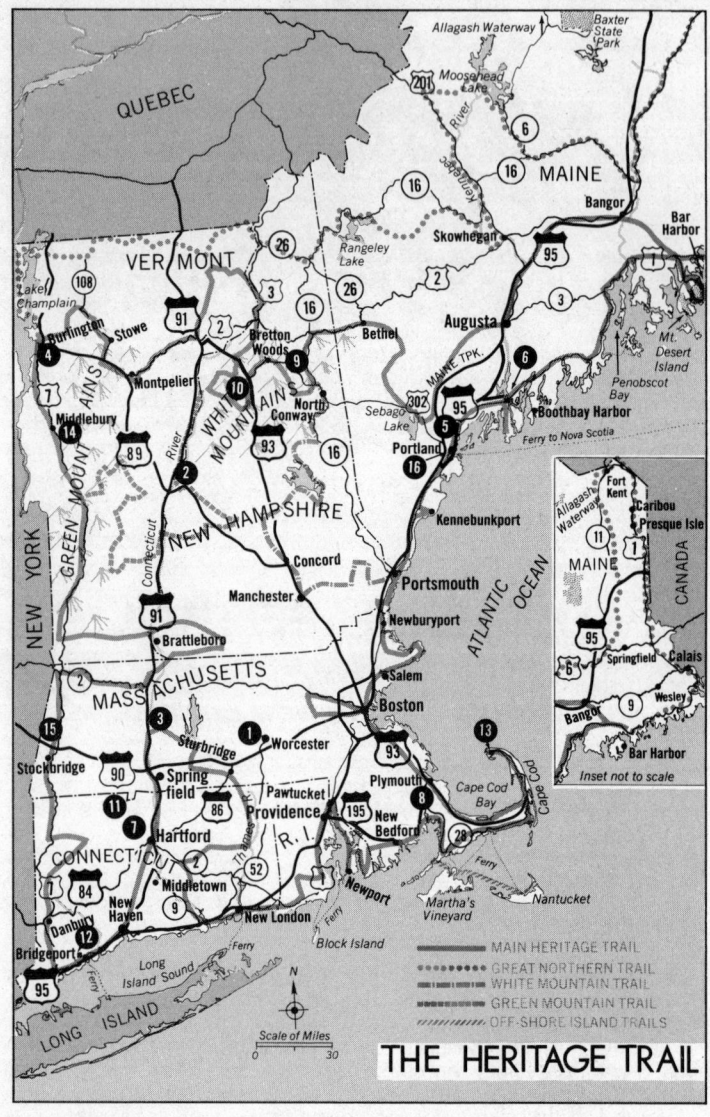

THE HERITAGE TRAIL

MAIN HERITAGE TRAIL
GREAT NORTHERN TRAIL
WHITE MOUNTAIN TRAIL
GREEN MOUNTAIN TRAIL
OFF-SHORE ISLAND TRAILS

Points of Interest

1) Centrum Civic Center
2) Dartmouth College
3) Emily Dickinson Home
4) Ethan Allen Burial Place
5) L.L. Bean
6) Maine Maritime Museum
7) Mark Twain Memorial
8) Mayflower II
9) Mt. Washington Cog Railway
10) Old Man of the Mountains
11) Old Newgate Prison
12) P.T. Barnum Museum
13) Provincetown Artist Colony
14) Robert Frost Farmstead
15) Tanglewood Festival
16) Wadsworth Longfellow House

Bar Harbor, on Mount Desert Island, with its adjacent and magnificent views.

You then proceed to Bangor and make your decision to either push on along the Great Northern branch or cut back east across the interior of the state continuing on the main trail. The northern route carries you almost to the Canadian line swinging into central Maine through virtual wilderness and small towns with names as appropriate as Caribou and Portage, and then skirts the shores of Moosehead Lake. The lower route takes you through Augusta, Lewiston, and Bethel. While the scenery is probably less spectacular than the northern route, it is the quicker and more prudent course during times of bad weather—or if your time is limited.

Both arms of the trail cross high in New Hampshire, through the beautiful White Mountains on the main trail and at the headwaters of the Connecticut River on the Great Northern Trail. From the main trail, you may take another detour along the White Mountain Trail, through North Conway and on down past the shores of Lake Winnipesaukee, cutting all the way back to Portsmouth. If you stay on either the main trail or the Great Northern, you will cross into Vermont, either on the state's border with Canada or across its midsection through the capital, Montpelier.

There is yet another detour available from the main trail at this point. It is the Green Mountain Trail and it winds across the Vermont–New Hampshire line, through mountains older than the Rockies, Alps, or Himalayas. The Green Mountains are worn down by time, round and relatively low and very easily traversed. Also, unforgettably beautiful.

The main trail crosses back into Massachusetts below Brattleboro, Vermont and then begins to meander through that state until it reaches Connecticut where it follows the coastline of Long Island Sound through Fairfield, Bridgeport, and West Haven until it turns abruptly inland to Hartford and then crosses back into Massachusetts. There is a brief loop through that state, touching Amherst and Sturbridge, before the trail swoops back down into Connecticut and swings once more up the coast through New London and Mystic. Then it moves into Rhode Island, touching both the coast at Newport and the capital, Providence, inland. Again, if you have time, you can take a detour onto the offshore island trail to visit Block Island off Rhode Island's coast.

The main trail then makes its final crossing into Massachusetts, passing through New Bedford on its way out to the Cape and Provincetown. There is another offshore detour here that will take you to Martha's Vineyard and Nantucket. Then it is back up the coast once more via the main trail, through Plymouth and on back to Boston where the journey began.

The Heritage Trail covers some 2,000 miles and there are over 1,000 specific points of interest along the way. That does not include those singular, spontaneous moments that occur to every traveler in this part of the country. With so much available, it is perhaps more enlightening to suggest than to catalogue what is there for the traveler along the Heritage Trail.

Say that you are especially interested in history. The richness of colonial and revolutionary history is abundantly available. You might visit Plymouth Rock and the *Mayflower II* in Plymouth, Mass., the Pioneer Village and the Witch Museum in Salem, Mass., and Old Newgate Prison in East Granby, Conn. You can walk the battlefields of Lexington, Concord, and Bunker Hill in Massachusetts and in Bennington, Vt. There are museums that preserve the region's nautical past such as the Mystic Seaport Museum in Connecticut, the Whaling Museum in New Bedford, Mass., and the Maine Maritime Museum in Bath. You could visit the birthplace of Daniel Webster in Franklin, N. H. or Ethan Allen's grave in Burlington, Vt. The entire New England region is redolent of history—so much so, in fact, that it is possible to specialize and tour according to what interests you most.

You could, for instance, use the trail for the purpose of taking a literary tour through the country. Never detouring too far from the main trail or from one of its branches, you could visit Henry David Thoreau's Walden Pond near Concord, Mass., the homes of both Mark Twain and Harriett Beecher Stowe in Hartford, Conn., Nathaniel Hawthorne's House of Seven Gables in Salem, Mass., Henry Wadsworth Longfellow's home in Cambridge, Mass. or the Wayside Inn in South Sudbury that he immortalized, Emily Dickinson's home in Amherst, Mass., Ralph Waldo Emerson's home in Concord, Mass. and a number of sites where Robert Frost lived and worked such as the Robert Frost Farmstead in Ripton, Vt. The region continues to be fertile literary ground and the trail passes a few miles west of Bread Loaf, Vt., the site of the most celebrated summer writing workshop in the nation, and perhaps the world.

Similarly, if one is interested chiefly in art there is more than enough along the trail to make the trip memorable. From the artist colony in Provincetown on Cape Cod to the Worcester Art Museum in central Massachusetts, the Museum of Fine Art in Providence, R.I., the Farnsworth Art Museum in Rockland, Maine, and the Southern Vermont Art Center in Manchester. There is something as well for those whose taste runs to the performing arts, especially in the summer when theater festivals are in progress all over the region—particularly the Tanglewood Music Festival in Lenox, Mass. and the Marlboro Music Festival in southern Vermont.

Sports lovers will find their share of opportunity along the trail. You may fish the surf off Cape Cod for blues or Maine's Penobscot River for the Atlantic salmon considered by many to be the prince of gamefish. For outdoor outfitting you can visit L.L. Bean in Freeport, Maine, which is open 24 hours a day. You can cast to rising brown trout on Vermont's famous Battenkill. You might also canoe some of the wild rivers of Maine, climb some of the challenging faces of New Hampshire's White Mountains, or sail off Newport, Rhode Island or Block Island.

Almost all of the best skiing and the most elaborate ski resorts in the East are within striking distance of the trail. Stowe in Vermont is the East's oldest ski resort and Mount Mansfield which looms over the town is the highest mountain in the state. The ski resorts range from world class to day trip affairs with prices varying accordingly. At the right time of year, you could virtually ski your way around the region.

Finally, it is possible to make the circuit of the Heritage Trail with nothing more than the view in mind. Even then—especially then—the traveler will not be disappointed. There is breathtaking beauty everywhere you look in New England and nowhere does one vista give way to another so totally different as it does in New England, where rocky sea coasts, tall mountains, and wide stretches of flat, timber covered lands are all within a few hours' drive of one another. Furthermore, the traveler will find the way eased by the kind of accommodations that are not available anywhere else in the country. The country inn survives in New England, making the end of a day's traveling something to anticipate as eagerly as any monument or museum.

The best time, of course, is in the Fall when the leaves are in their brilliant colors and the crisp air is full of harvest smells. Nights at the inn will be cold enough for a blanket and there will be frosts in the morning. And the countryside will be . . . it will be, quite simply, incomparable.

WHERE TO GO IN NEW ENGLAND

A Capsule View of New England States

by
GEOFFREY NORMAN

Although we always hear about "New England," it is important to remember that the area is comprised of six unique states. If you don't have time for a complete tour of each of the states, the following run-down may help you narrow down your choices of which to visit.

Connecticut

Connecticut is a small state, compact and efficient as the many industries that have sprung up and thrived there. The state is probably best known today for Fairfield County where New York executives return every night on trains to the prosperity of its bedroom communities. But there is much more to Connecticut—including even the farming of tobacco which is used in the making of cigar wrappers. Of more interest to the traveler, Connecticut is a haven for the performing arts and the site of numerous museums, some of general nature and some highly specialized. Among its theaters are the Yale Repertory Theatre in New Haven and the Eugene O'Neill Memorial Theater Center, a leading establishment for experimental work. Then there is the P.T. Barnum museum near Bridgeport, complete with all sorts of circus memorabilia. Mark Twain lived for 25 years in Hartford. (One wonders, fascinated, what Twain and Barnum might have had to say to each other.) Also, there is Mystic Seaport with its museum dedicated to the glory days of sailing. Best of all for the traveler, this richness is all available in a manageable area within easy driving range of New York, one destination yielding effortlessly to the next, almost as though it were planned with the traveler in mind.

Maine

The state of Maine is rugged—both in climate and topography. Its dense woods are latticed with rivers as formidable as the Penobscot and as wild as the Allagash. It is the largest of the New England states, nearly large enough to encompass the other five. It is famous for its lobsters and its blueberries; its lakes and its vast stretches of timber that cover fully eighty-five percent of the state; for its rocky coast and for L.L. Bean outfitters. Maine offers the finest wilderness canoeing in the East and, perhaps, in the nation. There is also excellent fishing with even the noble Atlantic salmon returning in good numbers to the once polluted waters of the Penobscot River. You can catch them now, within the city limits of Bangor. The skiing—both downhill and cross-country—is first rate. The coastal city of Bar Harbor is a famous resort, dedicated by the Rockefellers (among others) to preserving and celebrating the serenity of the old ways. Beyond these attractions, which are immediately available, there is that ineffable quality that has attracted so many artists and writers and brought them as visitors or permanent residents to Maine. A partial list would include Winslow Homer, Andrew Wyeth, E.B. White, and Rachel Carson for whom there is named a 4,000-acre wildlife refuge on the coast. No visitor, even the most casual, however, could remain unmoved by the sheer durable beauty of the State of Maine.

Massachusetts

Boston is the city that often overwhelms the state in which it resides. That is slightly unfair to Massachusetts but a testament to the enduring fascination of Boston. The city resonates with both the echoes of history and the electronic hum of the future. The famous Boston Common, the Town Hall, the *USS Constitution* resting at its pier, and many other soundly preserved monuments remind you at almost every turn of Boston's long and proud past. But the city is no relic. Its universities have trained the people who are leading the silicon revolution around Cambridge, across the Charles River from Boston. This new prosperity —coming a century and a half after Boston pioneered industrial manufacturing—has brought a boom in banking, restaurants, hotels, department stores, and the stuff of urban life.

Still, there is more to the state than its great city. Massachusetts has its remarkable coastal areas Cape Cod and the "islands"—Martha's Vineyard and Nantucket. The beaches and the sailing are among the most admired on the Atlantic coast. To the West, there are the Berkshires, generously called "mountains" but tall enough for skiing. They are lovely in the Summer when the theater festivals abound in Massachusetts, most notably the Tanglewood Festival in Lenox. Between the coast and the hills, there is farmland and woods dotted by all sorts of places that will quicken the blood of anyone who knows American history: Walden Pond, Lexington and Concord, Salem, and New Bedford. State and city are rich, indeed, in both beauty and history.

New Hampshire

A stranger might be excused for feeling a certain sense of intimidation about visiting New Hampshire. It is, after all, called the "Granite State" and its motto (taken from the words of native son, General John Stark of Rogers' Rangers) is "Live free or die." Even as he first approaches, the visitor will find something formidable about the state. Its short coastline is dominated by bustling Portsmouth and its northern border with Canada is densely wooded and barely populated. The summit of Mount Washington—highest mountain in New England and one of the most treacherous anywhere—rises well above the tree line and the winds there have been clocked in excess of 200 miles per hour. Then, there is Mystery Hill, site of some controversial stone constructions that recall Stonehenge and that may have been erected as long ago as 2000 B.C.

The fearsome aspect of New Hampshire is quickly softened when you see it up close and regard its small, lovely, and well preserved old towns; or Dartmouth which is probably the most beautifully situated university anywhere; or such loci of culture as Franconia where Robert Frost lived and Hawthorne would visit, and Peterborough, which is home of the Macdowell Colony, perhaps the most celebrated artists' refuge in the country. There is also Dublin, home of *Yankee Magazine,* which serves New England as reliably as the old *Saturday Evening Post* served the country, and the *Old Farmer's Almanac,* which is so much as part of America that you cannot imagine the nation without it. Finally, there is the score of modern ski resorts, especially those in the White Mountains around the town of North Conway, where the apparel shops and the restaurants match anything in any resort in the world. This, then, is New Hampshire. Both rugged and gentle; a place of the most extreme and beguiling contrasts.

Rhode Island

Founded by Roger Williams, a dissident among dissidents, Rhode Island is the smallest of the fifty states and the second most densely populated. But those numerical facts are deceiving. Rhode Island is neither excessively urbanized nor poor. Newport, in fact, is perhaps the most famous of the old summer spots for the rich, as evidenced by its spectacular mansions, and has continued to prosper while other famous spots such as Saratoga that once shared its glory have declined. The seventy-room house that Commodore Vanderbilt liked to call his cottage is still standing and open to the curious. Other elaborate homes are still there as are the beaches and the sailing that were their reason, originally, for being. Narragansett is a more earthy fishing village though it has its own fine homes, including "The Towers," designed and built by Stanford White. Then there is Block Island, about ten miles offshore, which you reach by ferry and find refreshingly primitive by Newport standards. Back on the mainland, the capital city, Providence, is charming and abundant with points of historical interest. The capital building is perhaps the loveliest in the country. Upstate (such as it is) there are the dignified towns that one expects of New England and which seem light-years away from the opulence of the beach, though in fact you can drive the distance between meals.

Vermont

In the imagination of outsiders, Vermont exists pretty much as Robert Frost wrote of it and Norman Rockwell painted it. Insiders labor mightily to keep it exactly that way. Though the state has no appreciable industry and its terrain and climate are inhospitable to most forms of modern agriculture, Vermont has written some of the most rigorous environmental legislation anywhere in the country. If most Vermonters had their way, it is the developers who would be endangered. But by their actions and attitudes Vermonters have insured the health of the state's greatest resource: its own beauty and, hence, tourism. People come to the state precisely for the exhilarating *Vermontness* of it. They admire the old ways of doing things in everything from making syrup to building barns, and they have no trouble finding what they are looking for in a state where even the covered bridge is protected. They will find it in graceful towns dominated by church steeples. Behind each church, or adjacent to it, there will inevitably be an old, scrupulously maintained graveyard. Often there will be, somewhere in town, a traditional inn. Usually a well kept village green or common. There are also, of course, the other things that attract people to the state: the fishing and the skiing and the craft and theater festivals. Also the resort life in general, which orbits around nuclei such as Stratton, Stowe, and Sugarbush. People come in the winter for the skiing—both cross-country and downhill. They come in the summer for golf and tennis. They come in the fall for the leaves. Spring passes too quickly it seems for anyone to plan a trip around it. But all of these things could be enjoyed some other place. What is unique about Vermont is something that cannot be catalogued and mercifully has not yet been corrupted.

NEW ENGLAND'S SPORTING LIFE

Year-Round Pleasures

by
PAUL ROBBINS

Paul Robbins, a freelance writer who is the sole member of the Vermont chapter of the Society of American Travel Writers, skied Vermont for years before moving there permanently in the mid-'70s. He is well published in major newspapers and national ski and travel magazines.

New England is six pounds of sports in a five-pound bag.

There are precious few patches on earth where a sports lover, either participant or spectator, is assured of being able to do whatever he or she wants when it comes to watching or doing—mostly doing.

Sports in New England? Oh sure, there are the Red Sox and Bruins, those golfers out at Pleasant Valley every summer, or over at Wethersfield with the Greater Hartford Open, and plenty of tennis action. You'll find athletes like Larry Bird, Marvelous Marvin, Wade Boggs, golf champions like Joanne Carner, Patty Sheehan, and Janie Blalock. You'll also find marathon winners like Bill Rodgers, Patti Catalano (although not in Boston, her hometown) and Joanie Benoit. Sure, all those high visibility, don't-need-AmEx card carriers are in New England—and let's not overlook many-time national kayaking king Eric Evans and world boardsailing queen Nancy Johnson, Olympic gold medalist equestrian Tad Coffin or Bill Koch, winner of an Olympic medal and a World Cup title in cross-country skiing.

Mostly, though, sports in New England means the Bosox (to some, the Boflops) and the Patriots (to some, the Patsies, especially after their collapse in Super Bowl XX), the Whalers, National Basketball Hall of Fame in Springfield, Mass., and the National Lawn Tennis Hall of Fame in Newport, R.I., right? You can also toss in those world sled dog championships in Laconia, N.H., each winter. Well, yes and no. There's no denying the professional and the world class amateur level, the headliners and front page events.

From the coastline to the ridgelines, from Newport, R.I., to Newport, Vt., just about every part of this six-state region is fertile ground for *doing something*. Maybe it's passive like riding a windjammer off the coast of Maine or on Lake Champlain, but it's probably something a little more active, although not necessarily running a marathon like Maine's Casco Bay run-around or that Josh Billings Run-aground each September out in the Berkshires which combines biking, canoeing and running.

Perhaps the best part of such a wide popularity of sports in New England is that you don't always have be a local to take part. True, you probably can't just show up and join the town softball team (or, depending on the town, maybe you can), but some of these activities revolve around tourists. Or, maybe you thought all those hikers, bikers, campers, skiers and others were simply out there for some neighborhood fun.

Perhaps we should better define what we mean by sports. Is it *watching* a horse race, auto race, tractor pull, jai alai or weightlifting competition? Is "playing" chess or backgammon a sport? Fishing—fresh water, deep sea or surf casting? For purposes of this look-see at sports in New England, let's try to break things down. First of all, there are participant and spectator sports and, yes, some definitely are both; there are professional and amateur sports; and there obviously are some sports that are pretty much unique to one locale, i.e., river rafting in Maine, or ski jumping in New Hampshire or Vermont.

If we toss out some of the more specialized activities such as biathlon, figure skating, fencing, gymnastics, motocross and Greco-Roman wrestling, there is still a heap of things to do—and an awful lot of places to do them in New England. Granted, some might be borderline "sports," but let's give 'em the benefit of the doubt and include them.

To give you a sampling of what sports are available in New England, consider the following. For the sports participant: camping, canoeing, diving, fishing, hiking, climbing, hunting, ice fishing, orienteering, rafting, skiing (alpine and cross-country), sky diving, sliding, snowmobiling, snowshoeing, soaring, swimming and windjammering. For the sports spectator: auto racing, baseball, softball, basketball, football, hockey, horse and greyhound racing, jai alai, and soccer. For either participants or spectators: biking, boardsailing, boating, bowling, chess, backgammon, golf, running, sailing, yachting, squash, tennis, and racquetball.

The list is fairly self-explanatory. While, yes, you can play soccer or hockey, the simple fact is most people wind up as spectators and chances are pretty remote, even if you're Mike Eruzione (New England born and bred), you're not likely to haul your skates and hockey stick on vacation with you, so that's a spectator activity, too. Auto racing and horse racing also are very popular sports but the same reasoning holds true: most people watch. On the other hand, how many times have you stood around and watched someone ice fish, camp or hike?

So, with the preliminaries discussed, here's a rapid rundown of a tourist's-eye view of sports in New England:

Auto racing

Not quite "The Brickyard" or Monte Carlo, but there are the drags and more than a few other notable events. Lime Rock in Connecticut has proven to have special attraction for Paul Newman, if you're a celebrity chaser; otherwise, Lime Rock still has an impressive slate of regional and national races. There is also a track in Thompson, Conn. Elsewhere, there are the drags at New England Dragway in Epping, N.H.; the stocks at two tracks in Vermont, Catamount Speedway in Milton and Thunder Road in Barre; Claremont (N.H.) Speedway; Salisbury and Waterford, in Connecticut; and Ellsworth, Oxford, Scarborough, Winterport, Wiscasset, or Unity, Maine.

Baseball/Softball

The Red Sox, of course, lead this parade, and their top farm team is in Pawtucket, R.I., but there is plenty of other action, including the Maine Guides, which are in the International League with the PawSox. The Eastern League has several teams in New England (Burlington, Vt.; Nashua, N.H.; New Britain and Waterbury, Conn.,) and there are other top organized leagues. The Northern League, for instance, is a semi-pro circuit based in Vermont and the Cape Cod League has been known for years as an incubator for top college prospects. And you can't overlook the quality of softball played in Stratford, Conn., home of the Raybestos Brakettes women's team.

Basketball

First place belongs to Boston's Celtics, and the rest of world is in a distant second place. Bird & Co. dominate the scene, of course, but there are the Bay State Bombardiers of the Continental Basketball League and some topflight college teams: Boston College, Holy Cross, Boston University, Providence, Connecticut, University of Rhode Island, American International College, Bentley, Assumption, among others.

Biking

Not to be confused with Motocross (at Bryar Motor Sport Park, Loudon, N.H.), there are some heavy-duty road races for intensive cyclists and some marvelous cruising routes for the vista-viewing vacationer. Among the top cycling events: the Mount Washington Auto Road Climb, usually in mid-September; and the Narragansett Wheelmen in Rhode Island hold a variety of events (for information write to Wheelmen, Box 1317, Providence RI 02901). And then there are the rest of us who'll hook on for a day or two of light touring, perhaps a weekend of pedaling between inns, but mostly just leisurely stuff. Vermont Travel Division (Montpelier 05602) can provide information on local tours; another source: New Hampshire Publishing, Box 70, Somersworth NH 03878, which has produced bike tour guides to several states.

Boardsailing

Again, the serious and the not-so. Also known as windsurfing, this isn't solely an ocean sport; in fact, Lake Champlain, Vermont's Lake Bomoseen and even the Charles River in Boston are becoming prime sailing spots, and Lake Winnipesaukee finally is developing. All you need is wind and water. Newport, R.I., is the ex-officio regional capital; Nancy Johnson helps run a local windsurfing school when she's not picking up trophies in some far-off regatta.

Boating

All kinds available, from cruising Lake Sunapee or Lake Winnipesaukee in New Hampshire to the harbor cruises in coastal areas, especially Hyannis or Provincetown on Cape Cod, to the longer journeys out of Haddam, Conn., daily. Or just try to find dock space on Winnipesaukee or Lake Champlain for your own tub. Best to call ahead, though, because mooring space is at a premium.

Bowling

It's been a couple of decades since the bowling craze died down, but New England remains prime territory for the keglers. Not only ten-pin bowling but they have duckpin, a pintsize version of ten-pin, and candlepins in which you'd swear you're rolling at a sixteen-ounce beer can. Seems like every village no matter what size its business district has some kind of lanes. You're never far from a chance to roll a few strings. One of the real cheap-date bargains.

Camping

Any time, almost anywhere. With all these mountains, state and national forests and parks, all these lakes and streams as well as coastline, it's only natural that New England be freckled with camping sites. Parks or forests usually have arrangements for campers or tents. Campsites can range from primitive to softball diamonds, volleyball courts, a beach and maybe even a small restaurant or at least a snack bar. Civilization is so near and yet so far; the parks and forests help keep "progress" at arm's length for a while. State tourism officials can provide details on private camping areas as well as public sites.

Canoeing/Kayaking

With all the lakes and rivers in this region, it's understandable that canoeists flock to the area. Whether it's paddling down the Saco River from New Hampshire into Maine or perhaps across Stockbridge Bowl in the Berkshires, New England has the quality and quantity for canoeists. Kayaking is less well-known but a kick of a sport, zipping across the water like an oversized waterbug. The Appalachian Mountain Club (5 Joy St., Boston 02108) has a canoe chapter and a fine guide (*New England Whitewater River Guide* $8.95).

Chess/Backgammon

Are these sports? Not really, although they are competitions; purists would allege chess is more the true contest since backgammon, involving the luck of the dice, relies on more than just your own resources. Do chess or backgammon players sweat? Where have you gone, Bobby Fischer? Boris Whosis? There are chess tournaments just about every weekend in New England: the New England Open is held over Labor Day weekend at a rotating site, the Down East Open is staged in Portland, Maine, in July every year; and, among others, the Central New England Open is held every Memorial Day Weekend in Leominster, Mass. For more details, contact the Massachusetts Chess Association, c/o Stephen Dann, 97 Granite St., Worcester MA 01604 (617–799–6290).

Diving

Southern New England, especially the Rhode Island–Cape Cod area, is especially active in scuba diving (SCUBA: self-contained underwater breathing apparatus). There are several national certifying authorities for instructors, so if you're interested, make certain to look for some sort of instructor's credentials other than "Hey, I've dived for years." Some diving goes on in lakes or rivers, but the vast majority takes place offshore along the coast. Dive shops, in many cases, serve as unofficial clubs, not so much in terms of membership and dues but by holding periodic outings, dives or other events. Two starting points for more information: Rhode Island Divers Supply (and Rhode Island Academy of Skindiving) in Providence (401–274–4482) and Cape Cod Divers in Buzzards Bay, Mass. (617–759–8665).

Fishing

More places than you could cast a worm or fly, or whatever, at. Deep sea fishing runs daily from several places on Cape Cod or Rhode Island (contact the Cape Chamber of Commerce, Route 6, Hyannis 02601 or Rhode Island Tourism Division, 7 Jackson Walkway, Providence 02903). You'll also catch surfcasters doing their drill at sundown throughout the Cape, out on the islands or in Rhode Island. There are also major tournaments in Rhode Island: striped bass in June (Warwick); billfish in July (Block Island); tuna, mid-July to late September (Galilee); striped bass and bluefish in August (Port Judith and Cranston), among others. For freshwater fans, it's a bonanza. Moosehead Lake in Maine is a superb trout bed, for starters, and then go find a quiet stream out in the Berkshires or perhaps up in Vermont's Northeast Kingdom, maybe near Island Pond or on Lake Willoughby, to drown worms or practice your fly casting.

Football

The U.S.F.L. Boston Breakers broke up, but the N.F.L. Patriots are still here as is college ball from traditional Ivy League powers Yale, Dartmouth and Harvard to independent strongboy Boston College, a resurgent Holy Cross and a battalion of smaller schools such as UNH and Plymouth State. If you want to revive your youth, catch a high school game one Saturday (or Friday night), then come back the next morning and watch (or join) the local sandlotters.

Golf

Big and small. The men pros come to Pleasant Valley near Worcester, Mass., and near Hartford, Conn.; the women pros visit Danvers, Mass.; and there are all sorts of state and regional tourneys. Beyond that, though, there are a gang of championship courses (Robert Trent Jones, for instance, did the courses at Woodstock and Warren, Vt.). Two southern Vermont resorts, Stratton Mountain (05155) and Mount Snow (05356), have golf schools.

Hiking

The Appalachian Trail terminates at Mount Katahdin in Maine and the route threads its way through New Hampshire, Vermont, Massachusetts and Connecticut. The Appalachian Mountain Club (5 Joy St., Boston 02108) does an admirable job of maintaining huts, marking trails and putting out guides. Possible backup for guides: New Hampshire Publishing, Box 70, Somersworth, NH 03878.

Hunting

Introduction of the moose season in Maine and doe season in Vermont has expanded this sport in the last few years. Bow and arrow hunting adds to the challenge. Each state's Department of Natural Resources, or the tourism office, can provide regulations concerning hunting dates, license fees, etc.

Ice fishing

It takes patience and plenty of warm clothing. Participants usually erect some sort of shelter, usually a small wooden shack, which serves as more of a windbreak than anything, over the hole that they've drilled in the ice. Then drop your line and wait.

Jai alai

It takes a sharp eye to follow the bouncing (and ricocheting) ball. These are the guys with the banana-shaped baskets strapped to one arm (and a crowd in the background legally betting on the winner). Frontons are located in Hartford, Bridgeport, Milford, CT, and Newport, RI.

Orienteering

Primarily a warm weather sport, you have a compass and map, and try to zip from here to there, following various directions. The key, of course, is not only to reach the correct final checkpoint but to do it by passing other "control" points. It's a combination of brains and brawn. They even hold national and world championships. Very big in Europe, orienteering has grown significantly in the U.S. in the past decade. New England Orienteering Club (57 Bent Rd., Sudbury MA 01776) holds weekend meets April through June and September through November at state parks. Family appeal is heightened by the fact that they have three or four courses for different level participants, from easy two-kilometer competitions to longer, harder ones. Recommended: *Orienteering* by NEOC President Hans Bengtsson ($9.95, Stephen Greene Press, Box 1000, Brattleboro VT 05301).

Rafting

Only in Maine, on the Penobscot, Kennebec and Dead rivers. One- and two-day trips, which can be a kick. There's always a guide on board, whether it's a four-man raft or larger vessel. The winter snow melt in spring provides a real river rush; otherwise, it's summertime rafting on rivers with dam-controlled runoff. Not as hellacious as rafting in the big rivers out West or the rivers in western Canada, but still a lot of fun (Contact: Maine Publicity Bureau, Hallowell 04331).

Running

The Boston Marathon and Falmouth Road Race get the headlines and media coverage, but there are road races throughout New England all year, including a "fun run" midweek by many clubs. Apart from the fact that vacationers can do their own running by simply taking a left or right when they go out the door of wherever they are, the amount of organized road races has increased dramatically—in quality and quantity—in recent years. Every state has one or more major races (for example, the Paul Bunyan Marathon in Bangor, Maine, each July; the New Haven 20-miler in Connecticut in September; or Vermont's Maple Leaf Half-marathon in Manchester, also September) and there are countless shorter local races year-round. If you want to compete, call ahead and check with chambers of commerce or tourism folks for races. The *Boston Globe* also has extensive race information in its Sunday sports pages.

Skiing

Plenty of terrain for both downhill or the overland variety. Snow-making enables alpine areas to produce snow "shot from guns," the machine–made crystals that are thicker than natural snow and more durable. There are ski areas in each New England state (even Rhode Island) but the most challenging, spicy skiing obviously takes place along the northern tier. Killington (Vermont) runs from Columbus Day or shortly thereafter into June while Sugarbush, about 40 miles north on Route 100, will start a week or so later and shut down around mid-May. Ski touring from inn to inn, that is, schlepping through woodlands and over meadows while someone transports your luggage by van to the next inn, has grown in popularity. Among the top cross-country ski centers: Stowe, Woodstock and Stratton Mountain, Vermont; and Franconia, Jackson and Waterville Valley, New Hampshire. Major areas such as Stratton, Bolton Valley, Burke Mountain, Stowe, and Woodstock in Vermont, Sunday River in Maine and Waterville Valley, The Balsams and Bretton Woods, New Hampshire, offer both alpine and cross-country. The New England Ski Museum is located at Cannon Mountain in Franconia, NH.

Sky diving

And if you want to jump out of a perfectly safe plane, that's available, too. The people to check with are at Parachutes Inc., Orange (Mass.) Municipal Airport (617–544–6961).

Sliding

Not much of a sport per se, but an awful lot of fun, whether it's riding down the terrain-tailored Alpine Slides (nine locations in New England) or the water slides.

Snowmobiling

A little bit of the cowboy appeal in this one: "saddling up" on the back of these snow machines and barreling across farmlands or through the woods. Most states require a registration fee and provide general, if not detailed, area maps of where to ride them critters. Check state tourism offices. One spot to rent snowmobiles: Sno-bug Village (20–plus miles of trails) in Danbury, NH, near Lake Sunapee.

Snowshoeing

There's no denying this sport lets you get out and about if you have a need to prowl some snowcovered landscape, or just a lust for building up body heat. The shoes are like lacework platforms that enable you to stay atop soft snow; the frame is usually made of ash (although aluminum models are being developed) and the lacing is made of leather thongs. For details, contact Vermont Tubbs, Forest Dale VT 05745 (802–247–3414).

Soaring

Unquestionably an elitist sport, if it's a sport, but if you've got the bucks, why not? Actually, it's more of a hobby. One starting point for information on riding the air currents without benefit of propulsion: Sugarbush-Warren Airport, Warren VT 05674 (802–496–2290).

Swimming

There is swimming and there is swimming. In New England, you've got the ocean and a legion of lakes. And then there are swimmin' holes, those romantic pools where freckle-faced kids, bouncing around in cutoffs or maybe even bare butts, swing out on a tire hung from a towering maple and drop into the water. A couple of suggestions: the popular spot along Route 313 where the covered bridge spans the Batten Kill in West Arlington, Vt.; Diana's Baths, part of the Swift River, off a dirt road outside of North Conway, N.H.; and Diana's Pool, an idyllic patch off Route 198 in South Chaplin, Conn. You can see the Batten Kill swimming hole from the road, but ask a local for directions to either of Diana's watery playpens.

Tennis

Many resorts, hotels and motels have one or more courts. You can dub around or get plenty serious. Vermont seems to have the largest share of major complexes, although New Hampshire can put forth the eighteen courts at Waterville Valley, the dozen at Bretton Woods and the indoor-outdoor layouts at the Mount Cranmore Tennis Club. In Vermont, Woodstock, Bolton Valley and Smugglers' Notch have ten courts each, Stratton Mountain has twelve (eight outdoor), the Sugarbush Inn has eleven and Topnotch at Stowe offers fourteen, ten out and four in. Major tournaments in the region include the U.S. Pro Championships at Longwood Cricket Club, near Boston, in mid-July; the Volvo International at its new site, Stratton Mountain Vt. in early August; the Stowe Grand Prix in mid-August; and the Hall of Fame Classic in July at the Casino in Newport, R.I. The women pros hit Newport in mid-July, right after Wimbledon.

Windjammers

A spinoff from the sailing crowd. These tall-masted beauties ply the coast of Maine (Camden is the preeminent port but they also sail weekly from Rockport and Rockland) and Lake Champlain. A pleasant mix of sunning and sailing, weather permitting. The Lake Champlain jaunts, which go for three or six days, are the only known inland windjamming in the U.S. and perhaps the world.

Yachting/Sailing

If you've got some kind of a tub, sailing—as with boardsailing—just needs wind and water. In New England, you've got a choice of ocean sailing or lake sailing. Just about every wrinkle of the coastline, from southwestern Connecticut to "down east," in Eastport, Maine, has some kind of marina or dock for ocean sailors. Newport R.I., Marblehead, Mass., and the central portion of Maine's coast—say, from Boothbay to Bar Harbor—are prime areas. Lake Winnipesaukee and Lake Champlain are the major inland spots, along with Lake Memphremagog in northern Vermont, New Hampshire's Lake Sunapee and a handful of smaller lakes. For spectators, the big yachting event used to take place in Newport, R.I. every three years in the form of the Americas Cup Races. The next race is scheduled for January 1987 off Perth, Australia (Newport r.i.p.).

So, there you go. Not quite sports from A to Z, but pretty close. New England is home to sports of all sorts, on land, in and on the water and in the air. And if anyone finds another way to do active things, you can be pretty sure that sport will show up here, too.

THE NEW ENGLAND STATES

Shakespeare Theatre

CONNECTICUT

The Constitution State

by
ALMA ESHENFELDER

A member of the Society of American Travel Writers and the New York Travel Writers Association, Alma Eshenfelder has had many travel articles published. Her radio program "Travel Time" has been broadcast weekly since 1971.

Connecticut is rich in history (the settlement dates back to the early 17th century) and equally rich in its continuous development of industry, educational institutions, health care, and cultural advantages. Its richness is probably most evident in its people—an amalgam not easily surpassed.

Connecticut is one of the smallest states in the Union, yet it has a rare cosmopolitan population. The colleges and universities throughout the state attract students from around the world; and in their wake come parents, friends, and contemporaries who also become enamored of the scenery, the climate, or the many advantages of the southern New England atmosphere.

Several branches of the military are represented in Connecticut including the U.S. Naval Submarine Base, the U.S. Naval Underwater Systems Center, the U.S. Coast Guard Academy, and the U.S. Coast

Guard Research and Development Center. Personnel and their families, from every state and numbering well over 100,000, establish their homes here during their tours of duty and often return after retirement.

Industrial employment is varied and includes shipbuilding, aeronautics, pharmaceuticals, electronics, and manufacturing, attracting trained and skilled labor, as well as the erudite researchers through whom the industries develop. Vast plants have been established in Connecticut and have brought to the state a wide variety of personalities and talents.

Fairfield County, in the southwestern part of the state, home to hundreds of New York City commuters, has lately become a magnet for the headquarters of major corporations. Stamford, Danbury, Greenwich as well as some of the smaller towns have been blessed by these additions to their tax rolls. The tide has turned in recent years, too, as commuters from Manhattan in increasingly large numbers come to Connecticut each day due to their employers' move to the suburbs.

There is easy access to Connecticut for visitors from all over. Amtrak has very good service from Washington, Baltimore, Philadelphia, and New York—through Connecticut to Boston on the Shoreland route and an inland route to Springfield via New Haven and Hartford. Metro North has frequent commuter trains to and from midtown Manhattan and New Haven.

Bradley International Airport, just outside Hartford in Windsor Locks, has daily arrivals and departures of both domestic and international flights. Commuter planes are available between Bradley International and smaller airports throughout the state.

Greyhound and Trailways have motorcoach routes throughout Connecticut, stopping in major cities, and other bus lines make regular trips between smaller cities and towns.

Access to Connecticut from Long Island, Fishers Island, and Block Island is provided by ferries. There are frequent trips, especially during warm weather, accommodating persons traveling with or without cars.

And Connecticut has fresh air—most likely because 75 percent of its 5,000 square miles is forest and woodland. The trees are thick and green in summer. In autumn, thousands of visitors are attracted to the Berkshire foothills and the Connecticut River area by the royal colors of the foliage.

Bordering Long Island Sound, each town has its boating fraternities, yacht clubs, charter fishermen, races, marinas, and facilities. The major rivers flowing into the Sound (the Housatonic, Connecticut, and Thames), as well as some smaller ones (such as the Saugatuck, Mystic or Pawcatuck), all add to a unique waterfront.

Connecticut is a four-season state. Visitors at any time of year will find interesting things to do, see, and hear. Natural ski areas are well equipped, and several are open and lighted in the evening, attracting family activity. Man-made snow supplements the God-given variety, so the slopes have an extended season. Lessons are usually available for adults and children. Winter sports for participants or spectators vary, depending on the area, but there is something of interest in nearly every part of the state.

Cultural activities during the year reach their peak in the winter, when there are concert series, theater performances, and ballet.

In spring and fall, of course, the foliage reigns supreme. Apple blossoms, dogwood, and mountain laurel give a true feeling of the reawakening of spring, while the earth colors of fall provide a proper backdrop for a good, crisp apple or a rousing football game.

Many public golf courses are open six or seven months of the year and are spotted throughout the state. Tennis courts, as well, are very popular during the pleasant weather in spring and fall.

State parks along the shore (Sherwood Island in Westport, Hammonasset in Madison and Rocky Neck in East Lyme) have immaculate beaches sloping gently into the Sound. Ocean Beach at New London, municipally owned and operated, is open to out-of-towners, and its mile of white sand is kept clean. There are amusements, restaurants, souvenir shops and snack bars offering a variety of treats.

Connecticut is never "out of season." The weather, like that of all New England, is changeable. But those who live here would not have it any other way.

The Colonial Tradition

The first cluster of settlements in the early 17th century included Hartford (named after Hertford, England), Windsor, just to the north, and Wethersfield, just to the south. These towns banded together informally and drew up a governing document called the "Fundamental Orders," which contained many provisions later incorporated into the U. S. Constitution. Connecticut proudly calls itself "the Constitution State."

After the first settlements, the New Haven Colony was established along the shoreline, and it grew rapidly. Until 1875, the capital of Connecticut was located alternately in Hartford and New Haven. Since then, Hartford has had the honor.

In the early days relations with the Indians were not especially good. A settler who paid an Indian for land assumed he received complete title. But private ownership of communal land, where once everyone had hunted and fished, was a concept the Indian did not understand. By his thinking, giving the settler title to the land in return for a handful of trinkets merely was extending to the stranger the courtesy of living on land used by everyone. It was, therefore, incomprehensible to the Indian when the white man erected fences and barriers and denied the Indian access to his traditional hunting and fishing lands.

Indian Words, Biblical Feelings

The Indian origin lives on in the name of the state, Connecticut, meaning "beside the tidal river." These early God-fearing settlers also drew heavily on the Bible when they named their settlements: there's Goshen, Sharon, Canaan and Bethlehem, to name a few. But most of the little stockade settlements were named as reminders of the homes they left behind: Cornwall, Norfolk, Hartford, New London, and the Thames River (pronounced in Connecticut as it is written, not Tems, as in London).

As was to be expected, the English made a large and lasting imprint on the culture, the way of thinking, the way of living of the people of Connecticut. A visible reminder is the classic, simple beauty of the white Congregational church. Many of these are seen throughout the state in communities that still treasure their Colonial heritage.

During the American Revolution, Connecticut soldiers were in the thick of every battle. It is said that General Israel Putnam would have led the American Army if George Washington had not accepted the assignment. Major battles of the Revolution were not fought in Connecticut—New York, New Jersey and Virginia can claim those honors —but the British on several occasions raided ports and some inland cities with fleet-based soldiers, burning private homes and destroying food and other supplies, then retreating to their ships before American regulars could reach the scene. The raid on New London was led by traitor General Benedict Arnold. It was a particularly dastardly affair. The American commander of the garrison at nearby Fort Griswold surrendered. When he had given up his sword, he and his men promptly were cut down in a senseless bloodletting.

When peace came, and Americans set about the business of building a new country, Connecticut assumed a unique role. There was nothing in its topography—a central river valley surrounded on both sides by rolling, irregular, forested hills dotted with lovely lakes—that would appear to have been a determining factor in its development, except that large-scale farming was not practical. The upper reaches of the valley, flat and fertile, were planted with tobacco, a strange crop for this Northern state where winters are rigorous. Yet, it was a fruitful decision. Tobacco—grown under wide cheesecloth tents, a colorful sight in summer—is now a less profitable and thus declining crop in Connecticut. The highlands, with their rocky fields, were suitable mostly for dairy farming, although fruit orchards and vineyards are scattered throughout the hills.

The Ingenious Yankees

Connecticut men, recognizing the limitations of farming, displayed an inventive genius that helped propel America right into the Industrial Age of factories and jobs for large numbers of workers. Perhaps the greatest debt is owed Eli Whitney—not for his own inventions, but for discovering the basic principle of mass production: the interchangeability of parts. Henceforth, manufactured goods no longer depended on the whims, the skills, the availability of individual craftsmen. This simple but basic discovery led directly to the assembly line. Almost anyone could stand at a machine and make one part over and over again. Manufacturing took its place alongside agriculture as a basis of the American economy, and Connecticut became known throughout the country for the skill of its factory workmen.

Connecticut factories turn out scores of products. The more intricate, the more detailed the item, the more likely it was "Made in Connecticut." Clocks, nails, screwdrivers, kitchen utensils, guns, ball bearings and numerous parts to fit other manufactured goods are made in this state. Latins cut their way through South American jungles with Collins machetes once made in Collinsville. The Pope Company made cars in Hartford before Detroit fashioned its first carburetor. Bicycles were made in Connecticut; hats, too, at Danbury.

Today in East Hartford, United Technologies' Pratt & Whitney division makes engines to power the world's airplanes. Its Sikorsky division in Stratford manufactures helicopters for world markets. In Groton, "The Submarine Capital," the Electric Boat Division of General Dynamics Corp. designs and builds the nation's powerful nuclear submarines. Pfizer, Inc.'s pharmaceutical plant and research laboratories share the Groton shoreline. Brass and copper roll from the mills at Waterbury, while tools and appliances, parachutes, textiles, marine hardware and hundreds of other items are fabricated, woven, designed, assembled or produced in hundreds of factories, big and small, throughout the state. In finance, too, Connecticut is a leader. Hartford is known as America's "Insurance City."

Culturally, the people of Connecticut look to both the past and the present. The Wadsworth Atheneum, in Hartford, was the first free public art museum in the country. Art associations dot the state, displaying the best work of amateurs and professionals. Connecticut has critically acclaimed theatres in Hartford (Hartford Stage Company), in New Haven (Long Wharf Theatre and Yale Repertory Theatre), East Haddam (Goodspeed Opera House), Chester (The Theatre of the Deaf), Stamford (The Hartmen), and Westport (Westport Country Playhouse).

Who are the Yankees of today? They are much changed from the Congregationalists who pushed their way through the woods from Newtown to Hartford with Thomas Hooker. Their lovely white churches still stand, but there are others. The great migrations of Europeans to the United States during the late 1800s and early 1900s saw large infusions of Latins, Germans, Eastern Europeans and others into Connecticut.

The influx of newer immigrants with different religions and cultures has had a large impact on a state that is conservative, but believes in justice and fair play.

If Connecticut still has one foot in its Colonial past, it has its other foot firmly in the future. Hartford and New Haven are good examples. The great American author and humorist, Mark Twain, came out of the Midwest and chose Hartford as his home, principally because his publisher was located there, but not only for that. He wrote that he found Hartford's wide, tree-lined streets pleasing and, in general, found its overall aspect attractive. (The unique house on Farmington Avenue in which he lived and worked for nearly twenty-five years is now maintained as a museum. Next door is the spacious home of Harriet Beecher Stowe, the woman Lincoln accused, in jest, of starting the Civil War.)

As the years passed, downtown Hartford and downtown New Haven became dreary slums. Like most American cities, they were not planned; they just grew. Back in the late '50s, however, under the leadership of farseeing Mayor Richard C. Lee, New Haven took the lead and embarked on a massive urban redevelopment plan that saw the wrecker's ball bash against building after building. Shiny new buildings started to rise when the rubble was cleared away. New Haven is now a pleasant place in which to live and work.

Hartford was a late starter. Its Front Street section, where Hartford was first settled, was completely razed and, with the backing of money from insurance companies, replaced with a new Constitution Plaza: a raised mall containing office buildings, a hotel, numerous shops and "landscaped" with trees in large planters. A striking glass skyscraper shaped like a ship houses the Phoenix Mutual Insurance Company. Beneath the mall is a large parking area. The completion of the Civic Center gave new life to downtown Hartford, and urban renewal projects have further changed the downtown skyline. More hotel rooms are becoming available to accommodate visitors and the conventions that crowd the Civic Center calendar. Numerous restaurants for all tastes and pocketbooks are scattered throughout the city.

Bridgeport, Connecticut's other major industrial city, is also undergoing a face-lifting. A civic center has risen on Golden Hill where the new city hall is located in a renovated high school. The P. T. Barnum Museum has undergone an extensive renovation. A portion of State

Street, in downtown Bridgeport, also has been redeveloped. The old city hall has been renamed McLevy Hall, in honor of the late Jasper McLevy, the Socialist who served as mayor of Bridgeport for a record of 25 years. The hall still houses some city offices.

The Connecticut story is not quite told. Shortly after the Pennsylvania Turnpike—the granddaddy of the big superhighways in the U. S.—was built, Connecticut laid down the Merritt Parkway. The superhighway led from the New York border, past Bridgeport to Milford, then becoming the Wilbur Cross, continued past Hartford on a diagonal route to Massachusetts and on to Boston. But if citizens of Hartford had a notion to visit the beaches and resorts in the greater New London area, they had to fight the traffic all the way to the coast. Likewise, citizens in the western part of the state had overcrowded Route 7 or Route 8 to take them down toward the shore and New York.

The next big highway project was the Connecticut Turnpike, which runs parallel to the Merritt Parkway until New Haven and, after that, helps speed visitors entering from New York across and out of the state toward Rhode Island and Massachusetts.

Travelers heading west out of Hartford toward the Berkshire Hills still take Route 44, alternately a rather congested thoroughfare and a scenic traverse of really beautiful rural areas. I-84, however, cuts through the Northwest hills across Connecticut horizontally, connecting Danbury and Waterbury to Hartford and then east toward Providence, Rhode Island.

In fact, Connecticut, tiny as it is, highly industrialized, a world center of insurance and a prime vacation state, has managed to strike a nice balance between city and country living. More concrete spanning the hills could only spoil it.

Since early times, the people of Connecticut have been compulsive about schools. Yale University and the fast-growing University of Connecticut head a long list of outstanding colleges and universities that attract students from all over the world. Equally important are its many excellent preparatory schools and community colleges.

Unlike some of their New England neighbors, the people of Connecticut may take a little longer to become fast friends, but then, in Connecticut, people choose friends carefully. Once you've been befriended by a Connecticut Yankee, you've made a friend for life.

EXPLORING THE HARTFORD AREA

Hartford, the capital of the state, is Connecticut's second largest city. For years, its skyline has been dominated by the skyscraper home of the Travelers Insurance Company, the tallest building in New England until the erection of the Prudential Tower in Boston in 1965. Hartfordites returning to their city at night know they are close to home when they spot the warm yellow glow of the Travelers Tower light. In recent years, other tall buildings—part of an extensive urban renewal project —have joined the Travelers in creating a new Hartford skyline. CityPlace, built on Asylum Street in downtown Hartford, has since supplanted the Travelers Tower as the city's tallest building. A mere 12 feet taller than the tower, its 38 stories sit on a plot of ground next to the Civic Center that is somewhat lower than the site of the Travelers Tower, giving the illusion that both buildings are of equal height.

The first building the visitor passes approaching the city from the south on Interstate 91 is only about five stories tall and is easily identified by its unique onion-shaped dome. The entire building once housed the Colt Patent Firearms Company, which manufactured the famous Colt revolvers that "won the West."

Proceeding north along the Connecticut River, a maze of intersections leads cars in and out of Hartford, across the river, and to north, south and east expressways.

Entering the city via State Street, Constitution Plaza—a complex of office buildings, stores, television studios, specialty shops, stockbrokers, and a hotel on a raised mall landscaped with trees—is on the right. At Christmastime, the trees are laced with tiny lights and musical groups perform frequently during the season. Architecturally unique is the ship-shaped Phoenix Mutual Insurance Company's skyscraper.

Just to the left of Constitution Plaza is the Old State House (1796). The Legislature met here until 1878 when the new Capitol became the seat of Connecticut government. It is a red brick Federal building with a white dome, designed by Charles Bulfinch, the designer of the State House in Boston. The building is now a public museum, furnished with period furniture, and holds Gilbert Stuart's only full-length portrait of George Washington to hang in its original setting. The Senate chamber and the graceful, unsupported spiral staircase are of special interest.

The Charter Oak Incident

South on Main Street are the Travelers Insurance Company buildings. The 527-foot-high tower may be visited. In May, June and September, the Travelers Tower is open by advance reservation only. Tours depart every half hour from 8:30 A.M. to 3:30 P.M., Monday through Friday in July and August. A plaque on the front of the tower building marks the spot of the old Zachary Sanford Tavern, locale for a dramatic incident that saw the colonists outwit the English governor of the New England colonies. On the night of October 31, 1687, Sir Edmund Andros, the Crown-appointed governor, arrived in Hartford with an armed escort. At a meeting in the tavern (throughout the colonies in those days, taverns played an important role in the political life of the people), he demanded the return of a liberal charter granted the Hartford Colony in 1662 by King Charles II. According to the story, the charter was produced; but before the governor could put his hands on it, all the candles in the tavern were suddenly blown out. The charter, which had given the Hartford Colony its independence, was stolen in the darkness by Joseph Wadsworth and hidden in the trunk of a great oak tree five blocks away. The irate Andros left Hartford without the precious document. Two years later, he was recalled to England, and the colony resumed government under the terms of the charter. The episode of the charter hiding was one of the first acts of resistance to Great Britain in the colonies, and its participants—including the tree—became legendary. Henceforth, the tree became known as the Charter Oak, and the name became a brand name for a variety of products.

A plaque on Charter Oak Place, in the south end of the city, marks the spot where the magnificent tree stood until 1856, when it crashed to the ground in a windstorm. Today, in various public buildings and

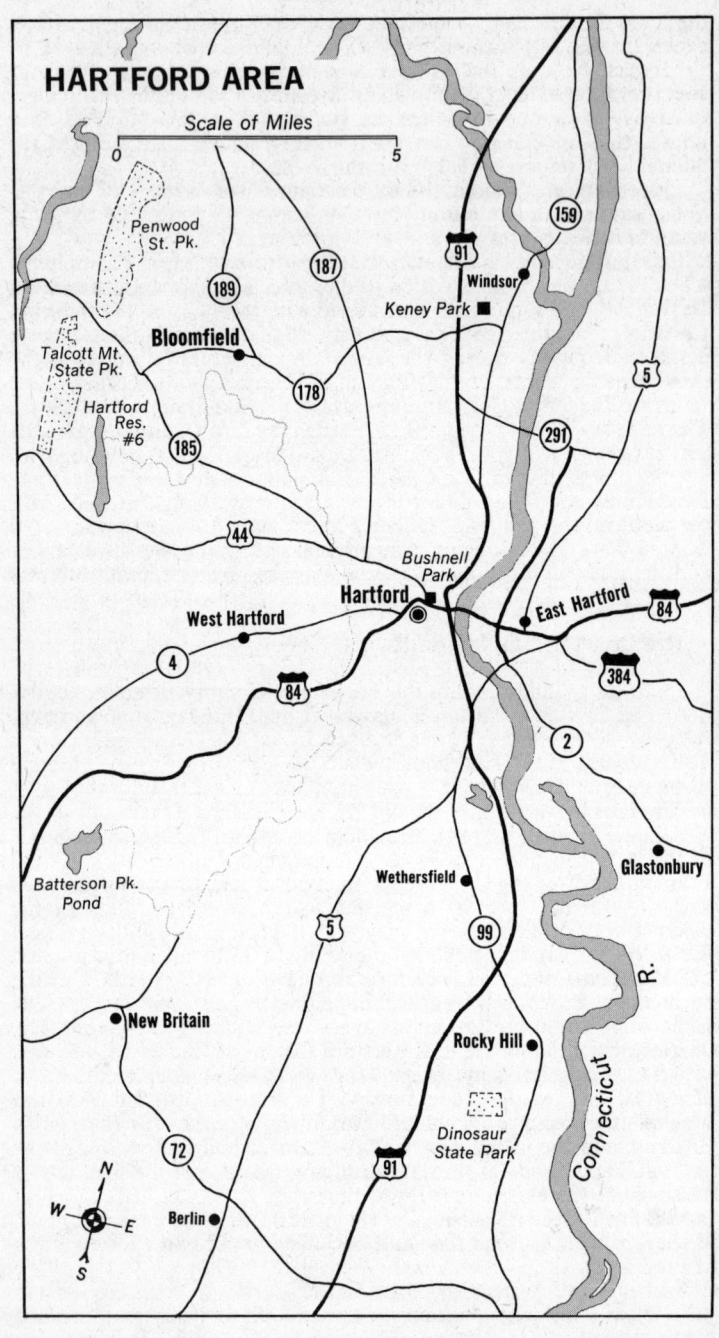

HARTFORD AREA

Scale of Miles

0   5

Penwood St. Pk.

(159)

(91)

Windsor

(187)

(189)

Keney Park

Talcott Mt. State Pk.

Bloomfield

(178)

(5)

Hartford Res. #6

(185)

(291)

(44)

Bushnell Park

Hartford

East Hartford

(84)

West Hartford

(4)

(84)

(384)

(2)

Batterson Pk. Pond

Wethersfield

Glastonbury

(5)

(99)

New Britain

Rocky Hill

Connecticut R.

(72)

Dinosaur State Park

(91)

Berlin

N
W   E
S

museums, there are on display gavels, chairs and other objects that were fashioned from the wood of the tree. Mark Twain commented on the subject. He said he had seen "a walking stick, dog collar, needle case, three-legged stool, bootjack, dinner table, tenpin alley, toothpick, and enough Charter Oak to build a plank road from Hartford to Salt Lake City."

Past the Travelers Building on Main Street is the Wadsworth Atheneum (America's oldest public art museum), which includes the Avery Art Memorial and the adjoining Morgan Memorial, a museum with an excellent collection of Middle Eastern and Oriental archeological relics, and one of the largest exhibits anywhere of Meissen china. A steel sculpture, *Stegosaurus,* by Alexander Calder rises high above the Burr Mall. It is a brilliant vermillion stabile that attracts the attention of even the most casual passerby. The Avery boasts paintings by Rembrandt, Wyeth, Daumier, Gilbert Stuart, Picasso, Goya, Giordano, Cézanne, Whistler and Sargent. Its many special exhibitions are the occasion for social evenings that bring out Hartford society. (Money for the Morgan Memorial was a gift from the famous financier J. P. Morgan, a Hartford boy who chose not to join his father's business, but went to New York to seek his fortune.)

The statue on the lawn in front of the Morgan Memorial honors Nathan Hale, the youthful Connecticut schoolteacher who was caught by the British while spying on Long Island for Washington's forces and hanged in New York City, uttering before his death words that have become immortal in American history: "I only regret that I have but one life to lose for my country."

South on Main Street is the city hall and next to it, resting on huge steel girders—among the largest ever fashioned—is the public library. The girders bridge four lanes of road that lead to the riverside super-highways. Thousands of cars pass beneath the library daily, but insulation muffles the sound.

Just a block past the library on Main Street is the oldest private home in the city. The Butler-McCook Homestead was erected in 1782 and is now operated as a museum of early life in Hartford. It contains an excellent collection of 18th- and 19th-century household artifacts as well as displays of American silver and furniture.

Beautiful Capitol Hill

The present state capitol sits dramatically atop the highest point in Bushnell Park. While the governor and top officials have their offices in the gold-domed capitol, most state workers are housed in the State Office Building at the edge of the park. Battle flags carried by Connecticut soldiers in many wars line the wall of the exhibition room of the capitol.

Across the street, the Raymond E. Baldwin Museum of Connecticut History has historical exhibits, including the original Connecticut charter (1662) and historical industrial displays, and a collection of early rifles and revolvers. The State Library has paintings by renowned Colonial artists. In an alcove off the museum room is the table upon which President Abraham Lincoln signed the Emancipation Proclamation that freed all slaves during the Civil War. A duplicate of the stolen Connecticut Charter is also on display.

Two other buildings of note stand in the capital complex: the State Armory and Bushnell Memorial at 166 Capitol Avenue. The armory, to the west of the capitol, is a large, imposing building, headquarters of the Connecticut National Guard and military reserve units. Across the street from the armory is the home of the *Hartford Courant,* the oldest daily newspaper in the country in continuous publication.

The Bushnell Memorial, on the east flank of the capitol, is a beautiful auditorium that serves as the cultural heart of a community that places a high premium on the theater and music. To the Bushnell come the world's top symphony orchestras, opera and ballet companies, Broadway plays, lectures, and movies. It is also the home of the Connecticut Opera Company. The Hartford Stage Company's productions are presented (October–May) at the John W. Huntington Theater, 50 Church Street.

With the completion of the Hartford Civic Center, New England's largest convention and entertainment center, downtown Hartford was reborn. The civic center has a vast variety of shops, boutiques, restaurants, food shops and a parking garage for 4,000 cars. It is also home for Connecticut's National Hockey League Hartford Whalers. The Greater Hartford Convention and Visitors Center is also located at the Civic Center.

Residential areas are opening up downtown, and once-neglected properties are being bought by people with innovative ideas and others interested only in restoration. Small discotheques and supper clubs have opened in the neighborhood and seem to be doing well.

Hartford is a large city, as New England cities go, but it does not have the more severe problems one associates with metropolitan areas. Its geographical location—about halfway between New York and Boston—is one of its greatest assets.

In the south end of the city at 300 Summit Street, high on a ridge of traprock, is Trinity College, one of the respected eastern colleges. Trinity's "Long Walk" is a lovely tree-shaded campus sidewalk bordered by school buildings. The 90-acre campus has the oldest Gothic-style buildings in the United States, with extraordinary stone sculptures and wood carvings. Housed in the Austin Arts Center are permanent and traveling exhibits as well as theatrical and musical productions.

Getting back to midtown Hartford, and heading west on Farmington Avenue, in the center of a small park is the red brick home office of Aetna Life & Casualty, the largest Federal-style structure in the country. The ultra-modern St. Joseph's Cathedral, which replaced the Roman Catholic cathedral destroyed mysteriously by fire, is across the street.

Mark Twain Lived Here

Farther out, 351 Farmington Avenue was once known as Nook Farm. On the few remaining acres of the tract are the old Victorian home of Mark Twain and the neighborning house in which Harriet Beecher Stowe lived and worked. For many years, the lower floor of the Twain house was used as a branch of the Hartford Public Library, with the upstairs rented out as private apartments. Interested residents raised sufficient money to take over the house, and a very active Mark Twain Memorial Commission started the long process of bringing back to Hartford furniture, furnishings and belongings of the author and his family. Today, except for a few rooms used as commission offices, the venerable old house is much as it was when the Twain family lived there. The great author built the kitchen on the street side so that the servants could watch the annual circus parade go by while continuing with their work. (The parade never got that far up Farmington Avenue.)

The south portico of the house is shaped much like the wheelhouse of a Mississippi River steamboat, recalling for Mark Twain the happy years he spent on the river as a pilot. In a top floor room is the pool table upon which he worked when he wanted to escape the hubbub of the family below. And in the basement is the typesetting machine Twain financed. It was never a success and eventually plunged the author into bankruptcy. Not one to escape his debts that way, Twain went on a world lecture tour, eventually paying back every creditor.

Of the Hartford house in which he lived and wrote for more than 20 years, Mark Twain once wrote: "Our house was not unsentient matter—it had a heart and a soul, and eyes to see us with; and approvals and solicitudes and deep sympathies; it was of us, and we were in its confidence and lived in its grace and in the peace of its benedictions. We never came home from an absence that its face did not light up and speak out in eloquent welcome—and we could not enter it unmoved."

The Harriet Beecher Stowe House, around the corner on Forest Street, is open to the public as a museum dedicated to the famous author. Operated in conjunction with Mark Twain's house, it is filled with Mrs. Stowe's furnishings, including some of her lovely floral paintings.

Many of the large office buildings you pass in Hartford (including this part of the city) are the homes of some of America's leading insurance companies. Because Hartford is known throughout the country as the "Insurance City," and because of the many other companies headquartered in the city, it is reputed to be the largest financial center in the U.S. Headquarters of major banks, with branches throughout Connecticut, are also located in the heart of the city. Connecticut National Bank and the Connecticut Bank and Trust Company are the two largest.

Elizabeth Park, on Asylum Street, is one of the many beautiful parks in the city. Its spectacular rose gardens annually attract thousands of visitors from all over the country.

West Hartford is a rather beautiful residential community, with miles of tree-shaded streets, attractive houses, and well-kept lawns and gardens. There are exclusive sections here, with expensive mansions. The modest little saltbox house in which Noah Webster (compiler of the first American dictionary) was born is at 227 South Main Street.

The University of Hartford is in West Hartford. It is a diverse university but has the campus atmosphere of a smaller institution. The University, founded in 1957, was the result of a merger of three long-established institutions: the Hartford Art School (1877), Hillyer College (1879), and Hartt School of Music (1920). Situated on 200 suburban acres, four miles from downtown Hartford, the university has over 4,000 full-time students from 40 states and 34 foreign countries.

The Children's Museum of Hartford is located in West Hartford. Youngsters will be fascinated with the numerous exhibits, ranging from Colonial artifacts to natural history displays and planetarium shows.

Touring the Suburbs

Metropolitan Hartford encompasses a number of interesting attractions. Immediately south of the city is the Webb House, close to the very beautiful Wethersfield Green. In the Webb House (1752), Washington and Count de Rochambeau, head of French forces in America, plotted the strategy that led to the victory at Yorktown over the British under Lord Cornwallis. Wethersfield was a natural meeting place for the two commanders, being about halfway between the Frenchman's headquarters in Newport, Rhode Island and Washington's command posts in upstate New York. Numerous Continental officers had been welcomed by Joseph Webb and his charming wife. The Webb House, a lovely mansion, became known as "Hospitality Hall." The story is told that Madame Webb, like any good hostess, rushed to have an expensive wallpaper, just arrived from France, put up in the room she had prepared for her distinguished American guest. The original gaily patterned red flock paper still looks down on the canopy bed in which Washington slept. Of interest, too, are the kitchen, the graceful stairway, and the council room in which the fateful battle plans were laid.

Researchers for the Connecticut Historical Commission discovered in Washington's diary his own account of the visit to the Webb House. The general left his headquarters on May 18 "for interview at Wethersfield with the Count de Rochambeau and Admiral Barras." On May 19, he wrote: "Breakfasted at Litchfield (at the Sheldon Tavern, where he spent the night), dined at Farmington and lodged at Wethersfield, at the house of Joseph Webb." May 20: "Had a good deal of private conversation with Governor Trumbull." May 21: "Count de Rochambeau with Chevalier de Chastellux arrived about noon. The appearance of the British fleet off Block Island prevented attendance of Count de Barras." May 22: "Fixed with Count de Rochambeau the plan of campaign."

The rest is history.

If the Webb House reflects the life of a wealthy Connecticut family during the Revolution, the nearby Buttolph-Williams House, built in 1692, shows how the Colonists lived under much sterner conditions nearly a century earlier. Additions were made to the original building, a common practice in Colonial times, but they were made to harmonize with the basic clean design of the dwelling. Most interesting in this house are the numerous artifacts in the big kitchen. The fire seat, a curved settee, the back of which acted as a heat reflector, looks inviting but actually is quite uncomfortable.

Other interesting old buildings in Wethersfield are the Silas Deane House (1776), home of one of the special envoys sent to Europe by the Continental Congress, and the Old Academy Museum (1801), where household tools, utensils and a loom are on display.

Across the Connecticut River, fast-growing East Hartford is the home of the Pratt & Whitney division of United Technologies, makers of American airplane jet engines. UT, which also maintains its headquarters here, has other divisions in Connecticut—Hamilton Standard in Windsor Locks (now engaged in aircraft and aerospace life support projects) and Sikorsky Helicopters in Stratford—and is one of the largest employers in the state.

Fields of Tobacco

Across the river again, over one of the five bridges that span the Connecticut River to the Hartford area, the route to the north leads to East Granby, the Old Newgate Prison, and the first chartered copper mine which dates back to 1707. Visitors may enter the main shaft to the mine. The site was once a prison for "British sympathizers" and war prisoners during the American Revolution and served as Connecticut's state prison until 1827.

Nearby Windsor is a town which probably has more well-preserved, pre-Revolutionary War houses than any other town in the state. Only a few buildings are open to the public. The Tyler House and Wilson Museum, at 96 Palisade Ave., is a typical mid-17th-century farmhouse with period furnishings and is one of the oldest in the state. The adjoining Wilson Museum is known for its genealogical records.

Farmington, on Route 4 west of Hartford, is a delightful old community with many Colonial homes set on quiet streets and shaded by graceful elms. It's the home of Miss Porter's, an exclusive preparatory school for girls housed in a building that was originally a hotel when the Farmington Canal opened. The Stanley-Whitman House (1660), now a museum, is one of the oldest frame houses in Connecticut. Prize of Farmington, however, is the Hill-Stead Museum (1901), a lovely mansion overlooking the valley. The front porch is somewhat reminiscent of Mount Vernon, but the real attractions of the museum are the paintings collected by its wealthy owners during their world travels: works by Monet, Manet and Whistler, and many Japanese wood-block prints.

Surrounding the city of Hartford are country suburbs with historic and legendary backgrounds. Most are typical small towns and villages with village greens and well-kept, restored houses, many with white picket fences. Around these small towns are the farms, forests and country landscape for which Connecticut has always been famous.

PRACTICAL INFORMATION FOR THE

HARTFORD AREA

HOTELS AND MOTELS. Urban hotels in Hartford, as well as motels and inns located in the capital region, offer accommodations suited to every circumstance. All rooms are air conditioned and have TV, unless specified otherwise. Pools are outdoor, unless noted. Accommodations are listed by average price for double occupancy, as follows: *Deluxe:* $70 and up; *Expensive:* $50–$69, *Moderate:* $30–$49; *Inexpensive:* $29 and under. Inquire concerning Family Rates, Senior Citizen Rates and wheelchair access.

AVON. Avon Old Farms Motel. *Moderate.* On Rte 44 (677–1651). Medium sized, with New England decor. Pool, pets. Across street from Avon Old Farms Inn. Tennis, golf, skiing nearby. Restaurant and lounge.

EAST HARTFORD. Holiday Inn. *Expensive.* 363 Roberts St. (528–9611). Branch of chain. Restaurant, bar, indoor pool. Special family rates.

Ramada Hotel. *Expensive.* 100 E. River Dr. (528–9703). Adjacent to Founders Bridge. Branch of chain. Dining room, bar. Entertainment nightly. Indoor heated pool, sauna, exercise room.

Howard Johnson's Motor Lodge. *Moderate.* 490 Main St. (569–1100). About 10 min. from downtown Hartford. Branch of chain. Restaurant. Pets. Nearby golf and tennis.

Imperial "400" Motel. *Moderate.* 927 Main St. (249–7781). Medium-sized with restaurants nearby, heated pool. 10 min. from downtown Hartford.

FARMINGTON. Marriott Hotel. *Deluxe.* 15 Farm Springs Rd., I-84, Exit 37 (1–800–228–9290; 678–1000). Conference Center and hotel, 10 minutes from downtown Hartford. Lounge, restaurant, health club, indoor/outdoor pool, tennis.

Farmington Motor Inn. *Expensive.* 827 Farmington Ave. (677–2821). Restaurant, cocktail lounge. Pool, golf. Pets. Nearby golf and tennis.

HARTFORD. Holiday Inn. *Deluxe.* Morgan & Market Sts. (549–2400). High-rise branch of chain. Restaurant, bar, pool.

Parkview Hilton. *Deluxe.* 10 Ford St. (249–5611). Newly refurbished downtown hotel; two restaurants, lounges, health club. Parking in adjacent garage.

Sheraton-Hartford. *Deluxe.* Trumbull St. (728–5151). Centrally located at Civic Center. Restaurants and lounge with entertainment. Cafe open for lunch and after-theater supper. Indoor pool, health club.

Summit Hotel. *Deluxe.* 5 Constitution Plaza (278–2000). Main entrance overlooks the Connecticut River. Free parking in large adjacent garage. Restaurants for lunch, dinner, and after-theater supper. Bar.

Howard Johnson's Motor Lodge. *Moderate.* There are two in the Hartford area, both off I-91. One is about 1½ miles from downtown, at 7 Weston St. (525–4441) with special rooms for non-smokers, meeting rooms, and airport limo service. The other branch is technically in Rocky Hill at Exit 24, 1499 Silas Deane Hwy. (529–7446). Both have restaurants and pool.

Ramada Inn. *Moderate.* 440 Asylum St. (246–6591). Urban. Family and weekend plans. Restaurant. Pets. Sauna.

Susse Chalet Motor Inn. *Inexpensive.* 185 Brainard Rd. I–91 Exit 27 (800–258–1980; 525–9306). About 5 min. from downtown. One of chain.

WETHERSFIELD. Ramada Inn. *Expensive.* 1330 Silas Deane Pwy. (563–2311). Restaurant. Lounge, entertainment. Sauna. Playground. Pets. Golf and tennis nearby.

WINDSOR. Sheraton Tobacco Valley Inn. *Expensive.* I–91, Bloomfield Ave. (688–5221). New England atmosphere and menu in dining room. Bar. Pool. 7 mi. to airport; 5 mi. to Hartford.

Windsor Towne House. *Moderate.* 19 Maple Ave. (688–6261). Coffee Shop.

American Motor Lodge. *Inexpensive.* 29 Windsor Ave. (525–1461). Restaurant and coffee shop.

WINDSOR LOCKS. Airport Ramada Inn. *Expensive.* Airport Rd. near Bradley International Airport (623–2441). Seafood restaurant, bar. Sauna. Airport limo service. Golf and tennis nearby.

Howard Johnson's Conference Center. *Expensive.* I–91 and Center St. (623–9811). Red Coach Grill restaurant, cocktail lounge with entertainment. Indoor pool, sauna. Airport limo service. Parks, museums, shopping, theaters nearby.

Koala Inn. *Expensive.* 185 Turnpike Rd. (623–9417). Complementary Continental breakfast; wine and cheese on arrival.

HOW TO GET AROUND. By air: Fourteen airlines serve Hartford at Bradley International Airport in Windsor Locks, 13 miles north of the city.

By train: *Amtrak* between Springfield and New York City stops in Hartford on the inland route.

By bus: Interstate bus lines make stops in Hartford, and there are intercity buses operating between many Connecticut cities and Hartford. Intercity bus services: *Greyhound, Arrow Line, Short Line, Vermont Transit* and *Bonanza* all depart from the Greyhound Terminal, 409 Church St., Hartford. Phone 547–1500. For speech- and hearing-impaired travelers, call 800–345–3190.

By car: There are several good interstate roads: I–91 runs from New Haven north through Hartford and continues to Massachusetts; I–84 from New York State through Hartford and east toward Rhode Island.

Car rental: *Avis, Hertz, Budget Rent-a-Car, National Car Rental, Thrifty,* and *Dollar* all have conveniently situated offices throughout the area.

INFORMATION SERVICES. For information on tours and other events, contact the *Greater Hartford Convention and Visitors Center,* One Civic Center Plaza, Hartford 06103 (728–6789). Open Mon. to Fri., 8:30 A.M. to 4:30 P.M.; *Visitor Information,* Old State House, 800 Main St., Hartford 06103 (522–6766). Open Mon.-Sat., 10 A.M.-5 P.M., Sun. noon-5 P.M. For *Civic Center* ticket information: box office open daily 10 A.M. to 6 P.M. and until showtime on events nights. Phone 727–8080.

TOURS. Hartford abounds in historic houses, open to the public, state buildings and museums, all offering tours. *The Hartford Civic Center,* One Civic Center Plaza, in the heart of downtown Hartford, could take a full day to explore. Connecticut Transit distributes a guide to the bus system and has its own information center at Main and State Sts., Hartford. Phone 525–9151 for information.

Special Interest Tours: *Elizabeth Park,* 915 Prospect Rd., (246-7950), has 99 acres of the most beautiful municipal rose gardens in the country. No guided tours.

Bus Tours: *Gray Line* has a 1½-hour tour of the city. Call 246–7950. *Heritage Trails,* Box 138, Farmington CT 06034 (677–8867), for historical homes and sites; half-day, full-day and dinner tours with narrations, and maximum ten people. Information on other bus tours from Greater Hartford Convention and Visitors Center.

PARTICIPANT SPORTS. Golf: In Hartford, there are two public 18-hole golf courses: Keney (722–6548) at the north end of the city and Goodwin (722–2561) at the south. Goodwin also has a flat 9-hole course, picnicking facilities, playgrounds and swimming. In the Greater Hartford area, Tunxis Plantation C. C., (677–1367) and Westwoods C. C., (677–9192)Farmington. Bel Compo C.C., (678–1358)in Avon. Rockledge C. C., (521–3156) and Buena Vista C. C., (523–1133) W. Hartford, and Niepsic C. C., (633–6435) in Glastonbury. Greens fees range from $8–$12. Country club courses are usually available to the public only on weekdays during playing season.

Boating: There are boat launching sites at E. Hartford, Windsor and Wethersfield; on the Connecticut River, on Farmington River and on Rainbow Reservoir; in New Hartford, on West Hill Pond. Canoe trips on the Connecticut River are offered by Main Stream Outfitters of Canton and include smooth water, white water, or weekend trips.

SPECTATOR SPORTS. Professional soccer and basketball games are played at the Civic Center, home of the N.H.L. Hartford Whalers, where ice-skating spectaculars also take place; lawn bowling in Elizabeth Park; polo at the Farmington Polo Grounds. *Greater Hartford Open Golf Tournament,* in July, at Edgewood C. C. in Cromwell (attracts many international celebrities). Jai alai is played at 89 Weston St., just off I–91, north of the downtown area (525–8611).

HISTORIC SITES. *Mark Twain Memorial Building* (1874), 351 Farmington Ave. (525–9317) home of the famous author when he wrote his best sellers. Next to it is the *Harriet Beecher Stowe Home,* also open to the public. *The Butler-McCook Homestead* (1782), in the heart of downtown Hartford at 396 Main St. (522–1806) was occupied by four generations of one family and is furnished with original family possessions. An 1866 carriage house is a museum of vehicles, military uniforms, and sports equipment. *Hatheway House,*

Main St. (Rte 75), Suffield, built 1760–1795, considered one of the finest examples of Connecticut architecture. Beautifully furnished. (247–8996). *Oliver Ellsworth Homestead,* 778 Palisado Ave., Windsor, (688–8717); *Noah Webster Birthplace,* 227 S. Main St., W. Hartford (521–5363), a salt-box house (about 1676) now a town museum.

Wethersfield: *Buttolph-Williams House,* Broad and Marsh Sts., (529–0460 or 247–8996); *Silas Deane House,* 209 Main St.; *Joseph Webb House* (1752), 211 Main St. (529–0612). General Washington and Count de Rochambeau planned the Battle of Yorktown here in May, 1781.

 **LIBRARY.** The *Connecticut State Library/Supreme Court Building,* across from the State Capitol, 231 Capitol Ave. (566–3056), houses the Raymond E. Baldwin Museum of Connecticut History. The collections include the state's original Royal Charter (1662), a collection of clocks manufactured in Connecticut, and the renowned Colt firearms collection among the State's other memorabilia. (Includes Museum of Connecticut Library.)

 MUSEUMS AND GALLERIES. *Wadsworth Atheneum,* 600 Main St. (278–2670) with 5 connecting buildings, 36 galleries, conservation studio, 300-seat theater, art library, galleries for handicapped, and shops. *Old State House* (1796), 800 Main St. (522–6766) Bulfinch-designed brick and brownstone museum of state's legislative, executive, and judicial branches. A National Historic Landmark (1961). *The Children's Museum of Hartford,* 950 Trout Brook Dr. (236–2961) in West Hartford, has a planetarium, with daily shows, and an aquarium. *Real Art Ways,* 100 Allyn St. (525–5521). Multimedia alternative art center. Varied schedule; special events. *Connecticut Historical Society Museum,* 1 Elizabeth St. (236–5621); *Hill-Stead Museum,* 671 Farmington Ave., Farmington (677–9064); *Old Newgate Prison & Copper Mine,* Newgate Rd, East Granby (566–3005); *Farmington Museum* (Stanley-Whitman House, c. 1660), 37 High St., Farmington (677–9222); *Old Academy Museum,* 150 Main St., Wethersfield (529–7656).

 **MUSIC.** *Bushnell Symphony Series,* distinguished orchestras, Bushnell Memorial, 166 Capitol Ave. (246–6807); (Oct. through Mar.); *Connecticut Opera Association Series,* Bushnell Memorial; *Hartford Symphony Series,* guest artists throughout the winter, at the Bushnell. *Symphony band concerts* at Elizabeth Park (June through Sept.); Trinity College Campus *Carillon concerts,* (527–3151) (June and July); *Chamber music concerts* on summer Wednesday evenings, with a tour of the chapel following.

 **THEATER.** *Hartford Stage Company,* John W. Huntington Theater, 50 Church St. (527–5151), directly across the street from the Hartford Civic Center, is a professional repertory company, providing classics, modern works and occasional tryouts in its handsome theater. *Bushnell Memorial,* near the capitol, schedules operas, concerts, plays, films, recitals, lectures and ballet. *Hartford Ballet Co.* 308 Farmington Ave. (525–9396), performs at the Bushnell and often may be seen during tours to other parts of the state. *The Coachlight Dinner Theatre,* Rte. 5, E. Windsor (522–1266), offers top musicals and comedies following a grand buffet dinner. Colleges and universities in the area have ongoing theatrical and musical programs throughout the year, many of which are free. Little theater or community theater groups, also present dramatic productions of public interest. Foreign films and revivals of classic films are shown at the *Atheneum Theatre* at the Wadsworth Atheneum (278–2670). The *Atheneum* is very popular.

SHOPPING. Department stores, specialty shops and shopping centers have always been distinguished in the Hartford area. *The Hartford Civic Center* has many top-quality shops and boutiques, offering everything from petit fours to the wooden spoons to mix the batter, clothes for every occasion or the fabrics to make them and the accessories to suit them, plus sports and recreational merchandise. There are 13 restaurants in the Civic Center with a wide variety of specialties, including grinders, light food, fast food, ice cream, bar snacks, crepes or elegant gourmet food in the atmosphere and with the service that are the rightful supplements. The shops typify what one finds throughout the downtown area, whether shopping in department stores or the many specialty shops. Suburban shopping centers have been developed in Glastonbury, Avon, Simsbury, Wethersfield, West Farms and Bishop's Corner in West Hartford. Most of the suburbs have at least one special shopping center to attract visitors. *Constitution Plaza,* one of the first redevelopment projects in the city, started as a shopping mall, but today investment houses make this section Hartford's "little Wall Street," of interest to those shopping the money market.

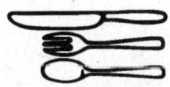

DINING OUT. Restaurants of every description may be found in the Hartford area. With the redevelopment of the city, there are many new eating places. The supper club is back; and seafood, as always, is prevalent in most area dining rooms. Ethnic restaurants run the gamut of nationalities. Almost any kind of speciality can be found here. Country inns in the capital region contribute another kind of ambiance. Price ranges, based on a full meal, exclusive of alcoholic beverages, tax and tip: *Expensive:* $25 and up; *Moderate:* $15–$24; *Inexpensive:* under $15.

AVON. Avon Old Farms Inn. *Moderate.* Jct Rtes. 44 and 10 (677–2818). A typical Connecticut country restaurant. Several small dining rooms. Antique furnishings in this restored historic building. Award-winning Sunday brunch.

FARMINGTON. Reading Room. *Moderate.* Mill Lane (677–7997). Located in a restored grist mill reputed to be the oldest in Connecticut. Gourmet. BYOB.
Benihana of Tokyo. *Moderate.* 270 Farmington Ave. (677–8548). Japanese Cuisine. Preparation of food and hibachi cooking at your table.

HARTFORD. L'Américain. *Deluxe.* 2 Hartford Sq. W. (522–6500). A handsome surprise in Hartford's South End. The décor is supplemented by soft music. Inspired French and American cuisine. Closed Sunday.
Gaetano's Restaurant. *Expensive.* Civic Center Plaza (249–1629). French and Northern Italian Cuisine. Elegant surroundings and distinctive service. Menu reflects quality ambiance.
Brownstone. *Moderate.* 124 Asylum St. (525–1171). Continental. Pleasant atmosphere in this restored brownstone, with its antiques and stained glass. Special hors d'oeuvres at dinner.
Carbone's Ristorante. *Moderate.* 588 Franklin St. (249–9646). Italian Cuisine. Pleasant surroundings and good service in this family-owned and operated restaurant, featuring unique Italian specialties.
Frank's. *Moderate.* 159 Asylum St. (527–9291). Popular downtown restaurant. Continental atmosphere, extensive Italian-American menu.
Honiss Oyster House. *Moderate.* 440 Asylum St. (246–5100). Open for breakfast, lunch, and dinner. Seafood specialties. A historic name among Hartford's best known restaurants. Lounge with entertainment Fri. and Sat.
Brown, Thomson & Co. Food & Drink Emporium. *Inexpensive.* 942 Main St. (525–1600). With something for everyone, prices included. Open from 11:00 A.M. until midnight. Three levels. Specializes in American and Mexican foods.
Valle's Steak House. *Inexpensive.* 165 Brainard Rd. (278–2555). Member of chain of family restaurants, well known for its quality beef and daily luncheon specials. Breakfast served. Free parking.

Civic Center. Downtown Hartford. There are numerous restaurants here, ranging from *Gaetano's Restaurant* to *The Ice Cream Scene* (featuring ice cream cones, sundaes, and other frozen desserts). On the first level, *Chuck's Steak House*, serving char-broiled specialties. Glass-enclosed area overlooking downtown streets. On the lower level are *La Crêpe* (110 varieties), *Ludlow's Seafood Restaurant* and *Shelly's Downtown Deli*. Prices range from expensive to very inexpensive, depending on the restaurant and the service provided.

MANCHESTER. Cavey's of Manchester. *Expensive.* 40 East Center St. (643–2751). First-class, family-operated restaurant. French cuisine downstairs in Cavey's Restaurant Français, with choice wines. Italian menu upstairs in Cavey's Northern Italian, with good veal saltimbocca and pastas.

WEST HARTFORD. Pancho McGee's. *Inexpensive.* 904 Farmington Ave. (233–5556). Texas/Mexican food. Barbecued ribs, chicken.

WETHERSFIELD. Steak Club, Ramada Inn. *Moderate.* 1330 Silas Deane Hwy. (563–2344). Open seven days for breakfast, lunch, and dinner.

 **NIGHT LIFE AND BARS.** Evening entertainment has been on the increase. Taking the place of the old-style nightclubs are the discotheques and small cocktail lounges found throughout greater Hartford.
Esplanade, Parkview Hilton, One Hilton Plaza (249–5611). Open 24 hours. Today's popular music for the over-35 crowd. *Le Jardin.* 121 Allyn St. (547–1190). 4:00 P.M.–3:00 A.M. Music from 1950s on. Sound system. Interesting ambiance here. *Shenanigan's,* Bushnell Plaza (522–4117). Mon. through Thurs. and Sun until 1:00 A.M.; Fri. and Sat. until 2:00 A.M. Reservations suggested. Live music and jukebox. *Mad Murphy's.* 22 Union Place. (247–9738). Mon.–Thurs. and Sun. until 2:00 A.M. Fri. and Sat. until 3:00 A.M. Barbecued chicken and ribs. *Rendezvous Room* Summit Hotel 5 Constitution Plaza. (278–2000, Ext. 268). Mon.–Thurs. and Sun. until 1:00 A.M. and Fri. and Sat. until 2:00 A.M.

EXPLORING THE REST OF CONNECTICUT

A tour of Connecticut should include both the superhighways and the country roads. Since Connecticut is a small state with much to see, it is difficult to chart a circular tour that would be artistic and geometric without missing some of the more interesting sights. Consequently, the routing suggested here is a double circle—one loop touching the cities and towns in the western half of the state and the other the eastern half.

Entry into the state from the west is possible via both the scenic Merritt Parkway and the Connecticut Turnpike (I–95). Toll gates are at either end of the Merritt Parkway (Greenwich and Milford); there are no tolls on the Connecticut Turnpike.

Greenwich to New Haven Area

Visitors will enjoy stopping in Greenwich and walking along the self-guided trail in the Greenwich Audubon Nature Center, 613 Riversville Road, or examining the 20,000 exhibits and the natural history dioramas in the Bruce Museum, Museum Drive. At the Pryory, International Doll Library, Pear Lane, there is a fine collection of over 8,000 dolls, puppets, electric cars, and antique sleighs. The U. S. Tobacco Company Museum, 96 West Putnam Avenue, presents the story of

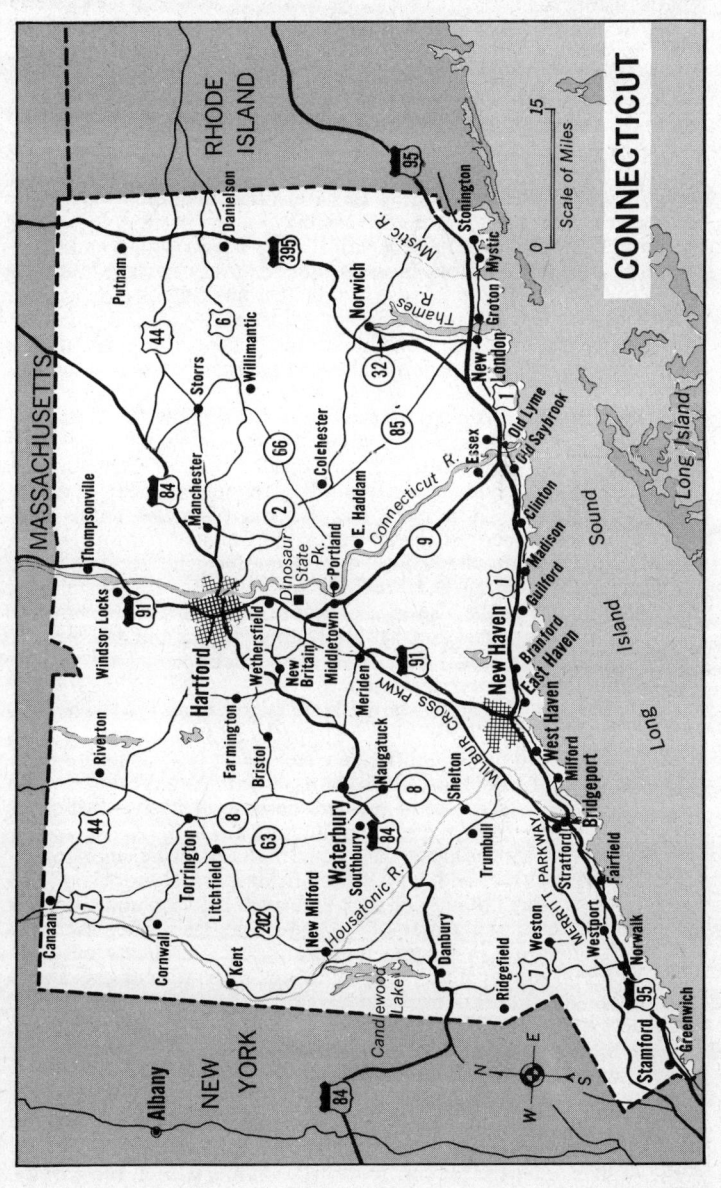

tobacco through the centuries and on five continents with tobacco-related artifacts.

North of Exit 5 on the Turnpike is Mianus, a nature preserve that still has stands of virgin timber, rarely found elsewhere in the state.

The Stamford Museum and Nature Center, at High Ridge and Scofieldtown Roads in Stamford, has a wide range of exhibits, including minerals, Indian relics, a nature center, and a planetarium.

Darien is the next town, easterly; veering off from it are highways leading to New Canaan. Both towns are exclusive residential communities. There are two attractions in this area other than the lovely towns themselves. One is the famous Silvermine Guild of Artists, located off Route 123 at 1037 Silvermine Road. It is open year-round and stages regular exhibits of the work of its members, mostly artists who live in Fairfield County. The guild also conducts a fine school. The number of artists, sculptors and ceramicists in residence swells in the summertime, during which a small exodus of artists takes place out of New York City. Another attraction is the bird sanctuary in New Canaan's Mead Park.

In 1978, by act of the state legislature, the famous Revolutionary War song "Yankee Doodle" was adopted as the state song. Legend has it that the lyrics were written in a Norwalk house on East Avenue. Unlike the "Battle Hymn of the Republic," the solemn, heavy, ponderous marching song of the Civil War, "Yankee Doodle" had a light-hearted lilt which buoyed the spirits of the Colonial patriots.

Although there are some New York commuters who live deeper into Connecticut, Westport (the next town up the line) is about as far out as most will go. For the visitor, the Nature Center for Environmental Activities, 10 Woodside Lane, has interesting exhibits and nature trails. To the south, Sherwood Island State Park offers picnicking, fishing, and swimming in Long Island Sound.

Along the coastal roads toward Rhode Island, access to the bathing beaches on the Sound is through state parks and an occasional town beach that allows non-residents (for a fee). Most beachfront property is in private hands, and most shore towns close to New York City have closed their beaches to out-of-towners because of over-crowding by carloads of people from the metropolitan area.

A spectacular sight during the spring is the dogwood in bloom at Greenfield Hill in Fairfield, just outside Bridgeport. Hundreds of dogwood trees put forth masses of pink and white flowers, and the effect is almost as breathtaking as the Potomac River Basin when the Japanese cherry trees are in bloom.

Bridgeport is principally a manufacturing center, with diverse manufacturing plants that produce a wide variety of things, from electrical appliances and equipment to clothing for all members of the family. The city's Museum of Art, Science, and Industry at 4450 Park Avenue should be of special interest to space-age visitors. On display is a huge scale model of the moon, showing the area where our astronauts landed and made their explorations. The jai alai fronton is an important recreational facility here.

P. T. Barnum, the circus man who immortalized the phrase, "There's a sucker born every minute," made a large impact on Bridgeport. His elaborate mansion stands opposite Seaside Park, his gift to the town. He established the P. T. Barnum Museum, 820 Main Street, which houses mementos of Jenny Lind (the Swedish Nightingale), clothes of Tom Thumb and his wife (the famous midget couple) and

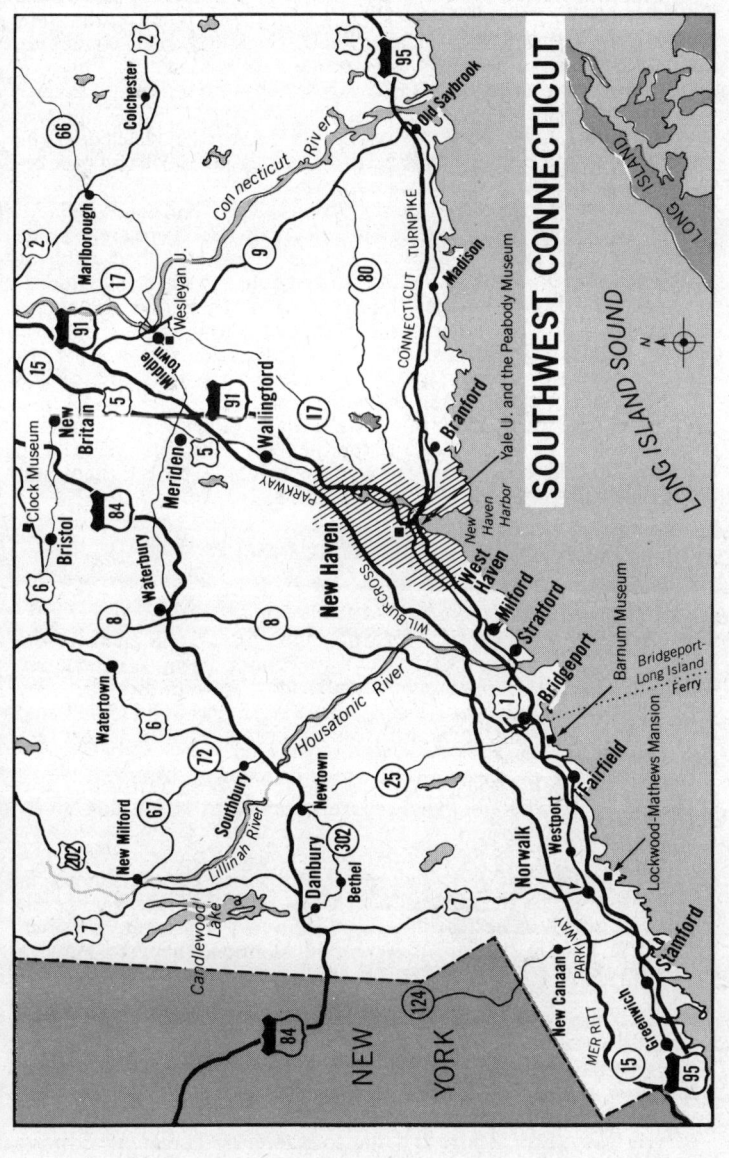

SOUTHWEST CONNECTICUT

other circus memorabilia collected by Barnum during his colorful career.

A Bridgeport tour should include a visit to Beardsley Zoological Gardens, Noble Avenue, Connecticut's largest zoo. The collection includes a variety of animals and a Shakespearean garden containing plants mentioned in the plays. At Captain's Cove Marina, 1 Bostwick Ave., *HMS Rose,* a replica of a British warship from the Revolutionary War, is a tourist attraction.

At Stratford, the American Shakespeare Theatre (modeled after the Globe Theatre in England) has been the setting for theatrical productions, often including Shakespearean plays.

The Judson House and Museum, 967 Academy Hill, built in 1723, is now a museum worth visiting while in Stratford. There are exhibits of clothing worn by the Colonists and dolls that amused their children.

The prime sightseeing attractions throughout the state of Connecticut are the many preserved old houses, many of them once the homes of historically prominent persons. Some are open to the public, but only in what is generally regarded as the regular vacation season. This can vary from early or late spring, through the summer into early or late fall. Few remain open during the winter months.

North of the Housatonic Bridge on the Merritt Parkway at Stratford, on the west bank of the river, is the Sikorsky helicopter plant. The adjoining tarmac usually has several of the machines parked there, and often they can be seen lifting off or landing.

Greater New Haven

Milford has the distinction of being the crossover point from the Merritt Parkway going east to the Connecticut Turnpike, (or going west vice versa). It is a shoreline town, a short drive midway between New Haven and Bridgeport. The Milford Jai Alai, 311 Old Gate Lane, is open from May to October on weekday evenings and matinees several days each week.

From Milford, it's a short drive east to New Haven, a treasure trove of things to see and do. Many of them are connected with Yale University.

While Hartford has its extensive collection of Colt revolvers, New Haven is proud of a gun made here that joined the six-shooter in winning the West—the famous Winchester repeating rifle. The development of the Winchester rifle, from 1866 to the present, is shown through models in the gun museum. In addition, there's a massive collection of 5,000 pieces of war and hunting equipment, ranging from guns of every variety to bullets, bayonets and bandoliers.

There's hardly a Connecticut town without a wildlife sanctuary, refuge, formal garden or nature trail. New Haven is no exception. On Wintergreen Avenue, the West Rock Nature Center has a zoo, ponds, picnic area, trails—and the Judges' Cave. And therein lies a tale. The story is told on a plaque bolted to a boulder:

"Here, May 15th, 1661, and for some weeks thereafter, Edward Whalley and his son-in-law William Goffe, members of parliament, General Officers in the Army of the Commonwealth and signers of the death warrant of King Charles I, found shelter and concealment from the officers of the Crown after the Restoration." Then the final sentence: "Opposition to tyrants is Obedience to God!"

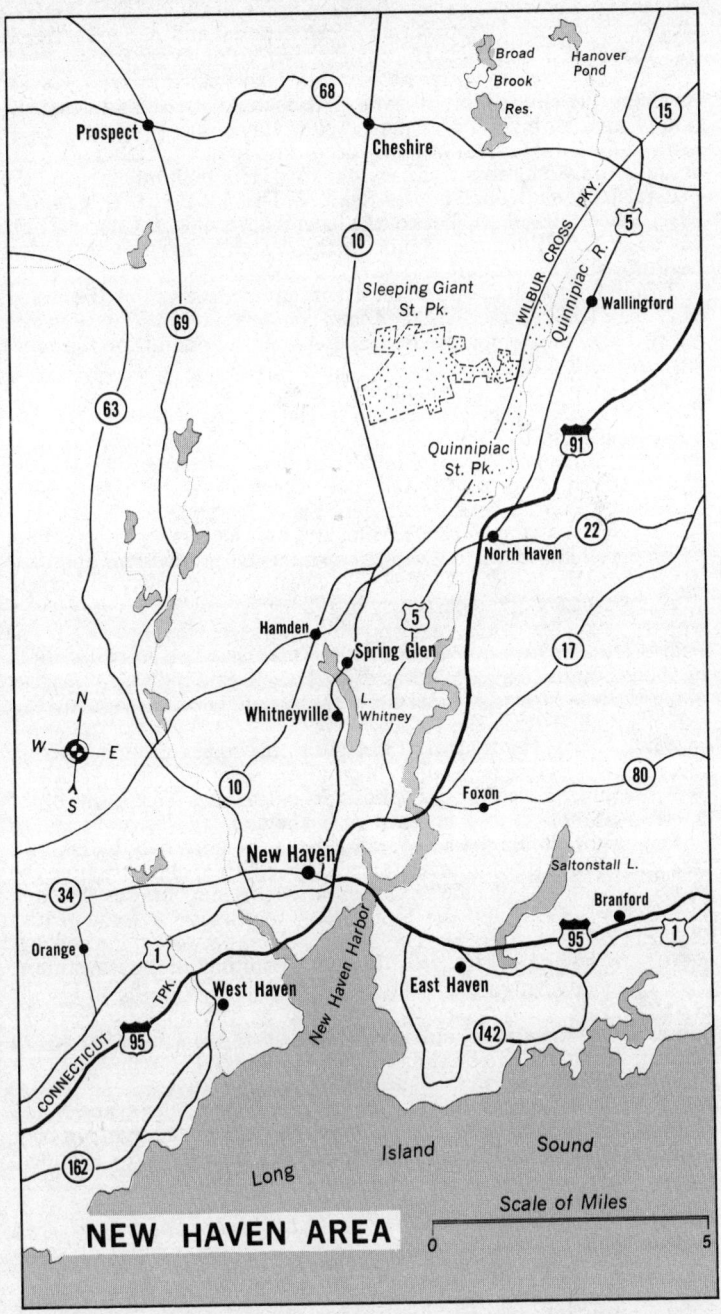

NEW HAVEN AREA

Scale of Miles
0   5

The two men who had sent the king to his death had fled England when their leader, Cromwell, had been deposed and King Charles II had mounted the throne. The cave is high up on West Rock.

A sweeping midtown face-lifting has taken place in New Haven, involving the elimination of slums and blighted streets and construction of modern buildings. The new New Haven has risen close to its historic Green, 16 acres of land laid out by founding fathers in 1638 and graced by churches, a library, the City Hall, built in 1861, and the Federal Building, which houses the U. S. District Court, U. S. Attorney's Office, and other offices of the federal government. Charles Dickens described Hillhouse Avenue in the center of town as the "most beautiful street in America."

Throughout the year, special events are scheduled on the green. There are free summer weekend jazz concerts, and in May, Powderhouse Day commemorates Benedict Arnold's demand for the city's keys to the Powderhouse.

In suitable weather, New Haven's *Liberty Belle* offers a lunchtime harbor cruise, weekend cruises, and special evening cruises. At the only horse-racing theater, Teletrack, near Long Wharf, you may place a bet and then watch your favorite horse race on a wide screen. Lunch and dinner served. A turn of the century Carousel has been restored at Lighthouse Point — much to the delight of everyone.

New Haven's Long Wharf Theater and Yale Repertory Theater have become well known for both their experimental productions and their productions of classics. The Schubert Theatre, handsomely and expensively refurbished, reopened early in 1984. This was once a pre-Broadway tryout theater where many notable shows were first produced. The Palace Theatre, formerly the Roger Sherman, has also reopened. Both of these houses are part of the New Haven Entertainment District along College Street. A Museum of American Theatre, with rotating exhibits, is housed in the Palace lobby.

While New Haven's nearly 130,000 citizens go about the business of making things, close to the old Village Green several thousand students at Yale University go about the business of learning. Yale is one of the finest institutions of higher learning in the country.

The visitor should get an overall view of the university by taking a free guided tour (for information, call 436–8330); then, extra time can be spent in any one of Yale's excellent museums and libraries. The new Art Gallery (1953) and the Yale Center for British Art and British Studies (1973) have priceless collections of masterworks. Particularly prized are the original Jonathan Trumbull paintings of the Revolution. Yale's Peabody Museum of Natural History ranks with the best in the country. Yale has a collection of musical instruments and Beinecke Library, the rare book and manuscript library is connected by an underground tunnel to Sterling Memorial Library, the main Yale University Library.

Albertus Magnus, Southern Connecticut State College, and South Central Community College are in New Haven. The University of New Haven is in West Haven and Quinnipiac College is in nearby Hamden.

Wallingford/Meriden Area

From New Haven, the Wilbur Cross Parkway and I–91 head north to Hartford. A few worthwhile stops may be made en route.

Old furnishings and documents are on display in the Jonathan Dickerman House, built in 1770 and maintained by the Hamden Historical Society. It is located at 4016 Whitney Avenue, close to Sleeping Giant State Park, one of the largest in Connecticut with more than 1,000 acres devoted to hiking, camping and picnicking. There's an excellent view of the surrounding countryside from a tower atop Mount Carmel.

Wallingford, up the road, is the home of a well-known school. The school is Choate-Rosemary Hall and the campus is located in the center of town. Among its noted graduates were John F. Kennedy and Adlai Stevenson.

The Samuel Parson House on South Main Street, restored by the Wallingford Historical Society, dates to about 1759. It has six fireplaces, a library, a Civil War collection, Indian artifacts and other items connected with Wallingford's early history.

In Meriden's Hubbard Park (on Route 66) is Castle Craig, a great stone tower with battlements 1,007 feet above sea level. The view from this location south, in fine weather, extends to Long Island Sound.

The first place where the Episcopalians worshipped in Connecticut was the Moses Andrews Homestead (1760), 424 West Main Street in Meriden. It is under the aegis of the local historical society and may be visited by appointment.

Routes 5, 15, I–91, 66, 70 and 71 all lead into Hartford. A side trip between Meriden and Hartford leads to New Britain, the "hardware city," home of the Stanley Works and other factories that make small tools, appliances and other gadgets that help keep the wheels of the country turning. There are 13.8 square miles devoted to 32 public parks in New Britain, ranging from the A. W. Stanley Park (224.5 acres) to others with less than an acre. Its Museum of American Art at 56 Lexington Street, which also has a natural history section for children, features the Arts in Life in America murals by Thomas Hart Benton.

Walnut Hill on West Main Street has an outstanding rose garden and illuminated 97-foot war memorial; Stanley Quarter Park, North Stanley Street, includes an eight-acre lake for swimming and an 18-hole public golf course.

West of Hartford to Litchfield Hills

Traveling west from Hartford, Route 44 (Albany Avenue) goes over Avon Mountain and down into the town of Avon. Greater Hartford's growing population, already living on most of the available land in the Connecticut Valley, is pushing up the mountain. The most expensive and most fashionable estates are now perched on the mountainside, with magnificent views of the city in the distance below.

In Avon, the Avon Old Farms School for Boys resembles a small English school in the Cotswolds of the 15th century. There are no special events scheduled here for the public, but visitors are welcome and can arrange for guides at the alumni office.

Not far from Avon, on Route 44, is Canton, a small village with a lively art colony and the Roaring Brook Nature Center.

Route 181 leads into Peoples State Forest, popular in summer months for camping, hiking, fishing and picnicking. On the other side of the park, on Route 20, is Riverton, where the Hitchcock Chair Factory (founded in 1818) is still making chairs modeled on the original designs. Visitors may watch through glass windows the "rushing" operation on the seats of the chairs. The chairs and other Colonial reproductions may be purchased in the salesroom. Associated with the Hitchcock factory is the nearby John T. Kenney Hitchcock Museum, specializing in 19th-century furnishings and artifacts.

Farther south, on Route 8, is Winsted, a town known to sightseers for its Laurel Festival the third week of June. Route 8 leads through Torrington, where John Brown, the fanatical abolitionist, was born. The house, just north of town near Route 4, burned down some years ago, but a ring of foundation stones and a plaque mark the site. Halfway between Winsted and Torrington, on a side road off Route 8 leading to Burr Pond, Gail Borden concocted the world's first condensed milk. Only a plaque marks the spot where the creamery stood, the beginning of the giant Borden Corporation.

In December, Christmas Village attracts children and their parents. The village is a free, noncommercial venture in Alvord Playground, and each child who visits Santa Claus receives a gift.

Indian Lookout, in Torrington, is a privately-owned mountain field of laurel, a magnificent display of Connecticut's state flower when in bloom.

From the Torrington valley, Route 202 climbs sharply into the Litchfield hills, a beautiful rural section of Connecticut. It is six miles to Litchfield Green, dominated by the beautiful white-steepled Congregational Church. On both sides of elm-lined North and South Streets are some elegant white, clapboarded Colonial homes with traditional black or green shutters. The area has been declared an historic district by the state, and no exterior changes may be made.

On South Street (Route 63) stands the Tapping Reeve House, one of Litchfield's prizes. But the eye of history is on another building on the same property, a small tan structure that was America's first law school. Visitors can see the desks at which many distinguished American jurists studied: men like Aaron Burr (Tapping Reeve's brother-in-law) and John C. Calhoun, both vice presidents of the United States; former supreme court justices Henry Baldwin, Leir Woodbury and Ward Hunt; six cabinet members, more than 100 congressmen, 28 senators, and numerous governors and chief justices of states. All these, and others, went forth from a one-room building in a remote Connecticut village to help spread the law throughout the land.

The birthplaces of three more famous Americans—Harriet Beecher Stowe, Henry Ward Beecher and Ethan Allen—all are on North Street.

A classical brick building houses the Litchfield Historical Society. It contains four galleries of exhibits depicting life in Litchfield during the past two centuries. A special "Please Do Touch" room is an exhibit for children.

The Haight Vineyard & Winery, on Chestnut Hill off Route 118 in Litchfield, is Connecticut's first vineyard/winery. Tours and tasting appointments may be made for certain days, May through October.

Route 202 leads to Bantam. Bantam Lake, on Route 209 to the south, is the largest natural lake in the state and a popular summer playground. While there is much private property on the lakeside, there's public swimming at Sandy Beach. At least half of the lake is bordered by the 3,500-acre White Memorial Conservation Center, Route 202, a bird and animal sanctuary that invites the public to hike, swim, picnic, camp and ride through its 27 miles of bridal paths. There's also a launching ramp for boats.

White Flower Farm, Route 63S has more than 25 acres of vari-colored flowers in bloom in mid-summer—a sight to behold! Giant begonias and other hothouse plants are in vast greenhouses. Open from April through December, it is a browser's paradise.

South on routes 209 and 61 is Bethlehem, a pleasant rural community of old Colonial homes, including the Bellamy House (1738), where the Rev. Joseph Bellamy taught classes on religion. The Glebe House (1600s) was a minister's farm or "glebe," and in 1783, in this living room, the first Episcopal Bishop in the United States was elected. The public spotlight was focused on Bethlehem in 1948, when the story of its Regina Laudis Abbey was made into a popular movie, starring Loretta Young, entitled *Come to the Stable*.

Washington (north again on Route 61 and then west on Route 109) has exquisite houses around a small green. The American Indian Archaeological Institute is on Route 199. It is a research and educational museum center for the study of prehistoric and historic man in Connecticut and New England. There are numerous exhibits, including a Paleo-Indian campsite, an indoor life-size reconstructed longhouse, and an Indian garden. There are regularly scheduled weekend programs open to the public as well as courses and field trips.

New Preston is north of Washington, via routes 45 and 202. Nearby is Lake Waramaug and its spacious state park. The area boasts fine country inns. Hopkins Vineyard welcomes visitors with samplings of its award-winning wines in a 19th-century—restored barn. The vineyard also maintains a hayloft gallery of works by local artists and craftsmen.

Throughout this area are many of the prep schools that draw their enrollment from every U.S. state and many foreign countries.

Still farther up Route 7 is Kent Falls State Park, a 275-acre preserve, with a beautiful waterfall.

Kent is the home of a prestigious preparatory school and the Sloane-Stanley Museum, which contains the Eric Sloane collection of early American tools. On the museum grounds are the remains of an early 18th-century blast furnace that once served the iron industry here.

Bull's Bridge in Kent crosses the Housatonic River, connecting Connecticut with New York State.

Little Goshen, a farming village on Route 4, has a pretty main street lined with white clapboard houses. Commercial hard-cheese-making in America started in Goshen and, in early days, its "pineapple" cheese was known throughout the country. The house that cheese built, a beautiful brick mansion, can be seen off Route 4 near the Torrington Country Club. Large farms abound in this area. In fact, half of all Connecticut's dairy farms are in the Litchfield area, but they, too, are slowly disappearing.

In this part of the country, democracy in its purest form (as practiced in the early days of the country) is still a way of life. Rules, regulations and ordinances are proposed by selectmen, but approval must be obtained from the voters assembled in traditional town meetings, where each has his say. Visitors may watch a town meeting in action from the balcony or the rear.

A short way from New Preston, on Route 202, is New Milford. There is an abandoned mica quarry near Merryall, where samples of columbite, gem garnet, aquamarines, beryl and other stones may be found by rockhounds, if permission is obtained to poke around.

Cornwall Area

Cornwall, on Route 4, just off Route 7, is another classic Colonial town that belongs on a calendar or postcard. Cornwall has attracted artists, writers, critics and poets, and is a delightful, congenial community. The photogenic, historic Cornwall covered bridge, one of the few remaining originals, spans the Housatonic River here.

The far northwestern corner of Connecticut is dotted with lakes, mountains, state parks, forests and lovely, old Colonial towns such as Sharon, Lakeville, Salisbury and Canaan. Each has charming inns, an historical society of some interest, perhaps the ruins of an early forge or foundry, a ravine, a gorge or a hiking trail. There are often art shows, antique shows and auctions.

Mohawk Mountain State Park, a popular ski area with tows, lifts, ski school, shops and a warming house, is in Cornwall. Since the area is in the lower snowbelt of New England, snow-making machines supplement nature. The tows and lifts do not operate for sightseeing in summer, although picnicking and hiking are popular.

Danbury Area

Route 7 north, past Danbury, Brookfield and New Milford, continues to Gaylordsville and Bulls Bridge and crosses the Housatonic River. Bulls Bridge is one of the few remaining covered bridges in Connecticut. Although covered bridges originated in the East, most have either rotted away or have been replaced by more modern bridges.

From New Milford, Route 7 south leads to Danbury. Alongside the highway, to the west, is a wooded area, behind which is man-made Candlewood Lake, the largest lake in the state. Much of the shore property is in private hands, but there are public beaches and marinas. Squantz Pond State Park is nearby, a popular swimming, boating and picnicking area.

Danbury, once the country's hat city, has an increasing number of corporate headquarters for major industries that have moved out to the suburbs from metropolitan areas.

Danbury was one of the cities burned by British raiding parties during the Revolution. Several buildings, now part of the Scott-Fanton Museum and Historical Society, 43 Main Street, escaped the torch and may be visited. Huntington Exhibition Hall has frequently changing exhibits of art, science and history. The rural Route 33 becomes the quaint, tree-lined Main Street of Ridgefield, one of Fairfield County's oldest and loveliest towns. Incorporated in 1709, its 35 square miles are home to about 20,000 people, including scientists, farmers, nurserymen, artists, writers and other professionals, as well as many corporation executives who have chosen their homes in country surroundings.

Bethel, southeast of Danbury, is the birthplace of Phineas T. Barnum, the great circus impressario. Putnam Memorial State Park is on Route 58 on the way to Redding Ridge. During the winter of 1778–9, New Hampshire and Connecticut regulars, under the command of General Israel Putnam, suffered from the cold, snow and lack of provisions. Two blockhouses and a museum recall the hardships that earned this tract the designation, "Valley Forge of Connecticut."

Bristol and Waterbury

From Litchfield, Route 254 angles down toward Thomaston, Terryville and Bristol. This is clock country, with two of the towns taking their names from pioneer clockmakers. Seth Thomas started his clock works in Thomaston in 1812, after learning the trade with Eli Terry, who patented a clock with wooden works that became hugely successful. In Terryville, where Terry started ticking, one of his original wooden clocks still tells time in the tower of the Congregational Church. But the real clock bonanza is in Bristol, the next city along the way. Here, more than 1600 clocks, some dating back to 1680, are on display in the American Clock & Watch Museum at 100 Maple Street. In Terryville, there is the Lock Museum of America, 130 Main Street, with over 18,000 locks and keys manufactured in Connecticut over a century ago.

Hershey Lake Compounce, on Route 229, just outside of Bristol, is a "turn of the century" amusement park. There are good swimming and picnic areas for family fun on any summer day.

Interstate 84 leads directly to Waterbury, the city that brass built. Its Mattatuck Historical Society Museum, 119 W. Main Street, has Whistler etchings, as well as a collection of pioneer relics. Children enjoy playing druggist in the miniature apothecary shop of its junior museum.

Route 8, southward toward the shore, passes through Naugatuck State Forest to Beacon Falls, where there's a covered bridge and a ravine for hikers. Old-home buffs will want to visit the unusually large saltbox house in Ansonia, built in 1748 by Reverend Richard Mansfield —first minister of the local Episcopal church—who served his parishioners for 72 years.

From Derby, Route 34 goes into New Haven and to the Connecticut Turnpike, which leads, then, into the eastern part of the state.

Branford to New London

In East Haven, signs lead to the Shoreline Trolley Museum, located on River Street near the Green. During the warm season, youngsters have an opportunity to ride old-fashioned horse-drawn streetcars, the first electric cars and many models in between—even the most modern trolleys, with cushioned seats and airflow design.

Bittersweet Handcraft Village, 779 E. Main Street (between Exits 56 and 57, I–95) an 85-acre farm—a working farm for over a century—has artists and craftsmen occupying the converted barns and coops. There is an extensive herb garden, Christmas tree plantation, chickens and a resident goat.

Also at Branford, there are roads leading from the Turnpike to the shore. It is possible, in the summer, to ride the mailboat around and through the Thimble Islands. On Money Island, legend has it that Captain Kidd buried some treasure. The islands are all privately owned and are not open to the public.

Guilford is a town of history and beauty. The Henry Whitfield House (1639–1640) Whitfield Street, is believed to be the oldest stone house in the state. Now a museum, it has an excellent exhibit of antiques, and an herb garden is replanted in the yard each year. The village has about 50 old houses of various design on original sites, many of them on the green. Among other buildings of interest are the Hyland House (1660),

84 Boston Street, whose five big old fireplaces are a feature, and the Thomas Griswold House (1774), 171 Boston Street.

The Guilford Handcrafts Center, 411 Church St. (Exit 58, I–95), is a gallery with shops and instruction in fine arts and crafts. The Congregational Church (1829), on the green, is a perfect example of Greek Revival architecture.

In Madison, the 18th-century Allis-Bushnell House at 853 Boston Post Road, has been restored and furnished by the Madison Historical Society. One room is furnished as the office of Dr. Milo Rindge, a physician who resided and worked out of the house early in this century. Children's toys, antiques and 18th-century costumes are on display. Madison also has a great many individually restored early houses that are owner-occupied.

Clinton, the next town along Route 1, has for many years been known as the home of Chesebrough Pond, makers of Vaseline and Pond's Cold Cream. The historic house to see here is the Stanton House, (c. 1790), 63 E. Main Street. It was originally a home and general store, now open to the public June through September.

At the mouth of the Connecticut River, where the river joins Long Island Sound, is the town of Old Saybrook, a flourishing center for boating and fishing. Yale University had its beginnings in Old Saybrook, and the story of the moving of the Yale library from its original location to New Haven caused such a local fight that the story was referred to as "The Battle of the Books." The United States' first submarine was built here during the Revolution, by David Bushnell. It carried one man, who propelled the craft by hand.

Across the Baldwin Bridge, over the Connecticut River, Exit 72 off the Connecticut Turnpike, leads into the beautiful, unspoiled town of Old Lyme. Its Congregational church has appeared in many architectural books, on calendars, and has been a very popular subject for the many artists who, over the years, have congregated in Old Lyme. The wide main street, with lush green trees and shrubs and historic old houses, gives the appearance of that typical New England country town everyone imagines.

The Florence Griswold House, 96 Lyme Street, is an art museum, once home to several 19th-century American painters. Also on Lyme Street, the Lyme Art Association Gallery has changing exhibits, and the Lyme Academy of Fine Arts has a faculty of recognized professional artists.

A unique museum, probably the only one of its kind, is the Nut Museum at 303 Ferry Road. It is housed in a Victorian house, home of the owner of the collection of nuts, nutcrackers, nut art and even nut music. The admission is one nut plus a contribution. From the Nut Museum, turn right on Route 156 toward Niantic. Two miles or so from Ferry Road is the Hall Mark Ice Cream Place, a landmark in this area. Sandwiches and snacks are available but the homemade ice cream is worth a stop (open May to October).

Route 213, which intersects Route 156 in Jordan Village, Waterford, leads to two important points of interest. The Harkness Memorial State Park has a beautiful beach, although, ironically, no swimming is allowed because the state does not provide lifeguards. There are acres of grassy lawns for picnics or just strolling, and, during the summer, exquisite flower gardens. The mansion, once the summer home of the late philanthropist Edward Harkness and his wife, is not furnished, but on exhibit in the rooms are some of the 900 life-size bird paintings in water color, bequeathed to the state by the Brooklyn-born artist, Rex Brasher.

New London

Still farther along on Route 213 is the Eugene O'Neill Memorial Theater Center, which has become one of this country's most renowned experimental theaters. This is the home of the National Playwrights Conference, the National Drama Critics Institute and the National Theatre Institute. Visitors are always welcome and readings from the plays of new playwrights during the summer have become increasingly popular for the public. An adjunct to the O'Neill, owned and operated by the Theater Center, is the Monte Cristo Cottage, 325 Pequot Avenue, New London, facing the Thames River. This property, once owned by James O'Neill, father of Eugene, the famous playwright, was the family's summer home and became the setting for "Long Day's Journey into Night" and "Ah Wilderness," two of Eugene O'Neill's better known plays. Open to the public at specified times.

A short distance away is Ocean Beach Park, in New London. It is maintained by the City of New London and open to all visitors. It was created after the 1938 hurricane, when beachfront properties were severely damaged. The beach plan was derived from Jones Beach, on Long Island, but on a much smaller scale. It is one of the most popular beaches in this part of the state and has an amusement park area and picnic grove, as well as a wide sandy beach.

New London, a six-mile-long waterfront city and one of the earliest towns in Connecticut, has historically looked to the sea for its sustenance. Along with Nantucket and New Bedford, New London put forth whaling ships that penetrated deep into the South Pacific in search of the elusive giants of the sea. Sealing, as well, was an important industry for ships out of New London.

Whaling from New England ports declined shortly after the Civil War, when Americans started pumping oil out of the ground in Pennsylvania, precluding the need for whale oil.

During the heyday of sealing and whaling, however, fortunes were made in New London. The public library began through a whaler's bequest to the city, and the building was opened in 1892; the Lawrence & Memorial Associated Hospitals began through the philanthropic interest of Sebastian Lawrence; and a few homes of the more prosperous are today reminders of this historic past. Although redevelopment in the city has taken many of the older buildings, a few remain to memorialize New London's days of glory.

Continuing its long tradition as a seafaring town, New London has been, since the early part of this century, the home of the U. S. Coast Guard Academy, one of the country's four military academies. Visitors may tour the grounds, some buildings, and—when she's in port—the bark *Eagle,* a tall ship used for cadet training cruises. *Eagle,* a former German ship named *Horst Wessel,* was a prize of World War II. She was renovated, renamed and turned over to the Coast Guard for training purposes. She is a magnificent sight as she leaves the mouth of the Thames River and heads out to sea, her sails filled with wind.

Battalion reviews attract visitors to the academy parade grounds during seasons when it is comfortable to drill outdoors.

The New London County Historical Society is located in the Shaw Mansion, on Blinman Street. Built in 1756 for Captain Nathaniel Shaw, a wealthy shipowner and trader, the collections in the house are primarily related to his son, Nathaniel, Jr., who, at the outbreak of the Revolution, was named naval agent for Connecticut. The Shaw Mansion became the naval office for Connecticut, and it was here that the first naval expedition under the Second Continental Congress, in 1776, was outfitted.

The two Hempsted houses at 11 Hempstead Street are among the few remaining 17th-century houses in Connecticut. Joshua Hempsted House (1678) survived Benedict Arnold's burning of New London, and Nathaniel Hempsted house (1759) is one of two surviving mid-18th-century cut-stone houses in Connecticut. The house stands on part of the original six-acre land grant received in 1645 by Robert Hempsted. It is owned and cared for by the Antiquarian and Landmarks Society of Connecticut, an organization that supports the restoration and maintenance of several historic buildings in towns throughout the state.

Nathan Hale Schoolhouse stands on Captain's Walk next to the Municipal Building. Sons of the American Revolution care for this historic site.

The Old Town Mill, built in 1650 by John Winthrop, Jr., as a grist mill, rebuilt in 1800 and restored more recently, is in its original location on Mill Street, under the Gold Star Memorial Bridge (I–95).

North from the Old Town Mill, and across from the U.S. Coast Guard Academy on Mohegan Avenue, is the Lyman Allyn Museum, an art museum with other collections of early American furniture, porcelains, silver, costumes, Greek and Roman artifacts, Oriental sculpture and 19th-century dollhouses, dolls and toys.

Connecticut College, also on Mohegan Avenue, is a coeducational, liberal arts college and is the cultural center of the city. It adjoins the museum property to the north. Dance, drama, music, and sports programs attract many people from within and outside the local community.

The 70-acre Connecticut College Arboretum is a stand of virgin forest, where there are 400-year-old trees. The Thames Science Center, nearby, is a center for environmental interests in this area, with nature trails, lecture series and a small museum.

Mitchell College on Pequot Avenue, New London, is a two-year community college attracting a student body from many parts of the U. S. as well as abroad. It also contributes to the cultural scene in the city and offers day and evening classes of special interest to area residents.

The expansive U. S. Naval Submarine Base, across the Thames River, is the headquarters of the North Atlantic fleet. Regulations concerning visitors to the base should be checked in advance. There is a submarine library and museum on the base. The first nuclear-powered submarine, *Nautilus,* is enshrined here.

The Submarine Memorial Association at 350 Thames Street is in Groton, just north of the Electric Boat Division of General Dynamics Corporation (builders of the Navy's nuclear submarines). The World War II submarine *Croaker* is open to the public here. The complex includes a small museum.

The 135-foot Groton Monument, offering a panoramic view of the harbor, marks the spot where American soldiers at Fort Griswold surrendered to traitor Benedict Arnold and his British cohorts—then were treacherously cut down to the last man.

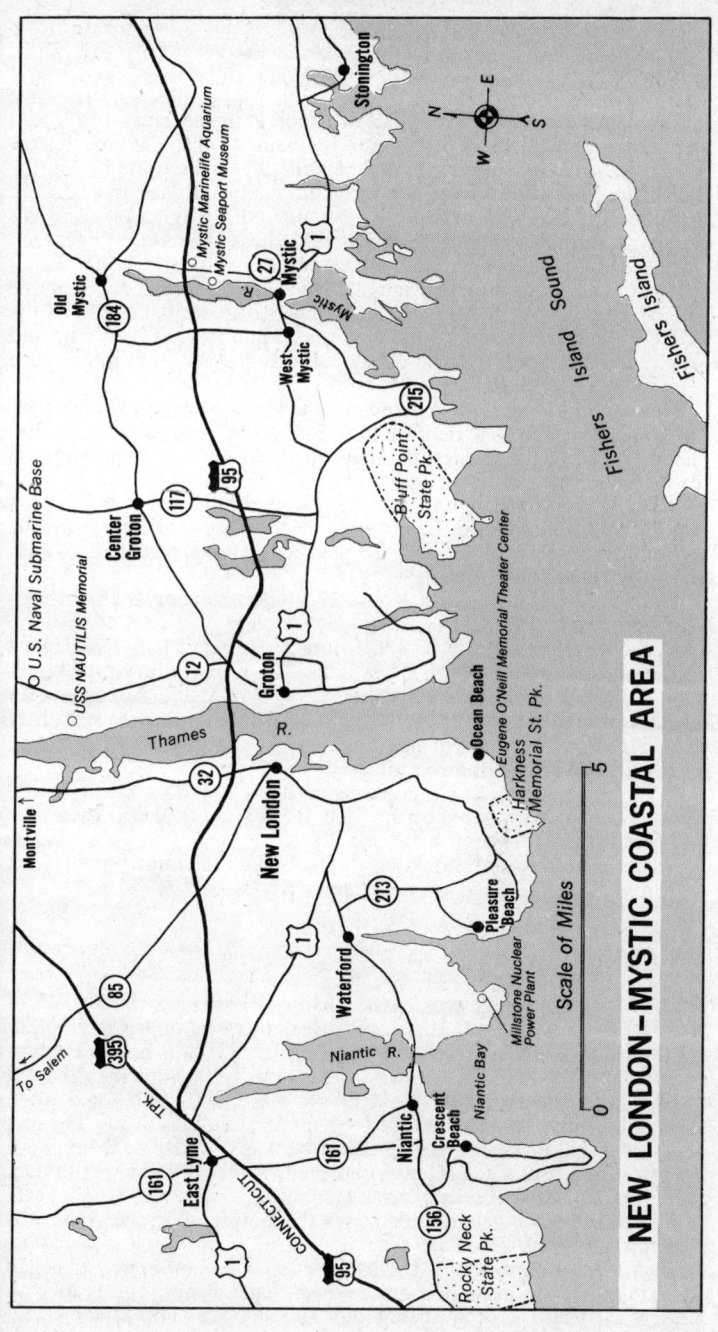

NEW LONDON–MYSTIC COASTAL AREA

Mystic

The community of Mystic, half of which is in the Town of Groton and half in the Town of Stonington, is divided by the Mystic River.

Mystic Seaport Museum, Greenmanville Avenue (Route 27) on the Stonington side of the river, is one of the major outdoor museums in this country. It is a recreated 19th-century New England coastal village, with authentic buildings and period ships. The Geo. Greenman & Bros. Shipyard, which built many of the record-breaking sailing vessels of the past century, originally stood on the site of the Seaport. The Marine Historical Association, chartered in 1930, developed the "village" by moving some buildings from other parts of New England and by building architectural reproductions of others that might have been in such a village.

The mid-19th-century American wooden whaleship, *Charles W. Morgan,* last of the New Bedford fleet, is the focal point of the museum. She is typical of the whaleships that sailed out of New England ports to the far corners of the world.

Other storied sailing ships are berthed at the wharves, and several major exhibition galleries have vast collections of maritime artifacts, including figureheads, scrimshaw, paintings and prints, half models and fully rigged ship models.

The Seaport is located on Route 27, the connecting road between I–95 and Route 1.

At the intersection of I–95 and Route 27 is Olde Mistick Village, a unique shopping center with shops housed in 19th-century-type buildings. Adjacent to the village is the Mystic Marinelife Aquarium, an outstanding tourist attraction. A section devoted entirely to seals is of special interest. Several seal and dolphin shows are presented daily and are especially fascinating to children.

A small museum of Stonington memorabilia, portraits, weapons and whaling gear is maintained by the Stonington Historical Society in The Old Stonington Lighthouse, on the Point.

North of Mystic and Stonington, interesting old country roads lead to Norwich, at the head of the Thames River.

Norwich

The Montville bridge crosses the Thames River a few miles south of Norwich. Montville is of interest because of its rich Indian lore, including the story of Uncas, chief of the Mohegans, who was born a Pequot.

Outsiders, the Pequots invaded Connecticut and conquered the local Indians; then, fearing the threat of the white settlers, turned upon them. The Indians were provoked. Misunderstandings arose. The end result, war and massacre, was the same here as it would be throughout the rest of the country in later years wherever the white man put down roots and squeezed the Indian off his lands.

When the fighting had ended and the power of the Indians was broken, this spot would be remembered as Connecticut's bloodiest battleground. Reminders of Uncas are everywhere: at huge Cochegan Rock, a 6,000-ton mass of granite where, legend says, Uncas used to hide; at Fort Hill, Uncas' stronghold; and at Uncas Hill in Mohegan, where the cellar of Uncas' cabin can be seen.

Uncas, it should be noted, disagreed with the Pequots and became "a friend to the whites."

Near the Mohegan Congregational Church is a small museum of Indian relics, the Tantaquidgeon Indian Museum, on Route 32. In the yard are the frames of both a long house and a round house, dwellings common to eastern Indians, who did not live in the buffalo-hide teepees favored by the western Indians.

Norwich, one of the earliest settlements in the state, shares with its sister cities the unique Connecticut distinction of being first in the design of an item that changed the entire business world.

On August 26, 1843, Charles Thurber perfected and patented the first typewriter for business correspondence. (The portable typewriter was patented by G. C. Blickensderfer of Stamford in 1892.)

Visitors to Norwich should visit the town's most historic house, the Leffingwell Inn (1675), 348 Washington Street at the junction of Routes 2 and 169. It was the home of Norwich industrialist Christopher Leffingwell, and it has been authentically restored and furnished with fine antiques. Continental officers met here to plot war plans and George Washington visited frequently.

The Slater Memorial Museum and Converse Art Gallery, 108 Crescent Street, is particularly noted for its Indian and Japanese collections. It is located on the grounds of Norwich Free Academy, a privately operated city high school. A memorial near the academy honors Samuel Reid, the soldier who, in 1818, designed one of the versions of the Stars and Stripes.

The Yantic and Shetucket Rivers join at Norwich to become the Thames River, which then flows southward to the sea. Indian Sachems are buried in a special graveyard set aside by President Andrew Johnson and marked by the Uncas Monument on Sachem Street.

Near the Yantic River Falls is Indian Leap, so named because the Mohegan Indians drove the Narragansetts over the cliff in 1643 during the Battle of Great Plain.

Mohegan Park and Memorial Rose Garden on Mohegan Road, has a small zoo, picnic area and a profusion of roses in bloom in June. The Rose Arts Festival, an annual event in Norwich, was inspired by this array.

North of Norwich, via the Connecticut Turnpike to Exit 85 and then on Route 138, roads from Voluntown lead to Pachaug State Forest, a 22,000-acre lake and one of the largest forest preserves in the state. Little known to most Connecticut residents from other parts of the state, it is inked in brightly on the maps of fishermen.

Danielson-Putnam Area

Travel north on the Connecticut Turnpike through Danielson and west on Route 6 to Brooklyn, and Israel Putnam surfaces again. This area is his country, his home. Putnam, a doughty farmer-soldier, served the state and the country so well during the Revolutionary War that his memory is surrounded by legends and fanciful stories which, if not necessarily true, have the basis of truth.

From Brooklyn, Route 6 in a westerly direction goes into Willimantic where a World War II Museum is at 64 Willowbrook Street, (which is Route 6). Route 195 leads to Mansfield and Storrs, the location of the main campus of the University of Connecticut. (Mansfield, incidentally, is where America's first silk mill (1829) was located. The building is now located at the Greenfield Village Museum in Dearborn, Michigan.) "U-Conn" is a bustling, ever-growing institution with many facilities. The campus buildings are set on landscaped rolling hills, with ponds and streams between. The agricultural school is one of the oldest and most respected in the country. There are several branches of the university in cities throughout the state, including medical, dental and law schools.

Farther west on Route 44A is Coventry, where Nathan Hale's family homestead is open to the public. Hale was hanged by the British in Manhattan and buried in an unknown grave. The body of his brother, Richard, is in a grave on St. Eustatius, Dutch West Indies, where he died of consumption. While both brothers were separated in death by many miles, they were united in the heart of their father, Deacon Hale, who expressed his love for his sons on a cenotaph he erected in a burial ground in Coventry, now known as the Nathan Hale Cemetery. The Revolutionary War collection in the Hale house is of historic significance.

Caprilands Herb Farm on Silver Street has an 18th-century dwelling right in the middle of herb gardens that have about every variety of herbs (said to be more than 300 types). Open to the public from April to December, an herb luncheon may be available if you reserve in advance.

Lebanon, another village with a classic green, is southeast of Coventry via Route 87. Jonathan Trumbull's home was on the green. He was a towering figure in the Revolution, who won this praise from Washington: "But for Jonathan Trumbull, the war could not have been carried to a successful conclusion."

Trumbull was governor of the Connecticut Colony when war broke out. His sympathies were with the revolutionaries, and he lent his prestige, his money and his efforts to further the war effort. From a building near his house, the "war office" of the Revolution, Trumbull marshalled supplies, men and war material to keep the army fighting. So efficient and effective was this man, Washington was often heard to say, "Let us consult Brother Jonathan."

Trumbull succored Washington's starving troops at Valley Forge, when he mounted a cattle drive of 300 steers from Connecticut to that sorely pressed winter encampment.

Trumbull's house and the "war office" may be visited. Trumbull became first governor of the state of Connecticut. His son was a noted Colonial artist.

Heading in a southwesterly direction, Route 16 will lead into Colchester, where the restored Nathaniel Foote House (1702), on the south side of Norwich Avenue, has an interesting exhibit of Colonial relics.

En route to Middletown, a sidetrip to the Salmon River State Forest includes a beautiful drive along the Salmon River. The Comstock Covered Bridge is one of the few remaining in Connecticut, although this one is closed to traffic.

South of the Salmon River is Day Pond State Park, with facilities for swimming, fishing, and picnicking.

At Westchester, Route 149 veers off toward Moodus Hills, a summer vacation area with a sprinkling of resorts similar, in a smaller way, to those of New York's Catskills and Pennsylvania's Poconos.

Portland is on the east side of the Connecticut River, opposite Middletown. From its brownstone quarries came most of the stone for the brownstone houses in New York City. Rockhounds flock to the nearby

Strickland Quarry, carefully chipping out beautiful specimens from the wide variety of minerals.

Middletown has several historic homes and an excellent historical society, but its major attraction is Wesleyan University. The home of the Honors College, built in 1828 by the Russell family, was one of the grandest mansions in the state. The General Mansfield House has a furniture collection.

The campus overlooks the town and the river. Once the largest city in the state, Middletown was soon surpassed by Hartford, New Haven, and Bridgeport. Today, its major industry is the manufacture of marine hardware.

From Middletown, south on Route 9, take Exit 7 to Route 82 across the Connecticut River to Goodspeed's Landing, an Historic District of East Haddam. The Goodspeed Opera House, an architectural gem built in 1876 and "Home of the American Musical Theatre," is open from April through November presenting new and revival musicals. Here is where several shows began their Broadway runs. Tours July and August on Mondays from 1 to 3. Walk to shops, craft co-ops in historic houses, and East Haddam Historical Society Museum. For a side trip, take Route 149 past the one mile of 18th- and 19th-century houses to Johnsonville Village, a private Victorian restoration. From Route 149 take Route 151 to Moodus Center to the Amasa Day House, an historical home open May 15 to October 15.

Route 82 leads to the Gillette Castle State Park, in Hadlyme, where one of the few authentic castles erected in America still stands. It was built by William Gillette, the actor who made a fortune playing the role of Sherlock Holmes.

Farther down Route 9 are signs directing the tourist to the Chester-Hadlyme Ferry. This little ferry is one of two plying the Connecticut River and dates back to the days before bridges spanned the river. It is now operated by the state and, for a minimal fee, one crosses in about five minutes—car and all. From the ferry, continue on Rte. 148 into Chester, a village of shops and restaurants. The National Theatre of the Deaf and the Goodspeed Opera House satellite, "Goodspeed at Chester," are here.

For a country road to New Haven, take Route 80 from Deep River over to I-91. Route 80 winds through farm country, the communities of Winthrop, Killingworth, North Madison, North Branford and Foxon before connecting with I-91. By taking this route one avoids the turnpike driving on Routes 9 and I-95 to New Haven, but also misses the historic little town of Essex.

Route 9A, from Chester through Deep River, is a beautiful rural road. It leads directly to the town of Essex, where bustling marinas are home ports for magnificent yachts. The main street, although filled with interesting shops and restaurants, appears primarily residential. Old sea captains' houses, which have been perfectly maintained throughout the years, give the town a prosperous air. Essex has been the home of the E. E. Dickinson Witch Hazel manufacturing plant for years. The Valley Railroad Steam Train, a popular tourist attraction, begins its trip north from tracks nearby.

Route 9 south dissolves into the Connecticut Turnpike (I-95), at Old Saybrook, running west to New York via New Haven, Bridgeport and Stamford, or east to Rhode Island and Massachusetts via New London.

There are some state parks and recreation areas and scores of lovely old towns and villages—each with its own history and appeal—that may seem to have been omitted. However, the cities, towns and attractions included in this routing are fairly representative of what to see and do when visiting Connecticut, while attempting to follow a somewhat logical pattern on the map.

This guide can be followed to the letter or side trips to other towns may be made impulsively. Either way, Connecticut is a traveler's delight.

 **SIGHTSEEING CHECKLIST.** Connecticut, a state for all seasons, has something to interest visitors of all ages at any time. Several ski areas located throughout the state have fine up-to-date lifts and trails; autumn leaves are superb, summer boating and swimming, theater, museums, sports for participants and spectators. Some of the experiences we would suggest during your visit to this state might include:

Theater. Attending a dramatic performance at Long Wharf Theatre or Yale Repertory Theater in New Haven; the Hartford Stage Company's series during the winter months; the Goodspeed Opera House in East Haddam which is dedicated to revivals and new musical comedies. Performance dates vary from late March through November but reservations in advance are absolutely necessary at whichever theatre you wish to go.

Castles and Ferries. Near East Haddam, in Hadlyme, is the Rhenish castle built by actor William Gillette on a high promontory overlooking the Connecticut River. Below the castle is the historic little Hadlyme-Chester ferry which will take you and no more than five automobiles across the river for a small fee in about five minutes. From Chester, down to Essex—all picturebook country—to the Valley Steam Train and a riverside/countryside ride up the river, returning if you wish by sightseeing boat.

Yale University in New Haven has a magnificent campus in the heart of the city that invites a stroll or guided tour. Yale's many museums and libraries are sources of vast information and pleasure.

Hartford. A visit to Hartford should include the Old State House (1796) on Main Street, the oldest in the nation; Mark Twain House and Nook Farm, home of Harriet Beecher Stowe (1870s), both nicely restored and furnished; the Civic Center, downtown; and in the summer the rose gardens at Elizabeth Park.

Air Museum. At Bradley International Airport in Windsor Locks, just outside of Hartford, New England Air Museum has aircraft from 1909 to the present.

Litchfield. The town of Litchfield has been designated an historic district—and the white clapboard houses on the wide main street reflect the early history for which each is known.

Stonington and Mystic in the southeastern corner of the state have natural, restored, and more recently created attractions. Stonington's streets of homes—some more lavish, the former homes of ship owners and captains of another century, are intermingled with the homes of draggermen and lobster fishermen. Present owners zealously guard the immaculate appearance of their town.

Mystic is sought out for what has been known for decades as the number-one tourist attraction in the state: Mystic Seaport Museum, a recreated, mid-19th-century New England coastal village with, in addition, numerous ships afloat and ashore and galleries of maritime treasures. The Mystic Marinelife Aquarium close by has vast displays of sea animals and daily seal, whale and dolphin shows.

Submarine. A few miles west, in Groton, "the submarine capital of the world," has a Submarine Memorial Association and the *USS Croaker,* a "mothballed" World War II submarine, now restored and open to visitors. The first nuclear-powered submarine, *Nautilus,* is enshrined at the U.S. Naval Submarine Base here.

Cruises. There are numerous day cruises from East Haddam, New London, Mystic, New Haven, Bridgeport and Norwalk, on many types of vessels—sail, motor ships, ferries . . . a wide choice here . . . and charter fishing, out of New London particularly, is becoming better known and more popular all the time.

Historic houses, restored and refurbished, are located throughout the state, usually owned and maintained by local historical societies. These graphically describe Connecticut living from the first settlements to the present. Most are open to the public in summer at specific times.

Etcetera. Football games in autumn, Jai alai, National Hockey League games, golf and tennis championship tournaments, and even folk dancing clubs are other features for the visitor to investigate.

And Connecticut restaurants, some of the best in the world, are waiting to provide some of their most interesting cuisine . . .

PRACTICAL INFORMATION FOR
THE REST OF CONNECTICUT

Note: Large Practical Information sections are organized by touring area for your convenience. Practical Information for the Hartford area is given earlier in this chapter.

 **FACTS & FIGURES.** Connecticut derives its name from the Algonquin Indian word *quinnehtukqut,* meaning "beside the long tidal river." In 1959, the General Assembly officially designated it "The Constitution State." The state flower is the mountain laurel; state tree, the white oak; state bird, the robin; state animal, the sperm whale; state insect, the praying mantis. *Qui transtulit sustinet* ("He who transplanted still sustains") is the state motto. The General Assembly designated "Yankee Doodle" the state song in 1978.

Hartford is the capital and largest city in the state, with a population just less than 150,000. The population of the whole state is over 3 million.

The climate is moderate. Naturally there will be differences between the hills of the northwestern corner and the shores of Long Island, but year-round average conditions are as follows:

	Jan.	Feb.	Mar.	Apr.	May	Jun.
Average Temperature (F)	25	27	36	48	59	68
Average Temperature (C)	−4	−3	2	9	15	20
Days of Rain or Snow	11	11	11	11	12	11
	Jul.	Aug.	Sept.	Oct.	Nov.	Dec.
Average Temperature (F)	73	72	63	53	42	28
Average Temperature (C)	23	22	17	12	6	−2
Days of Rain or Snow	10	10	10	8	11	12

Connecticut is approximately 100 mi. long and 50 mi. wide from the Massachusetts border to Long Island. The total area is 5,009 square miles. Connecticut was the fifth of the original thirteen states to ratify the Constitution, on Jan. 9, 1788. The Connecticut River flows southward towards Long Island Sound, dividing the state roughly in two. There are 6,000 lakes and ponds and 8,400 mi. of streams.

 **HOW TO GET THERE. By air:** Within the state there are 27 commercial airports, 8 commercial heliports and 3 commercial seaplane bases. The major airports are: Bradley International (Windsor Locks), Tweed–New Haven (New Haven), Trumbull (Groton), Bridgeport (Stratford) and Waterbury-Oxford. Direct flights out of many cities are operated to Bradley by *USAir, American, Delta, Eastern, TWA, United, Bar Harbor, Pan Am, Piedmont, Ransome, Empire, Northeastern, People Express,* and *Pilgrim.*

Connecticut Limousine Service, Inc. serves air travelers between various points in Connecticut and New York's airports (Kennedy, LaGuardia and Newark airports). Telephone within Connecticut, 800–922–6161 for information on rates, schedules, departure points and reservations. Senior citizen rates.

By train: *Amtrak* trains serve Connecticut from New York's Pennsylvania Station, either along the shoreline route via New Haven to New London, or the alternate route via New Haven to Hartford. *Metro North* commuter trains leave New York's Grand Central Terminal, making local stops from Greenwich east to New Haven and north to Danbury. For Amtrak information call 800–523–5700; for Metro North, 800–223–6052. Also try local railroad stations.

By car: More than 8,000 miles of state, interstate and local roadways crisscross the 5,000 square miles of Connecticut. Most motorists drive in from New York on the Merritt Pkwy., Conn. Tpke. (I–95), or I–84.

By bus: *Greyhound, Bonanza* and *Trailways* buses depart for Connecticut destinations from the Port Authority Terminal, 41st Street and 8th Ave., New York. Schedules and rate information at local bus terminals. Inquire about senior citizen rates.

By boat: Nautical-minded travelers arrive on yachts and motor boats at marinas dotting the 253 miles of the Long Island Sound shoreline.

Ferries: Bridgeport–Port Jefferson, L.I. Ferry, from Union Sq. dock in Bridgeport (Exit 27 off Conn. Tpke. to State St. to dock). Daily April to December. Car reservations suggested, extra fare and deposit required. 90-minute sail. For reservations/information in Connecticut, call 334–5993 or 367–3043; in New York, 516–473–0286.

New London–Block Island, R. I. Ferry, from Ferry St. downtown New London, near railroad station. Car reservation must be made in advance with deposit required. Service from mid-June to mid-Sept. only. Three hour sail. For reservations/information, call 442–7891 or 442–9553.

New London–Fishers Island, N.Y. Ferry, from City Pier, New London. Service year round. 45-minute sail. Telephone 443–6851; on Fishers Island 516–788–7463 or 800–358–5804.

New London–Orient Point, L. I., N. Y. Ferry, from Ferry St., downtown New London. Reservations for car required with deposit. Year-round service. 90-minute sail. Call 443–5281 or 443–5035. Orient Point phone 516–323–2545.

TELEPHONES. All Connecticut has the area code 203. Listings throughout this chapter therefore do not carry the area code. For out-of-local area, within Connecticut, simply dial "1" and the number. Telephone booths are conveniently located and some highways have intermittent emergency telephones.

HOTELS AND MOTELS. Hotels, motels, motor inns and country inns throughout Connecticut offer overnight accommodations comparable to better-than-average facilities in cities and towns throughout the United States. Most rooms are air conditioned and have TV in the rooms. Pools are outdoor, unless noted. Accommodations are listed by average price range for double occupancy, as follows: *Deluxe* $70 and up; *Expensive* $50–$69; *Moderate* $30–$49; *Inexpensive* under $30. Always check for family or senior citizen rates.

GREENWICH TO NEW HAVEN AREA

BRIDGEPORT. Sheraton-Bridgeport. *Expensive.* 815 Lafayette Blvd. (366–5421). Downtown, adjacent to shopping plaza. Restaurant. Lounge entertainment. Pets. Sauna. Indoor pool. Airport limo. Handicap access.

DARIEN. Holiday Inn. *Expensive.* 50 Ledge Rd. Exit 10 I–95 (655–8211). Restaurant, cocktail lounge with entertainment weekends. Room svc. Pets. Babysitting, valet svc. Airport limo. Handicap access.

Howard Johnson's Motor Lodge. *Expensive.* Exit 11 off I–95 (655–3933). Two-story motel, member of chain. Oversized family rooms. Restaurant with cocktail lounge. Room svc. Pool. Pets. Babysitting available. Nearby tennis and boating. Coin-op laundry on premises, valet svc. Handicap access.

FAIRFIELD. Fairfield Motor Inn. *Expensive.* 417 Post Rd., Exit 22 off I–95 (255–0491). Attractive colonial-style motel. Restaurant, lounge with entertainment and dancing weekends. Pool. Extra charge for pets. Handicap access.

GREENWICH. Homestead Inn. *Deluxe.* 420 Field Point Rd., Exit 3 off I–95 (869–7500). Fine old 18th-century colonial-style inn in residential area near Sound. Excellent restaurant with small lounge.

Showboat Inn. *Expensive.* Steamboat Road, Exit 3 off I–95 (661–9800), or (800) 243–8511. Large, modern motel on the water. Docking space available. Good restaurant, two lounges with entertainment. Room svc. Pool. Babysitting available. Airport limo service. Handicap access.

Note: At presstime construction had begun on a **Hyatt Regency.** Call worldwide reservations, 800–228–9000.

NEW CANAAN. Roger Sherman Inn. *Expensive.* Rte. 124 (966–4541). Charming New England inn with fine restaurant and lounge. Breakfast available to guests. Airport limo. Handicap access.

The Maples Inn. *Moderate.* Rte. 124 (966–2927). Breakfast only. Fine restaurants close by. Within walking distance to railroad station and shops.

NORWALK. Holiday Inn. *Expensive.* On U. S. 1 at Exit 13 off I–95 (853–3477). High-rise, restaurant, lounge with entertainment, room svc. Indoor pool. Pets. Babysitting available. Health spa and sauna. Handicap access.

Silvermine Tavern. *Moderate.* Perry & Silvermine Aves., 2 mi. north of Merritt Pkwy. (847–4558). Authentic 200-yr.-old New England inn. Rooms furnished with antiques, some with canopy beds and porches overlooking pond. TV in parlor. Rural locale. Fine restaurant, bar. Continental breakfast included. Some pets allowed. Country store adjacent.

STAMFORD. Le Pavillon Hotel. *Deluxe.* 60 Strawberry Hill Ave., Exit 8 off I–95 (357–8100). A large, luxurious downtown hotel catering especially to business travelers. Restaurant, bar, laundry, beauty parlor. Limousine service arranged. All accommodations are 2-room suites. Handicap access.

Stamford Marriott. *Deluxe.* 2 Stamford Forum. Exit 8 off I–95 (357–9555, or 800 228–9290). Strikingly modern, maximum service. Restaurant, coffee shop, cocktail lounge with nightly entertainment. Indoor-outdoor pool, health club. Laundry and valet svc. Pets. Babysitting and doctor available. Family rates and weekend package plans. Handicap access.

Ramada Inn. *Expensive.* 19 Clark's Hill Rd., Exit 8 off I–95 (327–4300). Restaurant, lounge, and sauna. Tennis and boating nearby. Handicap access.

STRATFORD. Marnick's Restaurant-Motel. *Moderate.* 10 Washington Pkwy. (I–95 Exit 30). (377–6288). Small, but access to beach is a plus here. Nearby tennis courts, golf course, and boat rentals. Handicap access.

Stratford Inn. *Moderate.* 6905 Main St., Exit 53 off Merritt Pkwy. (378–7351). Large, attractive motel, overlooking Housatonic River. Good restaurant, cocktail lounge with entertainment. Pool, playground. Pets. Babysitting available. Laundry on premises. Valet svc. Shuttle to airport limo.

WESTPORT. Westport New Englander Motor Hotel. *Expensive.* 1595 Post Rd. (259–5236). Restaurant. Airport Limo. Near shops.

GREATER NEW HAVEN AREA

HAMDEN. Howard Johnson's Motor Lodge. *Moderate.* Exit 10 off I–91. Just outside New Haven (288–3831). Near Sleeping Giant State Park and minutes from Yale Bowl and New Haven Coliseum. Pets. Airport limo.

Sleeping Giant Motel. *Inexpensive.* 3400 Whitney Ave., Exit 10 off I–91 (288–2502). Small motel near State Park and Quinnipiac College. Indoor pool. Airport limo.

MILFORD. Holiday Inn. *Expensive.* U. S. 1 (Exit 39B on I–95) (878–6561). Branch of chain. Convenient. Restaurant. Pool. Pets. Nearby tennis, golf, jai alai.

Howard Johnson's Motor Lodge. *Expensive.* 1052 Boston Post Rd. Exit 39A, I–95 (878–4611). Restaurant, lounge entertainment, playground, indoor pool and sauna. Handicap access.

Inn on the Parkway. *Moderate.* Wheelers Farms Rd., Exit 55 off Merritt Pkwy. (878–3521). Restaurant and coffee shop with full service.

Shoreline Motel. *Inexpensive.* 735 Boston Post Rd. (874–9975). Small facility with family units. Pool.

NEW HAVEN. Colony Inn. *Deluxe.* 1157 Chapel St. (776–1234). Continental breakfast. Gourmet restaurant, lounge. Nearby sport facilities.

New Haven Inn and Conference Center. *Expensive.* 100 Pond Lily Ave. (387–6651). Indoor pool, health club. Restaurant nearby.

Park Plaza Hotel. *Expensive.* 155 Temple St. (772–1700). High-rise midtown hotel near the Green. Rooftop restaurant. Elevator from garage to lobby and guest floors. Free parking. Pool.

Holiday Inn at Yale. *Moderate.* 30 Whalley Ave., across from Broadway and Yale (777–6221). Good Restaurants, bars, and pools.

Howard Johnson's Long Wharf. *Moderate.* 400 Sargent Dr. Off I–95 (562–1111). A multi-story branch of chain, with restaurant. Pool. Room service. Rooms for nonsmokers. Car rental available.

BRANFORD TO NEW LONDON AREA

BRANFORD. Branford Motor Inn. *Moderate.* On U. S. 1, Exit 55 off I–95 (488–8314). Sauna. Nearby golf and tennis. Coffee shop, pool. Restaurant and cocktail lounge adjacent. New Haven and Yale nearby.

MacDonald's Motel. *Inexpensive.* On U. S. 1, Exit 56 off I–95 (488–4381). Some family units. Near Hammonassett State Park, swimming, boating. Near restaurants.

CLINTON. Clinton Motel. *Inexpensive.* 163 East Main St. Exit 63 off I–95 (669–8403). Small. Restaurants nearby. Pool. Outdoor game courts. Nearby water sports.

GUILFORD. Tower Motel. *Inexpensive.* 320 Boston Post Road (453–9069). All efficiencies. Pets. Beach privileges. Nearby tennis, golf, saltwater swimming.

MADISON. Madison Beach Hotel. *Expensive.* 94 W. Wharf Rd. Exit 61, I–95. (245–1404). Restaurant, lounge, entertainment, beach swimming. Seasonal.

NIANTIC (EAST LYME). Howard Johnson's Motor Lodge. *Moderate.* Exit 74 off I–95 (739–6921). 24-hour restaurant, bar. Indoor pool. Family rates. Saunas.

Starlight Motor Inn. *Moderate.* Exit 74 off I–95 (739–5462). Coffee shop. Pool.

TraveLodge. *Moderate.* Exit 74 off I–95 (739–5483), or (800) 255–3050. Restaurant, bar. Pool. Babysitting available. Near charter fishing and saltwater beaches.

Susse Chalet Motor Lodge. *Inexpensive.* Exit 74 off I–95 (739–6991 or 800–258–1980). Member of chain. Pool. Restaurant adjoining. Golf and beaches nearby.

Morton House. *Inexpensive.* On Rte. 156, Main St., Niantic (739–8564). Large Victorian hotel facing L. I. Sound. Bar. Restaurant.

OLD LYME. Bee & Thistle. *Moderate.* 100 Lyme St. (Rte. 1), Exit 70, I–95 (434–1667). Relaxed atmosphere in Colonial rooms. Restaurant serving breakfast, luncheon and dinner.

Old Lyme Inn. *Moderate.* 85 Lyme St., Exit 70 off I–95 (434–2600). A most charming renovated Victorian house with antique furnishings. Continental breakfast included. French restaurant, bar; closed Mondays.

OLD SAYBROOK. Admiral House Motel. *Expensive.* Exit 66 off I–95 (399–6273). Minutes away from summer theaters. Charter fishing nearby. Beach privileges, pool. Seasonal rates. Walking distance to restaurants.

Howard Johnson's Motor Lodge. *Moderate.* Ferry Point Rd. Exit 69, I–95, then Exit 1 off Rte. 9 (388–5716). 24-hour restaurant. Bar. Indoor pool. Sauna.

Old Saybrook Motor Hotel. *Moderate.* U.S. 1 (388–3463). In center of town, set back from highway. In-room refrigerator. Pool. Beach privileges. Restaurants nearby. Cable TV.

WATERFORD. Blue Anchor Motel. *Moderate.* 563 Boston Post Rd. (442–2072). Rooms in main house, cottages and motel. On Niantic River, convenient to boating and fishing. Beach privileges available. Pets limited. Seasonal.

Lamplighter Motel. *Moderate.* I–95, Exit 81, 3 mi. west of New London (442–7227). Some efficiencies. Pool. Miniature golf. Near historic sites, colleges, and U. S. Coast Guard Academy.

NEW LONDON/GROTON/MYSTIC AREA

NEW LONDON. Lighthouse Inn. *Deluxe.* Lower Blvd. 443–8411. Rooms in mansion restoration and in adjacent lodge. Restaurant, lounge. Live band and dancing Saturday nights.

Holiday Inn. *Expensive.* On I–95 opposite New London Shopping Center (442–0631). Restaurant. Bar with entertainment most evenings. Beach, tennis, golf, and racquetball nearby. Pets.

Red Roof Inn. *Inexpensive.* I–95 and Colman St. (444–0001). One of a nationwide chain, opened here in spring, 1986. Complimentary morning coffee and newspapers; restaurants nearby. Convenient to business areas.

Queen Anne. *Moderate.* 265 Williams St., Exit 83N, 84S, I–95 (447–2600). Central location. Full breakfast and afternoon tea. Beautifully restored Victorian house with period furniture.

GROTON. Best Western Olympic Inn. *Moderate.* 360 Rte. 12 (445–8000). Located near U. S. Submarine Base and within easy driving distance of tourist attractions.

Groton Motor Inn. *Moderate.* At Jct. I–95 and Rte. 184 (445–9784). Medium-sized motel with restaurant, bar, rm. svc. Spacious grounds overlooking Thames River. Near historic sites and U.S. Submarine Base.

Thames Botel and Harbor Inn. *Moderate.* 193 Thames St. (445–8111). On the Thames River. Docking facilities. Charter boats, fishing from motel pier. Some efficiencies available.

Quality Inn. *Moderate.* 404 Bridge St., Exit 85N, 87S, I–95 (445–8141). Restaurant. Bar. Entertainment nightly. Near tourists attractions and shopping centers. Golf and beach nearby.

Shore Inne. *Inexpensive.* 54 East Shore Ave. in Groton Long Point (536–1180). A shore front property. Family style breakfasts. Privileges for use of Long Island Sound beach nearby. Restaurants close by.

MYSTIC. The Inn at Mystic. *Deluxe.* Jct. U. S. 1 and Rte. 27 (536–9604). A refurbished Victorian mansion overlooking coves and Mystic Harbor. On property of Mystic Motor Inn and award-winning Flood Tide Restaurant.

Howard Johnson's Motor Lodge. *Expensive.* At I–95 Exit 90, across from Old Mystic Village and Marinelife Aquarium. (536–2654). Restaurant. Bar. Indoor pool. Sauna. Some efficiencies. Golf nearby.

Ramada Inn. *Expensive.* Exit 90, Jct. I–95 and Rte. 27 (536–4281). Restaurant. Bar. Playground. Indoor pool. Pets. Family rates.

Seaport Motor Inn. *Expensive.* At Jct. I–95 and Rte. 27 (536–2621). A few family units. Located on hill overlooking Old Mystick Village. Restaurant. Lounge. Pool.

Old Mystic Motor Lodge. *Moderate.* Exit 90, I–95. (536–9666). Restaurant and tourist attractions nearby.

Days Inn. *Inexpensive.* Rte. 27 (800–241–7200). New 122-room unit of Days Inn of America chain. Pool. Restaurant.

NORWICH AREA

NORWICH. Norwich Inn. *Deluxe.* On W. Thames St. (886–2401). A Sonoma Mission Inn & Spa (Calif.) affiliate. Elegance describes the public and private rooms. Excellent restaurant. Afternoon tea served daily. Spa in separate building overlooking public golf course.

Sheraton Inn-Norwich. *Deluxe.* Rte. 82, Exit 80 off Conn. Tpke. (889–5201). A "city hotel" in a country setting. Restaurant and lounge with entertainment. Indoor and outdoor pools. Sauna. Tennis courts nearby. Children's playground.

MOOSUP/PUTNAM AREA

MOOSUP. Plainfield Motel. *Inexpensive.* Rte. 14, Exit 89, Conn. Tpke. (564–2791). Coffee shop. Lounge. Pets. Sauna.

PUTNAM. King's Inn. *Moderate.* Exit 96 off Conn. Tpke. (928–7961). Restaurant, bar, pool. Golf, tennis, skiing, boating nearby.

MIDDLETON TO ESSEX AREA
(The Lower Connecticut River Valley)

CHESTER. The Inn at Chester. *Expensive.* On Rte. 148 at the Chester-Killingsworth Line (526–9541). A late 18th-century home, expanded (1982–83) to include guest rooms. Facilities available for small conferences. Restaurant serving American cuisine. Reservations.

CROMWELL. Treadway Lord Cromwell Motor Inn. *Expensive.* Rte. 72, exit 21 off Rte. I–91 (635–2000). Between Hartford and Middletown. Restaurant. Indoor pool. Fine golf course nearby. Handicap access.

EAST HADDAM. Bishopsgate Inn. *Moderate.* Rte. 149 at Goodspeed's Landing (873–1677). Once the home of a wealthy shipbuilder. Period furnishings and country kitchen. A short walk to Goodspeed Opera House.

ESSEX. Griswold Inn. *Moderate.* Main Street, in center of town (767–0991). A country inn in operation since 1776. Fine restaurant, bar. Complimentary continental breakfast. No TV. Extraordinary marine art collection on restaurant walls.

MOODUS. Banner Lodge & Country Club. *Deluxe.* On Banner Rd. Rte. 2, Exit 16 (873–8652). Comprehensive resort facilities. Lodge and cottages. Nightly entertainment and dancing. American Plan. Snack bar. Open May to Nov. 1. Free transportation to station. Tennis, 18-hole golf, fishing, horseback riding. Miniresort for children. Huge pool.

Frank Davis Resort. *Moderate.* Rte. 151 (873–8681). A popular resort on 600-acre site with pool, stream, and sports facilities. American plan. Open May 1 thru Labor Day.

WALLINGFORD/MERIDEN AREA

MERIDEN. Yale Inn. *Moderate.* 900 East Main St. (238–1211). Restaurant, cocktail lounge. Pool. Pets. Airport limo.

NEW BRITAIN. Holiday Inn. *Moderate.* 65 Columbus Blvd. (224–9161). Restaurant, cocktail lounge. Indoor pool, sauna; golf nearby. Handicap access.

SOUTHINGTON. Howard Johnson's Motor Lodge. *Moderate.* Exit 32 off I–84 (628–0291). Restaurant, bar. Pool, sauna. Near cross-country and downhill ski areas and golf course. Airport limo service.

WALLINGFORD. Yale Motor Inn. *Moderate.* 1040 N. Colony Rd. Exit 66 off Wilbur Cross Pkwy. (269–1491). Large, well-run motel with family rates. In-room coffee. Pool, sauna, putting green. Heliport. Yankee Silversmith Inn (restaurant) is across road, same ownership. Pets.

LITCHFIELD/TORRINGTON/SALISBURY AREA

LITCHFIELD Tollgate Hill Inn. *Deluxe* Rte. 202 & Tollgate Rd. (482–6116). Mid-18th-century renovation; in National Historic Register. Some rooms with fireplace. Pets. Restaurant, breakfast.

Litchfield Inn. *Expensive.* On Rte. 202 (567–4503). An "18th-century" inn with 32 guest rooms, conference facilities and American regional cuisine. Handicap access.

NEW MILFORD. Homestead Inn-Midtown Motel. *Moderate.* 5 Elm St. (354–4080). On the Green. Lovely old building (1816) with additional rooms in modern motel section. Restaurant nearby. Continental breakfast.

NORFOLK. Mountain View Inn. *Moderate.* On Rte. 272 (542–5595). Victorian house with veranda. Restaurant, bar. Continental breakfast.

Blackberry River Inn. *Moderate.* Rte. 44 (542–5100). An 18th-century country inn. Cross-country ski rentals. Unusual menu for discerning guests.

RIVERTON. Old Riverton Inn. *Moderate.* Rte. 20 (379–8678). Small inn across from Hitchcock Chair Factory in center of town. Antique furnishings. Restaurant with excellent cuisine, bar. Breakfast for house guests and fishermen.

SALISBURY. White Hart Inn. *Moderate.* On the Village Green (435–2511). In a building almost 200 years old and for more than a century continuously operating as an inn. Restaurant, bar. Nearby golf, tennis and skiing.

TORRINGTON. Yankee Pedlar Inn & Motor House. *Moderate.* 93 Main St. (Jct. Rtes. 8, 202, 4) (489–9226). Tradition-laden hostelry in center of Torrington. Excellent restaurant, bar. Nearby sports facilities.

LAKEVILLE/NEW PRESTON AREA

KENT. Club Getaway. *Moderate.* S. Kent Rd. (927–3664). Adult resort. May through October. Restaurant and lounge. Lake swimming, disco, horseback riding, films, mountain climbing. Indoor rollerskating, tennis instruction.

LAKEVILLE. Interlaken Inn. *Deluxe.* Rte. 112 (435–9878). 20-acre site between two lakes. Contemporary style. Restaurant. Cocktail lounge with entertainment and dancing. Heated pool, fishing, swimming, boats, tennis, pitch & putt, sauna, game room, adjacent to golf course. Cross-country skiing.
    Wake Robin Inn. *Expensive.* Rte. 41 (435–2515). Small lakeside community. Charming guest rooms and dining room in Colonial inn (completely restored 1978); motel accommodations also available. Pool and private beach; boating and fishing; tennis and golf nearby.
    Iron Masters Motel. *Moderate.* Rtes. 44 and 41 (435–9844). Attractive building and grounds. Efficiency units. Courtesy coffee. Nearby golf, tennis, cross-country skiing.

NEW PRESTON. Boulders Inn. *Deluxe.* On Rte. 45 (868–7918). Furnished with antiques. Set on 250 acres, lake front. Some efficiency cottages. Restaurant, bar. Beach, boats, fishing, tennis, playground. Cross-country skiing.
    The Inn on Lake Waramaug. *Expensive.* N. Shore Rd. (868–0563) or (212)-724–8775). Charming 1790 lakeside colonial country inn with 25 guest rooms, some with working fireplace. Restaurant. Beach, watersports, sleigh rides, cross country skiing, special events, tennis, golf. Indoor pool.
    The Birches Inn. *Moderate.* West Shore Rd.; (868–0229). 1847, Federal-style summer guest house. Overlooks Lake Waramaug. April–November. Austrian and Swiss specialties in restaurant.
    Hopkins Inn. *Moderate.* Hopkins Rd., Lake Waramaug (868–7295). Quaint and cozy. Overlooks lake. Restful. Beach, fishing. Restaurant, bar. Terrace dining.

SHARON. Sharon Motor Lodge. *Moderate.* On Rte. 41 (364–0036). Attractive, medium-sized motel. Lovely setting. Restaurant across street. Pool.

WASHINGTON. Mayflower Inn. *Moderate.* On Rte. 47 (868–0515). Three buildings, some rooms with fireplace. Attractive grounds. Restaurant, bar. Golf, tennis and swimming nearby. Continental breakfast.

CORNWALL AREA

CORNWALL. Cornwall Inn. *Inexpensive.* Rt. 7 at Cornwall Bridge (672–6884). 150-year-old building. Picturesque inn with good country dining. Pool in garden setting. Handicap access.

DANBURY AREA

BETHEL. Stony Hill Inn (Best Western). *Moderate.* On Rte. 6, Exit 8E, 9W off I–84 (743–5533). Medium-sized motel with good restaurant, bar, pool, playground, landscaped grounds and pond. Efficiencies available.

DANBURY. Danbury Hilton & Conference Center. *Deluxe.* 18 Old Ridgebury Rd. (794–0600, 800–633–0600). An extensive property with 14 meeting rooms. Indoor pool and saunas. Restaurant and coffee shop.
    Ethan Allen Inn. *Expensive.* 21 Lake Ave. Exit 4 off I–84 (744–1776, 800–742–1776). New. Colonial-style motel decorated with Ethan Allen furniture. Good restaurant; bar with entertainment nightly. Indoor pool, saunas, valet svc. Babysitting available. Airport limo. Handicap access.

Ramada Inn. *Deluxe.* Danbury-Newtown Rd. Exit 8 off I–84 (792–3800). Large branch of chain near Candlewood Lake. Restaurant, bar. Indoor pool. Nearby tennis, golf, boating. Handicap access.

NEWTOWN. Hawley Manor Inn. *Moderate.* 19 Main St. (426–4456). Rambling colonial inn with a few rooms for overnight guests. Good restaurant. Peaceful country location.

RIDGEFIELD. Stonehenge. *Deluxe.* On Rte. 7 (438–6511). Small, elegant inn in rural setting. Early American decor. Gourmet restaurant. Room svc. Breakfast included. Tennis arrangements made at nearby clubs.
  West Lane Inn. *Deluxe.* 22 West Ln. (438–7323). Continental breakfast. Pantry menu afternoons and evenings. Restaurants of distinction nearby.

SOUTHBURY. Harrison Inn. *Deluxe.* Heritage Village, Exit 15 off I–84 (264–8200). Restaurant, cocktail lounge, weekend entertainment and dinner dancing. MAP packages. Conference facilities. Pool, tennis, golf. Bicycles, health club, fishing, skiing. Handicap access.

WOODBURY. Curtis House. *Inexpensive.* On Rte. 6 (263–2101). Connecticut's oldest inn in continuous operation dates to 1754. In "antique center." Fine restaurant with country cooking. Continental breakfast available.

BRISTOL/WATERBURY AREA.

PLAINVILLE. Holiday Inn. *Expensive.* Exit 34 off I–84 (747–6876). Large branch of chain. Restaurant, coffee shop, lounge. Nearby tennis, golf. Handicap access.

WATERBURY. Best Western Red Bull Motor Inn. *Moderate.* Schrafft's Dr., Exit 25 off I–84 (756–8123 or 800–528–1234). Restaurant, cocktail lounge with nightly entertainment. Pool.
  Holiday Inn of Waterbury. *Moderate.* Union & So. Elm Sts., Exit 22 E off I–84 (575–1500). Restaurant, lounge. Handicap access.
  Howard Johnson's Motor Lodge. *Moderate.* 2636 S. Main St. (756–7961). Branch of chain. Restaurant, lounge.
  Waterbury Motor Inn. *Inexpensive.* 91 Scott Rd. and I–84 (756–7925). Lounge entertainment. Playground.

HOSTELS. *American Youth Hostels,* AYH Yankee Council, Box 10392, West Hartford, CT 06110. For up-to-date information on availability of hostels in the state, call 247–6356. Accommodations at very low rates for hikers and bicyclists. Basic overnight facilities. Advance reservations are required.

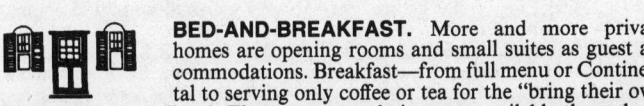

BED-AND-BREAKFAST. More and more private homes are opening rooms and small suites as guest accommodations. Breakfast—from full menu or Continental to serving only coffee or tea for the "bring their own food" clientele—are offered. These accommodations are available through established referral agencies that handle all arrangements, including financial. Owners vary—some take children, pets or smokers. Some don't. Some have resident dogs or cats or both. Business people in process of relocation are finding these accommodations comfortable and practical for interim periods. Application to the services help match preferences with those offered at the bed-and-breakfast locations. For details, write or telephone: *Covered Bridge Bed & Breakfast,* W. Cornwall, CT 06796 (672–6052); *Bed & Breakfast, Ltd.,* Box 216, New Haven CT 06513, tel. 469–3260; *Nutmeg Bed & Breakfast,* 222 Girard Ave., Hartford, CT 06105, tel. 236–6698; *Four Seasons International Bed & Breakfast,* 11 Bridlepath Rd., West Simsbury, CT (658–2181). also *Pineapple Hospitality,* 384 Rodney French Blvd. New Bedford, MA 02744.

PETS. All dogs must have rabies inoculations, health certificates and be licensed according to Connecticut statutes. Town or city clerks will provide details in each locality.

NEWSPAPERS. There are approximately 115 daily and weekly newspapers published in Connecticut.

RADIO AND TV. There are 40 AM and 37 FM radio stations and 12 television stations in the state.

HOW TO GET AROUND. By air: Commuter air carriers operate between Bradley International Airport (Windsor Locks), Tweed-New Haven (New Haven), Bridgeport Airport (Stratford), Waterbury-Oxford and Trumbull (Groton).

By train: Local service along the shore between Greenwich and New Haven and north between Stamford and Danbury on Metro North. (800–223–6052; in New York (212–532–4900). Express service along coast between Stamford and Mystic and from New Haven north to Hartford via Amtrak (800–872–7245).

By car. The Conn. Tpke. (I–95) enters at Greenwich and continues along the coast to Waterford, becoming Rte. 395 and turning north to the Mass. border. I–95 continues east along the coast through New London to Rhode Island and beyond. I–84 goes from Danbury northeast to Union. I–91 runs from New Haven north to Hartford and the Mass. border. Other good roads are Rte. 5, paralleling I–91 from New Haven to the Mass. border; Rte. 7, running north from Norwalk to the Mass. line; US 1, running along the entire coastline; US 202, northeast from Danbury to the Mass. line; Rte. 8, beginning at Bridgeport, travels north through Waterbury and Torrington and to the Massachusetts border; Rte. 9, from Old Saybrook to Hartford; and Rte. 2, from Hartford to the Conn. Tpke. at Norwich. *Car rental:* Rental car agencies have bureaus at airports and other convenient locations throughout the state.

By bus: *Greyhound, Trailways* and *Bonanza* offer limited point-to-point service within the state.

By Connecticut River Ferries: Rocky Hill—Glastonbury, oldest known ferry service in U.S. (started about 1650) and Chester-Hadlyme Ferry, both operated by Department of Transportation (566–5280) from Apr. 1 to Dec. 1, from 7 A.M. to 9 P.M., river conditions permitting. Modest fares for crossing, which takes less than 5 min. Ferries take passengers, cars and motorcycles.

On foot: The Appalachian Trail enters Conn. from New York two miles south of Kent and crosses to Mass. at Taconic, Conn., near Rt. 41.

TOURIST INFORMATION SERVICES. Connecticut Division of Tourism, 210 Washington St., Hartford CT 06106 (566–2496), has a free *Vacation Guide* with special listings: attractions by classification and community, campgrounds, recreation, lodgings and seasonal interests. For a schedule of fairs, write *Association of Connecticut Fairs,* 190 South Rd., Box 363, Somers CT 06071. *The Parks and Recreation Division,* State Dept. Environmental Protection, 165 Capitol Ave., Hartford, CT 06103 (566–2304), provides a list of parks, forests, snowmobiling, campsites and camping applications. *State Board of Fisheries & Game,* Dept. of Environmental Protection, 165 Capitol Ave., Hartford, CT 06103 (566–2304), has information concerning fishing and game preserves.

Information is readily available from the *Greater Hartford Convention & Visitors Bureau, Inc.,* One Civic Center, Hartford CT 06103 (728–6789) and the *New Haven Convention & Visitors Bureau,* 155 Church St., New Haven, CT 06510 (787–8367). A list of roadside areas, motorists' hints and information booth sites and a Conn. State map may be obtained from the *Department of Transportation,* Bureau of Highways, 24 Wolcott Hill Road, Wethersfield CT 06109 (566–5280). For information on art shows, crafts, plays, concerts, etc. *Connecticut Commission on the Arts,* 190 Trumbull St., Hartford, CT 06106

(566–4770). The *Connecticut Division of Tourism,* 210 Washington St., Hartford CT 06106 (566–2496), will provide a list of industrial tours in the state.

Travel information may be obtained in the New York City area at the *New England Vacation Center,* 630 Fifth Ave., Concourse No. 2, New York NY 10020 (212–307–5780).

Travel information centers within the state are located at Bradley International Airport, Windsor Locks; Greenwich, Merritt Parkway northbound; Danbury, I–84, eastbound; Mystic, at Olde Mistick Village (536–1641); North Stonington, I–95, southbound; Wallingford, I–91, southbound; Southington, I–84, eastbound; Westbrook, I–95, northbound; Plainfield, Rte. I–395 southbound; Willington, I–84, east and westbound.

Litchfield Hills Travel Council P.O. Box 1776, Marbledale, CT 06777 (868–2214) issues a comprehensive tour guide of the area.

 **SEASONAL EVENTS.** Information may be obtained either from the Tourism Division, Connecticut Department of Economic Development, 210 Washington St., Hartford CT 06106 (566–2496), or each town's chamber of commerce.

January (Middle): *New Haven*—Annual Winterfest, Yale Repertory Theatre; *Norwalk*—Norwalk Armory Antiques Show.

February (Early): *East Haven*—Winter Trolley Festival; *Salisbury*—N.E. Ski Jumping (Late): *New Preston*—Old fashioned ice harvest. *Stonington*—Annual Antiques Show at Stonington Community Center.

March (Middle): *Hartford*—Spring Antiques Show; *New Haven*—Spring Antiques Show, St. Patrick's Day Parade; *Stamford*—Doll House and Miniatures Show; *New Preston, Woodbury and Litchfield*—Maplesugaring.

April (Early): *New Haven*—Cherry Blossom Festival in Wooster Square; *Westport*—Westport–Southport Antiques Show at Fairfield Hunt Club; *New Preston*—Colonial muzzle-loading and firing. (Middle): *Meriden*—Daffodil Festival; *Hamden*—Forsythia Festival.

May (Early): *New Canaan*—N.E. Exhibition of Painting, Sculpture, Drawings at the Silvermine Guild Gallery (to mid-June). (Middle): *Fairfield*—Dogwood Festival; *Farmington*—Children's Services Horse Show & Country Fair; *Windsor*—Shad Derby & Festival. (Late): *Lime Rock*—Automobile racing season begins.

June (Middle): *New London*—Yale-Harvard Rowing Regatta; *West Torrington*—Laurel Display at Indian Lookout; *Winsted*—Laurel Festival; (Late): *Bridgeport*—Barnum Festival (to Early July); *East Haven*—Trolley Festival at Shoreline Trolley Museum; *Hartford*—Elizabeth Park Rose Garden Display; *Norwich*—Mohegan Park Rose Garden Display & Rose Arts Festival. (Weekends); *New Haven*—Symphony and Jazz Concerts on the Green.

July (Early): *Cromwell*—Canon-Sammy Davis, Jr., Greater Hartford Golf Tournament; *Stonington*—Blessing of the Fleet; *New Haven*—Jazz on the Green, weekends. *Hartford*—July 4 River Festival; *Bridgeport*—Barnum Festival continues from June; *Litchfield*—Open House Tour; *New London*—International Sail Festival at City Pier. (Middle): *Deep River*—Ancient Muster, Fife & Drum Corps; *Falls River*—Music Mountain Chamber Concerts; *Guilford*—Handcrafts Exposition on Guilford Green. (Middle to Late): *New London*—Pillar Polkabration at Ocean Beach Park.

August (Early): *New London*—U. S. Coast Guard Anniversary Celebration. (Middle): *Clinton*—Bluefish Festival; *Mystic*—Mystic Outdoor Arts Festival; *New London*—Lyman Allyn Outdoor Antiques Show & Flea Market, Ocean Beach Arts & Crafts Show; (Late): *Brooklyn*—Country Fair.

September (Early): *Farmington*—Antiques Weekend at the Polo Grounds; *Mystic*—Schooner Races; *Niantic*—Bluefish Tournament (to mid-Oct.); *Norwalk*—Oyster Festival, International In-water Boat Show at Cove Marina. (Middle): *New Haven*—Antiques Show in Coliseum. (Late): *Bristol*—Chrysanthemum Festival; *Lebanon*—Outdoor Antiques Show on Town Green. *New Haven*—Yale-Harvard Football Game; Octoberfest.

October (Early): *Glastonbury*—Apple Festival; *Hartford*—Autumn Antiques Fair; *Riverton*—Riverton Fair; *Salisbury*—Antiques Fair and Fall Festival;

Southington—Apple Harvest Festival on the Town Green. (Middle): *Litchfield* —Litchfield Arts and Crafts Show; *New Haven*—Columbus Day Parade; *East Haven*—Fall foliage trolley trips at Shore Line Trolley Museum. (Late): *Mystic* —Dyer Dhow Derby at Mystic Seaport Museum.

November (Late): *Hartford*—Constitution Plaza Festival of Lights (to Jan. 1); *Middletown*—Wesleyan Potters Annual Craft Show & Sale; *New Canaan* —Silvermine Guild Christmas Exhibition & Sale; *New Preston*—Turkey Olympics. Other Christmas bazaars and tree-lighting ceremonies throughout the state, also in December.

December (Early to Middle): *Bethlehem*—Special Christmas Postmark (Post Office 06751). (Middle): *Mystic*—Lantern-light tours and Carol Sing at Mystic Seaport Museum; *Old Saybrook*—Torchlight Parade, Muster & Carol Sing; *Torrington*—Christmas Village displays.

TOURS. At Yale University (New Haven), there are free tours available whether one is interested in arts and architecture, engineering, science or the general tour of the university. Arrangements may be made for special group tours. Information available from the Yale Information Office, 436–8330. New Haven Convention and Visitors Bureau (787–8822) will arrange special tours of the city.

To arrange a tour of the U.S. Naval Submarine Base in New London, call 443–1831.

By boat. *Project Oceanography Tours* (2½ hours exploring and obtaining samples from the nearby waters) from Avery Point, Groton (448–1616), Mystic River cruise on *Sabino* from Mystic Seaport Museum, Mystic (572–0711). Overnight cruises on *Mystic Whaler,* 7 Holmes St., Mystic (536–4218, 800–243–0416). *American Eagle* and *Independence* cruises from Haddam (345–8551, 800–243–6755). Harbor cruise aboard *Liberty Belle,* Long Wharf Steamship Lines, P. O. Box 2054, New Haven CT 06521 (562–4163). Cruises to Block Island, R I, from Ferry St., New London (442–7891 or 442–9553); to Orient Point, L.I. from Ferry St., New London, (443–5281/443–5035 or 800–358–5804); and Fishers Island from City Pier, New London, (443–6851). Cruise on Lake Waramaug, New Preston, on "Showboat," sternwheeler, from Inn at Lake Waramaug (868–0563).

By train: Valley Railroad, Essex, features an old-time train and boat ride along the Connecticut River (767–0103). Housatonic R.R., Canaan Union Depot. Scenic ride along Housatonic River (824–0339).

By bus: Tour operators feature bus trips throughout the year. *Heritage Trails,* Box 138, Farmington, CT 06034 (673–3778), offers a variety of tours throughout the state. Limit 10 persons each tour. *Gray Line* operates tours to local points of interest. *Anderson Mini-Tours.* 53 Bank St., New Milford, CT 06776 (354–3177 or 800–354–8155).

By balloon: *Venture Flights* (485–0555) Balloon, glider or open cockpit biplane.

Fall foliage tours: The height of the season usually comes in mid-October, when spectacular scenery attracts leaf-lookers and camera buffs. Highways through the Berkshires, Mohawk Valley, Litchfield, Sharon and Canaan, with routes along the Connecticut River combining riverboat cruises, are featured as autumn tours.

INDUSTRIAL TOURS. Inquiries and reservations should be made in advance. Suggestions might be: Haddam Neck: *Conn. Yankee Atomic Power Plant;* Norwalk: *Pepperidge Farms* (748–6095), U.S. 1 at Westport border, bakery; New Haven: *Southern New England Telephone Co.,* 277 Church St. (786–3100). Central office operations. One month advance notice. West Haven: *Lender's Bagel Bakery, Inc.,* Post Rd. (934–9231). Tour through bakery with explanation of bagel baking. Hartford: *M. Swift & Sons, Inc.,* 10 Love Lane (522–1181). Observe gold leaf beating and hear the story of this fine art.

Also, the newspapers offices of: *New Haven Register Journal-Courter,* 40 Sargent Dr. (772–3700). *Waterbury Republican-American,* 389 Meadow St.

(574–3636). *Meriden Record-Journal,* 11–16 Crown St. and *Hartford Courant,* 285 Broad St. (241–6549).

VINEYARDS AND WINERIES. Vineyards in several parts of the state are open to visitors but be sure to call ahead. *Haight Vineyard & Winery,* Off Rte. 118 on Chestnut Hill Rd. Litchfield (567–4045). Visitors welcome to taste samples of the wines at this small, producing vineyard, open year round. *St. Hilary's Vineyard,* Rte. 12. North Grosvenordale (935–5377). Fruit wines of several kinds are produced and tours and samples are offered. *Hamlet Hill Vineyards,* Rte. 101, Pomfret (928–5550). The largest winery in the state. Guided tours weekends by advance reservation. *Stonecrop Vineyards,* Taugwonk Rd., Stonington (535–2497). A small vineyard. Tours available May through Oct. by appointment. *Hopkins Vineyard,* Hopkins Rd., Warren (868–7954). Tours and tastings during summer and fall. Picnic facilities. Open weekends year-round, daily May–Jan. *Clarke Vineyard,* Taugwonk Rd., Stonington (535–0235). Tours and tasting year-round Tues.–Sun.

PARKS AND FORESTS. Connecticut, unlike other states, has neither a national park nor a national forest. Therefore, large sums of federal funds for park-forest purposes do not come to this state. Highly industrialized Connecticut, which is nearly 75 percent wooded, boasts 88 state parks (29,922 acres) and 30 state forests (137,782 acres in all). They are well marked and in good condition for hiking, picnicking, and camping. Within drives of from one-half hour to not more than 2½ hours, there are parks with saltwater and freshwater bathing facilities. Varied in appeal and facilities, they range in size from one-acre *Minnie Island* in Salem (no public facilities) to sprawling *Macedonia Brook Park* of 2,300 acres in northwestern Litchfield County (927–3238). At Macedonia, three miles of excellent trout streams and two hills (over 1,200 ft.) offer scenic trails and panoramic views.

Hammonassett Beach, at Madison (245–2785), attracts about 1 million people annually along its sandy beaches. There is camping, fishing and swimming. *Gillette Castle Park,* Hadlyme, off Rte. 9 near Middletown (526–2336), features a fortress-like castle, built by actor William Gillette from 1914 to 1919, overlooking the Conn. River. *Harkness Memorial Park,* in Waterford (443–5725), consists of about 235 acres, with a 42-room mansion displaying watercolors of American birds by Rex Brasher. *Fort Griswold State Park,* Groton (445–1729), is highlighted by a granite obelisk commemorating one of the only Revolutionary War battlefields in Conn. (Sept. 6, 1781); *Sherwood Island State Park,* a 233-acre island on Long Island Sound at Westport (226–6983), offers fishing and swimming. *Mohawk Mt. State Park and Forest,* in northwestern Conn. (672–6100), is a year-round playground where skiing and hiking trails have been developed. *Sleeping Giant State Park,* 3500 Whitney Ave., Hamden (789–7498). Small campsite for minimum number of trailers but with water and fireplaces. Fishing and hiking trails.

Recreation and picnic areas in state parks and forests are open from 8 A.M. to one-half hour after sunset.

Write to The Parks & Recreation Div., State Dept. of Environmental Protection, 165 Capitol Ave., Hartford CT 06106 or telephone (566–2304), for a list of parks and forests, showing what each has to offer. State Highway Dept. maintains about 150 roadside areas (from one-quarter acre to four acres) with picnic tables; fireplaces at some areas.

MUNICIPAL PARKS. Meriden. *Hubbard Park,* a municipal park of 1,200 acres, is located on West Peak, 1,007 feet above sea level. Good facilities for a day's outing. (For information, contact the Greater Meriden Chamber of Commerce, 17 Church St., Meriden, CT 06450; 235–7901.)

New Britain. *Walnut Hill Park,* between Hart St. and West Main St., this park of 98 acres was designed by Frederick Law Olmsted, designer of Central

Park in Manhattan. Music shell, ball fields and tennis courts. *Stanley Quarter Park,* 141-acre city park, off Eddy-Glover Blvd., has nature trails, picnic area and ball fields. (For information on these municipal parks, contact the New Britain Chamber of Commerce, One Central Park Plaza, New Britain, CT 06051; 229–1665.)

New London. *Ocean Beach Park,* is a mile-long white-sand beach on Long Island Sound with an amusement park, restaurants, picnic tables, and snack bars. The park is owned and operated by the City of New London. (447–3031.)

ZOOS. *Beardsley Zoological Gardens,* Noble Ave., Bridgeport (576–8082). Often referred to as "the biggest little zoo in New England," and the largest in Connecticut. Children's rides on zoo animals. Many animals from all over the world. *Mohegan Park and Memorial Rose Garden,* Mohegan Rd., Norwich. (886–2381 Ext. 242). This is a small zoo near the famous rose gardens. Picnic area. Lake swimming. *West Rock Nature Center,* Wintergreen Ave., New Haven (787–8016). A small zoo with native birds, reptiles. 40 acres of trails. Insect exhibits. *Moran Nature Center & Zoo,* Chester St., New London (443–2861). A municipal park with small zoo. Some farm animals. Picnic facilities.

CAMPING. The following state parks and state forests are open for camping from April 15 to Sept. 30; *Black Rock,* Watertown; *Burr Pond,* Torrington; *Devil's Hopyard,* E. Haddam; *Hammonasset Beach,* Madison; *Hopeville Pond,* Griswold; *Housatonic Meadows,* Sharon; *Macedonia,* Kent; *Kettletown,* Southbury; *Lake Waramaug,* New Preston; *Mashamoquet Brook,* Pomfret Center; *Rocky Neck,* Niantic; *American Legion State Forest,* Barkhamsted; *Sleeping Giant,* Mt. Carmel; *Cockaponset State Forest,* Haddam; and *Pachaug State Forest,* Voluntown; *Squantz Pond,* New Fairfield.

Detailed information on fees and regulations may be obtained from the Dept. of Environmental Protection, 165 Capitol Ave., Hartford CT 06103 (566–2304).

GARDENS AND NATURE CENTERS. *White Flower Farm,* Rte. 63 S., Litchfield (567–0801). Forty acres of growing fields; ten acres of display gardens (April to Nov.). Mountain laurel, the state flower, is in bloom throughout the state's woodlands during the latter part of June. The most spectacular display is *Indian Lookout,* an extensive private garden atop a mountain in West Torrington, off Rte. 4. *Harkness Memorial Park,* Rte. 213 (443–5725) in Waterford, is a gardener's paradise during the summer when the roses, and the old-fashioned cut-flower gardens are at the height of bloom. Rose gardens in *Elizabeth Park,* Prospect Ave., Hartford (722–6490) and *Mohegan Park and Memorial Rose Garden,* Mohegan Rd., Norwich (886–2381), are well worth a visit in mid-June. *Audubon Center,* 613 Riversville Rd., Greenwich (869–5272). Nature trails over the 485-acre property. Exhibits. Admission charged, but National Audubon Society members are admitted free. *Nature Center for Environmental Activities,* 10 Woodside Lane, Westport (227–7253). Nature trails including one especially for the blind. Museum and small aquarium. *Roaring Brook Nature Center,* 70 Gracey Rd., Canton (693–0263). Nature trails over 115 acres. Small museum with changing exhibits. Wildlife refuge. *White Memorial Conservation Center,* Rte. 202, Litchfield (567–0857). The largest nature center in Connecticut. Nature trails over 4,000 acres. Small museum with natural displays of sanctuary wildlife. Good library for research. *Pinchbeck Greenhouse,* 929 Boston Post Rd., Guilford (453–2186). A 1,200-foot-long greenhouse devoted primarily to roses. No tours. *West Rock Nature Center,* Wintergreen Ave., New Haven (787–8016). A small zoo and 40 acres of nature trails. *Caprilands Herb Farm,* Silver St., Coventry (742–7244). Twenty-eight herb gardens on the property of an 18th-century restored home. *H. S. Barnes Memorial Nature Center,* 175 Shrub Rd., Bristol (589–6082). Trails through 70-acre preserve. *Devil's Den Preserve,* Pent Rd., Weston (226–

4991). Twenty miles of nature trails in the 1,500 acres of forest. Cross-country skiing. Registration at parking lot.

QUARRIES. Rock hounds interested in digging for gemstones can look into possibilities at: *Walden Gem Mine* and *Strickland Quarry,* Portland (*Walden Rock Shop,* Cotton Hill Rd., Portland, 342–3852); and *Ottawa Silica Mines,* (536–2618), Old Mystic. Check with each mine in advance.

PARTICIPANT SPORTS. Golf: There are 77 public golf courses in Connecticut, ranging from 9 holes to the 27-hole courses in Farmington (Tunxis Plantation C.C.), (677–1367) in Hartford (Goodwin Park C.C.), (722–2561) and in New Britain (Stanley Park C.C.), (223–9870), and the 36-hole course in Bridgeport (Fairchild Wheeler C.C.), (372–6265). Nine semiprivate courses are open to the public at specified times, and advance inquiry is required. Golf tournaments are staged throughout the summer. The most widely known is the Greater Hartford Open at the Edgewood C.C. in Cromwell in late July. Many tourneys are sponsored by the Conn. State Amateur Golf Association. Write to Tourism Div., Dept. Economic Development, 210 Washington St., Hartford CT 06106 (566–2496), for complete list of golf and country clubs with addresses and telephone numbers.

Boating: About 70,000 motor boats are registered with the Conn. Boating Safety Commission, and there are a multitude of other sailboats, rowboats and dinghies. In state parks, there is boating at: Beaver Brook, Bigelow Hollow, Burr Pond, Haddam Meadows, Hopeville Pond, Indian Well, Mansfield Hollow, Quaddick, Stoddard Hill, Sqauntz Pond (Candlewood Lake), Cockaponset and Pachaug State Forest. Bantam Lake is noted for its sailboat regattas. Boat launching sites, with access to salt water, are at: Branford, Bridgeport, Groton, Guilford, New Haven, Old Lyme, Stonington and Waterford. Along the Conn. River, there are launch ramps at E. Haddam and Saybrook.

Fishing: Trout, bass, pickerel and shad can be caught in lakes and streams; bluefish in salt water. Fishing boats for charter are located at marinas along the shore. There are many headquartered on the Thames River in New London and on the Niantic River in Waterford.

Down-hill skiing: Although Conn. doesn't have the high slopes of other New England states, skiing and affiliated winter activities are increasingly popular. *The Connecticut Vacation Guide,* issued by the Tourism Div., Dept. Economic Development, 210 Washington St., Hartford CT 06106 (566–2496), has a complete list of the skiing areas in the state, with descriptions of facility, addresses and telephone numbers. Of the six ski areas, the largest is Mohawk Mt., near Rte. 4, at Cornwall (672–6464). It has a 750-ft. drop and 24 trails to challenge both the novice and the expert. Sundown, New Hartford, is Connecticut's largest night ski area (379–9851), with a 570-ft. drop and 14 trails; (800–622–3321, CT, and 800–243–3377 other states), Powder Ridge, Middlefield, Woodbury Ski & Racquet Area (263–2203) with a 500-ft. drop and 21 trails; and Mount Southington, Southington, with a 425-ft. drop and 7 trails. For the novice-intermediate skier, try Woodbury Ski & Racquet Area (263–2203) with 3 trails; Ohoho, So. Woodstock, (974–1040), with 4 trails.

Cross-country skiing: Cross-country skiing has become extremely popular throughout Connecticut in all state parks and forests.

Sleighriding: When weather obliges, sleighriding in horse-drawn sleighs has become a winter specialty, especially for group projects. (Hay wagons substitute in milder weather.) The Connecticut Department of Economic Development issues a schedule of sleigh rallies and stables offering sleighrides.

Snowmobiling: Areas have been opened up in the following state forests: Cockaponset, Housatonic, Mohawk, Naugatuck, Natchaug, Nipmuck, Pachaug, Peoples, Pootatuck and Shenipsit. *Ice Skating:* There are rinks at Mohawk Mountain and Powder Ridge ski areas. *Tobogganing:* At the Powder Ridge ski area.

Hunting: Much small game is found in the Connecticut fields and forests; waterfowl in lakes and marshes, along rivers and Long Island Sound. Nov. and Dec. is the bow-and-arrow deer season. Rules and pertinent information are available from the Dept. of Environmental Protection, Hartford (566–2304), free.

SPECTATOR SPORTS. Yale Bowl, at West Haven, is used for *College football* games while the New Haven Coliseum has *basketball* and is home to the New Haven Night Hawks AHL Hockey Team. The Hartford Civic Center is the home of the NHL Hartford Whalers. *Jai alai* frontons are in Bridgeport, Milford and Hartford; *greyhound racing* in Plainfield. *Sports car races:* National and regional races are staged during the summer at Lime Rock Track, in western Conn., and Thompson, in the eastern section. There is also stock car racing at Salisbury and Waterford. The Yale-Harvard *rowing races,* held every June on the Thames River in New London are among, if not the, oldest sports competition between universities in the U.S. New Haven Teletrack simulcasts horse racing. Post times vary depending on track location. Parimutuel betting and food services available. (789–1943).

CHILDREN'S ACTIVITIES. The carousel in Hartford's *Bushnell Park* is truly a magnet for children visiting the capital. *Keney Park* has Sherwood Forest, a children's zoo. *The Old State House,* at 800 Main St., and the *Mark Twain Memorial,* 351 Farmington Ave., both interest children. Manchester has the *Lutz Children's Museum* and West Hartford has a *Children's Museum,* at 950 Trout Brook Dr., with planetarium shows. The best amusement parks (open Memorial Day through mid-September) are at Lake Quassapaug, U.S. 6A, Middlebury, and Lake Compounce, 3 miles south of Bristol's center. Both lakes have excellent swimming areas, boating, rides and picnic groves. *Ocean Beach Park,* in New London, has an amusement park with rides, a picnic area, and an excellent beach. *Mystic Seaport Museum* on Rte. 27 between I–95 and U.S. 1, in Mystic, is a recreated 19th-century coastal village with historic ships and exhibition buildings, all relating to New England's seafaring heritage; planetarium shows daily, a maritime research library, and restaurant. *Mystic Marinelife Aquarium* is nearby. *Pequotsepos Nature Center,* Pequotsepos Rd. in Mystic, has nature trails and exhibit building. *Stamford Museum and Nature Center,* 39 Scofieldtown Rd., Stamford; *Nature Center for Environmental Activities,* 10 Woodside Lane, Westport; *Beardsley Zoological Gardens,* Bridgeport; *Thames Science Center,* Gallows Lane, Waterford, nature center and trails; *Bates Woods,* New London, has a small zoo and picnic areas. In Greenwich, the *Audubon Center,* 713 Riversville Rd. and the *Bruce Museum of Natural History,* Steamboat Rd. In New Haven, *West Rock Nature Center,* Wintergreen Ave.; the *Peabody Museum of Natural History,* Whitney Ave. and Sachem St., the carousel at *Lighthouse Park* and the *Children's Museum,* State St. The *American Indian Archaeological Institute,* Washington, emphasizes Northeast Indian history. The *Shoreline Trolley Museum,* near U.S. 1, in East Haven, and the *Warehouse Point Trolley and Fire Museum,* Rte. 140, North Rd., E. Windsor. *Gillette Castle,* off Rte. 148, East Haddam, is fascinating to children.

A replica of Jerusalem and Bethlehem, *Holy Land* at Pine Hill, is off U.S. 84 in Waterbury. *Mattatuck Junior Museum,* 119 West Main St., Waterbury; *P. T. Barnum Museum* in Bridgeport, which has a large model of a circus and memorabilia of Jenny Lind and Tom Thumb. *The Conn. State Fish Hatchery* in Burlington is interesting for the little ones. *The Submarine Museum,* 359 Thames St., Groton, is a memorial to submarine history. Visitors may go aboard the submarine *Croaker,* berthed at the museum on the Thames River. The first nuclear-powered submarine, *Nautilus,* is enshrined at the U.S. Naval Submarine Base, Groton. *The State Capitol,* in Hartford, should be a source of interest to children because of the displays and exhibits in the lobbies and halls. Older children may wish to visit the legislative halls and other rooms. *Dinosaur State Park* in Rocky Hill where there are dinosaur tracks said to be 200 million years old.

 **HISTORIC SITES AND HOUSES.** Most of the historic houses, monuments and sites are either owned, operated, or both, by local historical societies. Open hours, usually seasonal, depend on the availability of volunteers to act as host or hostess. When telephone numbers are not listed, a call to the local Chamber of Commerce would be the quickest way to obtain information or ways in which to contact an historical society member for information.

Some of Connecticut's history will be found in visits to any of the following:

GREENWICH-GREATER NEW HAVEN AREA

DARIEN. *Bates-Scofield Homestead,* 45 Old Kings Hwy. (655–9233). Mid-18th-century saltbox, authentic antique furniture.

GREENWICH. *Bush-Holley House,* Strickland Rd., Cos Cob (622–9686). Mid-17th-century saltbox, colonial furnishings.

HAMDEN. *Jonathan Dickerman House,* Mt. Carmel Ave. (288–4901). A fully and nicely restored and furnished pre-Revolutionary house (1770).

NEW CANAAN. *Hanford-Silliman House,* 13 Ocnokc Rd. (966–1776). Mid-18th-century house museum with other exhibit buildings on the property. National Historic Landmark . New Canaan Historical Society.

NEW HAVEN. *Fort Nathan Hale,* on the harbor's edge (787–6970). *New Haven Colony Historical Society Museum,* 14 Whitney Ave. (562–4183). *Pardee-Morris House,* 325 Lighthouse Rd. (562–4183). Restored and authentically furnished mid-18th-century home. Interesting gardens.

NORWALK. *Lockwood-Mathews Mansion,* 295 West Ave. (838–1434). Mid-19th-century home, chateau-inspired design. National Historic Landmark.

STRATFORD. *David Judson House and Museum,* 967 Academy Hill (378–0630). Mid-18th-century farmhouse, well furnished.

BRANFORD TO NEW LONDON AREA

CLINTON. *Stanton House,* 63 E. Main St. (669–2132). Late 18th-century house. Original furnishings.

EAST LYME (Niantic). *Thomas Lee House* (1660) and *Little Boston School* (1734), Rte. 156 (739–6070). Original property had one room called "Judgment Hall" said to be the one-time courtroom of Judge Thomas Lee. 17th-century furnishings.

GUILFORD. *Thomas Griswold House,* 171 Boston St. (453–3176). Late-18th-century saltbox.
Hyland House, 84 Boston Post Rd. (453–9477). Mid-17th-century colonial saltbox with period furnishings and walk-in fireplaces built for cooking purposes.
Whitfield House Museum, Whitfield St. (453–2457). 1639–1640 dates suggest it might be the oldest stone house in the settlement. Local history here.

MADISON. *Allis-Bushnell House and Museum,* 853 Boston Post Rd. (245–4567). Late-18th-century house with exhibits of antique dolls, toys, and early household utensils.

NEW LONDON-MYSTIC AREA

GROTON. *Groton Monument and Fort Griswold* (Fort Griswold State Park). Monument St. and Park Ave. (445–1729). Memorial obelisk; museum of Revolutionary War memorabilia.

NEW LONDON. *Nathan Hale Schoolhouse,* Captain's Walk (No telephone). Where Nathan Hale taught prior to enlisting for service in the Revolutionary War.
    Joshua Hempsted House (1678), 11 Hempstead St. (443–7949). One of the oldest 17th-century houses in the state. Early American furnishings.
    Nathaniel Hempsted House (1759), Hempstead and Truman Sts. (443–7949). A mid-18th-century cut-stone house often referred to as The Huguenot House.
    Monte Cristo Cottage, 325 Pequot Ave. (443–0051 or 443–5378). Late-19th-early-20th-century summer "cottage," once owned by family of playwright Eugene O'Neill. Appropriately furnished. Theater library.
    Olde Towne Mill (1650), Mill St. (444–2206). Built originally for Gov. John Winthrop, Jr. and was later a grist mill. Restored several times over the years.
    Shaw Mansion, 11 Blinman St. (443–1209). Mid-18th-century stone mansion, home of Nathaniel Shaw. Served as Connecticut naval office during the Revolution. Local historical records and local history library.

STONINGTON. *Denison Homestead* (1717), Pequotsepos Rd. (536–9248). The history of a family representing several generations and furnished with their belongings.
    Old Lighthouse Museum (1823), On the point (535–1440). One of the oldest lighthouses in U.S. Miscellaneous historical exhibits.

NORWICH AREA

NORWICH. *Leffingwell Inn* (1675), 348 Washington St. (889–9440). An historic, accurately restored and furnished house. Originally home of Thomas Leffingwell.

COLCHESTER. *Nathaniel Foote House,* Norwich Ave. (No telephone). An early 18th-century house (1702), now restored and a museum of Colonial antiquities.

COVENTRY. *Nathan Hale Homestead,* South St. (742–6917). Built by the father of Nathan Hale, 1776. Well furnished.

EAST HADDAM AREA

EAST HADDAM/MOODUS. *Amasa Day House* (1816), Rtes. 149 and 151 (873–8144 or 247–8996). Period furniture, ceramics and pewter.

WALLINGFORD-MERIDEN AREA

MERIDEN. *Moses Andrews Homestead,* 424 W. Main St. (237–5079). First place of worship for Connecticut Episcopalians. May be visited by appointment.

WALLINGFORD. *Samuel Parson House,* South Main St. (No telephone). A mid-18th-century house, restored. Local history exhibits and library.

LITCHFIELD/TORRINGTON/SALISBURY AREA

LITCHFIELD. *Tapping Reeve House and Law School,* South St. (567–5862). The first law school in America (1784), its graduates include some of the great names in American colonial history.

LAKEVILLE. *Holley-Williams House* (1808), Rte. 44 (435–2878). Greek Revival house with especially fine 19th-century furnishings.

DANBURY AREA

RIDGEFIELD. *Keeler Tavern,* 132 Main St. (438–5485). Mid-18th-century. A restored tavern with period furnishings.

FAMOUS LIBRARIES. *The Beinecke Rare Book and Manuscript Library* (436–8438) at Yale University is a $6-million windowless, six-story building with 250 huge marble slabs comprising the facade. The building (capacity 800,000 volumes and 1 million manuscripts on 21.3 miles of shelves) connects with *Sterling Memorial Library* (436–8330) through an underground tunnel. Gothic-styled Sterling Library is worth visiting for timely exhibits in the corridors and exhibition rooms. *Submarine Library and Museum,* 440 Washington St., Middletown (346–0388). World War II memorabilia. *G. W. Blunt White Library,* Mystic (572–0711). Mystic Seaport Museum, maritime research. *Mark Twain Library* (938–2240) Redding Road, Redding. *USS Nautilus Memorial and U.S. Submarine Force Library and Museum,* near U.S. Naval Submarine Base, Groton (449–2011).

MUSEUMS AND GALLERIES. Museums and galleries in Connecticut reflect the lives of the people throughout more than three centuries of the state's history through exhibitions of fine art, decorative arts, furniture and many of the industrial products for which Connecticut is well known. A stop at any one of the museums or galleries listed (and they are listed according to the routes outlined in the foregoing), will attest to the industrious, talented people whose descendants will not let them be forgotten.

GREENWICH-GREATER NEW HAVEN AREA.

BRIDGEPORT: *Bridgeport Museum of Art, Science, and Industry and Planetarium,* 4450 Park Ave. (372–3521). Art, industry, some antiques, planetarium shows.
P. T. Barnum Museum, 820 Main St. (576–7320). A collection of memorabilia reminiscent of this great circus founder. A 5-ring model circus among other things here.

EAST HAVEN. *Shore Line Trolley Museum,* 17 River St. (467–6927). A variety of "street cars." Rides on trolleys along 3-mile track near the shore. Numerous displays describing history of this form of urban transportation.

GREENWICH. *Bruce Museum,* Museum Dr. (869–0376). A mixture of art, natural science, history and anthropology in the exhibits here.
U. S. Tobacco Company Museum, 100 Putnam Ave. (869–5531). A museum depicting the history of tobacco and some of the accoutrements relating to its use, including snuff boxes, pipes, cigar store Indians.

NEW CANAAN. *Silvermine Guild Center for the Arts,* 1037 Silvermine Rd. (966–5618). A school of fine arts and crafts. Special shows and sales throughout the year. Open 12:30 P.M.–5 P.M. Closed Monday.

NEW HAVEN. *New Haven Colony Historical Society Museum,* 114 Whitney Ave. (562–4183). Local antiques, including dolls and toys; research library.
Peabody Museum of Natural History at Yale, 170 Whitney Ave. (436–0850). A vast collection of exhibits; minerals, animal displays; ecological exhibits.
Yale Center for British Art, 1080 Chapel St. (436–3909). Paintings, prints, sculpture, rare books from Elizabethan times to 1800s.

Yale Collection of Musical Instruments, 15 Hillhouse Ave. (436–4935).

Yale University Art Gallery, 1111 Chapel St. (436–0574). American, European, African, pre-Colombian, Near and Far Eastern art collections on display.

STAMFORD. *Stamford Museum & Nature Center,* 39 Scolfieldtown Rd. (322–1646). Art and artifacts; 19th-century farm; nature trails and planetarium.

WALLINGFORD-MERIDEN AREA

NEW BRITAIN. *New Britain Museum of American Art,* 56 Lexington St. (229–0257). Outstanding American art collection.

Copernican Space Science Center Planetarium and Observatory. Central Connecticut University. Wells St. (827–7419) Scheduled shows and special programs.

LITCHFIELD AREA

KENT. *Sloane-Stanley Museum & Kent Furnace,* Rte. 7 (566–3005). Tools and farm implements, some from 17th century, interestingly displayed. Museum is on the site of the remains of the 19th-century Kent iron furnace.

LITCHFIELD. *Litchfield Historical Society Museum,* Litchfield Green on Rte. 202 (567–5862). Exhibits describing Litchfield's history.

RIVERTON. *Hitchcock Museum,* Rte. 20 (379–1003). Near the Hitchcock Chair Factory. 19th-century Hitchcock originals on display.

WINCHESTER. *Winchester Center Kerosene Lamp Museum.* 100 Old Waterbury Tpke. (379–2612). Private collection dating from 1850–1880.

DANBURY AREA

DANBURY. *Scott-Fanton Museum,* 43 Main St. (743–5200). Collections on display in John Rider House (an 18th-century restoration), include furniture and accessories, Danbury hats, and a parlor named for composer Charles Ives. Includes Huntington Exhibition Hall with changing historical exhibits.

BRISTOL-WATERBURY AREA

BRISTOL. *American Clock & Watch Museum,* 100 Maple St. (583–6070). Connecticut-made clocks and watches dating back to the late 17th century.

TERRYVILLE. *Lock Museum of America,* 130 Main St. (589–6359). About 18,000 locks and keys from earliest types to present.

WATERBURY. *Mattatuck Historical Society Museum,* 119 W. Main St. (753–0381). Local colonial and Victorian history; fine and industrial arts.

BRANFORD-NEW LONDON AREA

OLD LYME. *Florence Griswold House Museum,* 96 Lyme St. (434–5542). Once the home of the Old Lyme Art Colony. Changing exhibits during the summer. Local history. Decorative arts and paintings.

Lyme Art Association Gallery, Lyme St. Summer gallery shows.

The Nut Museum, 303 Ferry Rd. (434–7636). Nut lore; nuts in great variety, nutcrackers. Admission includes one nut.

WASHINGTON. *American Indian Archaeological Institute,* Rte. 199 (868–0518). A research and education museum center for the study of prehistoric and historic man in Connecticut and New England. Courses, exhibits, demonstrations, films.

WOODBURY. *The Glebe House.* Hollow Rd. (263–2855). Ministers' farm or "glebe" in 1771. First American Bishop of Episcopal Church was elected here.

EAST HADDAM. *East Haddam Historical Society Museum,* Rte. 149. (No phone). A collection of local history. Household furnishings, photographs, etc.

NEW LONDON-MYSTIC AREA

MYSTIC. *Mystic Art Association Gallery,* Water St. (536–7601). Changing exhibitions throughout the summer. Lectures and special events.
Mystic Marinelife Aquarium. Old Mistick Village (536–3323). Sea animals in appropriate tanks and backgrounds. Seal and dolphin shows daily for visitors.
Mystic Seaport Museum, Greenmanville Ave., Rte. 27 (572–0711). Emphasis on mid-19th-century maritime history; historic ships; re-created seacoast village; research library and planetarium.

NEW LONDON. *Lyman Allyn Museum,* 625 Williams St. (443–2545). Connecticut silver and furniture. American, European and Oriental art. Visiting exhibitions. Doll houses and toys.
Thames Science Center, Gallows Lane, near the Connecticut College campus (442–0391). Nature trails and exhibits of chiefly environmental subjects. Films and lecture programs.

GROTON. *U.S. Submarine Force Library and Museum* located on Thames River adjacent to U.S. Naval Submarine Base. Artifacts, memorabilia, development models of submarines and a library of submarine literature. First Nuclear-powered USS *Nautilus* is enshrined here.
Submarine Memorial Association, 359 Thames St. (448–1616). A submarine, USS *Croaker,* veteran of World War II with creditable history. Displays of submarine memorabilia.

NORWICH-WILLIMANTIC AREA

MONTVILLE. *Tantaquidgeon Indian Museum,* Rte. 32 (848–9145), Indian memorabilia from Mohegan Indians. Wigwam, longhouse and stockade.

NORWICH. *Slater Memorial Museum and Converse Art Gallery,* 108 Crescent St. (887–2506). American, Oriental, Egyptian, African, and Indian paintings and sculpture.

WILLIMANTIC. *World War II Victory Museum,* 64 Willowbrook St., Rte. 6 (423–8194). A collection of souvenirs, uniforms and weapons from World War II.

DANIELSON-PUTNAM AREA

BROOKLYN. *New England Center for Contemporary Arts,* Rte. 169 (774–8899). Changing exhibits of living artists. Resident artists. Instructions in art and music. Lectures.

MUSIC. In every city in Connecticut, there are musical events throughout the year. Summer concerts vary from chamber music to pop to rock. During the winter, the symphonies in various locations present series of concerts, some including operatic soloists or ballet. Colleges and universities sponsor series of major internationally known concert orchestras and chamber music ensembles. Inquire locally.

THEATER. Because of their unique schedules, inquiries should be made to each of the theaters for information concerning performance dates and times and tickets. *Goodspeed Opera House,* East Haddam (873–8668); *Jorgenson Theatre,* U. of Conn., Storrs (486–4226); *Oakdale Music Theatre,* Wallingford (265–1501); *Southbury Playhouse,* Southbury (264–8215); *Westport Country Playhouse,* Westport (226–0153); *Candlewood Theatre,* Rte. 37, New Fairfield (746–6431); *Yale Repertory Theatre,* Chapel & York Sts., New Haven (436–1600); *Long Wharf Theatre,* Sargent Dr., New Haven (787–4282); *Shubert Performing Arts Center* (562–5666) and *Palace Theater* (624–8497) College St., New Haven, *Sharon Playhouse,* Rte. 343, Sharon (364–5909); *Eugene O'Neill Memorial Theater Center,* Rte. 213, Waterford (443–5378); *Hartford Stage Company;* John W. Huntington Theatre, 50 Church St., Hartford (527–5151); *Hartman Theatre Co.,* Atlantic St., Stamford (323–2131); *Darien Dinner Theatre,* Tokeneke Rd., Darien (655–7667). *National Theater of the Deaf,* Chester (526–4971).

SHOPPING. Connecticut offers a variety of shopping experiences, whether in city-centered department stores or in the smaller towns and suburbs where novel shopping centers have developed. *The Civic Center* in Hartford has an extensive covered mall filled with boutiques offering a wide range of merchandise. *The Olde Mistick Village,* I–95 and Rte. 27 (536–4941) has been created with a colonial architectural design for individual shop buildings. In New Haven is the *Chapel St. Mall,* newly renovated with numerous small shops and a branch of Macy's. Many new boutiques have opened on Upper Chapel St. Stamford's *Town Center* with 125 stores, said to be "the largest shopping mall in the New York metropolitan area," is the focal point of Stamford's redeveloped downtown area. *Cannon Crossing,* in Wilton (Cannondale), is a small shopping area adjacent to the Cannondale railroad station—restored in 1978 by actress June Havoc. At *Bittersweet Handcraft Village* on Rte. 1 in Branford, the barns and coops on the 150-year-old working farm have been transformed into studios and shops. *Sono,* the rehabilitated historic area of South Norwalk, has shops, galleries, restaurants, and waterfront activities. *Crystal Mall* in Waterford, is the largest shopping mall in the state with more than 125 stores, and over 850,000 square feet of store space on 80 acres. *The Heritage Village Bazaar,* Southbury, has unique shops, three restaurants and arts and crafts galleries.

Throughout the state, properties have been put to ingenious use by transforming factory buildings, homes, barns and other lapsed-use buildings, into boutiques, antique shops, craft shops, restaurants, ice cream parlors or whatever the creative mind produces. Antique shopping in Connecticut is a way of life. The shops are sufficiently abundant in that they are easy to find. Antique shows, too, are held at various times throughout the year, when the best of the inventories of the shops may be seen and purchased in a group atmosphere.

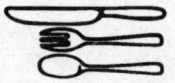

DINING OUT. The menus in Connecticut restaurants are, by and large, as varied and extensive as those in moderately priced restaurants in New York City or other metropolitan areas, usually at lower prices and often in attractive country or seaside establishments. Many old homes have been converted into "inns" which serve meals. For relaxed, comfortable dining—with a cheery fireplace in winter, a green pasture view, or a window overlooking the sea—back roads will lead to some of the more picturesque locations listed here. Restaurants are listed by price range, based on a full meal exclusive of alcoholic beverages, tax, and tip: *Deluxe,* $30 and up; *Expensive,* $25–29; *Moderate,* $15–24; *Inexpensive,* $14 and under.

To simplify locating, the restaurants are listed in the same area order as hotels, motels and inns, and within the areas alphabetically by towns.

GREENWICH-NEW HAVEN

BRIDGEPORT. Ocean Sea Grill. *Moderate.* 1328 Main St. (336–2133). Operating since 1934. Lobster specialty heading menu of fresh seafood. Proprietor also owns large wholesale seafood market. Meat dishes available.
Fitzwilly's. *Inexpensive.* 2536 East Main St. (334–1775). Sandwiches, soups, salads as well as entrées. Open late daily.

DARIEN. Chuck's Steak House. *Moderate.* 1340 Boston Post Rd. (655–2254). Part of chain specializing in char-broiled steaks and lobster tails.
Harper's. *Moderate.* 119 Boston Post Rd. (655–7481). Chili and seafood head the menu here, served in early American atmosphere.

FAIRFIELD. Fredericksburg. *Expensive.* 1201 King's Highway (333–1201). Five different restaurants here, the most lavish the Governor's Palace of Fredericksburg. Colonial decor. Continental cuisine.

GREENWICH. Homestead Inn. *Deluxe.* 420 Field Point Rd. (869–7500). This lovely Colonial inn dates back to 1759. Traditional French cuisine, unusual specialties daily. Small cocktail lounge and organist on Saturday evenings. Proper dress and reservations.
Tapestries. *Deluxe.* 554 Old Post Rd. (629–9204) Dining here is in an elegant ambience.
Boodles. *Expensive.* 21 Fieldpoint Rd. (661–3553). Dine on the glassed-in sunporch or in the cozy dining room with a fireplace in this large Victorian house. Varied American menu, with fresh seafood specials and good steaks. Daily specials. Sunday brunch.
Cinquante-Cinq. *Expensive.* 55 Arch St. (869–5641). Started as private businessman's club, The Greenwich Club. Two of the three floors are still private at luncheon. French cuisine, braised salmon in red wine with grapes, breast of chicken with champagne sauce. Clubby atmosphere. Small bar.
Jardine's. *Expensive.* 3 River Rd. (Cos Cob) (661–0204). Nouvelle cuisine served in a two-story restaurant overlooking Mianus River.
Showboat Restaurant. *Expensive.* 500 Steamboat Rd. (661–9800). The showboat is the riverboat "Mark Twain." Lobster, seafood and steak are featured, with music and dancing on the weekends. Breakfast available.

MILFORD. The Gathering. *Expensive.* 989 Boston Post Rd. (878–6537). Seafood, poultry, specialties. Noted for steaks. Dinner only, from 5 P.M.
Scribner's. *Expensive.* 31 Village Rd. (878–7019). Noted for seafood in very simple servings that may be shared with extra plate charge. Rustic decor with country lighting.

NORWALK. Higgins Restaurant & Groggery. *Expensive.* 148 Rowayton Ave. (853–6062). Mainly a seafood restaurant. Favorites at this friendly pub in Rowayton are lobster, stuffed shrimp and double-cut lamb chops. Homemade desserts. Children's portions are available.
Skipper's Restaurant. *Expensive.* Cove Marina, Beach Rd., East Norwalk (838–2211). On the harbor, with yachts docked just outside. Decor is nautical. Fresh seafood, steaks and prime ribs. Pick your lobster from the tank. Lounge on lower deck, with music and dancing on weekends.
Hunan U.S. 1. *Moderate.* 80 Connecticut Ave. (838–9111). Extraordinarily large menu of Chinese specialties. Reservations.
Silvermine Tavern. *Moderate.* Silvermine Ave. (847–4558). A 200-yr.-old inn, decorated with American antiques and primitive paintings. Rural setting next to mill pond and waterfall. Patio dining in summer, cozy fireplaces in

winter. Trad. American fare, with fresh seafood featured. Thursday buffet. Sunday brunch. Children's menu. Country store nearby.

STAMFORD. The Inn at Mill River. *Deluxe.* 26 Mill River St. (325–1900). Whether lunch in the Promenade, a formal English tea in the Library or a sumptuous dinner in The Swan Court, the French cuisine changes according to season. Champagne brunch on Sunday. Reservations required.

Aux Beaux Jardins. *Moderate.* In the Pavillon Hotel, 60 Strawberry Hill Ave. (357–8100). Linen, crystal and fresh flowers compliment Oriental objets d'art. French-inspired cuisine. Reservations recommended. Open daily breakfast through dinner.

Pellicci's. *Moderate.* 98 Stillwater Ave. (323–2542). Family-run Italian restaurant for over 30 years. Very popular for good reason. Homemade bread. Excellent dinners and pizza.

Sterling Ocean House. *Moderate.* 1349 Newfield Ave. (322–6244). Dining room overlooking Sterling Farms golf course. Fresh seafood. Daily specialties.

STRATFORD. Fagan's. *Moderate.* 946 Ferry Blvd. (378–6560). Overlooks Housatonic River. Near Shakespeare Theater. Fine seafood, steak and other New England specialties.

WESTON. Cobbs Mill Inn. *Deluxe.* Rte. 57, near Merritt Pkwy. (227–7221). Pre-Revolutionary inn beside a millpond and waterfall. Delightful place for cocktails, dinner and browsing in the country store. Varied menu, with venison and game in the fall. Dinner only.

NEW CANAAN. Roger Sherman Inn. *Deluxe.* 195 Oenoke Rd., Rte. 124 (966–4541). A country inn with five individually-decorated dining rooms. Superb continental cuisine. Cocktail lounge with pianist. Old New England charm. Summer dining al fresco on the terrace.

WESTPORT. Le Chambord. *Deluxe.* 1572 Post Rd. E. (255–2654). Distinguished French fare, with fine service. Excellent canard à l'orange, rack of lamb and beef Wellington. Daily specials fresh from the market.

Ocean House. *Expensive.* 1563 Post Rd. E. (259–4005). Not fancy, but freshest seafood poached or broiled. Crisp vegetable salad and fresh fruit bowl for dessert.

The Three Bears. *Expensive.* Rte. 33 (227–7219). Westport's oldest eating establishment, originally a stagecoach stop. An outstanding Tiffany lamp and glass collection. Seafood, steak, duckling and veal dishes expertly prepared. Excellent value. Children's portions. Pleasant cocktail lounge.

Chez Pierre. *Moderate.* 146 Main St. (227–5295). Charming, informal bistro centrally located among Westport's shops and boutiques. French provincial menu.

GREATER NEW HAVEN AREA

HAMDEN. Valentino's. *Expensive.* 2987 Whitney Ave. (288–7707). S. Italian style food served in high-style surroundings—crystal, linen, fresh flowers; daily specials.

Victorian Too. *Moderate.* 1642 Whitney Ave. (288–7688). Daily specials. Interesting antique clock collection.

Sanford Barn. *Moderate.* Sanford Ave. off Dixwell Ave. (288–3309). Dining room, once the sawmill, overlooks a pond. Cosmopolitan cuisine—American, French, Italian.

NEW HAVEN. Basel's. *Expensive.* 993 State St. (624–9361). Authentic Greek cuisine and wines. Live Greek music and dancing weekends. Warm, friendly atmosphere. Closed Sundays during summer.

Casa Marra. *Expensive.* 321 East St. (777–5148). Popular Italian restaurant. Well-prepared beef, veal, pasta. Al fresco dining in garden room.

Delmonaco's. *Expensive.* 232 Wooster St. (865–1109). Prepared-to-order Northern Italian food, expertly served. Located in restored Wooster Sq. area. Nicely decorated white stucco inside, fresh flowers and plants add to ambience. Closed Tuesdays.

Shawn's. *Expensive.* 150 Wooster St. (624–8837). Seafood, lamb and veal prepared to suit the Continental menu offered here. Interesting decor.

Blessings. *Moderate.* 45 Howe St. (624–3557). Northern Chinese cuisine with over 100 dishes served, each served generously. Exotically named cocktails.

500 Blake Street. *Moderate.* 500 Blake St. (378–0500). Plenty of late-19th-century atmosphere and fine Italian cuisine—pasta made here. Open late for after-theater snacks.

Leon's. *Moderate.* 321 Washington Ave. (777–5366 or 785–9901). Famous Italian restaurant. Pasta, meat and seafood specialties, served in attractive Mediterranean setting. Popular in New Haven and for good reason—the menu, prepared as you like.

Louis' Lunch. *Inexpensive.* 263 Crown St. (562–5507). Reputedly the home of the original hamburger.

Picnic on the Green. *Inexpensive.* 900 Chapel St. (777–6661). Eighteen eateries at Chapel Square. Ethnic, finger food, deli, natural and raw bars, desserts, ice cream, and so on.

Pepe's at 157 Wooster St. (865–5762). *Inexpensive.* Noted for pizza. "The best in the U.S.A." some New Haveners report.

NORTHFORD Millpond Taverne. *Moderate.* Rte. 17 (484-9316, 484-9260). Enter via a bridge to "days-gone-by" atmosphere. Rustic wood, fireplaces, and antiques provide the decor. Varied menu includes steaks, chops, veal, seafood.

MERIDEN-WALLINGFORD AREA

WALLINGFORD. Yankee Silversmith Inn. *Moderate.* 1033 N. Colony Rd. (269–8771). Family-operated for over 25 years. Costumed waitresses and piping hot popovers. Traditional American menu, with seasonal specialties. Bread and pastries baked on premises. Gift shop. Bar is an 1894 railroad coach. Varied-size portions available. Facilities for the handicapped.

LITCHFIELD/TORRINGTON/SALISBURY AREA

KENT. Fife & Drum Restaurant, Inn and Gift Shop. *Expensive.* Main St. Rte. 7 (927–3509). Tableside preparations. French and Italian cuisine. Live music with dinner. Colonial decor with candlelight.

Bull's Bridge Inn. *Moderate.* Rte. 7 (927–3263). An old New England inn with two dining rooms in a country setting. Continental cuisine, French specialties and paella a la Valenciana.

LITCHFIELD. Litchfield Inn. *Expensive.* Rte. 202 (567–4503). A new (1983) "18th-century-inspired" inn, serving French inspired menu in a terrace-side dining room. A light bill of fare is served in the bar after 3:00 P.M.

NORFOLK. Blackberry River Inn. *Expensive.* Rte. 44 (868–0229). 18th-century inn, nicely restored. Interesting and unusual cuisine. Closed Mon. & Tues. Reservations.

Mountain View Inn. *Moderate.* Rte. 272 (542–5595). New England cooking, soups and homemade bakery. Dinners only, Thursday through Sunday. Reservations requested.

RIVERTON. Old Riverton Inn. *Moderate.* Rte. 20 (379–8678). In center of town. Homey, friendly place. A stagecoach stop c. 1796 in rolling hill country. Floor in Grindstone Terrace Room is made of old grinding wheels. Traditional American fare. Across road from Hitchcock Chair Factory.

SALISBURY. White Hart Inn. *Moderate.* On Village Green (435–2511). A true country inn serving breakfast, lunch, and dinner, and special snacks afternoons and evenings. Tap room. Patio dining.

TORRINGTON. Yankee Pedlar Inn. *Moderate.* 93 Main St. (489–9226). An adjunct of Yankee Pedlar Motor Inn. Charming atmosphere. Breakfast and late supper available. Fine American/French cuisine for lunch and dinner. Children's menu. Cocktail lounge.

WASHINGTON DEPOT. The Pantry. *Inexpensive.* Titus Rd. (868–0258). Blackboard menu for lunches served amid racks of kitchen utensils and gourmet packaged foods. Takeout deli with bakery, desserts, cheeses, soups, salads.

LAKEVILLE-NEW PRESTON AREA

NEW PRESTON. The Inn on Lake Waramaug. *Expensive.* N. Shore Rd. (868–0563). A lakeside resort featuring traditional American cooking in the restaurant. Open daily. Sunday brunch.
  The Birches Inn. *Moderate.* W. Shore Rd. (868–0229). Overlooks Lake Waramaug. Continental cuisine, German specialties. Lunch and dinner. Sunday brunch. Closed Tuesdays.
  Le Bon Coin. *Moderate.* Rte. 202 (Woodville) (868–7763). A small country inn serving French cuisine; lunch and dinner. On seasonal schedule. Telephone ahead for reservations.

CORNWALL AREA

CORNWALL. Freshfields Restaurant. *Moderate.* Rte. 128. West Cornwall (672–6601). Menu features wood-burning grill preparations.

DANBURY AREA

BROOKFIELD. Christopher's Restaurant. *Moderate.* Rte. 7 (775–4409). A restored early 19th-century home. Chef's specials include seafood, beef, veal or poultry. Lunch Monday through Friday. Dinners daily. Sunday brunch.

DANBURY. 1848 House. *Expensive.* Danbury-Newtown Rd. (744–0918). Several attractive dining rooms lend a cozy atmosphere to this old New England inn. German-American food, tasty sauerbraten and stuffed baked mushroom caps.
  Bella Italia. *Moderate.* 2 Padanaram Rd. (743–3828). Ornate Italian décor. Same menu in three dining rooms—one formal, one trattoria, one pizzeria. Excellent Northern Italian food prepared to order.
  Fairfield's. *Moderate.* Danbury Hilton, 18 Old Ridgebury Rd. (749–0600 Ext. 118). Continental cuisine.
  Fitzwilly's. *Inexpensive.* 5 Ives St. (749–6688). Sandwiches, soups, salads, entrees.

NEWTOWN. Newtown Inn. *Expensive.* 160 S. Main St., (426–2325). Continental cuisine, especially French and Italian dishes. A 1787 Colonial inn filled with Early Americana.
  Hawley Manor Inn. *Moderate.* 19 Main St. (426–4456). A picturesque country inn with three fireplaces in the dining room. Prime ribs, steak and seafood, with some continental selections. Cocktail lounge. Guest rooms.

REDDING RIDGE. The Spinning Wheel. *Moderate.* Rte. 58, Exit 45N from Merritt Pkwy. (938–2511). An old saltbox house in rural setting. Several attractive dining rooms and lounge. Traditional American fare, steaks and ribs, pot roast and turkey. Sunday brunch. Music and dancing on weekends. Dinner only.

RIDGEFIELD. The Inn. *Deluxe.* Rtes. 33 & 35 (438–8282). Outstanding European cuisine, with French emphasis. Menu changes seasonally; game, venison, wild boar in winter; fresh fish, squab in summer. Lounge. Piano music.

Stonehenge. *Deluxe.* Rte. 7 (438–6511). Famous country inn (1823) in rural setting beside a pond. Renowned continental cuisine and service. Live brook trout, game in season.

The Elms. *Expensive.* 500 Main St. (Rte. 35) (438–2541). An inn since 1799, full of fine antiques. Excellent continental menu and an extensive wine cellar. Duckling and game in season. Lounge.

Le Coq Hardi. *Expensive.* Big Shop Lane (431–3060). Small but distinctive. French cuisine. Daily specials. Closed Mondays. Early reservations required.

WEST REDDING. The Country Emporium. *Inexpensive.* Station Pl. (938–2484) Small, informal restaurant adjacent to country store. Unusual pancakes (apple chip, lingonberry) and burgers on homemade "dilly buns," sarsaparilla and orange crush. Perfect for brunch or lunch. Reservations suggested. Takes you back in time!

WOODBURY. Curtis House. *Moderate.* 506 Main St. (263–2101). Reputedly Connecticut's oldest inn (1754). American menu, with emphasis on seafood. Charming locale.

BRISTOL-WATERBURY AREA

PLAINVILLE. Cooke's Tavern. *Expensive.* 143 New Britain Ave. (747–6813). An 18th-century property.

WATERBURY. 1249 West. *Moderate.* 1249 West Main St. (756–4609). An Italian restaurant known as a landmark in the city. Large servings and great variety. Closed Mondays.

BRANFORD-NEW LONDON

BRANFORD. Chez Bach. *Moderate.* 1070 Main St. (488–8779). Vietnamese cuisine. Reservations. Closed Mondays.

Claudio's of Branford. *Moderate.* 225 Montowese St. (481–6211). Italian menu of a wide variety of pasta, seafood and meats.

EAST LYME (NIANTIC). Fatone's Ristorante. *Expensive.* Rte. 156. (739–8141). Owned and operated by the Fatone family since 1901. Classic Italian fare. Outdoor garden for summer dining.

The Chopping Block. *Moderate.* Rte. 161 (739–5515). Casual, country atmosphere. Noted for aged Western beef and seafood specialties. Open daily for dinner.

Connecticut Yankee. *Moderate.* Exit 74, I–95 (739–5483). In the Travelodge Motel. Extensive menu, with daily specials. Seafood a specialty. Bar, with entertainment and dancing most evenings. Children's menu. Breakfast served.

Morton House Restaurant. *Moderate.* 215 Main St. (739–8564). Continental menu served in seashore hotel overlooking Long Island Sound. Open 7 days year-round.

GUILFORD. Century House. *Expensive.* 2455 Boston Post Rd., Exit 57, I–95 (453–2216). Fine French cuisine served in a renovated foundry. Excellent service, linen, crystal and fresh flowers. Entertainment in the lounge, evenings.

Sachem Country House. *Expensive.* 111 Goose Lane (453–5261). Convenient stop just off I–95 at Goose Lane Exit. Country ambience. Seasonal specialties. Closed Mondays.

Chello's Oyster House. *Moderate.* Boston Post Rd. (453–2670). American fare, with breads and pastries made on premises. Excellent seafood, steaks, chops and chicken. Children's portions.

The Happy Wok. *Moderate.* 633 Boston Post Rd. (453–4936). An interesting menu, featuring Vietnamese and Chinese specialties. Children's portions.

MADISON. Woodlawn. *Moderate.* 438 Boston Post Rd. (245–2616). A family restaurant with American-continental menu. Bar. Children's portions.

Friends & Company. *Inexpensive.* 11 Boston Post Rd. (245–0462). Specializing in foods prepared to order.

OLD LYME. Old Lyme Inn. *Expensive.* 85 Lyme St. (Rte. 1), Exit 70 on I–95 (434–2600). A restored 1850 mansion, with floor-to-ceiling windows overlooking Old Lyme's Main St. The decor is French inspired, punctuated by white linen, crystal and roses. The menu is in French, and the limited selections change seasonally. Homemade soups, pastry, and desserts.

Bee & Thistle Inn. *Moderate.* 100 Lyme St. (Rte. 1) Exit 70 on I–95 (434–1667). An old, restored country inn serving three meals daily. Reservations requested, especially for breakfast. Classical harpist on Saturday evenings. Closed Tuesdays.

OLD SAYBROOK. The Whitehouse Restaurant. *Expensive.* Boston Post Rd., Exit 66, I–95. (399–6291) Hungarian menu served in a restored white house. Hosts and kitchen knowledgeable in this cuisine and wines.

Dock 'n' Dine. *Moderate.* At Saybrook Point, overlooking the mouth of the Connecticut River (388–4665). Seafood is the specialty. Entertainment nightly in the Captain's Lounge. Same owner, Griswold Inn, Essex.

WATERFORD. Charley's Eating & Drinking Saloon. *Moderate.* Crystal Mall (447–3320). Decor of British pub. Light lunches or special dinner menu.

Poor Richard's. *Moderate.* 49 Boston Post Rd. (443–1813). A museum of stained glass in an old Victorian mansion. Specialties include bouillabaisse, veal papillotte, stuffed shrimp, seafood and steaks. Entertainment and dancing nightly. Bar. Popular Sunday brunch.

NEW LONDON-GROTON-MYSTIC AREA

NEW LONDON. The Bulkeley House. *Expensive.* 111 Bank St. (443–9599). A colonial home (1790) handsomely restored. Serving American/English menu. English ale on draft a specialty.

Lighthouse Inn. *Expensive.* (443–8411). A renovated Victorian mansion overlooking Long Island Sound. Traditional New England menu with beef and seafood specialties. Live music and dancing Saturday nights.

Ye Olde Tavern. *Expensive.* 345 Bank St. (442–0353). Family-owned and operated restaurant serving charbroiled steaks and chops and fresh-caught seafood. Bar.

Chuck's Steak House. *Moderate.* 250 Pequot Ave. (443–1323). Part of a chain of cozy small steak houses serving charbroiled meats and fish. This dining room has windows on three sides overlooking the Thames River.

The Gondolier. *Moderate.* 92 Huntington St. (447–1781). Italian fare. Bar. Dinner only.

Paisano's. *Moderate.* 655 Bank St. (443–3275). Italian home cooking. Small but attractive bistro in downtown New London.

Nameaug Seafood Market and Restaurant. *Moderate.* Cor. Bank & Howard sts. (443–4458). Typical shoreside restaurant with water view. Seafood specials, fish market and takeout.

Thames Landing Oyster House. *Inexpensive.* 2 Captain's Walk near City Pier (442–3158). Pleasantly informal seafood restaurant. Raw shellfish bar.

GROTON. Fisherman. *Moderate.* On Groton Long Point Rd. (Noank) (536–1717). On the water at Groton Long Point. Seafood restaurant, primarily serving fresh-caught local fish and prime beef. Cocktail lounge. Reservations suggested on weekends.

Brian's. *Moderate.* Plant St. (448–1770). "Just off the Green at Shennecossett Golf Club." A country club restaurant atmosphere serving lunch, dinner year round. Shore dinners and "super platters."

The Flame. (Best Western Olympic Inn) *Moderate.* 360 Rte. 12 (445–8000) American and Continental menu with daily specials. Located near USS *Nautilus* Memorial and area tourist attractions.

The Gathering Place. *Moderate.* 314 Rte. 12 (449–0748). A cafe specializing in hors d'oeuvres, gourmet, French, Greek, Italian; special coffees and desserts.

The Golden Cup. *Moderate.* Rte. 184 (443–6228). In the Groton Motor Inn, overlooking the Thames River. Traditional menu. Entertainment and dancing weekends.

MYSTIC. Flood Tide. (At The Inn at Mystic) *Expensive.* Rtes. 1 & 27 (536–8140). Overlooking Mystic Harbor. Serving throughout the day. Award-winning French-inspired menu.

J.P. Daniels. *Expensive.* Rte. 184, Old Mystic (572–9564). Provincial French cuisine. A restored barn with simple country decor. Linen and crystal service.

Seamen's Inne. *Expensive.* Greenmanville Ave., Rte. 27 (536–9649). At Mystic Seaport on the Mystic River. Typical New England menu for luncheon and dinner. Oyster bar. Sunday brunch. Children's menu.

The Steak Loft. *Expensive.* At Olde Mistick Village (536–2661). Steakhouse with salad and antipasto bar.

Margaritaville. *Moderate.* 12 Water St. (536–4589). Mexican foods are the specialties in this barnwood restaurant. Fireplaces and hanging plants. Salad bar. Located in historic downtown Mystic in a renovated factory building. Bar.

STONINGTON. Harbor View. *Deluxe.* 60 Water St. (535–2720). Overlooks Stonington Harbor and dragger docks. Typical New England waterfront scene. French influence on seafood specialties. Coquilles St. Jacques, bouillabaisse. Bar.

NORWICH-WILLIMANTIC AREA

NORWICH. Norwich Inn. *Deluxe.* Rte. 32 (886 2401). Elegance prevails throughout this inn, and the menu, changing daily, reflects the general ambiance.

Huntington's Restaurant. (at Sheraton Inn Norwich) *Moderate.* Rte. 395, Exit 80 (889–5201). Interesting menu with frequent buffets. Nightly entertainment in the cocktail lounge.

WILLIMANTIC. The Clark's. *Moderate.* Cor. North & Meadow Sts. (423–1631). Small, family restaurant since 1949. Imaginative American cooking. Baked stuffed lobster and duckling à l'orange are specialties. Cocktail lounge.

PUTNAM AREA

BROOKLYN. The Golden Lamb Buttery. *Deluxe.* Hillandale Farm, Rte. 169 (774–4423). Luncheon daily. Dinners Fridays and Saturdays only, by reservation. Imaginative gourmet menu uniquely served. Numerous fresh farm vegetables. Open June to Dec. only.

PUTNAM. Chuck's Steak House. *Moderate-Expensive.* Rte. 12, off 395 (928–3900). Connected with the King's Inn. Dinner only.

STAFFORD SPRINGS. Chez Pierre. *Deluxe.* 190 W. Main St. (684–3283). A restored Victorian mansion houses one of Connecticut's best French restaurants. Seasonal. Reservations required.

LOWER CONNECTICUT RIVER VALLEY
(From Middletown)

CENTERBROOK. Fine Bouche. *Deluxe.* Main St. (767–1277). An unusual French menu prepared with care and distinction. Unpretentious surroundings. Luncheons and *prix fixe* dinners. Reservations required. Closed Sundays and Mondays. Patisserie.

CHESTER. John B. Parmelee House. *Expensive.* Rte. 148 (526–4961). The restaurant in the Inn at Chester. Barn board interior, fresh flowers, Steinway grand piano music, American cuisine.

Restaurant du Village. *Expensive.* 59 Main St. (526–5301). Provincial and unadorned in the heart of the village. Simple but fine luncheons and dinners. Excellent homebaked breads and desserts. Daily specials. Reservations recommended.

The Chart House. *Moderate.* W. Main St. (526–9898). A restored, mid-19th-century brush factory building adjacent to the Pheaconk River. Cocktail lounge by a rushing waterfall. Dinner only. Sunday brunch.

EAST HADDAM. Gelston House. *Deluxe.* Goodspeed's Landing (873–1411). Dining room overlooks the Connecticut River, and Goodspeed Opera House is next door. Prime ribs, veal dishes and duckling featured.

ESSEX. Griswold Inn. *Moderate.* Main St. (767–0991). Catering to travelers for 200 years in rooms mellow with age. Walls covered with ship paintings, prints and maritime memorabilia. New England fare, especially seafood and prime ribs. Piano in tap room nightly and banjo music weekends.

HIGGANUM. Glockenspiel. *Moderate.* Rte. 81 (345–4697). Bavarian ambience and menu. All well-known German specialties. Two dining rooms, one overlooking running brook. Closed Mondays. Reservations requested.

IVORYTON. Copper Beech Inn. *Deluxe.* Main St. (767–0330). Restored inn, maintaining high standards. Fresh flowers, real china, crystal, and snowy linen please the eye; a creative chef prepares French-inspired dishes from the freshest ingredients. Closed Mondays.

MIDDLEBURY. Green Fields. *Moderate.* Lyman Orchards, Rtes. 147 & 157 (349–9355). Restaurant overlooks golf course. Country specialties include poultry, fruits and vegetables from nearby farms.

MIDDLETOWN. Harbor Park. *Expensive.* 80 Harbor Ave, Rte. 9 (347–9999). A historic landmark on the Connecticut River located in a converted boathouse. Contemporary menu at lunch and dinner. Seafood specialties.

Town Farms Inn. *Moderate.* River Rd. (347–7438). A gracious country inn located directly on the Connecticut River and operated by the same owner as The Inn at Chester and the Gelston House, East Haddam. Continental cuisine featuring seafood and milk-fed veal. Luncheon and dinner daily; hunt breakfast and dinner on Sundays. Bar. Piano and harp or string quartet with dancing some evenings.

 **NIGHT LIFE & BARS.** Most hotels and large motels have cocktail lounges that provide live entertainment on weekends—some every night. Other bars that are popular with the "locals" and truly "finds" for visitors to the area are listed below. Some of the better known are:

Cromwell. *The Treadway Cromwell Inn,* Rte. 72 (635–2000). Live entertainment Tues.-Sat. Bar and disco dance floor.

Hartford. *The Goodwin.* 219 Asylum St. (549–5568). International pub open Fri. until 1:00 A.M., Sat. until 2:00 A.M.

Mad Murphy's. 22 Union Pl. (247–9738). Open until 2:00 A.M. and Fri. and Sat. until 3:00 A.M. Lounge with nightly entertainment and specializing in barbecue chicken and ribs.

Le Jardin. 121 Allyn St. (547–1190). Reservations advisable. Open from 4:00 P.M. to 3:00 A.M. featuring music from 1950s on.

Shenanigan's. Bushnell Plaza. One Gold St. (522–4177). Open from 7:00 A.M. weekdays to 2:00 A.M. Open later Sat.; and Sun. closes at 1:00 A.M. Live music and juke box.

New Haven. *Basel's,* 993 State St. (624–9361). Greek entertainment and dancing until 2:00 A.M. *Bistro Eduardo* at Casa Marra. 321 East St. (777–5148). Jazz on Fri. and Sat. nights.

Norwich. *Sheraton-Norwich.* Exit 80, Rte. 395 (889–5201). Live entertainment in the lounge Tues. and Sat.

New London. *Lighthouse Inn.* Lower Boulevard (443–8411). Dinner dancing to "big band" sound live on Saturday nights.

Westport. *Dameon,* 30–32 Railroad Pl. (226–6580). Mon. through Thurs. 11:30 to 1:00 A.M.; Fri. and Sat. until 2:00 A.M.; Sun. to 11:00 P.M. Piano live jazz. A special place for commuters as it is directly across from the railroad station. Junior executive types. *The Inn at Longshore,* 260 S. Compo Rd. (226–3316). Mon. through Thur. 11:00 A.M. to 1:00 A.M.; Fri. and Sat. until 2:00 A.M. and Sun. until 11:00 P.M. Dinner dancing in the Longshore Bar overlooking Long Island Sound.

DRINKING LAWS. Beer, wine and liquor are sold in package stores and some drugstores in nearly all cities and towns. Grocery stores are permitted to sell beer. No package liquor sold on Sundays, Good Friday, and Christmas. Liquor served by the drink in licensed bars, restaurants and hotels at local option, according to existing statutes. Minimum drinking age in Connecticut is 21.

MAINE

A Triumph of Nature

by
JANE E. ZAREM

Jane E. Zarem, a born-and-bred New Englander, has been a free-lance travel editor for several years. She has traveled extensively throughout the New England states and currently lives with her family in Connecticut.

If you crave a vacation by the sea, waves smashing on the rocky shore, views of fishing boats bringing home the day's catch, lighthouses blinking at passing gulls, islands dotting the horizon—that's Maine! If you dream of crystal-clear lakes nestled among the mountains—or roaring rivers and rushing streams—of fishing and canoeing, hiking and mountain-climbing, skiing and snowmobiling, that's Maine, too! If you're an adventurer anxious to explore and camp in the great wilderness, or a hunter yearning to stalk game in the remote north woods, Maine's for you. Or if you're looking for a little cottage on a quiet cove where you can read, write, or paint, Maine's the perfect place for that, too.

Maine is a four-season vacation paradise—whatever your pleasure. There is a part of this marvelous state that will appeal to nearly everyone at one time of year or another.

Perhaps New England's most ruggedly scenic state, Maine owes its dramatic beauty to eons of geologic action. Such action during the Ice Age some 11,000 years ago determined the coastline of New England and laid a bedrock of sandstone, limestone and shale in the area we now know as Maine. Over the subsequent centuries, the soft rock eroded into valleys and lowlands; but the hard, more resistant rock stayed put, forming Maine's western mountains and the random peaks found elsewhere in the state—Mt. Katahdin in north–central Maine and Cadillac Mt. on Mt. Desert Island, for example.

The melting glaciers caused the ocean to seep into the area, forming thousands of lakes and ponds and several mighty rivers. From the Kennebec River east, the resulting shoreline is rugged and rocky, with scores of craggy peninsulas jutting into the ocean and countless off-shore islands. The shoreline from the Kennebec River west is quite different—quiet coves, long stretches of sandy beaches, tidal pools and marshy lowlands.

The First Settlers

Burial mounds found in the south–central part of Maine and shell heaps found along the coast near Damariscotta indicate Indians inhabited the area well over 2,000 years ago. These early residents were the ancestors of the Abnaki Indians, descendents of whom are represented now on the Penobscot and Passamaquoddy Reservations.

It is believed that Norsemen were the first explorers to visit Maine, followed by British, French and Spanish sailors and explorers. Pierre du Guast, le Sieur de Monts, and Samuel de Champlain established the first French colony at the mouth of the St. Croix River in 1604. Shortly after arriving, Champlain explored the area to the immediate west, naming it Mt. Desert Island (Isle des Monts Desert).

The French colony was cut short when England's James I included the Maine region in the grant given the Plymouth Colony. The French then moved east to Nova Scotia and founded Port Royal, the chief town of Acadia.

The first English settlers, led by George Popham, arrived in 1607 at what is now Phippsburg, at the mouth of the Kennebec River. A devastating winter of harsh weather and disease forced the few survivors to abandon the settlement in the spring of 1608. They took the time, however, to construct the first English ship to be built in North America—a thirty-ton "pynnace" called *Virginia*.

In 1613, the French established a new colony and Jesuit mission on Mt. Desert Island, but they were expelled by the British soon after. The "Province of Maine" was subsequently granted to Englishmen Ferdinando Gorges and Capt. John Mason, by the Council for New England, in 1620. It was at this point that the region formally became known as "Maine." By agreement with Mason some time thereafter, Gorges became the sole owner of the territory.

In 1639, Gorges received a charter from England's Charles I. York, in 1641, became the first city chartered by England in the New World and the capital of the Province of Maine.

In 1652, five years after Gorges died, jurisdiction over the province passed to Massachusetts Bay Colony. Title was disputed for many years until Massachusetts finally purchased the rights from Gorges' heirs.

Struggles between the British and the French and Indians continued for several years, with half a dozen very bloody wars fought over French positions in the area east of the Penobscot River. Even the Dutch were involved, but the British eventually prevailed, driving the French northward and eastward into Canada and wresting control of the land from the Indians.

This strife slowed down the settlement of Maine considerably. Widespread devastation left only the settlements of Kittery, Wells and York intact.

In 1691, Massachusetts received a new charter for the Province of Maine. Sir William Phipps, a native of Maine, became governor. Despite the war-ravaged years and Indian raids, fishing, lumbering and shipbuilding proved to be important resources leading to a relatively quick economic recovery.

Independence and Statehood

In the American struggle for independence, Maine men distinguished themselves by their leadership, their fortitude and their sense of purpose. The first naval battle of the Revolutionary War, in fact, took place unceremoniously off Machias, when local townspeople captured the armed British cutter *Margaretta.*

Along with the new nation, however, came local agitation for statehood. The displeasure of Maine residents over absentee ownership of land and a basic political polarization were coupled with general dissatisfaction with Massachusetts over what Maine felt was inadequate military protection during the War of 1812. It wasn't until the Treaty of 1814 that British troops finally removed themselves from Maine soil.

The Missouri Compromise, of course, hastened the separation from Massachusetts, when Maine was admitted to the Union as a free state in 1820 to balance the power between north and south on the issue of slavery. Portland became Maine's first capital. After several years and much discussion, however, Augusta was made the permanent capital.

The final controversy in the establishment of the state of Maine was the northern border dispute, which nearly led to an "Aroostook War" in 1839 between Maine and New Brunswick, Canada. The dispute was peacefully settled, however, by the Webster-Ashburton Treaty with Great Britain in 1842, which set the present northern boundary of Maine and successfully averted a war.

With statehood, Maine's prosperity and population increased. Timber, trade and shipbuilding were primarily responsible for drawing new residents to the coastal and river areas.

Maine made sizeable contributions to the Union in the Civil War, both in manpower and financially. Hannibal Hamlin, a native of Paris, Maine, was Vice President of the United States in Abraham Lincoln's first term.

Lumber, Boats, and Fishing

Today, Maine's population is still centered along the coast and major rivers. Shipbuilding is still an important industry. In the early days, the proximity of harbor to forest encouraged the extensive building of clipper ships.

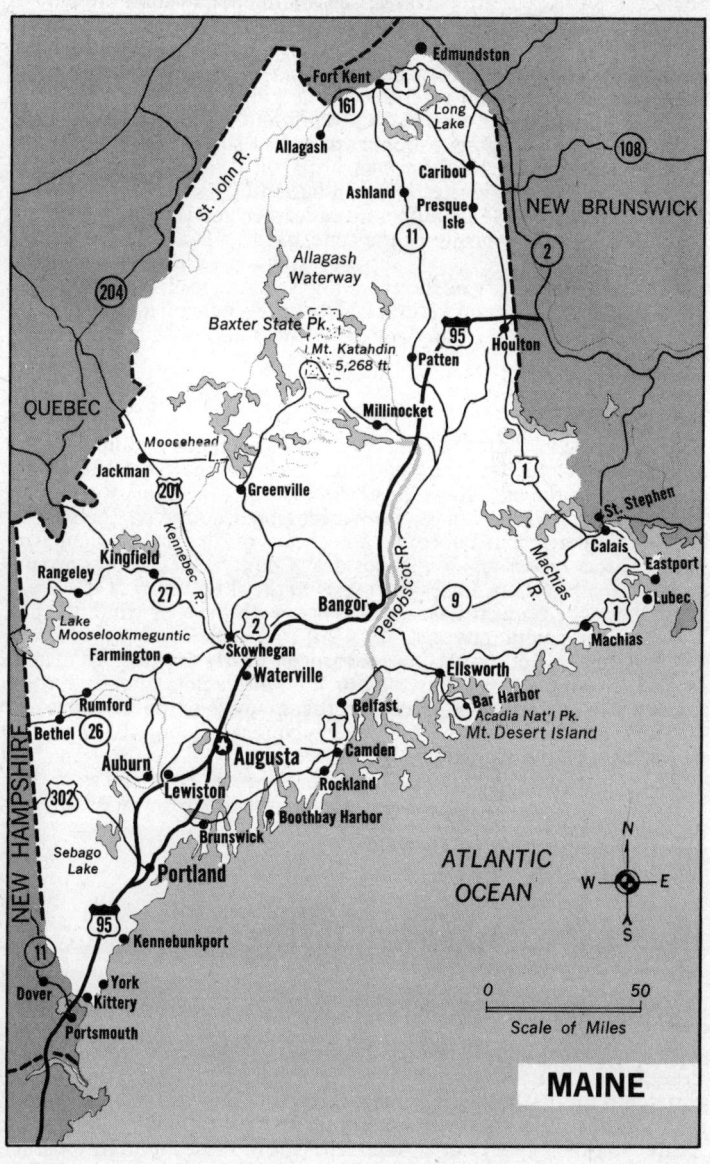

MAINE

More recently, the industry has turned to the construction of fishing boats and pleasure craft. Naval vessels and merchant ships are built at Kittery and at Bath.

And the timberlands continue to contribute greatly to the industrial wealth of the state. Maine is a leading producer of lumber and of wood and paper products that emerge from its pulp and paper mills.

The abundance of protected deep-water harbors ensures an involvement with the sea. Fishing continues to make a substantial contribution to the economy. Maine fishermen bring in a varied catch, but the incomparable Maine lobster is world-famous!

Agriculture and the manufacture of leather goods and textiles also add to the economic health of the state, but to a lesser degree than in the past.

An important factor in the economy is Maine itself—tourism. The unspoiled wilderness and natural beauty of the state offer the vacationer enormous diversity, abundant experiences and lasting pleasure.

Touring Maine

The routing in the following text has been arranged by touring areas as follows: Starting on the Southern Coast (at the New Hampshire border), it continues "Down East" through the Mid-Coast Region and Penobscot-Acadia to Lubec, in Washington County on the Maine-Canada border. From Lubec, the tour heads north through rich farmland to the wilderness of Aroostook County, then loops around through the Northern Lakes & Forests to the ski country of the Western Lakes. The Central Lakes area is last, with the tour winding up in Augusta, the capital city.

There are several opportunities throughout this routing to change direction and tailor the tour to your time available and your specific interest. Do keep in mind, of course, that many tourist attractions and facilities are seasonal—summer being high season along the coast and at some inland lake areas.

The tour begins where most travelers to Maine enter the state, just beyond Portsmouth, New Hampshire, on the north shore of the Piscataqua River.

EXPLORING THE SOUTHERN COAST

Kittery and The Berwicks

Instead of using I–95 (which becomes the Maine Turnpike, a 100-mile tollway extending from York to Augusta), take Route 1 north through Kittery, the southernmost town in Maine on the New Hampshire border. You will want to stop at the large Maine Information Center and the factory outlets characteristic of those found throughout this manufacturing state. Kittery is probably most widely recognized for its major industry, shipbuilding and submarine refitting. Many residents are currently employed by the Kittery-Portsmouth Naval Shipyard, which was established in 1800 (no visitors). You may, however, visit the Kittery Historical & Naval Museum, on Rogers Road off Route 1, which is open during the summer season. John Paul Jones set sail from Kittery on the 18-gun *Ranger,* defeating the British man-of-war *Drake* during the Revolution.

Across the Spruce Creek Bridge, follow Route 103 to Kittery Point. The Lady Pepperell House (1760) is here—a Georgian-style mansion built by Sir William Pepperell, the first native American to be made a baronet by the British crown. Farther along is Fort McClary (1690), a restored hexagonal blockhouse.

Here is an opportunity to make a swing inland. Route 91 heads west from Route 1 (just before the Yorks) to South Berwick, the site of the first (1631) permanent settlement in Maine. The earliest sawmill run by water power was built here, on the Great Works River, in the 1640s. Long before the Revolutionary War, Maine timber was being transformed in the Berwicks into pipe staves and ships. And on the slopes along the riverside, you can still see the terraced land where 17th-century colonists tried to grow grapes in the New World. In and around the Berwicks (North Berwick, South Berwick and Old Berwick), echoes of the industrial and mercantile past mingle with signs and sounds of the present.

The Berwicks are rich with fine old homes and other historic structures. Hamilton House (1787), on Vaughan's Lane off Route 236 in South Berwick, is a magnificently restored Georgian mansion with period furnishings. Nearby, at 101 Portland Street, is the Sarah Orne Jewett Memorial (1774). The home of the famed writer is lovingly preserved and worthy of a woman who so brilliantly chronicled the lives and changing times of these people. Both buildings are open to visitors during the summer season.

And now, back to Route 1. Head north to Route 1A and . . .

The Yorks

Charming, colonial York Village was the first city to be chartered in America (1641). Several of the town's 17th- and 18th-century structures are included in a National Historic District and are open to the public. The Old York Gaol (1720) contains dungeons, cells and jailer's quarters. It was built as the King's Prison for the Province of Maine. Other buildings to visit are: the beautifully furnished Emerson-Wilcox House (1742); Jefferd's Tavern (1750); the Old School House (1745); and the Elizabeth Perkins House (1731), a colonial home furnished as it was by its last occupants during the Victorian era.

While touring the Yorks, you're sure to cross Sewall's Bridge, a replica of the original built in 1761. It was the first pile drawbridge in America. Samuel Clemens (Mark Twain) used to summer at a house near the bridge. He spoke at York's 250th anniversary.

At the foot of Lindsay Street in York Village, you'll find the John Hancock Warehouse, once owned by the bold signer of the Declaration of Independence.

Farther along Route 1A, beyond York Harbor where boats are available for cruising and fishing, is York Beach. Short Sands and Long Sands Beaches are both popular, hardpacked sand beaches that slope gently to the ocean. There are shops and restaurants here and rides for the children at Wild Kingdom Amusement Park.

Just past Long Sands Beach is Nubble Road, the turnoff for Cape Neddick and a fine view of the Atlantic, picturesque "Nubble Light" (1879), the northward-reaching Maine coast, and Boon Island and Light.

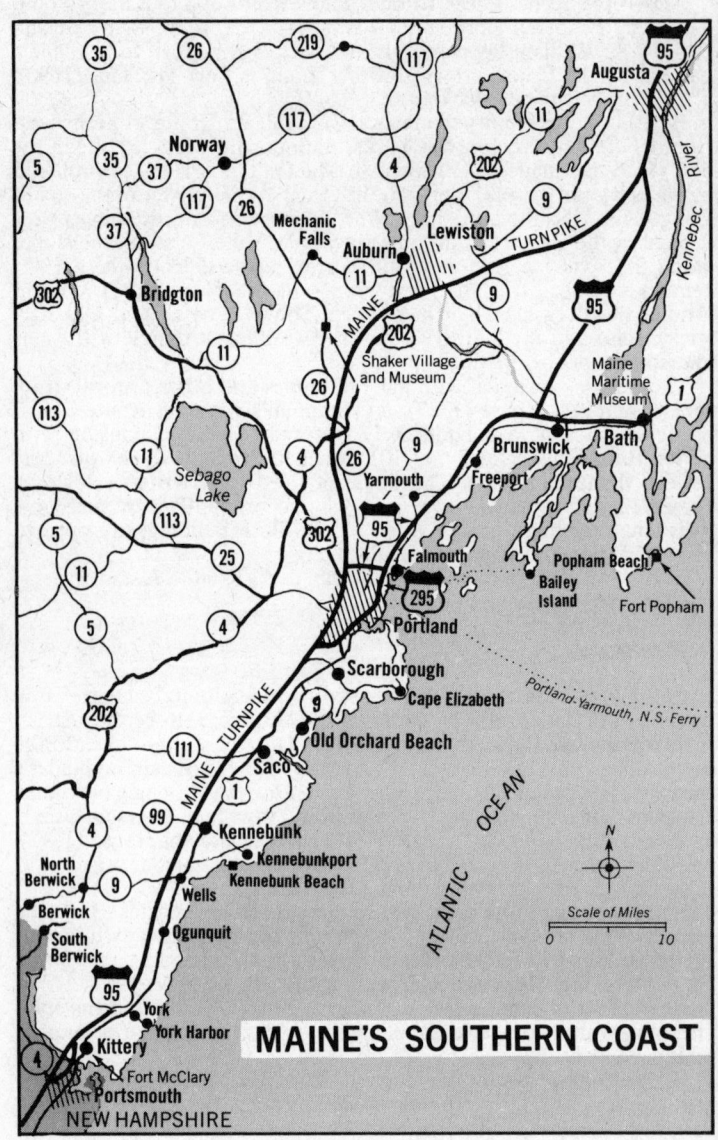

MAINE'S SOUTHERN COAST

Ogunquit and Wells

Following the shore road to Ogunquit, you will come to majestic Bald Head Cliff, where on a rough day you can see some fantastic surf—and on any day you can marvel at the view and the huge rough-grained rocks towering 100 feet above the ocean.

Ogunquit is an Indian name, meaning "beautiful place by the sea." Its beaches and natural beauty annually draw thousands of summer visitors to this charming coastal village. The town has become world famous as an artists' colony and as the home of the Ogunquit Playhouse.

Quaint Perkins Cove is here to explore, with its art galleries and artists' studios, gift shops and fishing boats. Or take a walk by the sea along Ogunquit's Marginal Way—a mile-long footpath that winds along the ocean and rocky cliffs. Sea gulls soar over the beaches and tidal pools along the way.

Wells, a seaside resort popular with families, has miles of fine sandy beach. Shoppers will find a concentration of brand-name factory outlet stores here, as well as flea markets, antique shops and second-hand stores.

Wells is also the site of the Rachel Carson National Wildlife Refuge, a total of 4,000 acres of marshland that is a sanctuary for many species of migrating birds. There is an excellent opportunity here for bird-watching and photography.

The Kennebunks

Just beyond Wells on Route 1, turn right onto Routes 9A/35 to visit the Kennebunks. The Kennebunk region (Kennebunk, Kennebunkport, Kennebunk Beach, Cape Porpoise, Goose Rocks Beach and Arundel) is a very popular summer vacation spot with more than its share of natural resources: fine, clean sandy beaches; rocky coastline; calm harbors; and picturesque off-shore islands. The beachcomber, the golfer, the fisherman (river or deep-sea), the yachtsman, the artist, the sightseer, and the shopper—all can keep quite busy here.

On Main Street in Kennebunk, the Brick Store Museum (1825) exhibits early local ship-building history and marine artifacts.

Follow Summer Street and drive toward the sea and Kennebunkport. The magnificent homes in the central residential area date back to 1724. The architecture spans the Colonial, Federal, Greek Revival and Victorian periods. Certainly the most unusual house you will pass is the Wedding Cake House (privately owned—no visitors) built by a sea captain as a wedding present for his bride. Note that early Maine farmhouses have barns attached, making tending the animals easier for the farmers during cold winters.

Kennebunkport is a colorful coastal community, a magnet for many famous artists and writers over the years. Here you will find a variety of tourist facilities, including comfortable inns, good restaurants, and a busy shopping area.

About three miles out of town, on Log Cabin Road, be sure to take the kids (of all ages) to Seashore Trolley Museum and "ride back to yesteryear." The museum's collection represents a variety of mass transit technology—from the classic horsecar to latter-day streetcars. You can take a trolley ride—an adventure for the young, nostalgia for the young at heart. A restoration facility is on site, where artisans and aficionados return antique cars to working order.

Ocean Avenue, a scenic ocean drive, winds past stately seaside "cottages" on the way to Cape Porpoise and Goose Rocks Beach. You will pass "Spouting Rock," a spectacular ocean fountain, and "Blowing Cave," a favorite rock formation where the waves roar in with an explosive crash. (Look closely, they're unmarked.) Cape Porpoise is a quaint fishing village, the center of the area's lobstering activity.

Old Orchard Beach

Follow the coast to Old Orchard Beach, the "Coney Island of Maine" and one of the longest beaches on the Atlantic. It is a favorite of youngsters, who love the several amusement parks and the fast-paced atmosphere.

Back on Route 1, continue north to Route 207. Turn right to Scarborough.

Scarborough and Prout's Neck

This is Winslow Homer country. It is also where Maine's first governor, William King, was born. His rags-to-riches story is a classic Maine —and American—tale. When his father died, William, at seven, worked in a sawmill. At nineteen, he took his only possessions, two steers (legend says he still didn't own a pair of shoes), and drove them to Bath. Starting at a sawmill there, he went on to acquire a mill of his own, then timberland, and in a few years was building his own boats and shipping his own cargoes. Rising to great wealth and prestige, he was a staunch advocate of statehood, and after Maine's separation from Massachusetts, he became the first governor upon Maine's entry into the Union in 1820.

Just beyond Scarborough, on the western side of this peninsula, is a beautiful stretch of marshland, ever changing its color and shape as light and shadow play across it. At sunset, the reflections are magnificent. Just beyond, at Prout's Neck, Winslow Homer used to live and paint. The Prout's Neck Bird Sanctuary here was given to the town by Winslow's brother, Charles, in memory of the great painter.

Following Route 77 north from Prout's Neck, you'll come to Cape Elizabeth. The shoreline here is awe-inspiring, with the Atlantic pounding relentlessly at a jumble of rocks; many people visit after a storm, when the surf is at its wildest. Crescent Beach State Park has a 4,000-foot-long white sand beach. Farther along is Two Lights State Park, with scenic picnic sites. Cape Elizabeth Light (1827) overlooks a rocky promontory. In clear weather, there's a fine view of famous Portland Head Light. Constructed between 1785 and 1790, the light was ordered into commission in 1791 by George Washington. It is the oldest lighthouse on the Maine Coast and the first lighthouse placed into service in the United States.

Continue on Route 77 to reach the city of Portland.

Portland

Route 77 crosses the Million Dollar Bridge from South Portland into Portland. Turn left beyond the bridge onto High Street and go to the top of a hill. Turn right here and you'll be on Congress Street, the main shopping street of the downtown area. The Wadsworth-Longfellow House, at 487 Congress Street, was the boyhood home of the poet and the first brick building to be built in Portland (1785). The home of the author of *Tales of a Wayside Inn, The Song of Hiawatha,* and *Evangeline* has great charm, from its old-fashioned kitchen to its lovely garden and manuscript collection. The Maine Historical Society is next door.

Portland, surrounded on three sides by water, was once a great shipbuilding city and port. Present-day Portland is the largest city in Maine and the state's cultural and commercial center. The city has been undergoing an economic surge, coupled with extensive redevelopment and revitalization over the past few years. Many major new buildings have been erected, yet historical integrity has been preserved in the Old Port district. Here, 19th-century buildings and warehouses have been painstakingly restored and converted to house a seemingly endless variety of shops, boutiques, book stores, arts and crafts shops, antiques, theaters, and several cafes and restaurants. Brick sidewalks, benches for tired shoppers and strollers, trees, and gaslights add to the ambiance—and this is all just a couple of blocks from the bustling waterfront.

From Custom House Wharf, Casco Bay Lines runs daylight, sunset or moonlight cruises to neighboring islands. Or you can take an overnight ferry to Yarmouth, Nova Scotia. Nearby, boats are available for rent or charter for sightseeing or fishing.

The 9,000-seat Cumberland County Civic Center, on Free Street, is the home of the *Maine Mariners* professional hockey team, but also presents a complete program of sports, music and special events. Symphony Hall, at the City Hall building, houses the world-famous Kotzschmar Memorial Organ and is home ground for the Portland Symphony Orchestra. A full series of concerts is offered each year, including a Pops concert.

Definitely worth a stop is the Portland Museum of Art on Congress Square. The museum is in a fascinating building and has beautifully displayed exhibits of American art—particularly that of Maine artists, including a fine collection by Winslow Homer.

At the junction of North and Congress Streets in the eastern end of town, the octagonal Portland Observatory rises 82 feet above Munjoy Hill (and 223 feet above sea level). The last of the 19th-century signal towers on the East Coast, it kept the city informed of approaching vessels and ships in distress. From its lantern deck, one gets a sweeping view of Casco Bay and, looking inland, one can see the Presidential Range of the White Mountains.

Stroudwater Village, three miles west of downtown, is worth a look. Unlike the part of Portland that was destroyed and rebuilt, much of the heart of Stroudwater has survived as an architectural unit. On a direct route to the Portland Jetport, and within earshot of the jets' roars, are the remains of mills, canals and homes that date back nearly 250 years. In the center of the old village is Tate House. Built in 1755 (with paneling brought from England), it overlooks the old mastyard where George Tate, Mast Agent to the King, prepared tall pines for the ships of the Royal Navy. In those years, the king claimed all white pines in Maine measuring over 24 inches in diameter. No matter whose land a tree was on, once the royal agent put the "broad arrow of the king" on it, down it would come. The Tate house, restored by the Maine Society of Colonial Dames, is furnished as it was from 1755 to 1800.

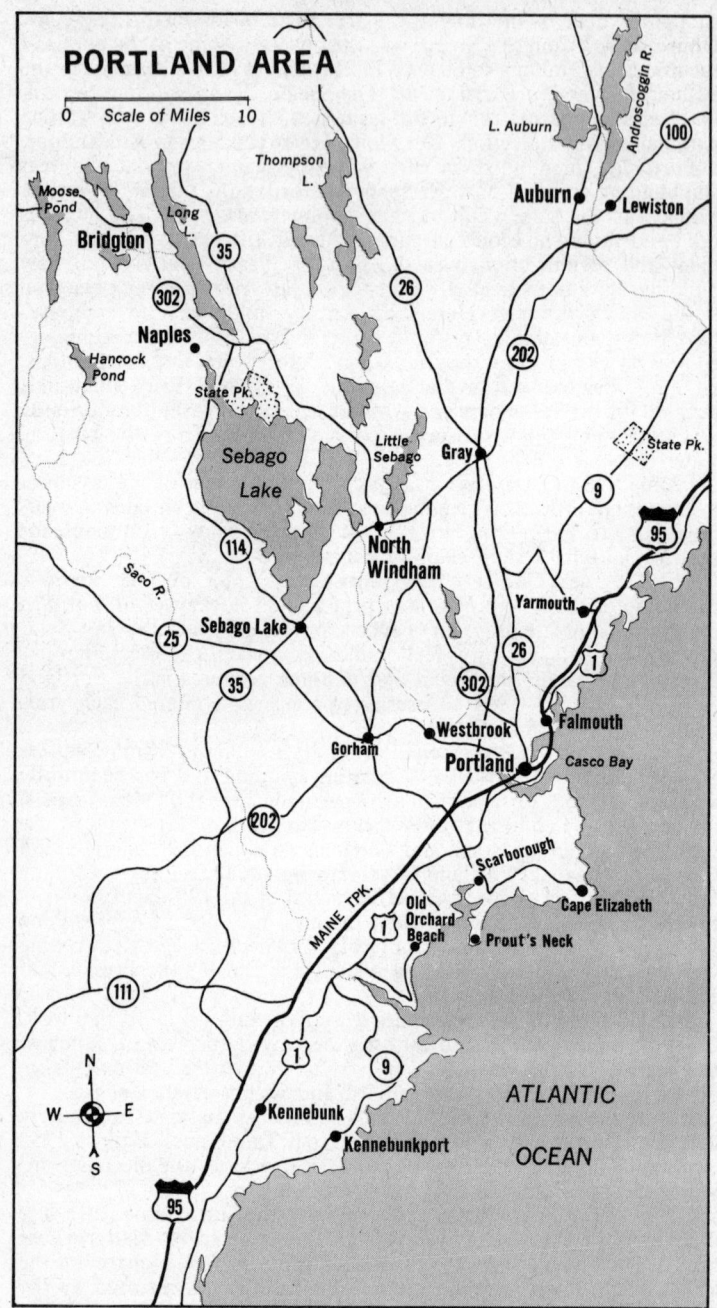

PORTLAND AREA

Scale of Miles
0   10

Moose Pond

Long L.

Thompson L.

L. Auburn

Androscoggin R.

100

Auburn   Lewiston

Bridgton

35

302

Naples

Hancock Pond

State Pk.

Little Sebago

26

202

Sebago Lake

Gray

State Pk.

9

114

North Windham

95

Saco R.

Yarmouth

25

Sebago Lake

26

35

302

1

Westbrook

Falmouth

Gorham

Portland

Casco Bay

202

Scarborough

MAINE TPK.

Cape Elizabeth

1

Old Orchard Beach

Prout's Neck

111

ATLANTIC

N
W   E
S

1

9

OCEAN

Kennebunk

Kennebunkport

95

Leaving Portland on Route 1, just south of the junction with Route 88 in Falmouth, is Gilsland Farm, headquarters for the Maine Audubon Society. The 6,000-square-foot building is heated by a prototype solar and wood energy system. There are educational displays and natural history exhibits. Guided tours and nature walks are available.

Route 88 provides an 8-mile loop from Route 1 (Falmouth to Yarmouth) past many fine residences and occasional ocean views. After about six miles, keep your eyes peeled for a small stone designated "B 136." The inscription indicates 136 miles to Boston along the 18th-century "King's Highway" and is one of the few original milestones. At Yarmouth, Route 88 again meets Route 1, and you pass through this quiet village that built over 300 sailing vessels during the early 1800s.

Freeport

Freeport is called "the birthplace of Maine." In 1820, the documents were signed here that officially separated Maine from the Commonwealth of Massachusetts and made it a state of the Union.

In the heyday of wooden ships, this town more than held its own. Today, residents make shoes and pack crabmeat; and world-famous L. L. Bean remains open day and night selling wilderness outfitting from clothing to canoes. Several rather posh factory outlet stores have sprung up adjacent to L. L. Bean, making the area a magnet for shoppers. Freeport was the home town of Commander Donald B. MacMillan, who began his Arctic explorations with Admiral Robert E. Peary on the North Pole Expedition in 1908–09. And for birdwatchers, a visit to the Audubon Wildlife Sanctuary on Lower Mast Landing Road is definitely worthwhile.

Brunswick

Just out of Freeport, take the Maine Turnpike to Brunswick—site of Bowdoin College. Henry Wadsworth Longfellow, President Franklin Pierce, Nathaniel Hawthorne, Admiral Robert E. Peary and Admiral Donald B. MacMillan were graduates of Bowdoin. The Peary-MacMillan Arctic Museum, in Hubbard Hall on the Bowdoin campus, has exhibits and displays relating to their polar explorations.

When Bowdoin was founded in 1794, Maine still belonged to Massachusetts. The founders chose the name of the state's then current governor, James Bowdoin. (His grandfather had arrived in Maine in 1687 as Pierre Baudouin, but the governor anglicized the name.) The governor's son, also named James, collected some excellent paintings by Dutch and Italian masters during his tenure as U. S. Minister to Spain and France. These, plus some valuable works by Winslow Homer, form the nucleus of the collection at the Walker Museum of Art (1894) on the Bowdoin campus. Special shows are arranged each summer.

Brunswick began as a fur-trading post known by the Indian name "Pejepscot." The Pejepscot Historical Society Museum, on Park Row, is rich in regional Americana. The Society is also accumulating a growing collection of military articles associated with General Joshua L. Chamberlain, the Civil War hero who later became president of Bowdoin and governor of Maine.

The Stowe House (1806), nearby on Federal Street, is where Harriet Beecher Stowe lived while writing *Uncle Tom's Cabin.* The Stowe House is now an inn.

Bailey Island

A pleasant side trip is to travel down one of Maine's lovely peninsulas—and here is an opportunity!

From Route 1 in Brunswick, travel east a few miles to the Cooks Corner section of town, where Route 24 south will take you on a 16-mile drive through Great Island and Orr's Island to Bailey Island. The area is a popular—but quiet—summer colony dotted with picturesque fishing villages.

A short bridge leads from Great Island to Orr's Island, where you can see the little white cottage where Harriet Beecher Stowe summered. Out of this stay came her book, *The Pearl of Orr's Island.*

From Orr's Island, cross the world's only cribstone bridge from Will's Gut to Bailey Island. The 1,200-foot span, built in 1928, is constructed of great granite blocks laid lengthwise, then crosswise, in a honeycomb pattern. The blocks are held in place by their own weight without cement or mortar. This unique design allows heavy tides and spring thaws to flow through freely.

At Bailey Island, tuna fishing has become a major summer industry. The annual Tuna Tournament takes place in late July. Giant tuna, occasionally weighing 700 pounds or more, are landed and displayed.

Just off the coast, between Bailey Island and Harpswell to the west, you will spot Eagle Island, home of Admiral Peary. There is a pier available to boaters, who can bring a picnic lunch and visit Peary's residence.

Bath and the Kennebec

Returning along Route 24 to Route 1, turn right for Bath and the mighty Kennebec River. This great river, flowing 150 miles from Moosehead Lake in the north to the Atlantic Ocean at Phippsburg, was one of the first to be explored by European newcomers. A main waterway for early settlers, it became a lifeline for the commerce and industry that followed. About a century ago, one of the main cargoes carried down the Kennebec was the chunks of the frozen water itself. Ice harvests of the 1880s brought Kennebec ice to markets far and wide.

The city of Bath is twelve miles inland on the Kennebec. Since its earliest days, Bath has been called "the City of Ships." The area's maritime tradition goes back to 1607, when the 30-ton *Virginia,* first ocean–going English sailing vessel built in America, was launched at nearby Popham Colony. Since then, over 5,000 ships (wood, iron and steel) have been built at Bath. During World War II, 244 Liberty ships were launched from Bath Iron Works alone. The Bath Iron Works still turns out a number of steel-hulled vessels each year—guided missile frigates and other U. S. Navy vessels, as well as containerized merchant ships. The successful America's Cup defender *Ranger* was built here, as was the 125-foot bow section of the experimental tanker *Manhattan* that sailed to Alaska in 1969 via the Northwest Passage.

The Maine Maritime Museum, four separate buildings along the river, houses an outstanding collection of artifacts related to over 300 years of Maine shipbuilding. A boat ride along the Kennebec River on the 50-foot motor vessel *Sasanoa* is included in the admission during the summer months. The museum buildings are on Washington Street, alongside great 19th-century homes that have made this street famous. The homes were built by prosperous shipbuilders and sea captains. A four-block walking tour along Washington Street, between Front and Pearl, includes historic architecture representative of all major styles of the 1800s. The Grand Banks schooner *Sherman Zwicker* is on permanent display at the museum. You can tour the entire 142-foot dory schooner, one of the last of its kind.

The waterfront has undergone a facelift in recent years, attracting new shops and restaurants to the area. The Performing Arts Center, in an 1846 Gothic Revival church building dubbed "Chocolate Church," offers a wide range of music and dance programs on weekends.

Popham Colony

From Bath, take Route 209 south through Phippsburg to the mouth of the Kennebec River and the site of the Popham Colony. This first attempt by about 100 English to settle permanently on Maine's coast was short-lived. Disease and the winter weather caused the few survivors to return to England post-haste.

Beyond this site is Popham Beach and Fort Popham, partially constructed in the year 1861. A climb to the top of the fort offers a sparkling view of the Kennebec's sweep. Down below you will find sandy salt marshes and lovely beaches in Popham Beach State Park. On the way back, side trips along Routes 216 and 217, touching West Point and Sebasco Estates, will reward the traveler with a variety of interesting views and sights, including an active resort area and a typical Maine fishing village.

EXPLORING THE MID-COAST REGION

Five Islands

Returning to Route 1, you cross the Kennebec and come immediately to Route 127. Turn right here toward Reid State Park, a beautiful sandy beach and picnic area on the ocean, and Five Islands, at the end of the peninsula. The warm scent of pines will greet you as you come upon placid little coves edged with evergreens. Though you know you're at the coast, the pines and the still, reflecting waters give a backwoods feeling. At Five Islands, the Maine coast becomes wilder. Here you begin to get an idea of the great tides and currents that affect the Down East coastline. Five Islands is at the mouth of the Sheepscot River, and its stilt-legged wharf is the center of the peninsula's life. Moored lobster boats bob on the sapphire and silver waters; a speedboat zooms past on its way to some privately owned island; a sleek schooner dips its sails as it rounds submerged rocks at the harbor entrance; sea gulls screech their complaints, while the scent of wood smoke drifts about you.

Round-trip, the drive to Five Islands is about 30 miles. For those who love woodland and sea beautifully interwoven, it's well worth the trip. Returning to Route 1, turn right, toward . . .

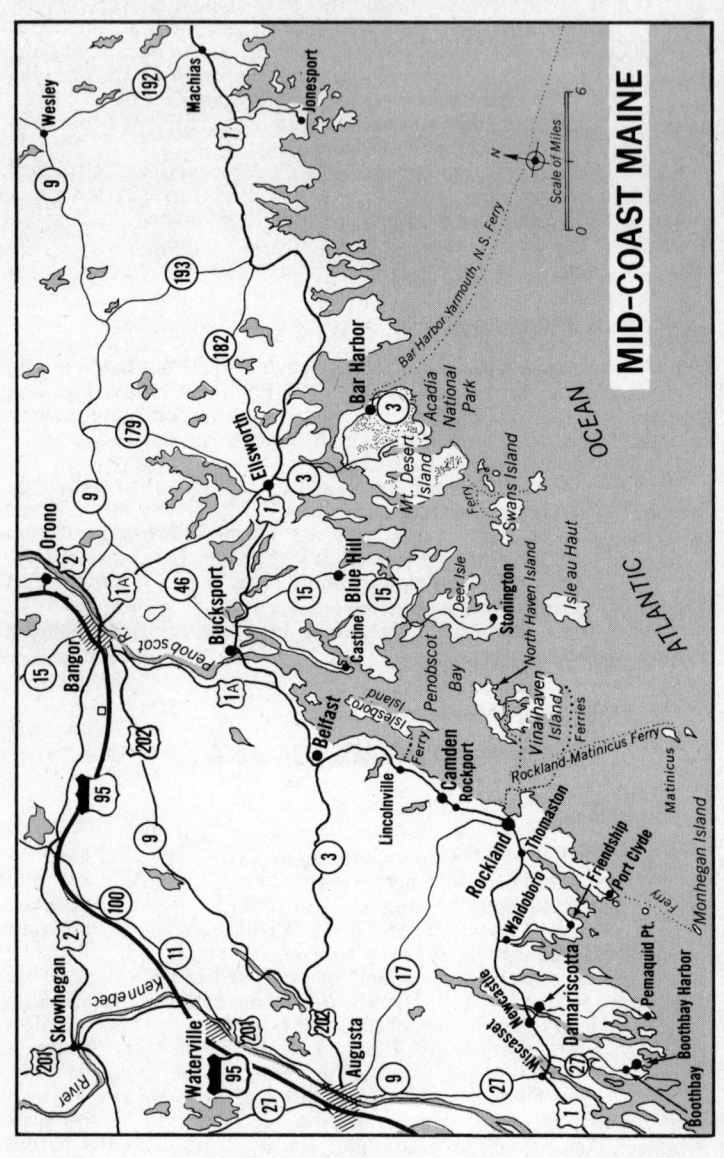

MID–COAST MAINE

Wiscasset

Wiscasset, a white, green, and brick-red town of great charm is nestled on a western hillside of the Sheepscot River a dozen or so miles from the sea. Wiscasset, too, was once a seafaring town and many of its fine old homes were built by seafaring families.

Wiscasset is a prime example of the birth-death-rebirth cycle of so many Maine communities. In the 18th century, it was busy building ships and shipping cargoes. Despite disease, war and embargoes, trade in lumber and ice and the building of clipper ships carried Wiscasset through until new technology and disastrous fires destroyed it all. For a time, Wiscasset was almost as derelict as the obsolete four-masted schooners, *Luther Little* and *Hesper,* that still lie in the harbor. Where schooners once loaded lumber and ice, there is now new industry— from the Maine Yankee Atomic Power Plant to the gathering and shipping of bloodworms and sandworms from the Wiscasset flats to sportsmen all over the nation.

The town has been lovingly preserved, and walking tours are offered by the Lincoln County Cultural and Historical Association.

The Lincoln County Fire Museum contains a collection of some of the country's oldest fire-fighting equipment, including an old hand tub dated 1803. The last of Maine's old-time stagecoaches is here, too. This museum is in the barn of the Nickels-Sortwell house, on the corner of Main and Federal Streets (Route 1), which is also open to visitors. One of Maine's most beautiful old homes, it was built by Captain William Nickels, a prominent shipmaster.

The old Lincoln County Jail (1811), made of three-foot-thick granite blocks, took over two years to build. The museum next door in the jailer's house displays 200 years of Maine arts and skills, as well as work of contemporary Maine craftsmen: weaving, pottery, toys, silk–screen prints, etc.

At the Wiscasset Musical Wonder House, you'll find a nostalgic collection of antique music boxes, gramophones, pipe organs, player pianos, and many other such items in an 1852 sea captain's home.

Castle Tucker, on Lee Street, an 1807 mansion with original Victorian furnishings and wallpaper and a free-standing elliptical staircase, is also open to the public.

Before continuing your coastal trip, take a jaunt north on Route 27 to the lovely tree-shaded village of Dresden Mills on the Eastern River. For those interested in our architectural heritage, the Pownalborough Courthouse (1760) is a must. The Lincoln County Cultural and Historical Association has done much to refurbish this oldest court building in Maine and the only one left from before the Revolution. It is interesting not only for its architectural details, but for many of its exhibits, including one on the Kennebec ice industry. And if you have time, stop off (Route 218) at the Old Alna Meetinghouse (1789), also filled with fascinating architectural details, including a pulpit leveler— a mechanism for elevating short-statured preachers.

The Boothbays

On the east side of the river at Wiscasset, turn right onto Route 27 through North Edgecomb and Edgecomb to the Boothbays and Cape Newagen. Fort Edgecomb's two-story octagonal blockhouse (1808–09) was built to protect Wiscasset's shipping industry from harassment by the English. Though this type of fortification proved inadequate during the War of 1812, it has been fully restored as an historic site.

North Edgecomb almost shared with Wiscasset the distinction of a royal visitor. Marie Antoinette was to have sailed here with one Captain Samuel Clough. But the Queen was beheaded before Clough's *Sally* could take her from France. Just why this North Edgecomb captain had been singled out to whisk her away is tauntingly obscure; in any case, once the guillotine had plunged, the captain hastily set sail.

Mrs. Clough, who had been promised a royal guest, had to be content with trunks containing Marie Antoinette's personal belongings and articles that friends had sent along with Clough. Many of the articles have disappeared; some are in New York's Metropolitan Museum of Art.

Farther south on Route 27 is Boothbay Railway Village. Items relating to steam railroading are on display in a pair of restored railroad stations, and you may take a ride on a narrow-gauge steam train. Several antique autos are exhibited, as well.

For the theater buff, the Boothbay Theater Museum has a collection of theater memorabilia from the 18th century to the present—costumes, autographs, portraits, playbills, models, etc.

Next come Boothbay and Boothbay Harbor, heart of a most busy summer resort area. The narrow streets are clogged with visitors to the shops, art galleries, marinas, restaurants, and many special events. Boothbay Harbor, "The Boating Capital of New England," is a pretty sight—sprinkled with sleek sailboats and backdropped by burly, stilt-legged wharves, pleasant homes, pine-clad peninsulas, and slim church spires. In mid-July, Boothbay Harbor celebrates "Windjammer Days." It is a festive event each year, with a beauty pageant, a street parade, and a "pass-in-review" parade of a dozen or so of the windjammers that cruise the Maine coast during the summer months.

Probably the best way to view the whole area—an intricate network of islands, coves, rivers, harbors, and peninsulas—is by boat. A number of excursion boats take passengers on morning, afternoon, and evening trips. Points of interest on the various cruises may be Ocean Point (where at one spot, you can see the lights of five lighthouses), Bath (up the Kennebec River), Five Islands, Seguin Light, Damariscove, Squirrel Island (where the movie *Carousel* was filmed), Ovensmouth, Burnt Island Lighthouse and Cape Newagen. One evening cruise, on the *Linekin II,* incorporates a Down East clambake into the trip. Take the *Balmy Days* cruise to Monhegan from Boothbay Harbor for a pleasant day trip. (Reservations are requested for this popular cruise.)

Back on land, take a trip down to Cape Newagen, on Southport Island, where Scottish settlers first landed in the early 1600s. After many years of the settlers fleeing Indian raids, resettling the area, then abandoning it still again, the town finally, in 1764, was incorporated into the town of Boothbay. At the Town Wharf, you can watch the sea and the tides busily at work.

En route back to the mainland, turn right in Southport just before crossing the drawbridge and proceed to McKown Point. (The drawbridge, incidentally, is the "most-often-opened" drawbridge in the State of Maine.) Here, you can visit the Sea and Shore Fisheries Aquarium, maintained by the State of Maine Department of Marine Resources. You can see all manner of sea creatures, including minute, newly hatched lobsters and playful seals in an outdoor pool.

Next door to the seaquarium is the Bigelow Lab, a marine life research facility known throughout the country as the authority on "Red Tide."

From Boothbay Harbor go east on Route 96 to see the many boatyards where you can watch sailing vessels under construction. Continue around to Ocean Point for further brilliant seascapes.

Damariscotta—Newcastle

Now, heading north on Route 27, look for River Road and a sign pointing to Damariscotta and Route 1. A few miles ahead, take "Business Route 1" or you will miss the many enjoyable things the twin villages of Damariscotta and Newcastle have in store. Damariscotta is separated from Newcastle by the Damariscotta River (famous for the running of alewives each spring), but they blend together so the traveler can see the attractions of both in one visit.

There are notable churches and homes in this area. St. Patrick's, in Newcastle, was finished in 1808. It is the oldest Catholic Church in Maine. In the summer, services are sometimes held outside among the tall pines and flowering bushes.

There are figureheads and other pieces by two famous early carvers, William Southworth and Edbury Hatch, on display at the Chapman-Hall House. Believed to be Damariscotta's oldest remaining dwelling, the Chapman-Hall House was constructed in 1754 and is one of the few early houses that escaped the torch of Indian raiders. After looking at grander homes elsewhere, you'll find a charm in the early craftsmanship displayed here, especially as the house manages to retain a lived-in look.

Prehistoric oyster-shell heaps east of the villages, on a state-owned archeological site, suggest a long tradition of good eating. More than a million cubic feet of shells were piled up here during the summer encampments of successive generations of Indians over the past 2,000 years.

The Pemaquid Peninsula

During the summer of 1965, amateur archeologists, spades and pick-axes in hand, attempted to unearth an area just to the south of Damariscotta near Pemaquid Beach. Old records indicated there had been a substantial trading post here in the mid-1600s.

They found an old customs house, a tavern, and what was probably a forge. One of the group came upon several skeletons. One was thought to be that of an Indian. Another skeleton brought experts flying from all parts of the U.S.—for the second figure was dressed in armor and sewn in a shroud of animal hide. The time of the burials could not be immediately determined, but archeological experts say the armor indicates the man was a Viking, a fact further suggested by the ancient Norse custom of sewing bodies in animal hide prior to burial.

Some fourteen foundations, believed to be those of 16th- and 17th-century settlements, have been uncovered, along with hundreds of artifacts indicating earlier Indian settlement. Adjacent to the Fort William Henry State Memorial is a private museum displaying much of this material. The State of Maine acquired Colonial Pemaquid for preservation and restoration.

To get to this site and all the beauties of the Pemaquid Peninsula, including famous Pemaquid Point Light (1824), turn off Damariscotta's Main Street onto Route 130 south.

Fort William Henry is unique in having been a succession of four different forts. The first, built about 1630, fell to the pirate Dixey Bull two years later. The second, erected in 1677, was destroyed by Indians in 1689. Sir William Phipps built the third (the first one to be called Fort William Henry) in 1692, during King William's War. Four years later it was leveled by Indians under Baron de Castin. In 1729 the fourth fort was built, and it, too, was destroyed during the Revolutionary War by locals who didn't want the British to occupy it. The present fort is a replica of the one Phipps built.

Returning to Route 130 and continuing south you'll come to one of the most-painted, most-photographed lighthouses in all America—Pemaquid Point. The Atlantic tosses its mane and pounds sonorously against the fascinatingly stratified rocks that form the shoreline here.

Christmas Cove, at the tip of the western fork of this peninsula (on Route 129), is a lovely unspoiled area. Christmas Cove was named by Captain John Smith, when he anchored here on Christmas Day in 1614. In his report on the area he noted "more than 200 Iles overgrowne with good timber, of divers sorts of wood, which do make so many harbors as requireth a longer time than I had, to be well discovered . . ." Present-day travelers, too, have the same complaint.

Waldoboro

Back at Route 1 turn right for Waldoboro. The earliest settlers here were Germans, led by General Samuel Waldo. This baleful inscription appears on a gravestone in the local cemetery: "This town was settled in 1748 by Germans who immigrated to this place with the promise and expectation of finding a prosperous city, instead of which they found nothing but wilderness." The Old German Church (1772), nearby on Route 32, is well-preserved—with square-benched pews and a pulpit shaped like a wine glass.

On Route 220, near its junction with Route 1, the Waldoboro Historical Society Museum is a complex of three buildings—a country school, a cattle pound, and a farm kitchen.

Friendship

Confirmed shunpikers and those interested in sailboats will want to take Route 220 and dip south to the village of Friendship, famous for its Friendship sloop. A charming, natural seaport proud of its trim boats, the town has a reputation that fishing vacationers would like to keep to themselves. The old (1851) schoolhouse, at the junction of Route 220 and Martin's Point Road, is now the home of the Friendship Museum, where you can find historical information on the Friendship sloop. The annual Friendship Sloop Regatta is held in Boothbay Harbor in July. Vintage sloops and present-day models join in the boat race.

From Friendship, on Route 97, head toward Route 1 and Thomaston, but make a point of stopping along the way at Cushing, a lovely summer community you may recognize from the paintings of Andrew Wyeth.

Thomaston

Continue east to Thomaston, a village of lovely homes. Thomaston, which flourished after the Revolution, grew into a major port and shipbuilding center in the first half of the 19th century.

High on a hill at the east end of town stands Montpelier, a reproduction of the magnificent Federal mansion built here in 1794 by General Henry Knox, one of Washington's closest advisers.

General Knox was an artillery commander during the Revolution, the first Secretary of War, and instrumental in founding the U.S. Military Academy at West Point.

Imposing Montpelier contains a bookcase of Marie Antoinette's (Knox purchased it after her execution), a traveling chest given him by Lafayette, and many pieces of rare china, family silver, and other personal effects of the general and his wife. The kitchen has great charm, and the house is especially noteworthy for its "flying staircase."

At the other (west) end of town is the Maine State Prison. At the Prison Store, visitors (open daily) can buy furniture and other articles made by the prisoners.

Thomaston is also the location of the largest cement plant in New England.

Port Clyde and Monhegan Island

Before exploring Rockland, consider the following side trip: from Thomaston, take Route 131 south to Tenants Harbor and Port Clyde, farther south, which are primarily fishing villages. There are fine shops and galleries to visit in Port Clyde; and nearby, Marshall Point Light overlooks splendid views of the ocean and nearby islands. You can take a boat to some of the nearby islands, including Monhegan—11 miles out at sea.

Monhegan Island, long a haven for artists, was discovered by Capt. John Smith in 1614. There are dramatic cliff formations here, a lighthouse and museum, and majestic Cathedral Woods. There are inns and guesthouses on the island. Many of the hardy year-round residents are engaged in the hazardous occupation of winter lobster fishing.

From Port Clyde, drive back on Route 73. Take the road that branches right to see Owl's Head Light. The proud little lighthouse, only 26 feet high, stands 100 feet above the sea on a red-and-yellow streaked headland. Nearby is the Owl's Head Transportation Museum. On many summer weekends, you can see old planes fly and antique cars and engines run; but the display is almost as interesting on weekdays, when things are quiet.

If this little peninsula intrigues you make a note to read Sarah Orne Jewett's *The Country of the Pointed Firs.* Her deceptively simple tale of a summer spent here is worth reading.

Rockland

Rockland is a busy place. It is Maine's largest fishing port and lobster-distribution center—the most active retail center of the Mid-Coast Region—and the birthplace of the great poet, Edna St. Vincent Millay. You will find swimming, sailing, fishing, an art colony, arts and crafts shops, festivals, and lovely vistas of harbor and city. There are several seafood processing and packing plants around the harbor, but safety rules prohibit visitors.

The four-day Maine Seafoods Festival is an annual event that takes place the first weekend in August. There are exhibits and demonstrations, pancake breakfasts and seafood dinners, a carnival, and King Neptune and his Court.

A most impressive attraction in Rockland is the William A. Farnsworth Library and Art Museum and adjoining Farnsworth Homestead. One of the largest collections of the paintings of Andrew Wyeth, including *Her Room,* is in the gallery. The museum has dedicated one gallery to display works of Maine artists, including Winslow Homer and the elder Wyeth. Another gallery has a fine collection of works by other American artists.

The Shore Village Museum, in the Grand Army Hall on Limerock Street, has a permanent Coast Guard exhibit of lighthouse equipment, buoys, and life-saving gear from search and rescue boats, coupled with a large collection of Civil War uniforms and artifacts.

Although deeply involved in its commercial pursuits, Rockland has, in recent years, initiated many civic improvement projects—including the renovation of its beautiful harbor. There are anchorages over 40 feet deep, with facilities for anything from a freighter to a small pleasure cruiser. Windjammers, which take passengers on week-long cruises along the Maine Coast, sail from Rockland (as well as from nearby Camden, Rockport, and Belfast, farther north).

Day trips depart from the Maine State Ferry Terminal to the offshore islands of Vinalhaven, a busy fishing community with some tourist facilities and North Haven, with a rugged shoreline and wooded headlands but no accommodations for tourists or campers.

Camden—Rockport

Approaching the Camden Hills, which rise to the northeast, you come to Rockport and Camden. Their pasts and presents are so closely interwoven, they are virtually twin communities. Yachtsmen claim this area of Penobscot Bay is among the best cruising waters anywhere in the world. You can visit Rockport first by turning right off Route 1 at Route 90—or you can tour Rockport during the course of your Camden visit.

Rockport, mainly a residential village, has a delightful harbor, assorted shops, and boatbuilding yards. Mrs. Efrem Zimbalist, one of the area's best-known summer residents, was responsible for the landscaping of the Rockport waterfront, as well as that of the inviting Vesper Hill Chapel, which was landscaped according to Biblical script.

The historic lime quarries, next to the Goose River bridge, and the abandoned lime kilns have been designated landmarks.

And at Rockport's Public Landing, take the children to see Andre the seal who performs tricks each summer afternoon at 4 P.M. from his pen in the harbor.

Camden, with its incredible long-distance views of Penobscot Bay and its many islands, is a popular yachting center and a delightful town through which to meander. Visitors to Camden are charmed by the pretty flower baskets on the lampposts.

Camden's Information Bureau is at the public landing; nearby there's a captivating view of the Camden River's waterfalls, whose waters cascade into the harbor after running beneath the main street.

This is home port for several windjammers that sail the Maine coast each summer, and there are boats on which you can cruise to nearby islands for the day.

Musicians and music lovers have found Camden a favorite place to visit or spend a summer. There are frequent musical programs, as well as theater productions and other events, at the outdoor Amphitheater behind the Public Library on Atlantic Avenue. The Camden Shakespeare Company presents an exceptional classical repertory each summer.

Those interested in authentic Colonial Maine farmhouses and barns will not want to miss Conway House (1780). Restored by the Camden-Rockport Historical Society, the house and barn have fascinating architectural details and old farm implements.

In the western part of town, off Hosmer Pond Road, is Ragged Mt., where the Camden Outing Club maintains the Camden Snow Bowl—Maine's oldest ski area—for wintertime skiing, both Alpine and cross country, daytime and nighttime, on a 4,500-foot trail.

The Camden Hills, rising abruptly from Penobscot Bay, are a unique physical feature of the area. Camden Hills State Park has a family picnic area, and camping is permitted at the foot of the mountains. You can drive (toll road) or hike up to the 1.4-mile summit of Mt. Battie for a splendid panoramic view of the bay, the islands, and the peninsulas beyond. This view is breathtaking at night, too—a point to keep in mind at many places along the coast.

Lincolnville Beach—Islesboro

Continuing northeast on Route 1, you'll come to Lincolnville Beach. Besides the sandy beach, there are several seafood restaurants, antique shops and gift shops.

From the Maine State Ferry Terminal, boats come and go between Lincolnville Beach and Islesboro. The *Governor Muskie* takes 25 minutes and accommodates 24 cars and 125 passengers. The island is worth visiting. There are miles of rough country road and many snug harbors to explore. Warren Island State Park, reached only by private boat, is at the tip of Islesboro.

Belfast

Farther along on Route 1, Belfast is the next community. Follow the route marked "Business District" to see some of the lovely old Federal and Greek Revival homes, built by merchant sea captains, along the Bay. If time allows, drive down a few of the cross streets to see others. One of the centers of the state's poultry industry, Belfast is known as the "Broiler Capital of Maine." A fifteen-acre city park slopes to the shores of the bay. This is where the annual Belfast Bay Festival is held in mid-July, highlighted by a gigantic chicken barbecue.

Searsport

Seven miles east of Belfast on Route 1 is the lovely old sea town of Searsport, Maine's second largest deep-water port. Still busy with maritime commerce, Searsport is rich in the traditions of the sea.

In the Penobscot Marine Museum, there are portraits of 284 sea captains, all from Searsport. Indeed, 10 percent of all the nation's

deep-water sea captains hailed from this town of 2,500 in the 1870s and
'80s. The museum's exhibits, in four buildings, include a whaling room
and treasures from faraway lands where captains (and often their families, too) visited and traded. There are paintings of famous ships, a
collection of ship half-models, charts, logs, navigational instruments,
and other mementos of the days of the tall ships.

Today, Searsport's harbor is still very active. Modern freighters ship
lumber from the northern woods through Searsport to destinations far
and wide.

Searsport is known as the antique capital of Maine because of the
concentration of antique shops and flea markets found here.

Fort Knox State Park

Taking Route 1 out of Searsport, turn left at Route 1A; then, a few
miles beyond, right onto Route 174. Driving through hill, pine, and
meadow country, you come to Fort Knox State Park. Fort Knox was
built of granite by master craftsmen starting in 1844. It is one of the
largest forts of its type in the U.S. It was named for the same General
Knox who used to live at Montpelier and was Washington's Secretary
of War. Some parts of the fort are underground and dark, so if you wish
to see most of this huge structure, get out your flashlight or rent one
near the park entrance!

From the fort there are impressive views of the Penobscot River. The
mill on the opposite bank, in Bucksport, is the St. Regis Paper Company, the area's main industry.

EXPLORING THE PENOBSCOT/ACADIA AREA

Bangor Area

Turning north on Route 1A some ten miles north of Belfast will take
you on a journey inland to Bangor and environs. Bangor, 24 miles up
the Penobscot River, was once a bustling shipping center. Fortunes
were made in lumber cargoes.

A trip to the Bangor Historical Society's museum, the Thomas Hill
House (1834), recalls those bygone days when Bangor was the lumber
capital of the world. The 31-foot statue of the legendary Paul Bunyan,
at Bass Park near Bangor Auditorium and Civic Center, suggests the
brawn of those Maine lumbermen.

Present-day Bangor, the "Queen City of Maine," is the commercial,
financial and cultural center of northern and eastern Maine. The logging town of the past has given way to modern shopping malls and
industrial parks. The city's heritage has been retained, however, in the
carefully restored lumber barons' mansions located in the Broadway
Historic District.

At Bangor's Salmon Pool (opposite beautiful Grotto Cascade Park),
each May and June, 10- to 30-pound sea salmon fight their way up-
stream. With proper licensing, fishermen can try for that big one!

The Bangor State Fair takes place at Bass Park for ten days in early
August. Along with the midway and the cotton candy, there are
agricultural exhibits, animal judging, and ox and draft horse contests.

Orono, just north of Bangor on Route 2, is where you'll find the University of Maine's beautiful campus along the Stillwater River. There is a planetarium on campus, and the university's Anthropology Museum has special exhibits on Maine Indians and Maine prehistory.

Following Route 1A north along the river a few more miles will bring you to Old Town, hometown of the Old Town Canoe Company. Visitors are permitted to watch craftsmen construct sleek-hulled canoes. Old Town is also the location of the Penobscot Indian Reservation. The Penobscot National Historical Society Museum has items depicting the history of the Penobscot Indian tribe, members of the once-powerful Abnaki Nation.

Now, take Route 178 south to Brewer, Bangor's twin city, then Route 15 south to Bucksport.

Bucksport

Whether you have taken the northern sidetrip and come down Route 15 from the Bangor area or have followed coastal Route 1 from Belfast and crossed the Waldo-Hancock Bridge, you are now in Bucksport. Turn left just over the bridge for the Jed Prouty Tavern. Some writers, describing the tavern as a 1798 hostelry, have misled more than one traveler into expecting vestiges of the 18th century. None remain. But it was a stop on bygone stage runs. William Henry Harrison, Andrew Jackson, John Tyler, Martin Van Buren and Daniel Webster are known to have been guests.

Just beyond Bucksport, Route 175 south will take you into a whole wonderland of Maine life. This area is the East Penobscot Bay Peninsula, sometimes called the Naskeag Peninsula.

Castine

Those who seek the untrammeled byways will delight in the Naskeag Peninsula. Though people have been writing and talking about it for many years, there is so much to see that few travelers know this most extensive peninsula on the Maine coast in its entirety.

When you reach Route 166A on the peninsula, follow it to Castine. This calm, peaceful settlement belies its pugnacious past. For almost 200 years it was the object of dispute by English, French, Dutch and Colonial armies. Almost 100 signs are posted throughout the town, recounting various events which occurred here. Perhaps you can piece together its past from these. You'll find reading the signs an amusing pastime.

No one is quite certain how early Castine's Fort George was built, but there were fortifications on this site about 1626. It was razed and rebuilt many times over a period of 200 years.

Just opposite Fort George and Witherle Park is the Maine Maritime Academy. The academy, which has been here since 1941, is one of five institutions in the United States training young men and women for careers as officers in the Merchant Marine. Visitors can tour the *State of Maine,* training ship of the academy, when it is in port.

Nearby, the Wilson Museum has exhibits on the Stone and Iron Ages of Europe, plus artifacts dating back to prehistoric times.

Route 166 and Route 199 loop the Castine cape, so that you will arrive back on Route 175 (southbound). At the junction of Routes 175 and 176, turn right on Route 176. At Brooksville, a tiny settlement, have a look at Buck's Harbor, a favorite of yachtsmen. It's one of the deepest along the Maine coast, with a beauty all its own.

Farther south, cross Deer Isle Bridge at Eggemoggin Reach and head for Stonington.

Stonington

Stonington is the archetypical "Down East" fishing village. The magnificent harbor, with the town climbing the little hills that border it, exemplifies the beauty of the Maine coast. Stonington once had a flourishing granite quarry, the source of the granite used in New York's Triborough Bridge. Now the town is geared to the waterfront and the sardine-packing factory.

There are several boat trips to take in this area. For instance, there's a morning mail boat to Isle au Haut, a portion of which is part of Acadia National Park. Other cruises go periodically to Vinalhaven and Swans Island. Stonington is a quietly busy harbor, and likely as not you'll see one of the windjammers that cruise Down East in the summer months. Just west of Stonington, you'll see Ames Pond, a lily pond covered with a galaxy of pink and white blossoms in the summertime.

Blue Hill

From a distance you'll have no trouble recognizing Blue Hill. It not only dominates much of the scenery in the northern section of the peninsula—it is also often blue. But in late summer and fall, much of it becomes a brilliant soft red. This is when the leaves of the blueberry bushes turn, and it presents a dramatic sight.

Blue Hill, and the surrounding area, is a lovely unspoiled tract dotted with fine estates and summer cottages. The highly creative parson Jonathan Fisher, whose house can be visited, lived here in 1814. The home, on Main Street, contains the minister's own homemade furnishings.

An ancient Norwegian coin was found in Blue Hill recently. As a result, archeological digs have been undertaken to determine if there was a visit to Maine by the Vikings 900 years ago.

Kneisel Hall, a summer school for string and ensemble music now directed by Marianne Kneisel, presents weekly chamber concerts during the summer season. At Rackliffe Family Potters and at Rowantrees Pottery, you can see potters working at their wheels, firing the pottery, etc.

Ellsworth

Ellsworth is a major crossroads and the business center of Hancock County. From here, you can head toward Bangor and the wilderness and farmlands to the north; or go "way down east" to rugged Washington County with its 700 miles of magnificent coastline and its 2,628 square miles of woods, lakes and mountains; or you can turn south to popular Acadia National Park on Mount Desert Island.

Heading north on Route 172, be on the lookout for the Colonel Black Mansion (1828), on your left, at the outskirts of Ellsworth. An elegant red-brick mansion of modified Georgian architecture, the Colonel Black Mansion is fully furnished, and a visit gives one more the feeling of having paid a call than of having visited a museum.

Another point of interest in Ellsworth is the Stanwood Homestead Museum (1850), a memorial to Cordelia J. Stanwood, pioneer ornithologist. Adjacent is a 40-acre woodland sanctuary, including 8 trails and 3 ponds.

Mount Desert Island and Acadia National Park

Follow Route 1 a short distance beyond Ellsworth to Route 3 south, which will take you to Mount Desert Island.

In 1604, the French explorer Samuel de Champlain, noticing the bald mountain peaks on the island, called it L'Isle des Monts Deserts. In the mid-1800s, vacationers began coming to Mount Desert Island by rail and steamboat. Soon it became a colony of spacious summer homes owned by wealthy people. As more and more families arrived, followed by merchants to serve them, privacy became threatened. In 1919 President Wilson was persuaded to preserve much of the island as a national park. Children and grandchildren of those who once owned the great estates still come to Mount Desert Island.

Among the first summer residents of Bar Harbor, back in the 1800s, were artists who were attracted by the area's incredible natural beauty. The artists were followed by prominent east coast families, such as the Astors and the Rockefellers, who built "cottages" to rival some of those in Newport.

For almost 100 years, Bar Harbor was a society resort. The Great Depression, followed by the Great Fire of 1947, brought the dream to an abrupt halt. Although several mansions were burned, many still exist; and some have become lovely inns. The Bar Harbor Historical Museum, in the basement of the Jesup Memorial Library on Mount Desert Street, has on display a large collection of photographs and other memorabilia of those early days.

Today, Bar Harbor is the commercial center of the island—its attractive village center is chock full of shops and restaurants, with a wide variety of accommodations available. There are festivals, concerts, and special events scheduled throughout the summer season.

The car/passenger ferry *Bluenose* leaves from the terminal on Eden Street (Route 3), north of the center of town, for the 6-hour journey to Yarmouth, Nova Scotia. Shorter excursions (sightseeing trips, sunset cruises, and deep-sea fishing charters) leave from the Municipal Pier at West Street.

About 3 miles south of the village center, on Route 3, you will come to The Jackson Laboratory, world-famous center for mammalian genetics research. Here scientists study inbred lab animals (mainly their own specially bred mice) for insight into behavior problems and human diseases—cancer, diabetes, birth defects, aging, etc. A one-hour lecture and film program is available to the public free of charge on certain afternoons each week during the summer.

These days, almost 2,500,000 motorists annually visit this area. Although Bar Harbor is lovely and busy, often the main interest is exploring Acadia National Park. The region has an air of vast, timeless beauty—mountains, sea and shore. It is Maine unmasked and the face revealed is majestic!

Acadia is a natural paradise, with 100 miles of hiking trails, 50 miles of car-free paths for bicycling (or cross-country skiing), over 40 miles of bridle paths, 26 lakes and ponds, several picnic areas and campsites.

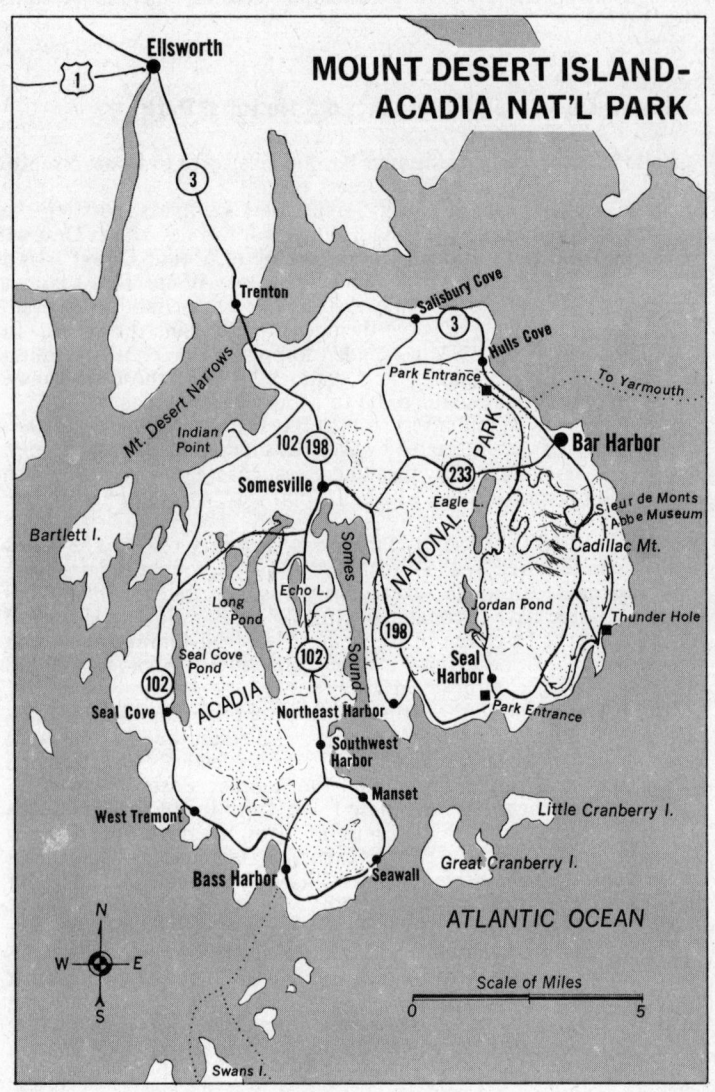

MOUNT DESERT ISLAND-
ACADIA NAT'L PARK

Ellsworth

1

3

Trenton

Salisbury Cove

3

Hulls Cove

Park Entrance

To Yarmouth

Mt. Desert Narrows

Indian
Point

102 198

Somesville

Bar Harbor

233

Eagle L.

NATIONAL PARK

Sieur de Monts
Abbe Museum

Cadillac Mt.

Bartlett I.

Somes

Echo L.

Long
Pond

Jordan Pond

Thunder Hole

Seal Cove
Pond

198

102

Sound

102

ACADIA

Seal Cove

Northeast Harbor

Seal
Harbor

Park Entrance

Southwest
Harbor

Manset

West Tremont

Little Cranberry I.

Great Cranberry I.

Bass Harbor

Seawall

ATLANTIC OCEAN

N
W E
S

Scale of Miles

0   5

Swans I.

At Sieur de Monts Spring, near the beginning of Ocean Drive, you will enjoy the Robert Abbe Museum of Stone Age Antiquities, with its dioramas of early Indian life and Indian artifacts. There is a nature center here and gardens of lovely wildflowers.

Drive along scenic Ocean Drive (which is one way). In and among the 33,000 acres of the park, you can stop to poke about, see Thunder Hole and great ragged cliffs and coves. Take the road north from Seal Harbor to the 1,532-foot summit of Cadillac Mt.; marvel at magnificent Jordan Pond.

Seal Harbor and Northeast Harbor are both coastal villages where yachting is the main attraction. The summer residents and visiting yachtsmen gather for races, for regattas or for cruises. Hundreds of boats of every size and shape can be seen at anchor in both these harbors throughout the summer season.

From the public wharf in Northeast Harbor, there is ferry service to the nearby Cranberry Isles. The Islesford Historical Museum, on Little Cranberry Island, has exhibits on the early history of Acadia.

Out of Northeast Harbor, take Sargent Drive (passenger cars only) to see the fjord at Somes Sound. It is the only natural fjord on the east coast, and the view is breathtaking.

Route 198 north brings you around the head of Somes Harbor to Route 2. Turn south to Somesville, the first village on the western lobe and the oldest settlement on Mount Desert Island. The Acadia Repertory Theater performs several plays here each summer at the Masonic Hall on Route 102.

Following Route 102 south as it loops around the island, the next community to visit is Southwest Harbor. This is another authentic Maine fishing village, its harbor crowded with lobster boats and its main street dotted with shops and galleries.

The Mount Desert Oceanarium, on Clark's Point Road in Southwest Harbor, has tanks filled with all manner of live local sea animals and presents fishing and lobstering demonstrations. There are hands-on exhibits and workshops. Kids will especially love the Oceanarium.

The ferry between Northeast Harbor and the Cranberry Isles also stops at Southwest Harbor, at the Coast Guard Depot.

Leaving Southwest Harbor, Route 102A veers off to the left and hugs the coast through the villages of Manset, Seawall (aptly named, as you will see) and Bass Harbor, then rejoins Route 102.

For a change of pace (from boats to cars), follow Route 102 west and north through the Tremonts to Seal Cove. The Seal Cove Automobile Museum has a collection of 150 or more antique autos, spanning the years from early 1900s to the 1940s. There are also several restored fire trucks and pumpers.

Follow the coast north until Routes 102 and 198 meet Route 3 and the causeway that will take you back to Route 1.

For those who wish to know more about this area, read *The Story of Mount Desert Island,* by distinguished historian Samuel Eliot Morison.

Hancock—Sullivan

Back on Route 1, turn right for Hancock, which, as music-lovers know, is the location of the Pierre Monteux School of Music. Summer chamber concerts are held regularly. Begun in 1965, the Monteux Memorial Festival is an annual event.

Farther east on Route 1, just beyond Hancock and near Sullivan, look for a sign marking a scenic turnoff. From this spot, you can look out on one of the most magnificent views of coastal America. You can see a splendid panorama of Mount Desert Island, Cadillac Mountain, pine–clad islands, and the far reaches of Frenchman's Bay.

Gouldsboro Peninsula

Farther along the coast (about five miles), be on the lookout for signs for Route 186 and Winter Harbor. This is the Gouldsboro Peninsula. Generally unfamiliar to travelers, it is a quiet place with a peaceful, pretty harbor.

Winter Harbor is the gateway to the 2,080-acre Schoodic Point, a section of Acadia National Park. A one-way road leading to the point is lined with pine and spruce forests. Pink granite rocks, caught between blue water and evergreened shore, make for some memorable scenes. Schoodic Mountain rises to an elevation of 500 feet above a terraced ledge. The surf here is always spectacular; following a storm, it is awesome. The view from Schoodic Head stretches all the way east to the Bay of Fundy.

Returning from Schoodic, take Route 186 east to serene Prospect Harbor (home of the state's largest sardine canning factory), then Route 195 about three miles to Corea. The village of Corea has a simple charm. It's a working harbor, with trim little lobster boats and long-legged wharves. But despite the peaceful scene, you sense it isn't so simple, for lobstering and fishing on this stern coast, at times, takes its toll.

Corea has two main paved streets. Each becomes a little dirt road which peters out at the harbor's edge. Here is where you should decide whether to continue your journey farther Down East to Washington County, head north to the great north woods in Aroostook County, or turn back west to visit Maine's lake and mountain regions.

EXPLORING WASHINGTON COUNTY

Washington County is as close as you can get to a frontier feeling and still be on the east coast. It's big (2,628 square miles, larger than the states of Delaware and Rhode Island combined) and wild (1.47 million acres of woods, 133,000 acres of lakes and ponds, the rest cropland and pasture). This easternmost county in the U. S. is still a place where you can "get away from it all" to beachcomb, fish, hike, hunt, boat, swim, paint, take pictures, seek antiques, study rocks and wildflowers, or camp out in the wilderness.

Machias Area

Route 1 east from Cherryfield to Machias (pronounced Match-EYE-iss), the county seat, passes by the headlands of several bays. The miles of meandering shoreline vary from stark rocky ledge to quiet coves, making the area one of the most picturesque sections of the Maine coast.

There are broad stretches of blueberry barrens, starting between Columbia Falls and Machias and extending deep into the central part of the county. Ninety percent of the nation's crop is harvested right here. And this is spectacular fishing country! There are 46 troutfishing streams in Harrington. The Pleasant River, in Columbia Falls, and the Machias River, in Whitneyville, are centers for Atlantic salmon fishing.

Fort O'Brien, overlooking Machias Bay, is five miles south of Machias on Route 92. It is the site of the first naval engagement of the Revolution (five days before the Battle of Bunker Hill), when the British schooner *Margaretta* was captured in 1775.

Burnham Tavern (1770), at Main and Free Streets in Machias, is the oldest building in eastern Maine. It has been restored and is operated by the Daughters of the American Revolution as a museum. It contains period furnishings and items relating to the capture of the *Margaretta*.

If you follow Route 191 along the coast to Lubec, you will pass through Cutler. This is the location of Radio Cutler, the U. S. Navy's Radio Transmitting Station. There are 26 towers, soaring up to 1,000 feet in the air, on the 2,800-acre site. It is the most powerful radio transmitting station in the world.

Lubec—Eastport

Lubec is a fishing and sardine-canning town—and is the gateway to Campobello Island and Roosevelt Campobello International Park. The park, on Route 774 in Welshpool, New Brunswick, Canada, is a 2,600-acre nature area, with picnic sites, vistas and a lookout at Friar's Head. The summer home (1897) of President Franklin D. Roosevelt has been preserved and contains many original family furnishings.

A main attraction of the Lubec area is a drive down to Quoddy Head State Park. Candy-striped West Quoddy Head Light (1807) stands on the easternmost point of land in the United States. (Hence, the county's nickname, "Sunrise County.") Tides here are the greatest in the nation, a variation of some 20–28 feet between high and low tide.

Lubec and Eastport sit opposite each other, about three miles apart, at the mouth of Cobscook Bay. But to travel from one town to the other by land, it is a 40-mile trip. The bonus for making the circuit is a stop midway at Cobscook Bay State Park, which was developed from part of the Moosehorn National Wildlife Refuge.

Eastport, located on Moose Island, is the birthplace of Maine's sardine business. Fishing and canning are still major industries here. Just north of town, on the mainland, is Quoddy Village, a project built during the 1930s to harness the great ocean tides of Passamaquoddy Bay to generate electric power. Although there are hopes that a great quantity of inexpensive power can still result, the project has never been fully developed.

The Pleasant Point Indian Reservation, home of the Passamaquoddy Tribe of the Abnaki Indian Nation, is on Route 190 south of Perry. Perry, incidentally, is located halfway between the equator and the North Pole! There is a small stone marking the point at a roadside picnic area on Route 1.

Calais

Calais is a busy port of entry at the border between Maine and New Brunswick, Canada. If you're planning to visit Calais, the first thing you should know is that it is pronounced CAL-lus (not cal-LAY).

Calais and its sister city in Canada, St. Stephen, New Brunswick, have an unusually close community bond. They share essential municipal services, such as police and fire protection, and there is cooperative trade and commerce. The close bond is celebrated each August with a week-long International Festival.

From Calais, you can make a bee-line 90 miles west on Route 9 to Bangor through heavily wooded central Washington County. Or you may head north on Route 1 through sparsely populated timberland. Central and northern Washington County has few roads, but you will find the area a perfect place for a hunting or wilderness vacation or a canoe expedition. There are several lodges and sporting camps among the winding streams and sparkling lakes.

EXPLORING AROOSTOOK COUNTY

"The County," as it is referred to Down East, is the largest county of Maine. It is bounded on three sides by Canada and covers an area of 6,453 square miles. Most of the population lives along the eastern edge of the county and in the St. John River Valley in the north.

In southern and eastern Aroostook, from Houlton to Presque Isle and on up to Fort Kent, the low rolling countryside, rich and green, yields 50 million bushels of potatoes per year. Besides the economic importance of the harvest, the potato fields in summer burst forth acres of vari-colored blossoms—a sight to behold!

Nearly all the northwestern portion of the county is unspoiled wilderness. There are some four million acres of forest, nearly all privately owned by several large paper companies. The pulp and paper mills produce lumber, wood and paper products. With proper permits and licensing, the wilderness area is a sportsman's paradise: fishing, hunting, camping, hiking, canoeing, swimming, boating, skiing and snow-mobiling.

Houlton

About 100 miles north of Calais, at the junction of Route 1 and I-95, is Houlton, the county seat and the center of the southern Aroostook potato farming area. It is the primary port of entry to Canada's Maritime Provinces.

The oldest community in the county, dating back to 1805, its quiet residential neighborhoods are filled with fine old homes. The Amos Pearce Home (1820), on Court Street, is the oldest residence in town. Built by Houlton's first postmaster, it housed the post office on the main floor and a smokehouse in the basement. Much of the original meat-curing equipment is still there.

Presque Isle Area

Presque Isle, Aroostook's largest city, is the business, industrial and cultural center—and the primary potato shipping point—of the county. It is also where the first successful transatlantic hot air balloon, *Double Eagle II,* was launched in August, 1978.

Each August, the Northern Maine Agricultural Fair is held at the fairgrounds. It is a week-long event, with agricultural exhibits, horse shows, contests and harness racing. Adjacent to the fairgrounds is the Northern Maine Forum and Civic Center, where special events are regularly scheduled.

Nearby, south of town, 430-acre Aroostook State Park offers camping, swimming, boating, nature walks and skiing. Or follow the hiking trail to the 1,213-foot summit of Quoggy Joe Mountain.

The Nylander Museum, in Caribou (13 miles north of Presque Isle), has exhibits of Indian items, shells and marine life—and over 6,000 specimens of native animals and plants.

St. John River Valley—Fort Kent

The area from Van Buren to Fort Kent was settled during the mid-18th century by Acadian refugees expelled from Nova Scotia. The Acadian Village, on Route 1 in Van Buren, preserves the spirit of those Acadians in a group of 16 reconstructed buildings. Period furnishings are in the houses; there are barns, a railroad station, a school, a blacksmith shop, a general store, and several other restored structures.

Van Buren itself is a small manufacturing (tennis racquets), farming (potatoes and sugar beets), and lumbering town.

Madawaska, an industrial community, is the northernmost town in Maine. Just south, on Route 162, Long Lake is a major recreation area famous for landlocked salmon fishing, hunting, canoeing and snowmobiling. There are many sporting camps here.

Fort Kent is probably best known as the beginning of U. S. Route 1, which ends in Key West, Florida. It is also a port of entry to Maine from Quebec City, just 169 miles away. There is fishing in the St. John and Allagash Rivers and hunting for bear, deer and grouse in the vast hinterlands. Fort Kent is the downstream terminus of the famous St. John-Allagash canoe trip, which begins 156 miles away at Moosehead Lake.

The Fort Kent Blockhouse (1838) was built to protect timber interests during the "Aroostook War" with Britain. The fort was never used, as the border dispute was settled peacefully by the Webster-Ashburton Treaty of 1842.

Fort Kent is the gateway to northwest Aroostook's vast wilderness and recreation region. This is wild country, some of it still not thoroughly explored. With the exception of a route that goes to Allagash out of Fort Kent, there are no public roads in this remote area—only private logging roads. For information regarding permits for use of north woods roads, write: North Maine Woods, PO Box 382, Ashland, ME 04732 (435–6213).

Allagash Wilderness Waterway

About 40 miles west of Fort Kent, at the confluence of the St. John and Allagash Rivers, the small village of Allagash marks the terminus of the Allagash Wilderness Waterway. This 92-mile-long corridor through 200,000 acres (30,000 of them water, the rest woods) is the result of creative cooperation. The state and federal governments funded the project jointly, with the Maine Department of Parks and Recreation administering it. Access to this area is limited, and all parties must be registered. Although Allagash has been very popular for canoeing, camping, and fishing in the warmer seasons, the snowmobile has now increased winter use. The area can only be enjoyed if there is advance planning about entry, registration, rules and regulations. If you plan to visit the area or make the canoe trip, write: Maine Dept. of Conservation, Bureau of Parks & Recreation, State House, Augusta ME 04333 (289–3821).

Portage—Ashland—Patten

From Fort Kent, Aroostook Scenic Highway (Route 11) is a 50-mile drive south through a wooded paradise. There are dense forests, mirror lakes, and turbulent streams.

Portage is a lumbering and recreation center, with sporting camps and float plane service to remote areas. It is the southern terminus of the Fish River chain of lakes canoe trip.

Ashland, just ten miles south on Route 11, is a lumbering town. The three-day Lumberjack Roundup, in early July, is a festival of competitive contests, where lumbermen can show their skill and stamina.

Patten, on the border between Aroostook County and the Northern Lakes Region of Maine, is about 50 miles south of Ashland. It is a commercial center and a logging town. The outstanding Patten Lumberman's Museum, on Route 159, is a group of eight buildings that tells the story of Maine's logging history. There are more than 2,000 artifacts, log haulers, tractors, a re-creation of an 1820 logging camp, and several other machines and exhibits.

Patten is just a few miles north of I–95, permitting easy access to the rest of Maine. Or Route 159 west leads to the northern entrance to Baxter State Park, 30 miles away.

EXPLORING THE NORTHERN LAKES

AND FORESTS

Millinocket—Baxter State Park

From Patten, Routes 11 and/or I–95 lead south to Millinocket some 40–45 miles away. Millinocket, in the heart of timber country, is a large newsprint manufacturing center, as well as the home of Great Northern Paper Company. It is also the primary gateway to Baxter State Park and Mt. Katahdin.

From Millinocket, drive northwest on Baxter State Park Road. Don't be disturbed that much of the road skirting the park is marked "private" on the map; it belongs to Great Northern, but the public has access.

Baxter State Park, a wilderness preserve that covers more than 200,-000 acres, was given "for the benefit of the people" by former governor Percival P. Baxter, who for more than 30 years personally collected parcels of this unique land. In 1930, he deeded the land to the state to be held in trust "as a state forest, public park, and for public recreational purposes . . . to be kept in its natural wild state and as a sanctuary for wild beasts and birds."

And a true wilderness it is. Roads in the park are narrow, winding dirt roads, with tall stands of pines on either side. Moose, white-tail deer and bear roam freely here.

Mt. Katahdin, in the park, is the highest point in Maine (5,268 feet above sea level) and one of the highest points in the U. S. east of the Rockies. The mountain marks the northern terminus of the Appalachian Trail, which extends 2,050 miles south to Mt. Oglethorpe in north Georgia.

There are several campgrounds in Baxter State Park, some accessible by car, others only by foot. Large house trailers are not permitted in the park, because they cannot traverse the narrow roads. Reservations for camping must be made and paid for in advance. Hikers and other park visitors must have permits to use or to travel through the park. No food, fuel, or supplies are available once inside, so visitors must be sure to come fully equipped. Write or stop by the park office for information regarding park rules: Baxter Park Authority, 64 Balsam Drive, Millinocket, ME 04462 (723–5140).

Moosehead Lake—Greenville—Rockwood

For the adventurous traveler, take Great Northern's private road (open to the public except when closed by winter weather) southwest to Moosehead Lake and the resort town of Greenville at the southern tip of the lake.

An alternative routing would be to follow Route 11 from Millinocket southwest through Brownville Junction, Route 6/15 west through Dover-Foxcroft, and on up to Greenville. This trip is considerably longer, but you can visit the Katahdin Iron Works (six miles down a gravel road just north of Brownville Junction) en route. The "works," once a mine and smelting mill, now has a restored stone blast furnace and charcoal kiln on site. Dover-Foxcroft is a thriving business and industrial town.

Greenville is the starting point for trips into big fishing and hunting country. The lake front is busy with the pontoon planes of local air services, which fly people to even more remote sites. There are ample accommodations and restaurants in and around the town.

The Moosehead Marine Museum, on Pritham Avenue, is home for the restored lake steamer *Katahdin* (1914). There are artifacts and photographs of the steamboat era and the logging industry at Moosehead Lake.

Crystal-clear Moosehead Lake is Maine's largest. Over 40 miles long and, in some places 20 miles wide, it has many islands and bays. The shorefront, owned almost entirely by paper companies, is virtually uninhabited and inaccessible, except by boat or canoe. The area is great for fishing, cruising, camping, and hunting, as well as for finding fossils and Indian artifacts. Moose watching is also a popular sport—particularly in the evening!

North on Route 6/15 takes you past Squaw Mountain (3,267 feet), with its panoramic view of Moosehead Lake, and Squaw Mountain Ski Area, with resort facilities and downhill or cross-country ski trails.

A few miles farther north is Rockwood, a resort village for nature lovers. The rivers here are a fly-fisherman's paradise—trout and salmon abound. The wildlife areas are among the best hunting grounds for deer, bear, partridge and small game. There are well-maintained snowmobile trails, plus snowshoeing and ice fishing for the cold-weather vacationer. During the warmer months, canoe trips or white-water rafting provide a way to travel to the picturesque remote areas.

One of the great sights for travelers in this area is Mt. Kineo, a sheer cliff that rises out of the lake to a height of 1,860 feet. A geological oddity, it is a solid piece of green flint. Indians sought out the flint to make arrowheads and stone tools. There is a boat tour available.

Jackman

If you love wilderness scenery and want to see more than you have so far, Route 15, after nearby Rockwood, is a very pleasant road. It connects with Route 6/201 some 30 miles beyond. If you head north on Route 201 you'll be in Jackman in minutes and only 16 miles from the Canadian border.

Like Greenville, Jackman is a jumping-off place for deepwoods fishing, hunting, ski touring, and snowmobiling, and a station on both the Moose River and Attean Lake canoeing routes. With many mountain ranges forming a backdrop, Jackman caters to outdoor interests and casual vacationers year-round. There are several sporting camps, restaurants and accommodations available in the region.

Route 201 south from Jackman becomes a Maine Scenic Highway from The Forks (so named because it marks the confluence of the Dead River with the mighty Kennebec) to Solon, 32 miles away. Back in 1775, this route was a portion of the trail Benedict Arnold and his men followed on their march to Quebec. There are several commemorative markers along the roadside.

EXPLORING THE WESTERN LAKES

Kingfield—Carrabassett Valley

Now, continue south on Route 201 at Solon (bear right) to North Anson, where you pick up Route 16 to Kingfield. Along Route 16, there are placid riverside scenes and ever-changing farmland vistas.

Kingfield is a busy little town in the Carrabassett River Valley. It is the hometown of F. E. and F. O. Stanley, inventors of the first steam-driven automobile, the Stanley Steamer.

The Carrabassett Valley area has become one of the East's leading four-season recreation spots. A few miles north of Kingfield, on Route 16, Sugarloaf USA at Sugarloaf Mountain (at 4,237 feet, Maine's second highest peak) is the largest winter resort in Maine. There are superb ski trails: novice, intermediate and "super steep." There is a 45-meter ski jump and a modern Alpine village at the base. Enclosed four-passenger gondolas take you for the 9,000-foot ride to the summit of the mountain and back, allowing magnificent views winter, summer and fall. Hunting and fishing opportunities are also popular in the area; and there are diversified winter activities in addition to skiing.

Rangeley Area

Scenic Route 16 takes you through Bigelow and Stratton to Rangeley, 20 miles away. The sweeping mountain views are breathtaking. If you're traveling late in the afternoon, you might spot a moose by the side of the road.

Rangeley, the center of this beautiful region, has a frontier quality—sort of a last outpost before the pure wilderness that lies beyond. The chain of lakes and connecting streams create an area of more than 450 square miles of playground for sportsmen and lovers of the great outdoors: flyfishing, hunting, sailing, canoeing, swimming, hiking, camping, golfing, skiing, and snowmobiling. In and around the town of Rangeley, there are all manner of accommodations (resorts, hotels, lodges, camps, cottages, etc.) and a variety of restaurants.

Rangeley Lake State Park, 691 acres of fragrant fir trees and mountain views, is on the south shore of Rangeley Lake. Campsites are available; and there is a boat-launching ramp, as well as a swimming and picnicking area.

About eight miles southeast of Rangeley, the Appalachian Trail cuts across Rte. 4, then through the wilderness several miles where it crosses scenic Route 17 southwest of Rangeley Lake.

From December through April, you can ski Rangeley's Saddleback Mountain (4,116 ft.). There are slopes and trails appropriate for all levels of competence from beginner to expert and including downhill racing. The Ski Nordic Touring Center, at Saddleback, offers 40 kilometers of scenic groomed trails through the wilderness.

More than 100 miles of groomed trails are marked for safe, exciting snowmobiling. Rangeley Lake freezes solid in the winter, creating an invitation to snowmobilers as well.

More and more travelers are visiting Rangeley each March to join in the excitement of the two-day, 30-mile Sled Dog Race. Contestants and teams come from all over northern New England, upper New York State, and Canada. Spectators come from far and wide.

From Rangeley, Route 4/16 west follows the northern edge of Rangeley Lake to the small town of Oquossoc. Turn left onto Route 17 to the "Height of Land." A roadside turnoff provides a truly exquisite view. Lake Mooselookmeguntic, other lakes, islands, mountains, golden shores, patches of pines, the blue sky and water, form an unforgettable mosaic in a sight that would be hard to beat anywhere. This is possibly the most extensive panoramic view in the state.

Rumford—Bethel Area

Route 17 south to Rumford follows the rocky Swift River through woods, meadow, and sleepy towns. At Byron you are likely to see people wading among the rocks, sifting the sand of the river bottom as they pan for gold. Rent a kit along the roadside and try your luck!

Rumford is the largest community in the area, with a sizable business district. The Oxford Paper Company, Rumford's predominant employer, has one of the largest book-paper mills in the world here, which looms over the downtown landscape. The Ellis, Swift, and Concord rivers flow into the Androscoggin River at Rumford, and Pennacook Falls can be viewed from the downtown business section of town.

Traveling westbound on Route 2 brings you to Newry. The "Artist's Covered Bridge" (1872), which crosses the Sunday River near Newry, is the most photographed, most painted covered bridge in Maine. Grafton Notch State Park, farther north on Route 26, is a fine area in which to drive or hike to drink in some lovely natural sights. There's Old Speck Mountain (4,150 feet), on the Appalachian Trail, with the highest forest lookout tower in Maine; and Screw-Auger Falls is where the Bear River has drilled holes as deep as 25 feet into the rock riverbed.

By going southwest on Route 2, you'll come to Bethel, an authentic 19th-century village—quiet and unpretentious—nestled in the Oxford Hills. It is the regional center of a thriving wood-products industry. Bethel is typically New England, with a Common and handsome homes lining its streets.

The Bethel Inn, on the Common, has put together a brochure outlining a walking tour of the town. Some of the highlights are: Moses Mason Museum, a fully restored Federal-style house (1813); Gould Academy, one of the finest preparatory schools in the state; Dr. John G. Gehring Clinic, a Queen Anne-style house (1896) where Dr. Gehring studied and practiced the treatment of nervous disorders; several of the lovely homes located in the Broad Street Historic District and around the Common; and, of course, The Bethel Inn (1833), a thriving year-round resort.

You will discover four-season recreation in the Bethel area: lake swimming and boating, golfing, hiking, fishing, rock hounding, or skiing at Sunday River and Mount Abram Ski Areas. There are dramatic views of New Hampshire's White Mountains, as Bethel is near the edge of White Mountain National Forest.

From Bethel, drive south on Route 26 to Trap Corner in West Paris. Here is Perham's Maine Mineral Store, attracting over 70,000 visitors annually who come to see and buy from the mineral and gem collection. Jane Perham, owner of this unpretentious but extraordinary shop, is a rock hound's friend and willingly allows collectors to visit and chip away at the five mines she owns in the area.

A few miles south of Trap Corner, be on the lookout for a small sign pointing left (an unnumbered route, east to Paris Hill). Paris Hill used to be a main stop on the stagecoach route between Portland and Montreal. It is one of the prettiest towns in New England, with handsome houses and a wide, peaceful village green. Virtually unknown to the present-day traveler, it was once the business center of this area, and it retains a certain dignity. Hannibal Hamlin, Vice President of the U. S. under Abraham Lincoln, was born here, and you can see his childhood home next door to the Old Stone Jail.

When you continue on Route 26, you'll reach Norway, a busy community famous for the manufacture of snowshoes and toboggans. Most of the snowshoes used by our armed forces in World War II were made here and Admiral Peary trod to the North Pole on a pair.

Long Lake—Sebago Lake Region

If you love lakes and forest, follow Route 117 from Norway around the head of Long Lake to Bridgton on its western shore. This lakeside resort area attracts vacationers year-round. You will find golf and tennis in the spring; swimming, fishing and boating in the summer; foliage viewing, antique-ing, and small game hunting in the fall; and skiing, snowmobiling and ice fishing in the winter. Bridgton has many waterfront campgrounds and cottage rentals available. The Pleasant Mountain Ski Area, on Route 302, has 20 miles of trails and well-groomed slopes. The 4,000-foot chair lift takes you to the summit for skiing in the winter. In summer, you can sweep down the mountain on an Alpine Slide.

Travel nine miles down Route 302, and you will come to Naples at the southern tip of Long Lake. It is here, via the Songo River, that Long Lake connects with Sebago Lake.

In the mid-1800s, the Cumberland-Oxford Canal was the important link between Portland and Harrison, at the northern tip of Long Lake. The railroad, coming into the area in the 1870s, made the canal obsolete. There is but one operating lock that survives, Songo Lock, located on the Songo River between the two lakes. Pleasure boats keep it active, and boat rides through the lock are available from Naples.

Crystal-clear Sebago Lake, second largest in the state, is about 14 miles long and 11 miles wide. There are points where it reaches a depth of 400 feet. Spectacular fishing awaits the angler—land-locked salmon, trout, bass, and perch abound.

A turn in Naples onto Route 114 will take you around the western edge of Sebago Lake, through several waterfront villages, until you reach Sebago Lake Village at the foot of the lake.

At the junction of Route 35, turn left to follow the eastern shore north to North Windham. Thousands of Indian relics have been discovered here, as well as an Indian burial ground said to be one of the largest in the U. S.

A left turn on Route 35/302 completes the circle and brings you to South Casco. Nathaniel Hawthorne's boyhood home (1812) is here on Hawthorne Road, off Route 302. Sebago Lake State Park, partly in South Casco and partly in Naples, is a 1,300-acre lakeside site that straddles the Songo River. The Casco side is for day use only, and the Naples side has camping facilities.

EXPLORING THE CENTRAL LAKES

The Central Lakes Region is located in the center of the most populated part of the state, making the major towns in the area jumping-off points for touring in and around the various regions outlined previously in this guide. In each of the geographic sections described below, routes have been indicated whereby the traveler can easily change course and visit an adjoining recreational region.

Poland Spring—Dry Mills—New Gloucester

If you take Route 11 east from the Naples-Casco area for fifteen miles or so, turn right on Route 26 to Poland and Poland Spring. Just off the road, you can drive through the grounds of this once-elegant resort and see the actual Poland Spring, source of the familiar mineral water. The State of Maine Building, originally built for the Chicago

World's Fair (1893), was reconstructed here on the grounds of the former Poland Spring Inn.

At the Cumberland/Androscoggin county line, on Route 26, you will find the Shaker Museum. Established in 1793, the members of this sect continue their traditional lifestyle. There is a store and museum, with furniture, textiles, folk art, wooden objects and farm tools on display and for sale.

At Dry Mills, south of Poland Spring on Route 26, the Maine Department of Inland Fisheries & Wildlife has a fish hatchery and, adjacent, a 1,300-acre game farm. The fish are used to restock Maine's lakes and ponds with salmon and trout; pheasants are raised at the game farm and released as game birds.

Just south of Dry Mills, at Gray, there is a Maine Turnpike interchange for access to southern coast towns.

Auburn—Lewiston

Auburn and Lewiston are twin cities on either side of the Androscoggin River, making up the second largest metropolitan district in Maine and a key commercial, industrial and cultural center.

Residential Auburn has a diverse economic base. It is the agricultural trading center for the area on the one hand; and, on the other, there are several industrial parks housing a variety of businesses. Auburn remains a major shoe-manufacturing center, as well. Lost Valley Ski Area is nearby and, just out of town, Lake Auburn is available for fishing, boating and peaceful refreshment.

Lewiston is Maine's principal textile manufacturing town. The Bates Manufacturing Company, makers of bedspreads, draperies and other linens, is located here. (There is an outlet store next door to the factory for you bargain hunters.) Bates College, the well-known liberal arts institution, is also located on 75 acres in Lewiston.

From Auburn and Lewiston, the Maine Turnpike connects with towns along the Southern Coast; Route 11 will bring you directly to the Sebago Lake Region; and Route 11 to Route 26 winds up in the Bethel area.

Livermore—Farmington—Skowhegan

North of the Auburn-Lewiston area, via Route 4, are Livermore and Livermore Falls, quiet communities situated among small ponds and streams in the hill country of Androscoggin County. It is primarily an agricultural area—apple country—although International Paper Company has enormous paper mills in Livermore Falls and in nearby Chisholm. Norlands Living History Center, on Norlands Road in Livermore, just a mile or so north of Route 108, is a 430-acre working farm operated just as it would have been around 1870. The grounds include the Washburn Mansion (1867), a one-room school (1823), a church (1828), and a stone library (1883).

From Livermore, Route 108 could take you to Rumford and then on up Route 17 to the Rangeley Lakes Region. Or follow Route 4 still farther north through Wilton (home of the famous G. H. Bass Company, shoemakers) to Farmington, commercial center of the area. The Nordica Homestead (1840), on Holley Road off Route 4, is the birthplace of the opera singer, Lillian Nordica (née Norton). The collection

includes displays of her costumes, music, programs and other memorabilia.

From Farmington, Route 4 goes directly to the Rangeley Lakes.
(Route 27, off Route 4, goes to Kingfield and the Carrabassett Valley.)

The Little Red Schoolhouse Museum (1852), at the junction of
Routes 4 and 2 in Farmington, serves as a local information center.
Pick up Route 2 here, though, and head east to Skowhegan, birthplace
of former U.S. senator Margaret Chase Smith, the first U.S. congress-
woman from Maine. The Skowhegan State Fair, in mid-August each
year, is one of the largest agricultural fairs in Maine. The major industry here is Scott Paper Company's vast paper mill. Tours are available
during the summer. You can't miss the 65-foot statue of an Abnaki
Indian in town. It was handcarved by the late Maine sculptor, Bernard
Langlais, and erected in 1960 to commemorate the area's first inhabitants.

Several touring alternatives are available from Skowhegan, the
northernmost point we will encounter on this tour of the Central Lakes
Region:

Scenic Route 201 extends north from Skowhegan to The Forks and
on up through Jackman, in the wilderness area beyond Moosehead
Lake, to the Canadian border.

Route 2 goes fifty miles east to Bangor, then north along the Penobscot River and on to Houlton on the eastern border with Canada.

Waterville—Belgrade Lakes—China Lake

Heading south on Route 201 brings you into Waterville, the "Elm
City," which has played a key role in the industrial development of the
Kennebec River Valley and is the medical center for central Maine.
Colby College, established in 1813, has its impressive 500-acre campus
on Mayflower Hill.

The Two-Cent Bridge, between Waterville and Winslow on Front
Street, is the only known footbridge in the country which, until recently, collected a toll.

Fort Halifax (1754), on Route 201 in Winslow, is one of the oldest
blockhouses in the United States. This was a stop on Benedict Arnold's
expedition to Quebec in 1775.

Waterville is the gateway to the popular summer and winter recreation areas of Belgrade Lakes to the west and China Lake to the east.
In both these regions, fishing (particularly for small-mouthed bass) is
the main attraction—but there is plenty else to do: exploring, boating
and canoeing, picnicking, swimming, hiking or golfing. There are several motels and campsites for vacationers, as well as weekly cottage
rentals.

From Waterville, Route 137 east is a secondary road to Belfast, on
Penobscot Bay, and coastal Route 1.

Route I–95 goes northeast to Houlton, on the far eastern border of
Aroostook County—or through Augusta and south, as the Maine
Turnpike, to the Southern Coast.

Augusta—Hallowell

Augusta, the capital city, and nearby Hallowell offer history and
antique buffs many hours of interesting exploration.

The State Capitol Building (1829), on State Street, was designed by Charles Bulfinch and was constructed of Hallowell granite. Next door, in the State Cultural Building, completed in 1971, are the State Archives, Library, and the Maine State Museum. The museum has exhibits relating to Maine's heritage and special natural history displays.

As far back as 1628, the Plymouth Colony of Massachusetts had a trading post near the present site of Fort Western, on Bowman Street.

Fort Western was built originally in 1754 for protection against Indian raids. Benedict Arnold's army of men regrouped and transferred to bateaux here while on their historic, unsuccessful march to Quebec. The barracks rooms are furnished in keeping with the early days, and there are exhibits devoted to military and naval articles. The fort was restored in 1921.

Though more than 30 miles from the sea, Hallowell, on the banks of the Kennebec, was once a busy port and shipbuilding center. Hallowell is an antique center today, with several antique shops along Water Street to browse. Many of the residences on the streets that branch uphill from the riverfront are fine examples of varied and interesting architectural styles—Federal, Greek Revival, Victorian, wooden row houses—which suggest something of Maine's cultural, economic and social heritage.

Many major roads pass through Augusta, linking the capital city with the coastal areas, the mountains and the wilderness areas. And here you are now at the northern terminus of the Maine Turnpike, the direct route south to the Maine-New Hampshire border.

SIGHTSEEING CHECKLIST. Maine is an enormous state with such a variety of attractions that it may be helpful to have some ideas on how to spend a limited amount of time there. The following is a short list outlining some possibilities.

Southern Beaches. Spend some time lazing on miles of sandy Atlantic beach in the busy resort towns along Maine's Southern Coast—from the Yorks to Old Orchard Beach.

Portland. Visit Portland, Maine's largest city and its cultural and commercial center. Besides the many historic sites and the marvelous Portland Art Museum, you won't want to miss the Old Port Exchange, a district of boutiques and bistros in refurbished buildings near the waterfront.

Cruise Maine's coastal waters and off-shore islands. Excursion boats depart from Portland, Boothbay Harbor and Northeast Harbor on day trips or moonlight sailings. Or set sail aboard a windjammer out of Camden, Rockport, or Rockland for a week-long cruise.

Acadia National Park, on Mt. Desert Island, is a 30,000-acre composite of the wonders of the rugged Maine coast—rocky shore, a mountain to climb (on foot or by car), miles of hiking trails, bikeways and bridle paths—and quaint fishing villages adjacent.

Baxter State Park. For campers and hikers, pack your gear and visit Baxter State Park, a 200,000-acre wilderness preserve. Come prepared to enjoy the unspoiled woodland, ponds and streams; and hike along the Appalachian Trail to its northern terminus on mile-high Mt. Katahdin. There are campsites and shelters available by reservation, and boats or canoes can be rented; but no supplies (food, fuel, sleeping equipment or cooking utensils) are available within the park.

PRACTICAL INFORMATION FOR MAINE

Note. Large sections in Practical Information have been organized according to touring area for your convenience.

 **MAINE FACTS AND FIGURES.** There are various theories about the origin of the state's name: that it came from the French province of "Maine"; that it refers to the "mainland," to set it apart from the offshore islands; that it simply means "important."

The state's nickname is "Pine Tree State." *Dirigo* ("I lead" or "I direct") is the state motto. "State of Maine Song" is the state song. The white pine cone and tassel is the state flower; white pine, the state tree; chickadee, the state bird; landlocked salmon, the state fish; tourmaline, the state mineral; the honeybee, the state insect; and the moose, the state animal.

Irregularly diamond-shaped, Maine is 320 miles from north to south, 210 from east to west at its widest point. The total land area is 33,215 square miles, 39th among the 50 states and just under half of all of New England, which totals 66,608. Maine has over 2,000 islands, 542,629 acres of state and national parks, and a mountain (Mt. Katahdin) that is a mile high (5,268 ft. above sea level). The population of 1,163,650 is 38th in the nation and about one-twelfth of New England's. Augusta, population 22,000, is the state capital; but Portland, with 62,000, is the largest city. Maine was the 23rd state to enter the Union, on March 15, 1820.

The only one of the contiguous 48 states bordering no more than one other state and the biggest of the six New England states, Maine is famous for the rugged beauty of its rocky, indented coastline dotted with countless small islands and dozens of popular beach resorts. Although the coast itself is 230 miles long, Maine has 3,500 miles of shoreline, much of it spectacular. Parts of the state are mountainous and heavily wooded (timber and wood lots comprise 87 percent of the state), with more than 6,000 lakes and ponds and 32,000 miles of rivers and streams. The forests and the sea contribute significantly to Maine's economy. Skilled fishermen bring in a varied catch, but it is the Maine lobster that has achieved international fame. Nearly 200 million pounds of seafood is harvested annually, including about 20 million pounds of lobster. And the Maine farmer is known for his excellent potatoes, grown in flat and fertile northeastern Aroostook County. Maine potato production and acreage ranks third nationally. Maine farmers also produce apples, corn, poultry, and 98% of America's low-bush blueberries. Ship-building remains an important industry, as does the manufacture of apparel, textiles, and leather goods. Maine also has considerable mineral wealth.

Maine has cool summers and long, cold winters. Specifically, year-round average conditions are:

	Jan.	Feb.	Mar.	Apr.	May	Jun.
Average Temperature (F)	20	23	32	43	54	63
Average Temperature (C)	–6	–5	0	6	12	17
Days of Rain or Snow	11	10	11	12	13	11

	Jul.	Aug.	Sept.	Oct.	Nov.	Dec.
Average Temperature (F)	70	66	59	48	37	27
Average Temperature (C)	20	19	15	9	3	–3
Days of Rain or Snow	9	10	8	9	12	11

HOW TO GET THERE. By air: There are flights to Augusta, Bangor, Portland, Waterville, Presque Isle, Bar Harbor, and Auburn-Lewiston from major cities in the northeast via Bar Harbor Airlines, Delta, People Express, United, or Air Vermont. (Portland and Bangor serve both domestic and international carriers.) In addition, general aircraft are accommodated at airfields throughout the state.

By car: I–95 enters at Kittery, Maine's southern tip, and continues northeasterly across the state to New Brunswick, Canada. From northern New Hampshire, Rte. 16 is a scenic entry to Maine's western mountains and northern wilderness areas. Primary access from Quebec is Canadian Rte. 173, which connects with U.S. Rte. 201 near Jackman. From New Brunswick, an exit at Woodstock on the Trans Canada Highway is just a few miles by connector to Houlton and the northern terminus of I–95. Also from New Brunswick, U.S. Rte. 1 continues along Maine's "Down East" coast.

By car ferries: Passenger/auto ferry service is available (May–October) on *Scotia Prince* between Portland and Yarmouth, Nova Scotia. The trip takes about 10 hours. (For information: Lion Ferry Portland Ltd., International Terminal, Portland, ME 04101. 800–341–7540. The *MV Bluenose Ferry* provides passenger-auto service (year-round) between Bar Harbor and Yarmouth, Nova Scotia, a 6-hour trip. (For information: CN Marine, Eden St.-Rte. 3, Bar Harbor, ME 04609. Tel. 800–341–7981.

By bus: Daily service via Greyhound or Continental Trailways from Boston, Mass., to Portland and along Rte. 1 to Caribou; Canadian service available from Montreal to Bangor and to Portland, between Quebec and Augusta, and from the Maritime Provinces along Rte. 1 to Bangor. Consult your telephone directory for numbers to call for bus schedule information for these national carriers.

TELEPHONE. The area code for the entire state of Maine is (207). The price of a local call in a pay phone in Maine is 20¢. Portland utilizes the 911 emergency telephone number. In other towns and cities, consult the local telephone directory or call "0" for emergency assistance.

HOTELS AND MOTELS. Accommodations in Maine range from the expensive and sometimes spectacular resorts on Maine's historic coast to the plain and simple inns, hotels and motels in the small towns. Many hotels and inns along the coast are closed from October to May. Some do remain open and lower their rates considerably during the winter months. Hotels and inns in resort areas often require a minimum stay during the high season. Travelers can often benefit from special weekly rates or package plans, especially at ski areas.

Many Maine inns are included in a central reservation system and can be booked by calling (800) 624–6380.

The Maine Publicity Bureau, 97 Winthrop St., Hallowell ME 04347, publishes an annual listing of cottage rentals, campgrounds, country inns, and bed-and-breakfast accommodations. American Youth Hostels are located in Blanchard (south of Greenville) and in Lincoln (southeast of Millinocket).

Rates are based on double occupancy, in season: *Deluxe* rates are $80 and up; *Expensive* $60–$80; *Moderate* $40–$60; *Inexpensive* less than $40. **Note:** Unless otherwise noted, accommodations are open year-round. There is a 5% Maine State Lodging Tax.

Bed & Breakfast. Guesthouses, delightful tourist homes, and "bed-and-breakfast" inns abound in Maine and are often the most charming and least expensive alternative. The Chamber of Commerce in the town or area you will be visiting will be happy to send you names and addresses, or contact the following: *Bed & Breakfast Down East Ltd.,* Box 547, Macomber Mill Road, Eastbrook, ME 04634 (565–3517); *Bed & Breakfast Registry of Maine,* RFD 4, Box 4317, Brunswick, ME 04011; Kennebunk-Portland-Yarmouth area (781–4528); Freeport-Brunswick-Bath-Damariscotta area (563–5519); Sebago Lake area (655–4075).

SOUTHERN COAST AREA

BAILEY ISLAND. Driftwood Inn. *Expensive.* Rte 24 (833–5461). On the ocean, boating, pool, restaurant, lovely views. June to Oct.

Dockside Motor Inn. *Moderate.* Mackerel Cove (833–6656). Small motel at water's edge. Marina, sun deck, snack bar and good restaurant.

BATH-BRUNSWICK. Stowe House. *Moderate-Expensive.* 63 Federal St., Brunswick (725–5543). Historic house (1807) near Bowdoin College with modern accommodations. Restaurant and Tap Room.

Grane's Fairhaven Inn. *Moderate.* N. Bath Rd., Bath (443–4391). A country inn (1790) nestled into the hillside overlooking the Kennebec River. Hike, cross-country ski or snowshoe, in 27 acres of surrounding woods. Boating, beach, golf, restaurants nearby. Full country breakfast available.

The New Meadows Inn. *Moderate.* Bath Rd., West Bath (443–3921). Motor hotel and cottages geared to family vacations. Spacious pine-paneled rooms, colorfully decorated. Good restaurant.

Maineline. *Inexpensive-Moderate.* 133 Pleasant St. off Rte. 1, Brunswick (725 8761). Comfortable rms. Pool.

KENNEBUNK. The Kennebunk Inn. *Moderate.* 45 Main St. (985–3351). Fine lodging and meals in restored inn (1799). Cocktail lounge. Centrally located in village.

KENNEBUNKPORT. The Colony. *Deluxe.* Ocean Ave. (967–3331). Grand white clapboard resort hotel, with motel annex and a spectacular ocean view. Summer sports. Pool, putting green, shuffleboard. Fine dining; cocktail lounge with entertainment. June through Sept.

The Nonantum. *Deluxe.* Ocean Ave. (967–3338). Large resort hotel overlooking the river. Dockage at private pier. Pool. Play area. Golf, tennis nr. Restaurant, cozy lounge. May to Oct.

Shawmut Motor Inn. *Deluxe.* Turbat's Creek Rd. (967–3931). 30-acre family resort. Main inn, cottages and motor lodge, all situated on bluff overlooking ocean. Beach, pool, play area. Golf, tennis, shopping nearby. Restaurant, bar, dancing. May to Oct.

Village Cove Inn. *Deluxe.* S. Main St., Chick's Cove (967–3993). Rustic elegance, peaceful and quiet, overlooks private cove. Restaurant, bar, dancing; beaches, golf, fishing, tennis and theater nearby. Indoor and outdoor pools.

The Captain Lord Mansion. *Expensive-Deluxe.* Cor. Pleasant and Green Sts. (967–3141). An intimate Maine coast inn, vintage 1812. Quiet elegance. Fireplaces. Walk to shops and restaurants. Sandy beaches close by. Breakfast included.

Old Fort Inn. *Expensive-Deluxe.* Old Fort Ave. (967–5353). Luxurious resort in a secluded area of town. All rooms have kitchenette. Pool, tennis, walk to ocean. Continental breakfast provided. Open May–Oct.

Cape Arundel Inn. *Expensive.* Ocean Ave. (967–2125). A small, intimate inn directly on the ocean. Excellent dining. Open Apr. to Dec.

The Captain Jefferds Inn. *Expensive.* Pearl and Pleasant sts (967–2311). Hospitable country inn, beautifully furnished, built in 1804 by a wealthy sea captain. Close to Dock Square.

English Meadows Inn. *Expensive.* Rte. 35 (967–5766). Victorian farmhouse and carriage house with antique furnishings. Lovely grounds. Casual country setting. Easy walk to Dock Sq., shops, waterfront, 1 mi. to beach. Full breakfast included. Apr. to Oct.

Tides Inn By-the-Sea. *Expensive.* Goose Rocks Beach (967–3757). 6 miles N.E. of Kennebunkport. "Homey" country inn overlooking the beach. Casual, relaxed atmosphere. Sports nearby. June to Sept.

KITTERY. Chart House Motor Hotel. *Expensive.* Rte. 1 bypass (439–2000). Pool, summer sports. Pets. Restaurant next door. Large family rooms available. Open all year.

OGUNQUIT. Cliff House. *Deluxe.* On Bald Head Cliff, 2½ mi. S. of Ogunquit (646–5124). Original family inn and several motel units on 90 acres. Panoramic ocean views. Near beach, shops and theater. Tennis, water sports, pool, dining. Open Apr. to Nov.

Dolphin Post Motor Inn. *Deluxe.* Beachmere Lane (646–7586). Luxurious studio apartments, some with kitchens; balconies overlook ocean and scenic walk. Boating, fishing, beach. Open Apr. to Nov.

Sparhawk. *Deluxe.* Shore Rd. (646–5562). Fine accommodations, with ocean views. Tennis, play area, golf nr. Good restaurant. Open May to Oct.

Old Village Inn. *Expensive.* 30 Main St. (646–7088). In-town inn dates to 1833. Pleasant bedrooms and suites; TV in the living room; game room. Several comfortable dining rooms serve dinner. Closed Jan.

The Colonial Inn. *Moderate-Expensive.* 71 Shore Rd. (646–2438). Gracious Victorian coastal inn in the heart of town. Easy walk to beach and to Perkins Cove. Pool. Continental breakfast. Open May to Oct.

OLD ORCHARD BEACH. Diplomat. *Deluxe.* E. Grand Ave. (934–4521). Nicely furnished rooms in motel or lodge overlook ocean. Private sandy beach. Coffee shop, continental breakfast free. Open May through Sept.

Royal Anchor. *Deluxe.* E. Grand Ave. (934–4521). Private patios and balconies overlook ocean. Tennis. Pool. Restaurant, bar. Open May through Oct.

Windsor Cabins. *Inexpensive.* Ocean Park Rd., Rte. 5 (934–5514). 23 fully-equipped cabins located in pine grove. Pool, putting green, playground. Open May to Oct.

PORTLAND. Sheraton Inn. *Deluxe.* 363 Maine Mall Rd., So. Portland (775–6161). Large, modern hotel. Indoor pool, good restaurant, entertainment. Panoramic views. Convenient to airport and shopping.

Sonesta Hotel. *Deluxe.* 157 High St. (775–5411). Luxurious in-town hotel with high standards of personal service. Pool, two restaurants, and "Top of the East" rooftop lounge. Complimentary transportation to airport.

The Inn at Park Spring. *Expensive–Deluxe.* 135 Srping St. (774–1059). Very small hotel in a three-story townhouse. Personal attention in the grand style. Help yourself to breakfast; traditional tea at 4 P.M.

Executive Inn. *Expensive.* 645 Congress St. (773–8181). Pleasant rooms, centrally located near tourist attractions. Pool. Pets. Free parking. Children free. Restaurant and lounge.

Holiday Inn–Downtown. *Expensive.* 88 Spring St. (775–2311). Convenient to airport, golf, ocean and sightseeing. Indoor pool, sauna. Restaurant, bar, entertainment.

Holiday Inn West. *Expensive.* 81 Riverside St. (774–5601). Nicely kept, nicely furnished. Pool. Pets. Restaurant, bar, entertainment.

SCARBOROUGH. Atlantic House. *Deluxe.* Scarborough Beach. (883–4381). Large traditional family resort since 1850. 18 acres of grounds, a milelong beach, tennis and children's activities. Meals included. Plan to dress for dinner.

Black Point Inn. *Deluxe.* Prouts Neck (883–4311). Secluded oceanfront country inn. Elegant and impressive; good service. American Plan. PGA golf course, tennis courts, heated pool, sailing, beaches. Restaurant, bar, entertainment, dancing. Open late May to mid-Oct.

SEBASCO ESTATES. Sebasco Lodge. *Deluxe.* Rte. 217 (389–1161). Water sports, fishing, boating are featured at this 600-acre, informal resort on Casco Bay. Comfortable rooms in lodge, lighthouse or cottages. Saltwater pool, play area. Golf, tennis. Restaurant. Entertainment, dancing. Open late June through Sept.

Rock Gardens Inn. *Expensive.* Rte. 217 (389–1339). Casual family-style resort on a point of land on Casco Bay. Marvelous meals. Comfortable rooms in inn; cabins have fireplaces. Golf, pool, tennis, boat trips, play area. Open mid-June to late-Sept.

WELLS. Seagull Motor Inn. *Expensive.* Rte. 1 (646–7082). Overlooks ocean. Family resort with motel rooms plus housekeeping cottages. Pool. Pitch and putt golf course. Open mid-Apr.–Oct.

Sleepytown Motel & Resort. *Expensive.* Rte. 1 (646–5545). Resort motel and housekeeping cottages. Children's boating and fishing pond; pool and playground area. Restaurant and cocktail lounge. Apr. to Nov.

YARMOUTH. Homewood Inn. *Moderate–Expensive.* Rte. 115., Drinkwater Pt. (846–3351). Informal, family-owned country resort inn on Casco Bay. Some housekeeping cottages. Many guestrooms with fireplaces. Boating, tennis, excellent seafood restaurant, clambakes. Bar. Open June to Oct.

Down-East Village. *Moderate.* Rte. 1 (846–5161). Spacious grounds overlook Royal River. Pool, play area, swimming. Golf and marina nearby. Seafood restaurant. Open Apr. to Nov.

YORK AREA. Stage Neck Inn. *Deluxe.* Stage Neck Rd, York Harbor (363–3850). An inviting resort situated on a rocky point of land jutting into the ocean. Modern, attractive rooms with balconies. Saltwater pool and beach, golf, tennis and fishing. Open Apr. to Nov.

York Harbor Inn. *Moderate–Expensive.* Rte. 1A, York Harbor (363–5119). Authentic (1637) New England inn. Some of the charming rooms have ocean view, some fireplaces. English pub with entertainment for your dining pleasure.

Lilac Inn. *Moderate.* Ridge Rd., York Beach (363–3930). Bed & breakfast inn with Victorian charm. Attractively decorated, ocean views, and a large porch.

MID-COAST REGION

BELFAST. Colonial Gables. *Expensive.* Searsport Ave. (Rte. 1) (338–4000). Modern motel and housekeeping units. Private sandy beach; boating on Penobscot Bay. Children's playground. Lobster pounds nearby. Open April to Oct.

WonderView Cottages. *Inexpensive.* Searsport Ave. (Rte. 1) (338–1455). On Penobscot Bay. Efficiency cottages, some with fireplaces, screened porches. Private beach. Restaurant. Open April to Oct.

BOOTHBAY HARBOR AREA. Linekin Bay Sailing Resort. *Deluxe.* On Linekin Bay (633–2494). Five large lodges and several cottages create an informal setting for sailboat enthusiasts. A large fleet of sailboats are available for guest use; instructions for novices. Weekly regattas. Pool, tennis also. Full American Plan. Open June–Sept.

Spruce Point Inn. *Deluxe.* Spruce Pt. Rd. (633–4152). Picturesquely situated on wooded peninsula. Rooms in lodge or inn. Pools, putting green, tennis, beach, boats, fishing. Golf nearby; lobster bakes. Cocktail lounge, entertainment. Play area. Family units avail. Meals included. Open June to Sept.

Fisherman's Wharf Inn. *Expensive.* 42 Commercial St. (633–5090). Large motel built on pier. Nicely decorated rms. overlook bay and dock. Downtown location, center of boating and shopping activity. Seafood restaurant, bar. Open April to Nov.

Ocean Gate Motor Inn. *Expensive.* On Rte. 27, Southport (633–3321). Modern motel nestled alongside harbor. Nicely decorated rms. Boating, fishing. Pool. Pets. Restaurant, bar. Open May to mid-Oct.

Rocktide Motor Inn. *Expensive.* 46 Atlantic Ave. (633–4455). On pier, with own dock. Attractive rooms with balconies over the water. Harbor views. Restaurant, bar. Open June to Oct.

Smuggler's Cove Motor Inn. *Expensive.* Rte. 96, E. Boothbay (633–2800). Resort-motel, right on the ocean, with fine accommodations. Boating, beach, pool. Restaurant. Open May to Oct.

Top Side. *Expensive.* McKown Hill (633–5404). Inn and newer motel. Picturesque setting—highest point in town, overlooking harbor and bay. Walk to all tourist and sporting activities. Open late-May to Nov.

Captain Sawyer's Place. *Moderate.* 87 Commercial St. (633–2474). "The yellow house" in the heart of town. An old sea captain's house remodeled into a charming guesthouse. Open April to Oct.

Lake View. *Moderate.* Lakeview Rd. off Rte. 27 (633–5381). All rooms face the water. Private sandy beach on freshwater lake. Boating, fishing. Play area. Restaurant and cocktail lounge. Open May to Oct.

Ocean Point Inn & Motel. *Moderate.* Rte. 96, E. Boothbay (633–4200). Charming seacoast inn. Down East Hospitality, home-cooked food. Boat trips leave from wharf. Pool. Open May to Oct.

The Thistle Inn. *Moderate.* 53 Oak St. (633–3541). Old sea captain's home in center of town converted to a New England inn, Scottish-style. Good food, friendly bar.

CAMDEN. Norumbega. *Deluxe.* Rte. 1 (236–4646). Victorian stone castle overlooking Penobscot Bay. Distinctive service, elaborate public rooms, 7 bedrooms with period furnishings, porches and balconies. Adults only.

Whitehall. *Deluxe.* 52 High St. (236–3391). Historic Colonial inn. Tennis, boat trips, concerts, entertainment. Gracious dining, cocktails. Open June to mid-Oct.

Camden Harbour Inn. *Expensive-Deluxe.* 83 Bayview St. (236–4200). Spectacular harbor view. Authentic Victorian inn (1892) exudes old-fashioned charm; quiet and comfortable. Dining porch, lounge, entertainment.

Aubergine. *Expensive.* Belmont Ave. (236–8053). Cozy rooms available in lovingly restored Victorian inn. Swimming, boating and golf nearby. Small, quiet and classy. Excellent French restaurant. Open Apr. to Nov.

Beloin's on the Maine Coast. *Expensive.* Rte. 1 (236–3262). Shorefront lodging on picturesque cliffs. Modern motel, mini-kitchen units available. Private beach. Nearby golf, shops and restaurants. Open May to Oct.

Goodspeed's Guest House. *Moderate-Expensive.* 60 Mountain St. (236–8077). Small Federal-style (1879) guesthouse within walking distance of harbor. Attractively decorated rooms. Continental breakfast included. Open July - Oct.; weekends only in winter.

CHRISTMAS COVE. Coveside Inn. *Moderate.* Cove Rd., Rte. 129, (644–8282). Shorefront inn-motel, marina, moorings. Restaurant and bar. Open April to Oct.

ISLESBORO. Islesboro Inn. *Expensive.* Dark Harbor (734–2222). Guestrooms have dramatic views of the bay; some have fireplaces. Lovely public rooms. Relaxed atmosphere. Tennis, some swimming. Meals included—picnic lunches prepared. Yachtsmen welcome. Ferry from Lincolnville Beach. Open June to Oct.

MONHEGAN ISLAND. The Island Inn. *Moderate.* (596–0371). Rather plain food and furnishings. Peace and quiet. No smoking. Appeals to birdwatchers, artists and fishermen. Open June to Sept.

NEWCASTLE. The Newcastle Inn. *Expensive.* River Road off Rte. 1 (563–5685). A small, comfortable inn on the Damariscotta River, with cozy rooms. Breakfast served. Cross-country skiing nearby. Some water activities available. Close to Boothbay Harbor; walk to Damariscotta.

ROCKLAND. Trade Winds. *Expensive.* 303 Main St. (596–6661). Modern units overlooking harbor. Indoor pool. Restaurant, bar, entertainment on wknds.

ROCKPORT. The Samoset Resort. *Deluxe.* Warrenton Ave. (594–2511). Modern resort bounded on two sides by the Atlantic Ocean. Indoor and outdoor tennis and pools; golf course, health club, game rooms; restaurants and entertainment. Meals included.

SEARSPORT. The HomePort Inn. *Expensive.* Rte. 1 (548–2259). Bed and breakfast in an elegant New England sea captain's mansion, circa 1863. Warm, homey atmosphere. Open all year.
Yardarm Motor Inn. *Inexpensive.* Rte. 1 (548–2404). Personalized hospitality has made this motel popular. Beautiful view of bay, attractive landscaping. Open mid-May to mid-Oct.

SPRUCE HEAD. The Craignair Inn. *Expensive.* Clark Island Rd. (594–7644). In a small village at water's edge. Hiking, bicycling, birdwatching, fishing, boating and swimming. Other sports nearby. Breakfast and dinner included.

TENANTS HARBOR. The East Wind Inn. *Moderate.* (372–6366). Restored 19th-century inn. Lovely view of the waterfront from the veranda. Perfect for a relaxing vacation. Weekly rates available. Hearty New England meals.

WESTPORT. The Squire Tarbox Inn. *Moderate-Expensive.* Rte. 144 (882–7693). Very small restored country inn. Delightful and friendly. Antique furnishings. Sumptuous dining. Open April to Oct.

PENOBSCOT-ACADIA AREA

BANGOR AREA. Bangor Hilton. *Expensive-Deluxe.* Rte. I–95, Bangor (974–6721). At Bangor Int'l Jetport. Beautiful rooms and suites in this large, modern hotel. All amenities: summer and winter sports, excellent service, near shopping. Good restaurant, cocktail lounge. Pool and sauna.
Holiday Inn. *Expensive.* Two locations: 404 Odlin Rd., Bangor (947–0101) and 500 Main St., Bangor (947–8651). Comfortable motel. Restaurant, bar. Pets accepted. Pool. Open all year.
University Motor Inn. *Expensive.* 5 College Ave., Orono (866–4921). Nicely decorated with patio or balconies. Restaurant, bar. Pool. Walking distance to Univ. of Maine.
The Phenix Inn. *Moderate-Expensive.* West Market Sq. (947–3850). Recently restored downtown hotel with "Old World" ambiance. Convenient to business district and shopping.

BAR HARBOR. Atlantic Oakes. *Deluxe.* Eden St. (288–5218). Handsomely decorated rooms, each with ocean view. Elegant, yet informal. Built on former estate. Pebble beach, boats. Tennis. Game rm.
Bar Harbor Motor Inn. *Deluxe.* Adjacent to Town Pier (288–3351). Luxurious motor hotel, built in 1887, on the shore of Frenchman's Bay. Pool and sundeck. Restaurant and lounge. Open May to Oct.
Manor House Inn. *Expensive-Deluxe.* 106 West St. (288–3759). Guesthouse. Turn-of-the-century decor in restored Bar Harbor "cottage." In-town location. Privileges at Bar Harbor Club across street—pool, tennis. Quiet, comfortable, convenient. Continental breakfast included. Open Apr. to Nov.
Park Entrance. *Expensive.* Rte. 3, across from Nat'l. Park Hdq. (288–3306). Pleasant rooms with patios or balconies overlooking the ocean. Pool, beach, putting green, boats. Picnic area. Open May to Oct.
Stratford House Inn. *Expensive.* 45 Mt. Desert St. (288–5189) Small, English Tudor Inn styled after Shakespeare's birthplace and furnished with Jacobean-period antiques. Short walk to town center and waterfront. Continental breakfast included. Open June to Oct.

Wonder View Motor Lodge. *Expensive.* Eden St. (288–3358). Hilltop view of Bar Harbor and Frenchman's Bay. Pool. Restaurant, cocktail lounge. Close to town. Open May to Oct.

Cleftstone Manor Motor Inn. *Moderate-Expensive.* On Rte. 3 (288–4951). Historic English-style mansion at foot of Cadillac Mountain. Gracious rooms, a well-stocked library, and a game room. Continental breakfast and afternoon tea included. Open May to Oct.

Thornhedge Inn. *Moderate-Expensive.* 47 Mt. Desert St. (288–5398). Reminiscent of early Bar Harbor elegance. Downstairs sitting rooms. Spacious guestrooms. Congenial atmosphere. Complimentary breakfast. Walking distance to all town facilities. Open Apr. to Nov.

Cadillac Motor Inn. *Moderate.* 336 Main St. (288–3831). Pleasant motor inn close to town. Ideal for families. Convenient, comfortable, cordial. Some kitchenettes. Free transportation to and from airport, bus or ferry terminal with prior arrangement.

BLUE HILL. Arcady Down East. *Moderate-Expensive.* South St. (374–5576). This elegant Victorian manse exudes Old World Charm. Bicycles available to guests. Continental breakfast included. Open May–Oct.

Blue Hill Inn. *Moderate-Expensive.* Main St. (374–2844). Very pretty landmark inn (1840) in the town center. Golf, tennis and beaches nearby. Excellent dining.

BROOKSVILLE. Breezemere Farm Inn. *Deluxe.* Rte. 176, S. Brooksville (326–8628). Lovely 1850 farmhouse plus cottages on Orcutt Harbor. All amenities and numerous sports. Excellent restaurant. Open June to Oct.

BUCKSPORT. Jed Prouty Motel. *Moderate.* Rte. 15 (469–3113). Historic inn and new motel overlooking Penobscot Bay. Modern rooms, comfortably furnished. Restaurant.

CASTINE. Castine Inn. *Moderate.* Main St. (326–4365). Traditional New England country inn (1898). Friendly service, comfortable accommodations. Complimentary home-baked breads and pastries for breakfast. Open May to Oct.

Pentagöet Inn. *Moderate–Expensive.* Main St. (326–8616). Small, comfortable Victorian inn, right on the coast. Full dinner service. Open Apr.–Dec.

DEER ISLE. Goose Cove Lodge. *Expensive.* Sunset, 4½ mi. from Deer Isle Village (348–2508). Rooms in the lodge or in rustic cottages. Miles of nature trails on grounds overlooking Goose Cove. Private beach for swimming and boating. Sports nearby. Weekly rates; family-style meals included. Open May to Oct.

Pilgrim's Inn. *Expensive.* Main St., Deer Isle (348–6615). Quiet Colonial inn (1793), overlooking a millpond. Comfortable accommodations. Swimming and boating available. Weekly rates include meals. Open May to Oct.

The Captain's Quarters Inn & Motel. *Moderate.* Main St., Stonington (367–2420). Harborside location offers a panoramic view of the bay. Close to village. Rooms, suites, efficiencies or apartments. Coffee shop.

Eggemogin Inn. *Moderate.* Little Deer Isle (348–2540). A secluded inn perched on a point of land on Eggemogin Reach. Oceanfront rooms, some with shared bath. Enjoy sailing, fishing, boating and privacy! Continental breakfast available. Open June–Sept.

NORTHEAST HARBOR. Asticou Inn. *Deluxe.* Rtes. 3 & 198 (276–3344). Rambling, formal, turn-of-the-century resort inn and modern housekeeping cottages. Pool. Cozy rms., some with fireplaces. Open June to Sept.

Kimball Terrace Inn. *Expensive.* Huntington Rd. (276–3383). Large motor inn overlooking the harbor. Golf, tennis, boating. Pool. Elevator. Children free.

SOUTHWEST HARBOR. The Claremont. *Expensive.* Clark Point Rd. (244–5036). Mt. Desert Island's oldest summer hotel and adjacent rustic cottages. Tennis, deepwater dock and moorings. Public dining. Open June to Sept.

SURRY. Surry Inn. *Moderate.* Rte. 172 (667–5091). Lovely, sprawling inn (1834) with a 60-ft. porch. Swimming, boating and lawn games in summer; cross-country skiing in winter. Delicious dining. Near Acadia National Park and Deer Isle.

WASHINGTON COUNTY

CALAIS. Heslin's Motel & Cottages. *Moderate.* Rte. 1 (454–3762). Informal family resort overlooking the St. Croix River and Canada. Fine dining; lounge. Canoeing, fishing and wilderness expeditions available. Open May to Oct.

DENNYSVILLE. Lincoln House Country Inn. *Moderate.* Rte. 1 (726–3953). Restored (1787) Georgian colonial. Choice birdwatching and Atlantic salmon fishing. Fine dining. Open Apr.–Dec.

GRAND LAKE STREAM. Leen's Lodge. *Expensive.* On West Grand Lake (796–5576). From freshwater fishing to cocktail get-togethers, this family resort offers variety. Boats and guides available. Nicely furnished cottages have fireplaces or Franklin stoves. Excellent meals included. Open mid-May to mid-Sept.

LUBEC. Eastland Motel. *Moderate.* Rte. 189 (733–5501). At the airport. Comfortable, large rooms. Just ten minutes from Roosevelt-Campobello International Park.
Home Port Inn. *Inexpensive-Moderate.* 45 Main St. (733–2077). Pleasant accommodations and fine dining in a comfortable home in a historic section of town.

AROOSTOOK COUNTY

CARIBOU. King Henry's Motor Inn. *Moderate.* Access Hwy. (493–3311). Modern motel. Miles of snowmobile trails nearby. Restaurant, cocktail lounge, entertainment.

FORT KENT. Jalbert's Allagash Camps. *Moderate.* (P.O. Box 126, Ft. Kent 04743 for info.) (843–5015). Located in Allagash Wilderness Waterway area. Comfortable cabins, tasty food. Camps reachable by canoe only; equipment and guides provided. Variety of "deepwoods" vacation trips available—mainly trout fishing and canoeing. Open May to Oct.
Rock's Motel. *Moderate.* Main St., opp. International Bridge at beginning of U.S. Rte. 1 (834–3133). Convenient resting place in hunting, fishing, canoeing, and snowmobiling area.

HOULTON. Shiretown Motel. *Moderate.* North Rd. at jct. Rtes. 1 & I–95 (532–9421). Full service motor inn, comfortable and convenient. Kitchenettes available. Indoor pool, sauna, exercise room.

PATTEN. Mount Chase Lodge. *Expensive.* Shin Pond Rd., at N. entrance to Baxter State Park (528–2183). Family accommodations in the wilderness country of northern Maine. Bathing, fishing, canoeing, hiking and float plane service. Family-style meals. Open May to Nov.

NORTHERN LAKES & FORESTS AREA

GREENVILLE. Penobscot Lake Lodge. *Expensive.* Penobscot Lake, N. of Greenville near Quebec border (695–2786). Wilderness sporting camp reached by float plane from Greenville, a 50-mile trip. No direct access by road. Full meal service and use of boats, canoes, fishing tackle. Accommodations are in private log cabins, with lodge for socializing and dining. Fishing is the main attraction. Open from late May to Sept.

Chalet Moosehead. *Moderate.* On Moosehead Lake, just off Rtes. 6 and 15 (695–2950). Chalet-style efficiencies. Attractive grounds overlook the lake. Offers private beach, boating, fishing, and hiking. Free use of canoes. Golf and tennis nearby.

Squaw Mountain at Moosehead. *Moderate.* Greenville Jct. (695–2272). Four-season mountainside/lakeside resort specializing in family vacations. Offers full range of water sports, plus tennis, riding, lawn games in summer; snowmobiling, skiing and hunting in winter. Play area. Restaurant, bar, entertainment, dancing wknds.

Greenville Inn. *Inexpensive-Moderate.* Norris St. (695–2206). Former lumber baron's home (1895). Ten cozy guestrooms, two with fireplaces. Snowmobile trails, skiing, golf and tennis nearby; boating and watersports at Moosehead Lake. View of the lake from dining room.

JACKMAN-MOOSE RIVER. Sky Lodge and Motel. *Deluxe.* Rte. 201 (668–2171). Massive log lodge in remote back country. Rustic and very attractive. Mountain and lake views. Excellent food. Pool, archery, rifle range.

Attean Lake Resort. *Moderate.* Off Rte. 201 on Attean Lake (668–3321). Rustic log cottages with fireplaces. Fishing, mountain climbing, water sports, hiking and nature walks all at your doorstep. Great family vacation spot. All meals included.

ROCKWOOD. Moosehead Motel. *Expensive.* Rtes. 6 and 15 (534–7787). On Moosehead Lake, with magnificent view of mountains and lake. Pool, boating, fishing, hunting, skiing and snowmobiling. Good restaurant and cocktail lounge.

The Birches. *Moderate.* 2 mi. N. of Rockwood on Moosehead Lake (534–7305). Main lodge and several log cabins situated among the birch trees. Housekeeping facilities or full meal service. Private marina, all water sports—miles of cross-country skiing and snowmobiling in winter. Weekly rates available.

Rockwood Cottages. *Moderate.* On Moosehead Lake opp. Mt. Kineo (534–7725). Housekeeping cottages—neat, clean and comfortable. Perfect for quiet, peaceful North Woods family vacation—or hunting and fishing. All water sports in summer; ice fishing, skiing and snowmobiling in winter.

Tomehegan. *Inexpensive.* Box A (534–7712). Woodland hideaway. Main lodge (1910) and nine hand-hewn cottages located down a 10-mile private road on Moosehead Lake. Expert outfitters and guides for hunting, hiking, cross-country skiing, and ice fishing. Meals provided.

WESTERN LAKES AREA

BETHEL. Bethel Inn & Country Club. *Expensive-Deluxe.* On the Common (824–2175). Classic country inn with fine furnishings and lovely grounds. Excellent cuisine, modern comforts, personal service. Meal and package plans. Winter skiing, summer boating, tennis, golf, fishing, swimming in the lake or pool, and more.

The Sudbury Inn. *Moderate-Expensive.* Lower Main St. (824–2174). The two-room suites and dorm-style bunkrooms are attractively decorated, and the restaurant serves delicious homemade New England fare. Closed Apr. and Nov.

Sunday River Inn. *Inexpensive-Moderate.* At Sunday River Ski Area, off Rte. 1 (824–2410). Hostel-like accommodations; families and groups welcome. Family-style meals included. Housekeeping units and dorms available. Open Nov. to April.

L'Auberge. *Inexpensive.* Mill Hill Rd. (824–2774). Home-like country inn at edge of village. Spacious lawns and gardens lie just beyond the front porch. Mountains, lakes and golf course nearby. Continental breakfast included.

BRIDGTON. Pleasant Mountain Inn. *Expensive.* Off Rte. 302, W. Bridgton (647–2431). Small, secluded Alpine inn on Moose Pond, offering boating, beach, fishing, hunting, ice skating, tennis. At base of Pleasant Mt. ski slopes. Restaurant.

    Tarry-A-While Resort. *Moderate-Expensive.* Ridge Rd. (647–2522). Hospitable lakeside resort—like stepping into Switzerland! All water sports available, plus golf and tennis nearby. Fine Swiss cuisine in famous Switzer Stubli Dining Room. Open June to Sept.

CENTER LOVELL. Westways. *Expensive-Deluxe.* Rte. 5 (928–3663). On Kezar Lake, at the edge of the White Mountain National Forest. Rustic main lodge and surrounding cottages offer woodsy seclusion and magnificent lake views. Meals included; sports activities available. Closed Apr. and Nov.

KINGFIELD. Sugarloaf Inn. *Expensive-Deluxe.* At the foot of Sugarloaf Mountain (237–2701). Modern full-service inn. Exceptional skiing at your door in winter; pool and tennis in summer. Dining room and cocktail lounge.

    Winter's Inn. *Expensive.* Winter's Hill (265–5421). Restored Georgian mansion offering beautifully decorated guest rooms and a fine French restaurant. The view overlooks surrounding mountains and is spectacular. Meals included. Pool, tennis and skiing available. Closed Apr., May, and Nov.

    The Herbert. *Moderate.* Main St. (265 2000). Gracious hotel restored and refurbished to its original 1913 style. Classic New England dining.

NAPLES. Chute Homestead. *Expensive.* Harrison Rd., Rte. 35 (693–6452). Family resort on Long Lake, with a lively schedule. Chalet rooms and cottages, some with private wharves. Summer sports, beach, boating. Play area. Entertainment. Clam and lobster bakes, as well as excellent dining rm. fare. Golf nr. Open mid-June to Sept.

RANGELEY. Country Club Inn. *Expensive-Deluxe.* Country Club Rd., off Rte. 4 (864–3831). A delightful resort perched high on a hill overlooking Rangeley Lake. Magnificent view, personalized attention. Good restaurant, golf, pool, fishing, water sports, winter skiing.

    Pleasant Island Lodge and Cottages. *Expensive.* On Cupsuptic Lake, Oquossoc (864–3722). A family camp in Rangeley Lakes region. 13 comfortable, modern log cottages with maid service. Home-cooked meals in central dining room included. Rustic and informal. Pets. Family rates. American Plan only. Open May through Sept.

    Saddleback Lake Lodge. *Expensive.* Saddleback Lake (864–5501). Individual log cabins nestled in the woodland at the base of Saddleback Mountain. Swim or fish in the lake outside your door. Delicious Maine food. Open mid-June–Oct.

    Rangeley Inn and Motor Lodge. *Moderate.* Main Gt. (864–3341). Turn-of-the-century inn or modern motel units on lake. All sports available nearby. Old-fashioned comfort and hospitality. Restaurant, bar. Open all year.

    Town & Lake Motel. *Moderate.* Main St. (864–3755). On Rangeley Lake. Pleasant family resort with motel units and housekeeping cottages. Beach area, boating, canoeing, play area. Winter skiing and snowmobiling.

RUMFORD. Madison Motor Inn. *Moderate-Expensive.* Rte. 2 (364–7973). Nicely decorated, pleasant rms., some with balconies or steambaths. Views of river. Restaurant, bar, dancing. Boating, fishing, hunting, skiing available nearby.

    Kimball's Motel & Cabins. *Inexpensive.* Rte. 2 (364–4495). On scenic Androscoggin River. Small motel with pool and housekeeping units. Tourist attractions, shopping and skiing nearby.

SOUTH CASCO. Migis Lodge and Cottages. *Deluxe.* Rte. 302 (655–4524). On Sebago Lake amid pine tree forest. Small lodge and 25 cabins. Learn water skiing and enjoy boating at this waterfront resort. Fine beach. Open June to Oct.

WATERFORD. Kedarburn Inn. *Moderate-Expensive.* Rte. 35 (583–6182). Small country bed-and-breakfast inn on the shore of Lake Keoka. Winter and summer sports. Full breakfast included; dinner served.

WILSON'S MILLS. Bosebuck Mountain Camps. *Expensive.* On Azicohos Lake (243–2945). Rustic cabins surrounded by 200,000 acres of remote wilderness. A choice area for hunters and fishermen. All meals included; guide service available.

CENTRAL LAKES AREA.

AUGUSTA. The Senator Inn. *Moderate-Expensive.* 284 Western Ave. at I–95 (622–5804). Large, comfortable Best Western motor inn. Pool, restaurant, evening entertainment in lounge.

BELGRADE LAKES AREA. Castle Island Camps. *Moderate.* Mt. Vernon Rd., Long Pond (495–3312). Fully furnished cottages ideal for a family vacation. Beautiful pine forest setting. Community building for dining and recreation. Excellent fishing and swimming in lake at your doorstep. Boats available. Weekly rates, meals included. Summer only.
    Whisperwood Lodge & Cottages. *Inexpensive.* On Salmon Lake (465–2497). Mddern cottages with wood-burning stoves. Bass and trout fishing, private docks, raft, water sports; indoor games; pony rides. Meals in central dining room included. Summer only.

CHINA LAKE AREA. Willow Beach Camps. *Moderate.* Rte. 202 (968–2421). Cozy, fully equipped cabins among the trees on the shore of China Lake. Home-cooked meals in the dining room. Fishing, swimming, and varied recreational facilities. Weekly rates. Summer only.

FARMINGTON. Farmington Motel. *Moderate.* Rtes. 2 and 27 (778–4680). Comfortable, spacious rooms in modern motel. Good location for visitors interested in fishing or sightseeing, ski country or snowmobiling. Restaurant and gift shop.

SKOWHEGAN. Breezy Acres. *Inexpensive.* Rte. 201, Waterville Rd. (474–2703). Family units. Fishing in private pond. Pool, play area. Pets. Open mid-May to late-Oct.

WATERVILLE. Holiday Inn. *Expensive.* 375 Upper Main St. (873–0111). The usual pleasant accommodations, with all amenities available.

HOW TO GET AROUND. By air: Intrastate flights are available on scheduled airlines between cities via Bar Harbor Airlines, Valley, Delta, and Bangor International. Float planes are available in Rangeley, Greenville, Jackman, Brewer, Millinocket, Patten and Portage to carry fishermen and hunters to sporting camps in remote areas.

By car: Maine has about 22,000 miles of public highway, over 300 miles included in the U.S. Interstate Highway System. The major routes are: I–95, which runs from the southernmost tip of the state northeasterly to Houlton, and U.S. 1, which follows the entire coast, then turns northward—linking Kittery in the south with Ft. Kent in the far north. Other roads you may wish to travel are: Rte. 2, which goes from Bethel and the White Mountains in the west through Bangor and along the Penobscot River to Houlton; Rte. 3 from Augusta to the coast, then through Bucksport to Acadia National Park; Rte. 9, a bee-line through the blueberry barrens and timberland of Washington County between Bangor and Calais; Rte. 11 from Fort Kent in the far northern wilderness south to Portage and on through Ashland to Patten; Rte. 26 through the Grafton Notch State Park area north of Bethel; Rte. 27 from the mountains in

Kingfield northwest through the woods to the Canadian border; Rte. 201 from Portland and Augusta north along the Kennebec River thrbugh the wilderness to Jackman and across to Quebec; Rte. 202 from the New Hampshire border in southern Maine through Augusta to Bangor. There are very few public roads in the northern wilderness areas. Logging roads are privately owned, but many are available for public use (weather permitting). Some require permits, some have road access fees. For information: North Maine Woods, P O Box 382, Ashland, ME 04732 (435–6213).

Car rental: Major car rental companies are represented in Augusta, Bangor, Bar Harbor, Brunswick, Camden, Portland, Presque Isle, Rockland, Saco, Sanford, Trenton, Waterville, and York.

By boat: It's as easy to rent a boat as a car in Maine. Up north, much of the boat service is handled by sporting camps. At docks along the waterfront in most coastal towns, boats are generally available for rent or charter. Car ferry service to coastal islands is available at Rockland, Lincolnville, Bass Harbor, Bar Harbor and Portland. Passengers only between Boothbay Harbor and Monhegan, and on the mailboat between Stonington and Isle au Haut or Port Clyde and Monhegan. Ferry service between Rockland and Matinicus runs only one day each month. For schedules, write Maine State Ferry Service, P O Box 645, 517A Main St., Rockland, ME 04841 (594–5543).

TOURIST INFORMATION SERVICES. A variety of colorful folders and brochures are available from *The Maine Publicity Bureay,* 97 Winthrop St., Hallowell ME 04347 Tel. (207) 289–2423; *New England Vacation Center,* Shop #2, Concourse Level, 630 Fifth Ave., New York NY 1-020 Tel. (212) 307–5780; and *InfoRoute USA,* Centre Capitol, 1200 McGill College Ave., Montreal, Quebec, Canada H3B4G7 Tel. (514) 861–0481.

The Main Publicity Bureau operates a major Tourist Information Center in *Kittery,* accessible from both I–95 and U.S. Rte. 1. Regional Tourist Information Center locations are: *Portland,* 142 Free St.; *Bangor* (summer), Bass Park, 519 Main St.; *Calais* (summer), Main St.; *Houlton,* Ludlow Road near Jct. I–95 and U. S. Rte. 1; *Bethel* (summer), Jct. Rtes. 2 and 113, *Fryeburg* (summer), U.S. Rte. 302.

About 40 local tourist information offices are affiliated with the Maine Publicity Bureau and are located strategically in towns throughout the state.

In addition local Chamber of Commerce offices will gladly provide you with information about the town or area in which you are interested.

Tourist attractions are well marked by small roadside directional signs. The Official Maine State Map is an excellent, up-to-date resource (available from the Maine Publicity Bureau).

SEASONAL EVENTS. Write to the *Maine Publicity Bureau,* 97 Winthrop St., Hallowell ME 04347, for a current listing of events, fairs, expositions, etc.

January. *Augusta*—Maine State Agricultural Show (civic center); *Kingfield*—Winter Carnival (Sugarloaf USA).

February. Winter Carnivals take place in *Augusta, Bethel, Caribou, Bridgton,* and *Bangor; Rangeley*—Rangeley Village "100" Snowmobile Race; *Caribou*—Dog-sled races.

March. *Rangeley*—Annual Rangeley Lakes 30-mile dog-sled races; *Greenville*—Squaw Mtn. Winter Carnival.

May. *Eustis* (Sugarloaf area)—Upper Dead River Whitewater Canoe Race.

June. *Portland*—Old Port Festival; *Madawaska*—Acadian Festival.

July: (early) *Bath*—Heritage Days (antiques, crafts, parade), *Ashland*—Northern Maine Lumberjack Roundup (log rolling, canoe tilting, tree cutting contests), *Camden-Rockport*—Schooner Days (2-day celebration); *Jonesport*—Lobsterboat races. (mid) *Belfast*—Belfast Bay Festival (mammoth chicken barbecue, exhibits, professional entertainment); *Boothbay Harbor*—Windjammer Days; *Ft. Fairfield*—Maine Potato Blossom Festival; *Yarmouth*—Yarmouth Clam Festival (3-day event: beauty pageant, parade, clambake, arts & crafts); (late) Art shows and festivals in *Norway, Bar Harbor, Millinocket; Bailey*

Island—Tuna Tournament (prizes, lobster & clambakes); *Boothbay Harbor*—Friendship Sloop Regatta; *Portland*—Deering Oaks Family Festival; *Oxford*—Annual Bean Hole Festival; *Lewiston*—Franco-American Festival.

August. (early) *Bangor*—Bangor State Fair; *Calais*—International Festival; *Boothbay Harbor*—Tuna Tournament; *Rockland*—Maine Lobster Festival (4-day affair, beauty pageant, seafood suppers, crafts, professional entertainment); *Brunswick*—Maine Festival of the Arts (exposition of Maine arts and crafts, information on fishing, boatbuilding, food, etc.); (mid) *Skowhegan*—Skowhegan State Fair; *Union*—Maine Antique Festival; *Castine*—Retired Skipper's Race; (late) *Union*—Union Fair & Blueberry Festival; *Camden*—Downeast Jazz Festival; *York Harbor*—Seacoast Crafts Fair.

September. *Blue Hill*—Hancock County Agricultural Fair; *Phillips*—"Fall Foliage Days"; *Cumberland Center*—Cumberland Farmers Club Fair.

October. *Boothbay Harbor*—Fall Foliage & Country Fair Weekend; *Fryeburg*—W. Oxford Agricultural Fair (largest fair in Maine).

November. *Portland*—League of Maine Craftsmen Exposition.

December. *Jackman*—Annual International Snowmobile Races.

FALL FOLIAGE. Country fairs, apples and pumpkins at roadside stands, and a crispness in the air mark autumn in Maine and spectacular foliage viewing from mid-September through early October. The sweeping views one gets in the mountains of western Maine offer the most striking panorama of brilliant fall colors. The 9,000 ft. (round-trip) gondola ride at Sugarloaf/USA, Kingfield, operates daily in the fall and gives a perfect vantage point.

TOURS. By boat. For a week's tour of the Maine coast, windjammers sail from Rockland, Rockport and Camden during summer season. Write Chamber of Commerce, P. O. Box 246, Public Landing, Camden ME 04843 (236–4404), or Maine Windjammer Association, Box 317, Rockport ME 04856 (236–4867) for a list of cruises. *Casco Bay Lines,* Custom House Wharf, Portland ME 04112 (774–7871) offers several daily cruises around the islands in Casco Bay, some with lobster and clambakes included. Out of Boothbay Harbor, excursion boats cruise the harbor islands and sheltered coves in the area. Some cruises are nature-oriented (whale watching or seal watching), others include a lobsterbake, and still others venture farther out in the ocean to the outer islands. For brochures: Boothbay Harbor Region Chamber of Commerce, Rte. 27, P. O. Box 356, Boothbay Harbor ME 04538 (633–4232). Excursion boats also depart from Bangor, Kennebunkport, Machias, and Jonesport for river or ocean cruises or whale and seal watching.

Acadia National Park features *Naturalist Sea Cruises* during summer, accompanied by a park naturalist. Contact the Park Information Center, Hull's Cove, Rte. 3, Bar Harbor ME 04609 (288–3338). Boats also leave from the Municipal Piers in Bar Harbor and Northeast Harbor for sightseeing trips around Mt. Desert Island.

In the Sebago Lakes area, a cruise through the Songo Lock for a half day trip along the Songo River departs daily from the Causeway, Rte. 302, Naples ME 04055 (693–6861). A two-hour afternoon or evening cruise around Sebago Lake departs from Pt. Sebago Outdoor Resort, Casco ME 04015 (655–3821).

Walking tours: Self-conducted tours have been outlined for the capital city of Augusta, the Old Port section of Portland, the Marginal Way in Ogunquit, the Cliff and River Walk in York Village, and the historic districts of Bethel, Bath, Wiscasset, and Camden. Information can be secured at your hotel, the local Chamber of Commerce, or from a local tourist information service booth.

By bus. A variety of bus tours are available in popular touring areas around the state. For example:

Maine Coast Jitney Sightseeing. 104 Limerock St., Rockland (594–4478) conducts summer and fall tours of mid-coast Maine in the Camden-Rockport-Rockland area.

Great Atlantic Tour Company in Portland (775–7700) departs from area hotels daily for city tours of Portland and for tours of Boothbay Harbor, Ogunquit or Kennebunkport.

Marjorie Windsor Guide Service, Southport (633–5307) offers bus tours in and around the Boothbay Harbor area.

Executive Tours and Charter Tours, Bar Harbor (288–4505) conducts half-day tours of Mt. Desert Island by reservation only.

National Park Tours conducts a 2½-hour bus tour of Acadia National Park that leaves daily from Testa's Restaurant, Main St., Bar Harbor, and is fully narrated by a local naturalist. Inquire at the restaurant for particulars (288–3327).

By air: Sightseeing flights can be arranged at Bar Harbor for an air tour over Acadia National Park and Cadillac Mountain, and at Rangeley for a seaplane flight around Rangeley Lake.

Industrial Plant Tours. The Maine Publicity Bureau publishes a brochure listing several Maine businesses offering tours, such as: *Rackliffe Pottery,* Blue Hill 04614 (374–2297), and *Rowantrees Pottery,* Blue Hill 04614 (374–5535)—pottery and dinnerware; *Bradbury Barrel Co.,* Main St., Bridgewater 04735 (429–8141)—cedar barrels and barrel furniture; *Anderson & Sons, Inc.,* Cumberland Center 04021 (829–3374)—lobster traps; *Old Town Canoe Co.,* 58 Middle St., Old Town 04468 (827–5513)—canoes & kayaks; *G. H. Bass & Co.,* Weld St., Wilton 04294 (645–3131)—shoes. Advance notice is requested but not always necessary. Products are often available for sale. For tours of pulp and paper mills, contact *Paper Industry Information Office,* 133 State St., Augusta 04330 (622–3166).

 **WILDLIFE REFUGES.** *Maine Audubon Society,* 118 U.S. Rte.. 1, Falmouth (781–2330) and the Maine chapter of the *Nature Conservancy,* 20 Federal St., Brunswick (729–5181) organize field trips to offshore islands to view the native vegetation and wildlife.

Rachel Carson National Wildlife Refuge, Wells (646–9226) has 4,000 acres of coastal marsh area—habitat for a variety of birds, mammals and plants.

Birsacre Sanctuary, adjacent to the Stanwood Homestead Museum, Rte. 3 (east of town center), Ellsworth (667–8683), is a small wildlife refuge of about 40 acres. The museum, a memorial to Cordelia J. Stanwood, pioneer ornithologist, has an excellent collection of bird specimens; the sanctuary has trails, wild flowers, bird nesting areas, ponds and picnic grounds.

Bird-watchers will sight many species in *Acadia National Park,* on Mt. Desert Island, the most important observation point for the Atlantic Flyway. Nature walks are scheduled morning and afternoon; inquire at Park Information Center, Hull's Cove, Rte. 3, Bar Harbor ME 04609 (288–3338).

Moosehorn National Wildlife Refuge, Calais (454–3521) consists of 22,775 acres. There are miles of trails and logging roads; 200 species of birds and 39 species of mammals have been recorded here.

Baxter State Park, in north-central Maine, is a 200,000-acre wildlife preserve —"a sanctuary for wild beasts and birds." There are many hiking trails, including the last few miles of the Appalachian Trail, and camping is permitted. For information and permits: Baxter State Park Authority, 64 Balsam Dr., Millinocket ME 04462 (723–5140).

Bigelow Game Preserve, off Rte. 27 in Bigelow (west of the Carrabassett Valley), is a vast wooded area where large and small game roam free.

Hunter Cove Wildlife Sanctuary, opposite Dodge Pond on Rte. 4 north, Rangeley, has walking trails where you can view the region's wildlife and natural history.

Aquariums open to the public are: *Seaquarium,* McKown Pt., West Boothbay Harbor ME 04575 (633–5572), *Mt. Desert Oceanarium,* Clark Pt. Rd., Southwest Harbor ME 04679 (244–7330, and *Maine Aquarium* Rte. 1, Saco ME 04072 (284–4511).

NATIONAL PARKS. *Acadia National Park* encompasses more than 30,000 acres near Bar Harbor on Mt. Desert Island. Along scenic drives, visitors pass great ragged cliffs and coves. A drive to the 1,530-ft. summit of Cadillac Mt. provides a 360° view of coastal and inland Maine. At Thunder Hole, the surf crashes with a fury into a rocky ravine. There are miles of hiking trails and car-free carriageways for bicycling, horseback riding, and cross-country skiing. Camping, trailer sites and picnic areas, are plentiful. Nature guide service offers varied daily programs. Swimmers have a choice of salt or fresh water. Birdwatchers will spot everything from herons to eagles. Lots of wildlife too—deer, beaver, raccoon, fox. Additional sections of Acadia National Park are on Isle au Haut (boat from Stonington) and on Schoodic Peninsula. For information, contact: Acadia National Park, Hulls Cove, Rte. 3, Bar Harbor ME 04609 (288–3338).

White Mountain National Forest is partly in Maine, southwest of Bethel. There are campsites, hiking trails, picnic grounds, and magnificent mountain scenery. For information, contact: Ranger, White Mountain National Forest, Bethel ME 04217 (824–2134).

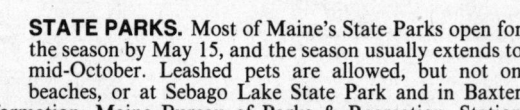

STATE PARKS. Most of Maine's State Parks open for the season by May 15, and the season usually extends to mid-October. Leashed pets are allowed, but not on beaches, or at Sebago Lake State Park and in Baxter State Park. For information: Maine Bureau of Parks & Recreation, Station #22, Augusta 04333 (289–3821).

Southern Coast. *Bradbury Mountain* (Pownal)—Camping, picnicking, hiking, play area, fun for families; *Crescent Beach* (Cape Elizabeth)—Picnicking, swimming, fishing, snack bar; *Popham Beach* (Phippsburg)—Picnicking, swimming, fishing; *Scarborbugh Beach* (Scarborbugh)—Picnicking, swimming, fishing; *Two Lights* (Cape Elizabeth)—Picnicking, swimming, fishing (only 9 mi. from Portland), magnificent scenery; *Wolf Neck Woods* (Freeport)—Picnicking, hiking.

Mid-Coast. *Camden Hills* (Camden)—Camping, picnicking, snowmobiling, hiking, trails, scenic drive; *Damariscotta Lake* (Jefferson)—Picnicking, swimming, fishing; *Fort Point* (Stockton Springs)—Picnicking, fishing; *Lake St. George* (Liberty)—Camping, picnicking, swimming, boating, fishing, snowmobiling; *Moose Point* (Searsport)—Picnicking; *Pemaquid Restoration* (Pemaquid)—Picnicking, fishing, snack bar; *Reid* (Georgetown)—Picnicking, swimming, fishing, snack bar; *Warren Island* (Islesboro)—Camping, picnicking, fishing.

Penobscot-Acadia. *Holbrook Island Sanctuary* (Brooksville)—Picnicking, hiking, nature study; *Lamoine* (Ellsworth)—Camping, picnicking, fishing, boating.

Washington County. *Cobscook Bay* (Dennysville)—Camping, picnicking, fishing, snowmobiling, hiking, boating, day trips to Moosehorn National Wildlife Refuge; *Quoddy Head* (Lubec)—Picnicking, hiking, beautiful spot for photography (easternmost point of land in U.S., with tides ranging from 20–28 feet); *Roque Bluffs* (Roque Bluffs)—Picnicking, swimming, fishing.

Aroostook County. *Aroostook* (Presque Isle)—Camping, picnicking, swimming, boating, fishing, snowmobiling and hiking.

Allagash Wilderness Waterway is a 92-mile corridor of lakes and rivers extending from Moosehead Lake to the far north near Fort Kent. The Waterway is famous for canoeing, but visitors can enjoy picnicking, swimming, fishing and snowmobiling. If you plan to visit or make the canoe trip, write for information: Maine Dept. of Conservation, Bureau of Parks & Recreation, State House, Augusta ME 04433 (289–3821).

Northern Lakes & Forests. *Lily Bay* (Greenville)—Camping, picnicking, swimming, fishing, boating, snowmobiling; *Mattawamkeag Wilderness* (Mattawamkeag)—Camping, picnicking, swimming, hiking; *Peaks-Kenny* (Dover-Foxcroft)—Camping, picnicking, swimming, fishing, hiking.

Baxter State Park (Millinocket) is a 200,000-acre wilderness preserve where visitors enjoy camping, fishing, snowmobiling, and hiking; roads are narrow, dirt, and winding. The Appalachian Trail terminates in the park at Mt. Katahdin, at 5,267 ft. the highest point in Maine. For visitor permit, camping, or other information, write: Baxter State Park Authority, 64 Balsam Dr., Millinocket, ME 04462 (723–5140).

Western Lakes. *Grafton Notch* (Upton & Newry)—Picnicking, fishing, hiking, spectacular scenic drive; *Mt. Blue* (Weld)—Camping, picnicking, swimming, fishing, boating, snowmobiling, hiking, nature study; *Rangeley Lake* (Rangeley)—Camping, picnicking, swimming, fishing, boating, snowmobiling; *Sebago Lake* (Naples)—Camping, picnicking, swimming, fishing, boating, snack bar; Songo Lock operated daily for Sebago Lake-to-Songo River boat trips.

Central Lakes. *Peacock Beach* (Richmond)—Picnicking, swimming, fishing; *Range Ponds* (Poland)—Picnicking, swimming, fishing, boating.

CAMPING. About half of the state parks in Maine, as well as Acadia National Park, allow camping. There are no trailer hookups in any of the parks, however. Except for Baxter State Park, reservations are not accepted, but are on a first come, first served basis. There are about 90 wilderness campsites, mostly on lakes and rivers, maintained by the Maine Forest Service and available at no charge. For information on these sites and on fire permits, write: *Maine Forest Service,* State House, Augusta ME 04333 (289–2791).

Facilities in privately owned campsites range from simple basics in the wilderness to deluxe cabins and cottages for rent—sometimes including tennis and shuffleboard courts, canoe and boat rentals, automatic laundry equipment, restaurants and snack bars, swimming pools, or recreation halls.

Sporting camps catering to hunters and fishermen abound from Rangeley and Greenville north through the Allagash Wilderness Waterway. The prime wilderness area in northeastern Maine is the Forest City-Carrol-Grand Lake Stream triangle, with camps run by people whose way of life is the great outdoors. Lodgings in the sporting camps may consist of housekeeping cabins or a central lodge with sleeping cabins. Meals are generally included. Float plane service is often necessary, and guide service is usually available.

Maine Publicity Bureau, 97 Winthrop St., Hallowell ME (289–2423) will provide a current listing of cottage rentals, trailer parks, campsites and conveniences available.

SUMMER SPORTS. Boating. Maine's seemingly endless coastline and hundreds of miles of inland waterways offer perfect opportunity for boating of all sorts—cruising, sailing or even rowing. The coast is dotted with towns where boats are for hire, excursion boats embark and charter fishing boats are available. Windjammer cruises for a week at a time are thrilling, while day or hourly cruises on excursion boats or ferries are delightful.

Flat-water and **white water canoeing** are popular sports for the beginner and for the expert. Popular canoe trips traverse the St. John, St. Croix and Machias Rivers, although first and foremost for canoeing is the Allagash Wilderness Waterway, from Moosehead Lake north to Fort Kent. Information and a list of canoe rental agencies are available from Maine Publicity Bureau, 97 Winthrop St., Hallowell ME 04347 (289–2423).

Maine has, undoubtedly, the best wilderness **white-water rafting** in the East. Premier locations are the upper reaches of the Kennebec and the west branch of the Penobscot Rivers. All trips are operated by trained guides. A list of raft-trip operators is available from the Maine Publicity Bureau (address above).

Many state parks offer saltwater br lake **swimming.** Miles of white sandy beach on the Atlantic attract surf swimmers to the Southern Coast, from York Beach to Old Orchard Beach. Swimming has a short season in the sometimes bone-chilling Atlantic Ocean farther "Down East." Water skiing is popular on the inlnd lakes.

Horseback riding. There is a 40-mile system of bridle paths in Acadia National Park, on Mt. Desert Island, open to horseback riding. Horses are available for hire in the Park. Inquire at the Park Information Hdq., Hull's Cove, Rte.

3, Bar Harbor ME 04609 (288–3338). Several of the state parks have riding trails. A list of riding stables is available from the Maine Publicity Bureau.

Golf. There are 27 18-hole courses in Maine open to the public, a 27-hole course in Portland, and about 75 9-hole courses. Greens fees range from $10–$15. Among the best courses are: Bar Harbor—*Kebo Valley C.,* a narrow, tree-lined course of Scottish design; Bethel—*Bethel Inn G. C.,* a short 9-hole layout; Kennebunk Beach—*Webhannet G.C.,* lush seaside links, level fairways; Poland Spring—*Poland Spring G.C.,* the oldest 18-hole resort course in the U.S.A.; York—*York G. & Tennis C.,* a fine seaside course.

Mountain Climbing. Maine boasts 10 peaks of 4,000 feet or higher. In Baxter State Park, *Mt. Katahdin* (5,267 ft.) has many trails, some very treacherous and suitable only for expert climbers. State parks in the western mountains have marked trails. Climb *Mt. Blue* in Mt. Blue State Park, Weld, for a 3,000-feet-above-sea-level view.

Hiking. Trails in the White Mountains National Forest, near Bethel, connect with the 280-mi. stretch of the Appalachian Trail that traverses Maine northeast to its terminus at Mt. Katahdin, in Baxter State Park. (For information: Maine Appalachian Club, P.O. Box 283, Augusta 04330.) Acadia National Park and most state parks have marked hiking trails.

Bicycling. There are few designated bicycle paths, but there are plenty of beautiful country roads. Acadia National Park on Mt. Desert Island has 50 miles of car-free carriage paths—a cycler's paradise. Bike shops, especially in coastal towns, rent bicycles and mopeds.

 **WINTER SPORTS.** Downhill skiing begins in mid-Nov. in Maine and lasts until May at more than 30 major ski areas, many lighted at night. Slopes are less crowded and lift lines shorter than in neighboring states, and snow conditions and facilities can compete easily.

Some major areas, which have both aerial and surface cable lifts, are: *Camden Snow Bowl,* Ragged Mt., Camden ME 04843 (236–4418). *Squaw Mountain,* Rtes. 6/15, Greenville ME 04441 (695–2272), *Mount Abram,* Rte. 26, Locke Mills ME 04250 (875–2601); *Pleasant Mountain,* Rte. 302, Bridgton ME 04009 (647–2022); *Saddleback Mountain,* Rte. 4, Rangeley ME 04970 (864–3380); *Sugarloaf USA,* Rte. 27, Kingfield ME 04947 (237–2000)—Maine's only gondola; *Sunday River,* Rte. 26, Bethel ME 04217 (824–2187). For information on Maine ski conditions, call 237–2000.

Cross-country skiing is booming in Maine. Major touring centers are located in *Acadia National Park, Sunday River* (Bethel), *Carrabassett Valley, Squaw Mountain* (Greenville), and *Saddleback* (Rangeley). Local Chambers of Commerce and the Maine Publicity Bureau, 97 Winthrop St., Hallowell ME 04347 (289–2423) will provide colorful brochures with detailed information.

Snowmobiling is very popular for exploring the untouched woods in the north. Thousands of miles of marked and groomed trails interconnect throughout Maine and into Canada and New Hampshire. *Allagash Wilderness Waterway* offers 100 miles of trails for experienced riders or with guides. For trail maps and information, contact Maine Dept. of Inland Fisheries & Wildlife, Snowmobile Section, 284 State St., Augusta, ME 04333 (289–2043).

 **FISHING.** If you want rugged and challenging year-round saltwater fishing, countless bays and inlets offer cod, Atlantic smelt, mackerel, halibut, flounder, pollock (the adult is noted for fighting spirit), haddock, striped bass, and tuna. There are extensive boat rental facilities available (advance reservations are recommended). A list of charter and head boats for deep-sea fishing is available from Maine Publicity Bureau (address above under Winter Sports). No license required for saltwater fishing, although there are some bag limits and restrictions on equipment.

Freshwater fishermen will find trout and bass in the lakes and rivers. For all nonresidents 12 years old or over, a fishing license is required; several types (3-day, 7-day, 15-day and season) are available. Maine is the only state where Atlantic salmon may be caught, and a special license is required. Write to Dept.

of Inland Fisheries & Wildlife, State House, Augusta ME 04333 (289–2043). The assistance of a guide can be invaluable on a trip to the north woods. Contact Maine Professional Guides Association, Box 265, Medway ME 04460.

 **HUNTING.** Hunting wild birds and animals is a major autumn attraction in Maine's millions of acres of wilderness. Strict regulations are enforced for hunting with bow and arrow, firearms, and traps in order to manage the abundant wildlife: pheasant, grouse, duck, and woodcock; fox, bobcat, lynx, and coyote; deer, bear, and moose. Moose hunting is limited to 1,000 hunters (only 100 nonresident) drawn by lottery. Licenses are required for all hunters 10 years old or over. Applicants for adult firearms licenses must show proof of having previously held an adult license or having successfully completed an approved hunter safety course. Hunting on certain Indian territories is regulated by the tribes, and special permission must be obtained. For information bn hunting licenses and regulations, contact Dept. of Inland Fisheries & Wildlife. Maine Guide service is recommended for wilderness trips. (See "Fishing" above for addresses.)

 **SPECTATOR SPORTS. Hockey.** At the Cumberland County Civic Center, on Free Street in Portland, the Maine Mariners play professional hockey from October through May. For information, call 775-3458.

Basketball. The Maine Lumberjacks, a professional basketball team, play at the Bangor Auditorium, 100 Dutton St., from Dec. through March. Call 947–5252 for details.

Baseball. The AAA Maine Guides, Maine's only professional baseball team, make their home at The Ballpark, Old Orchard Beach from Apr.–Sept.

Stock car racing. Maine has racing ovals that seat from 2,000 or 13,000 spectators. Most of the tracks have hot top surfaces and are a third of a mile in length. The season goes from early spring through October. The eight race tracks are located at Scarborough, Wiscasset, Ellsworth, Unity, Winterport, Oxford, Hermon and Caribou. All offer stock-car racing except Winterport, which has drag racing. Speedway Inc., at Oxford, also has added a drag strip.

Boat races. Spectators may watch regattas during the active boating season, spring through Nov. In April, The Carrabassett Whitewater Canoe Race is held at Sugarloaf USA, Kingfield. Friendship Sloop Races are held in Boothbay Harbor at the end of July.

Horses. Horse shows are scheduled from July through Oct., or you may attend horse races at: Lewiston Raceway, 729 Main St., Lewiston ME 04240; Scarborough Downs, Scarborough ME 04074; Aroostook & Northern Raceways, P. O. Box 43, Presque Isle ME 04769; Cumberland Raceway, Blanchard St., Cumberland ME 04021. Harness racing, with parimutuel betting, is a main attraction at the Bangor State Fair and the Skowhegan State Fair, as well as at many county fairs.

QUARRIES. Rockhounds can pan for gold or search for beryl, garnet, topaz, quartz and tourmaline. One of the most popular spots for gold panning is the Coos Canyon area of the Swift River, along Rte. 17 in Byron. Perham's Maine Mineral Store, at the junction of Rtes. 26 and 219, W. Paris (674–2341), is a rockhound's mecca. Perham's has several quarries in the area, five of which are open to collectors free of charge. Maps are distributed at the store.

 **PHOTOGRAPHY.** For the photographer, there's the wonderland of rugged coast and primeval wilderness, waves smashing on the rocky shore "Down East" and the beauty of potato fields in blossom in Aroostook County. *Acadia National Park* boasts some of the most beautiful coastal scenery and interesting plant life in the country. *Stonington* and *Northeast Harbor* are photogenic New England fishing ports. *Camden* is the home of the windjammers. The lighthouse at *Pemaquid Point,* Bristol, is much photographed, as is

the Wedding Cake House on Summer St. in *Kennebunk*. Gulf Hagas, near *Brownville Junction,* is known as the Grand Canyon of the East. The signpost at *Lynchville* is a good subject (listing Paris, Poland, Peru, Mexico, etc.). There are 10 covered bridges remaining in Maine, but the most photographed is the "Artist's Bridge" (Sunday River Bridge) near *Newry*.

 **INDIANS.** The Maine *Penobscot Indians* are part of the Algonquin linguistic group. The Penobscots were the largest tribe in Abnaki Nation and were very helpful to the American patriots during the Revolution. Indian crafts are sold at the Penobscot Indian Reservation on Indian Island near Old Town. The *Penobscot National Historical Soceity Indian Museum* (827–2271), also on Indian Island, has artifacts, photos and religious items detailing the complete history of the Penobscot Tribe.

The *Passamaquoddy* tribe, also part of the Abnaki Nation, have the Pleasant Point Indian Reservation in Perry, just north of Eastport, in Washington County. Their beautifully handcrafted baskets and souvenirs may be purchased at the reservation.

 **CHILDREN'S ACTIVITIES.** One of the beauties of Maine is that it is a great place to take the family. There are many special interest museums and amusements that capture children's imagniation and make their trip to Maine memorable. Along Maine's southern coast, from York Beach to Saco, kids can enjoy ocean swimming at white sand beaches and thrilling rides at several amusement parks. State parks—and especially Acadia National Park on Mount Desert Island—are wonderful places for children, boating, hiking, nature walks and swimming generally available. Kids will have a wonderful time, too, at any of the state or county fairs held in several communities (see *Seasonal Events*). The Maine Publicity Bureau has compiled a listing of activities especially suited to children.

SOUTHERN COAST AREA

Bath. *Maine Maritime Museum,* Washington St. (443–6311). Includes displays for children marked "Please Touch" in the museum area, a working boatyard, a boatride along the Kennebec River, and the Grand Banks dory schooner *Sherman Zwicker*.

Old Orchard Beach. Noted for its large amusement area, *Palace Playland,* on Rte. 1 (934–2001).

Portland. *Children's Museum of Maine,* 746 Stevens Ave., off Rte. 9 (797–3353). "Hands-on" educational exhibits on the arts, sciences, and natural history.

Saco, *Funtown USA,* Rte. 1, Maine's largest amusement park, and *Aquaboggan Water Park,* Rte. 1, with waterslides, miniature golf, and a gigantic wavepool.

York Beach. *York's Wild Kingdom Amusement Park,* Rte. 1, (363–4911). Tame animals for petting and feeding, as well as rides for the kids.

MID-COAST AREA

Boothbay. *Boothbay Railway Village,* Rte. 27 (633–4727). Steam-railroad exhibits plus a ride on a narrow-gauge train.

Owls Head. *Owls Head Transportation Museum,* Rte. 73, Knox County Airport (594–9219). Collection of early planes and cars; demonstrations on weekends.

Rockport. *Andre the Seal,* Public Landing. Afternoons at 4 P.M., Andre performs tricks from his pen in the harbor.

PENOBSCOT-ACADIA AREA

Bar Harbor. *Aqualand Wildlife Park,* Rte. 3 (288–3898). Fun and exciting animal shows; petting farm and picnic area.

Natural History Museum. College of the Atlantic, Eden St. (Rte. 3). Displays on whales, birds, plants, and land mammals of Mt. Desert area.

Southwest Harbor. *Mt. Desert Oceanarium,* Clark Pt. Rd. (244–7330). Live sea creatures and lobstering demonstrations.

WESTERN LAKES AREA

Bridgton. *Pleasant Mountain Ski Area,* Rte. 302 (647–2022). Chair lift/Alpine slide during the summer season.

Rumford. *Rumford Zoo,* Rte. 2 (364–7043). Wild animals and birds from around the world.

CENTRAL LAKES AREA

Augusta. *Fort Western,* Bowman St. Built to defend the Kennebec River during the French & Indian War; costumed guides.

Gray (Dry Mills). *Maine Dept. of Inland Fisheries and Wildlife,* Rtc. 26 (657–4977). State fish hatchery and game farm.

 **HISTORIC SITES.** In order to recreate its long history for present-day visitors, Maine has preserved and restored many old homes and designated several historic districts throughout the state. Call for days and hours before visiting to avoid disappointment.

SOUTHERN COAST AREA

BRUNSWICK. *Stowe House* (1806), 63 Federal St. (725–5543). Where Harriet Beecher Stowe wrote *Uncle Tom's Cabin;* now an inn.

HARPSWELL. *Eagle Island,* Casco Bay. Adm. Robert E. Peary's boyhood home, accessible by private boat only and available to picnickers.

KITTERY. *Fort McClary* (1846), Kittery Pt. Rd. (Rte. 103). Restored hexagonal blockhouse. (No tel.)

Lady Pepperell House (1760), Rte. 103 Georgian mansion built by Sir William Pepperell, first American baronet. (No tel.)

POPHAM BEACH. *Fort Popham* (1861), Rte. 209. Granite fort built during Civil War; near site of Popham Colony, early English settlement. (No tel.)

PORTLAND. *Portland Observatory,* 138 Congress St. (773–5779), 19th-century signal tower; extensive views of Casco Bay and White Mountains from the Lantern Deck.

Tate House (1755), 1270 Westbrook St., Stroudwater Village (774–9781). Built by George Tate, King's Mast Agent. Exceptional paneling and fine collection of 18th-century furnishings.

Victoria Mansion, 109 Danforth St. (772–4841). Victorian Italian villa with most of its original decoration and furnishings intact.

Wadsworth-Longfellow House (1785), 487 Congress St. (772–1807). Boyhood home of the famous poet containing many original furnishings.

S. BERWICK. *Hamilton House* (1787), Vaughan's Lane (off Rte. 236) (384–5269). Magnificently restored Georgian mansion with period furnishings.

Sarah Orne Jewett Memorial (1774), 101 Portland St. (384–5269). Preserved home of the famous writer, furnished with 18th- and 19th-century antiques.

YORK VILLAGE. *Elizabeth Perkins House* (1731), Sewall's Bridge (363–4974). Colonial home with Victorian furnishings.

Emerson-Wilcox House (1742), York St. (363–3872) Museum of local history and American decorative arts.

Jefferds Tavern (1750), 5 Lindsay Rd. (363–4974). 18th-century saltbox inn with period furnishings.

John Hancock Warehouse, Lindsay Rd. (363–4974). 18th-century warehouse with exhibits on local river history.

Marshall Store, Lindsay Rd. (363–4974). 19th-century store with many locally crafted items.

Old Gaol Museum (1720), York St. (363–3872). King's Prison for Province of Maine, containing dungeons, cells and jailer's quarters.

Old Schoolhouse (1745), Lindsay Rd. (363–4974). One-room school with 18th-century furnishings.

MID-COAST AREA

ALNA. *Old Alna Meetinghouse,* Rte. 218 (586–5536). 18th-century meetinghouse (1789), with fascinating architectural details, including a pulpit leveler and original box pews.

BRISTOL. *Colonial Pemaquid Restoration,* Rte. 130, Pemaquid Pt. Building foundations and artifacts indicating 17th-century Indian settlements. (No tel.)

CAMDEN. *Conway House,* Conway Rd. (off Rte. 1) (236–2257). Authentic Colonial (1770) Maine farmhouse and barn, with period furnishings and utensils.

DAMARISCOTTA. *Chapman-Hall House,* Main St. Oldest remaining dwelling in Damariscotta (1754), with period furnishings, exhibits of local artisans, and an adjacent herb garden. (No tel.)

DRESDEN MILLS. *Pownalborough Court House,* Rte. 128. Oldest court building in Maine (1761), with interesting architectural details and an exhibit on the Kennebec ice industry. (No tel.)

N. EDGECOMB. *Ft. Edgecomb* (1808), Old Fort Rd., Davis Island. Two-story octagonal blockhouse built to protect Wiscasset. (No tel.)

PROSPECT. *Fort Knox,* Rte. 174. Maine's largest fort, with underground stairways and interesting construction techniques. (No tel.)

ROCKLAND. *Wm. A. Farnsworth Homestead,* 21 Elm St., (596–6497). Victorian residence, fully furnished and preserved; adjacent to renowned Farnsworth Art Museum.

THOMASTON. *Montpelier* (1794), High St., Rte. 1. Replica of mansion built by Gen. Henry Knox, advisor to George Washington and his Secretary of War. (No tel.)

WALDOBORO. *Old German Church* (1772), Rte. 32. Well-preserved church with square-benched pews and a pulpit shaped like a wine glass. (No tel.)

WISCASSET. *Castle Tucker,* Lee St. (882–7364). An 1807 mansion built by Judge Silas Lee, with original Victorian furnishings and wallpaper and a free-standing elliptical staircase.

Lincoln County Museum and *Old Jail,* Federal St. (Rte. 1) (882–6817). Museum is in the jailer's house (1837) and has on exhibit examples of Maine arts and skills over the past 200 years; jail, next door, has granite walls more than three feet thick.

Nickels-Sortwell House (1807), Cor. Main and Federal Sts. (Rte. 1) (882–6817). One of Maine's most beautiful old homes, built by Capt. Wm. Nickels, a prominent shipmaster.

PENOBSCOT-ACADIA AREA

BLUE HILL. *Jonathan Fisher Memorial,* Main St. (Rte. 15). Home of town's first minister (1814), with many of his homemade furnishings on display. (No tel.)

CASTINE. *Ft. George* (1779), Rte. 166A. British-built fort with interpretive panels chronicling fort's history. (No tel.)

WASHINGTON COUNTY

COLUMBIA FALLS. *Ruggles House* (1818), ¼ mi. off Rte. 1. Federal-style residence with intricately carved mouldings and a flying staircase that is a masterpiece. (No tel.)

MACHIAS. *Burnham Tavern* (1770), Main and Free Sts. (Rte. 192) (255–4432). Pre-revolutionary tavern with period furnishings and items relating to initial naval battle of Revolutionary War.

Fort O'Brien (1775), Rte. 92. Overlooking Machias Bay. Site of first naval battle of Revolutionary War. (No tel.)

AROOSTOOK COUNTY

FORT KENT. *Fort Kent Memorial* (1840), Block House St. (off Rte. 1). Blockhouse built in preparation for Aroostook War; never used, since dispute was solved by treaty. (No tel.)

HOULTON. *Amos Pearce Home,* Court St. Oldest residence in town, with post office on main floor and smokehouse in the basement. (No tel.)

NORTHERN LAKES & FORESTS AREA

BROWNVILLE JCT. *Katahdin Iron Works* (1843), 6 mi. down gravel road off Rte. 11 (5 mi. N of Brownville Jct.). Once a mine and smelting mill, now has a restored stone blast furnace and charcoal kiln on site. (No tel.)

WESTERN LAKES AREA

NAPLES. *Songo Lock,* on Songo River. Single surviving operating lock of Cumberland-Oxford Canal; boat trips available. Call 693–6861 to arrange a boat trip.

PARIS HILL. *Hannibal Hamlin Memorial Hall* and *Old Stone Jail.* Jail now houses a library and museum of American primitive art, local minerals, and artifacts from the Hamlin family. (No tel.) Hamlin Home next door is now privately owned and not open to visitors.

S. CASCO. *Nathaniel Hawthorne's Boyhood Home* (1812), Hawthorne Rd. (off Rte. 302). Boyhood home of the famous author, now furnished as a community hall. (No tel.)

CENTRAL LAKES AREA

AUGUSTA. *Fort Western* (1754), Bowman St. (622-1234). Built to defend the Kennebec River during French & Indian War; stopping place for Benedict Arnold on his march to Quebec. Restored blockhouse and stockade.
State Capitol Building, State St. (289-1110). Designed by Charles Bulfinch (1829) and constructed of Hallowell granite; displays of Maine battle flags, portraits of Maine's governors, office of the governor and legislative chambers.

FARMINGTON. *Nordica Homestead,* Holley Rd. (off Rte. 4) (778-2042). Birthplace of the opera singer, Lillian Nordica (nee Norton); home dates from 1840 and houses displays of her costumes, music, programs and other memorabilia.

WINSLOW-WATERVILLE. *Fort Halifax* (1754), Rte. 201 (near bridge) (872-2706). One of the oldest blockhouses in the U.S.; another stopping place during Benedict Arnold's march to Quebec.

 MUSEUMS AND GALLERIES. No matter where you travel in Maine, you'll find a museum or art gallery at which you'll want to stop and browse. Maine's rich history centers around its shipping industry so you will find an emphasis on maritime exhibits from the early days before statehood up to modern times. No matter what your interest is, though, Maine is bound to offer an exhibit somewhere that will pique your interest. Call ahead for days and hours.

SOUTHERN COAST AREA

BATH. *Maine Maritime Museum,* Washington St. (443-6311). Four historic sites, including exhibits of marine artifacts, a working boatyard, an apprentice shop, an impressive multimedia/multilevel exhibit on *Lobstering and the Maine Coast,* the Grand Banks dory schooner *Sherman Zwicker,* and a boatride along the Kennebec River.

BRUNSWICK. *Bowdoin College Museum of Art,* Walker Art Bldg. (1894), Bowdoin Campus (725-8731). Collection of Old Masters, American Colonial and Federal portraits, works of Andrew Wyeth and an extensive collection of Winslow Homer memorabilia and paintings.
Peary-MacMillan Arctic Museum, Hubbard Hall, Bowdoin Campus (725-8731). Exhibits and memorabilia relating to Arctic explorations of Adm. Robert E. Peary and Adm. Donald B. MacMillan.
Pejepscot Historical Society Museum, Park Row (729-4622). Americana and military exhibits displayed in the Skolfield-Whittier House (1863).

KENNEBUNK. *Brick Store Museum* (1825), 117 Main St. (Rte. 1) (985-4802). Local shipbuilding history and marine artifacts.

KENNEBUNKPORT. *Seashore Trolley Museum,* Log Cabin Rd. (off Rte. 1) (967-2712). Vast collection of streetcars, including a restoration facility; ride on open trolleys.

KITTERY. *Kittery Historical & Naval Museum,* Rogers Rd. (off Rte. 1) (439-3080). Exhibits of local maritime history.

PORTLAND. *Portland Museum of Art* (1882), Congress Sq. (775–6148). Important works of American art, much of it by Maine artists, beautifully displayed in a fascinating building.

WELLS. **Wells Auto Museum,** Rte. 1 (646–9064). Antique cars dating from 1900 are displayed; additional exhibits of motorcycles, bicycles, license plates, and antique toys.

MID-COAST AREA

BOOTHBAY. *Boothbay Railway Village Museum,* Rte. 27 (633–4727). Steam-railroading exhibits housed in two restored railway stations; ride on a steam train.
   Boothbay Theater Museum, Corey Lane (633–4536). Collection of theater memorabilia, costumes, playbills, posters, etc.

FRIENDSHIP. *Friendship Museum* (1851), Jct. Rte. 220 & Martin's Point Rd. Historical information on the Friendship Sloop. (No tel.)

MONHEGAN ISLAND. *The Monhegan Museum,* Lighthouse Hill. Former lightkeeper's house includes displays of island plants, flowers and wildlife and an art gallery. (No tel.)

OWLS HEAD. *Owls Head Transportation Museum,* Rte. 73, Knox County Airport (594–9219). Collection of antique aircraft and automobiles (1900–1940s), all in operating condition; weekend demonstrations.

ROCKLAND. *Wm. A. Farnsworth Art Museum,* 19 Elm St. (596–6457). Renowned collections of American and European art; changing exhibits.
   Shore Village Museum, 104 Limerock St. (Grand Army Hall) (594–4950). Coast Guard exhibit of lighthouse equipment, buoys, and life-saving gear from search-and-rescue boats, coupled with a large collection of Civil War uniforms and artifacts.

SEARSPORT. *Penobscot Marine Museum,* Church St. (548–6634). Collection of marine paintings, shipbuilding tools, and whaling memorabilia dramatically exhibited in several sea captains' homes.

WALDOBORO. *Waldoborough Historical Society Museum,* Rte. 200 (near Jct. Rte. 1). A complex of three buildings: a country school, cattle pound, and a farm kitchen. (No tel.)

WISCASSET. *Lincoln County Fire Museum,* Federal St. (Rte. 1) (882–6817). Contains a collection of some of the country's oldest firefighting equipment, dating from 1803.
   Musical Wonder House, 18 High St. (882–7163). Antique music boxes and player pianos in a restored house (1852). Summer candlelight concerts.

PENOBSCOT-ACADIA AREA

BANGOR. *Bangor Historical Society Museum,* 159 Union St. (942–5766). Exhibits of local memorabilia housed in historic Thomas Hill House (1834).

BAR HARBOR. *Bar Harbor Historical Society Museum,* 34 Mt. Desert St. (Jesup Mem. Library) (288–3838). Early photographs and memorabilia of Bar Harbor in the golden days before the fire of 1947.
   The Jackson Laboratory, Rte. 3 (3½ mi. South of Bar Harbor) (288–3371). Active center for mammalian genetics research.

Robert Abbe Museum of Stone Age Antiquities, Sieur de Monts Spring, Acadia National Park (288–3519). Exhibits of stone age tools and early Indian life.

CASTINE. *Wilson Museum,* Perkins St. Geology, maritime, and North American Indian collections, plus artifacts dating back to prehistoric times. (No tel.)

ELLSWORTH. *Col. Black Mansion,* West Main St. (667–8671). Georgian home furnished with period furniture; lovely gardens.

Stanwood Homestead Museum, Bar Harbor Rd. (Rte. 3) (667–8683). A memorial to pioneer ornithologist Cordelia J. Stanwood, with many bird specimens on exhibit; adjacent is a 40-acre bird sanctuary with picnic grounds and marked trails.

ISLESFORD. *Islesford Historical Museum,* Little Cranberry Island. Exhibits on the early history of Acadia. (No tel.)

OLD TOWN. *Penobscot National Historical Society,* Indian Island (827–2271). Exhibits detail the entire history of the Penobscot Indian Nation.

ORONO. *Univ. of Maine Anthropology Museum,* South Stevens Hall, (581–1901). American Indian exhibits, especially Maine Indians and Maine prehistory; rotating exhibits from other museums.

University of Maine Planetarium, Wingate Hall (581–1341). Spectacular star shows available to the public.

AROOSTOOK COUNTY

ASHLAND. *Ashland Logging Museum,* Garfield Rd. (435–6663). Exhibits relating to lumbering industry, including several buildings and heavy equipment.

CARIBOU. *Nylander Museum,* 393 Main St., (493–4474). Exhibits of Indian items, shells and marine life—and over 6,000 specimens of native animals and plants.

VAN BUREN. *Acadian Village,* Rte. 1 (868–2691). 16 buildings depicting the Acadian culture, all with period furnishings.

NORTHERN LAKES & FORESTS AREA

GREENVILLE. *Moosehead Marine Museum,* Pritham Ave. (695–2716). Home of the lake steamer *Katahdin* (1914); exhibits of logging industry in Moosehead Lake area.

PATTEN. *The Lumberman's Museum,* Rte. 159 (West of Patten) (528–2650). 2,000 artifacts related to Maine's lumbering industry, including heavy equipment and an 1820 logging camp.

WESTERN LAKES AREA

BETHEL. *Moses Mason Museum,* 15 Broad St., (824–2908). A fully restored Federal-style house (1813), with special exhibits and programs year-round.

LIVERMORE. *Norlands Living History Center,* Norlands Rd. (N of Rte. 108) (897–2236). 430-acre 19th-century working farm, including school, church, library and homestead.

NEW GLOUCESTER. *The Shaker Museum,* Rte. 26 (926–4597). Exhibits of furniture, crafts, and folk art depict an active Shaker community dating back to 1794.

NEWFIELD. *Willowbrook at Newfield,* Main St., off Rte. 11 (793–2784). Re-creation of a 19th-century village; 27 buildings illustrate village life, tools, vehicles, household implements, and "trades of yesteryear."

CENTRAL LAKES AREA

AUGUSTA. *Maine State Museum,* State St. (Capitol complex) (289–2301). Various exhibits depicting Maine's history, including special displays related to Maine's industries.

FARMINGTON. *Little Red Schoolhouse Museum,* Jct. Rtes. 2 and 4. Restored 19th-century schoolhouse (1852), which also served as a local information center. (No tel.)

THEATER. Maine, the birthplace of summer theater, offers professional productions of Broadway hits as well as non-Equity companies performing contemporary drama and comedy. Among the professional theaters are: *Hackmatack Playhouse,* Rte. 9, Berwick 03901 (698–1807); *Ogunquit Playhouse,* Rte. 1, Ogunquit 03907 (646–5511); *The Performing Arts Center at Bath,* 804 Washington St., Bath 04530 (442–8455); *Brunswick Music Theater,* Pickard Theater, Bowdoin Campus, Brunswick 04011 (725–8769); *Camden Shakespeare Co.,* Amphitheater, Atlantic Ave., P. O. Box 786, Camden 04843 (236–8011); *Acadia Repertory Theatre,* (winter) Main St. at Union, Bangor 04401 (942–3333); *Acadia Repertory Theatre,* (summer), Masonic Hall, Somesville 04679 and Bar Harbor Club, Bar Harbor 04609 (244–7260); *The Theater at Monmouth,* Cumston Hall, Monmouth 04259 (933–2952); *Lakewood Theater,* Rte. 201, Skowhegan 04976 (474–3331); *Thomas Playhouse,* Rte. 302, S. Casco 04077 (655–7728); *Waterville Summer Music Theater,* Waterville Opera House, Waterville 04901 (872–2707). *Maine Theatre,* Civic Center, P.O. Box 15002, Portland 04101 (871–7101).

SHOPPING. Local crafts are offered in many galleries and gift shops throughout the state. At the Maine Prison Store, Rte. 1, Thomaston (open daily), furniture and other items handcrafted by prisoners are for sale.

Antique shops are scattered throughout the state, but especially in Searsport, near Belfast on the coast, and in the Hallowell area, near Augusta. For a listing of antique dealers, write to the Antique Dealers Assoc., Inc., P. O. Box 144, Kezar Falls 04047 (625–3207).

Factory outlets are situated at mills throughout Maine. Kittery, Wells, and Freeport have a concentration of outlet stores. The *G.H. Bass & Co.* outlets, in several towns, offer fine men's and women's sandals, moccasins, dress shoes, boots, ski boots and golf shoes at discount prices. The *Hathaway Shirt Co.,* 10 Water St., Waterville, and in Wells, Freeport, and Ellsworth, has the renowned men's and women's shirts at reduced prices. Wells, in fact, is well-known for its concentration of brand-name factory outlet stores. *Quoddy* moccasins are sold at outlet stores throughout the state and at many gift shops in resort areas.

There are several knitting mills and fabric shops where you can still find a bargain. The *Bates Factory Outlet,* Canal St., Lewiston (784–7311), and on Rte. 1, Wells (646–5256), has good buys on bedspreads, draperies, and other linens.

And for the hunter, camper, and outdoorsman and woman the world-famous *L.L. Bean Store,* Freeport, (865–4761) is a must, open 24 hours every day.

But for the most delicious souvenir of your visit to Maine, many lobster pounds in coastal towns will ship lobsters or pack them for travel.

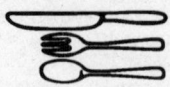

DINING OUT. Once you taste a Maine lobster, you will never forget that ocean-fresh flavor. Seafood, fresh from the sea, is a specialty—clams, salmon, trout and the ubiquitous lobsters. Chowders are features at most restaurants. Reasonably priced seafood tops the list on just about all menus.

During your tour, you may have noticed establishments called lobster pounds. The pound, a "Down East" institution, supplies local residents with fresh live lobster and also serves boiled lobster. At most pounds, you pick your own lobster and watch it go into a pot of boiling water. The lobsters are cooked in the open air, and most pounds have tables and benches outside where you can eat. (Many also have an indoor dining room for cold or rainy days.) Most diners order either New England clam chowder or steamed clams. Then come the bibs, claw-crackers, picks, melted butter—and the lobster.

Several cruises incorporate a clambake or shore dinner on an island. A real Down East Clambake is cooked in seaweed covered with tarpaulins and rocks. This retains all the flavor of the Maine lobsters and clams. Clambakes and shore dinners begin with a hot cup of chowder, then the steamed lobsters, steamed clams, corn on the cob, Maine potatoes, and baked onions. Blueberry cake is dessert, followed by hot coffee.

During the high season (summer at coastal resorts), we recommend that you call ahead for reservations. Also, most restaurants take credit cards, but it's always wise to telephone before you go to be sure credit cards are accepted and which ones they take.

For the restaurants listed below, average price per person for a complete dinner, exclusive of cocktails and wine, is as follows: *Deluxe:* $30 and up; *Expensive:* $20–$30; *Moderate:* $10–$20; *Inexpensive:* under $10.

Note: Unless otherwise indicated, the restaurants below are open year-round.

SOUTHERN COAST AREA

BAILEY ISLAND. Dockside Steak & Lobster House. *Moderate.* Mackerel Cove (833–6656). Dine or have cocktails overlooking the water. Open June to Oct.

BATH-BRUNSWICK AREA. 22 Lincoln. *Expensive.* 22 Lincoln St., Brunswick (725–5893). The atmosphere is casual and friendly; the gourmet cuisine is artfully prepared; the elegant service is attentive, yet unobtrusive. Light suppers at the Side Door Lounge.

The Grapevine. *Moderate–Expensive.* 1 Elm St., Bath (422–7422). Attractive, airy setting for well-prepared seafood and other menu items using the freshest ingredients. Pleasant, prompt service.

Stowe House. *Moderate–Expensive.* 63 Federal St., Brunswick (725–5543). Near the Brunswick Music Theater. Enjoy prime ribs, steaks, Maine seafood and German specialties in this historic home of Harriet Beecher Stowe.

Montsweag Farm. *Moderate.* Rte. 1, Woolwich (443–6563). Charcoal-broiled steaks, lobster, and other seafood. Casual nautical atmosphere. Cocktails.

New Meadows Inn. *Moderate.* Bath Rd., W. Bath (443–3921). Varied menu includes steaks, and vegetarian entrées. Fine view of cove from dining rooms.

FALMOUTH. The Galley. *Expensive.* 215 (rear) Foreside Rd., Rte. 88 (781–4262). Overlooks Casco Bay. Chowder, salads, crêpes, and seafood. Casual dress, boaters welcome.

KENNEBUNK. The Kennebunk Inn. *Moderate-Expensive.* 45 Main St., Rte. 1 (985–3351). Gracious dining in classic Maine coast inn (1799). International menu. Breakfast, lunch and dinner.

The Unicorn and Lion. *Moderate-Expensive.* Portland Rd. (Rte. 1 N.) (985–2985). Restored turn-of-the-century barn. Piano bar in loft; dancing. Fine evening dinner.

KENNEBUNKPORT. Olde Grist Mill. *Expensive.* Mill Lane (967–4781). Historic mill filled with antiques. Traditional Maine dishes from chowder to Indian pudding. Children's portions. Lunch, dinner. Country store adjacent. Open May to Oct.

Cape Arundel Inn. *Moderate-Expensive.* Ocean Ave. (967–2125). Country inn overlooks spectacular rocky coast. Hearty New England breakfasts; native seafood, steaks, and numerous veal and chicken dishes beautifully prepared for dinner. Open April to Dec.

The Lobster Claw. *Moderate.* Ocean Ave. (967–2562). Delicious home cooking in a charming, informal atmosphere. Sidewalk café in summer. Seafood is the specialty; homemade soups, chowders, breads, and desserts. Children's menu.

KITTERY. Warren's Lobster House. *Expensive.* Rte. 1 (439–1630). Lovely atmosphere and very fine seafood. Summer season only.

OGUNQUIT. Whistling Oyster. *Expensive-Deluxe.* Perkins Cove (646–9521). Established 1907. Elegant seafood and continental dishes cooked to order; own baking. Proper dress required.

Barbara Dean's. *Moderate.* Shore Rd. (646–2241). Delicious seafood specialties, prime ribs, pot roast. Chef owned and operated since 1929. Children's portions. Open May to Oct.

Julie's Ristorante. *Moderate.* Rte. 1 (646–7859). Family-run Italian restaurant; authentic Neapolitan cooking: Homemade pasta (prepared al dente), mouth-watering entrees and freshly made Italian cheesecake.

Ogunquit Lobster Pound. *Moderate.* Rte. 1 N. (646–2516). Lobster, clams, steaks, deep-dish pies outdoors or in the rustic dining room. Open May–Sept.

Barnacle Billy's. *Inexpensive.* Shore Rd., Perkins Cove (646–5575). Dine outside on the deck or inside by the hearth. Sandwiches, salad plates, seafood, chicken, boiled lobster, lobster stew. Scenic cruises from the wharf. Open May to Oct.

OLD ORCHARD BEACH. Joseph's by-the-Sea. *Expensive.* 55 W. Grand Ave. (934–5044). Oceanview dining. Seafood, steaks, roast beef, buffets. Delightful atmosphere. Open all year.

PORTLAND. L'Antibes. *Expensive-Deluxe.* 47 Middle St. (722–0453). Elegant, intimate dining. French cuisine.

The Vinyard. *Expensive-Deluxe.* 111 Middle St. (773–5424). Intimate French restaurant with limited menu. Exquisite meal and service. Extensive wine list.

The Baker's Table. *Expensive.* 434 Fore St. (775–0303). An informal bistro where imaginative entrees using the freshest Maine ingredients are presented.

Boone's. *Expensive.* On the waterfront at #6 Custom House Wharf (774–5725). Ocean-fresh lobster, fish, chowders and stews—as well as steaks. Children's portions.

DiMillo's Floating Restaurant. *Expensive.* 121 Commercial St. (772–2216). Dine on a former car ferry, right on the waterfront. Fresh fish, lobster, shore dinners, steamers. Very popular.

The Marketplace Restaurant. *Moderate.* 100 Maine Mall Rd., S. Portland (772–3754). Designed as a turn-of-the-century city market. Prime beef and seafood, New York-style cheesecake.

Cap'n Newick's Lobster Hbuse. *Inexpensive.* 740 Broadway, S. Portland (799–3090). Complete seafood menu at family prices. Also steaks and chicken. Informal.

Carbur's Restaurant. *Inexpensive.* 123 Middle St. (772–7794). Delectable— and unusual—sandwiches, built to order.

SACO. Three Thieves Inn. *Moderate-Expensive.* 63 Storer St. (284–5500). Fine food in 19th-century tavern. Varied continental menu. Lunch, dinner and Sunday brunch. Intimate bar.

WELLS. The Grey Gull Inn. *Expensive.* 321 Webhannet Dr., Moody Point (646–7501). Quaint Maine coast inn serving lobster, seafood and cocktails. Spectacular ocean views.

YARMOUTH. Camp Hammond. *Expensive.* 74 Main St. (846–3895). Formal dining in elegant historic (1888) home. Continental specialties, including lamb, veal, bouillabaisse and lobster.

Homewood Inn. *Expensive.* Drinkwater Pt. (846–3352). Shore dinners, chowders, delicious soups and desserts. Clambakes every Monday night. Open Mid-June to mid-Oct.

YORK HARBOR. Nubble Light Dining Room. *Expensive.* Nubble Rd., York Beach (363–4054). Choose your own lobster from the tank. Home baking. Lunch, dinner. Open June to Labor Day.

Bill Foster's Down East Lobster & Clambake. *Moderate.* Rte. 1A (363–3255). Clams, lobster and all the "fixin's" (or steak or chicken). Features an old-fashioned sing-along. Reserve ahead. Summer only.

York Harbor Inn. *Moderate* Rte. 1A (363–5119). Dining room overlooks the harbor. Continental menu—pasta, beef and seafood. Children's portions.

MID-COAST REGION

BOOTHBAY HARBOR AREA. Brown Bros. Wharf. *Expensive.* Atlantic Ave. (633–5440). Complete menu. Lobster from the tank, native seafood. Breakfast, lunch, dinner. Cocktails. Open April to Dec.

Fisherman's Wharf. *Expensive.* 42 Commercial St. (633–5090). Hotel dining room at water's edge. Fresh seafood, steaks and chops. Daily specials. Children's portions. Open May to Nov.

The Lawnmeer Inn Dining Room. *Expensive.* Rte. 27, Southport (633–2544). Traditional "Down East" cooking, excellently prepared and served in the spacious dining room. Open May to Oct.

Tugboat Inn Restaurant. *Moderate-Expensive.* 100 Commercial St. (633–4434). Dine aboard the tugboat *Maine.* Fine seafood dinners, steak, and prime rib. Deckhouse lounge.

Blue Ship. *Moderate.* At Foot Bridge (633–4074). Seafood, steak, sandwiches and chowder. Homemade breads and pastries. Wonderful cinnamon buns for breakfast. Open May to Oct.

Lake View's Greenhouse Restaurant. *Moderate.* Lakeview Rd. (633–5381). Gourmet restaurant featuring lobster, steak, seafood, and Continental-style specialties. Open May to Oct.

Robinson's Wharf. *Inexpensive.* At the drawbridge, Southport (633–3830). Lobster, clams, and sandwiches to eat on the wharf or take out. Homemade pies. Beer and wine. Open June to Sept.

CAMDEN. Aubergine. *Expensive.* 6 Belmont Ave. (236–8053). Intimate dining in beautifully renovated inn, or light supper in the bar. Classic French cuisine with seasonal local ingredients. Open May to Nov.

Whitehall Inn. *Expensive.* 52 High St. (236–3391). Gracious dining, memorable meals; historic country inn. Open June to Oct.

Lobster Pound. *Moderate-Expensive.* Rte. 1, Lincolnville (789–5550). Pick your own lobster from the pool, then eat it on deck overlooking bay. Shore dinner, sautéed lobster, steak, ham or turkey also. Children's portions. Open May to Oct.

Peter Ott's Tavern & Steakhouse. *Moderate.* 12 Bayview St. (236–4032). Dinner only, offering excellent steaks and seafood. Home-baked bread and homemade desserts. Informal. Children's menu. Open April to Dec.

Waterfront Restaurant. *Moderate.* Bay View St. (236–3747). Situated on a deck on Camden Harbor. Lunch and dinner feature regional seafood entrees, but steaks and sandwiches, too. Cocktails and raw bar. Outdoor dining in summer.

DAMARISCOTTA. Cheechako. *Expensive.* Lewis Point (563–3536). Gracious dining along the Damariscotta River. Fine treatment of regional foods. Try the coho salmon or shore dinner and the lemon chiffon pie. Open Apr. to Oct.

ISLESBORO. Islesboro Inn. *Expensive.* Dark Harbor (734–2221). Marvelous view of the harbor. Extensive, varied menu. Cocktails. Open June to Oct.

ROCKLAND. The Black Pearl. *Moderate-Expensive.* Harbor Park (594–2250). Informal seafood and steak restaurant on the pier. Docking available. Nightly entertainment in the lounge. Open Apr. to Oct.

ROCKPORT. Sail Loft. *Moderate.* At the Public Landing (236–2330). Harbor view restaurant specializing in seafood for luncheon and dinner.

SEARSPORT. Yardarm Restaurant. *Expensive.* Rte. 1 (548–2404). A Victorian sea captain's home. Elegant dining—"Continental" dishes, seafood, homemade soups, bread and pastry. Open mid-May to Oct.
Th' Lobster Shack (Superior Shellfish Inc.) *Inexpensive.* Trundy Rd. (548–2448). Lobster cooked in seawater; a platter of fresh seafood in a truly Maine setting. Open early spring to late fall.

VINALHAVEN. The Haven. *Moderate.* Carver's Harbor (863–4969). Restaurant overlooks the harbor. International cuisine served at dinner. Informal family atmosphere. No liquor license. Open for breakfast and lunch, too.

WISCASSET. Le Garage. *Expensive.* Water St. (882–5409). Dock and dine overlooking the Sheepscot River and the hulks of famous old shipwrecks. Traditional New England fare and Continental specialties using local ingredients. Homebaked breads and pastries.

PENOBSCOT-ACADIA AREA

BANGOR AREA. Murphy's Steakhouse & Butcher Shop. *Moderate-Expensive.* Bar Harbor Rd. (Rte. 1A), Brewer (989–1474). Quality western beef and fresh Maine seafood. Excellent value. Mahogany paneling and paintings by Maine artists lend a club-like atmosphere. Children's menu.
Pilot's Grill. *Moderate.* 1528 Hammond St. (Rte. 2 W.). Bangor (942–6325). Family-owned and operated. Home-style cookery, headed by delectable lobster, steak and roast beef. Well-rounded bill of fare. Bar. Children's portions.
Town Farm Restaurant. *Moderate.* 28 Mill St. Orono (866–5515). International menu, including vegetarian, meat, and seafood specialties. Homemade soups and baked goods.

BAR HARBOR. The Garden of Eden. *Expensive.* 102 Eden St. (288–5750). Dinner served in four cozy dining rooms and in the garden. Fresh seafood, finest cuts of meat, and vegetarian specials.
Lorenzo Creamer's Lobster Pound. *Expensive.* West St., at Golden Anchor Inn (288–5033). On the harbor. Very good food: lobsters, of course, shore dinners, seafood and charbroiled steaks.
Jordan Pond House. *Moderate-Expensive.* Park Loop Road, in Acadia National Park (276–3316). Enjoy a lovely luncheon—or enormous popovers and homemade ice cream on the lawn for afternoon tea. Dinners are served in front of a crackling fire with classical music accompaniment. The view is magnificent during the day, and the mood is memorable in the evening. Open June to Oct.
Acadian Restaurant. *Moderate.* Rte. 3, Hulls Cove near Natl. Park Hdq. (288–5493). Seafood, chops, steaks. Home-baked pies. Enjoy the panoramic water view while dining. Summer only.

Brick Oven Restaurant. *Moderate.* 21 Cottage St. (288–3708). Six cozy, uniquely decorated dining rooms. Varied menu: lobster, seafood, beef, great salads and tasty desserts. Open May to Oct.

Testa's. *Moderate.* 53 Main St. (288–3327). Grill Room and Garden Room. Steaks, shellfish, Italian specialties, inspired green salads; fresh fruit pies. Breakfast, lunch, dinner. Children's portions. Summer only.

BLUE HILL. Firepond. *Expensive.* Main St. (374–2135). Gourmet dining in this historic building "by the old mill stream." Entrées prepared Continental style, with fresh seafood daily. Summer only.

DEER ISLE. Pilgrim's Inn. *Expensive.* Main St. (348–6615). 200-yr.-old antique-filled inn serving international specialties. Fixed price menu. Children half price. Open May–Oct.

ELLSWORTH AREA. Le Domaine. *Expensive.* Rte. 1, Hancock (422–3395). Classic French country cuisine. Superbly prepared entrees and pastry. Open May to Oct.

Surry Inn. *Moderate-Expensive.* Rte. 172, Surry (667–5091). The French cuisine served in the pleasant dining room of this country inn is enhanced by the view over the sweeping lawn to Convention Cove.

Michael's Pineland Diner. *Moderate.* 156 Main St., Ellsworth (667–9257). A vintage (1932) diner refinished in classy mahogany and stainless steel. Soup, sandwiches, more elaborate entrées. Not the usual diner fare—and not the usual diner!

NORTHEAST HARBOR. Asticou Inn. *Expensive-Deluxe.* Rtes. 3 & 98 (276–3344). Attractive dining room overlooks the harbor. Prix fixe dinner. Traditional American dining. Jackets and ties required.

The Mast & Rudder. *Expensive.* Huntington Rd. at Kimball Terrace Inn (276–5857). Perfect view of Northeast Harbor from your table. Specialties include steak, lobster and local fish.

SOUTHWEST HARBOR. Long's Downeast Clambakes. *Moderate.* Rte. 102 (244–5255). Lobster, clams and corn, steamed in rockweed and served outdoors, with chips, lemonade, and blueberry cake. Evenings daily from June–Sept.

WASHINGTON COUNTY

CALAIS. Bottling Plant Restaurant. *Moderate.* 33 North St. (454–7658). Former bottling plant with a copper bar. Mostly steaks and seafood, salad bar.

DENNYSVILLE. Lincoln House. *Expensive.* Rte. 1 [726–3953]. Restored 18th-century colonial, now an inn with two small dining rooms. Limited menu changes nightly. Open Apr.–Dec.

EASTPORT. Cannery Wharf Restaurant. *Moderate.* N. Water St. (853–4800). Former cannery on the wharf. Lobster, Maine seafood, and steaks. View of Campobello Island.

MACHIAS. 5 Water Street. *Moderate.* 5 Water St. (255–4153). Fine food and drink served by candlelight. Varied menu includes steaks and chops as well as vegetarian dishes.

Micmac Farm. *Moderate.* Rte. 92, Machiasport (255–3008). Candlelight dining in restored 1776 farmhouse on Machias River. Continental cuisine. No liquor license; setups provided.

MILBRIDGE. Blueberry Goose Inn. *Moderate.* Main St. (546–7533). Continental cuisine served in New England inn with a view of the ocean.

AROOSTOOK COUNTY

Given the sparsely populated nature of much of Aroostook County, the best bet for dining out is to patronize the restaurants in motels or inns in which you're staying. Most serve breakfast, lunch and dinner. The other alternatives are small, in-town restaurants and grills or quick-lunch stops. Most travelers to this area are campers and are self-sufficient. Sporting camps provide meals.

NORTHERN LAKES & FORESTS AREA

DOVER-FOXCROFT. Brown's Mill Restaurant. *Moderate.* 16 Vaughn St. (564–8614). Upstairs in an old mill on the Piscataquis River. Simple, traditional New England fare, from hot dogs and beans to steamed salmon steak.

JACKMAN-MOOSE RIVER AREA. Sky Lodge. *Moderate-Expensive.* Rte. 201 (668–2171). Pleasant dining room with gorgeous view of Moose River mountain region. Continental and New England-style cuisine. Features steaks and Maine lobsters. Homemade bread and desserts. Bar. Breakfast, lunch, dinner.

GREENVILLE. Lake View Manor Restaurant. *Expensive.* Lily Bay Rd. (695–3810). French "haute-cuisine" in cozy dining room before crackling fire. Wed. through Sun. only.
Greenville Inn. *Moderate.* Norris St. (695–2206). A former lumber baron's home on Moosehead Lake. Changing menu includes Continental-style entrées. Reservations requested.

WESTERN LAKES AREA

BETHEL AREA. Olde Rowley Inn. *Expensive.* Rte. 35, N. Waterford (583–4143). A restored 1790s country inn. Gourmet dining or Sunday brunch.
Bethel Inn. *Moderate-Expensive.* On the Common (824–2175). Superb cuisine served in elegant dining rooms, in the Mill Brook Tavern downstairs, or on the veranda. Sunday brunch.
The Sudbury Inn. *Moderate-Expensive.* Lower Main St. (824–2174). Tasty, home-cooked, full-course meals in the New England tradition. Light, airy dining room with lovely service.
The Boiler Room. *Moderate.* Rte. 26, Bryant Pond (665–2500). The 19th-century powerhouse of a clothespin mill has been converted into a striking restaurant serving excellent German-American food. Open all year (except April and Nov.).
Mother's. *Inexpensive–Moderate.* Upper Main St. (824–2589). Gingerbread house with wood stoves and bookshelves in the dining room. Summer dining on the porch. Soups, salads, and sandwiches at lunch; lobsters and steamers featured in the evening.

BRIDGTON-SEBAGO LAKE AREA. Switzer Stubli Restaurant. *Moderate-Expensive.* In Tarry-A-While Resort on Highland Lake, Bridgton (647–2522). Specialties prepared by Swiss chef; wiener schnitzel, raclette, fondue. Home-baked breads and pastries. Open June to Sept.
Barnhouse Tavern. *Moderate.* Boody's Corner, Jct. Rtes. 302 and 35, N. Windham (892–2221). The rustic barnhouse (1872) has been carefully restored, with lots of exposed wood and windows. Dine in the main dining room or in the loft. Cocktails at the mahogany bar or (weather permitting) on the patio. Steaks and seafoods (lobster in summertime) mainly, with daily luncheon and dinner specials.
The Highlander Restaurant. *Moderate.* Rte. 302, Bridgton (647–8003). Dine overlooking scenic Highland Lake. Complete menu with daily specials. Entertainment weekends.

Pleasant Mountain Inn. *Moderate.* Mountain Rd. (off Rte. 302), W. Bridgton (647–2431). American cooking specializing in steaks, salmon, and shellfish. Sunday buffet.

KINGFIELD. One Stanley Avenue. *Expensive.* 1 Stanley Ave. (265–5541). Continental cuisine includes interesting preparations of veal, chicken, pork and beef, as well as seafood. Delicious desserts.

The Winter's Inn. *Expensive.* Winter's Hill (265–5421). Lovely inn with marvelous mountain views. French cuisine, prepared with care. Reservations required.

The Herbert. *Moderate.* Main St. (265–2000). Traditional American fare served in three dining rooms of hotel restored to its 1913 ambiance.

RANGELEY LAKES AREA. Country Club Inn. *Expensive-Deluxe.* Rtes. 4 and 16 (864–3831). Fine dining, pleasant service, magnificent view of lake and surrounding mountains. Traditional American fare. Nightly specials.

Rangeley Inn. *Expensive.* Main St., Rangeley (864–3341). Fine food served in dining room of turn-of-the-century inn. Live entertainment and dancing.

The Oquossoc House. *Moderate.* Rtes. 17 and 4, Oquossoc (864–3881). Family restaurant, rustic decor. Charcoal-broiled steaks, seafood, daily specials.

CENTRAL LAKES AREA

AUBURN-LEWISTON AREA. No Tomatoes Restaurant. *Moderate.* 36 Court St., Auburn (784–3919). Fine Continental cuisine. Lunches and light dinners available in Garden Lounge.

Steckino's. *Moderate.* 106 Middle St., Lewiston (784–4151). Italian specialties, plus lobster and steak. Children's portions. Bar. Lunch, dinner.

AUGUSTA-HALLOWELL AREA. Hazel Green's. *Moderate.* 349 Water St., Augusta (622–9903). Informal pub. Steak, seafood, fine prime ribs, salad bar.

Mariah's. *Moderate.* 222 Water St., Hallowell (622–4554). Fine cuisine with a French touch. Veal, duckling, steaks and seafood. Luncheon and dinner.

Slate's. *Moderate.* 167 Water St. (622–9575). Attractive, candlelit dining room. Varied menu with a French touch.

WATERVILLE. Silent Woman. *Moderate.* Kennedy Memorial Dr. (873–4522). Renowned restaurant with Colonial atmosphere. Full menu for lunch and dinner, including fresh seafood and roast beef. Children's portions. Bar.

 **NIGHT LIFE AND BARS.** Much of the appeal of Maine to visitors is the no-nonsense ability to commune with nature, either through active (or even rigorous) participation in, say, a long hike or by simply watching the sunrise against the craggy shore. The popular pattern, therefore, is "early to bed, early to rise," with nightlife taking runner-up position.

Many of the large resorts, country inns, and restaurants have cocktail lounges (some with entertainment on weekends), especially in Portland, in the resort towns along the Southern Coast, in the Boothbay area, and in Bar Harbor. For suggestions, refer to the Hotels and Motels and Dining Out sections.

Some other popular nightspots are: Kennebunkport: *The Landing,* Dock Sq.; Portland: *F. Parker Reidy's,* 83 Exchange St.; Boothbay Harbor: *Gepetto's,* On the Byway; *McSeagull's,* Pier 1, *Tugboat Lounge,* On the Waterfront; Camden: *Peter Ott's Tavern,* Bay View St.; Bar Harbor: *The Mary Jane,* Main St.; *The Garden of Eden,* 102 Eden St.; Bryant Pond: *The Boiler Room,* Rte. 26; Bethel: *D. W. McKeen's,* Sunday River Ski Area; Kingfield: *Longfellow's Riverside Pub,* "On the Corner"; *Maxwell's,* Sugarloaf Ski Resort.

In addition, there are two dinner theaters in Boothbay Harbor: *Boothbay Dinner Theater,* McKown Hill (633–6186), is a professional music theater, with contemporary Broadway shows, a backstage deli and bar or full dinner (mid-

June–Sept.); *Carousel Music Theater,* Rte. 27 (633–5297), has live Broadway entertainment, including old favorites, dinner and cocktails.

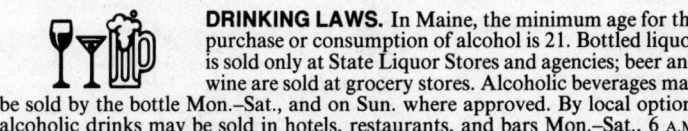 **DRINKING LAWS.** In Maine, the minimum age for the purchase or consumption of alcohol is 21. Bottled liquor is sold only at State Liquor Stores and agencies; beer and wine are sold at grocery stores. Alcoholic beverages may be sold by the bottle Mon.–Sat., and on Sun. where approved. By local option, alcoholic drinks may be sold in hotels, restaurants, and bars Mon.–Sat., 6 A.M.–1 A.M.; Sun. and Memorial Day, noon–1 A.M.

A mandatory deposit on beer and soft drink bottles and cans is returned when empties are returned to stores or redemption centers.

Maine has instituted very strict drunk driving laws, with stiff fines and penalties. Do not drink and drive.

MASSACHUSETTS

A Contrary and Creative Spirit

by
WILLIAM G. SCHELLER

William G. Scheller, a freelance writer, lives in Newbury, Massachusetts. He is the author of Country Walks near New York, More Country Walks near Boston, *and* Train Trips: Exploring America by Rail.

Massachusetts in the late eighties: it is a place of lobster pots and logarithms, crullers and *nouvelle cuisine.* Walk through Brockton or Lynn, and you might wonder if there can be life after the shoe factories leave; drive down Route 128 between Danvers and Dedham—"America's Technology Region," the signs say—and you will see dozens of brand-new buildings where they fashion the slivers of silicon that add, subtract, digest, file, remember and amuse, and drag us, like it or not, into the twenty-first century. Then head up the coast to Salem or Newburyport, and ask yourself if there is any place in America that husbands its history this carefully.

The idea of a "place of contrasts" is surely the oldest cliché in the business of regional image-building, yet it remains singularly apt for Massachusetts. It extends beyond appearances to the temper of the people themselves, a people fiercely adept at arguing with each other and the rest of the nation. The men and women of Massachusetts will demand fine services while slashing local taxes, build missile guidance systems and shout loud and clear for disarmament, elect a conservative governor and then replace him with his liberal predecessor.

Massachusetts is well-educated, proudly inconsistent, and thoroughly contentious. It answers to powerful and quirky traditions, whether rural Yankee, Boston Brahmin, Cambridge counterculture, or immigrant Irish. And it is never quiet for long.

Puritan Origins

Students of Massachusetts' changing economy point out that the state has shifted from an industrial role to one emphasizing "research and development"—that modern activity predicated not only upon manufacturing but deciding what ought to be manufactured. There is a local history of figuring out new ways to do things. Today, this translates into a brisk business in paper and ink, as well as a lively climate for bankers.

But in the broadest sense, Massachusetts has always been involved in research and development. The research was conducted in the contrary and inquisitive spirit of the 17th and 18th centuries, and the development was seen through with the capital and enthusiasm of the 19th and 20th. It is an old place, Massachusetts. To look at the earliest architecture and study the ways of the first settlers, you might say that it is the only part of the country to live through the late Middle Ages. But there was an important difference: the men and women who came to Plymouth and Boston in the early 1600s were the vanguard of a new spirit in the West, as far removed from the world of kingship and fiefdom as we are from the first settlers themselves.

There are two popular postures among those who reflect on these first white New Englanders. Some choose to look on them as a race as benign and noble as Thanksgiving itself; at the opposite extreme, there are those who revile them as hypocrites of the worst sort, ever ready to deny others the rights they had traveled so far to secure. But to learn about colonial and modern Massachusetts it is necessary to see the first immigrants for what they were.

For the most part, the passengers on ships like the *Mayflower* and *Arbella* were the members of a new social order: the middle class. The tremendous surge of mercantile activity which had followed the breakdown of the European feudal order had created this class; but, as always, the political scheme of things had not kept pace with the economic, and many of these merchants, professionals and yeoman farmers felt socially disenfranchised in a system which made few allowances for a middle.

This disillusioned class embraced a religion which was morally conservative yet politically radical. The Puritans' reaction to the lax, quasi-Romanized Anglican establishment of their day was largely a reaction against the king and aristocracy, who equated communion with loyalty to the political status quo. Reformers within the Reformation, these middle-class rebels practiced their fundamentalist creed in individual congregations beholden to no archbishop in Canterbury or pope in Rome. For a while, their triumph in England was total, with the head of Charles I the price paid by the old order for its intransigence. But even before this temporary victory had been won, the most zealous and impatient of the Puritans had left for Massachusetts, where neither political nor religious hierarchies could impede their establishment of a "New Canaan," whose chosen people were themselves, and whose promised land was the vast American continent.

The details of the colony's history during the 17th century and in the years preceding the Revolution illustrate the way in which the Puritans' view of themselves and the world shaped immediate events. The Mayflower Compact, drawn up by the Pilgrims as their ship lay at anchor in Plymouth harbor in 1620, respected the will of the majority as the foundation of governmental authority. This agreement was a profound departure from the way men had heretofore formed societies. Instead of consenting to surrender their power to a ruler in return for his governance—thus making the ruler the source of power—they combined by mutual consent into a "civil Body Politick" whose cement was the promise, "in the Presence of God and one another," to "enact, constitute, and frame" the laws and apparatus of government—thus retaining sovereignty in the people. It took more than 150 years of political and social evolution before the divorce from kingship could become final and the relationship with democracy consummated.

The foothold at Plymouth led to further Puritan immigration that quickly flowered into a host of new, experimental communities. Seeds of independence were planted in the charter creating the Massachusetts Bay Colony, organized in 1628 as the New England Company by one of the several Puritan groups granted a land patent for New England settlements. The charter gave them control of a grant of land between the Charles and Merrimack rivers, extending indefinitely inland or westward to "the South Sea." They settled in Salem under John Endicott, but others soon gained control of the young organization, obtaining a royal charter officially designating it as the Governor and Company of the Massachusetts Bay in New England.

These Puritan leaders emphasized religious and political considerations over trade. One group, under the leadership of John Winthrop, met at Cambridge University, agreeing to go to New England on the key condition that the government and charter be entrusted solely to the settlers. They came, establishing Boston and many of the surrounding communities and laying the basis for religious, political and economic patterns that were to follow. The new charter, by setting the precedent for removal of royal control, foreshadowed the coming erosion of England's hold. At the same time, the forms of colonial government the charter advanced, arising from new conditions, suggested the governmental forms that would emerge in the American republic.

The Massachusetts legislature today is still called the General Court, because under that original charter the colony was to be administered not by a royal governor or agents of Parliament, but by two general courts. One was to be comprised of freemen (stockholders in the company), who met quarterly; they selected a governor, deputy governor and 18 aides, who made up the other general court, serving as the administrative power over the colony.

New Homeland

Within four years, 10,000 Puritans had settled here. By the end of the century, 80,000 settlers had arrived. There were 50,000 more in Connecticut, Rhode Island, and New Hampshire, three colonies which to some degree arose out of discontent with Bay Colony rule, just as the Bay Colony was a consequence of discontent with English rule.

Despite the beginnings of democratic forms, the premises of independence, and the adoption of most of the safeguards of English law that later became the basis of the Bill of Rights, the Puritan clergymen created a theocracy as intolerant as the Anglican society from which they had fled. It is not difficult to understand how this dictatorship of the theologically sophisticated took hold. Although universal education was emphasized a great deal more in America than it had been in Europe, only a handful of the New England populace could hope to attend Harvard for a thorough grounding in Hebrew, Latin and scriptural interpretation. Those who did assumed leadership, and were alarmed at the prospect of sharing or losing it. Add to this the zeal which traditional-minded Puritans felt for the righteousness of their experiment and the absolute necessity of its success, and the inflexibility of the elders, though no more commendable, appears much more plausible.

The stage had been set for another series of battles between authoritarianism and righteous dissent. The Reverend Thomas Hooker, uncomfortable under the spiritual pressures of the Puritan fathers, left to join the founders of Connecticut. Others, like Anne Hutchinson, the first of many Massachusetts women to play leading roles in the struggle for human rights, and her brother-in-law John Wheelwright, were banished for their defiance of Puritan orthodoxy. She removed to the region just north of Dutch New Amsterdam, where she and her followers were killed by Indians; he went north to found Exeter, New Hampshire. How fierce was the absolutism of the Puritan theocracy is demonstrated by the case of Quaker Mary Dyer, a supporter of Anne Hutchinson. Mrs. Dyer, twice banished from Boston for her activities as a Quaker, returned to test the validity of the law that repressed these ardent believers in equality. She was hanged in 1660 for her nonconformity; her statue now stands before the State House in Boston.

The most shocking instance of the misuse of power among the ruling elite, however, grew out of the panic over witches in the 1690's. In the peak year of 1692, colonial leaders put to death as witches fourteen women and six men.

It was Roger Williams, banished from the Bay Colony in 1685 for heresy, who saw that safety for believers resided not in state-enforced religion but in a state that insured freedom for all religions. The challenge to orthodoxy in his arguments for religious freedom and the separation of church and state are still fresh today. He challenged the theocracy's claims by maintaining it was not the king who held true title to the land but the Indians. Moreover, he held one could not argue with absolute surety that Indian religions were not as acceptable to God as Christianity or any other faith.

Repression, Relaxation, and Enlightenment

The fortunes of the Bay Colony waxed and waned in the early years, often affected by events in Europe. The colony was delighted by the Puritans' victorious revolution in England, but after the restoration of Charles II, the euphoria passed and with it went the original charter, revoked in 1684 and replaced in 1686 by the person of Sir Edmund Andros as royal governor of all New England. This was just what the colonists had managed to avoid from the beginning. James II, fearing encirclement of British holdings by the French, combined all the northern colonies into a dominion under Andros, whose actions (taxes without representation, excessive payments to the crown, etc.) set a precedent for the violation of local and individual rights which, nearly a hundred years later, would spark the Revolution.

When James II was deposed and William and Mary assumed the throne in the "Glorious Revolution" of 1688, the aroused people of Boston were quick to stage a revolt of their own, tossing the hated Andros into jail. And thanks to the efforts of Increase Mather, they also got a new charter that made administrative reforms, ended church membership as a requirement for voting, and united the Bay Colony with Plymouth and Maine. But by providing for a royal governor, the charter reset the time bomb that was to go off a half-century later after William and Mary's amity gave way to royal enmity.

Now it is time to examine the second great influence on the character of Massachusetts and, subsequently, that of the United States—the intellectual movement known as the Enlightenment, which incorporated the scientific revolution. The Enlightenment drew its sustenance from a renewed interest in the liberal learning of the classical world, as well as from the revived respect for man's potential, which had begun in the Renaissance, but its effects, particularly upon the New World, concern us here more than its origins. The Enlightenment brought a new secular spirit, contrary to that which motivated Puritan divine Jonathan Edwards when he called men "sinners in the hands of an angry God." The spirit of scientific inquiry naturally followed in this age in which reason was respected most among all man's attributes, and it was Massachusetts which produced one of America's great scientists, and one of the towering figures of the Age of Reason—a Boston printer's apprentice named Benjamin Franklin. Franklin's own precocious embracing of the rationalist spirit somewhat preceded that of other Bostonians. Discussing the reasons for leaving Boston in his *Autobiography,* he writes

. . . and further . . . my indiscreet disputations about religion began to make me pointed at with horror by good people as an infidel or atheist.

But the hold of religion on the "good people" grew weaker, and the calls of science and commerce stronger. Education, of course, had always been a Puritan imperative. Schools were established in Boston in 1636 and in Salem in 1639. In 1642, an edict of the General Court made the selectmen of each town responsible for training all boys whose parents could not afford their schooling. By 1647, towns of 50 or more were required to establish elementary schools and towns of 100 or more to set up grammar schools similar to those in England. This was the first time anywhere that education of the young was established as a public responsibility. From this grew our present concept of free public education—bolstered over the years by such Massachusetts schoolmen as Horace Mann—which ranks with the development of democracy itself among New England's enduring gifts to America.

Harvard University, established in 1636, has been a leader in higher education ever since. Other colleges followed, emphasizing religion at first, then expanding to become centers of all learning. Just a partial listing of the more than eighty Massachusetts institutions of higher learning is impressive: Massachusetts Institute of Technology, Tufts, Brandeis, Radcliffe, Boston University, Wellesley, Williams, Mount Holyoke, Amherst, Smith, Clark, Simmons, Northeastern, Holy Cross,

Boston College, and the University of Massachusetts. Education and research are among the leading enterprises of modern Massachusetts.

In the realm of commercial enterprise, the new secular atmosphere went hand in hand with Yankee acquisitiveness. Although the early Puritans had a distaste for ostentation and had even penalized tradesmen suspected of earning too great a profit, there had always been a belief that the Lord might demonstrate approval of one of his "elect" by the material success he allowed him to enjoy in life. The religious relaxation, and the removal of the early hardships, allowed the Yankees to seek wealth and enjoy it. Thanks to the abundance of good wood and good harbors, the New Englanders soon became shipbuilders and leading sea traders. A profitable triangular trade emerged. Sugar and molasses were brought from the West Indies in return for lumber, codfish, and livestock; the molasses was made into rum and sent to Africa in return for slaves who were sold in the Indies for gold used to buy English luxuries. By 1740, Boston was the largest town in the colonies, while places like Salem, Newburyport, Marblehead and Nantucket shared in the prosperity as shipping and whaling centers.

The final legacy of the Enlightenment was the dissemination of bold new political ideas throughout Europe and in America. Men were beginning to question the divine right of kings, and writers such as Rousseau went so far as to suggest that man was noblest in his natural state, unfettered by the conventions of society. The revolutionary spirit reached its zenith in France in 1789, although it quickly degenerated there into a climate of vicious recrimination. Democratic ideals were assimilated more cautiously in New England, where secession from the crown was first looked upon as a last resort by all but the most fervent revolutionaries. But England eventually pushed the colonies over the brink.

More and more, the crown sought to reimpose the authority it had ceded to the colonists—and more and more the colonists resisted. England imposed a long series of restrictions on colonial trade. First came the Acts of Trade and Navigation that, among other things, required colonists to ship products from America only to England or her colonies and to buy goods only through English sources. The reaction was the great Massachusetts smuggling era that flourished until the end of the French and Indian Wars in 1763.

As England turned the screws of control ever harder—the Stamp Act of 1765, the Townsend Acts of '67, the Tea Act of '73, the Intolerable Acts of '74—the voices and actions of the American patriots grew louder and more radical. That consummate technician of revolutionary propaganda, Samuel Adams, joined with the brilliant lawyer James Otis and the practical, influential, and popular merchant, John Hancock ("The Prince of Smugglers") to agitate among the colonists and exploit the king's intemperate efforts at coercion.

A clash of arms became inevitable. Lexington, Concord and Bunker Hill gave rise to the rallying cries of revolution. Militiamen hurried from all over the thirteen colonies to join General Washington, who took command in Massachusetts of the Continental Army, the likes of which the world had never seen before. Heretofore, wars were fought between hosts of professionals; now, free men voluntarily formed themselves into battalions to march against the regulars.

The British holed up in Boston, but left in 1776, never to return. The war that began in the Bay State and in which many of its people fought on all levels resulted in the inevitable separation.

It was fitting that this state of so many great beginnings should also have been the first to elect a convention to draft a constitution to be ratified by the people after intensive discussion in town meetings. This constitution was a departure from the other colonies' systems in that it allowed for the checks and balances provided by a bicameral legislature, a well-defined executive and a strong judiciary. (John Adams, a moving force behind the new system, was the first of four presidents from Massachusetts. The others: his son, John Quincy Adams, Calvin Coolidge—also claimed by Vermont—and John F. Kennedy.) Once more, the Commonwealth had set an example for the growing nation. Although much amended, this constitution is still operative.

Stress and Prosperity in the Federal Period

The period immediately after the Revolution was one of severe growing pains. Shay's Rebellion, an uprising of farmers outraged over mortgage foreclosures and high taxes, was symptomatic of the difficulties facing the young republic as it groped its way toward nationhood. The soaring growth of commerce and industry aided in the state's stabilization. Yankee traders, sailing their New England-made ships, found their way around Cape Horn to China to open lucrative routes that would boost the economies of state and nation. By 1812, Salem was a key shipping port and Boston accounted for a third of all the sea trade in the United States.

The prosperity of those times is evident in the buildings of Charles Bulfinch and Samuel McIntire. Many of Bulfinch's structures are long gone, but among those remaining are the statehouse in Boston (1799), University Hall at Harvard (1815), Massachusetts General Hospital (1820), and the three Harrison Gray Otis houses (1796–1804). From 1818 to 1830, Bulfinch completed the capitol at Washington, creating the style that has influenced state capitols ever since. Many of McIntire's houses still stand in Salem. Designed for the affluent sea traders, they are noted less for their facades than for their interiors, featuring magnificently carved cornices, mantelpieces, and other examples of fine wood sculpture.

Massachusetts nurtured many architectural innovators. Their work can be seen today—from the remaining seventeenth-century salt boxes and Cape Codders built by anonymous craftsmen to the glass, steel and concrete structures of Walter Gropius, longtime chairman of Harvard's architecture department, and the geodesic and tensegrity creations of Buckminster Fuller, born in Milton.

Whether it was a McIntire mansion in Salem or a frontier barn, buildings were made out of New England gold—wood. Houses and ships, spoons and plates, barrels for fuel and beverages, all grew on trees. Wood kept farmers, trappers and townspeople warm through the severe winters; it fueled the locomotives that came later; and it was used to obtain salt to preserve cod and other fish vital to the state's economy. It took one and a half cords of wood to get a bushel of salt from 400 gallons of sea water. During one year in the late eighteenth century, 100,000 cords of wood were burned to produce 70,000 bushels of salt for New England's fishing industry. And even more quantities of wood were consumed in such processes as glassmaking, distilling turpentine, firing brick kilns and smelting metals. Massachusetts was largely forested when the Pilgrims came. There were some natural open spaces, as well as fields cleared by the Indians for crops. The open area quickly increased, however, as wood was harvested in such quantities. Vast sections of coastal pine forest as well as thousands of acres of western upland woods were denuded.

Trees have reclaimed much territory in Massachusetts; in fact, there are far more trees in the state now than before the Civil War. But the reforesting is recent enough so that it is not unusual to hear an older Berkshire resident a refer to a thickly wooded tract as "the old west meadow."

The Commercial Revolution

After the revolution, Massachusetts politics became strongly Federalist. The Federalists favored amicable relations with Britain. Jefferson's embargo and the War of 1812 were so unpopular that rumblings of secession were heard at the Hartford Convention of 1814–15. But the restrictions on trade turned out to be a boon for the Yankee businessmen, and the dissidents who so vehemently opposed the administration and the war could not prevail over the majority that favored the union.

Out of the war with England thus emerged the golden age of New England trade and industry. It was a time of phenomenal indusrial expansion. The great 19th-century industrial revolution exploded in the new as well as the old world, with Massachusetts contributing much in research, technology and manufacturing. The English had got off to an early start, jealously guarding the secrets of their new manufacturing methods. But despite rigid controls, enterprising young men persisted in their piracy. Harvard-educated Francis Cabot Lowell (1775–1817), for example, studied the British machines for making textiles and not only reconstructed them from memory, but improved the whole process of turning raw cotton into cloth. He was among those who led the way in turning Massachusetts into the nation's leading textile center, a role the Bay State played until the 1920's when southern competition, through reliance on cheap labor and new synthetics, forced the closing of mills throughout New England. The Massachusetts textile industry is no longer pre-eminent, but it has revived somewhat and now employs nearly 30,000 people in raw manufacturing and some 40,000 others in the production of apparel and finished goods.

Today, high technology has captured the imaginations of those concerned with the state's economic development. In the years immediately following the Second World War, Edwin Land pioneered with his Polaroid Corporation, still headquartered in Cambridge where the retired Dr. Land has built a private research laboratory for the pursuit of pure science. Then came the sixties and the growth of Wang Laboratories, Digital Equipment Corporation, Raytheon, and a host of other high-tech firms. Today Boston's suburbs rival California's silicon valley in the manufacture of information-processing equipment, a pursuit that has helped make Massachusetts's unemployment figures the lowest of any state in the Union.

Despite the ups and downs of commodities ranging from ax heads to minicomputers, fishing has always played a role in the Bay State's economic life. The whale, of course, is safe now from New Bedford harpooneers. But haddock and cod still arrive at piers along the coast each morning, and New Bedford is now a leading port for sea scallops. Massachusetts fishermen enthusiastically greeted the United States' recent 200-mile fishing limit, which reduces the toll taken by foreign fleets. A rivalry with Canada continues, however, with rights on rich Georges Bank the main point of contention.

Influx of Immigrants

The opening of the west in the 19th century drew people off the Massachusetts farms; others went into factories where they were soon joined by new immigrants. Oppressed by British rule like the Pilgrims before them, the Irish formed a large part of the influx. The mid-19th-century potato famine drove tens of thousands of Irish immigrants to Boston. Here, too, they were exploited and discriminated against, but just as the Pilgrims had prevailed over the hardships imposed by nature and man, so did the Irish prevail over hard conditions and Yankee antipathies. They came to terms with the place and the people to play leading roles not only in Massachusetts, but throughout the nation. The Irish were followed by French Canadians, Italians, Poles, Portuguese, and others, all seeking new ways of life and making contributions that generated further progress.

But progress brought its own counterpoint of new demands and conflicts. Not everyone praised the machine. As more and more men and women joined the assembly lines in factories and mills, where they were known reductively as "hands," conditions there spawned waves of strikes foreshadowing the building of the modern labor movement. On the cultural front, themes of individualism were sounded in the influential essays of Emerson, while Thoreau counseled resistance to the Mexican War in "Civil Disobedience." Other literary figures, less involved in the social struggles of the day but equally repelled by the emerging industrialism, sought alternative societies in organizations such as Brook Farm at West Roxbury. This was a group experiment in "plain living and high thinking" based on the principles of Charles Fourier, the French utopian socialist whose ideas continue to echo in modern communal ventures.

The most successful of those who turned away from the world, at least in the short run, were the Shakers. Like the Pilgrims who had so efficiently combined religion with craftsmanship, husbandry, and other worldly talents, the Shakers mixed religious fervor with remarkable material accomplishments in the crafting of everything from machinery to medicine and furniture. The failure of Shaker societies to persist past the first generation is most directly attributable to their practice of celibacy.

One of the best outdoor museums in the country is the Shaker Village in Hancock, site of one of the most important Shaker settlements. Lovingly restored through the initiative of Mrs. Laurence Miller, wife of the publisher of the *Berkshire Eagle,* this is a must stop for families touring western Massachusetts. The *Eagle,* by the way, runs a useful occasional supplement called *Up Country,* a magazine and calendar of regional events.

The spirit of reform ran deep in 19th-century Massachusetts. This state, whose ships and mills helped support slavery, also produced such leading abolitionists as William Lloyd Garrison, Wendell Phillips, and John Greenleaf Whittier.

This state that hanged women and girls as witches also produced women who played leading roles in the struggles for women's recognition and emancipation. At first there were women like Anne Hutchinson and Mary Dyer. Anne Bradstreet, the colonies' first woman poet, published *The Tenth Muse* in 1650. Later, there were women's suffrage leader Susan B. Anthony, abolitionist Lydia Maria Child, educator Mary Lyon, reformer Mary Livermore, women's rights leader Lucy Stone, Red Cross organizer Clara Barton, and the controversial writer and critic Margaret Fuller.

New Faces—Same Traditions

The issues at stake in Massachusetts today, and the individuals who plead the arguments they involve, would be only partly recognizable to the builders of the old colony. A Lexington yeoman of the 18th century might well grasp the question of how much a person should be taxed, and how much government he should receive in return. But he could think only of the fishes in the sea, and not of the oil that lies beneath its floor. The town meetings that survive to this day are equipped to deal with matters of immediate local concern, but much of the world and its problems have run away from them. Still, they provide a useful forum, as can be seen in local votes on issues such as the nuclear freeze.

Still, the same old passions enliven debates large and small. And it is this very love of argument that has made Massachusetts such an interesting place for so many years. An atmosphere charged by the clash of ideas is a healthy one for thinking men and women. Consider even this partial list of the state's notables: Horatio Alger, Richard Henry Dana, Emily Dickinson, Nathaniel Hawthorne, Ralph Waldo Emerson, Henry David Thoreau, Bronson and Louisa May Alcott, James Russell Lowell, Henry Wadsworth Longfellow, John Greenleaf Whittier, the Oliver Wendell Holmeses, John Singer Sargent, Winslow Homer, James McNeill Whistler, Henry Adams, Francis Parkman, William H. Prescott, William and Henry James, Julia Ward Howe, Louis Agassiz, Samuel Eliot Morison, Bernard DeVoto, George Santayana, John Dos Passos, Amy Lowell, T.S. Eliot, Conrad Aiken, Van Wyck Brooks, Archibald MacLeish, Jack Kerouac, Fannie Farmer, the Arthur Schlesingers, Theodore White, John P. Marquand, Bette Davis, Leonard Bernstein, George Lyman Kittredge, Julia Child, and Norman Rockwell.

The physical face of Massachusetts has changed with the years. Parts of cities recently thought obsolete are being refurbished for new uses. The suburbs, which marched from Boston to the drawn lines of Routes 128 and 495 like children on a dare, grow more temperately now as energy and resource limitations couple with wiser land use decisions to brake the boom of the sixties. With the help of new state legislation that makes sale and subdivision of tilled land less attractive, family farming makes a last-ditch stand in a state that must import over 80 percent of its produce. The lovely and varied terrain, along with the more judicious changes man has worked on it during his long stay here, continues to attract travelers. And the people are still hard at work on their newest occupation and their oldest: research and development.

EXPLORING BOSTON

Although modern Boston sprawls far to the north and south of its downtown section, the area containing the most historical and architectural points of interest is quite compact. All of these sites are accessible either by foot or by using the convenient public transit. The old city (from the Common to the harbor wharves) was laid out hundreds of years before the coming of the automobile, and its streets still wind and twist like the cowpaths they once were. For this reason, there is no advantage whatever to be derived from touring the downtown, Beacon Hill, or North End sections by auto. Traffic is chaotic and parking nearly impossible. You will enjoy Boston much more if the car is left at your hotel or in a garage. With this in mind, let's begin a walking tour of Boston by following the Freedom Trail, a mile-and-a-half route which leads through the heart of the historic old city linking 16 famous colonial, revolutionary and historic sites. As you follow the trail, which is marked by a red line, you will walk not only into the past of Boston, but into some of the most exciting chapters in the early history of the United States.

The walk begins at the Freedom Trail Information Center located on Boston Common, about 100 feet from the Park Street Massachusetts Bay Transportation Authority (MBTA) Station. There you can obtain a booklet with descriptions of the famous historic sites and a map of the Trail, as well as other information and literature about things to do and see in Boston. The commentary that follows is designed to supplement the MBTA guidebook, though it can be used alone.

From the Station the Trail leads through Boston Common up the base of Beacon Hill to the gold-domed "new" State House. The oldest public park in the country, the Common was originally the town cow pasture. Along with the Public Garden, located west of the Common across Charles Street, it is a pleasant place for a stroll and provides a refreshing island of green in the center of the city. The Common is suitable for active recreation; the Public Garden, which is actually the nations's oldest botanical park, should be treated a little more gently. Enjoy its statuary, flowers, specimen trees, and—in summer—swan boat rides on the lagoon; but try to remain on the paved walkways.

Along with the far newer Prudential and Hancock Towers, the gold dome of the "new" State House is one of the landmarks of the Boston skyline. The central domed section, built in 1795 of red brick (actually painted yellow through much of the 1800s!) with a classical portico of white Corinthian columns, was designed by Charles Bulfinch and is considered his finest work. While the graceful dignity of the original building was not reflected in the massive gray marble wings added on either side in 1918, they are plain enough to provide a contrasting frame to the beautiful Bulfinch section. The familiar shining dome was originally built of wood and then covered with copper by Paul Revere to protect it from the weather. It was not gilded until 1861. The dome was painted grey during World War II to keep it from presenting a shining nighttime target in the event of enemy bombing raids.

Free guided tours of its interior depart from Doric Hall, inside the main entrance, and are well worth taking. Points of interest include: the Hall of Flags; the House of Representatives Chamber, built in 1895, with its Sacred Cod hanging over the public gallery to commemorate the importance of the codfish industry to the colonial settlers; the classical Senate Chamber, part of the original Bulfinch building and located directly beneath the Dome; and the Archives museum, containing important historical documents such as Bradford's *History of Plimoth Plantation,* the original plates and engravings by Paul Revere of the Boston Massacre and the landing of the British troops, and the Massachusetts Bay Company Charter.

From the State House, the Trail proceeds along Park Street down Beacon Hill to the Park Street Church, the scene of many events of note in the nineteenth century. Built in 1809 and designed by Peter Banner, its architecture reflects an earlier style than the classic State House and its contemporaries. The lovely spire, in particular, was influenced by the work of English architect Sir Christopher Wren. The American Temperance Society was founded in the church in 1824, and here, five years later, on July 4, 1829, William Lloyd Garrison gave his first public speech in Boston against slavery. The church, founded by a Trinitarian congregation in protest against the Unitarian movement, declined toward the end of the 19th century, but was revived in 1905 and continues with an active membership.

Pre-Revolutionary Problems

Continuing north along Tremont Street, you come to the Old Granary Burying Ground, which contains the graves of many famous Bostonians, including John Hancock, Robert Treat Paine, and Samuel Adams, all signers of the Declaration of Independence; Paul Revere and Peter Faneuil; the parents of Benjamin Franklin; nine early governors of Massachusetts; and the victims of the Boston Massacre, five members of an angry mob fired upon by Redcoat sentries on March 5, 1770. The British regretted the incident and found two of their soldiers guilty of manslaughter, but Samuel Adams and Paul Revere utilized the event for revolutionary propaganda in the form of an inflammatory Revere engraving of the massacre.

At the corner of Tremont and School streets, turn right down the hill to historic King's Chapel, Boston's first Episcopal Church. The congregation was formed in 1688, but the present structure was not built until 1749. Peter Harrison, who designed it, was trained in the school of Wren but produced an original and distinctive monument. The austere Quincy granite building was intended to support a steeple, which was never built due to lack of funds. The present chapel's severity would probably have been softened by the addition of the proposed steeple. The beautiful Colonial interior, harmonious and simple in design, yet rich and warm with its high enclosed pews upholstered in red damask, is one of the finest in New England. The graceful carved pulpit and the governor's pew, designed originally for the royal governors, are of particular interest.

King's Chapel is as interesting historically as it is architecturally. Founded by the Crown to serve British soldiers stationed in Boston and supported financially by William and Mary and King George III, it was resented by Puritan anti-royalist Boston, which dubbed it "Stone Chapel." Then in 1789, after most of its royalist congregation had fled from the Revolution to Great Britain or Nova Scotia, King's Chapel became the first avowedly Unitarian church in the United States.

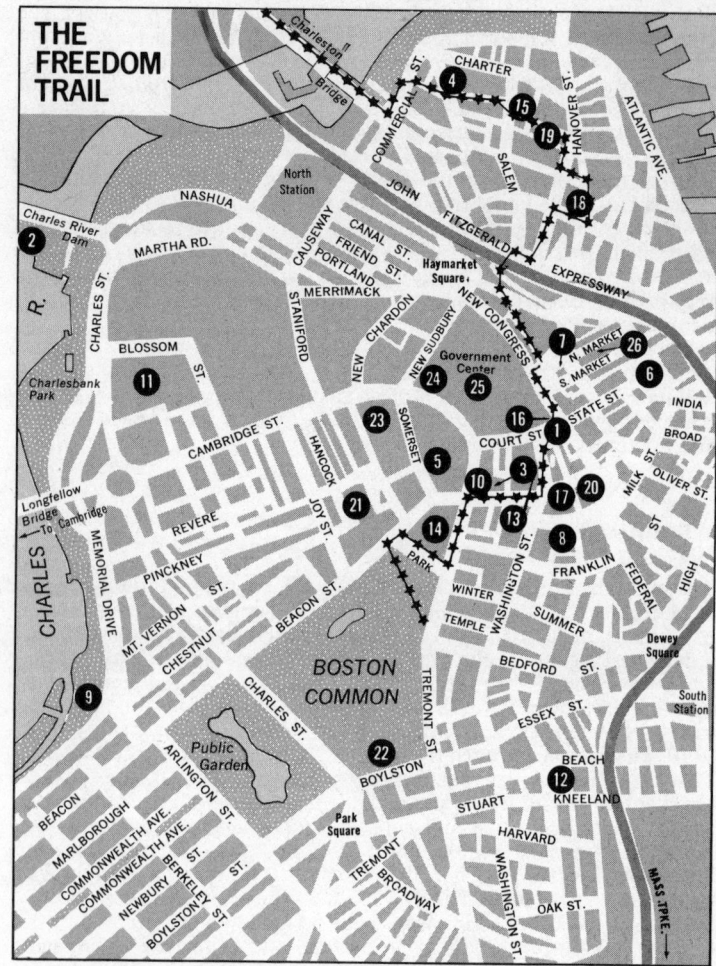

THE
FREEDOM
TRAIL

Points of Interest

1) Boston Massacre Site
2) Boston Museum of Science
3) Old City Hall
4) Copp's Hill Burying Ground
5) Court House
6) Custom House
7) Faneuil Hall
8) Franklin's Birthplace Site
9) Hatch Memorial Concert Shell
10) King's Chapel
11) Massachusetts General Hospital
12) Tufts New England Medical Center
13) Old Corner Book Store
14) Park Street Church and Old Granary Burying Ground
15) Old North Church (originally Christ Church)
16) Old State House
17) Old South Meeting House
18) Paul Revere's House
19) Paul Revere Statue
20) Post Office
21) State House
22) Central Burying Ground
23) State Office Building
24) John F. Kennedy Federal Building
25) New City Hall
26) Quincy Market

The Burying Ground located behind King's Chapel, the oldest in Boston, contains the tombs of several of Massachusetts' governors and other notables. As you stroll through it, notice the carvings on the headstones, primitive and sometimes amusing, but powerfully direct with their winged death's heads. Near the church entrance, a stone bearing a French inscription commemorates a sad event of the Revolution. In 1788, the first contingent of French regulars arrived in Boston to help the colonists in their war effort. The Frenchmen set up their own bakery using imported stores of wheat, a commodity then extremely scarce in Boston. When the townspeople were told they could not buy the bread (a situation made worse by the language barrier), a riot ensued and a young French officer, the Chevalier de Saint-Sauveur, was killed. He was buried in the King's Chapel vault, and, according to Esther Forbes in her book *Paul Revere and the World He Lived In,* his funeral was probably the occasion of the first Catholic Mass said in Boston.

The Freedom Trail continues down School Street past the old city hall, built on the original site of the Boston Public Latin School (1635), the first public school in the country and the alma mater of many famous Americans. The school is presently located on Avenue Louis Pasteur, off the Fenway.

One of the school's best-known alumni is Benjamin Franklin, whose statue, sculpted by Richard S. Greenough in 1856, stands on the lawn of city hall.

On the left, where School Street meets Washington Street, is the Old Corner Bookstore, one of the oldest brick buildings in Boston. Built around 1718, the building was first used as an apothecary's and then in 1829 as a bookstore. Under the ownership of William D. Ticknor and James T. Fields, who published some of America's greatest writers, it became Boston's pre-eminent literary salon and center of the New England Renaissance. The roster of American writers who met there during the mid-19th century is truly extraordinary: Emerson, Hawthorne, Longfellow, Holmes, Harriet Beecher Stowe, Whittier and Julia Ward Howe. Today the building is maintained by the Boston *Globe,* which restored it in 1960 and operates it as the Globe Corner Bookstore. The store has a fine selection of books about New England and by New Englanders.

Convention of Liberty

Across Washington Street and slightly to the right from in front of the bookstore you will see the Old South Meeting House (1729) with its plain brick exterior and graceful wooden steeple. Along with Faneuil Hall, the meeting house was the center for the impassioned series of anti-British speeches and gatherings that culminated in the American Revolution. The best-known of these took place on the night of Dec. 16, 1773, when Samuel Adams and the radical Sons of Liberty summoned a convention that set off the Boston Tea Party. After the British governor refused the convention's demand that British tea be shipped back to England, a mob of disguised radicals emptied the precious tea into the Boston harbor to protest British taxation and trade practices. The British were so irritated that they blockaded Boston harbor and passed punitive measures known as the Coercive or Intolerable Acts. The colonists in turn were angered at what they considered an overreaction to a prank, and the confrontation that Sam Adams and the other radical leaders wanted was well on its way.

During the Revolution, the British tore out the pews of Old South and used the space to practice equestrian maneuvers. It was restored in the 19th century and now holds a collection of Revolutionary relics. It is still available to the public as a meeting house.

From the Old South Meeting House, the Freedom Trail winds through Boston's financial district to the old State House, another building rich in Revolutionary history. Built in 1713 on the site of the Boston Town House, it served as seat of government for the royal governors and was the place where the British proclaimed the acts that so angered Boston. After the Revolution, it became the seat of the Commonwealth of Massachusetts until the completion of the new State House. The building has been restored and now houses a collection of local and maritime historical artifacts maintained by the Bostonian Society. The colorful lion and unicorn adorning the building's front cornices were once the symbols of British imperial power. The original figures were pulled down during the Revolution. The old State House looks out over the site of the Boston Massacre, marked by a circle of cobblestones in the street.

After passing Government Center, the trail turns right into Dock Square and leads to Faneuil Hall, which stands in the center of this open area. Faneuil Hall is named after Peter Faneuil (generally pronounced "Fan'l" or "Fan-yuel"), a wealthy Boston merchant who gave the building to the city in 1742 to be used as a market and a town hall. It was nearly destroyed by fire in 1761 but was soon rebuilt. The present third story, galleries, and Doric columns were designed by Bulfinch and added in 1805. Atop the building is a unique grasshopper weathervane; there are several stories to account for this unusual decoration. One version merely states the grasshopper was an old agricultural symbol, making it a fitting figurehead for the market. But Hector Campbell, late superintendent of the artillery museum located on the top floor, preferred another explanation. According to his account, a group of children were chasing grasshoppers in a field outside London in 1519 when they found an abandoned baby lying in the grass. They took the infant to a nearby church, where he was sheltered. The child grew to become Sir Thomas Gresham, financial advisor to Queen Elizabeth and founder of the Royal Exchange of London. In gratitude, Sir Thomas had a grasshopper placed on the Exchange Building.

Two centuries later, Peter Faneuil became a member of the exchange. He was fascinated by both the shape of the building's weathervane and the accompanying legend. When he gave Faneuil Hall to the Town of Boston, he had a large grasshopper placed above the cupola.

During the War of 1812 the grasshopper became the secret password to the port. Strangers who did not identify it as the symbol of Boston were questioned as spies.

The second floor of Faneuil Hall has always been a free meeting hall, opened whenever a sufficient number of citizens want to gather there to discuss and debate. And so, starting in 1763, it became the prime site for the stirring Boston town meetings where Sam Adams and James Otis proclaimed the rights of the colonists. Although new shops dominate the restored first floor of Faneuil Hall, the great balconied room above is still used as a forum for discussion, and is available to any legitimate citizens' group upon petition.

Here begins the large market complex which spreads around Dock Square, so named because it was originally Boston's waterfront, before landfill projects moved the shoreline back beyond the ramps of the Fitzgerald Expressway. You may wish to leave the trail for a look at this colorful, bustling area, especially on a Friday or Saturday when the outdoor as well as indoor markets of Haymarket Square are open. Stalls with carefully arranged pyramids of fruits and vegetables extend along two narrow parallel rows which are crowded with shoppers and noisy with vendors' cries.

The grasshopper atop Faneuil Hall has today become the symbol of the Faneuil Hall Marketplace, one of the most ambitious building "recycling" projects yet undertaken on the East Coast. More a restoration than a recycling, the marketplace has brought a thriving retail trade back to the three long, arcade-like buildings behind Faneuil Hall. These were built in the early-19th century by Mayor Josiah Quincy, and have since been known as Quincy Market. For many years the long hallways of the market were lined with the displays of butchers and produce dealers. After a long period of decline, a combination of city and private interests restored the market to its original bustle and color. At the entrance, plants and flowers are sold in glass greenhouses. The main building, with its central dome and rotunda, is home to an appealing array of specialty food and housewares shops, craft stalls, exotic snack bars and fine restaurants. The north and south market buildings house clothing shops, offices, and still more restaurants.

Past the Marketplace, in the direction of the harbor, lies a new park and lattice-canopied walkway. To your left are newly redeveloped Lewis and Constitution wharves, with their chic shops and cafes. To the right rises the United States Custom House, originally built in the Greek Revival style of its neighbors, but transformed in 1915 into Boston's first skyscraper. A balcony on the top provides a fine panorama of the harbor and the city.

Italian Influence

The Freedom Trail passes around Haymarket Square and under the Fitzgerald Expressway to emerge in Boston's North End, once the home of wealthy sea captains and Revolutionary patriots and now a miniature Italy, abounding with bakeries, Italian groceries and restaurants. You will often hear Italian being spoken in this neighborhood. During the summer, the feasts of patron saints are celebrated in the streets of the North End. There are bands, processions and sidewalk stands dispensing everything from calamari (fried squid) to manicotti (cheese-stuffed pasta).

The Freedom Trail heads up Hanover Street, the main shopping area, and turns right on Richmond Street and left on North Street to the most popular attraction along the route, the Paul Revere House, where Revere and his large family lived from 1770 to 1780. This house delights visitors because it provides a direct and intimate link to our revolutionary past and allows us to visualize the lives of the men who shaped our country. You enter by the same door through which Paul Revere left for the Boston Tea Party dressed as an Indian; and, two years later, in April 1775, for his midnight ride to have signal lanterns put in the steeple of the Old North Church and to warn John Hancock and Sam Adams in Lexington. The interior is warm and snug with wide chimneys and low ceilings. Inside you can see the old kitchen with its huge fireplace, brick ovens and antique utensils; Paul Revere's bedroom; and a collection of his engravings and belongings.

Revere's house, which was already a century old when he moved into it, is the oldest wooden dwelling in Boston. It was built around 1677. The overhanging second story and windows are typical of English cottages of that period.

From the Revere House the Trail leads to the Old North Church via the Paul Revere Mall, where there is a statue of the patriot on horseback by Cyrus Dallin. Built in 1723 as Christ Church, the Old North today houses the second Episcopal Congregation in Boston (King's Chapel was the first) and is the oldest house of worship in Boston. Paul Revere ordered two signal lanterns lit in its steeple on the night of his historic ride, April 18, 1775, to inform the Charlestown patriots that the British were crossing the Charles to Cambridge, thereby shortening their route to Lexington and Concord. While the lanterns were being lit, Revere himself set out on horseback to warn his fellow patriots to the west. In the steeple are the colony's oldest bells, rung by Paul Revere himself as a boy. The bells were cast by England's historic Whitechapel foundry, and were completely restored in 1983. Later in his life, Paul Revere himself became involved in the casting of bells, the largest of which is the one in King's Chapel. It tolled for its maker when he died in 1818.

Just down Hull Street from the Church is Copps Hill Burying Ground. It offers a vista of the Charles River and Charlestown and is a pleasant place for walking with its fine old trees and 17th- and 18th-century gravestones. During the Revolutionary War, the British stationed cannon there which were used to set Charlestown on fire and to attack Bunker Hill. Members of the famous Mather family are buried here, as is Edmund Hartt, who built the *U.S.S. Constitution,* "Old Ironsides," the oldest commissioned ship of the U.S. Navy.

Before leaving the North End for Charlestown, where the *Constitution* is moored, walk back down Salem Street for a look at the wonderful displays in the windows of Italian butcher shops and the bins of olives, capers, spices and dried beans outside the grocery stores. Sample a *cannoli* or *sfogliatella* in one of the pastry shops here or on Hanover Street.

The site of the *Constitution* in Charlestown—last official stop on the Freedom Trail—can be reached by foot (2½ miles), by automobile, by MBTA (take the orange line from Haymarket or North Station to City Square and walk down Chamber Street and right on Water Street), or by the MBTA bus from South Station in Boston (schedules change; call the MBTA for details). The ship was built in 1797 and sheathed in copper milled by Paul Revere. She acquired her nickname during the War of 1812. The old navy yard itself has been restored as a historic site.

Beyond the navy yard you can see the shaft of the Bunker Hill Monument, built in the early-19th century to commemorate the famous battle fought on June 17, 1775. The monument actually stands on Breed's Hill, where the misnamed battle took place; Bunker Hill is just north of it. Diorama exhibits explain the fighting, and the tower may be climbed for an excellent view.

Beacon Hill

No visit to Boston would be complete without at least a brief walk through the beautiful gas-lit, tree-lined streets of Beacon Hill, past the shuttered brick townhouses where many of Boston's wealthy, socially prominent families lived throughout the 19th century. Although many of the houses have been broken up into apartments, some are still owned by old Boston families, and all have changed little outwardly. The residents have tried to ensure that this lovely old-fashioned section will retain its restrained elegance and harmonious architecture.

The hill takes its name from a harbor beacon installed atop it shortly after Boston was settled in 1630. Beacon Hill originally stood considerably higher than it does now. Along with Copp's Hill and Fort Hill its top was leveled in the early-19th century to provide the earth for filling in the area around Charles Street. The Back Bay itself was later filled with gravel from suburban Needham.

A good place to start is on Beacon Street opposite the new State House. There, on the edge of the Common, you will see the Robert Gould Shaw Memorial, sculpted by Augustus Saint-Gaudens to commemorate Shaw and his regiment of black soldiers, who fought valiantly in the Civil War. From here continue west along the edge of the Common so that you can view the townhouses that line the far side of Beacon Street. The twin mansions at numbers 39 and 40, mirror images of each other, belong to the Women's City Club of Boston. Beacon Hill began to be a fashionable residential area after the completion of the state house in 1798. At that time, the estate of exiled Tory artist John Singleton Copley was subdivided into the building lots on which today's townhouses stand. Around 1814 or 1815, Nathan Appleton, a textile manufacturer, and Daniel Parker, a shipping merchant, engaged the architect of the state house, Charles Bulfinch, to design homes for them. After completing plans for their exteriors he was called to Washington to assist in designing the Capitol. His associate, Alexander Parris, finished the designs for Appleton and Parker and is responsible for most of the interiors, with their Greek Revival touches.

The graceful bow fronts of the two houses both contain original panes of the fashionable purple glass of Beacon Hill. Its mauve tint was produced accidentally, by the action of strong sunlight on a batch of defective glass purchased abroad for these homes. The distinctive shade was coveted by others but, owing to its accidental origins, it could not be duplicated exactly. In its rarity, the glass became a sign of age, wealth and distinction.

The houses are open to the public; members conduct guided tours for visitors, by appointment. Call the Women's City Club for schedules. Those who take the tour may also dine in the members' cafeteria roof garden on the second floor. The interiors, splendid examples of the Greek Revival style, have changed little since the houses were built. There is a beautiful curved Bulfinch staircase in Number 40, and both houses show careful attention to symmetry and harmony with details such as curved walls and curved mahogany sliding doors designed to reflect the curves of the bow windows.

Continue down Beacon Street past Number 45, also designed by Bulfinch, and turn right on Charles Street, Beacon Hill's main shopping area. Here you will find Boston's main concentration of antique stores, along with establishments selling everything from nautical paintings to dollhouse furniture. Wander off Charles onto the shady, peaceful side streets, with their brick-walled gardens, blooming windowboxes, and unexpected courtyards. Many of the houses are noteworthy for their architecture or their former residents. Admiral Richard E. Byrd lived at 7–9 Brimmer Street, and 44 Brimmer was the lifelong home of historian Samuel Eliot Morison. In Morison's youth, around the turn of the century, the waters of the Charles washed the

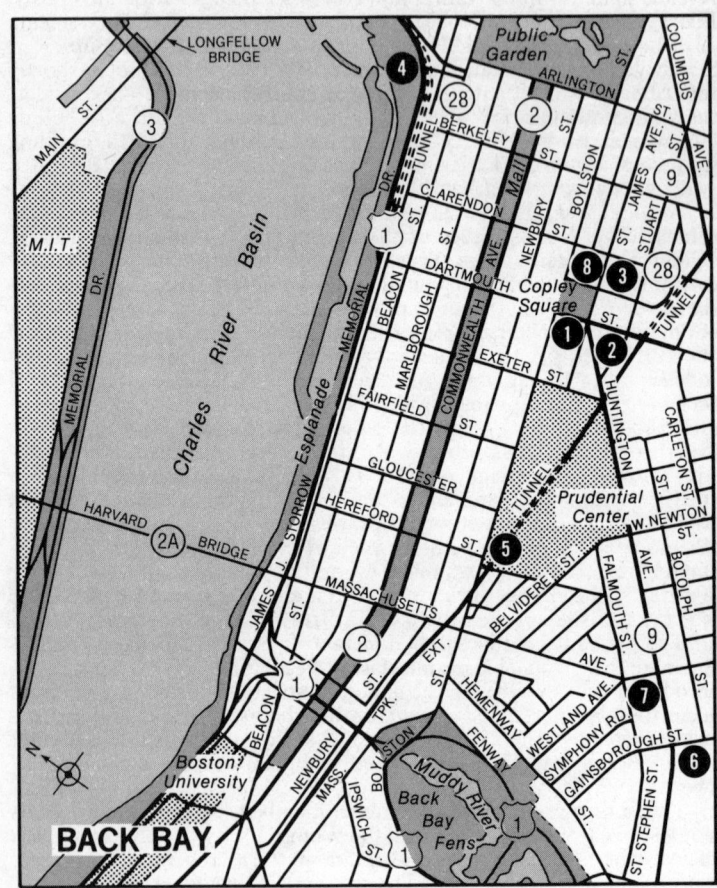

Points of Interest

1) Boston Public Library
2) Copley Place
3) Hancock Tower
4) Hatch Memorial Shell
5) Hynes Auditorium
6) New England Conservatory of Music (Jordan Hall)
7) Symphony Hall
8) Trinity Church

opposite side of this street. (Morison is now commemorated, by the way, in a beautiful new bronze life-size statue on the Commonwealth Avenue mall.) Number 29A Chestnut Street was the home of Edwin Booth, the Shakespearean actor, and Julia Ward Howe lived at number 13. The home of Charles Francis Adams, Sr., at 57 Mount Vernon Street, is a dignified mansion set back from the street. You may visit the Nichols House Museum at 55 Mount Vernon Street, furnished in the original style. The Sears House at 85 Mount Vernon was designed by Bulfinch. Number 83, next door, was the home of William Ellery Channing, Unitarian clergyman and author.

Make sure your walk includes a tour of Louisburg Square, whose sedate elegance epitomizes the spirit of Beacon Hill. The square, which runs between Mount Vernon and Pinckney streets, was built up in the 1830s. The central green, surrounded by a wrought-iron fence, is owned by the people who live on the square. Small statues of Aristides the Just and Columbus stand at either end. Among the well known who once lived on Louisburg Square are Louisa May Alcott, Jenny Lind and William Dean Howells.

The area north of Pinckney Street and extending to Cambridge Street is the oldest section of Beacon Hill and the one which developed most slowly. In the early 19th century many of Boston's black families lived in this area. An early black meeting house, on Smith Court off Joy Street, has been restored and serves as the starting point for the Black Heritage Trail. Narrow courtyards of this type contain some of the most delightful examples of domestic architecture on this side of the hill. Near the foot of Joy Street, at 141 Cambridge Street, is the Harrison Gray Otis House, one of Boston's finest old mansions. It was designed by Bulfinch in 1795 for Otis, a prominent Bostonian and one of the original developers of Beacon Hill. It is the first of three Bulfinch homes Otis owned on the hill. The Society for the Preservation of New England Antiquities, which restored the house and has established its headquarters there, has furnished part of it in the Federal style of the late 18th century.

Just beyond the Harrison Gray Otis house stands the Old West Church, designed by Asher Benjamin, a contemporary of Bulfinch. These two structures are among the few that survived the West End urban renewal project of the 1950s, which replaced the old neighborhoods with expensive high-rise apartment buildings.

Emerald Necklace

Boston's multitude of parks, large and small, wooded or grassy, are a source of constant and often unexpected delight to both its residents and visitors. They do much to give the city its special human quality, and to make it a beautiful and inviting place to live or visit. Among the finest are those planned by Frederick Law Olmsted, designer of many of the great parks of the United States, and of the grounds of the U.S. Capitol. (Olmsted lived and worked in nearby Brookline; his home and studio are now a National Historic Site.) In the late 19th century Olmsted created a chain of beautiful, semi-rustic parks stretching from Back Bay south to the Arnold Arboretum and Franklin Park which has come to be known as the Green Belt, or less prosaically, the Emerald Necklace.

The visitor on foot can begin a tour of the parks with the Back Bay Fens or Fenway, as it is generally called. Now circumscribed by Park

Drive and the Fenway, the Back Bay Fens were originally a marshy, unappreciated backwater of the Charles River. Under Olmsted's direction the land was drained and transformed into a lovely and varied landscape of water, trees and grass designed to serve the people of Boston without completely losing its original natural identity. In one section marsh reeds still grow. But nearby, avid Boston gardeners tend their vegetable plots. Across from the Museum of Fine Arts there are scenic footpaths, and off Park Drive there is a formal rose garden.

The Fenway area is home to some of Boston's leading cultural, athletic, educational and medical institutions. To the north is famous Fenway Park, home of the beloved Boston Red Sox. During home games, the streets in the area become clogged with the cars of Red Sox fans. The western edge is lined with schools and colleges: Simmons, Emmanuel, Wheelock and Boston State Colleges; the Wentworth Insitute and Northeastern University; Boston Latin High School; and Harvard Medical School. Children's Hospital, the Boston Hospital for Women and Beth Israel Hospital are all located near the latter. For visitors, the high points of this area are the Museum of Fine Arts and the Gardner Museum, situated near each other along the Fenway.

The Museum of Fine Arts, whose main entrance is on Huntington Avenue, is one of the country's finest art museums, noted for its collections of Impressionists and post-Impressionists, colonial American painting, furniture, and silver, and Greek, Roman, and Egyptian art. There are always interesting special exhibits, as well as a museum store selling books, prints, jewelry and reproductions.

The Isabella Stewart Gardner Museum, at 280 The Fenway, is far more intimate than the massive Museum of Fine Arts. Both the Venetian mansion and the fine collection of European paintings, sculpture, and furniture within it belonged originally to Mrs. John Lowell Gardner, a wealthy, cultured socialite whose independence and spirited lifestyle fascinated the reserved late-19th-century Boston society with its Puritan heritage and Victorian morals. Free chamber music concerts are presented each week at the museum.

From the Fenway, the rest of the Emerald Necklace is best reached by automobile. It narrows to a thin strip of woodland and water along the Riverway, which gives a suburban air to this city road. It widens after crossing Huntington Avenue and becomes Olmsted Park, which contains three small ponds and is bordered by the Jamaicaway. Next comes lovely Jamaica Pond, in the midst of an attractive residential area. After the pond, the Necklace becomes no more than a line of green along the Arborway, but it broadens out shortly to form the gem of the Park System, the Arnold Arboretum. Open every day from sunrise to sunset and free to the public, the arboretum is owned by Harvard and contains the world's largest collection of trees and shrubs, all labeled by name and date. But it is not only a superb horticultural museum, it is also a magnificent park with a maze of lovely walks winding among its varied flora, with open spaces where dogs and children romp, and quiet secluded corners for peaceful meditation. It is worth visiting at all times of the year. You may catch the breathtaking collection of lilacs in flower in the spring or enjoy the autumn leaf display. The seemingly endless variety in the huge evergreen collection will astound you whenever you visit, and bonsai fanciers have a special treat in store. Parking facilities are limited, but it can be reached via the MBTA's Green Line.

The Arborway continues past the Arboretum to Franklin Park, the last and largest link in the chain. It is beautifully landscaped with rolling hills, lush vegetation, and large stone outcroppings, and is well worth driving through. It's probably best known for its zoo, open daily, and particularly the children's zoo. The walk-through aviary is exceptionally well stocked. There are also picnic sites with tables and fireplaces. The park also offers a golf course and horseback riding. As for safety—avoid all parks after dark, and keep in pairs when exploring remote areas.

Back Bay and the Prudential Center

West of the Public Garden is Back Bay, which abuts Copley Place and Prudential Center to form one of Boston's major shopping and residential areas. Until the 1850s, when it was filled in to provide more land for the growing city, this area was indeed a marshy tidal bay that extended all the way east to Washington Street, which then formed the thin neck that attached Boston Peninsula to the mainland. Streets in the newly-created district were laid out in a formal grid pattern, making a distinct contrast to old Boston's twisting, random streets that followed old footpaths and cowpaths. Commonwealth Avenue was designed with a spacious central mall of grass and trees that made it an especially desirable place to live, and which affords a fine place for strolling and appreciating the surrounding architecture. While much of Boston is said to resemble London, the tone here is French. This is not surprising since Commonwealth Avenue was laid out in conscious imitation of Baron Haussmann's plans for Paris which had been executed only a few years before. The Back Bay has remained a fashionable and conveniently located residential area, although most of the single family townhouses have been converted into apartments and condominiums. Needless to say, it is no longer true that Marlborough Street is for people with an old Boston pedigree, Commonwealth Avenue is for people with money, and Beacon Street is for those with both. That's what used to be said, and 19th-century Boston's social traditions were just hidebound enough to make it stick.

Originally, development concentrated upon the eastern end of the Back Bay, closest to the Public Garden, and gradually moved westward. The careful observer, walking west toward Massachusetts Avenue, where the last buildings were erected at the turn of the century, will note the townhouse building styles altering in order to meet successive changes in specifications of height and setback.

Copley Square, named after the colonial portrait painter, is distinguished by two of the finest buildings in Boston. Trinity Church, built in 1877, was designed by H.H. Richardson, one of America's foremost architects. The Boston area is a mecca for admirers of his neo-Romanesque works, which include not only churches, but also buildings at Harvard, public libraries and private houses. As in many of his buildings, Richardson used colored stones for the exterior of Trinity Church. The design of the church, with its dominant central tower, round arches, and compact, massive shape, was inspired by the 11th-century Romanesque buildings that preceded the emergence of the Gothic style in Europe.

On the west side of Copley Square stands the Boston Public Library, completed in 1895, and one of the largest and finest libraries in the country. The architects, McKim, Mead, and White, intended the classical simplicity of its exterior to harmonize with nearby Trinity Church. The interior contains murals by Puvis de Chavannes, Edwin

A. Abbey and John Singer Sargent, bronze bas-relief doors designed by Daniel Chester French, and a lovely inner courtyard. The old library is complemented by a modern extension, designed by Philip Johnson.

Copley Square is bounded on the south by the elegant old Copley Plaza Hotel, and by Copley Place, a retail, hotel, and apartment complex completed early in 1984. Westin and Marriott are the hostelries, and Nieman-Marcus is the anchor store. There are also such names as Gucci, Tiffany, and Godiva, and Boston's largest cinema complex is here as well. Also in Copley Square is I. M. Pei's John Hancock Tower, a striking rhomboid with sheer glass walls reflecting a constantly changing cloudscape, as well as the buildings around it. Watch as the image of Trinity Church undulates along the side of this great blue slab, and then head to the Hancock's top floor for a fine view of the city and its suburbs.

The other skyscraper which dominates this section of the Boston skyline is the Prudential Tower, a massive 52-story building rising out of the 31-acre Prudential Center, a redevelopment project completed in the mid-60s. Since then, the tower has become a new Boston landmark which, along with the Hancock, can be seen for miles from vantage points among the hills that surround the Boston basin. The tower itself has a skywalk on the 50th floor that provides another spectacular view of Boston and the surrounding country. On a clear day one can see as far as New Hampshire's Mount Monadnock, 63 miles away. The Prudential Center also contains apartment buildings, a shopping plaza and department stores. The shopping area continues into Back Bay and along Newbury Street, which is lined with art galleries, boutiques, and elegant stores.

Southwest of the Prudential Center, on Huntington Avenue, is the Christian Science Church Center, world headquarters of the Christian Science faith. The most renowned building in this complex is the "Mother Church" of Christian Science, consisting of the smaller gray granite First Church built in 1894 and the great domed Italian Renaissance extension added in 1904. The church offers guided tours of the center, one of the highlights of which is the "maparium," a walk-in translucent globe.

Across Massachusetts Avenue from the Christian Science Center is Symphony Hall. Designed by McKim, Mead and White in 1900, this is the proud home of the outstanding Boston Symphony Orchestra. The distinguished New England Conservatory of Music is located farther out on Huntington Avenue. The area south of Huntington and east of Massachusetts avenues is undergoing a change of identity as decaying South End townhouses are renovated by young, professional Bostonians intent on restoring the middle-class character originally envisioned by the area's 19th-century developers. The displacement of the poor in such neighborhoods, however, has become a growing urban problem and has resulted in the coining of the term "gentrification."

One of Boston's most fascinating neighborhoods is frequently overlooked by travelers. This is tiny Bay Village, so named because it originally occupied the shores of a bay, now long-since filled in. Bay Village lies just to the north of the South End, in a pocket bordered by Park Square and the Massachusetts Turnpike. The toy-like brick houses which line the narrow streets of Bay Village were built by French Huguenot refugees at the end of the 18th century; today, they have become desirable as homes and apartments. It was here that Edgar Allen Poe spent part of his early years.

Government Center

Government Center began in 1961 as a federally aided urban renewal project designed to address several major problems at once. New office space was needed for city, state and federal government facilities. This need became apparent at a time when Boston's downtown, especially parts of the historic old section, was beginning to deteriorate. By centralizing the office construction in a notably seedy, decaying area known as Scollay Square, the Boston Redevelopment Authority hoped to improve the district—which was also convenient to existing shopping, financial, residential and government areas—and at the same time to revitalize the ailing downtown. The architectural firm of I.M. Pei was hired to submit a master plan for the project, and the designs for individual buildings were awarded to various other architects.

The completed project has not only answered the specific needs that inspired it, but through the masterful planning of Pei and the other architects' work it has become an integrated and harmonious part of Boston's downtown and an inviting locale for the citizens who deal with or work for the many government agencies located there. For pedestrians and visitors the heart of the complex is City Hall Square, an eight-acre plaza surrounding the prize-winning brick and concrete Boston City Hall building and linking it with surrounding buildings, both new and old. Continuity with the historic Boston of the Freedom Trail and Beacon Hill is emphasized by the use of red brick paving to create a flowing open space. This sense of openness is also fostered by the buildings' placement and design, as specified by Pei. The plaza contains a sunken fountain and an array of benches and retaining walls which are put to constant use by lunching office workers, footsore pedestrians and the many who simply enjoy sitting and looking. During the summer the plaza is also the scene of various city hall–sponsored community activities, including evening entertainments.

If you stand in the plaza in front of city hall and look around, you will see that although the plaza is ringed by massive buildings, they are arranged at intervals that offer wide vistas. Beyond city hall to the right rises the pink granite tower of the New England Merchants National Bank Building. The low curved brick building forming the square's southern boundary is the Sears Crescent, built in the early 1800s, a publishing center throughout the course of the century. The curve of the Sears Crescent is echoed on a larger scale in the brick and concrete Center Plaza Office Building directly opposite city hall. This private office building is one of the longest in the country. An arcade of shops extends along the street, and staircases lead up through it to the higher interior of the curve, an area known as Pemberton Square and containing the Suffolk County Court House.

Looking down Cambridge Street past Center Plaza, you can see the twenty-two-story Leverett Saltonstall State Building on the left. The north end of City Hall Plaza is framed by the John F. Kennedy Federal Office Building, consisting of a low four-story section joined to twin 26-story towers with a tree-lined plaza and benches in front of it. The building was designed by Walter Gropius and the Architects Collaborative and Samuel Glaser Associates. It houses the offices of the late President's brother, Senator Edward Kennedy, and of numerous other federal officials and agencies. Nearby, a plaque on the New England Telephone Building marks the birthplace of Charles Bulfinch.

A wide open space in the plaza between the Kennedy building and city hall provides a striking view of the structures of old Boston framed by the very newest. You can see past Haymarket Square and the Fitzgerald Expressway to the brick rooftops of the North End. Steps descend down the back side of Beacon Hill past city hall to provide easy pedestrian access to this area. I.M. Pei designed Government Center so that the historic buildings of old Boston would be visible from city hall. Shortly before its completion, a rectangular section was excised from the base of the New England Merchants National Bank Building in order to furnish city hall with a view of the Old State House.

City hall itself is the central building in Government Center, and one of the most exciting. Its architects, the New York firm of Kallman, McKinnell and Knowles, were chosen by a national design competition. The lower floors house city agencies which do daily business with the public; the upper floors contain administrative offices and the fifth floor is headquarters for the mayor and the city council. Because city hall is built into the base of the north slope of Beacon Hill, it is actually a split-level building which is entered from the City Hall Square side on its third floor. The lower floors extend down the hill to the rear of the building. Free guided tours of city hall depart from the main lobby on the third floor and are indispensable for full appreciation of its ingenious and brilliant architecture. The lobby and gallery areas of city hall are also the site of frequent exhibits of art and photography.

Boston's Waterfront: The Harbor and the Charles

Massachusetts Bay and protected Boston Harbor were among the earliest sections of the North American coastline visited by European explorers. The first permanent settlement on Boston Harbor was made in 1623, at what is now Weymouth. Then, two years later, three men moved to the area where the Charles and Mystic rivers flowed into the sea. One of them, William Blackstone, an Anglican clergyman, built his home on the west slope of Beacon Hill. The other two settled in Charlestown and Chelsea. The settlements grew, and the rivers and harbor became centers of trade, commerce and the codfishing industry that supported many of the early colonists. Not long afterward, a process began which was to continue for two centuries: marshes and swamps were filled in as maritime activity increased, and Boston's shoreline gradually edged outward. The original maritime center was located at Dock Square, near Faneuil Hall. Today the shoreline extends another third of a mile east.

Boston's waterfront continues to change and develop. The working docks are primarily located in east and south Boston, but the Boston Redevelopment Authority has found new uses for the old docks on the peninsula. A good place to start a tour of Boston's waterfront is Central Wharf, now the site of the New England Aquarium, which houses a fascinating and very well displayed collection of fish and marine animals. There are seals and sea lions in a pool on the first floor. A giant ocean tank housing sharks, sea turtles, and many different varieties of fish can be viewed from above and through its thick glass walls along a circular descending ramp. Special display tanks line the outer walls.

South of the aquarium, at Rowes Wharf, Boston Harbor sightseeing boats depart for tours of the harbor and some of its many islands. Other harbor tours depart from Long Wharf, just to the north of the aquarium; here you may also take a passenger ferry for Provincetown on the Cape.

Continuing north along Atlantic Avenue, you come to Commercial and Lewis wharves. From here Commercial Street curves around the North End, past North Station and Boston Garden, home of the Celtics and Bruins, to the mouth of the Charles River. The Charles River Dam, built in 1910, created the freshwater Charles River Basin by keeping out the harbor tides. On the wide dam, which connects Boston with East Cambridge, are located the Museum of Science and the Hayden Planetarium, favorites with children and adults and good places to spend rainy days.

On the Boston side of the Charles River Basin, stretching from the Dam to Boston University Bridge, is the Charles River Embankment, a park and recreation area bordered by Storrow Drive. This is a fine area for walking. You can watch sailboats in the basin and crew shells and sculls from Boston's universities and colleges practicing on the Charles. There are fine views of Beacon Hill, Back Bay and the buildings of M.I.T. across the river. Opposite the foot of Mount Vernon Street is the Hatch Memorial Shell, where free open-air Esplanade concerts by the Boston Pops are sponsored by the city during the summer. Concerts are also held at other Boston locations as part of "Summerthing," a summer arts and recreation program sponsored by the City of Boston.

You can cross over the Charles to Cambridge on foot, using Longfellow, Harvard or Boston University Bridges, and continue walking along the Charles to Harvard and beyond that to the beautiful and historic Mount Auburn Cemetery. The Dr. Paul Dudley White bicycle paths parallel this stretch of the river. The Cambridge side of the Charles affords fine vistas of the Boston skyline, especially at sunset and on clear nights.

Cambridge

Cambridge, located across the Charles River from Boston, is best known as the home of two great American universities, Harvard and the Massachusetts Institute of Technology (M.I.T.). Originally known as New Towne, Cambridge was settled by farmers in 1630 in an area southeast of the present Harvard Square. It began to take its present shape as early as 1635, when the main roads to Menotomy and Concord to the northwest and to the neck of Boston Peninsula were worn down along the route still followed by Massachusetts Avenue, the major artery of modern Cambridge.

The history of Harvard is almost as old as that of the city. In October 1636, the General Court of the Massachusetts Bay Colony decided to subsidize a college and New Towne was selected as the site. John Harvard, a Puritan minister educated at Cambridge University in England, died shortly after and bequeathed half of his library and half of his estate to the new college. In recognition of his generosity, the court named the college after him and changed the name of the village from New Towne to Cambridge. In its colonial days Harvard was primarily a divinity school; during the early 18th century its reputation and finances were weakened by religious conflicts. But as Cambridge prospered and wealthy landowners transformed the small farms into elegant country homes, Harvard recovered from its slump.

Cambridge was a stronghold of the Patriots during the Revolution. No battles were fought there, but soldiers were quartered in the homes of Tories who had been forced to evacuate, and in 1775 Cambridge became headquarters for the American militia and Minutemen. A bronze plaque on Cambridge Common commemorates the spot where George Washington stood to take command of the American Army on July 3, 1775. Boston, meanwhile, was held by the British until they were routed by Washington's artillery, placed strategically atop Dorchester Heights.

After the Revolution, Cambridge and its university began to develop into a great American intellectual center. Among the 19th-century scholars who contributed to its growth were Oliver Wendell Holmes, Henry Wadsworth Longfellow, Louis Agassiz, James Russell Lowell and Margaret Fuller, who edited the *Dial,* a transcendentalist magazine, and was one of the earliest advocates of women's rights. It took Harvard until 1879 to create Radcliffe College, which began as an informal association of Harvard instructors who agreed to teach women. Radcliffe did not become an official part of Harvard until 1894. Wellesley College, in the Boston suburb of the same name, had begun to educate women nearly 20 years earlier.

Another great educational institution, the Massachusetts Institute of Technology, having outgrown its original site in Boston, was established in Cambridge in 1916. M.I.T., one of the world's major centers of scientific and technological research and learning, is located in Cambridgeport along the Charles River. Perhaps more than any other influence, it is the presence of the faculty and students of MIT which made possible the Boston area's ascendancy in high-technology industries.

During the 19th century, the city of Cambridge expanded geographically and commercially as well. After the construction in 1793 of the West Boston Bridge (precursor of today's Longfellow Bridge), an industrial center known as Cambridgeport began to develop in the southeastern section of Cambridge that had formerly consisted of farms and swampy lowlands. East Cambridge next became a commercial area. The area between Harvard Square and these new centers consisted of large estates until the 1830s and then became a residential suburb known as Mid-Cambridge. Because of this decentralized pattern of urban development, the old part of the city consisting of the University, Harvard Square and West Cambridge has changed quite slowly and retains many fine residential streets and old buildings.

Harvard University now consists of Harvard College and a complex of graduate and professional schools, including schools of law, divinity, medicine, architecture, education, dentistry, public health, business, government, and graduate arts and sciences. Visitors to Harvard may obtain maps of the campus—which spreads from North Cambridge through Harvard Square across the Charles—from the Harvard Information Center in Holyoke Center, Harvard Square. This is also the place to go if you would like information on guided tours of the university; they leave twice each weekday and once on Saturdays from the Admissions Office on Garden Street (Saturdays from Holyoke Center).

If you would like to visit Harvard on your own, the place to start is Harvard Yard, the college's original center and, with its series of red brick Georgian buildings and fine old trees, one of its most beautiful spots. The yellow clapboard Colonial house to the right of the entrance opposite Holyoke Center is Wadsworth, built in 1726 as the residence for Harvard presidents. It is now the alumni office. If you walk north from there to the center of the yard you will be surrounded by some of the oldest structures in the university. Massachusetts Hall was built in 1720, Harvard Hall in 1766. Across from them is beautiful University Hall, designed by Bulfinch in gray granite ornamented with white pilasters. In front of it stands a statue of John Harvard sculpted by Daniel Chester French. Holden Chapel, north of Harvard Hall, was built in 1744 and is an outstanding example of Georgian architecture. The other buildings in this half of the yard are nearly all dormitories.

The quadrangle beyond is of later date. It is dominated by the imposing staircase and Corinthian arcade of the massive Widener Library, donated in memory of Harry Elkins Widener, a collector of rare books and 1907 graduate of Harvard who lost his life on the *Titanic*. Widener's own incomparable collection is housed in a special room in the library designed to create the atmosphere of a wealthy gentleman's study. The Widener, along with the nearby Lamont Library for undergraduates, the Houghton Rare Books Library, and the various departmental and college libraries, comprises the largest university library and one of the most important research libraries in the world. Opposite Widener stands Memorial Church, constructed in 1932 as a war memorial. On the walls inside are listed the names of Harvard men who died serving their country in both the First and Second World Wars. Among the World War II names, listed with the class of 1904, is President Franklin Delano Roosevelt. The east side of the quadrangle is dominated by Sever Hall, a finely proportioned and beautifully crafted building designed by H. H. Richardson in 1880 and built of red brick to harmonize with the 18th-century architecture of the yard. Notice the recessed Syrian arch which frames the entrance.

Art and Memorial

Across Quincy Street is the Fogg Art Museum, housing Harvard's principal art collections; down the street to the left is the new Sackler Museum of Oriental and Islamic Art. To the right of the Fogg stands the Carpenter Center for the Visual Arts (1963), designed by Le Corbusier. Just north of the Yard is multicolored brick Memorial Hall. It was built in 1878 as a memorial to Harvard men who died in the Civil War. Some see it as an example of Victorian Gothic gone too far; others love its striped polychrome roof and Gothic windows and towers. Memorial Hall houses Sanders Theater, a small, acoustically superb hall where concerts and plays are frequently presented. At the end of Quincy Street is the Busch-Reisinger Museum, which contains a collection of Germanic art. During the school year, free organ concerts are offered here each Thursday at noon. Nearby is the tall white tower of William James Hall. North of these two buildings are the divinity school campus and the classroom buildings and laboratories of the science departments. Near here are the university museums, which include the Peabody Museum of archeology and ethnology, and separate collections devoted to comparative zoology, minerals and geology and botany (be sure to see the glass flowers).

Across Oxford Street is Harvard Law School, founded in 1817 to offer an alternative to the then-current apprenticeship approach to legal education. It achieved a lasting place in history in the latter part of the 19th century when Professor (later Dean) Christopher Columbus Langdell revolutionized American legal education with the introduction of the "case method," which has since predominated in American law schools. The law school buildings include Austin Hall (1883), a Richardson Romanesque masterpiece with an impressive arched entrance porch, massive Langdell Hall (1907), built of Indiana limestone, and two modern buildings of poured concrete and plum-colored brick on Massachusetts Avenue. North of the law school, note the award-winning dormitory and graduate center complex designed by Walter Gropius and constructed in the late 1950s.

Several blocks to the north and west of the law school are the Radcliffe dormitories, now occupied by Harvard men as well, the new Hilles Library (1967), and the Harvard College Observatory. This is the beginning of the area known as North Cambridge or Cambridge Heights, which contains many fine late-19th- and early-20th-century houses. Radcliffe Yard, the Loeb Drama Center and the graduate school of education are nearby. The Harvard houses—undergraduate dormitories and social units—stretch from the Charles north to Massachusetts Avenue. Their red brick Colonial exteriors were intended to harmonize with the buildings of the yard and they appear quite old, although construction was not begun until 1930. The more recent houses are modern in design.

If you walk down John F. Kennedy Street (formerly Boylston Street) from Harvard Square you will pass Kirkland and Eliot Houses. The Kennedy School of Government occupies the opposite corner. In 1981, the Cambridge City Council objected to Harvard's playing down of the Kennedy name in connection with its government school; it was said that the university wished, by so doing, to stand in better stead with the new conservative federal administration. The council reacted by changing the school's address, renaming Boylston Street after the late president. Walk to the end of Kennedy Street and cross the Larz Anderson Bridge to reach the Harvard Business School (diplomatically named after no one in particular), the football stadium, and other athletic fields.

Harvard Square is the heart of Old Cambridge. Technically it includes only the MBTA station, news kiosk and surrounding buildings, but in fact "the square" is used to designate the entire shopping center in the university area. It is worth a long and leisurely stroll. The square has a flavor all its own, displaying in a concentrated and striking form that special fusion of old and new, European and American, that characterizes all of Boston. Side by side are traditional department stores, high-fashion boutiques and blue-jean emporiums. There is a tempting array of good things to eat and drink, ranging from fine continental restaurants and gourmet shops to inexpensive European-style cafes where you can sit and talk over espresso or cold drinks; you'll also find hamburger and sandwich joints, ice cream parlors, supermarkets and college bars. And, as one might expect in a university town, there are bookstores of all types, copying centers, record stores and movie theaters.

Visitors to Harvard Square who were familiar with the subway construction chaos of the past few years will be happy to find that the mess has been cleaned up, and even the old cast-iron MBTA station has been put back in place. The T's Red Line no longer comes to an end at the Square, but extends on to Porter Square and will eventually reach Arlington. We should hope that this will relieve traffic pressure on ever-crowded Massachusetts Avenue.

The City of Cambridge publishes an excellent visitors' pamphlet called *Old Cambridge Walking Guide*. It is free at the information center near Harvard Square. The tour includes Cambridge Common,

Christ Church, the Longfellow House and some of the historic buildings of Harvard. Supplement it, if possible, with visits to the Cooper-Frost Austin House, the oldest house in Cambridge, located on Linnaean Street, and a stroll out Brattle Street, where some of the most beautiful 18th- and 19th-century homes in greater Boston stand amidst landscaped gardens. The Lee-Nichols House at 159 Brattle Street is owned by the Cambridge Historical Society and is open to the public on Thursdays.

Massachusetts Institute of Technology: M.I.T. can be reached from Harvard Square by taking a bus or driving southeast on Massachusetts Avenue. Along the way you will pass through Central Square, the main shopping district of Cambridgeport. Free guided tours of the M.I.T. campus depart weekdays from Building 7, on the Institute's Massachusetts Avenue campus. Two outstanding buildings are the Kresge Auditorium and the M.I.T. Interdenominational Chapel, both designed by Eero Saarinen.

PRACTICAL INFORMATION FOR
THE BOSTON AREA

 **HOTELS AND MOTELS.** Once there were only the Ritz, Copley, Parker House and a few others; now new hotels rise all over Boston. Truly inexpensive lodgings are found only in the suburbs, but the downtown hotels offer freedom from driving hassles. Even expensive hotels have reasonable weekend packages; call for details.

The following ranges pertain to double occupancy in both Boston and Cambridge hotels and motels: *Deluxe,* $140 and up; *Expensive,* $95–$140; *Moderate,* $75–$95; *Inexpensive,* $45–$75.

BOSTON

Deluxe

Back Bay Hilton. Dalton and Belvedere Sts. (236–1100). Opened fall 1982, this high-rise hotel near Prudential Center, Hynes Auditorium, and new Copley Place features pool, shops, restaurants, and lounges.

Bostonian. At Quincy Market, Dock Sq. (523–3600). One of Boston's newest and smallest hotels; fireplaces, jacuzzis, an excellent restaurant, easy access to Faneuil Hall, North End, and business district.

Colonnade. 120 Huntington Ave. at Prudential Center (424–7000). Pool in season, sauna. Restaurants, bars, entertainment, dancing.

Copley Plaza. 138 St. James Ave. at Copley Sq. (267–5300). Grand hotel opulence is the order here. Restaurants, Plaza Bar, entertainment. Small pets. Excellent Back Bay location between Public Library and Trinity Church, near Copley Place. Reasonable weekend pkg.

Four Seasons. 200 Boylston St. (338–4400). Splendid new hotel overlooking Public Garden—spacious rooms, indoor pool and health club, outdoor cafe, fine dining.

Lafayette. 1 Ave. de Lafayette (451–2600). In new Lafayette Place development; a sedate oasis in Federalist style but with convenient downtown location. Opened 1985. Outdoor pool and terrace; excellent restaurant.

Long Wharf. 296 State St. (227–0800). A Marriott Hotel, on the waterfront. 5-story atrium, Viennese café, terrace dining overlooking harbor. Indoor pool.

Marriott at Copley Place. 236–5800. Over 1100 rooms, 77 suites. Health club, indoor pool. Full meeting and convention facilities and Boston's largest ballroom. 3 restaurants, cocktail lounges.

Meridien. 1 Post Office Sq. (451–1900). Member of fine French hotel group. In renovated Federal Reserve Bldg., financial district. Airy, well-lit rooms, all with mini-bars; some loft suites. Concierge service. Excellent restaurant. 24-hour room service.

Parker House Hotel. 60 School St. (227–8600). Restaurants, bar, entertainment. Boston's oldest hotel, the recently renovated Parker House is also its most centrally located. Weekend plans avail.

Ritz-Carlton. Arlington & Newbury Sts. (536–5700 or 800–952–7495). Elegant and understated as always, despite a recent doubling in size. Many rooms overlook Public Garden; older section has fireplaces in suites. Splendid dining room.

Sheraton-Boston, 39 Dalton St. at Prudential Center (236–2000). Luxurious hotel. Rooftop pool. Some rms. have private poolside patios. Restaurants, bars, entertainment, dancing.

Westin. Copley Place (262–9600). Brand-new highrise hotel. Full health club, indoor pool, concierge, 24-hour room service. Bars, 3 restaurants.

Expensive

Hilton Inn at Logan. Logan Int'l Airport. (569–9300). Outdoor pool. Restaurants, bar, entertainment. Dancing wknds. Airport car avail. Pets.

Holiday Inn-Government Center. 5 Blossom St. (742–7630). Outdoor pool. Restaurant, bar, entertainment, dancing. Pets. Nr. Mass. Gen. Hosp., Gov't Center.

Howard Johnsons's. 200 Stuart St. (482–1800). Indoor pool, sauna. Restaurant, bar, entertainment, dancing.

Park Plaza. Park Sq. at Arlington St. (426–2000). Restaurants, bars. Rooms on lower floors considerably less exp. than Towers. Family rates avail.

Moderate

Eliot. 370 Commonwealth Ave., Cor. Mass. Ave. (267–1607). Small, convenient Back Bay hotel. Most rooms have kitchenettes.

Howard Johnson's-Fenway Commonwealth. 575 Commonwealth Ave. at Kenmore Sq. (267–3100). Indoor pool, romantic rooftop lounge. Free parking. Nr. Boston U., Lahey Clinic.

Lenox Hotel. 710 Boylston St. at Prudential Center. (536–5300 or 800–225–7676). Restaurant, bars, entertainment.

Ramada Inn-Airport. 225 McClellan Hwy., E. Boston. (569–5250). Indoor pool, play area. Restaurant, bar, entertainment.

Inexpensive

Copley Square. 47 Huntington Ave. at Exeter (536–9000). Free coffee in many rms. Restaurant, bar. Economy rooms without bath are one of city's great bargains.

Fenway Howard Johnson's. 1271 Boylston St. (267–8300). Pool. Restaurant, bar, entertainment. Next to Fenway Park. Free parking.

Howard Johnson's. Howard Johnson Plaza, Dorchester (288–3030). Restaurant, bar. Away from downtown but nr. Kennedy Library, Bayside Expo Ctr.

Howard Johnson's Motor Lodge. 407 Squire Rd. Revere (near Logan Airport) (284–7200). Outdoor pool. Lounge, 24-hour coffee shop, Japanese steak house. Free parking.

Ramada Inn. 1234 Soldiers Field Rd., Brighton (254–1234). Outdoor pool, play area nr. Pets. Restaurant, bar, entertainment, dancing.

Susse Chalet. 800 Morrissey Blvd. (287–9100). Outdoor pool, play area. Restaurant nr. Plain, basic. Member of regional chain.

Terrace. 1650 Commonwealth Ave., Brighton (566–6260). All rooms with kitchenette. Restaurant nr. Low weekly rates.

CAMBRIDGE

Deluxe

Charles. Bennett and Eliot sts. 864–1200. Brand new; rooms feature bathroom TVs and phones; computer modems. Computer rental avail. Restaurant; bars; entertainment. Near Harvard Square.

Hyatt Regency. 575 Memorial Dr. (492–1234). Continuing the Hyatt reputation for striking modern design, this hotel features a 14-story atrium lobby in which glass elevators ascend, two restaurants and a revolving rooftop lounge.

Expensive

Sheraton-Commander. 16 Garden St. opp. Common (547–4800). Restaurant, bar, entertainment, dancing. Just renovated. Quiet location yet convenient to Harvard Square.

Royal Sonesta. 5 Cambridge Pkwy. (491–3600). Recently doubled in size. Pool. Restaurants, bar, entertainment, dancing. Pets.

Moderate

Harvard Motor House. 110 Mt. Auburn St. (864–5200). Practically in Harvard Square. Direct access to public transportation.

Howard Johnson's. 777 Memorial Dr. (492–7777). Outdoor pool, outdoor platform tennis. Par course, stretching guide for joggers. Japanese steak house.

Inexpensive

Quality Inn. 1651 Massachusetts Ave. (491–1000). Near Harvard Law School. 10 min. walk from Harvard Sq., on bus line. Parking. Restaurant, lounge.

BED AND BREAKFAST. There are now a number of bed and breakfast homes within a 10 to 20 minute drive of downtown Boston. Rates vary from $27 to $47 double occupancy. Reservations available through New England Bed and Breakfast, Inc., 1045 Centre Street, Newton, MA (498–9819); or Bed and Breakfast Areawide Cambridge & Greater Boston by Riva Poor, 73 Kirkland St., Cambridge, MA (576–1492).

YOUTH HOSTELS. Hostels affiliated with the A.Y.H. are located throughout Massachusetts. All are coed. The following is a list of towns in which A.Y.H. hostels currently operate: Amherst, Boston, Brookline, Cedarville, Charlestown, Dudley, East Bridgewater, East Brookfield, Eastham, Granville, Hyannis, Littleton, West Tisbury (Martha's Vineyard), Nantucket, Newburyport, Northfield, Orleans, Springfield and Truro. For details on facilities provided at these hostels, write the Greater Boston Council, American Youth Hostels, 1020 B Commonwealth Ave., Brookline MA 02146 (731–5430).

HOW TO GET AROUND. From the airport: Logan International Airport, about 3 miles from Boston, is served by all major airlines. Facilities have been designed with handicapped travelers in mind. Bus, subway, or taxi to downtown Boston (taxi fare about $7). Ferry to downtown May–Oct.

By train: Boston is the northern terminus of *Amtrak's* northeast corridor, and is served several times daily by trains from Washington and New York. South Station is the point of arrival and departure for these trains, and for *Lake Shore Limited* to western Mass., Albany, and Chicago.

By bus: *Greyhound* terminal is at Park Square (423–5810); *Trailways* is at South Station (482–6620). The MBTA operates local and suburban bus, subway and trolley lines. Maps available at Park St. station. Call 722–3200 for information.

By boat: Service from Boston to Provincetown from Commonwealth Pier. Weekends only Memorial Day to late June, and Labor Day through Columbus Day; daily late June through Labor Day. Bay State Cruises (723–7800). (See "Special Interest Tours.")

TOURS. *Gray Line of Boston* offers tours of greater Boston and historic suburbs leaving from the Park Plaza, Sheraton Boston, and Copley Plaza hotels. Tour No. 1, 3 hrs., covers highlights of old and new Boston; Tour No. 2, 3 hrs., takes sightseers to Lexington and Concord, including battlefields, by way of Harvard Square; Tour No. 3, 7 hours, is a "grand combination" of the above excursions, with a lunch stopover (price of meal not included) at Longfellow's Wayside Inn in Sudbury. For schedules and prices, call or write the Gray Line, 420 Maple St., Marlboro, MA 01752 (426–8805).

SPECIAL INTEREST TOURS. Bay State Cruises, 20 Long Wharf (723–7800), offers cruises around Boston Harbor and to George's Island, where there is a Civil War fort. From George's, take free water taxi to other harbor islands. Also boats to Provincetown; lunch cruises. Weekend schedule begins Memorial Day, ends Columbus Day. Daily schedule June through Labor Day. *Mass. Bay Lines,* 344 Atlantic Ave. (749–4500), offers similar itineraries from Rowe's Wharf (no Provincetown service); also, lunch, dinner and sunset cruises. Weekend schedule Memorial Day to Labor Day; daily schedule starts 4th of July. Private charters are available.

Beacon Hill tours: tours of some homes may be arranged through the Women's City Club of Boston, 40 Beacon St. (227–3550).

Black Heritage Tour covers Beacon Hill's black historical sites. Call 445–7400 for information. *Harborwalk* highlights maritime and mercantile history; brochures are available at the information center on Boston Common.

Bicycle Tour: Planned and frequently ridden by famed heart specialist Dr. Paul Dudley White, marked 11-mi. path begins and ends at Eliot Bridge across Charles River. Bike rentals at Community Bike Shop, 490 Tremont St., Boston (542–8623).

GARDENS. *Public Garden,* next to Boston Common, has formal gardens, rare trees and in spring a wondrous display of tulips. *The Arnold Arboretum,* Jamaica Plain, offers a non-stop, year-round show of flowers, shrubs, trees—one of the best in the country. You can pick up a pamphlet at the office for a self-guided tour.

SPECTATOR SPORTS. Suffolk Downs Race Track, Rte. 1A, E. Boston (567–3900) has thoroughbred racing Mar. to mid-July and from mid-Oct. to early Dec. Post time is 1:45. Greyhounds are raced at Wonderland Park, Revere (284–1300).

The Red Sox play baseball at Fenway Park; the Celtics, basketball, and Bruins, hockey, at Boston Garden; and the Patriots, football, at Sullivan Stadium in suburban Foxboro. For information: *Red Sox,* 267–8661; *Celtics,* 523–3030; *Bruins,* 227–3200; and *Patriots,* 262–1776.

HISTORIC SITES AND HOMES. *Freedom Trail.* Booklet outlining walking tour is available at Tremont St. Information Center; the Greater Boston Chamber of Commerce, Prudential Plaza, Box 490 (338–1976), from The Greater Boston Convention and Tourist Bureau, Prudential Plaza, (267–6446), and at points along the way.

John F. Kennedy National Historic Site, 83 Beals St., Brookline (566–7937). Birthplace of Pres. Kennedy. Closed Jan. 1, Thanksgiving, Dec. 25.

Bunker Hill Monument, Monument Sq., Lexington & High St., Charlestown (241–8220). Spiral staircase to top off 221-ft. obelisk. Closed Christmas.

Longfellow House National Historic Site, 105 Brattle St., Cambridge (876–4491). Closed Jan. 1, Thanksgiving, Dec. 25.

Dorchester Heights National Historic Site, 456 W. 4th St., South Boston (269–4275).

Frederick Law Olmsted National Historic Site, Warren St., Brookline (566–1689). Landscape architect's home and studio.

State House, Cor. Beacon and Park Sts. (727–3676). Classic Bulfinch structure is seat of Massachusetts government. Free tours Mon. through Fri.

Park St. Church, 1 Park St. (523–3383). Built in 1809; site of Garrison's anti-slavery speeches. Open daily; services Sun.

Old Granary Burying Ground, Tremont St., adjacent to Park St. Church. Burial site of Paul Revere, Sam Adams, other patriots. Open daylight hours.

King's Chapel, 58 Tremont St. (523–1749). Earliest home of Church of England in Boston; historic graveyard. Open daily; services Sun.

USS Constitution. Charlestown Navy Yard, across Charlestown Bridge from North End (242–5601). "Old Ironsides" is star attraction of decommissioned Navy Yard, now a National Historic Site featuring museum, maritime history exhibits. Open daily. Free tours of ship; museum $2 adults; $1 seniors; 50 cents children.

Old South Meeting House, Cor. Washington and School Sts. (482–6439). Where the Tea Party began. Free daily lectures on the half hour during summer months.

Faneuil Hall, Dock Sq. (523–2980). "Cradle of Liberty" has shops on first floor, great hall above. Open daily.

Paul Revere House, 19 North Sq. (523–1676). Home of patriot and oldest wooden house in Boston. Open daily Apr. through Dec.; closed Mondays Jan. through March. $1.50 adults; 75 cents children 7 to 16 and senior citizens; 25 cents children under 6.

Old North (Christ) Church, 193 Salem St. (523–6676). One if by land, two if by sea: this is the church. Free tours daily year round.

Copps Hill Burying Ground, Hull and Snowhill Sts., North End. 1659 graveyard is burial place of Mather family, other Colonial notables. Open daylight hours.

Appleton House, 40 Beacon St. (227–3550). Home of Women's City Club of Boston. Tours Weds. by appt., year round. $2.00 fee.

Harrison Gray Otis House, 141 Cambridge St. (227–3956). 1796 home of patriot and Beacon Hill developer, designed by Bulfinch. Tours Mon. through Fri. year round. $2.00 adults; $1.00 under 12; under 7 free.

Old West Church, 131 Cambridge St. (227–5088). Designed by Asher Benjamin. Open daily.

Boston Massacre Site, in front of Old State House, at the head of State St. Circle of cobblestones marks site where five colonists died in hail of British gunfire.

Trinity Church, Copley Sq. (536–0944). Richardson's Romanesque masterpiece. Tour guides available daily in summer, 10:30 A.M. to 3:30 P.M.; call for appt. rest of year. No set charge; donations accepted.

City Hall, 1 City Hall Sq., 725–4000. Striking modern structure at heart of Government Center. Tour guides available for groups.

Lee Nichols House, 159 Brattle St.,. Cambridge (547–4252). Home of Cambridge Historical Society. Open Thurs. 3 P.M. to 5 P.M.

 **LIBRARIES.** *Boston Public Library* at Copley Square is an impressive Italian renaissance building with rare book collections, priceless paintings and the only Chavannes murals outside of France. Closed Sun. See the library's beautiful enclosed courtyard, with its fountain and formal garden. *Bapst Library,* Boston College, has a rare book section, a collection of Irish literature. Free. *John F. Kennedy Library,* overlooking the harbor at Columbia Point, Dorchester, houses late president's papers and effects; film on JFK's life shown daily; Library also houses Hemingway papers, accessible to scholars.

MUSEUMS AND GALLERIES. *Museum of Fine Arts,* 465 Huntington Ave. (267–9300). American, European, Oriental collections; period rooms, musical instruments, silver. Lectures, films, special children's programs. Closed Mon., Jan. 1, July 4, Christmas. Fees, hours subject to change. The Museum is proud of its fine new West Wing, designed by I. M. Pei.

Isabella Stewart Gardner Museum, 280 The Fenway (734–1359). Home of Mrs. Gardner, patron of arts. Paintings, sculpture, concerts. Closed holidays.

Busch-Reisinger Museum, Kirkland Ave., Cambridge (495–2338). Germanic art, medieval through modern periods. Closed legal and academic holidays.

Fogg Museum, 32 Quincy St., Cambridge (495–2387). Paintings, sculpture; all periods. Closed legal holidays. Adjacent is new Sackler Museum; Oriental and Islamic art.

Peabody Museum, 11 Divinity St., Cambridge (745–1876). Artifacts from ancient civilizations. Closed Thanksgiving, Christmas, New Year's.

Museum of Science, Science Park (723–2500). Do-it-yourself exhibits, Talking Transparent Woman, physical science demonstrations, medical science displays. Closed Mondays Sept. through Apr., also closed holidays.

Charles Hayden Planetarium, part of Museum of Science. 45-min. shows.

Children's Museum, Museum Wharf, downtown Boston (426–8855). Hands-on exhibits. Closed Mon., Thanksgiving, Christmas, New Year's.

Museum of Transportation, 15 Newton St., Brookline (522–6140). Old cars; public transportation exhibits.

New England Aquarium, Central Wharf (742–8870). Over 2,000 species; dolphin exhibit.

Nichols House Museum. 55 Mt. Vernon St. (227–6993). Home of Miss Rose Nichols, philanthropist; exquisite 19th-century furnishings. Also home of International Visitors Center. Open 1–5 P.M. Mon., Wed., Sat.

Bostonian Society Historical Museum. 15 State St. (State St. entrance, Old State House) (242–5610). Focus is on Colonial and early republican Boston. Open Tues. through Fri.

Computer Museum, 300 Congress St. (542–0476).

MUSIC. *Boston Symphony Orchestra.* Winter season begins the end of Sept. with concerts in Symphony Hall, Massachusetts & Huntington Aves., Fri. afternoon; Sat. evening and occasionally on Sun., Mon., or Tues. Several rehearsals open. *Pops Concerts* in Symphony Hall, late Apr. to late June, and Christmas season. Outdoor *Esplanade Concerts* in Hatch Memorial Shell, along Charles River, end of June to mid-July. For BSO and Pops information, call 266–1492. See Boston *Globe* Calendar, Thursdays, for programs concerts at John Hancock Hall, New England Mutual Hall, Boston University Concert Hall, Jordan Hall, Berklee College, New England Conservatory of Music, and museums. The *Opera Company of Boston,* under the direction of the renowned Sarah Caldwell, performs during winter opera season at the Company's new home, the Savoy Theater, 539 Washington St., in downtown Boston; check newspapers for schedules, or call 426–5300. Oldest U.S. active choral group, Boston's *Handel and Haydn Society,* performs in Boston and Philharmonic Hall, New York. Spring opera season at the *Wang Center,* 268 Tremont St. (482–9393), features New York's *Metropolitan Opera. Boston Ballet* has been widely acclaimed; tickets at 553 Tremont St., or call 542–3945.

There are frequent chamber music performances in Harvard's Sanders Theater; watch local papers for details.

STAGE AND REVUES. Boston has three major downtown theaters famous for pre-Broadway premieres. They are the *Wilbur,* 246 Tremont St. (423–4008); the *Shubert,* 265 Tremont St. (426–4520); and the *Colonial,* 106 Boylston St. (426–9366). The *Wang Center,* 268 Tremont St. (482–9393), offers occasional theatrical presentations as well as concerts. Smaller theaters include the *Charles Playhouse,* 74 Warrenton St. (426–6912); *Next Move,* 1 Boylston Place (423–5572); *Lyric Stage,* 54 Charles St. (742–8703); *Nucleo Eclettico,* 216

Hanover St. (367–8056); and *Theater Works,* 250 Stuart St. (338–6648). The *Boston Shakespeare Company* is at 52 St. Botolph St. (267–5600). Presentations by college drama groups, such as those at Tufts, Boston University, Emerson College, and *Loeb Drama Center* at Harvard, are scheduled throughout the year. The Loeb, 64 Brattle St., Cambridge (547–8300), is the home of the *American Repertory Theater.* For tickets, call box offices, *Ticketron* (542–5491), or stop at the Quincy Market kiosk of Bostix (723–5181).

 SHOPPING. *Filene's,* 426 Washington St., Boston's most famous store, includes *Filene's Basement,* a bargain-hunter's paradise. *Jordan-Marsh Co.,* 450 Washington St., has everything from records to designer dresses. Newbury St., in the Back Bay, is lined with art galleries, haute couture shops, and branches of exclusive New York stores such as *Bonwit Teller, Brooks Brothers* and *F.A.O. Schwartz.* On nearby Boylston St., you'll find *Louis* and *Roots,* two of Boston's best men's shops, and the venerable jewelry, tableware, antiques, and gift emporium of *Shreve Crump and Low.* The new *Copley Place* complex features *Nieman Marcus, Gucci, Charles Jourdan, Louis Vuitton, Tiffany, Rizzoli Books, Ralph Lauren, Saint Laurent Rive Gauche, Godiva Choclatier,* and several dozen other posh shops. In the Prudential Center, you'll find *Lord and Taylor, Saks Fifth Avenue,* and many smaller specialty shops.

The Faneuil Hall-Quincy Market complex is a colorful and eclectic bazaar; visit when you're hungry.

Downtown at 29 School St., near the old City Hall, is *Brookstone,* which sells ingenious, high quality tools and gadgets for home, car, and garden. Outdoorspersons will enjoy *Eastern Mountain Sports,* 1041 Commonwealth Ave. near Boston University and at Winthrop Sq. downtown.

The Harvard Coop, in Cambridge and downtown Boston, has outstanding record and book selections. Visit *Crate & Barrel,* Brattle Square, Cambridge, for housewares.

 **DINING OUT.** Boston's restaurants are heirs to a long tradition: the first was established by a French emigré in the 18th century, and "pot luck" in taverns and inns goes back long before that. You may have to look hard for the famous baked beans, but Parker House rolls are still served where they were invented, and everywhere there is fresh seafood. Ethnic dining is popular in Boston, and even more so in Cambridge. You will have no trouble finding the Victorian saloon-steakhouse establishments in Boston, and lately there has been a profusion of soup-and-salad bar places as well. At the other end of the price scale, Boston offers some of the country's finest hotel dining. Restaurants in Cambridge and suburbs follow Boston listings.

The cost of an à la carte dinner is the basis of our price range: *Deluxe,* $30 and up; *Expensive,* $22–$30; *Moderate,* $16–$22; *Inexpensive,* under $16. Remember that there are plenty of places with prices even lower than the "Inexpensive" category, and also deluxe establishments where dinner for 2 with wine and tip will cost well over $100.

Most restaurants accept credit cards; however, we strongly advise you to call ahead and double check, and it is also wise to make reservations ahead of time as Boston restaurants fill up quickly. A phone call, of course, will also tell you if reservations are not accepted—in which case you'll just have to expect a wait, especially on weekends.

BOSTON

American International

Apley's. *Deluxe.* Sheraton-Boston Hotel, Prudential Center (236–2000). Original treatments of traditional dishes. Pheasant in port sauce; scallop and shrimp mousse; loin of venison; dessert soufflés. Extensive wine list.

The Bay Tower Room. *Deluxe.* 60 State St. (723–1666). A thirty-third-floor enclave in the financial district; private at lunchtime but open for dinner. Filet of beef *en cocotte;* fine wines.

Locke-Ober. *Deluxe.* 3 Winter Pl. (542–1340). Locke-Ober has been here forever. Its food is traditional, featuring items such as oyster stew, plates of fresh asparagus, grilled lamb chops, and sweetbreads (all very good), and we would often choose it over more imaginative places for atmosphere alone. Locke's is the epitome of the Yankee Boston of legend.

Maison Robert. *Deluxe.* 45 School St., in old Boston City Hall (227–3370). Rack and saddle of lamb; striped bass with cream sauce; *crepes suzette* prepared at tableside. Excellent wine cellar.

Parker's. *Deluxe.* Parker House Hotel, Tremont St. (227–8600). A fine new menu—red snapper en croute, scallop of veal with kiwi fruit, medallion of veal Dijonnaise. Lots of seafood and, of course, Parker House rolls.

The Ritz. *Deluxe.* 15 Arlington St. (536–5700). Located in the hotel of the same name, with food and service in the great Ritz tradition. A serene and elegant oasis. Specialties include pâte en croûte with Cumberland sauce, lobster *etuvé au whiskey.* The wine list is unusually good.

Seasons. *Deluxe.* Bostonian Hotel, Dock Sq., 523–3600. Magnificent service and appointments, and one of the city's most imaginative menus. The offerings change with the seasons, with freshness of ingredients the prime concern.

Arne's. *Expensive.* Copley Place (267–4900). A new seafood place that has been very well received. The escargot ravioli in garlic butter is a big hit.

Devon on the Common. *Expensive.* 150 Boylston St. (482–0722). Excellent steaks, rack of lamb, seafood, all displayed raw for your selection. Downstairs is the *New Orleans Cafe,* less expensive, a Cajun spot with Dixieland band.

Gallagher. *Expensive.* 55 Congress St. (523–6080). One of downtown's best. Fresh cod in puff pastry; veal chop in parchment. Jazz in adjacent club Wed. through Sat.

Landmark Inn. *Moderate-Expensive.* North Market Bldg., Quincy Market (227–9660). Four restaurants—The Wild Goose (roast pheasant and goose, veal Stroganoff); Thompson's Chowder House; a lounge; and a glassed-wall café.

29 Newbury St. *Moderate-Expensive.* (536–5137). A small new restaurant with a large a la carte menu ranging from homemade pasta to sweetbreads to sashimi. Open till 12:30 A.M.

Chart House. *Moderate.* 60 Long Wharf (227–1576). Fine steaks and seafood in a fascinating, multi-level wharf building. Bar.

Durgin Park. *Moderate.* North Market, Faneuil Hall Marketplace (227–2038). Gargantuan slabs of roast beef served at long, communal tables by waitresses playing the "sassy wench" of popular Colonial tradition. Closed holidays. Durgin Park now has a branch in Copley Place (266–1964).

Legal Sea Foods. *Moderate.* Park Plaza Hotel, Park Sq. (426–4944). An old Cambridge landmark reborn in Boston. Strictly fresh seafood, including some unusual varieties like monkfish and shad. Also at Chestnut Hill Mall, Newton.

Tiger Lilies. *Moderate.* 23 Joy St. (523–0609). French country ambience in a Beacon Hill townhouse. "American nouvelle" menu changes with seasons. Fireplaces, patio dining in summer.

Brandy Pete's. *Inexpensive.* 82 Broad St. (482–4165). Plain and simple; a downtown bargain. Roast turkey; scallops and other seafood; veal parmigiana.

Souper Salad. *Inexpensive.* 5 locations in downtown, Back Bay, and Cambridge. Soups, sandwiches, quiche, a few hot specials and a salad bar rated best in Boston by the *Globe.*

Chinese

Hen Ho. *Inexpensive.* 266 Newbury St. (267–1157). Vietnamese actually. Beef and chicken with lemon grass; spring rolls; stuffed shrimp.

Imperial Tea House. *Inexpensive.* 70 Beach St. (426–8439). Great fun—it's one of those Chinese places where the *dim sum* (dumplings, etc.) cart makes endless rounds, diners pick what they want, and the waiter counts the plates to tally the bill.

French

L'Espalier. *Deluxe.* 30 Gloucester St. (262–3023). At or near the top of everyone's "best" list for Boston. All dinners are prix fixe and might include venison, quail salad, or *escalope de saumon,* depending on the chef's current interests and the availability of ingredients. A cheese course is served.

Julien. *Deluxe.* 1 Post Office Sq. (451–1900). Julien's approach to *nouvelle cuisine* is faithful without being dogmatic, and this new hotel restaurant (it's at the Meridien) is already one of Boston's best. Recent offerings have included salmon and sole mousse, veal kidneys with red wine butter, and medallions of duck. The desserts are excellent, as is the service.

Aujour d'hui. *Deluxe.* Four Seasons Hotel, 200 Boylston St. (338–4400). A new spot starting out strong—it's nominally French, but specialties run to imaginative "New American" as well as continental treatments.

Le Marquis de Lafayette. *Deluxe.* Lafayette Hotel, 1 Avenue de Lafayette (451–2600). An ambitious and successful offering of updated *haute cuisine;* duck and salmon dishes are exceptional.

Another Season. *Expensive.* 97 Mt. Vernon St. (367–0880). Popular with Beacon Hill neighborhood crowd. Menu changes every other week. A tasteful blend of ethnic cuisines, with a French bias. Good fish dishes, and always a vegetarian selection.

Icarus. *Expensive.* 540 Tremont St. (426–1790). An intimate South End spot. The food runs to revisionist French provincial or what's called "New American"—examples are artichoke and red onion tart with goat cheese, smoked tenderloin of pork braised in cider with cabbage and pears.

Lily's. *Expensive.* Faneuil Hall Marketplace (227–4242). Don't mistake the sidewalk cafe for the restaurant of the same name, located just indoors and a world away.

Maitre Jacques. *Expensive.* 10 Emerson Pl. (742–5480). Rack of lamb, duck with orange sauce, Dover sole, splendid desserts. Bar.

German

Jacob Wirth's. *Inexpensive.* 31 Stuart St. (338–8586). As much a bar as a restaurant, but the only place in town that serves up big platters of wurst, kraut and boiled meats Milwaukee style. It owes its old-time look not to a decorator, but to time itself.

Greek-Middle Eastern

Aegean Fare. *Moderate.* Faneuil Hall Marketplace (742–8349) and two other Boston locations. Boston loves Greek salad, and this restaurant is largely responsible. Baklava is also featured.

Red Fez. *Inexpensive.* 1222 Washington St. (338–8446). Cuisine of the Mideast—hummus; shish kebab; lamb and string beans. In South End.

Indian

Kebab-n-Kurry. *Inexpensive.* 30 Massachusetts Ave. (536–9835). Authentic Indian cuisine served at lunch and dinner.

Italian

Ciro and Sal's. *Expensive.* (437–0500). A spin-off of the famous Cape Cod restaurant. In Back Bay. Caponata, homemade pasta with at least a dozen different sauces, good seafood. To start, try *insalata di polpi,* a cold octopus salad.

Davio's. *Expensive.* 269 Newbury St. (262–4810). Easy to pass by, but don't. Extensive northern Italian menu. Fettucini Alfredo, *mozzarella in carozza.* Light, flavorful sauces.

Venezia. *Moderate-Expensive.* 20 Ericson, off SE Expwy. in Dorchester (436–3120). Great harbor views—it's even accessible by boat! Northern Italian cuisine, with fine repertory of veal and seafood dishes. Handy if you've been to Kennedy Library or Bayside Expo Ctr., but get directions first.

Felicia's. *Moderate.* 145A Richmond St. (523–9885). House specialty is Chicken Verdicchio, with artichoke hearts and dry white wine. Beer, wine. Closed holidays.

The Romagnolis' Table. *Moderate.* North Market Building, Faneuil Hall Marketplace (367–9114). Fine homemade pasta, including *tortellini*. A choice of sauces. Veal, chicken dishes. Nice desserts. Owned by famous TV cooks.

Pat's Pushcart. *Inexpensive.* 61 Endicott St. (523–9616). Not a pushcart exactly, but a cozy and inviting little spot. Good sandwiches at lunchtime; full dinner menu.

Japanese

Kai-Seki. *Moderate.* 132 Newbury St. (247–1583). Sushi bar. Also full dinner menu featuring authentic Japanese dishes. Steamed scallops, sauteed pork with ginger and sesame.

The Seventh Inn. *Moderate.* 272a Newbury St. (247–2475). Specializing in natural foods served Japanese style, emphasizing the freshest of fish and vegetables. Closed Mon.

Mexican

Casa Romero. *Moderate.* 30 Gloucester St. (536–4341). More sophisticated than tacos and tamales, although these are available, too. Bar, featuring Mexican beers.

Russian

The Hermitage. *Expensive.* 955 Boylston (247–8029). Located beneath the Institute of Contemporary Art, this imaginative restaurant features specialties from the French-inspired cuisine of Imperial Russia. Caviar. Bar stocked with exotic flavored vodkas, served shivering cold. Daily tea and Sunday brunch.

EAST BOSTON

Blazing Saddles. *Inexpensive-Moderate.* 940 Saratoga St. (569–2020). Tasty, hearty portions of baby back ribs, sirloin tips, steak. The onion ring loaf is superb—but make sure you're hungry. A good place to stop when you're early for a flight out of Logan.

BROOKLINE

Chef Chang's House. *Inexpensive.* 1004–1006 Beacon St. (277–4226). Mandarin, Szechuan, and Shanghai specialties, including Peking duck.

Sol Azteca. *Inexpensive.* 914A Beacon St. (262–0909). A small, chef-owned Mexican spot that does a creditable job with the standard south-of-the-border (and Tex-Mex) repertory.

CAMBRIDGE

American International

Voyagers. *Expensive.* 45½ Mt. Auburn St. (354–1718). Formal dining on main floor; upstairs, a greenhouse and harp music. Veal Brillat-Savarin; fresh game in season incl. smoked quail. Closed Mon.

Harvest. *Moderate.* 44 Brattle St. (492–1115). American nouvelle, featuring salmon in season, duck breast with papaya, homemade pâtés. Outdoor cafe.

Peacock. *Moderate.* 5 Craigie Circle (661–4073). French provincial dishes, such as roast duck with red cabbage. Excellent desserts. Closed Sun. and Mon.

Casablanca. *Moderate.* 40 Brattle St. (876–0999). Enter from the side alley. A cozy upstairs spot featuring good soups, steaks, pasta, daily specials. Bar. The murals depict scenes from a certain movie . . .

Pentimento. *Inexpensive.* 344 Huron Ave. (661–3878). Old oak furniture and down-home cooking in a quiet corner of Cambridge. Ratatouille, chicken pot pie, vegetable curry, rich desserts. No smoking.

Chinese

Hunan. *Moderate.* 700 Mass. Ave. (876–7000). Menu is an encyclopedia of dishes from the Chinese provinces of Szechuan and Hunan. The chef will tone down spices if requested; otherwise, dishes listed in red will bring tears to your eyes.

Lucky Gardens. *Inexpensive.* 282 Concord Ave. (354–9514). A restaurant with a following. Steamed and fried dumplings, chicken and peanuts in spicy sauce, Peking duck, plus many other authentic dishes.

French

Ferdinand's. *Expensive.* 121 Mt. Auburn St. (491–4915). Small, intimate. Simple things done well, like filet mignon with bearnaise sauce. Unusual selection of vintage wines.

Autre Chose. *Moderate.* 1105 Mass. Ave. (661–0852). Country-style French cooking, with atmosphere to match. The Sunday brunch is a local standout. Closed Mon.

Cajun

The Cajun Yankee. *Moderate.* 1193 Cambridge St. (576–1971). The real thing—gumbo, jambalaya, shrimp remoulade, crayfish etouffee. Small—reservations a must.

Greek

Athenian Taverna. *Moderate.* 567 Mass. Ave. (547–6300). Shish kebab, steaks, lamb dishes. Entertainment in evenings. Closed holidays and Greek Easter.

Averof. *Inexpensive.* 1924 Mass. Ave. (354–4500). Greek cuisine and entertainment; luncheon buffet is one of area's best bargains.

Indian

India. *Moderate.* 1780 Mass. Ave. (354–0949). An assortment of curries; Indian bread and desserts.

Oh Calcutta. *Inexpensive.* 468 Massachusetts Ave. (576–2111). Meat and vegetable curries; Indian breads and condiments.

Japanese

Bisuteki. *Moderate.* Howard Johnson Motor Lodge, 777 Memorial Dr. (492–7777). Japanese steak house features *tepinyaki* tableside cookery. Sakura lounge.

Little Osaka. *Moderate.* Concord Ave., off Fresh Pond Circle (491–6600). *Sushi,* traditional dishes. Popular with visiting Japanese.

Mexican

Chi-Chi's. *Inexpensive.* At the Orson Welles Theater, 1001 Massachusetts Ave. (491–2040). The usual Tex-Mex fare plus *chimichangas,* a sort of deep-fried burrito. Big strawberry margaritas.

Portuguese

Casa Portugal. *Moderate.* 1200 Cambridge St. (491–8880). An ethnic cuisine not to be overlooked. The Portuguese have an especially fine touch with pork and seafood dishes.

WATERTOWN

Le Bocage. *Expensive.* 72 Bigelow St. (923–1210). Tournedos of beef, French provincial cuisine. Informal and intimate.

Glenda's Kitchen. *Moderate.* Lexington St. (926–3222). Spanish/Mexican dishes, including enchiladas and seafood platters. Pitchers of sangria. Luncheon specials a good value.

 **COFFEE HOUSES AND OUTDOOR CAFES.** *Cafe Florian.* 85 Newbury St. (247–7603). Exotic coffees and teas; pastries; luncheon. Sidewalk cafe in summer. There are also several outdoor cafes in the Faneuil Hall Marketplace complex.

In Boston's North End, visit the *Pompeii* and the *Café Della Sport,* both on Hanover St., for espresso and Italian pastries.

In Cambridge, a popular folk spot is *Passim,* 47 Palmer St., Harvard Square (492-7679). Expect a modest cover charge. Two Cambridge coffee houses specializing in exotic brews and excellent desserts are the *Algiers,* in Brattle Square, and the *Pamplona,* on Bow St. near Massachusetts Ave.

 **NIGHT LIFE AND BARS.** *The Black Rose,* 160 State St. (523-8486), dispenses draft stout and offers Irish folk music nightly. Lunch and dinner. *Clarke's,* 21 Merchants Row (227-7800), with outdoor seating in summer, is a popular after-work spot in Boston's financial district. *Friday's,* Newbury at Exeter St. (266-9040), occupies a sidewalk greenhouse attached to the old Exeter Street Theater. The bar at the *Lenox Hotel,* 710 Boylston St. (536-5300) features popular piano singalongs. *Hampshire House,* 84 Beacon St. (227-9600), features two taprooms—an upstairs parlor decked out like a 19th-century mens' club, with a lovely view of the public garden, and the *Bull and Finch Pub,* a more informal (and louder) cellar bar. This is the bar on which the TV show "Cheers" is based. *The Last Hurrah,* at Dunfey's Parker House, Tremont St. (227-8600), also serving lunch and dinner, is hung with photos of old-time politicos. Swing orchestra often featured. *Lily's,* in the Faneuil Hall Marketplace (227-4242), has jazz in both cafe and bar settings. *The Ritz Bar,* in the Ritz Carlton Hotel (536-5700), is perhaps Boston's most famous spa and surely its quietest and most intimate. Luncheon and hors d'oeuvres served. Recently remodeled; looks more like it did pre-1970. The *Copley Plaza* (267-5300), also houses two fine drinking salons. *The Copley Bar,* more formal of the two rooms, features (except in summer) the superb piano artistry of Dave McKenna. Another quiet, dressy spot for cocktails—with a spectacular view— is the lounge at the *Bay Tower Room,* 60 State St. (723-1666). In *Cambridge,* the *Regatta Bar* at the new Charles Hotel, Eliot and Bennett Sts. (864-1200) offers local jazz Wed.-Sun. For jazz, try *Springfields,* 1369 Cambridge St. (354-8030) or *Ryle's,* 212 Hampshire St. (876-9330). The *Wursthaus,* 4 John F. Kennedy St. (491-7110), which features a German menu, is known for its selection of dozens of international beers. There are two elegant lounges at the Hyatt Regency Hotel, the *Pallysadoe* and the top-floor, revolving *Spinnaker.* Both offer entertainment. The Hyatt is at 575 Memorial Dr. (492-1234).

EXPLORING CAPE COD

by Bob Murphy and Helen Dalzell

Bob Murphy and Helen Dalzell have taught courses on New England history through the Boston Center for Adult Education, the Habitat Institute, and the Providence Learning Connection. They are also active environmentalists who have worked to preserve coastal Massachusetts.

The Cape, like Boston and much of Massachusetts' South Shore, has figured in American history from the start. It was explored in 1602 by the English navigator Bartholomew Gosnold, who named it after the great schools of codfish he found in the bay. Eighteen years later, the Pilgrims first landed in Provincetown before continuing on to Plymouth. Although the sand and marshes these early settlers found did not support much farming, prosperous whaling and fishing industries developed and flourished. Salt works had been established on the Cape during Pilgrim times, and in the early 19th century, came the glass industry of Sandwich. But the Cape never developed as a major indus-

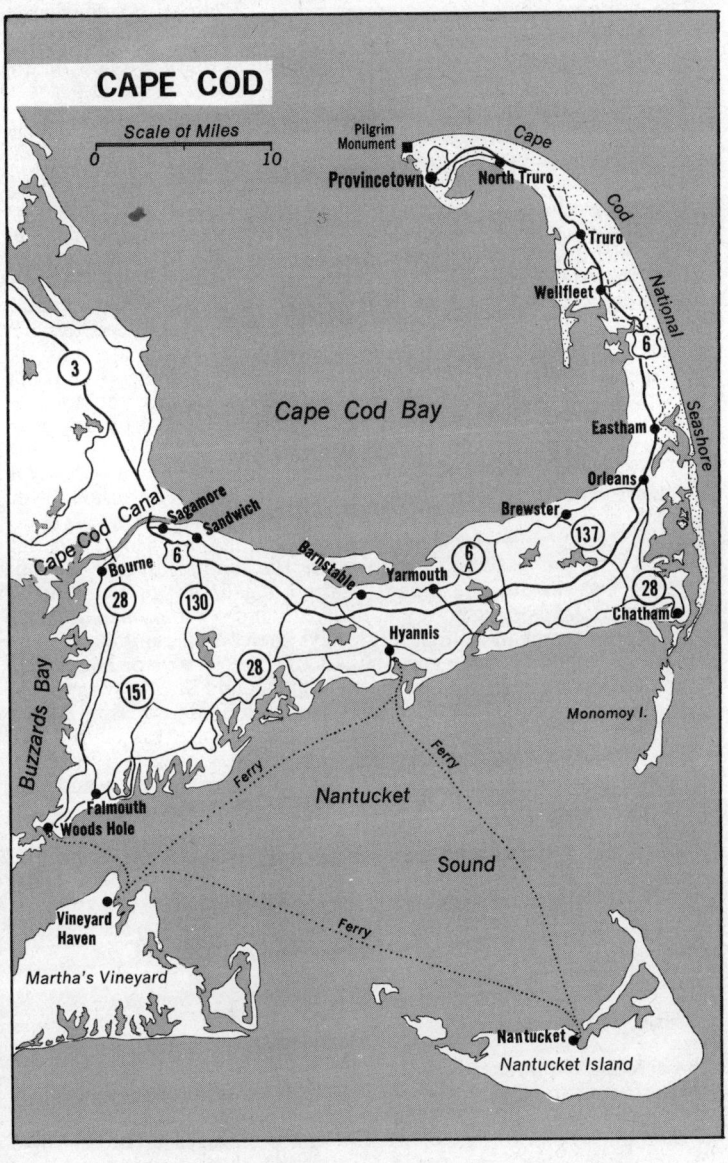

CAPE COD

Scale of Miles

0   10

Pilgrim Monument

Provincetown   North Truro

Cape

Cod

Truro

Wellfleet

National

6

Cape Cod Bay

Eastham

Orleans

Seashore

Brewster

Sagamore

Cape Cod Canal   Sandwich

Barnstable

137

3

Bourne

6

6
A

Yarmouth

28

Chatham

28

130

Hyannis

Buzzards Bay

151

28

Monomoy I.

Ferry

Ferry

Nantucket

Falmouth
Woods Hole

Sound

Vineyard
Haven

Ferry

Martha's Vineyard

Nantucket

Nantucket Island

trial center. Manufacturers began to decline in the mid-19th century, and the Cape entered a period of economic depression.

In the 1920s, this trend began to be reversed with the birth of a new industry and a new way of life—tourism. Although the fishing, lobstering and boatbuilding industries are still alive, tourism is by far the biggest industry on the Cape today. With its miles of varied beaches, its charming old New England villages of white clapboard mansions and churches and silver-shingled Cape Cod cottages; its pine woods, grassy marshes and rolling dunes; and its mild ocean climate, Cape Cod has been one of the country's most loved vacation spots for many years. Inescapably, the new prosperity brought by the tourists who flock there in ever-increasing droves has significantly altered the appearance, the way of life and the ecological balance of the Cape. The great danger is that the primitive natural beauty that draws travelers to the Cape will be destroyed by the very growth of tourism. Or, the Cape may gradually be transformed into a southern suburb of Boston, a process that has already begun in the burgeoning western sections. At any rate, the Cape is not what it was twenty years ago, and it will undoubtedly continue to change for some years to come. However, despite the summer crowds and the overdevelopment of the most frequented resorts, most of the Cape remains compellingly beautiful.

The Cape is convenient to Boston, and under ideal conditions you can travel by car to Provincetown in 2½ hours. However, although you can make a complete circuit of it in about two days, the Cape is really a place for relaxing—for swimming and sunning; for fishing, boating and playing golf or tennis; for attending the summer theater, antique hunting and making the rounds of the art galleries; or for leisurely walking and exploring. So if you like sand and sea and have time, it's a good idea to spend at least a few days there. You can find all sorts of accommodations, from guest houses to resort motels or housekeeping cottages and cabins. Summer travelers should always reserve several months in advance, and even off-season lodging is getting harder to come by without reservations. But there is still plenty of elbow room on the Cape in the fall and spring, and you may even find its visual appeal enhanced during those seasons, although swimming and sunbathing must be forsaken. A Cape Cod resort directory may be obtained at the Cape Cod Chamber of Commerce information booths at Bourne and Sagamore, where the two bridges cross the Cape Cod Canal. Or, write the Chamber of Commerce at Hyannis, MA 02601 (362–3225). If possible, it's a good idea to avoid travel to and from the Cape on crowded Fridays and Sundays when traffic jams sometimes occur on Route 3 from Boston and on Route 6 on the Cape.

Side Trips

There are two interesting side trips to historic sites off Route 3, the main road from Boston to the Cape. The first is to Quincy, the only city in America where you can see the birthplaces, homes and final resting places of two Presidents. On Hancock Street at the corner of Washington is the First Parish Church, which was built in 1828 of Quincy granite and contains the crypt of the Adams family. Here are buried the remains of John Adams and his wife, Abigail, as well as those of John Quincy Adams and his wife, Louisa Catherine. A little beyond the church on Hancock Street, turn right on Franklin Street for the Adams National Historic Site, the home of four generations of the Adams family. Filled with priceless heirlooms and antiques, it is open to the public. The family presented the home to the United States government in 1946. Also located on Hancock Street is the home of Dorothy Quincy, wife of John Hancock. The Quincy family, long prominent in colonial politics and trade, were prosperous New England shipbuilders. Visitors are welcome at the Quincy home.

Quincy, in its early days, was well known for its granite, with which the Bunker Hill Monument and King's Chapel were built. The first railroad in the U.S. was built to haul Quincy granite in the 1820s, but the motive power was draft animals rather than steam. You may return to Route 3 from here, or if you have time, remain on Route 3 Alternate, through the pleasant seaside towns of Hingham, Cohasset, Greenbush and Marshfield. This route runs close to the ocean, and many public beaches can be enjoyed by turning left on almost any of the small roads. The community of Duxbury was established by the Pilgrims shortly after the settlement of Plymouth, and you may visit the John Alden House there. Route 3 Alternate rejoins and crosses the superhighway (Route 3), but visitors should stay on the smaller road to Kingston. The history of this town almost coincides with that of Plymouth, of which it was a part until 1726. The Bradford House contains many of the original furnishings, dating back to 1674, when it was built. Route 3 Alternate continues four more miles to Plymouth, the second major attraction on the way to the Cape.

Plymouth

Plymouth was one of the first English-speaking settlements in the New World. Today, it is visited annually by thousands of Americans who want to know where and how it all began. Since that historic day in December 1620, when the weary, weakened Pilgrims landed there in the *Mayflower,* Plymouth has grown and thrived, and is now a busy city. But thanks to the many restorations and museums, the imaginative visitor to Plymouth will find that sense of the past he seeks. To enjoy this town you must first close your eyes and picture the 102 *Mayflower* voyagers sailing anxiously into the quiet harbor of an unknown region, to what they hoped would be their new home. The first winter was hard and took the lives of half the group. But when the *Mayflower* departed for England in the spring, not a single survivor returned with her.

With this picture in mind, turn off Route 3 Alternate, left on North Park Avenue, and continue to the waterfront, where Plymouth Rock now rests under a canopy of granite to protect it from souvenir hunters. Not far from the hallowed boulder is the *Mayflower II,* a replica of the original ship. It was built in England and sailed across the Atlantic in 1957. Visitors are welcome aboard. From the rock, climb the stairway leading to Cole's Hill. This is where the Pilgrims buried their dead by night, so that the Indians could not calculate the number of survivors. If it had not been for the friendship of Massasoit, the great chief of the Wampanoags, they would have all perished. A statue of him stands near the sepulcher. On Leyden Street is the First Parish Church, home of a congregation begun by the Pilgrims. The original building was erected in 1683 and the present church is the fifth on this site. Walk up the stone steps beside the church to Burial Hill, which overlooks the square. The fort was built in 1621 and contained five cannons. Nearby are the graves of such early settlers as Governor Bradford, Edward

Gray. Thomas Clark and John Cotton. Also of interest is the town brook, which furnished water to the Pilgrims. The town established Brewster Gardens nearby, on the site of the settlers' original gardens.

If you continue north along Water Street and turn left on Chilton Street you will arrive at the Pilgrim relics and paintings. Located nearby, off Court Street, is the visitor information booth. After leaving the Plymouth waterfront, follow Route 3 Alternate south about half a mile to Plimoth Plantation, a recreation of the original Pilgrim colony as it looked in 1627, based on early historical documents. The first census was taken in 1627; in that same year, the herd of cattle, which had previously been owned in common, was apportioned. Surviving records of these efforts tell us who lived in each of the houses. Costumed men and women today enact the day-to-day life of the Pilgrims. Information on American Indian life is also presented.

The Cape

Next, follow Route 3 to the Cape Cod Canal, which separates the Cape from the mainland and is crossed on the eastern side by the Sagamore Bridge and from Route 28 on the Buzzards Bay side by the Bourne Bridge. The canal was dug between 1909 and 1914 by the U.S. Army Corps of Engineers, 300 years after Myles Standish first proposed it to eliminate the dangerous trip around the shallows off Provincetown.

From the canal to the elbow (Cape Cod resembles a crooked arm) the Cape is traversed by three major roads: Route 6A on the northern side; Route 6, a two-lane highway, down the middle; and Route 28 to the south. They all join at Orleans and from there Route 6 continues up the forearm to Truro and Provincetown. The Cape's townships are oddly formed, often extending from the North Shore down to the South. The township of Dennis, for example, consists of the towns of Dennis and East Dennis on the North Shore, South Dennis in the center, and West Dennis and Dennis Port on the South Shore. Because of the multiplicity of similarly named villages, it's always a good idea to check your road map.

The three main highways traverse contrasting regions. Route 6 passes through the relatively unpopulated center of the Cape, which is characterized by an undulating landscape of scrub pine and scrub oak. It is generally the fastest route east and visitors with specific destinations on the North or South shores or who want to travel directly to the National Seashore Project are advised to take it to the appropriate exits. You may wish to drive east on Route 6 to the Yarmouth or Dennis exits and then swing south to Route 28, thereby avoiding the more congested areas around Falmouth and Hyannis.

The southern side of the Cape, reached by Route 28, is the more heavily populated and the major center for tourism. Its growth as a resort area has been abetted by its abundance of scenic harbors overlooking Nantucket Sound and its fine beaches with white sand and gentle surf. On the extreme southwestern corner is Woods Hole, where the car ferries for Martha's Vineyard and Nantucket depart. It is also the location of the Woods Hole Oceanographic Institute and the aquarium of the U.S. Bureau of Commercial Fisheries, among the world's largest centers for marine research. Falmouth and the surrounding villages comprise one of the Cape's main commercial and resort areas. It was settled in 1661 by a group of Quakers and was an active center of trade and shipping. The Congregational church, opposite the green, contains a bell made by Paul Revere.

Mashpee is the home of the Cape's Wampanoag Indians, and the newly developed South Cape Beach, open to the public. Hyannis, with its fashionable satellite resort towns, is the commercial hub of tourism on the Cape. Hyannis Port is famous as the site of the Kennedy family compound. Although tourists are not allowed near the compound, which is surrounded by a high fence, traffic is heavy with sightseers. Lewis Bay, farther east, is a focal point of boating activity and the point of departure for summer passenger ferries to Martha's Vineyard and Nantucket. The proliferation of motels, restaurants, and antique shops continues past Hyannis on the South Shore but thins out somewhat as you go east. There are fine sea captains' mansions in South Yarmouth. You may want to take Lower County Road from West Dennis to Harwich Port, where it rejoins Route 28 and passes by scenic Wychmere Harbor.

Noncommercial Chatham to Orleans

Chatham is a typical Cape Cod village, but free of the commercialism that mars many towns and villages on the South Shore of the Cape. It also boasts the largest public beaches on the Cape. You can watch the boats unloading their catch around noon at the Fish Pier. Every Friday night during the summer, the Chatham band gives a concert in a natural amphitheater located just off Main Street. Children will enjoy the concert, which is planned with them in mind.

The view of the ocean from the Chatham Lighthouse is spectacular. South of Chatham, trailing off from the "elbow" of the Cape, lies Monomoy, accessible only by boat. This fragile spit of land now enjoys protection as a federally-designated wilderness area—although this political distinction did nothing to mitigate the ravages of the freak tides which accompanied the blizzard of 1978 as well as more recent storms. In the words of an Audubon Society official, there are now "two Monomoys." The entire eastern coast, from Monomoy up past Chatham Light House to Nauset Beach and the Cape Cod National Seashore Project, has been the scene of countless shipwrecks and there are many stories of vessels helplessly dashed against the coast by the unchecked force of fierce northeasters. In one of the most famous of these wrecks, the British Man o' War *Somerset* ran aground in 1778. She figures in Longfellow's *The Midnight Ride of Paul Revere* as the ship Paul had to row past in order to reach Charlestown. Every half century or so, the sands shift to uncover the *Somerset's* remains.

From Chatham, Route 28 curves north and joins 6 and 6A at Orleans on the northern part of the Cape. In Orleans you can follow Rock Harbor Road to the town landing. Here, in 1814, the militia of Orleans routed a British landing party. The Captain Linnel House on this road resembles a country home in southern France. From Orleans go east on Nauset Beach Road to Nauset Beach, one of the finest along the east coast. It is the anchor end of a 40-mile stretch of beach extending to Provincetown. This is the "Great Beach" of which Thoreau wrote so movingly in *Cape Cod.* Visitors can still walk its length as Thoreau did, although the writer's path is now under water: each year, the Atlantic claims more of the Cape's eastern shore.

National Seashore

Three miles north on U.S. 6 is the town of Eastham; just beyond the village is the headquarters building of the Cape Cod National Seashore, established in 1961 to preserve the Cape's natural and historic resources. Four major areas of the park have been developed for visitors: Nauset, Marconi Station, Pilgrim Heights and Province Lands. Within them you can find superb ocean beaches; great rolling, lonely dunes; various types of swamps, marshes and wetlands; austere scrub and grasslands; and all kinds of wildlife. The headquarters building at Nauset Center in Eastham has displays, literature racks and an auditorium for nature lectures. Turn right here for the Coast Guard area and the Nauset Beach Lighthouse. The beach has parking and bathhouse facilities. During the season, park guides offer daily nature walks and lectures. There is a special Buttonbush Trail for the Blind with handropes and Braille inscriptions; other trails lead to a red maple swamp, a salt pond and to Nauset Marsh. The high bluffs in this area provide excellent views. Although these sand cliffs tempt visitors to make a quick, well-cushioned descent, climbing or sliding is discouraged because of its contribution to the already serious erosion problem.

Five miles beyond, on the same route, is the Marconi Station Area of the park. Here are the remains of the first transatlantic wireless station erected on the U.S. mainland. From here, Marconi sent a radio message to Europe on January 19, 1901. Most of the site has given way to the relentless waves which each year erode more of the shore, and which, hundreds or thousands of years from now, may break through to Cape Cod Bay. In 1717, the pirate ship *Widah* was blown ashore in the surf three-quarters of a mile northeast of the Marconi Area, spilling her crew and her ill-gotten wealth into Cape Cod waters. In 1984, divers began to recover the *Widah*'s gold.

Route 6 continues on through Wellfleet, once the location of a large oyster industry, and along with Truro to the north a colonial whaling and codfishing port. Wellfleet is one of the more picturesque and tastefully developed Cape resort towns. The village contains a number of fine restaurants, inns and historic homes. A foot trail leads through a sandy wilderness to the tip of Great Island, the promontory that forms Wellfleet Harbor. Truro, a town boasting huge dunes, is popular with artists and writers. The most prominent painter to have lived here was the late Edward Hopper, who found the Cape light ideal for his austere brand of realism. Up Route 6 a bit farther on the right is the Pilgrim Heights Area of the National Seashore. Lectures on the early history of this region are given daily at the shelter and there are parking and picnic areas. Close by is the spring from which the Pilgrims refilled their casks before sailing on to Plymouth. There is also a self-guided trail to Small's Swamp. From here you can follow U.S. 6 to the Province Lands Area of the Park or U.S. 6A to Provincetown. The Province Lands Area comprises Race Point and Herring Cove beaches, a picnic area, bicycle trails and the Beech Forest Nature Trail.

Provincetown

Provincetown, or P-town as Cape Codders call it, stands by itself and what attracts one visitor to Provincetown may cause another visitor to raise an eyebrow. The town enjoys spectacular, windswept beaches and dunes, offering opportunities for many forms of outdoor recreation, from surf-fishing to horseback-riding. In Provincetown's commercial district, Portuguese-American fishermen mix with whale-watchers from Boston and tourists from Quebec. The town has attracted a variety of painters, poets, and writers. P-town has also become a popular resort town for gays.

European fishermen and explorers first came to what is now Provincetown in the 1500s. In 1620, the Pilgrims' first landfall in the New World was at the tip of Cape Cod. The 252-foot stone tower called the Pilgrim Memorial, located at the juncture of Commercial Street and Beach Highway, commemorates the Mayflower's brief visit to the area, before sailing on to Plymouth. Provincetown has always been a bit unconventional, and by the early 1700s, Provincetown had gained its reputation for being an "outlaw town" - pirates, privateers, smugglers, and their doxies all found refuge close to the harbor. Later, honest fisherfolk - first Yankees, then Portuguese-speaking immigrants - arrived to tame the Cape's frontier.

During the early 1900s, Provincetown became known as "Greenwich Village North." Long before the 1960s and the age of "the counterculture," Provincetown Bohemians were shocking the more staid members of Provincetown society. Inexpensive summer lodgings, close to unspoiled beaches, attracted a variety of young rebels and artists - including Jack Reed, Mabel Dodge, Louise Bryant, Sinclair Lewis, and Eugene O'Neill. Many of O'Neill's early plays were presented in a tiny wharfside theater. The Provincetown Playhouse still builds its repertory around O'Neill's works.

Thousands of visitors still make the trek to Provincetown each summer. In mid-July, Commercial Street, in the center of town, is packed with sightseers. Rental fees for studio space soar into the stratosphere. Still, crowded or not, Provincetown is never dull. In the spring and fall, the rents are down and P-town regains its quiet charm.

There is an underlying stability to Provincetown: It is a fishing village, with classic Victorian homes, from which fishermen venture out each morning to confront the rough Atlantic. The artists, too, seem to be well rooted in P-town. And, in their own way, the summer crowds, the waitresses, and the candy-makers, all seem to be part of a familiar Provincetown pageant.

Bay Side

The northern shore of the main part of the Cape, reached by Route 6A, is quite different from the south shore and the forearm. This coastline, known as the Bay Side, tends to be marshy, and the water in the protected bay is far calmer than that of Nantucket Sound and the Atlantic. The Bay Side is generally far less developed than the other sections. Here restaurants and motels are fewer, and, for the most part, the only commercial establishments you will see along Route 6A are decorous craft and antique shops. The towns have retained more of their original quality; their main streets are lined with the stately white clapboard mansions of sea captains and the fine old shade trees that were planted to set them off. Brewster has several such mansions, as well as saltbox Cape Cod cottages. In West Brewster you can visit a working corn mill, a museum of natural history and Sealand of Cape Cod, which features a marine aquarium, seal pool and trained dolphins.

While you are driving along 6A, watch for signs pointing out town landings; if you have time, visit these and watch the local fishermen unload their catches. West of Brewster, Dennis, along with Sandwich, is one of the centers of cranberry culture on the Cape. In early autumn, travelers along 6A can see the berries being harvested in shallow, red-splotched bogs. It also boasts Scargo Hill, the highest spot in the mid Cape, all of 160 feet tall. The view of the bay from here is spectacular. Yarmouth and Yarmouth Port are particularly lovely old seafaring towns, and some of the captains' homes in the latter are open to the public.

Barnstable and Sandwich

As you continue west on 6A past fine views of meadows and the Bay, you will come to Barnstable, the site of the Liberty Pole. Here the Colonists held many freedom meetings. When the pole disappeared from the village green, suspicion centered on one Aunt Freeman, a defiant Tory, because of her previous threat of tearing down the patriots' pole. She was tarred, feathered and ridden out of town on a rail. Barnstable is now a lovely town of large old homes, many built when the town had a large trade in codfish, rum and molasses. Great salt marshes extend into the bay. Sturgis Library, dating to 1645, is a fine example of the Cape Cod house.

Sandwich is the oldest town on the Cape and one of the most interesting and charming. It remains famous for the beautifully colored glass that bears its name and was produced there from 1825 until 1888 when competition with glassmakers in the Middle West closed the factory. The Historical Museum on Main Street contains relics of the early history of the town as well as an outstanding collection of pressed and lace glass. You may visit the nearby Hoxie House, a 17th-century shingled saltbox cottage, and see the Dexter Gristmill in operation. Heritage Plantation, located on the beautifully landscaped grounds of the Dexter Estate, is a complex of various museums and craft exhibits housed in a collection of old buildings.

The Islands

Martha's Vineyard, Nantucket, and the Elizabeth Islands, known collectively as "the Islands," were formed some 100,000 years ago when a retreating glacier left behind its ragged collection of clay, sand and rocky debris. Most of this glacial moraine became Cape Cod, but the outermost protrusions formed a series of islands as the glacier melted and the sea level rose. Some of the Elizabeth Islands, a small chain located off Woods Hole and parallel to the west coast of Martha's Vineyard, remain much as they were then. They are for the most part privately owned, and not easily accessible.

Thomas Mayhew, after buying Martha's Vineyard, Nantucket and the Elizabeth Islands in 1641 for the grand sum of 40 pounds, settled the Vineyard the following year at what is now Edgartown. Nantucket was settled several years later largely by Quakers retreating from the repressive religious authorities of the Massachusetts mainland. For a while, the rolling grassy heath of the two islands was used for farming and raising sheep, but in the 18th century their economies shifted to whaling and both became major whaling centers. Mansions built by wealthy sea captains still stand in the ports of Edgartown and Nantuck-

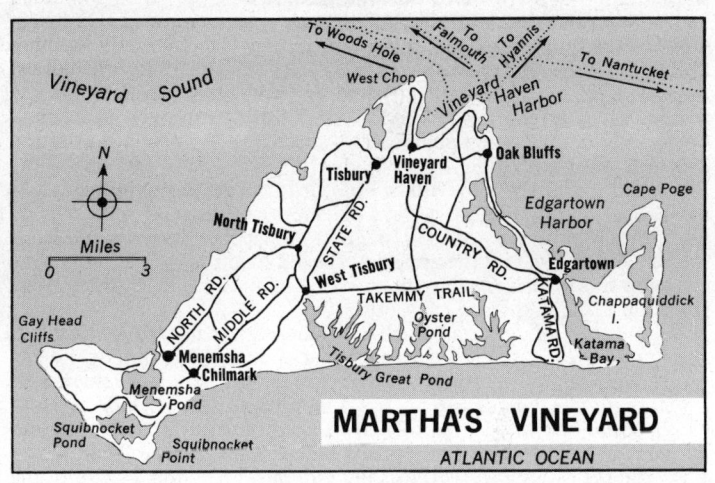

MARTHA'S VINEYARD

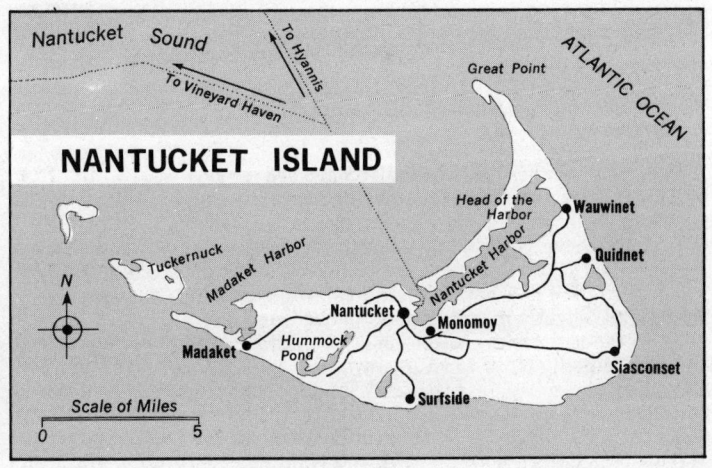

NANTUCKET ISLAND

et, giving these towns a brooding aura of the past. As the whaling and shipbuilding industries died out, the Islands were slowly depopulated and nearly forgotten. But, like Cape Cod, they were reborn as resort areas in the first decades of the twentieth century. However, because they are islands and reachable only by ferry, private boat or airplane, they have changed less radically and quickly. Many summer visitors return year after year, and close-knit summer communities have developed, each with its own character. Nantucket, 30 miles at sea and a 2½- to 3-hour ferry ride from Woods Hole, has succumbed less to the tides of tourism than Martha's Vineyard, thanks to extremely tight local zoning regulations as well as distance. Like the Cape, the islands attract visitors because of their magnificent beaches, harbors and bays; the lure of the sea, and the appeal of the old towns and weathered gray cottages. But the islands have distinctive qualities which set them apart from the Cape and from each other.

Each of the villages on Martha's Vineyard has its own personality and appearance, and tends to attract year-round and summer residents who have common interests and backgrounds. There is a remarkable diversity in the landscapes of the Vineyard, which include verdant heath, scrub oak woods, flat meadows, salt and fresh water ponds and marshes, clay cliffs, busy harbors and lonely ocean beaches pounded by surf. The sea is omnipresent, its salty dampness reaching even into the farming regions of the interior.

Nantucket is wilder and lonelier than Martha's Vineyard. Its hilly moors seem primitive, more open to the fury of the sea. The town of Nantucket, with its cobblestone streets, old captains' mansions and gray weathered cottages, hardly seems changed since whaling days. Salt breezes carry the smell and feel of the sea everywhere. Nantucket serves as a reminder that human settlement and natural beauty are not necessarily incompatible. Travelers eager to escape the summertime crowds on the Cape may enjoy making a day trip to Nantucket from Hyannis or Woods Hole. Leave your car on the Cape.

Martha's Vineyard

Passenger ferries to Martha's Vineyard depart frequently from Woods Hole, Falmouth, Hyannis Port, and, in summer, New Bedford, and land either in Vineyard Haven or nearby Oak Bluffs. Bus tours of the island leave from stations near the ferry landings and there is summer bus service between Oak Bluffs, Vineyard Haven and Edgartown. Bicycling is a popular and healthful way of getting around the island and bicycles may be rented in the three main towns or brought over on the car ferries. Automobiles are not essential, unless you wish to travel quickly from town to town. But why rush on the Vineyard? You may rent a car near the ferry landings or bring your own on the Woods Hole ferry. However, car space on the ferries is limited and you need to make automobile reservations well in advance; contact the Woods Hole, Martha's Vineyard, and Nantucket Steamship Authority in Woods Hole, MA 02543.

Most of the island's visitors land at Vineyard Haven, the main port, shopping center and winter community. Much of the old whaling and fishing town was destroyed by the Great Fire of 1883, and Vineyard Haven therefore lacks the architectural and historical interest of Edgartown, the other whaling port. But its busy harbor and a varied and attractive shopping district make it a pleasant place to visit. You may also visit a restored sailors chapel near the main wharf and discover a few old buildings that escaped the fire's destruction.

Oak Bluffs, where the rest of the ferries dock, is located across the harbor from Vineyard Haven. It, too, was settled in the 17th century, but its fascinating architecture dates from the 19th century, when it became the center for Methodist camp meetings. These began as tent revivals, but as more and more worshippers attended, permanent buildings were erected. A great conical ironwork tabernacle was built in the center of the campground. Around it, arranged in concentric circles, is a fantastic array of tiny Victorian gingerbread cottages, each striving to outdo its neighbors with the ornateness of its patterned shingles and colorful decorative moldings. The cottages are brightly colored and neatly kept. Once every summer, on the holiday known as Illumination Night, their owners festoon them with brilliant Japanese paper lanterns, turning the campground into a veritable fairyland.

Many of the other houses in Oak Bluffs were built around the same era as the campground cottages and were influenced by their design. The predominance of these whimsical, pastel-colored dwellings gives the whole community the look of a seaside toyshop. In addition to being a Methodist center, Oak Bluffs is also one of the oldest Black resort communities in the United States. Oak Bluffs has many of the island's restaurants and a popular harbor with berths for pleasure boats.

The oldest town on Martha's Vineyard, and a famous whaling port in the 18th and 19th centuries, Edgartown is now characterized by the beautiful old houses and tree-lined streets of its past and the elegant stores, fine hotels and restaurants that make it the most fashionable summer resort on the island. This combination makes it a superb spot for walking and window shopping. You might wish to start at the Thomas Cooke House on Cooke Street, headquarters of the Dukes County Historical Society. The house, built in 1765 by shipbuilders, now houses a whaling and historical musuem. At the end of Cooke, the island's oldest street, is the Edgartown Cemetery. North and South Water Streets are lined with captains' houses, some with widow's walks on their roofs. Main Street, lined with fine shops, ends at the town dock, where you catch the little ferry, *On Time,* to nearby Chappaquiddick, a sandy island with the Cape Poge Wildlife Reservation, a good spot for birdwatching. Chappaquiddick lacks stores and restaurants so pack a snack for your expedition.

The south shore of Martha's Vineyard faces the ocean, and along its entire length there are fine surf beaches with unusually warm water. The county beach extending across Katama Bay is open to the public. At the western end are smaller beaches reserved for residents of Chilmark. Behind the beaches are saltwater ponds and marshes.

The west end of Martha's Vineyard, known by residents as "up-island," is more rural and wild than the east end. The winter winds blow with such bitterness that some of the year-round islanders who live here in the summer move to sheltered Vineyard Haven when it gets cold, even though the moderating influence of the sea keeps Martha's Vineyard from getting much of the snow that falls farther north on the mainland. But in the summer, "up-island" is a favorite vacation spot for nature lovers, writers, educators and other professionals who return year after year and have established close ongoing summer communities.

West Tisbury, which occupies the central swath of the island, includes a charming New England village, a small settlement at Lambert's Cove and surrounding farms and summer homes. Visitors may go birdwatching or walk through the woods to a freshwater pond on Cedar Tree Neck, situated along the north shore. Chilmark, to the west, has always been less developed, although its oak woods now hide summer homes. Its roads afford a succession of scenic views of the ocean or Vineyard Sound and two beautiful ocean beaches are open to residents. To the north, on the stretch of cold, swift water called the Menemsha Bight, is the fishing village of Menemsha. A small collection of fishermen's weathered shanties and sturdy fishing boats ranged along either side of the channel which connects Menemsha Pond to the Bight, this little town makes what many consider the most picturesque scene on the island. But the piled-up lobster traps and fishy odor attest to the fact that this beautiful village has not been built for show. You may purchase fresh fish or eat in a nearby seafood restaurant. The Menemsha Beach, large, pleasant and open to the public, is located right next to the town.

Earliest Vineyard Inhabitants

When the first colonists came to Martha's Vineyard in the mid-17th century, they found the island's earliest settlers, the Wampanoag Indians, living at the western tip, which is now called Gay Head. The Indians taught the colonists how to kill whales and plant corn, and where to fish. Later on, the Gay Head Indians were hired by whalers; in *Moby Dick,* Melville describes Gay Head as "a village which has long supplied the neighboring island of Nantucket with her most daring harpooners." The descendants of the Wampanoags still live and work in the area. You may see some of them at the concessions on the way up to the Gay Head Cliffs, brilliantly colored clay bluffs on the extreme western tip of the island. Unfortunately, the sea that first carved out these bands of ochre, gray, rust, and white is now reclaiming them. Until recently, visitors could descend them to the colored beaches below, but their trampling hastened the process of erosion and now the cliffs must be enjoyed from a roped-in area above, or by walking around to the beach from a marked path to the south. The cliffs have greatly diminished in size in recent years, and since no feasible means of preserving them has been discovered, no doubt they will eventually melt away altogether in a few centuries.

Nantucket

The name Nantucket is a corruption of the Indian word *Nanticut,* "far-away land," a description which seems quite apt as you near the end of the long ferry ride there. Your first glimpse of the town, as the ferry pulls into the safe enclosure of Nantucket Harbor, is likely to be obscured by fog. You may be able to distinguish the silvery brown of weatherbeaten shingles. The oft-shrouded island has been called "the gray lady." You have to be on the island a while to understand another of its Indian names, *Canopache,* "the place of peace." Its small size and geographical isolation, along with the contrast between the snug brick-and-clapboard village of Nantucket and the bleak, exposed moors nearby, gives the island a dreamlike quality.

There are a number of summer colonies on the island, but Nantucket is the only real town. Its great whaling saga began when Nantucketers caught their first whale in 1672 off the shores of the island. Old South

Wharf still stands as a nostalgic emblem of the era when Nantucket was the greatest whaling port in the world. The best place to begin exploring Nantucket is the marvelous Whaling Museum on Broad Street. Its fascinating exhibits on whales and the various operations involved in catching and processing them, its displays of whaling artifacts, its collection of captains' portraits and a library of books about Nantucket will enable you to peer into the past and to see the town's cobblestone streets and historic dwellings as they were 150 years ago, when the town ranked third in commerce in Massachusetts.

From the museum walk back to Main Street in the center of Nantucket. Lined with white clapboard captains' mansions and shaded by elm trees, this beautiful street reflects the affluence enjoyed by the town at the peak of its whaling trade. The elegant Hadwen-Satler Memorial House at 96 Main Street is open to the public. It is one of the exhibits of the Nantucket Historical Association, which administers the whaling museum and maintains several original buildings as public museums. The historical museum at 8 Fair Street, just off Main Street, consists of a collection of primitive portraits and period furniture and a wing of the Friends Meeting House. The Jethro Coffin House was built in 1686 and is the oldest on Nantucket. It is located on Sunset Hill, at the northern end of the town, and contains period furniture. On Old Mill Hill, on the southwestern side of town, stands the Old Mill, built by Nathan Wilbur in 1746 from the wood of shipwrecks, and still used to grind corn. Nearby on Mill Street is the 1800 House, a restored early-American dwelling dating from Nantucket's early whaling days.

Other buildings of interest in Nantucket are the Maria Mitchell House, 1 Vestal Street, birthplace of America's first woman astronomer and discoverer of Mitchell's Comet; the adjacent Observatory and Mitchell Memorial Library; and the old jail, farther west on Vestal Street.

These buildings are restorations open to the public, but because of ironclad laws regulating the exteriors of both houses and businesses, the entire town of Nantucket is like a living musuem. The laws are so strict that permission is needed to make the smallest exterior changes and all signs must be approved. In addition to the houses maintained by the historical association, there are periodic tours of privately owned historic homes.

One new addition is the luxurious Nantucket Boat Basin, planned and constructed by Walter Beinecke, who, along with his father, established the Nantucket Historical Trust in the 1950s to restore the town's landmark buildings. He enlarged the docks and built little gray shingled houses on them, making an attractive facility for sailing and motor yachts.

Lonely Moors and Summer Colonies

Beyond the town are the moors, covered with bayberry, wild roses, brambles and cranberry vines, still colorful with flowers in the autumn. Scattered among them are the small summer colonies of Madaket Polpis and Wauwinet. Siasconset, the largest of these, is an artists' colony with little houses and delightful rose gardens. Like Martha's Vineyard, Nantucket has beaches for all tastes. The south shore looks out on the Atlantic, which crashes on the wide sandy beaches in powerful breakers. The ocean is wildest on the Madaket side. The water on

Nantucket Sound is calmer, and the harbor's beaches are the most placid of all. Great Point, the tip of the northern peninsula, is a good area for surfcasting and birdwatching. It is accessible only by four-wheel-drive vehicles or on foot, and makes a perfect destination for an all-day round-trip hike.

The last word on Nantucket belongs to Melville:

> The Nantucketer, he alone resides and riots on the sea; he alone, in Bible language, goes down to it in ships; to and fro ploughing it as his own special plantation. *There* is his home, *there* lies his business. . . . For years he knows not the land; so that when he comes to it at last, it smells like another world, more strangely than the moon would to an Earthsman. (*Moby Dick,* Chapter XIV, "Nantucket")

PRACTICAL INFORMATION FOR CAPE COD

HOW TO GET THERE. By air: *Provincetown-Boston Airline* (800–352–3132) flies from Boston and New York City to Cape Cod and the Islands. *New York Air* (800–221–9300), flies from New York and Boston to Hyannis and Nantucket. *Gull Air* (771–1247 or 800–222–4855) connects Hyannis with the islands.

By ferry: Car ferries are regularly scheduled to Martha's Vineyard and Nantucket from Woods Hole. Reservations well in advance are required. Write Steamship Authority. Box 284, Woods Hole, MA 02543 (540–2022). Pier parking is available for ferry passengers. Passenger ferries operate from Hyannis to Martha's Vineyard and Nantucket in season, and between West Falmouth and Oak Bluffs. Passenger service from Boston to Provincetown is also available during the summer. Contact *Bay State–Spray & Provincetown Steamship Co.,* 20 Long Wharf, Boston 02108 (723–7800). Passenger-only ferry service between New Bedford and Martha's Vineyard is provided from mid-May through mid-Oct. by *Cape and Islands Express Lines,* Box J-4095, Leonard's Wharf, New Bedford MA (997–1688).

By train: *Cape Cod and Hyannis Railroad* runs from Buzzards Bay to Hyannis, and Falmouth. Mid.-Apr. to Oct. 31. P.O. Box 57, Hyannis (771–1145). The *Plymouth and Brockton* bus company provides all-year service from Boston to Hyannis and Chatham (773–9400, 775–5524).

HOTELS AND MOTELS. The Cape offers a wide range of accommodations, from luxurious seaside resorts to the most basic motel. Many close down completely during the off season; others offer much lower prices. Our price rating is based on double occupancy, European plan, in season. *Deluxe,* $100 and up; *Expensive,* $75–$100; *Moderate,* $50–$75; *Inexpensive,* $35–$50.

An inexpensive lodging option for Cape vacationers is to stay at one of the many bed-and-breakfast homes in the area. For information, contact Bed and Breakfast Cape Cod, Box 341, W. Hyannis Port (775–2772); or House Guests Cape Cod, 85 Hokum Rock Rd., RFD Dennis (398–0787).

Note: Unless otherwise indicated, the accommodations below are open year-round.

CAPE COD

BARNSTABLE. Beechwood Inn. *Expensive.* Rte. 6A (362–6618.) Elegant bed-and-breakfast inn with stunning view of Great Marshes and Sandy Neck. Quiet surroundings.

Cobb's Cove. *Expensive.* Rte. 6A (362–9356.) Secluded bed-and-breakfast inn famous for gourmet cuisine. Close to north-shore beaches. Off-season rates.

Lamb and Lion. *Moderate.* Rte. 6A (362–6823.) Pleasant motel that tries to be "as non-commercial as possible." Efficiencies available. Large swimming pool and sundecks. Daily and weekly rates. Off-season rates.

BASS RIVER. Blue Water. *Deluxe.*

BASS RIVER. Blue Water. *Deluxe.* S. Shore Dr. (398–2288). Indoor and outdoor pools, private beach. Tennis, putting green. Some efficiencies. Color cable TV. Restaurant, bar, dancing wknds. No children under 12 in season.

Red Jacket Beach Motor Inn. *Deluxe.* S. Shore Dr. (398–6941). Indoor and outdoor pools, beach. Private balconies, color cable TV. Tennis, play area. Saunas, putting green. Restaurant. Open mid-Apr. to Nov.

Ocean Mist. *Expensive.* S. Shore Dr. (398–2633). Pleasant motel on private beach. Pool, play area. Kit. units avail. Color cable TV, shuffleboard. Open Apr. to Nov.

Riviera Beach. *Expensive.* S. Shore Dr. (398–2273). On private beach. Some efficiencies. Indoor heated pool, restaurant, bar. Off-season rates. Open April to Nov.

Surfcomber. *Expensive.* S. Shore Dr. (398–9228). On the ocean with private beach. Efficiencies available. Pool. Lawn games. Over 8 in season. Open mid-May to early Oct.

Village Green. *Moderate.* S. Shore Dr. (398–2167). Pleasant motel opp. beach. Pool, play area. Coffee shop. Some efficiencies. Over 6 in season. Open Apr. to Nov.

Windjammer. *Moderate.* S. Shore Dr. (398–2370). Beach just a step away. Pool. Cont. brkfst; pkg. plans avail. Open late March to Nov.

BOURNE. Mashnee Village.

BOURNE. Mashnee Village. *Moderate.* Mashnee Village Rd., 5 mi. E. of bridge, off Rte. 28 (759–3384). Pool, tennis, play area. Beach. Cottages with kits., fireplaces. Free movies. Fishing, boating. Bar. Pets. Open mid-May to mid-Oct.

Panorama. *Moderate.* Rte. 28 at S. Bourne Rotary (759–4401). Pleasant 2-story motor lodge with view of canal and bridge.

Windmill Motel. *Moderate.* Mid-Cape Hwy (888–3220). Pool. Restaurant. Cont. breakfast; miniature golf. Open May to Oct.

BREWSTER. Bramble Inn.

BREWSTER. Bramble Inn. *Expensive.* Main St. (896–7644). A pleasant restored building in a quiet village setting. Restaurant and art gallery on premises. Free cont. breakfast. Half mile to beach. Closed mid-Feb.

Captain Freeman Inn. *Moderate.* 15 Breakwater Rd. (896–7481.) Pleasant guest rooms. Free continental brkfst.

Old Manse Inn. *Expensive.* Rte. 6A (896–3149.) Handsome country inn. Off-season rates.

BUZZARDS BAY. Buzzards Bay Motor Lodge.

BUZZARDS BAY. Buzzards Bay Motor Lodge. *Moderate.* Rte. 6 (759–3466). On private beach with dock. Some cottages with kitchens. Restaurant nr. Open May to Nov.

Quinstar Motor Lodge. *Inexpensive.* Rt. 28 at Bourne Bridge (759–2711). Indoor pool, sauna, exercise room. Restaurant, lounge. Refrigerators in rooms.

CENTERVILLE. East Bay Lodge.

CENTERVILLE. East Bay Lodge. *Deluxe.* East Bay Rd. (428–6961). Excellent facilities. Tennis, playground. Café, bar. Off-season rates.

Trade Winds Inn. *Deluxe.* Craigville Beach Rd. (775–0365). Luxurious inn with private beach, lovely gardens. Dining rm. for breakfast, dinner. Bar, entertainment, dancing. Open Apr. to Nov. CP. MAP avail. in season; EP off season.

Centerville Corners Motor Lodge. *Expensive.* S. Main St. (775–7223). Heated pool, saunas, play area nr. Craigville Beach. Restaurant. Tennis near. Pets. Special pkgs. in fall and spring, inc. golf wknds.

CHATHAM. Chatham Bars Inn & Cottages. *Deluxe.* Shore Rd. (945–0096). All resort pleasures: beach, boating, tennis, lawn games. Dining rm., bar. Dancing, entertainment. Roomy cottages. No housekeeping. American plan avail. Open May to Nov. AP.

Wequasset Inn. *Deluxe.* Beautiful resort complex on Pleasant Bay (432–5400). Rooms and suites in cottages overlooking water. Tennis, sailing, pool, nightclub. Golf nearby. Windsurfing instruction. Fine food served in 18th-century mansion. Open May to Oct.

Dolphin of Chatham. *Expensive.* 352 Main St. (945–0070). Off hwy. Spacious grounds. Kit. units avail., also cottages. Heated pool, whirlpool bath. Play area. Open April to Dec.

Hawthorne. *Expensive.* 196 Shore Rd. (945–0372). Private beach. Efficiencies avail. Children over 8 welcome. Open mid-June to Oct.

Pleasant Bay Village. *Expensive.* Rte. 28 in Chathamport (945–1133). Lovely grounds with play area, pool, picnic area. Breakfast avail. Open May.-Oct. Wkly rates avail.

Chatham Wayside Inn. *Moderate.* 512 Main St. (945–1800). Comfortable 19th-century inn close to town center. Restaurant. Outdoor pool.

Seafarer. *Moderate.* Rte 28 and Ridgevale Rd. (432–1739). Spacious rooms, quiet location ½ mile from beach. Some 2-room efficiencies.

DENNIS. Dennis Bayside. *Moderate.* Rte. 6A (385–9770). Pool. Free morning coffee. Restaurants and beach nearby. Open mid-May to mid-Oct.

Dun Wandering. *Moderate.* Rte. 6A (385–3414). Family-oriented motel. All units are efficiencies. Pool. Color TV. Nr. beaches. Open late May to Labor Day.

Sesuit Harbor. *Moderate.* Rte. 6A (385–3326). Pool. Free cont. breakfast in season. Off-season rates.

DENNISPORT. Soundings. *Deluxe.* Chase Ave. Dennisport (394–6561). Nicely decorated. Large private beach. Pools, putting green; sauna. Free coffee. Restaurant nr. Open April through October; fall and spring pkgs. available.

Colonial Village. *Expensive.* Lower County Rd., Dennisport (398–2071). 2-story motel with kit. units and cottages with fireplaces. Pool. Open Apr. to Nov.

Cross Rip. *Expensive.* Chase Ave., Dennisport (398–6600). 2-story motel built around pool. Private beach. Sundecks overlook ocean. Nice view of Nantucket Sound. Nr. restaurants.

Sea Lord. *Expensive.* Chase Ave. and Inman Rd., Dennisport (398–6900). Pool, complimentary cont. brkfst. Restaurants near. Open mid-Apr. to late Oct.

Spouter Whale. *Expensive.* 405 Old Wharf Rd., Dennisport (398–8010). On ocean with private beach. Some efficiencies. Free breakfast and rolls. Children over 5. Open mid-May to mid-Oct.

Cape Pine. *Moderate.* Lower County and Capt. Chase Rds., Dennisport (394–8820). Restaurant nr. Bar. Entertainment. Sauna. Efficiencies available.

Corsair. *Moderate.* 41 Chase Ave., Dennisport (398–2279). 2-story motel with balconies on private beach. Pool. Free morning coffee. Refrigs. Bike and sailfish rentals. Restaurant nr. Children over 5. Open May to Nov.

Cutty Sark. *Moderate.* Old Wharf Rd., Dennisport (398–9116). Opp. town beach. Inn or motel rooms. Color cable TV. Pool. Restaurant nr. Open late May to Oct.

Gaslight. *Moderate.* Chase Ave., Dennisport (398–8831). Across street from ocean beach. Morning coffee. Restaurant adjacent. Open mid-May to Oct.

Jonathan Edwards. *Moderate.* Rte. 28, Dennisport (398–2953). Pool, play area, rec. rm. Coffee and rolls on the house. Open year round.

Lighthouse Inn. *Moderate.* W. Dennisport 1 mi. S off Rte. 28 (398–2244). Resort hotel designed for family pleasure. On beach. Pool, play area, tennis, boating, fishing. Special rec. program for the kids. Dining rm, bar, entertainment. Open mid-May to mid-Oct. MAP.

Sea Shell. *Moderate.* Chase Ave., Dennisport (398–8965). Private beach. Rooms in motel or main house. Kit. units avail.; refrig. in every room. Continental breakfast in season.

William & Mary. *Moderate.* Lower County Rd., Dennisport (398–2931). Pool. Coffee and rolls avail. Restaurant nr. Kit. units avail. Open mid-Apr. to Oct.

Ocean View Lodge and Cottages. *Inexpensive.* Depot St. (398–3412). One minute walk to Nantucket Sound. Motel and efficiency accommodations. TV lounge. Weekly rates avail. Open May to Oct.

EASTHAM. Sheraton Ocean Park Inn. *Expensive.* Rte. 6 (255–5000). Attractive modern resort. Health club, tennis, pools. Room service, café. Off-season rates.

Whalewalk. *Expensive.* Bridge Rd. (255–0617). Old sea captain's home. Antique furnishings. Room in inn or housekeeping cottages; some with fireplaces. Free breakfast for Inn guests. Open mid-March to late Nov.

Blue Dolphin. *Moderate.* Rte. 6, 3 mi. N of Nat'l Seashore entrance (255–1159). Comfortable quarters on wooded grounds. Pool, play area. Restaurant. Near hiking and bicycle trails.

Cranberry Cottages. *Moderate.* Rte. 6, ¾ mi. N. or Orleans Rotary (255–0602). Cape Cod cottages tucked away in shady grove. Wkly rates avail.

Town Crier. *Moderate.* Rte. 6 (255–4000). Enclosed heated pool, play area. Recreation room. Full breakfast avail. Nr. Nat. Seashore entrance. Pets.

FALMOUTH. Sea Crest Hotel. *Deluxe.* Old Silver Beach (548–3850). Large resort on private beach. Tennis, putting green, health club, pools. MAP available.

Sheraton Inn-Falmouth. *Deluxe.* 291 Jones Rd. (800–325–3535). New member of internat'l chain. Indoor pool, sauna, sundeck. Restaurant, lounge, entertainment. Pkgs. avail.

Cape Codder. *Expensive.* Cape Codder Rd. (800–352–7146). Oceanside resort. ¼ mile of ocean front, pools, play area. Restaurant, bar. Dancing, entertainment. MAP. Open June to mid-October.

Cape Colony. *Expensive.* Surf Dr. (548–3975). Pool, play area. Directly on beach. Morning coffee free. Restaurant nr. Open late Apr. to mid-Oct.

Coonamesset Inn. *Expensive.* Jones Rd. & Gifford St. (548–2300). Beautiful gardens, Cape Code-style buildings. Excellent restaurant, bar.

Falmouth Marina. *Expensive.* Robbins Rd. (548–4300). In attractive grounds overlooking harbor. Pool. Wknd. pkgs. avail. Open April to Oct.

Shoreway Acres. *Expensive.* Shore St. (540–3000). Beautiful grounds, 2 pools, sauna. Some efficiencies. Breakfast room. Off-season pkgs.

Capewind. *Moderate.* 34 Maravista Ave. Ext. (548–3400). Htd. pool, play area. Free in-rm. coffee. Boats avail. Some kitchenettes.

Falmouth Heights Motor Lodge. *Moderate.* 146 Falmouth Heights Rd. (548–3623). Heated pool. Play area. Free in-rm. coffee. Restaurant nr. 5-min. walk to beach. Open mid-April to Oct.

Green Harbor. *Moderate.* Acapesket Rd., E. Falmouth (548–4747). Pools. Private boating beach. Boats avail. Pkg. plans available. Some efficiencies.

Mostly Hall. *Moderate.* 27 Main St. (548–3786). A cozy inn serving copious breakfasts. Near ferries and beaches. Children over 16; no pets.

Red Horse Inn Motel. *Moderate.* 28 Falmouth Hghts. Rd. (548–0053). Nicely kept. Within walking distance of summer boats to Martha's Vineyard. Near restaurants, stores.

Sea Gull Lodge. *Moderate.* 41 Belvidere Rd. (548–0679). Small guest house near beaches, restaurants.

Studio Motel. *Moderate.* 113 Falmouth Heights Rd. (548–1513). Spacious rms. overlooking harbor. Restaurant nr. Free morning coffee and rolls.

Elm Arch Inn. *Inexpensive.* Elm Arch Way (548–0133). Small traditional hotel, centrally located. Colonial furnishings, beamed ceilings. Pool.

HARWICH. Seadar Inn. *Expensive.* Bank St. and Braddock Lane, Harwich Port (432–0264). Opp. Beach. Includes buffet brkfst. Open mid-May to Oct.

Commodore. *Moderate.* 30 Earle Rd. (432–1180). Pool, play area. Putting green, shuffleboard. Beach nr. Brkfst. and lunch served in season.

Country Inn. *Moderate.* 86 Sisson Road, Harwich Port (432–2769). Pool, tennis. Taproom with fireplace. Meals available, prepared by owner-chef.

Handkerchief Shoals. *Moderate.* At jct. Deep Hole Rd. and Rte. 28 (432–2200). Off hwy. Play area. Nr. golf, tennis, fishing. Open May to Oct.

Melrose Inn. *Moderate.* Harwich Port (432–0171). Rooms in inn or beach house annex. Pool, private beach. Old-fashioned resort atmosphere, fine seafood, bar. AP and MAP available. Open mid-June to Oct.

Moby Dick. *Moderate.* Main St., S. Harwich (432–1434). Pool play area. Croquet and shuffleboard. Nr. golf courses. Open April to Nov.

Red River Motel. *Moderate.* Rte. 28 (432–1474). One mile to beach. Off-season rates. Close to beaches and natural areas.

Lion's Head Inn. *Moderate.* 186 Belmont Rd., W. Harwich (432–7766.) Handsome bed-and-breakfast inn. Nr. beach, golf, shops. Two cottages can be rented on a weekly basis.

HYANNIS. Dunfey-Hyannis. *Deluxe.* West End Circle (775–7775). Resort hotel with golf, tennis, pools, play area. Restaurant, bar, dancing, entertainment. MAP avail.

Holiday Inn. *Deluxe.* Rte. 132, nr. airport (774–6600). Pool, tennis. Restaurant, bar, dancing, entertainment. Pkg. plans avail. Open June to Oct.

Howard Johnson's. *Deluxe.* Main & Winter Sts. (775–8600). Enclosed pool, saunas. Restaurant. Pkg. and family plans.

Sheraton Regal Inn. *Deluxe.* Rte. 132 (771–3000). Pools, play area. Tennis. Pets. Restaurant, bar.

Heritage House. *Expensive.* 259 Main St. (775–7000). Pools. Private balconies. Saunas. Restaurant, lounge. Package rates avail. A Best Western Motel.

Hyannis Harborview. *Expensive.* 213 Ocean St. (771–2625). Opp. pier. Pools. Indoor health center. Lounge. Wknd pkg. avail.

Lewis Bay Motel and Marina. *Expensive.* 53 South St. (775–6633). Restaurants, cocktail lounges. Some efficiencies. Pets. Nr. harbor, ferry, walk to town.

Breakwater. *Moderate.* 432 Sea St. (775–6831). Cottage units on beach. Heated pool. Play area. 7-day min. in season; 3-day off season. Open April to Dec.

Captain Gosnold Village. *Moderate.* Gosnold St. (775–9111). Motel rooms or efficiency cottages. Pool, play area. Beach short walk away. Free in-rm. coffee. Open Apr. to Oct.

Country Lake. *Moderate.* Rte. 132 (362–6455). On lake, with fishing, boating avail. Pool, play area. Restaurant nr. Open April to Nov.

Hyannis Star. *Moderate.* Rte. 132 and Pine Needle Lane (775–2835). Pool, play area. Pets. Restaurant nr. Motel rooms or full-kitchen cottages. Wkly. rates avail.

Hyannis Town House Motor Inn. *Moderate.* 33 Ocean St. (775–3828). Restaurant, nr. beaches Open May to Nov.

Hyannis Travel Inn. *Moderate.* 16 North St. (775–8200). Outdoor, heated indoor pools. Saunas. Free cont. brkfst. Restaurant nr. Open mid-Apr.–Oct.

Koala Inn. *Moderate.* 867 Iyanaough Rd. Outdoor heated pool. Free coffee and rolls. Pets. Off-season pkg. plan.

Park Square Village. *Moderate.* 156 Main St. (775–5611). Cottages, rooms, and efficiencies. Close to Hyannis center. Low off-season rates. Pool. Tennis. Picnic area.

Presidential. *Moderate.* Iyanough Rd. (362–3957). On pond with boats, fishing avail. Play area. Opp. new 18-hole golf course. Open late May to Oct.

Rainbow. *Moderate.* Iyanough Rd. (362–3217). On pond, with boats, fishing avail. Heated pool, play area, children's pool. Efficiencies available. Open June to Oct.

Captain Bearse Lodge. *Inexpensive.* 39 Pearl St. (771–2700). Small Victorian inn in center of town. Open late May to mid-Oct.

MASHPEE. New Seabury Inn. *Deluxe.* Shore Dr. West, New Seabury (477–9111.) Large oceanfront resort. Golf, tennis, marina.

Popponesset Inn. *Deluxe.* Shore Dr., New Seabury (477–1100). Resort. Restaurant. Tennis, marina. Cottages, kitchens. Open June to Oct.

NORTH TRURO. Anchorage. *Moderate.* Rte. 6A, Beach Point (487–0168). Motel units or efficiencies. Private beach, sundeck. Open Apr. to Nov.

Crow's Nest. *Moderate.* Rte. 6A (487–9031.) Efficiencies and motel units. Private beach. Scenic waterfront view. Off-season rates. Open April to Oct.

ORLEANS. Nauset Knoll Motor Lodge. *Expensive.* Nauset Beach (255–2364). Attractive rms. have ocean view. Open Apr. to late Oct.

Skaket Beach. *Expensive.* Exit 12, Rte. 6 (255–1020). Heated pool, play area. Attractive rms. have refrigerators. Picnic area. Continental brkfst. Open April to Nov.

Cove House and Cottages. *Moderate.* Rt. 6A (255–1312). Inn rooms or efficiency cottage with decks and fireplaces.

Governor Prence. *Moderate.* Jct. Rtes. 6A & 28 (255–1216). Pool, play area. Color cable TV. Breakfast avail. Bar. Package plans. Open Apr. to Nov.

Ridgewood Cottages and Motel. *Moderate.* Jct. Rtes. 28 and 39 (255–0473). Pool. Play area. Comfortable efficiencies. Picnic grounds with BBQs. Wkly. rates.

Ship's Knees Inn. *Moderate.* Beach Rd. (255–1312). Small country inn. Pool. Near Nauset Beach.

PROVINCETOWN. Hargood House. *Deluxe.* 493 Commercial St. (487–1324). Pleasant, modern efficiency apartments near the harbor. Fine view from rear units. Private beach. 1 unit with fireplace. 2-day minimum off season; weekly rentals, or longer, in summer.

Angel's Landing. *Expensive.* 353 Commercial St. (487–1420). Waterfront apartments, studios. Beach. Sundeck. Open mid-May to Nov.

Holiday Inn. *Expensive.* Snail Rd. at Jct. Rte. 6A (487–1711). Pool. Restaurant, bar. Nr. public beach. Entertainment, sitters available. Closed Jan. and Feb.

Provincetown Inn. *Expensive.* 1 Commercial St. (487–9500). Fine location nr. tip of Cape. Restaurant. Heated indoor pool, private beach. Cocktail lounge, nightclub. Dune tours and bike rentals avail.

Surfside Inn. *Expensive.* 543 Commercial St. (487–1726). Private beach. Open Easter to Mid-Oct.

Bradford Gardens. *Expensive.* 178 Bradford St. (487–1616). Small inn, cottages. Private patios. Free continental breakfast. Open April to Dec.

Land's End Inn. *Expensive.* 22 Commercial St. (487–0706). Lovely Victorian inn. Antiques. Beach, restaurants, and shops nearby.

Bradford House & Motel. *Expensive.* 41 Bradford St. (487–0173). Pool. Pleasant, centrally located. Nr. Restaurant. Open May to Oct.

Masthead. *Expensive.* 31 Commercial St. (487–0523). Cottages facing ocean, and attractive motel rms. Large sundeck, private beach. Nr. restaurant. Year round.

The Moors. *Expensive.* Beach Rd. and Bradford St. Ext. (487–1342). Restaurant. Free coffee and rolls. Pool. Open mid-April to mid-Oct.

Best Western Chateau. *Moderate.* Bradford St., Rte. 6A (487–1286). Heated pool. Comfortable rms. overlook dunes. Open May to Oct.

Meadows Motel & Cottages. *Moderate.* Bradford St. Ext. (487–0880). Motel and efficiency cottages. 3 min. to beach. Sightseeing and dune tours.

Tides Motor Inn. *Moderate.* Beach Point Rd. (487–1045). Pool. Most rms. on private beach with patio or balcony. Open mid-May to mid-Oct.

SANDWICH. Daniel Webster Inn. *Expensive.* 149 Main St. (888–3622). Handsome inn with good restaurant. Package plans available.

Spring Hill Motor Lodge. *Moderate.* Rte. 6A (888–1456). Wooded setting. Color TV. Free morning coffee. Off-season rates.

Earl of Sandwich Motor Manor. *Moderate.* Rte. 6A (888–1415). Charming small motel with Tudor decor. Free coffee and rolls. Pets. Nr. restaurant. Year round.

WELLFLEET. Holden Inn. *Moderate.* Commercial St. (349–3450). Cheerful rooms in restored home of Capt. Baker, one of Cape Cod's famous sea captains. Open June to Sept.

Inn at Duck Creek. *Moderate.* Main St. (349–9333). Traditional inn decorated with antiques. Restaurant, bar, dancing. Open May to Oct.

Southfleet Motor Inn. *Moderate.* Rte. 6 (349–3580). Indoor and outdoor pools, saunas. Restaurant, bar. Entertainment in season.

Even'Tide. *Moderate.* Rte. 6 (349–3410). Motel units and cottages. Color TV. Playground. Picnic area.

Wellfleet. *Moderate.* Rte. 6 (349–3535). Play area. Heated pool. Bar. In-room coffee and refrigerators. No pets. Open March to Dec.

WOODS HOLE. Nautilus. *Expensive.* Woods Hole Rd. (548–1525). Pool, bar, restaurant, tennis. Nr. island ferries. Open Apr. to Oct.

Sands of Time Motor Inn. *Expensive.* Main Rd. (548–6300). Overlooking harbor. Nr. island ferries. Pool, play area. Restaurant nr. Open Apr. to Oct.

YARMOUTH. Blue Rock Motor Inn. *Expensive.* Off High Bank Rd. (398–6962). Private balconies. Pool, shuffleboard court, tennis. Restaurant. Nr. golf. Open Apr. to mid-Nov.

Colonial Acres. *Expensive.* 114 Standish Way, W. Yarmouth (775–0935). Cottages on Lewis Bay. Coffee shop, private beach. Wkly rates. Open April to Nov.

Colonial House Inn. *Expensive.* Rte. 6A, Yarmouthport (362–4348). Vintage inn furnished with antiques. Quiet. Restaurant.

Green Harbor Village. *Expensive.* 182 Baxter Ave., W. Yarmouth (771–1126). Pool, private beach. Very attractive. Kit. units and cottages with sundecks. Open May to Oct.

Wedgewood Inn. *Expensive.* Rte. 6A, Yarmouthport (362–5157). Small country inn. Antiques. Fireplaces. Near beaches.

The Village Inn. *Moderate.* 92 Main St., Yarmouthport. (362–3182). Built in 1795. Relaxed. Continental breakfast. Reservations requested.

MARTHA'S VINEYARD

EDGARTOWN. Charlotte Inn. *Deluxe.* S. Summer St. (627–4751). Antique-filled, with superb restaurant. Some suites with fireplace. Art gallery.

Daggett House. *Deluxe.* N. Water St. (627–4600). Lovely traditional inn, gardens. Antique-furnished rooms.

Governor Bradford Inn. *Expensive.* 128 Main St. (627–9510). Gracefully restored inn. Continental breakfast. Lounge.

Harborside Inn. *Expensive.* S. Water St. (627–4321). Boating, with instruction available. Pool, play area. Excellent restaurant. Children over 6 only. Bar, dancing, entertainment. Open late April to Oct.

Kelley House. *Expensive.* Kelley St. (627–4394). Popular island inn. Good restaurant. Bar. Pool.

MENEMSHA. Beach Plum Inn. *Deluxe.* On hill above Menemsha (645–9454). Overlooking the sea, with country inn charm. Rates include breakfast and dinner. Open mid-May to mid-Oct.

OAK BLUFFS. Island Country Club. *Expensive.* Overlooking Farm Neck Golf Club (693–2002). Tennis, pool, golf. Dining room.

Wesley House. *Moderate.* On the Harbor. (693–0135). Old-style Victorian hotel. Comfortable. Open May to Sept.

VINEYARD HAVEN. Capt. Dexter House. *Moderate.* Main St. (693–3767). Handsome guest house, close to center of town. Antiques.

Lothrop Merry House. *Moderate.* Owen Park (693–1646). 18th-century guest house overlooking harbor. Rates include breakfast.

WEST TISBURY. Lambert's Cove Country Inn. *Expensive.* Lambert's Cove Road. (693–2298). Bed-and-breakfast inn. Beautiful gardens. Restaurant.

NANTUCKET

NANTUCKET. The Harbor House. *Deluxe.* South Beach St. (228–1500). Large villagelike complex. Pool, restaurant, meeting rooms. Open Apr. to Jan.
   White Elephant. *Deluxe.* Easton St. (228–2500). Putting green, tennis, sailing. Restaurant. Open mid-May to mid-Oct.
   Gordon Folger Hotel & Cottages. *Expensive.* Easton St. (228–0313). Restaurant. MAP, EP avail. Open mid-May to mid-Oct.
   Jared Coffin House. *Expensive.* Broad & Center Sts. (228–2400). Charming restored mansion with many antiques, handwoven fabric. Restaurant; bar, entertainment. Special Christmas celebration. Open May to January.
   Nesbitt Inn. *Moderate.* Broad St. (228–0156). Guest house, close to Steamboat Wharf.

 **SPECIAL-INTEREST TOURS.** The Mass. Audubon Society and the National Seashore sponsor *Spring Wildflower Pilgrimages,* usually late May. Also, walking tours for bird watchers can be arranged year round at Audubon sanctuaries in Hatchville (Falmouth) and Wellfleet. For information, contact Mass. Audubon at Box 236, S. Wellfleet MA 02663, or call 349–2615. *Mitch's Dune Tours,* which leave from the parking area of the Provincetown Inn, give passengers a close-up look at the unusual flora and topography of the Cape's tip. Call the Inn for information. For a different perspective, sail out of Provincetown harbor on the schooners *Olad* or *Hindu* for a 2-hour, windpowered circuit around Race Point. Call 487–9308 for the *Olad,* 487–0659 for the *Hindu.* One of the most fascinating cruises anywhere, though, is Captain Al Avellar's *Whale Watch.* During April and May, the Captain pilots his big, steel-hulled *Dolphin IV* and *Dolphin V* out of Provincetown Harbor in search of migratory whales. Experienced crewmembers help identify species; chances for sightings are excellent. Cruises take four hours in spring, 5 hours in summer and fall. Call 487–1900 in summer, 255–3857 rest of year for reservations.

 **SPORTS. Fishing:** Surf casting and deep-sea fishing are deservedly popular. Charter party boats can be hired for the day at Falmouth, Hyannis, Provincetown, Wellfleet, Oak Bluffs and Nantucket. No license needed.
   Surfing. Nauset Beach, East Orleans and White Crest Beach, Wellfleet, have special area for the surfer. Special sections of Coast Guard Beach and Nauset Light Beach, Eastham, are also set aside, no fee.
   Golf. Round Hill Country Club, E. Sandwich (888–3384); Chequesset Yacht and Country Club, Wellfleet (349–3704); Falmouth Country Club, E. Falmouth (548–3211); Highland Golf Club, Truro (487–9201); Iyanough Hills Golf Club, Rt. 132, Hyannis (362–2606); Bass River Golf Course, S. Yarmouth (398–9079).
   Tennis. Massasoit Crossing, Mashpee; Falmouth Sports Center, Highfield Dr., Falmouth (548–7433); Dennis Racquet Club, E. Dennis (385–2221); Oliver's Tennis Courts, Rt. 6, Wellfleet (349–3330); Mattakesett Tennis Club, Katama Rd., Edgartown; Nantucket Tennis Club, off Cliff Road, Nantucket.
   Sailing instruction and boat rentals are available throughout the Cape and islands. In Edgartown, try the Harborside Inn; on Nantucket, Nantucket Sail, Inc.; and check the wharves in East Orleans, Hyannis, and along the Bass River.
   The Cape is also a fine place for *bicycling.* Don't stray too far from paved roads; the deeper the sand, the slower the going.

 HISTORIC SITES AND MUSEUMS. If you find that there's a rainy day while you're visiting Cape Cod or "The Islands," don't worry that you may be wasting a day of your vacation. The area is full of wonderful museums and sites that chronicle the lives of the early settlers and the fishing and whaling business that became so much a part of the life and lore of Cape Code.

CAPE COD

BARNSTABLE. *Donald G. Trayser Memorial Museum,* Main St. (362–2092). Historical documents, marine exhibits. Open July to Sept. Tues. through Sat. *Cape Cod Art Association Gallery and Studios,* Rt. 6A (362–2909). Classes, exhibits. May to early Nov.

BOURNE. *Aptucxet Trading Post,* 24 Aptucxet Rd., off Shore Rd. (759–5755). Replica of Pilgrim trading post. Native American artifacts. Open mid-April to mid-Oct.

BREWSTER. *Drummer Boy Museum.* Rte. 6A (896–3823). Scenes from American Revolution, with life-size figures. Guided tours. Late May to mid-Oct. *Cape Cod Museum of Natural History,* Rte. 6A, (896–3867). Animal, marine exhibits, nature trails. Daily in summer; Tues. through Sat. in winter. *Sealand of Cape Cod.* Rte. 6A (385–9252). Dolphin and seal shows, aquariums, picnic area. Daily in summer; Thurs. through Tues. in winter. *New England Fire & History Museum,* Rt. 6A (896–5711). Early fire engines; other hist. exhibits. Picnic area. *Daily mid-June to mid-Oct.*

CENTERVILLE. *Centerville Historical Society Museum,* Jct. of West Bay Rd., Parker Rd. (775–0331). Sea captain's home. Doll collections, ship models. Open late June to late Sept. Wed. through Sun.

DUXBURY. *John Alden House.* Alden St. No phone. Open June 1 to Labor Day, Tues. through Sun. Here lived the *Pilgrim* who "couldn't speak for himself" but married Priscilla anyway.

EASTHAM. *Old Grist Mill* (1793), Grist Mill Park. opp. Town Hall, Rte. 6. Memorial Day to Labor Day. *Eastham Historical Society,* off Rte. 6 (255–0788). Early school house, Indian artifacts, farming tools. Also *Swift-Daley House.* Early June to Labor Day, Wed. through Fri.

FALMOUTH. *Historical Society Museum,* Palmer Ave. (548–4587). Whaling, period furniture, tools, costumes. Garden. Mid-June to mid-Sept. Closed Sun. *New Alchemy Institute,* 237 Hatchville Rd. (563–2655). Solar greenhouses, aquaculture, organic gardens. Open all-year. Saturday tours, May to Oct.

PLYMOUTH: *Plymouth Rock, the Mayflower II, Cole's Hill, Burial Hill,* and *Brewster Gardens* all clustered in same downtown area, at North Park Ave. and the waterfront. Burial Hill and Brewster Gardens, closer to the First Parish Church, at Town Sq. on Leyden St. No telephone numbers. With the exception of the ship, they may be visited at any time. *First Parish Church.* Town Sq. (746–2980). Open daily in summer; open for church services only rest of year. Building is the fourth successor to the original 1683 structure, and home to a congregation begun by the Pilgrims. *Pilgrim Hall Museum,* 74 Court St. (746–1620). Open daily year round. Artwork and artifacts depicting the Pilgrim experience. *Plimoth Plantation,* Rte. 3A (746–1622). Open Apr. 1 to Nov. 30, daily. The crafts and daily living of the Pilgrims, circa 1627, practiced in authentic recreated environments by costumed men and women. *Cranberry World,* Water St. (747–1000). Large cranberry trade exhibit. Free. Open April to Dec.

PROVINCETOWN. *Pilgrim Memorial Monument.* Town Hill (487–1310). Commemorates pilgrims' first landing. *Provincetown Heritage Museum,* Commercial and Center Sts. (487–0666), has marine relics. *Mayflower* diorama.

Provincetown Art Association, 460 Commercial St. (487–1750). Regional art museum, concerts. Open late May to Oct. *Fine Arts Work Center,* 24 Pearl St. (487–9960). Local painting, sculpture, pottery on exhibit during summer. Closed Thurs. *Nickerson House,* 72 Commercial St. Oldest house in Province-town. Daily June to Sept. No phone (private).

QUINCY. *Adams National Historic Site.* Three locations: Old House, 135 Adams St.; John Adams Birthplace, 133 Franklin St.; and John Quincy Adams Birthplace, 141 Franklin St. (773–1177). Open daily Apr. 19 to Nov. 10.

SANDWICH. *Historical Society, Sandwich Glass Museum,* Town Hall Sq. (888–0251). Examples of renowned Sandwich glass. Open April to Nov. *Hoxie House & Dexter Grist Mill,* Route 130, Sandwich Center. Restoration of 17th-century home and mill. Mid-June to early Oct. No phone. *Heritage Plantation,* Grove & Pine Sts. (888–3300). Round barn houses Barney Oldfield diorama, historic cars; Military Museum, contains Lilly collection of miniature soldiers, antique firearms; Arts & Crafts Bldg. exhibits Colonial tools, paintings. Open early May. *Thornton W. Burgess Museum.* Water St. (888–6870). Children's museum. Story-telling in July and August. Family nature trail. Open April to Dec.

YARMOUTH. *Captain Bangs Hallet House,* Rte. 6A (362–3021). Home of Yarmouth Historical Association. Garden. Trails. June to mid-Oct.

WOODS HOLE. *National Marine Fisheries Aquarium,* waterfront (548–5123). Free. Open mid-June to mid-Sept.

MARTHA'S VINEYARD

EDGARTOWN. *Dukes County Historical Society,* Cooke & School Sts., Ed-gartown (627–4441). Restored Thomas Cooke House (1765) with furnishings, scrimshaw, whaling relics. Herb garden, library. Tues. through Sat. in summer; Thurs. through Sat. rest of year. Donation. *Felix Neck Sanctuary,* off Vineyard Haven Road, has a small natural history museum. Open all-year. (627–4850). *Cape Pogue Wildlife Reservation* on Chappaquiddick Island. Open all year. No phone.

NANTUCKET ISLAND

NANTUCKET. *Jethro Coffin House* (1686) Sunset Hill. Beautiful restoration of island's oldest house. No phone. June to Sept. *Whaling Museum,* Broad St. (228–1736). Late May to mid-Oct. *Peter Foulger Museum,* Broad St., historical museum with reference library. No phone. *Old Windmill* (1746), Mill Hill. June to early Sept. *Maria Mitchell Assoc.* (1790), 1 Vestal St. Birthplace of famous astronomer, observatory, library, natural science museum. Mid-June to mid-Sept. Library open all year Mon. through Thurs. Observatory mid-June to mid-Sept., Weds. eve. only. Check local listings for phones of individual departments. *Hadwen House-Satler Memorial,* Main & Pleasant Sts. Early 19th-century furnishings. June to late Oct. No phone. *1800 House,* Mill St. 19th-century home. June to early Sept. No phone. *Lightship Nantucket.* Straight Wharf. Once served as harbor light. Nautical memorabilia aboard. Summer only. No phone.

 **STAGE & REVUES.** Cape Cod offers excellent summer theater, usually Broadway favorites with professional casts. Chatham: *Monomoy Theatre,* Rte. 28 (945–1589). Features student actors and young professionals. Dennis: *Cape Playhouse,* Rte. 6A (385–3911), July and Aug. *Falmouth Playhouse,* off Rte. 151 (563–5922). Early July to early Sept. West Harwich: *Harwich Junior Theatre,* Willow & Division Sts. (432–2002). Drama, musical for children. July and Aug. Hyannis: *Cape Cod Melody Tent.* W. Main St. (775–9100). Late June

to Labor Day. Provincetown: *Provincetown Playhouse* (487–0955). Repertory group specializing in O'Neill. July to Labor Day.

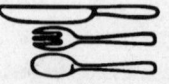 **DINING OUT.** Cape Cod is liberally dotted with interesting restaurants and inns. Although many restaurants are closed after the summer season, a growing number are open year round for those interested in seeing the Cape after the sun-worshippers have gone.

Our ratings are based on the price of an à la carte dinner. *Expensive,* $25 and up; *Moderate,* $15–$25; *Inexpensive,* under $15. Diners should keep in mind that lobster prices fluctuate considerably; when prices are up, expect to pay $15 or more for one of the creatures. The best bets for no-frills lobsters are often simple roadside establishments serving them boiled, on paper plates.

Call ahead to inquire about credit card and reservation policies.

Note: Unless otherwise noted, the restaurants below are open year-round.

CAPE COD

BARNSTABLE. Mattakeese Wharf. *Moderate.* Barnstable Harbor (362–4511). Seafood: baked stuffed lobster, native fish. Outdoor dining overlooking harbor. Fish market on premises. Open May to early Oct.

BREWSTER. Chillingsworth. *Expensive.* Rte. 6A, E. Brewster (896–3640). Award-winning restaurant in lovely Colonial inn. Seven-to-eight course dinners based around superb fish, lamb, veal, duck, and beef tenderloin entrees. Own baking; fine wine list. May be the Cape's best restaurant. Dinner by reservation only; 2 seatings nightly. Open late May to Dec.

Old Manse Inn. *Expensive.* Rte. 6A (896–3149). Modified table d'hote. Menu changes nightly. Open weekends year-round. Tues. through Sat. evenings in season.

Bramble Inn Gallery and Cafe. *Moderate.* Rte. 6A (896–7644). Carbonnade de boeuf flammande; other specialties. Wine and beer. Open mid-June to Sept.

BUZZARDS BAY. The Windjammer. *Moderate.* 3131 Cranberry Hwy. (759–7262). Seafood. Own baking: popovers, breads, pastries. Bar.

Lobster Trap. *Inexpensive.* 290 Shore Rd., Bourne (759–3992). Patio dining. Huge tasty portions of fried seafood; steamed clams; lobsters and lobster rolls. Open mid-June to mid-Sept.

Quintal's. *Inexpensive.* Scenic Hwy. (759–7222). Seafood, pot roast, daily specials, salad bar.

CHATHAM. Queen Anne Inn. *Expensive.* 70 Queen Anne Rd. (945–0394). Nouvelle and classic cuisine in stately 19th-century inn. Traditional decor. Lounge area with outdoor patio. Tues. night clambake. Extensive wine list. "Casual elegance."

Captain's Table. *Moderate.* 578 Main St. (945–1961). Yankee cooking: chicken pie, fish, orange bread. Open Apr. to Nov., Tues. through Fri. 4 to 8 P.M.; Sun. noon to 8:30. Closed Mon.; Tues. off season.

DENNIS. Columns. *Expensive.* Main St., W. Dennis (389–8033). Tournedos Rossini; frogs' legs; fettucini Alfredo. Entertainment under tent. Lovely old mansion.

Swan River Seafood Restaurant. *Inexpensive.* Lower County Road, Dennisport (394–4466). Good fresh fish; take-out avail. Open late May to Sept.

FALMOUTH. Flying Bridge. *Expensive.* Scranton Ave. at Marina (548–2700). Open-hearth cooking. Steaks, roast beef, seafood. Overlooks harbor. Bar, live music, dancing. Open Apr. to late Oct. for lunch, dinner.

Coonamessett Inn. *Moderate.* Jones Rd. and Gifford St. (548–2300). Lovely traditional dining room serving seafood, steak. Open for breakfast, lunch, dinner. Bar with pianist, trio, dancing.

HARWICH. Bishop's Terrace. *Expensive.* Main St., W. Harwich (432–0253). New England specialties; lobster, roast beef, steak. Terrace dining. Dinner nightly, lunch Mon. through Fri. Sun. Brunch. Open mid-June to mid-Oct.

HYANNIS. Asa Bearse House. *Moderate.* Main St. & Pearl St. (771–4131). Pleasant surroundings. Seafood. Jazz and piano.

Albertos. *Moderate.* 337 Main St. (771–6213.) Located behind an art gallery. Delicately prepared Italian food; interesting pastas. Wine, beer.

Mitchell's Steak and Rib House. *Moderate.* Rte. 28 opp. airport (775–6700). Filet mignon, prime rib, first-rate chowder. Irish music nightly.

MASHPEE. The Flume. *Moderate.* Nr. Rte. 130 (477–1456). Small country restaurant serving some of the best chowder and fish on the Cape. Informal.

ORLEANS. Orleans Inn Restaurant. *Moderate.* Rte. 6A (255–2222). Seafood. Lunch served on patio overlooking town cove. Bar. Open noon to 9:30 in season; Sat. 5 to 9. Open March to January.

PROVINCETOWN. Cafe at the Mews. *Expensive.* 359 Commercial St. (487–1500). Native seafood; duckling cassis; Chateaubriand. Bar with fireplace. Dinner nightly; Sunday brunch., June to early Sept.

Ciro & Sal's. *Expensive.* 4 Kiley Ct. (487–9803). Northern Italian specialties scallopine Marsala, saltimbocca. Intimate wine cellar atmosphere. Open daily in season; wknds only, Nov. to Apr.

The Moors. *Expensive.* Bradford St. (487–0840). Portuguese cuisine: kale soup; pork tenderloin with ginger, cumin, coriander, and garlic. Open April to Nov.

Poor Richard's Buttery. *Expensive.* 432 Commercial St. (487–3825). Continental dining. Music lounge. Open April to mid-Oct.

Napi's. *Moderate.* 7 Freeman St. (487–9703). Gallery. Popular with local artists, writers. Eclectic menu with nice surprises.

Cookie's. *Inexpensive.* Commercial St. (487–1800). Best down-home Portuguese food in town. Kale soup, squid stew, marinated pork and fish dishes.

TRURO. Whitman House. *Expensive.* Great Hollow Rd. (487–1740). Home baking. Lobster, roast beef. Entertainment. Open April to Nov.

WELLFLEET. Aesop's Tables. *Expensive.* Main St. (349–6450). Internat'l cuisine. 6 to 10, May to mid-Oct.

Sweet Seasons. *Expensive.* At Inn at Duck Creek (349–6535). Chilled poached lobster, homemade caviar mayonnaise, steak au poivre au chemise. Excellent, leisurely Sunday brunch. Open mid-May to mid-Oct.

Serena's. *Inexpensive.* Rte. 6 (349-9370). Italian specialties and seafood. Informal family restaurant.

WOODS HOLE. Fishmongers Café. *Inexpensive.* 56 Water St. Old-time waterfront café. Informal. Open April to Nov.

YARMOUTH. La Cipollina. *Moderate.* Rt. 6A, Yarmouthport (362–4341). Excellent Italian cuisine. Open late April to Oct.

Cranberry Moose. *Moderate.* 43 Main St. (362–8153). Internation'l cuisine in 200-yr.-old building. Paella, roasts, duckling a l'orange. Open May to Nov.

Old Yarmouth Inn. *Moderate.* Rte. 6A (362–3191). In historic inn. Curries, regional foods featured. Open April to Nov.

MARTHA'S VINEYARD

EDGARTOWN. Chez Pierre. *Expensive.* In the Charlotte Inn, S. Summer St. (627–8947). Lobster Pernod; braised quail. Dine indoors or on terrace. Good wine list.

Lawry's Seafood. *Moderate.* Upper Main St. (627–8857). Some of the freshest seafood on the island. Open April to Oct.

MENEMSHA. Beach Plum Inn. *Expensive.* On hill above Menemsha (645–9454). Overlooks the water. Striped bass with lobster sauce, veal piccata. Outstanding desserts.

The Homeport. *Moderate.* On the water in Menemsha (645–2679). Stuffed lobster, broiled swordfish, and other simple, satisfying seafood dishes. Lovely view. Bring own beer, wine, liquor; set-ups avail. Open June to mid-Sept.

VINEYARD HAVEN. Black Dog Tavern. *Expensive.* Beach Rd. (693–9223). Innovative cuisine; menu changes nightly. Exotic desserts. Hearty brunches. Bring own beer or wine.

NANTUCKET ISLAND

NANTUCKET. Chanticleer Inn. *Expensive.* Siasconset (257–6231). Classic French: foie gras; sea bass in sorrel, vermouth, and cream; raspberries grown on the premises. Lunch in rose garden. Open late May to Oct.

Company of the Cauldron. *Expensive.* 7 India St. (228–4016). Menu changes each week; features lamb, veal, salmon, local seafood. Reservations a must; no credit cards. Open June to Sept.

Lobster Trap. *Moderate.* 23 Washington St. (228-4041). Lobsters, scallops, and clams "without the frills." Open June to Labor Day.

Obadiah's. *Moderate.* 2 India St. (228–4430). A fine selection of fresh seafood, like stuffed lobster. Clam bar in courtyard. Early Apr. to mid-Dec.

EXPLORING THE REST OF MASSACHUSETTS

by William G. Scheller

Lexington and Concord

A popular one-day trip out of Boston takes you to Lexington and Concord—where the American Revolution began in April 1775—with a return stop at Sudbury. Cross the Charles River at the Massachusetts Avenue bridge and proceed through Cambridge, bearing right for Arlington at Harvard Square. You will come to Arlington center in about 15 minutes. Drive straight ahead on Massachusetts Avenue to the first traffic light beyond the center, turn left into Jason Street and stop at the Jason Russell House. As the Redcoats retreated from Concord on that April 19, they passed along Massachusetts Avenue and engaged a group of Colonists close by this house in the second major battle of that eventful day. A number of the Minutemen, nearly surrounded by the British, retreated to the Russell home. Russell and 11 others were killed on the first floor of the house, where bullet holes are still visible.

Continue west on Massachusetts Avenue, through Arlington Heights and East Lexington, where you will pass the Munroe Tavern, a colonial gathering place open to the public, and the entrance to the Museum of Our National Heritage, which houses exhibits illustrating

American history since independence. Massachusetts Avenue soon reaches Lexington Green, where the Minutemen faced the line of British march. A statue and a large boulder mark the Colonists' line. On the stone is inscribed the command: "Stand your ground. Don't fire unless fired upon. But if they mean to have war, let it begin here."

On the right side of the green is Buckman Tavern, where the Minutemen gathered and waited for the British. The Hancock Clark house, a short way from the green on Hancock Street, is also open to the public. John Hancock was staying here when Paul Revere rode into Lexington warning that the British were coming from Boston. Samuel Adams, also in the house at the time, fled with Hancock to avoid capture. The house contains a notable collection of historical articles and is open the same days and hours as the Buckman Tavern.

This quiet suburban town comes alive each Patriots' Day (the Monday nearest April 19) with a celebration of these events, including a colorful battle re-enactment at 6 A.M. and morning and afternoon parades. Volunteer regiments from area towns participate in these re-creations in authentic 18th-century dress and military equipage.

Leave Lexington on Massachusetts Avenue, which bears left from the green and connects with Route 2A to Concord (through Minuteman National Historic Park). Concord owes its distinguished place in American history not only to the events of April 19, 1775, but to the perseverance of the settlers who made it the first New England village to be situated away from the immediate seacoast, and to the remarkable literary figures who made their homes here during the early 19th century. Many of their homes survive, in period style, and are open to the public.

As you approach Concord center from Lexington on Route 2A, you will pass Grapevine Cottage, where Ephriam Bull developed the Concord grape from local strains. Just beyond the cottage (now a private home) is The Wayside, a late-17th-century building once owned by Nathaniel Hawthorne. Among its occupants during Concord's literary heyday were Bronson Alcott and Margaret Sidney, author of *Five Little Peppers*. Nearby is the house where Bronson's famous daughter, Louisa May Alcott, lived when she wrote *Little Women*.

The Lexington Road next intersects with the Cambridge Turnpike, and at the fork stands the Concord Antiquarian Museum, which contains several fully furnished early New England rooms. The museum is also richly endowed with personal possessions of Ralph Waldo Emerson and Henry David Thoreau, the two pre-eminent figures of Concord's Golden Age. Just around the corner from the museum is Emerson's own house, in which the writer's study and other rooms look as they did when he lived there.

Pass through Monument Square, the town's center, and head out Monument Street towards the battlefield. Along the way you will pass the Old Manse, built by Emerson's grandfather and later lived in by Hawthorne. Take special notice of the faint inscriptions on one of the ancient windowpanes, made by Mrs. Hawthorne with her diamond ring.

Just beyond the manse is the North Bridge. Here stands the Minuteman statue commemorating the farmers who stood their ground here against British troops in the opening engagement of the American Revolution. Here also are the graves of British soldiers who fell that day. A brief walk up the hill from the bridge will bring you to the visitors' center, a mansion built by descendants of one of Concord's founders and later donated to the National Park Service. There is an

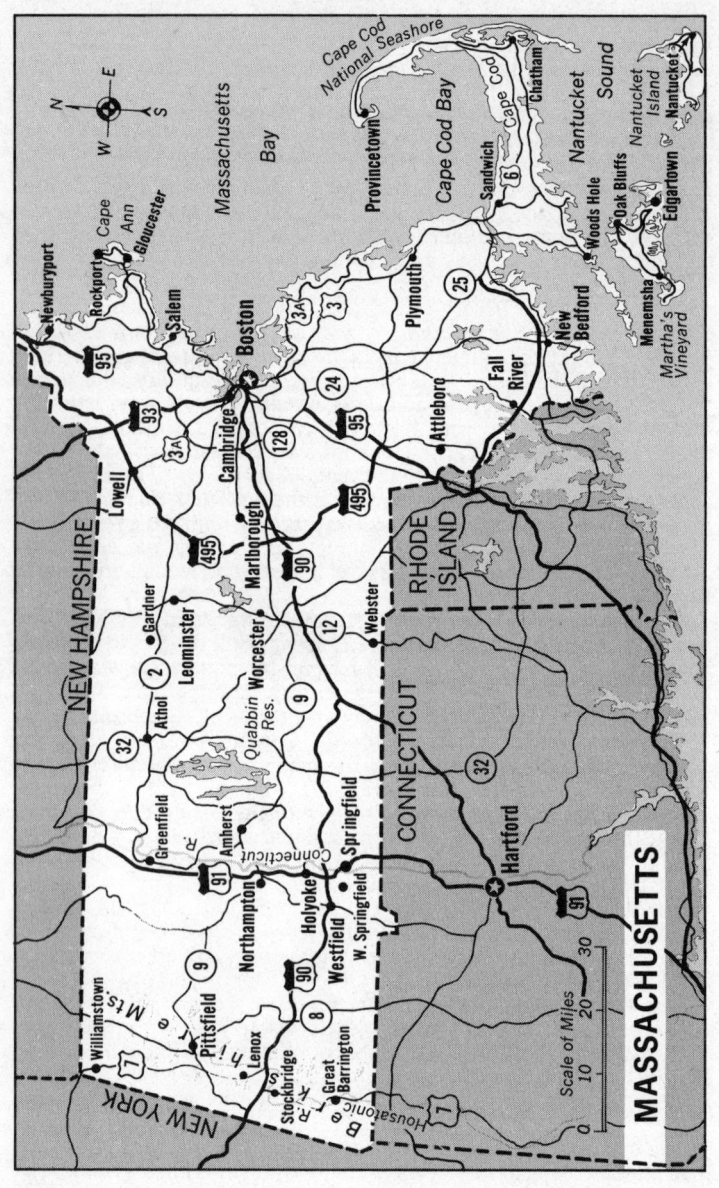

MASSACHUSETTS

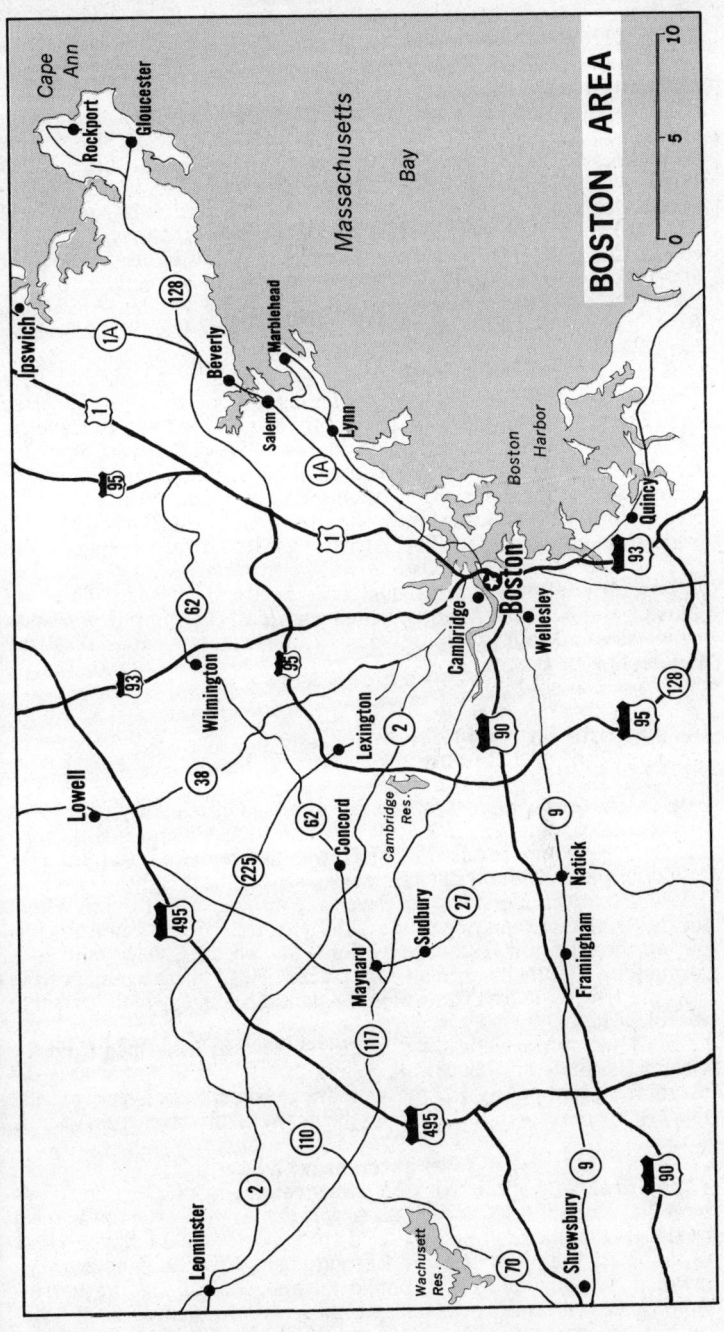

BOSTON AREA

informative slide show given every 15 minutes at the center, and the grounds are the site of frequent concerts and historical re-enactments every summer. The acrid smell of black powder drifting over this field at Concord is the very stuff of history.

Leave Concord the way you came (Route 2A); turn right on a connecting road marked "Wayland" and left on Walden Street. This crosses Route 2 and becomes Highway 126. On the right lies Walden Pond, where Henry David Thoreau lived from 1845 to 1847 at an expense of about eight dollars a year. His experiment in simple and natural living is described in the classic *Walden* (1854).

The site of Thoreau's cabin can be reached by walking to the right along a wooded path at the north end of the pond. Directly across the lake, in a lovely grove that is part of the 150-acre Walden Pond State Reservation, is a public picnic area. Another shore has a town bathing beach, and a large parking area is available.

Route 126 soon joins U.S. 20, where you should turn right and drive six miles to South Sudbury. A sign on the right points out the Wayside Inn. The inn, which has been providing food and lodging to travelers for almost 280 years, was originally known as Howe's Tavern and later Red Horse Tavern. It acquired its present name after Longfellow made it the scene of his *Tales of a Wayside Inn*. In 1923, it was bought by Henry Ford, who preserved it through a national trust. Burned in 1955, it has since been restored. The extensive gardens form a setting for the early 19th-century Old Redstone Hill School.

To return to Boston, turn around on U.S. 20 and head east. This road joins Commonwealth Avenue, which leads past the campus of Boston University and into Kenmore Square, after which it enters the Back Bay section of Boston.

The North Shore: Marblehead, Salem, Cape Ann, and Newburyport

The next tour combines fascinating glimpses into history with views of rugged coastline. Leave Boston on Route 1A, which leads through the Callahan Tunnel under Boston Harbor and borders Logan International Airport. At the traffic circle near Revere, bear right to continue 1A, which travels along Revere Beach and into the city of Lynn. Watch for the "Nahant" signs once you reach Lynn; this narrow peninsula juts out north of Boston Harbor and affords fine beaches, views, and rock formations, despite its residential character. Head north again, bearing always to the right, and you will join Atlantic Avenue, which leads into Marblehead.

The town of Marblehead was settled in 1629 by fishermen from the Channel Islands and Cornwall. While fishing is still important, the magnificent harbor has become a yachting center. Race Week, usually the last full week in July, brings boats from all over the Atlantic seaboard.

Abbott Hall, seat of town government, houses the famous picture, *The Spirit of '76*, considered America's greatest patriotic painting, done by A.M. Willard in 1876. Also on view is the original deed to the town by the Nanepashemet Indians, dated 1684. To get the full flavor of one of the finest examples of a pre-Revolutionary New England seacoast town, park your car in the public lot and walk along the narrow winding streets lined with ancient elms and the mansions of 18th-century sea captains. The Old Town House on Mugford Street was built in 1727, and St. Michael's Church (1714) still uses a bell cast by Paul Revere. Before leaving, visit Marblehead Neck and the lighthouse at the harbor entrance, reached by following Ocean Avenue Causeway from Atlantic Avenue. Still hugging the sea, leave Marblehead on Route 114 to Salem, just three miles away.

Salem, home of privateers and the sea captains who made fabulous fortunes in the China trade, was until about 1810 one of the nation's leading ports. That old glory is long gone, but its memory lives on in places like the Peabody Maritime Museum, the Salem Maritime National Historic Site with its Richard Derby House, the Old Custom House and Derby Wharf, and the Essex Institute, which incorporates a half-dozen homes built in the 17th, 18th, and 19th centuries. The Institute also houses a library, doll collection, and gardens. Many other, privately owned homes not open to the public are nonetheless easy to appreciate from the outside. Salem, like many other eclipsed shipping and industrial centers in the northeast, was allowed to slowly and unconscionably deteriorate during the middle years of this century. This process is happily being reversed, particularly in downtown Salem, with its attractive pedestrian mall, and in the Pickering Wharf restoration, which features shops, apartments, and marina. Also visit Chestnut Street, lined with the circa–1800 homes of Salem's merchant princes. It is one of the most beautiful streets in America.

The Chamber of Commerce has indicated many points of interest on a historic trail map and has erected signs to mark their location. A copy of the map may be obtained at information booths or at the chamber's office. Of particular interest in Salem, of course, are places—such as the restored "Witch House," home of Jonathan Corwin, judge of the witchcraft court—recalling notorious witchcraft trials that took place in nearby Danvers (then called Salem Village) in the late 17th century. The Salem witch museum tells the story.

The Salem episode was sparked by a West Indian slave named Tituba, a servant of the Rev. Samuel Parris. She had a talent for storytelling, particularly voodoo tales. Her listeners, frequently, were two impressionable young girls who would have nightmares after one of Tituba's better yarns. The girls were declared witches and shortly accused Tituba and two other unpopular old women in the town of acquainting them with the Devil. Given the example of widespread witch trials in Europe, no one was safe in Salem. Nineteen persons were hanged on Gallows Hill in 1693. (Contrary to popular belief, no one was burned at the stake.) The witchcraft trials came to an abrupt end when the wife of Governor Phipps and the saintly Mrs. Hale, wife of a minister, were accused.

Leaving Salem, go north on Route 1A, cross the bridge over the harbor, and turn right on Route 127 to Beverly, known as the birthplace of the American Navy. According to official records of the Library of Congress, the schooner *Hannah,* which was docked at Glover's Wharf, was converted to an armed vessel of war and set sail on Sept. 5, 1775. Two days later, the *Hannah* returned with its first British prize. A Beverly resident, George Cabot, was named as first Secretary of the Navy by President Adams. Also of interest in Beverly is the Balch House (1638), at 448 Cabot Street.

Continue on Route 127 to Beverly Farms, Pride's Crossing, Manchester-by-the-Sea and Magnolia, towns known for the stately summer retreats built by Boston Brahmins. By taking Hesperus Avenue in Magnolia you can see Norman's Woe Rock, made famous by Longfellow's "Wreck of the Hesperus." (The best view is from the castellated

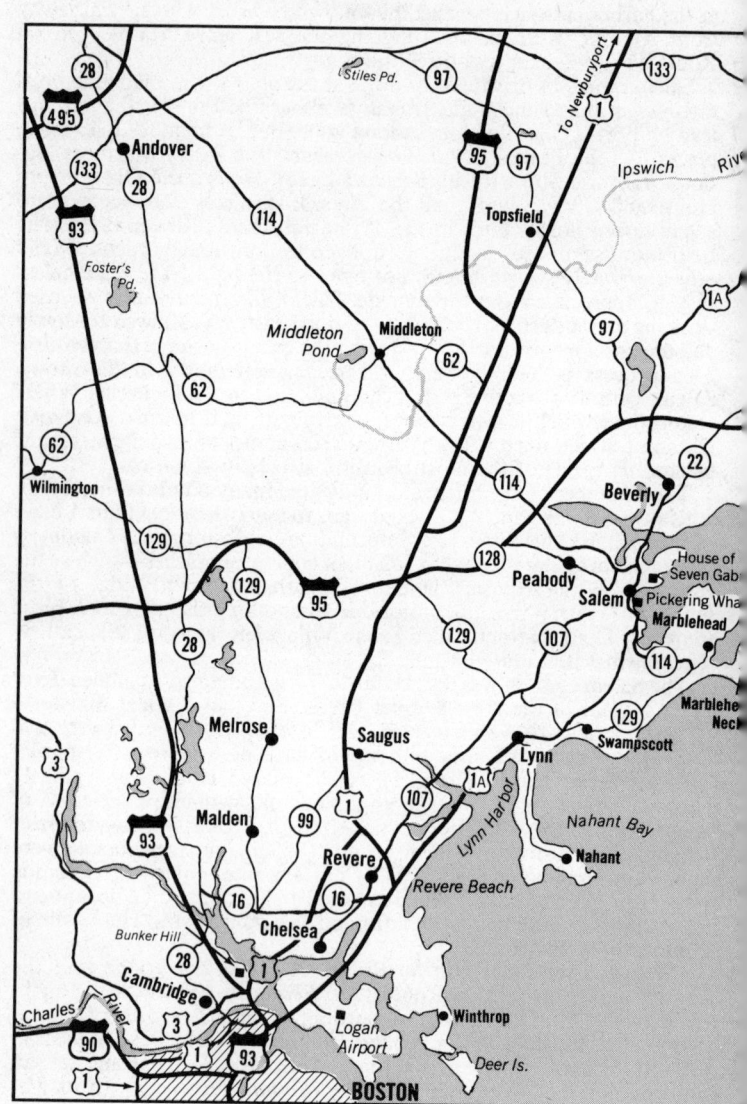

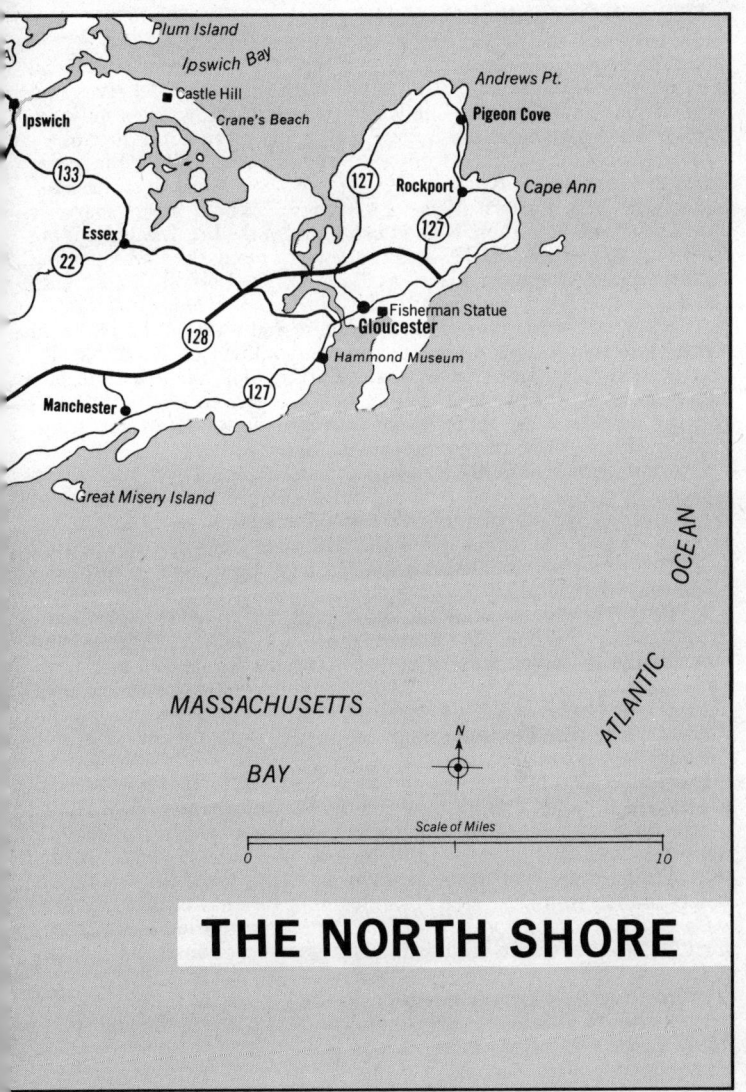

THE NORTH SHORE

top of the Hammond Museum, worth a visit.) Hesperus Avenue rejoins Route 127 and crosses the Annisquam River into Gloucester. Park your car along the seawall.

Facing the sea is the Gloucester Fisherman statue, a memorial to Gloucestermen lost at sea. Each August, a memorial service is held along the seawall; flowers are scattered upon the water to disappear on the outgoing tide. Beyond the statue on the right are wharves and picturesque fishing vessels. Gloucester is one of the world's most famous fishing ports, and the largest lobster distributor in America.

Instead of aiming directly for Rockport on Route 127, take the scenic shore drive, which is Route 127 Alternate. This leads down to East Gloucester and Eastern Point Lighthouse. When the stripers or bluefish are running, there is good fishing from the breakwater leading out from the light. Route 127 Alternate winds along the shore, passing such intriguingly named places as Bass Rocks, Loblolly Cove, Gap Head, Good Harbor Beach and Brier Neck.

At Rockport, park your car in the square and walk out on Bearskin Neck. Here stands the lobster shack jestingly known as "Motif No. 1," portrayed in paintings by generations of artists. The shack was heavily damaged during the blizzard of 1978, but has since been rebuilt. Rockport has numerous art galleries and souvenir shops and attracts thousands of people daily throughout the summer.

Continuing on Route 127, you will come to Pigeon Cove. Look sharp for a small sign on the left pointing out the Paper House. It is one of those strange structures utilizing cast-off material, like the famous Watts towers in California. The Paper House at Rockport was started in 1922; more than 100,000 newspapers have been used to form the house and its furniture.

Route 127 continues along the shore from Rockport. It passes Halibut Point and runs down the western shore of Cape Ann, affording fine views of the sea every mile of the way. It joins Route 128 at a large traffic circle. Turn right on 128, cross the Annisquam River, and turn right again (Highway 133) toward the town of Essex, which has an afternoon's worth of antique shops on its main street. Ipswich is four miles farther.

Ipswich, settled in 1633, is said to have more 17th-century Colonial houses still standing and lived in than any town in America. Whipple House, built around 1640, is the town showpiece and is furnished with many antiques. It is located at the junction of Route 133 and 1 Alternate. Argilla Road leads from the town square to the Crane Memorial Reservation, a 10-mile stretch of sandy public beach. Located here also is Castle Hill, a mansion where public concerts and lectures are frequently held in summer. And seafood lovers will, of course, have heard of Ipswich clams.

From Ipswich, continue north on Route 1A for 12 miles, past the salt marshes of Rowley and Newbury, until you reach Newburyport. Route 1A becomes High Street, which is lined with some of the finest examples of Federalist style (roughly 1790–1810) mansions in New England. You'll notice "widow's walks," which afford a view of the port and farther out to sea, perched atop many of these fine houses. Like those in Salem, they were built for prosperous sea captains who lived in this city, which also once thrived as a leading port and shipbuilding center. Although Newburyport's maritime significance ended with the day of the clipper ships, some of the best of which were built here, an energetic downtown renewal program has brought new life to the town's brick-fronted center. Renovated buildings now house an assortment of restaurants, taverns, and shops, selling everything from nautical brasses to fine antique oriental rugs. These civic improvements have been matched by private restoration of the town's housing stock, much of which dates from the 18th century with a scattering of 1600s homes in some neighborhoods.

A causeway leads from Newburyport to Plum Island, a narrow spit of land harboring a summer colony at one end and a fine, carefully managed wildlife refuge at the other. The beaches on the refuge are open to bathers and fishermen (gates close when parking lots are filled), and the self-guided trails through dunes and marshes offer the North Shore's most rewarding setting for birdwatching. U.S. 1 returns to Boston through Topsfield, scene of the country's oldest public fair.

Lowell's Industrial Past

You may return directly to Boston via Route 1 or Route 95, perhaps with a stop in Saugus to visit the restoration of America's first iron works. Or, take 95 north from Newburyport to Route 495 and head west toward Haverhill, Lawrence and Lowell, the great textile towns of the Merrimack Valley. Lowell is particularly fascinating; its central core has been designated a National Historical Park, the purpose of which is to commemorate and interpret the beginnings of the Industrial Revolution in America. The modern American factory system was conceived in Lowell in the 1820's; today, the great hulking textile mills, long abandoned, are being restored both for new uses and as interpretive centers. Canal tours reveal the ingenuity with which water power was used in Lowell; barges are used to take passengers through the old industrial district. There are also trolley rides. Interestingly, this old textile manufacturing town is now a computer manufacturing center.

From Lowell, return to Boston via Route 93, or continue on 495 if you are heading toward Route 2, the Massachusetts Pike, and the western part of the state.

Bristol County and New Bedford

For those who like the taste of the sea—fishing, surfing, sailing, maritime history and, of course, seafood—a visit to Bristol County will be rewarding on all counts. If you are coming off the Cape, follow U.S. 6 to Fairhaven and New Bedford. Out of Boston, follow State 24 into State 25 to U.S. 6. Although no longer a prime port, New Bedford is a busy center of fishing and textile manufacturing. From 1820 until the discovery of oil in Pennsylvania almost 40 years later, New Bedford vied with Nantucket for preeminence in American whaling. Today, the industry which once employed 10,000 seamen is commemorated in museums like the one on Johnny Cake Hill in New Bedford. Here you can see the square-rigged whaler *Lagoda,* a half-scale (89 feet) replica of the sort of ship that once crowded the docks of New Bedford. And there are prints and paintings, ship carvings and scrimshaw, and the world's largest collection of whaling gear. Nearby is the seamen's Bethel, vividly pictured by Melville in *Moby Dick.* The Bethel (chapel) was built in 1832 for the spiritual edification of the sailors who shipped out from New Bedford. Melville, whose brief whaling career began here, first visited the chapel when it was but eight years old. The pew where he sat is marked with a commemorative plaque.

New Bedford was once the home of a flourishing glass industry, the products of which are displayed in a recently opened glass museum, which occupies the restored Rodman House just one block from the Whaling Museum on North 2nd Street. New Bedford glass, however, is not just a well-kept memory—after a twenty-year absence, the Pairpoint Glass Company has returned to a new plant near the museum.

Fall River

Fall River is just a short ride west from New Bedford on Interstate 195. Here is a classic scene in the Massachusetts story, a once-booming textile town struggling to make a comeback from the southward movement of the mills. Like New Bedford, Fall River has a large Portuguese community as well as many French-Canadians.

Here is where the great veteran of World War II naval action, the USS *Massachusetts,* is berthed, along with other historic fighting ships. It's open all year from 9 to dusk. Just a short walk from the battleship is Fall River's Marine Museum, with an interesting collection of ship models, steam engines and material related to the old Fall River line and other ships of the steamboat era. Bargain hunters should note that Fall River has become a major factory outlet center—at last count, there were 51 outlets in the city, most concentrated in one area. If you'd like to see some lively dog racing, take State 24 north to Taunton Dog Track and Raynham Park. From Taunton, follow State 140 north to Interstate 95, south to the junction with Interstate 495, north to Interstate 90 (the Massachusetts Turnpike), and west into Worcester.

Worcester

Worcester (pronounced "Wooster"), in the heartland of Massachusetts, is a major educational, industrial and retail center with a history of uncommon achievements. Long ago, Isaiah Thomas worked here, printing chapbooks and starting, in 1770, a longlived patriotic newspaper, *The Massachusetts Spy.* Destined to become the country's leading printer and founder of the American Antiquarian Society (where his press can be viewed today), he gave the first reading of the Declaration of Independence to occur in New England, on July 4, 1776, in Worcester.

Worcester has been the birthplace of a number of ingenious inventions ranging from the first calliope to the first liquid fuel rocket. It was also the site of the first women's suffrage national convention. Notable figures associated with Worcester include General Artemus Ward, first commander-in-chief of the American forces in the Revolution; Clara Barton; Elias Howe and Eli Whitney; horticulturist Luther Burbank; baseball player and manager Connie Mack; and humorist Robert Benchley.

Worcester's attractions range from water sports, at nearby Lake Quinsigamond, to the fascinating exhibits of the Worcester Science Museum to the Higgins Armory Museum displays of arms, armor and art from the middle ages and Renaissance. The Worcester Art Museum houses one of the finest collections outside a major metropolitan area, and the American Antiquarian Society has amassed a priceless documentary record of American history and biography. Try to attend a concert at historic, restored Mechanics' Hall. Worcester's Centrum, at Foster and Commercial Streets, is a new and successful civic center drawing top entertainers from around the country as well as sporting events, exhibitions and conventions.

The city's horticultural society mounts colorful exhibits throughout the year. For details of these and other special events, check with the Central Massachusetts Tourist Council at Mechanics Tower, Suite 350, 100 Front St., Worcester 01608.

Old Sturbridge Village

New England has many villages which have been reconstructed to demonstrate the mode of life in the early days of the nation. Old Sturbridge Village, less than 20 miles southwest of Worcester, is among the most popular. A visit here—at any season—makes an interesting and pleasant side trip from Boston, about an hour away. (Write to the Tri-Community Chamber of Commerce, Southbridge MA 01550, for details about winter weekends and other attractions at Old Sturbridge.) It's just off the Massachusetts Turnpike (Exit 9). It can also be reached by way of the Merritt and Wilbur Cross Parkways (Routes 15 and I–86).

Visitors to Old Sturbridge meet history face to face. They can see an historic newspaper pulled from a 200-year-old printing press, a horseshoe shaped under a smith's hammer, or a traditional meeting house. Horses draw a carry-all for the visitors to ride. An oxcart plies the village lanes and a flock of photogenic geese guard the millpond. You can sit in the shade of a maple tree on the village green and listen to a strolling minstrel sing his story-songs. In the village are found the homes, shops, general store, schoolhouse, tavern and pillory of a typical New England village of the early 1800s. Craftsmen in period costumes recreate the life of the times, demonstrating spinning, weaving, printing, the making of pottery, and the skills of pewtersmith and tinsmith, as well as the domestic arts of fireplace cooking, herb gardening and candle dipping. The farm work and cottage industries recreated at the village depend upon the same sources of energy tapped by early New Englanders—wood, water and the muscle power of men and oxen. A visit to Old Sturbridge Village, then, is an object lesson in the use of many "renewable" energy options that are just being rediscovered today.

Many of the original buildings—there are nearly 40 in the village—were brought to Old Sturbridge from different parts of New England. Meals and lodging and a large parking lot are available. No cars are allowed within the village, but walking distances between the buildings are not great.

Springfield and the Pioneer Valley

Here, through Franklin, Hampshire and Hampden counties, flows the longest river in New England, called the Quinnitukqut ("Long Tidal River") by the Indians, the Connecticut by the English. The Connecticut was a major avenue of trade and transportation during the days of colonial settlement (as the Vermont villages named after downstream towns will attest) and later figured in the valley's industrial development. After years of abuse, the Connecticut is responding to anti-pollution treatment, and shad and salmon can again be found in its waters.

The Pioneer Valley is an area of rich harvests, not only in tobacco and apples but in industry and education. Interstate 91 runs from North Bernardston in the north to Longmeadow in the south. Off the turnpike, visitors can find everything from dinosaur tracks and trout streams to colleges and cities. On Rte. 20 between Sturbridge and Springfield, there seem to be antique shops at every turn in the road.

Springfield, New England's fourth largest city and home of the Springfield and Garand rifles, has long been commercially important. The cycle of boom, bust and renewal common to the state's industrial areas is in a new phase today as diversified tool, machine and appliance enterprises are thriving along with a revival in retail trade.

Springfield's attractions reflect the city's past accomplishments, a healthy present-day cultural appetite and its location at the geographical heart of New England. Undoubtedly this helps make the Eastern States Exposition, called the "Big E" and held here every September, one of the most popular fairs in the country. The exposition is a showcase of New England's industrial and agricultural accomplishments, and a longed-for destination for thousands of young people involved in livestock and homemaking projects with 4-H and other youth groups.

Not many cities can boast of giving birth to a major sport, but it was in a Springfield gymnasium in 1891 that Dr. James Naismith first organized teams to attempt stuffing a lively, unpredictable ball through hoops mounted tantalizingly out of reach. The Naismith Memorial Basketball Hall of Fame, on the Springfield College campus, commemorates this fact and the great players of the past. The museum at the Springfield Armory recalls more serious business, with a collection representing every firearm manufactured at the old installation from 1795 to modern times.

Important Springfield cultural institutions are located in the city's Museum Quadrangle. These include the Museum of Fine Arts, Science Museum, Connecticut Valley Historical Museum, and George Walter Vincent Smith Art Museum, housing an impressive collection of oriental rugs, armor, and decorative arts.

Five miles north of Springfield, on U.S. 5, is Holyoke. The fine college of Mount Holyoke is just four miles from this busy industrial city on Highway 116. The grounds and buildings of the college are spacious and attractive and the Dwight Memorial Art Museum, open weekdays, is worth visiting. Just north of the small town of South Hadley (the college's actual location) is Dinosaur Land, an interesting display of the fossil tracks of prehistoric animals who left imprints in the sandstone cliffs and river banks between Holyoke and Northampton.

Head from South Hadley on Highway 47 to the junction of the mountain road, about three miles from the village. The road leads through the Pass of Thermopylae, a narrow, winding road that goes under Titan's Piazza, an unusual trap rock formation on Mount Holyoke that local people deem one of the seven wonders of the world. From the summit of the mountain road, return to Highway 47 and continue to Hadley. Turn left to Northampton, site of Smith College (where there is a fine collection of contemporary paintings and prints) and the Massachusetts home of Calvin Coolidge, our 30th president. (The Coolidge Room at the Forbes Library on West Street houses a collection of Coolidge papers and memorabilia.) There are many interesting, antique-filled houses, such as the Cornet Joseph Parsons House (1658), Northampton's oldest.

A fair is held here in September, and during the last weekend in July, the nation's largest single-breed horse show, the Eastern National Morgan Horse Show, takes place at the fairgrounds. There are also a variety of outdoor activities, including boating, swimming, golf and snowmobiling. Three miles south, off U.S. 5, is Mt. Tom, a major ski center.

From Northampton, turn east on Route 9 to visit Amherst, site of the lifelong home of Emily Dickinson, the University of Massachusetts and Amherst College. Returning to U.S. 5 and continuing north, drive twelve miles to the village of Old Deerfield, a National Historic District with 30 buildings more than a century and a half old. The village's history goes back much further. Today, Deerfield is not so much a town as the ghost of a town, one of the most fascinating of its kind in America. Other New England communities have been important, but Deerfield stands as a classic statement of the tragic and creative moment when one civilization destroys and displaces another. Little of consequence has happened there for nearly 300 years since the grim time from 1672 to 1704 when it was the northwest frontier of New England. Although it formed part of Dedham in 1663, no Dedhamite had settled there until 1669, when Samuel Hindsdell, a squatter, began cultivation of the fertile soil where the Pocumtuck Indians had grown their corn, tobacco and pumpkins. By 1672, however, Samson Frary and others had joined Hinsdell; soon the population reached 125. This, according to the Pocumtucks, was carrying encroachment too far and one dark night three years later, they struck in what is called the Bloody Brook Massacre. They either killed or drove off to hamlets farther south every single white person. It was a foretaste of the coming 200 years of struggle between the intruders and those whose lands were relentlessly usurped from Plymouth to Puget Sound.

For seven years, Deerfield's houses were empty. Slowly, the settlers returned, and in 1686 Deerfield held its first town meeting. The Indians attacked again in 1704, putting to the torch more than half the town's buildings, capturing more than 100 men, women and children for slaves, and killing 50 others who tried to resist. With this great raid, Deerfield's active life ended. But its memory lingers. The Deerfield Historical Society has restored many of the original buildings. Memorial Hall contains, along with many relics of early days, the front door of one of the Deerfield homes which survived the raid of 1704. The door bears the mark of a tomahawk. The Frary House is well worth a visit, as is the Indian House with its second- and third-story overhangs, characteristic of the earliest Colonial architecture. Many other fascinating early homes are open for inspection along Old Deerfield St. Continue north from Old Deerfield on U.S. 5 to Greenfield and the start of the Mohawk Trail, going west into lovely Berkshire County. Drive through Greenfield for a preview of the gracious western New England town life you will find as you cross the Hoosacs into Williamstown on the New York—Vermont border. Follow Maple Street to the top of Rocky Mountain for good views of the Berkshires to the west and the farmlands to the east. On Leyden Road is one of the last covered bridges to be found in Massachusetts. Because of its proximity to I-91, Greenfield has become a summer and winter sports center for the Pioneer Valley area.

The Mohawk Trail and the Northern Berkshires

The Berkshires can be approached from several different directions: from Connecticut on U.S. 7 and Massachusetts 8; along feeder roads off New York's beautiful Taconic Parkway, through Columbia and Rensselaer Counties; or from Vermont on Routes 7 and 8 and other smaller roads. But the most spectacular approach is via the Mohawk Trail, running alongside the Deerfield River through upland towns, farms and woods and gorges that open up beautiful mountain views.

The 67 miles of Route 2 betwen Greenfield and the New York boundary have been officially recognized by the Massachusetts legislature as the Mohawk Trail. A key link between the great Hudson and Connecticut River transport systems of New York and Massachusetts, the trail has been significant since it was first an Indian path stretching from New York's Finger Lakes to the villages of western and central Massachusetts. This was the route taken by colonial forces marching west to defend British outposts on the New York frontier during the French and Indian Wars. One of the recruits was a young silversmith named Paul Revere, traveling for the first time from his native Boston. Later, as settlers streamed west in their covered wagons, the Mohawk Trail became the prime road over the mountains and the lifeline for garrisons along the Hudson. In 1786, the trail became America's first toll-free road. Before then, most roads were privately owned and a toll was charged. During the 19th century, the trail became a symbol of America's westward expansion and was the route followed by the stagecoaches. In 1913, it was engineered for auto travel, with many off-road parking areas for scenic vistas and historical markers.

The 4¾-mile Hoosac Railroad Tunnel, one of the engineering marvels of its time, crosses the trail north of the town of Florida. Completed in 1875—after 25 years, 196 lives and 21.2 million dollars—the tunnel cuts the distance and the grades between Troy and Boston.

Leave Greenfield on Route 2 West and take alternate route 2A into Shelburne Falls, an inadvertently but perfectly preserved "Main Street" town of the early 20th century. Watch for the signs directing you to the "Bridge of Flowers." Planted and maintained since 1929 by the Women's Association, the unique 400-foot bridge is a riot of color in spring, summer and early fall. Originally built in 1908 to carry trolley tracks across the Deerfield River between Shelburne and Buckland, the five-arch concrete bridge was abandoned in 1927 with the passing of the trolleys, which hold a faded but special place in Berkshire memory. The trolley was invented by Stephen Dudley Field, who operated the first car on his front lawn in Stockbridge in 1880. Ten years later, a trolley line ran through Pittsfield to Pontoosuc Lake. Soon, other towns had lines, along with inter-urban connections. A parlor car started running between Canaan, Connecticut and Bennington, Vermont, in 1903. The thought of these urban-style vehicles rumbling through the Berkshire Hills is intriguing.

In 1902, a Pittsfield trolley figured in a spectacular accident in which President Theodore Roosevelt was severely injured and a Secret Service man killed when Trolley Car 29, speeding guests to the Country Club for a presidential reception, rammed the landau carrying the President.

Visible in the riverbed at Shelburne Falls are glacial potholes, one of which is the world's largest. The town of Shelburne, established in 1756, was the birthplace of Linus Yale, founder of the Yale Lock

Company. Farther along the trail, on the right, is the old Oak Meeting Ground, a pre-Revolutionary War shrine.

Mid-point on the trail is Charlemont, with good views of the Deerfield River and many unusual off-trail drives north and south. The Indian statue, Hail to the Sunrise, is just west of the bridge at the junction of the road to Monroe Bridge and Monroe. The Bissel Bridge, a modern covered bridge, is located here. An interesting side trip along the trail is a pleasant ride via Monroe Bridge, south along the Deerfield River and past the entrance to the Hoosac Tunnel. Another side route takes you into Rowe, a once-thriving small community that has become a virtual ghost town. There is, however, a well-stocked Historical Society Museum in Rowe, open during the summer.

The trail now winds through the Mohawk Trail State Forest. Attractive scenery and numerous camping sites provide pleasant stopping places. Boy Scouts camp at the junction of the Cold and Deerfield rivers where Indians once held war councils. Several off-trail drives radiate from the top of Forbidden Mountain. One circles through the Savoy Mountain State Forest (follow local signs) and travels by Tannery Falls, Balance Rock and Beaver Pond. Cabins and camping facilities are available here.

Whitcomb Summit, highest point on the trail, offers fine views of the Deerfield River and overlooks the tunnel entrance. A short drive beyond is Western Summit, offering excellent views of North Adams, Williamstown, and Mt. Greylock. A memorable part of the trail is just ahead at the Hairpin Turn, a classic of its kind. The trail from here travels down the mountains to North Adams, once a leading mill town of western Massachusetts, now struggling to make a comeback after severe economic losses. North Adams might have continued to prosper, but its immediate environment could only have been the poorer if suburbs had spread throughout these hills as they have along Route 2 to Williamstown. Now, when patterns of desirable growth and land use are better understood, the town's revitalization should proceed without detracting from the rural landscape which borders so abruptly on this vestige of 19th-century industrialism.

North Adams is a gateway to the Berkshires, a region stretching from the Vermont line on the north to Connecticut on the south, bordering what the old-timers refer to as "York State" along the west. Here, on the outer edge of the Boston and New York megalopolis, is a region that treasures the values of slow growth even as pressures from outside for explosive change become increasingly difficult to withstand. It is a place of some of the most appealing landscapes on our continent, a place, like the Ile de France, whose beauty has been shaped by a long-standing, compatible relationship between man and nature. Here are the elm-shaded streets of gracious New England villages; meadows and wooded hills; winter and summer resorts; cultural riches and a long history of agriculture, diversified commerce and industry.

An exploration of the Berkshires can begin with a short drive south to Mt. Greylock, which lies within an 8,660-acre state reservation with bridle paths, picnic facilities, hunting, and camping. A scenic road leading to the top can be reached from just west of North Adams, off Route 2 to the left. At 3,491 feet, Greylock is the state's highest peak, overlooking magnificent panoramas of western Massachusetts, the Hudson River Valley of New York and the Green Mountains of southern Vermont. Many foot trails, including the Appalachian Trail, cross the summit. The more hardy tourists will find an hour's wandering of the trails close by the summit quite rewarding.

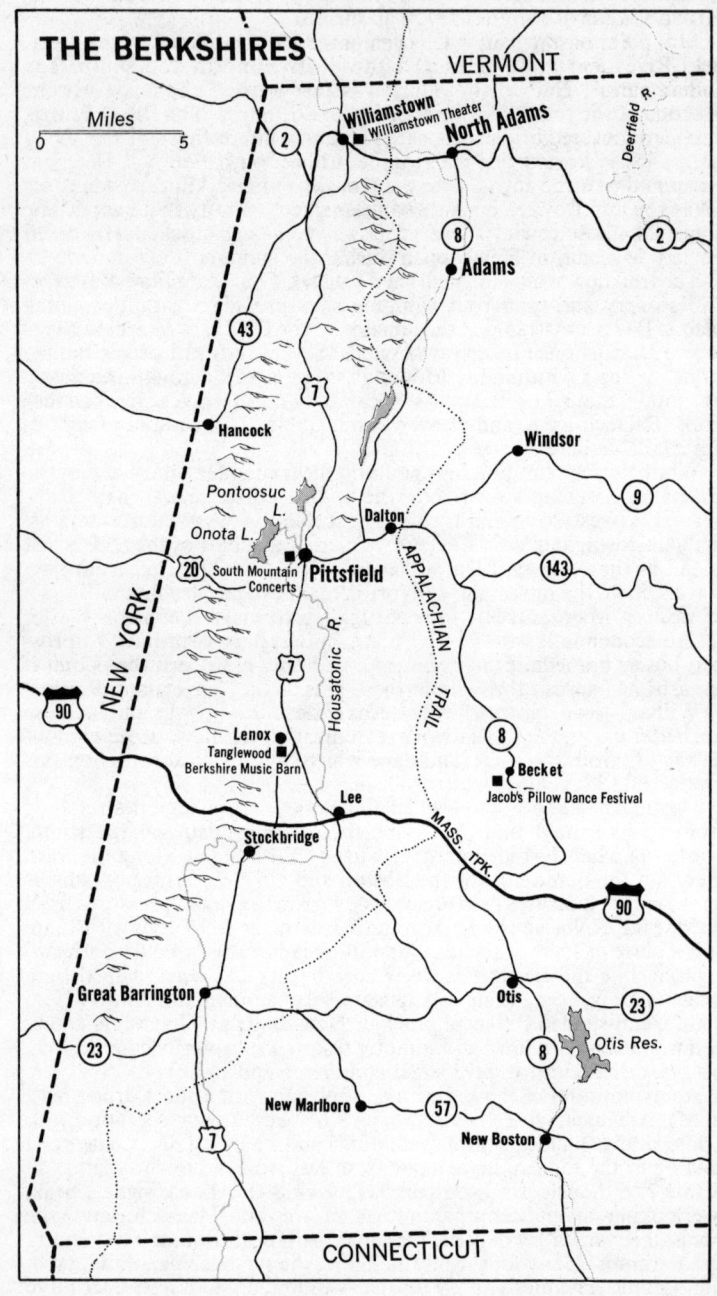

THE BERKSHIRES

VERMONT

Miles
0   5

Williamstown
Williamstown Theater
North Adams

Deerfield R.

2

8

Adams

2

43

7

Hancock

Windsor

9

Pontoosuc L.
Onota L.
Dalton

20

South Mountain Concerts
Pittsfield

143

APPALACHIAN TRAIL

NEW YORK

7

Housatonic R.

90

Lenox
Tanglewood
Berkshire Music Barn

8

Becket
Jacob's Pillow Dance Festival

Lee

MASS. TPK.

Stockbridge

90

Great Barrington

Otis

23

23

8

Otis Res.

New Marlboro

57

7

New Boston

CONNECTICUT

After driving down the mountain, return to State 2 and continue west to Williamstown. Although only five miles from North Adams—indeed, the two towns are connected, as most close settlements unfortunately are, by a stretch of burger stands, shopping centers, gas stations, trailer parks and franchise operations—Williamstown is worlds removed. It grew up around a college rather than factories, and has weathered like old brick into one of the loveliest towns in New England.

Williams was started here as a free school, but became a college in 1793. The attractive campus is well worth a walking tour. The college's Thompson Memorial Chapel, a Gothic structure built in 1904, is on the north side of Main Street. Its stained glass windows are seen to best advantage from inside. Diagonally across the street is the Williams College Art Museum, in Lawrence Hall, identifiable by its octagonal form and Grecian rotunda. It houses fine collections of glass, pottery, bronzes and sculpture. On South Street, just west of the center of town, is the Sterling and Francine Clark Art Institute, one of the finest small art museums in America. It boasts great paintings (including a memorable collection of Renoirs), rare silver, furniture and china, most of which was collected by the Clarks, who founded the art institute to share their loved possessions with others. Williamstown, with good restaurants, motels and inns, is a delightful place to pause, with excellent skiing nearby. It has delightful areas for hiking, riding, snowmobiling, and foliage watching. The Adams Memorial Theater is regarded as one of the leading summer theaters in the nation, and the Taconic and Waubeeka Springs golf courses are fine ones.

There are three ways south from Williamstown to Pittsfield—Route 43, Route 7, and Route 8—and all are pleasant. Route 43 lies to the west through North Hancock and Hancock Center, a delightful valley "discovered" by newcomers who are rapidly transforming its character from back-hills farming to residential and resort. The understandable temptation for farmers to sell their land to developers, however, has been mitigated by a new Massachusetts law which allows the state to purchase development rights from farmers, thus assuring continued agricultural use of the land and a fair deal for those who work it.

Here, too, is Jiminy Peak, a popular ski facility just three hours from Boston and New York and less than an hour from Albany. Turn left at N.Y. 22 in Stephentown and left into U.S. 20 at Lebanon Springs.

Shaker Village

On the way into Pittsfield, as you come down the eastern slope of Lebanon Mountain, is the Hancock Shaker Village, open daily during the summer and early fall, weather permitting. This place has been fashioned into one of the nation's most popular and intriguing "living museums."

The Shakers first gathered at Hancock in the early 1780s when Mother Ann Lee, the English-born founder of the movement, an outgrowth of Quakerism, was still alive. They believed that religion should not be separated from the secular concerns which tend to dominate human life, but should permeate all thought and action. They organized according to four principles—separation from the world; common property; confession of sin; and celibacy, with separation but equality of the sexes. During the 1830s, there were six "families" at

Hancock, each with elders, eldresses and deacons. Total membership was about 300 men and women.

Each year, as more buildings are restored and opened to the public, more fascinating objects attesting to the genius of these spiritually motivated people for coping with the material world are revealed. The Round Stone Barn, scrupulously restored, is an architectural treasure. Those interested in Shaker architecture, by the way, should take a short ride west on Route 20. Just beyond the New York State line, look for signs on the left pointing to the Darrow School, a private school housed in the fine old buildings of what once was the Mt. Lebanon Shaker community. About 20 miles farther west, in Old Chatham, N.Y. is a private Shaker museum (in non-Shaker structures) with an outstanding collection of Shaker objects. The legacy of the Shakers in design is one of an austere elegance proceeding from function. Their classic inventions include the wooden clothespin and the flat broom.

If you go south from Williamstown on Route 7 you will be taking the faster, more direct road to Pittsfield, passing through New Ashford (home of the popular Brodie Mountain ski area). The hills on your right are the eastern slopes of the mountains enfolding the Hancock settlements.

The easterly road south, Route 8, goes through Adams and Cheshire. Vistas in these towns sometimes resemble the English Lake District and sometimes are reminiscent of the factories and row houses of a Dickens setting. The environs are lovely to drive through at foliage time, and the side roads off the main routes are always worth exploring. From the home of women's suffragist Susan B. Anthony (private) at Bowen's Corners and East Road, for instance, drive to Highway 116 and bear left to the mountain village of Savoy. To the south of town, a well-marked road turns right, leading to the Jambs in Windsor State Forest, a deep flume or gorge cut through solid rock. This forest road joins Route 9. Turn left on Route 9 to reach the William Cullen Bryant homestead, open to the public for a small fee.

If you turn right (west) on Route 9, the ride down the hills toward the town of Dalton offers excellent views, particularly during foliage season. The Crane Museum of paper making, housed in the Old Stone Mill on the banks of the Housatonic, offers an interesting look at one of the area's oldest industries. At the foot of the hills, a well-marked road on the left leads to Wahconah Falls, a state park created around a waterfall in a clear, cold mountain stream. Continue west on Route 9, through Dalton to Pittsfield.

Pittsfield and the Berkshires Cultural Scene

Pittsfield, the Berkshire County seat, is at the geographic center of the county. It is also a center of commerce and industry in a most inviting setting, surrounded by mountains, well watered and well forested. While Pittsfield has some of the problems of larger population centers, its saving grace is its reasonable size and lovely environs. The Berkshire Medical Center, superior to many hospitals serving much larger communities, meets the health needs not only of this large county but of neighboring areas in New York and Vermont. Pittsfield is a good stopping-place for travelers who want to be in town and still be near the cultural and outdoor facilities for which the Berkshires are so noted. Pittsfield itself has two fine lakes (Onota and Pontoosuc) with public swimming. There are fishing, hiking, camping, hunting, snowmobiling and other outdoor diversions in the Pittsfield State Forest. Bousquet's Ski Area, off U.S. 7 and 20, has excellent day and night facilities for novices and experts. At the southern edge of town, toward the great Berkshire cultural centers of Lenox, Lee, and Stockbridge, is South Mountain with its fine vistas and seasonal programs offered by the South Mountain Chamber Music Concerts. During the late 19th century, William Stanley built a plant here utilizing work done in Great Barrington on alternating current for lighting. This was the genesis of General Electric, now the major employer in this city of 57,000.

Pittsfield's Berkshire Museum has an interesting colletion of minerals and of Peary and Hawthorne memorabilia, as well as film programs. Students of New England history will find much of interest in a fine collection at the Berkshire Athenaeum, which houses, in its Melville Room, a matchless collection of papers and artifacts associated with the author. Melville's home, Arrowhead, is just outside Pittsfield on the Holmes Road. The old farmhouse has been restored and opened to visitors. Here is the room where, with a view of an undulating line of hills that reminded him of ocean waves, Melville wrote *Moby Dick*. Many other literary and prominent figures of the mid-19th century, including Hawthorne and Oliver Wendell Holmes, also lived or summered near here.

Lenox, Stockbridge and the Southern Berkshires

If you're in a hurry to get down to Tanglewood in Lenox for the great summer festival of the Boston Symphony, just scoot south on U.S. 7. If you have a bit of time, take U.S. 20 west about five miles to State 41 and come in the back way through Richmond. Now a prosperous farming area and popular bedroom community for Pittsfield, it was once an important mining center—the iron used in the *Monitor's* cannon was produced here. The ruins of the early foundry are still visible. Off 41, turn left into Lenox Road for a short ride through the forest to Tanglewood. Here, every summer, on a 200-acre estate, students and world-renowned performers, the Boston Symphony and just plain music lovers gather to learn, enjoy and perform. The main shed seats 6,000 for the major concerts (July and August) but there's plenty of room for delightful listening out on the great lawn; just bring a blanket or a folding chair—and a light sweater. The Theater Concert Hall is used for small orchestra and chamber concerts; the Chamber Music Hall seats 300 and accommodates chamber music groups, lectures, and large classes.

From Tanglewood, travel east on Highway 183 to Lenox. Nearby is the Pleasant Valley Wildlife Sanctuary, a Massachusetts Audubon Society facility sheltering many living specimens of regional plant and animal life. Other local attractions are the Avaloch Ski area and the Eastover year-round resort.

Continue south on U.S. 20 to Lee, with its interesting Congregational church dating from 1857. Here, too, are the lime and marble quarries that yielded the stone for the capitol in Washington and the headstones for the soldiers' graves at Arlington National Cemetery.

To the south are the Oak 'n' Spruce Ski Area and, in West Becket, the great Jacob's Pillow Dance festival and school, founded by the late Ted Shawn. Top dancers from all over the world give regular performances to packed houses. Also in Lee is the 14,000-acre October Mountain State Forest. The Appalachian Trail runs through it, and there are facilities for hunting, fishing, camping, snowmobiling and other outdoor activities. Return via U.S. 20 and State 102 to Stockbridge.

Stockbridge, to many the archetype of the New England small town, has a long history of attracting creative people. Here is where Jonathan Edwards spent the last eight years of his life, writing theological treatises and serving as missionary to the Indians. In more recent times, playwright Robert E. Sherwood summered here for many years. Playwright William Gibson and novelist Norman Mailer also have made their homes in Stockbridge, and Norman Rockwell moved here after spending many years in Vermont. Arlo Guthrie immortalized Stockbridge for many as the scene of his comic protest song "Alice's Restaurant." Over 50 of Rockwell's paintings of the American scene are on exhibit in the Norman Rockwell Museum, a 1790 Federal mansion. There's an inviting inn here (the Red Lion) and one of the nation's top summer theaters, The Berkshire Playhouse. Other places worth visiting are the Mission House, Naumkeag Gardens, and Chesterwood, a 150-acre estate containing the studio of Daniel Chester French, sculptor of the famed Lincoln Memorial and of Concord's Minuteman. French said, "I live here six months of the year—in heaven. The other six months I live, well—in New York." Chesterwood, a National Trust property, is located off State 183, two miles west of Stockbridge.

A short, scenic drive south from Stockbridge on U.S. 7 takes you to Great Barrington, largest town and economic center of south Berkshire. The townspeople seized the courthouse from the British in August 1774; it has been claimed that this was the first act of open resistance to the crown in America. There are lovely views from atop Mt. Everett, a nice place to hike and picnic. Butternut Basin, two miles east on State 23, has fine skiing, as do Catamount and Jug End in nearby Egremont, just a couple of hours away from the New York and Boston metropolitan areas.

Take Route 23 a few miles southwest to South Egremont and then left into Highway 41 to Bash Bish Falls Reservation. A large parking area is provided and a short, pleasant footpath leads to the falls and a picnic area. Following a gorge cut deep into solid rock, the Bash Bish Brook plunges 50 feet into a deep, clear, rock-bottomed pool. According to the story, seemingly told at every waterfall in North America, an Indian maiden, unhappy in love, jumped to her death from the rocks above. Her tortured spirit, of course, haunts the falls. The spirit known as Jack Frost is also most active here each fall, as the Berkshires are known for Massachusetts' most vibrant display of autumn leaves.

Streams, falls and historic houses are easy to find in this lovely south Berkshire farm country with its gentle mountains, inviting woods, and towns like Mount Washington, Sheffield, New Marlborough, Sandisfield, Monterey, Otis and Ashley Falls. Just to the west of Ashley Falls is nature's own rock garden, Bartholomew's Cobble, a protected public reservation noted for wildflowers and an extraordinary variety of ferns. Sheffield has the double falls of Sage's Ravine, as well as Glen Falls, Bear Rock Falls and Race Brook Falls. The first Berkshire town to be chartered, Sheffield is the only one left in the state with two covered bridges. From the flatlands of the Housatonic Valley in Sheffield to the uplands of Mt. Washington, this corner of Berkshire County comprises the essence of rural Massachusetts.

SIGHTSEEING CHECKLIST. There are hundreds of things to see and do in Massachusetts, and sorting out the "musts" is a difficult business. Nevertheless, we offer the following top ten:

Boston's Freedom Trail. Perhaps the most concentrated and important historical tour in the country, this relatively short urban walk includes the Old North Church, Boston Massacre Site, Faneuil Hall, Paul Revere's House, and much more. Bunker Hill and Old Ironsides are not far away.

Lexington and Concord. To stand at Lexington Green, or at the North Bridge in Concord, is to experience patriotism at its simplest, strongest, and most benign. And the towns and countryside the Middlesex yeomen fought for are still quite lovely in their own right.

Cape Cod National Seashore. The Cape is many things to many people, but first and foremost it is a place of great natural beauty. The National Seashore preserves it as Thoreau saw it: dunes, cliffs, heather, sea, and sky.

Old Sturbridge Village. The lingering popular image of Currier and Ives New England has largely been supplanted by modern realities. Here, you can see what life was like when that image *was* reality. One of the nation's finest early American restorations, staffed with working artisans and tradespeople.

The Coast from Marblehead to Newburyport. Drive the North Shore route described in this chapter, and enjoy both the rocky, irregular coast and the towns created by three and a half centuries of maritime commerce. A required trip for all aficionados of early American architecture.

Tanglewood and the Berkshires. Spend an evening under the stars, listening to one of the world's great orchestras. Put up at a country inn, take your choice of superb restaurants, and travel the back roads through pretty hill towns.

Plymouth: The Rock, the Plantation, and the Mayflower. If the story of Plymouth Rock did not exist, we would have to invent it, as a myth of our national origins. It's worth a visit, as is the vivid portrayal of Pilgrim life at Plimoth Plantation. As for the *Mayflower,* ask yourself: would you have made the trip?

Martha's Vineyard and Nantucket. The Vineyard is countryside surrounded by water; Nantucket, the "gray lady," is more like a ship at sea. Both have their partisans; both justify the time and expense of leaving the mainland. Our preference is off season, when the crowds are thin and the wind is chill.

Lowell. Visit an old factory town? Yes, because the Industrial Revolution in America started here, and it has been duly commemorated by the new National Historic Park. The men and women who worked amid the racket of power looms in these brick mills built this country as surely as did John Adams and Paul Revere.

Boston: Beacon Hill and Back Bay. Few cities in either the Old or New World can boast such beautiful residential districts so close to downtown. The finest visual aspects of 19th-century urban planning are accessible here within a two hours' walk—with the Public Garden and the river esplanade thrown in free.

PRACTICAL INFORMATION FOR THE REST OF MASSACHUSETTS

Note: Large sections in Practical Information have been organized according to touring area for your convenience. See previous sections for Practical Information for the Boston area and Cape Cod.

MASSACHUSETTS FACTS & FIGURES. Massachusetts derives its name from the Massachuset Indians, an Algonquian tribe. The word means "at the great hill." The state nickname is Bay State, or Old Bay State; its flower is the mayflower, or trailing arbutus; its bird, the chickadee; its tree, the American elm. *Ense petit placidam sub libertate quietem* ("By the sword she seeks peace, but peace only under liberty") is the state motto.

The state population is 5,737,037 (1980 estimate), which places it 11th in the nation.

Heavily populated in most areas, Massachusetts is one of the leading industrial and technological states in the U.S. The state's many historical sites and resort areas, particularly the Cape Cod peninsula, attract many visitors each year. From its low Atlantic coastline, Massachusetts rises to a hilly plateau in the center of the state and to the scenic Berkshire Hills and Taconic Mountains in the west. Massachusetts is irregular in shape. From north to south its dimensions vary from 50 to 100 miles; the greatest distance east to west is about 190 miles; and the total area is 8,257 square miles, 45th in size among the 50 states. Boston, with a population of about 563,000 (1980 census), is the state capital, the largest city and leading port and cultural center of New England, and the center of a 20-by-40 mile urban sprawl that is the beginning of the east coast megalopolis that ends at Norfolk, Virginia. Massachusetts was the sixth of the original thirteen states to ratify the Constitution, on Feb. 6, 1788.

It is a state of sharp climatic changes—cold winters and warm summers.

	Jan.	Feb.	Mar.	Apr.	May	Jun.
Average Temperature (F)	30	30	37	48	59	68
Average Temperature (C)	−1	−1	3	9	15	20
Days of Rain or Snow	12	11	12	12	11	10

	Jul.	Aug.	Sept.	Oct.	Nov.	Dec.
Average Temperature (F)	73	72	66	55	45	34
Average Temperature (C)	23	22	19	13	7	1
Days of Rain or Snow	9	10	9	9	12	11

HOW TO GET THERE. By car. The Massachusetts Tpke., I–90, runs E to W from Boston to the New York border at W. Stockbridge, where it leads to the New York Thruway. The Southeast Expwy. (Rte. 3) travels from Boston to Cape Cod's Sagamore Bridge; from there, Rte. 6 leads to Hyannis and Provincetown. Rte. 128 circles Boston from Gloucester on the North Shore to Braintree on the South Shore. I–84 links Hartford, Conn. with the Mass. Tpke. at Sturbridge.

I–91 runs north-south, roughly following the Connecticut River, and links Brattleboro, Vt., Holyoke, Chicopee and Springfield, Mass., Hartford and New Haven, Conn., where it joins the Connecticut Tpke. I–95, which heads south out of eastern Maine and New Hampshire, enters Massachusetts at Amesbury and circles Boston (same route as 128) on its way to Providence, RI, New London and New Haven, Conn., and on into New York City and points south.

In the western part of the state, Rtes. 7 and 2 provide scenic drives through the Berkshire Hills.

Avis, Hertz, National, and *Budget* have car rental offices in all key localities.

By air. Boston's Logan International Airport is served by major airlines. Springfield is served by Bradley International Airfield in Windsor Locks, Conn.

By train. *Amtrak's* Northeast Corridor service extends from Washington, DC to Boston by way of Philadelphia PA, New York, New Haven CT, and Providence RI; and to Springfield and Boston via Hartford CT. The Amtrak *Lake Shore Limited* runs between Chicago and Boston, serving Pittsfield, Springfield, and Worcester.

By bus. Both *Trailways* (482–6620) and *Greyhound* (423–5810) bus companies serve the state.

TELEPHONES. Massachusetts is divided into 2 telephone area codes. 617 is the code for Cape Cod, the Islands, the Greater Boston area, and eastern Massachusetts. 413 is the code for the western part of the state. Readers of this guide should assume that all numbers for hotels, restaurants, and attractions listed under the *Springfield and Pioneer Valley* and *Berkshires* headings have a 413 area code; other sections are 617.

The pay telephone charge in Massachusetts is 10 cents. In public areas throughout the state, there are coinless phones for use with collect and credit card calls.

Virtually all municipalities use the 911 Police Emergency Number.

HOTELS AND MOTELS. The high standard of Massachusetts hostelries is matched only by their general reputation for hospitality. The charming inns of western and southern Massachusetts, the comfortable resorts in the Berkshires and the up-to-date hotels and motels around the larger cities and along the "pikes" are considered among the best in the country.

The following ranges are based on double occupancy. *Deluxe,* $95 and up; *Expensive,* $70–$95; *Moderate,* $55–$70; *Inexpensive,* under $55. Remember that these figures take a quantum leap in the Berkshires during the summer concert season. At that time of year, $70 might buy you a spartan motel room 20 miles from Tanglewood.

Note the 413 area code, which applies in the Pioneer Valley and points west.

SOUTH SHORE AND NEW BEDFORD

DEDHAM. Comfort Inn. *Moderate.* 235 Elm St. (326–6700). Just off Rte. 128/I–95, near Rte. 1. Restaurant, lounge; entertainment.

NEW BEDFORD. Yesterdays. *Expensive.* 1 Merrill's Wharf (999–2700). In restored, historic Bourne Counting House. Harbor views. Restaurant, shops.

Skipper. *Moderate.* 110 Middle St., Fairhaven (997–1281). Pool. Pets. Restaurant, bar, entertainment. Marina, health spa.

QUINCY AREA. Howard Johnson's. *Expensive.* 150 Granite St., Braintree, Rte. 128 exit 68 (848–8500). Indoor pool, lounge, and restaurant.

Sheraton Tara. *Expensive.* Rte. 128, exit 68 (848–7890). Pools, sauna. Restaurant, bar, entertainment. Recently doubled capacity.

Boston. *Moderate.* 655 Washington St., Weymouth (337–5200). Pool, play area. Pets. Restaurant, bar.

Susse Chalet Motor Lodge. *Inexpensive.* 125 Union St. (at Rte. 3), Braintree (848–0600). Member of popular budget chain. Convenient to Boston and Cape.

PLYMOUTH. Howard Johnson's. *Expensive.* Rte. 3, exit 35 (585–3831). Pool. Pets. Restaurant.

Governor Bradford Motor Inn. *Moderate.* Water St. (746–6200). Overlooking bay. Pool. Free in-rm coffee. Nr. restaurant. Walk to historic sites.

Governor Carver Motor Inn. *Moderate.* 25 Summer St. (746–7100). Outdoor pool, Pets. Restaurant, bar.

Pilgrim Sands. *Moderate.* Warren Ave. (747–0900). Pool. Pets. Private beach with sundeck. Nr. restaurant. Opp. Plimoth Plantation.

TAUNTON. Town 'N Country Motor Inn. *Inexpensive.* Rte. 44, ¼ mi. W of Fall River Expwy., Raynham (824–8647). Pool. Pets. Breakfast coffee and rolls free. Nr. restaurant.

CONCORD-LEXINGTON AREA

CONCORD. Colonial Inn. *Expensive.* 11 Monument Sq. (369–9200). Traditional Colonial inn on village green. Main rooms date to 1716. Restaurant, bar.

Howard Johnson's. *Moderate.* Rtes. 2 and 2A (369–6100). Pool, restaurant, bar, entertainment wknds.

Concordian. *Inexpensive.* Rte. 2, Acton (263–7765). Pool. Pets. Morning coffee and rolls free.

LEXINGTON. Sheraton-Lexington Motor Inn. *Expensive.* Minute Man Nat'l Park Exit, Rte. 128 (862–8700). Attractive rms. Pool. Pets. Restaurant, bar.

Battle Green Motor Inn. *Inexpensive.* 1720 Mass. Ave. (862–6100). Restaurant. Right in town nr. Common.

Catch Penny Inn. *Inexpensive.* 440 Bedford St. (861–0850). Pool. Restaurant.

SUDBURY. Longfellow's Wayside Inn. *Inexpensive.* Wayside Inn Rd., off Rte. 20 (443–8846). America's oldest inn, c. 1686, restored by Ford Foundation. Fine period furnishings, public rooms, kitchen. Pets. Breakfast avail. Restaurant, bar.

NORTH SHORE AND MERRIMACK VALLEY

ANDOVER. Sheraton Rolling Green Motor Inn. *Deluxe.* Lowell St. at I–93 exit 31 (475–5400). Attractive rooms. Pools. Tennis, golf, cross-country skiing. Play area. Restaurant. Bar, entertainment, dancing wknds.

Andover Inn. *Moderate.* Chapel Ave. (475–5903). Restaurant, bar, entertainment, dancing. Play area, rec. rm. On campus of Phillips Academy.

Merrimack Valley Motor Inn. *Inexpensive.* Chickering Rd. (688–1851). Restaurant, bar, entertainment, dancing, pool, putting green.

DANVERS. Quality Inn King's Grant. *Expensive.* Trask Lane, Rte. 128 at Exit 21N (774–6800). Very inviting quarters. Good restaurant, bar, entertainment. Pool.

Sheraton Tara. *Expensive.* I–95 at Rt. 1 (777–2500). Country club setting. Restaurant, lounge. Golf, cross-country ski trails. Pkg. plans avail.

Village Green Motor Inn. *Moderate.* Rte. 1 (774–6500). Outdoor pool. Pleasant spacious rms. Restaurant, bar. CP.

GLOUCESTER. Bass Rocks Motor Inn. *Expensive.* 89 Atlantic Rd. (283–7600). Pool, beach nr. Private balconies overlook ocean. Nr. restaurant. Open Apr. to Oct.

Twin Light Manor Motor Inn. *Expensive.* Atlantic Rd. on Scenic Shore Dr. (283–7500). Pool. Restaurant, bar, entertainment. Play area, rec. rm, nr. beach. Open Apr. to Nov.

Vista. *Expensive.* Thatcher Rd. (281–3410). Private patios or balconies overlook ocean. Nr. restaurant.

The Anchorage. *Moderate.* 5 Hawthorne Lane, beyond Rocky Neck (283–4788). Overlooks harbor. Nr. beach. Free coffee and rolls. Nr. restaurant.

Gloucester Traveler. *Moderate.* 1 mi. W of Rte. 128 exit 14 (283–2502). Pool, play area. Hilltop wooded grounds with picnic area. Breakfast avail.

LOWELL. Lowell Hilton. *Deluxe.* 50 Warren St. (452–1200). Brand new hotel in heart of historic district. Health club, indoor lap pool; 2 restaurants; airport limo; car rental; pets welcome.

NEWBURYPORT. Garrison Inn. *Expensive.* Brown Sq. (465–0910). An 1809 inn, recently restored and reopened. 24 rooms, several suites. 2 restaurants, tavern. Nr. shops, waterfront.

Morrill Place. *Moderate.* 209 High St. (462–2808). An imposing Federalist mansion, filled with antiques. Daniel Webster slept here.

ROCKPORT. Captain's Bounty Motor Inn. *Expensive.* 1 Beach St. (546–9557). Private beach. Kit. avail. Nr. restaurant. Open Apr. 1 to Oct., wknds in Nov.

Ralph Waldo Emerson Inn. *Expensive.* Pigeon Cove (546–6321). Pool, play area. Traditional, quiet hotel. Restaurant. Mem. Day to mid-Oct. MAP; EP off season.

Seaward Inn. *Deluxe.* Marmion Way (546–3471). Attractive inn on beach with resort atmosphere. Golf, tennis nr. Planned entertainment. Nr. beach, bird sanctuary. Open mid-May to mid-Oct. AP, MAP avail.

Yankee Clipper Inn. *Expensive.* 127 Granite St. (546–3407). Popular quiet hotel overlooking ocean. Pool, beach. Restaurant serves dinner to guests during season; brkfst only rest of year.

Bearskin Neck. *Moderate.* Bearskin Neck (546–6677). Small 2-story motel on ocean. Restaurant. Open Apr. to mid-Nov.

Tuck-Inn Lodge. *Moderate.* 17 High St. (546–6252). Quiet area near town. Pool. Restaurant. MAP.

Turk's Head Motor Inn. *Moderate.* 283 South St. (546–3436). New motel located a short walk from beach. Pool. Coffee shop.

SALEM. Hawthorne Inn. *Expensive.* 18 Washington Sq. (744–4080). Homelike atmosphere, many antiques. Restaurant, bar, entertainment.

Coach House. *Inexpensive.* 284 Lafayette St. (744–4092). Old inn with memorabilia of clipper ship days. Kit. units avail.

WORCESTER AND CENTRAL MASSACHUSETTS

FRAMINGHAM. Sheraton-Tara. *Deluxe.* 1657 Worcester Rd. just off Tpke exit 12 (879–7200). Pools, sauna, health club. Play area. Restaurant, dining rm, bars, dancing.

Holiday Inn. *Expensive.* 30 Worcester Rd. (875–6151). Pools. Restaurant, bar.

Howard Johnson's. *Expensive.* 130 Worcester Rd. (872–8811). Pool, play area. Pets, Restaurant, bar.

Framingham Motor Inn. *Moderate.* 1600 Worcester Rd. at Tpke exit 12 (879–8400). Pool. Pets, Restaurant, bar, entertainment, dancing wknds. Spacious grounds with play area.

Koala Inn. *Moderate.* 1668 Worcester Rd. (620–0500). Complimentary coffee and r9lls.

STURBRIDGE. Sheraton Sturbridge Inn. *Expensive.* Rte. 20 (347–7393). Pool. Restaurant, bar, entertainment. Health club, cross-country skiing. Nr. Old Sturbridge.

American. *Moderate.* At jct. Rtes. 20 and 131 and I–86; Tpke exit 9 (347–9121). Pool. Pets. Restaurant, bar. Boating on Cedar Lake. Sauna.

Carriage House. *Moderate.* At jct. Rtes. 20, 131 (347–9311). Pool. Restaurant, bar nr. Paddleboating on lake.

Publick House. *Moderate.* I–86 Exit 3, 2 mi. S of Tpke exit 9 (347–3313). Charming late-18th-century inn. Pets. Restaurant, bar, entertainment. Also operates *Col. Ebenezer Crafts House,* restored farmhouse with pool, continental brkfst.

Sturbridge Coach Motor Lodge. *Moderate.* Rte. 20 (347–7327). Pool. Nr. Old Sturbridge.

Quality Inn Colonial. *Inexpensive.* Rte. 20 (347–3306). Pool, play area, tennis. Restaurant adjacent. Cable TV.

WORCESTER. Worcester Marriott. *Expensive.* 10 Lincoln Sq. (791–1600). Heated indoor/outdoor pools; health club. Restaurant, lounge, entertainment. Weekend package plans.

Best Western Centrum Inn. *Moderate.* 110 Summer St. (757–0400). Downtown location. Suites and efficiencies available. Weekly and monthly rates. Restaurant adjacent.

Howard Johnson's. *Moderate.* 181 W. Boylston St., W. Boylston (791–5501). Pools. Pets. Restaurant, bar.

Pleasant View Motor Lodge. *Inexpensive.* Worcester-Providence Pike; Tpke exits 10 & 11 (865–5222). Pets. Nr. pool. Coffee shop. Country club facilites.

SPRINGFIELD AND PIONEER VALLEY

AMHERST. Lord Jeffrey. *Expensive.* 30 Boltwood Ave. (253–2576). Centrally located hotel, with Colonial furnishings, charming gardens. Dining rm., bar.

Howard Johnson's. *Moderate.* Rtes. 9 & 116 (586–0114). Pool. Restaurant, bar. Pets.

University Motor Lodge. *Moderate.* 345 N. Pleasant St. (256–8111). Free in-rm. coffee. Golf nr. Convenient to colleges. Family plan.

DEERFIELD AREA. Deerfield Inn. *Expensive.* Main St. (774–5587). Lovely old inn is part of restoration. Restaurant, bar.

Howard Johnson's. *Moderate.* I–195 Ocean Grove exit (774–2211). Pool. Pets. Restaurant, bar.

Oxbow. *Moderate.* Rte. 2, Charlemont (625–6729). Restaurant, pub, game room. Theater, fishing, hunting, and ski pkgs. avail.

Rainbow. *Moderate.* 5 mi. S. on Rtes. 5, 10; I–91 exits 22 or 23 (665–8707). Play area. Pets. Restaurant nr. Pool.

Hilltop. *Inexpensive.* Rte. 2, Shelburne Falls (625–2587). Some rooms w. kitchen; also cottages. In-room coffee.

GREENFIELD. Candle Light. *Moderate.* 208 Mohawk Trail (772–0101). At I–91 exit 26. Pool, golf nr. Breakfast avail. Steak house and lounge.

Howard Johnson's. *Moderate.* 125 Mohawk Trail (774–2211). At I–91 exit 26. Pool. Restaurant, bar.

HOLYOKE. Holiday Inn. *Moderate.* 245 Whiting Farms Rd. (534–3311). Restaurant, lounge. Indoor pool. Pets.

NORTHAMPTON. Wiggins Tavern. *Expensive.* 36 King St. (584–3100). An historic inn, completely restored. Cable movies, room service, babysitting. Restaurant and lounge.

Hotel Northampton. *Moderate.* 36 King St. at jct. Rtes. 5 and 9, I–91, exit 18 (584–3100). Good restaurant, wine bar. Country shop in rear.

Northampton Hilton Inn. *Moderate.* Rte. 5 at jct. I–91, exit 18 (586–1211). Pool, play area. Restaurant, bar, dancing, entertainment.

Towne House. *Moderate.* Conz & Pleasant Sts. (586–1500). Pool. Free in-rm. coffee. Nr. restaurant.

NORTHFIELD. Bernardston Motel. *Inexpensive.* South St., Bernardston (648–9282). Comfortable. Cable TV. Nr. Greenfield and Rte. 91.

SPRINGFIELD AREA. Sheraton. *Expensive.* 1080 Riverdale Rd., W. Springfield (781–8750). Pool. Restaurant, lounge. Easy access to interstate.

Best Western Black Horse. *Moderate.* 500 Riverdale St., W. Springfield (733–2161). Pool, play area. Picnic area. Nr. fairgrounds.

Holiday Inn. *Moderate.* 711 Dwight St. (781–0900). Pool. Free in-rm. coffee. Restaurant, bar, entertainment, dancing.

Howard Johnson's. *Moderate.* 1150 Riverdale St., W. Springfield (739–7261). Restaurant, bar, pool. Convenient to exposition grounds.

Marriott. *Moderate.* 1500 Main St. (781–7111). Pool, saunas. Restaurant, bar, entertainment. Airport limo. Easy access to I–91, local attractions.

Ramada Inn. *Moderate.* 357 Burnett Rd., Chicopee, just off I–29 (592–9101). Pool, play area. Restaurant, bar, dancing, entertainment. Airport car avail.

Arrowhead. *Inexpensive.* 1573 Riverdale St., W. Springfield (788–9607). Pool, play area. Restaurant.

Best Western Chicopee Motor Lodge. *Inexpensive.* 463 Memorial Dr., Chicopee (592–6171). Pool. Restaurant adjacent. Near Mass. Pike.

Capri. *Inexpensive.* 1537 Riverdale St., W. Springfield (734–2176). Pool. Nr. restaurant.

Lantern Lodge. *Inexpensive.* 560 Riverdale St., W. Springfield (733–6678). Pool, play area. Pets. Coffee shop.

Seven Gables. *Inexpensive.* 1356 Boston Rd. (783–2111). Pool. Pets. Nr. restaurant. Bar. Swimming, fishing on lake.

Susse Chalet. *Inexpensive.* 6 Burnett Rd. (592–5741). At Mass Pike and I–291. Pool.

WARE. Wildwood Inn. *Inexpensive.* 121 Church St., off Rte. 32 (Main St.) (967–7798). A Victorian guest house, with cheerful appointments and family atmosphere. Tennis, volleyball, winter sledding. Breakfast served.

THE BERKSHIRES

GREAT BARRINGTON AREA. Jug End in the Berkshires. *Expensive.* S. Egremont (528–0434). Year-round resort. Pool, tennis, golf, riding, bicycling, skiing, skating. Rec. rm., planned entertainment. Free in-rm. coffee; breakfast, box lunches avail. MAP, ski pkg., family rates avail.

Egremont Inn. *Moderate.* Old Sheffield Road, S. Egremont [528–2111]. Built as a country inn in 1780. Tennis, pool. Gracious tavern, dining, and common rooms. MAP.

Windflower. *Moderate.* Rte. 23 (528–2720). A pleasant, rambling, antique-filled inn. Some rooms have fireplaces. MAP; excellent cuisine.

Liberty Cabins. *Inexpensive.* Albany Rd., Hancock (443–9431). Heated pool. Cottages. 5 miles from Pittsfield.

LEE. Oak N' Spruce Resort. *Expensive.* S. Lee (243–3500). Full-equipped resort. MAP. Golf, tennis. Pools. Nightclub. Skiing. Pkg. wknds., wkly, rates available.

Sunset. *Moderate.* 114 Housatonic St. (243–0302). Nr. restaurant.

Gaslight Motor Lodge. *Inexpensive.* Rte. 20, E. Lee (243–9701). On lake nr. Appalachian Trail. Swimming, boats, fishing, hiking.

LENOX. Eastover. *Expensive.* East St. (637–0625). Year-round resort for young adults. Pools, riding, tennis, canoeing, skiing, skating. Planned entertainment. Dancing, entertainment. Huge grounds.

Gateways Inn. *Expensive.* 71 Walker St. (637–2532). A large, elegantly restored mansion with many antiques. Chef-owned. An enormous suite is available. Continental breakfast.

Lenox Motel. *Expensive.* Pittsfield Rd. (449–0324). 2 miles from ski area. Pool. In-room coffee.

Quality Inn Lenox-Pittsfield Lodge. *Expensive.* Outdoor and heated indoor pool; sauna; tennis; play area. Restaurant, lounge.

Tanglewood Motor Inn. *Expensive.* Pittsfield-Lenox Rd. (442–4000). Pbbl, play area. Efficiencies avail. Nr. restaurant.

Village Inn. *Expensive.* 16 Church St. (637–0020). Cozy, cheerful inn. Restaurant, taproom with fireplace. 1 mile from Tanglewood.

PITTSFIELD. Berkshire Hilton Inn. *Expensive.* South St. (449–2000). Pool. Restaurant, bar, entertainment, dancing. Family rates avail.

Best Western Springs Motor Inn. *Expensive.* Rte. 7 New Ashford (458–5945). Pool. Nr. golf, skiing. Rec. rm. Free in-rm. coffee. Restaurant, bar.

The Huntsman. *Expensive.* 1350 W. Housatonic St. (442–8714). Nr. pool.

Heart of the Berkshires. *Moderate.* 970 W. Housatonic St. (443–1255). Pool, play area. Free in-rm. coffee.

SHEFFIELD. Ivanhoe Country House. *Moderate.* Undermountain Road (229–2143). A secluded inn set amidst rolling hills. One room has a corner fireplace. Continental breakfast brought to your door.

STOCKBRIDGE. The Inn at Stockbridge. *Moderate.* Rte. 7 (298–3337). A circa 1900 country inn, 1 mile north of town. Full breakfasts; dinner wknds and holiday wks. Cross-country skiing on grounds; outdoor pool.

Red Lion Inn. *Moderate.* Rte. 7 (298–5545). Pool. Pets. Traditional Colonial inn, beautifully restored with fine antique furniture, china, pewter collection. Excellent restaurant, bar. Airport car avail.

Williamsville Inn. *Moderate.* Rte. 41, W. Stockbridge (274–6580). 18th-century farmhouse. Quiet and secluded. Some rooms with fireplace. Restaurant features French country cuisine.

WILLIAMSTOWN. The Orchards. *Deluxe.* 222 Adams Rd. (458–9611). A lovely new 49-room inn filled with English antiques. All rooms with refrigerators, some with fireplaces. Restaurant, lounge, pool, sauna, ice skating; golf and tennis nearby. Outdoor dining in season.

Williams Inn. *Expensive.* On the green (458–9371). Traditional-college town atmosphere. Pool. Saunas. Pkgs. available.

Berkshire Hills. *Moderate.* At jct. Rtes. 7 and 2 (458–3950). Pool. Breakfast coffee and rolls on house. Nr. restaurant.

Carriage House. *Moderate.* Rte. 7 (458–5359). Free in-rm. coffee. Restaurant. Nr. tennis.

1896 Motel. *Moderate.* Cold Spring Rd. (458–8125). Quiet, secluded. Breakfast coffee and rolls free. Restaurant, bar.

Elwal Pines Motor Inn. *Moderate.* Cold Spring Rd. (458–8161). Pool, boating on pond. Pets.

YOUTH HOSTELS. Hostels affiliated with the A.Y.H. are located throughout Massachusetts. All are coed. The following is a list of towns in which A.Y.H. hostels currently operate: Amherst, Boston, Brookline, Cedarville, Charlestown, Dudley, East Bridgewater, East Brookfield, Eastham, Granville, Hyannis, Littleton, West Tisbury (Martha's Vineyard), Nantucket, Newburyport, Northfield, Orleans, Springfield and Truro. For details on facilities provided at these hostels, write the Greater Boston Council, American Youth Hostels, 1020 B Commonwealth Ave., Brbokline MA 02146 (731–5430).

BED AND BREAKFAST. Keep in mind the bed and breakfast alternative. For greater Boston and North Shore B&B information, contact New England Bed and Breakfast, 1045 Centre St., Newton (498–9819). In the Berkshires, the place to call is Berkshire Bed and Breakfast, P.O. Box 211, Main St., Williamsburg, MA 01096 (413–268–7244). For a brochure containing statewide B&B listings, write the Mass. Division of Tourism, Dept. of Commerce, 100 Cambridge, St., Boston, MA 02202.

HOW TO GET AROUND. Larger towns usually have bus service. Taxi service is no problem; local companies are listed in telephone directories.

By air. *Delta* flies to New Bedford and Worcester from Boston. *Will's Air* (800–352–7559) connects Nantucket with Hyannis and Boston. *Gull Air* (800–352–7191) connects Hyannis with the islands. *Provincetown-Boston Airline* (800–352–3132) flies from Logan Airport, Boston, to Provincetown and Nantucket. *Island Air Service* (994–1231) flies from Fairhaven to

Cuttyhunk. An air-taxi service. *New England Flyer's Air Service* (922–2220) is located at Beverly Airport, Beverly.

By boat. Summer excursions boats between Boston and Provincetown (Cape Cod). Daily steamer service between Woods Hole and Martha's Vineyard and Nantucket (Steamship Authority, 240–2022). Seasonal ferries to the islands leave from Hyannis but are passenger-only. To bring a car, you must leave from Woods Hole. Summer ferry service (passenger only) from Falmouth and New Bedford to Martha's Vineyard also available. Car ferry reservations are a must in summer, and a good idea year round. See Boston and Cape Cod Practical Information sections for addresses and phones of excursion and ferry companies.

Cuttyhunk Boat Lines (992–1432) sail daily from New Bedford to Cuttyhunk Island. Sailboats may be rented along the coast at Gloucester, Marblehead and Boston, as well as at numerous locations on Cape Cod.

On foot. Hiking trails in the Berkshires are bordered with laurel late June. The Appalachian Trail enters Massachusetts near Ashley Falls on the Connecticut border, and crosses into Vermont at Williamstown. Hiking is the only way to get to the top of Monument Mountain in Stockbridge—Great Barrington area. Two foot trails. Parking facilities are at foot of mountain. Climb to the tower at the summit of Mount Everett, S. Egremont. There are special historic walking tours of Boston, Cambridge and Salem. Maps available from local chambers of commerce. Best hiking guides are *Mass-R.I. Trail Guide* and More Country Walks Near Boston, Appalachian Mountain Club, 3 Joy St., Boston 02108 (523–0636).

TOURIST INFORMATION SERVICES. Free folders, brochures and maps may be obtained from the *Massachusetts Department of Commerce,* Divisivion of Tourism, 100 Cambridge St., Boston MA 02202 (727–3201). There is a Visitor Information kiosk at Tremont St., Boston Common. Write to the main Visitor's Information Center at Prudential Plaza, Bbx 490, Boston, or call 536–4100.

The following offices provide regional information: *Cape Cod Chamber of Commerce,* Hyannis MA 02601 (362–3225); *Berkshire Visitors Bureau,* Berkshire Common Plaza Level, Dept. MA, Pittsfield, MA 01201 (443–9186); *Pioneer Valley Convention and Visitors Bureau,* 1500 Main St., Suite 600, Dept. MA, Springfield, MA 01115 (787–1548); *Mohawk Trail Association,* P.O. Box 7, Dept. MA, North Adams, MA 01347 (664–6256); *Nantucket Chamber of Commerce,* Nantucket MA 02554 (228–1700); *Martha's Vineyard Chamber of Commerce,* P.O. Box 1698, Dept. MA, Martha's Vineyard MA (693–0085); *Plymouth County Development Council,* P.O. Box 1620, Dept. MA, Pembroke, MA 02359 (826–3136); *North of Boston Tourist Council,* P.O. Box 3031, Dept. MA, Peabody, MA 01960 (532–1449); *Springfield Convention and Visitors Bureau,* 1500 Main St., Springfield, MA 01105 (734–4959).

SEASONAL EVENTS. February: Boat Show, also Home Show, Bayside Expo Center, Boston; Winter Carnival Northampton.

March: Boxboro Outdoor Show; Flower Show, Bayside Expo Center, Boston.

April: Patriots' Day reenactments, Lexington and Concord; Boston Marathon, Hopkinton to Boston.

May: Liberty Pole Day, Wilmington; Antique Flea Market, Topsfield Fair Ground, Topsfield; Antique Fair, Brimfield (also held in July and Sept.); Porter Memorial Horse Draw, Fairgrounds, Westfield; Cambridge River Festival; Lilac Sunday, Arnold Arboretum, Boston.

June: Boston Art Festival, Boston Common; St. Peter's Fiesta and Blessing of the Fishing Fleet, Gloucester; Blessing of the Fleet, Provincetown; Muster Day, Old Sturbridge Village; Yankee Apaloosa Show, Coliseum, W. Springfield. Tanglewood Festival, Lenox, begins its 9-week season lasting from late June to late August.

July: Festivals of the Arts, Marblehead, Hyannis, and Provincetown; Yankee Homecoming, Newburyport; Antiques Fair, National Guard Armory, Hyannis; Acton-Boxborough Jamboree, Acton; Ould Newbury Horse Show, Plum Island Tpke., Newbury; All Arabian Horse Show, Exposition Grounds, W. Springfield; New England Morgan Horse Show, Northampton; Lily Show, Horticultural Society, Worcester; Laurel Week, Westfield; Flower Show, Chatham.

August: Shaker Kitchen Festival, Hancock Shaker Village, Hancock; Marshfield Fair, Marshfield; North River Art Society Festival, Marshfield; Bridge of Flowers Art Festival, Shelburne Falls; Cape Cod Antiques Expo, Orleans; Gladiolus Exhibition, Horticultural Society, Worcester.

September: Barrington Fair, Great Barrington; Eastern States Exposition, Springfield; TriCounty Fair, Northampton; Franklin County Fair, Greenfield; Berkshire County Fair, Pittsfield; Rehoboth Fair, Dighton; Cranberry Festival, Carver; Foliage Festivals, Greenfield and North Adams; Annual Art Show, Art Center, Lexington; Dressage Show, Andover Riding Academy, N. Andover.

October: Topsfield Fair, Topsfield; Rockport Amateur Art Festival, Rockport; Festival in the Hills, Conway; Scallop Festival, Buzzards Bay; Harvest Home Festival, Plimoth Plantation, Plymouth; 17th-Century Day, Ipswich; Lenox Open House, Lenox; Myopia Hunt Club Four-in-Hand Event, Topsfield; Harvest and Chrysanthemum Show, Horticultural Hall, Boston.

November: Boston Globe Antiquarian Book Fair, Boston; Thanksgiving Day Pilgrim Procession, Plymouth.

December: Antique Show, Commonwealth Pier, Boston.

For information on county fairs and other agriculturally-oriented events, contact the Fairs Department at the Mass. Dept. of Food and Agriculture, 100 Cambridge St., Boston (727–3037). Flower show information is available from the Massachusetts Horticultural Society, 300 Mass. Ave., Boston (536–9280).

FOLIAGE. Massachusetts shares with the rest of New England a reputation for magnificent autumn foliage. The colors are not equally vivid every year, but the spectacle is always worth seeing. Trees begin to turn color in late September, with the "peak" of the foliage season usually reached by the second week of October. The season arrives somewhat earlier at higher inland elevations than in the south and along the coast; local radio and television stations will give foliage reports. The best viewing locations are along the Mohawk Trail and other highways and back roads of western Mass.; also along the North Shore and Merrimack Valley.

TOURS. Gray Line, 420 Maple St., Marlboro MA 01752 (426–8805), *Plymouth Pilgrimage,* 4 hours; visit Adams Mansion in Quincy; Mayflower II; Plymouth Rock; historic houses; Brewster Gardens. *Cape Cod Bay and Villages,* 8½ hours; visit Sandwich; Dexter Grist Mill; Hyannisport, Kennedy Memorial. *North Shore Dinner tour,* 6 hours. Explore Gloucester and Rockport at the tip of Cape Ann; visit Bearskin Neck shops and dine at harborside. *Martha's Vineyard,* 9 hours: includes ferry trip and coach circuit of island. *New England Seacoast,* 8 hours. To Portsmouth, New Hampshire and York, Maine, by way of beautiful Newburyport. *Salem, the Witch City,* 4 hours, incl. Marblehead and Salem Witch Museum.

Yankee Holidays, 20 Spring St., Saugus, MA 01906 (231–2884). *Boston Experience,* 4 days, 3 nights. Tour historic sites, modern attractions. Drinks, dinner inc. *Yankee Doodle,* 3 days, 2 nights. Highlights of Boston and Cambridge. *Yankee Sightseeing,* 4 days, 3 nights. Boston; Lexington and Concord; South Shore and Cape; Martha's Vineyard. Concert or museum pkgs. available.

Peter Pan Lines, 1776 Main St., Springfield MA 01103 (781–3320). *Bus and Boat Cruise to Provincetown,* 1 day. Summer only. Via Boston. *Eastern States Exposition,* 1 day. Departing from Boston, late Sept. *Historic and Modern Springfield,* 1 day. Leaves twice wkly. Also service to Old Sturbridge Village from Springfield and Boston.

Travelers planning to take bus trips should remember that itineraries are subject to alteration. Check with your travel agent for details of latest offerings.

NATIONAL PARKS. Spectacular *Cape Cod National Seashore* in Eastham was authorized as a national park in 1961. Eventually the National Seashore will encompass 27,000 acres from Chatham to Provincetown. Now five areas are open to the public all year round, accessible by paved roads from Rte. 6. Although camping is limited, inquiries may be addressed to: Superintendent, Cape Cod National Seashore, Rte. 6, S. Wellfleet MA 02663 (349–3785).

Visitors to the National Seashore will enjoy the guided walking tours and evening lectures July through Oct. Self-guided trails are open all year for a good look at wildlife and birds.

Visitors' information centers are located in Orleans on Rte. 6, and in Provincetown (summer only) on the Province Lands Rd.

Picnicking is allowed on all the beaches, protected by lifeguards in summer from morning to 6 P.M.

Seasonal hunting must conform to regulations. Freshwater and shell fishing require license; not necessary for saltwater fishing.

The National Seashore is off limits to beach buggies, except along prescribed routes in a limited area near Provincetown. See Cape Cod section for guided-tour information.

STATE PARKS. From May to Oct., the approximately 50 state parks and forests are open daylight hours. Usually trailer and tent sites are available; picnicking is allowed. There's a two-week limitation on campsites. *Beartown State Forest,* access from State 23 or 102, near Great Barrington. Camp and swim at Benedict Pond. Ski in winter. More than 8,000 acres include Mt. Wilcox, Sky Peak, Livermore Peak, Beartown Mountain. *Brimfield State Forest,* U.S. 20, near Worcester and Springfield. Fish in Woodman Pond. Swim in Dean Pond. Hike on Mt. Waddaquadduck. *Erving State Forest,* State 2, near Erving and West Orange. Hunting, fishing, camping, and swimming here. *Horseneck Beach Reservation,* access from U.S. 6 and State 88, near Fall River. Stroll on sand dunes; enjoy surf-fishing and swimming. Camping. *Mohawk Trail State Forest,* State 2, near Charlemont. Fish for trout; take outstanding scenic photographs. Camping. *Mount Greylock State Reservation,* near N. Adams. Mt. Greylock highest Massachusetts mountain, is here, with Masachusetts War Memorial Beacon. Hunt, ride, camp, and ski on more than 8,000 acres. *Mount Tom State Reservation,* access from U.S. 5, Holyoke. Good fishing. Excellent, privately owned ski area open to public. *October Mountain State Forest,* near Lee. Good camping (trailers). Visit Schermerhorn Gorge; fish in Shaker Mill Pond. Largest Massachusetts forest, almost 15,000 acres. *Myles Standish State Forest,* near Plymouth. Swim in ponds; hunt, fish. Camping (trailers); cabins for rental. *Pittsfield State Forest,* near Pittsfield. Sports galore, including skiing. *Salisbury Beach State Reservation,* access on state 1A, near Newburyport. Miles of ocean for swimming. Camping. *Spencer State Forest,* State 31, Spencer Monument to inventor Elias Howe and family here. Swim, fish in Howe Pond. *Walden Pond State Reservation,* State 126, near Concord. Summer sports in pond area. Thoreau lived here. *Willard Brook State Forest,* State 119; near Fitchburg. Scenic waterfalls; Damon Pond Beach. Camping (trailers). The *Boston Harbor Islands* have recently been given state park status. Georges Island, site of a Civil War fort, is served by regularly scheduled ferries from Rowe's and Long wharves, Boston. Water taxis ferry visitors from George's to other islands, some of which have camping facilities.

Contact the Metropolitan District Commission, 20 Somerset St., Boston (727–5215), or the Dept. of Environmental Management, 100 Cambridge St., Boston (727–3180), for details and camping permits.

INDIANS. Massachusetts is named for the Massachuset Indians, who occupied the Massachusetts Bay Territory in the early 17th century. The Massachuset tribe also owned and occupied the site of Boston. Although they numbered about 3,000, the tribe was reduced to fewer than 500 by 1631. Soon after, the Indians converted to Christianity and their tribal life diminished. Now there are approximately 11,500 Indians living in Massachusetts; in addition to the descendants of the native tribes, Massachusetts' Indian population has been augmented by emigrants from Canada's Maritime provinces. Indian day is Aug. 12 in Massachusetts, a quiet observance. That was the date in 1676 when the famous Indian leader King Philip was killed by an Indian informer. King Philip was the son of Massasoit. A powerful Indian ruler and chief of the Wampanoag tribe, Massasoit signed the peace treaty of 1621 with the Pilgrims of Plymouth. He kept his vow faithfully. Neighboring Indians participated in the first Thanksgiving Day feast with the Pilgrims in 1621. The colonists were grateful for all that the Indians taught them about farming and survival in New England.

One of the original Massachusetts tribes was the Wampanoags. Their recent claim to lands in Mashpee, on Cape Cod, involved arguments as to whether or not the present-day bearers of the Wampanoag name constitute a legitimate tribal group. The Wampanoags were unsuccessful in reclaiming any land. However, the chief medicine man of their tribe currently serves as the state's commissioner of Indian affairs, and is working hard to correct lingering injustices.

GARDENS. Stockbridge. *Naumkeag Gardens,* Prospect Hill (298–3239). Exotic, with Chinese motif, moongate. Mansion belonged to Joseph Choate, ambassador to England. Open July to Labor Day. Closed Mon. Sat. and Sun. only from Labor Day to Oct. 1. *Berkshire Garden Center,* Rtes. 102 and 183, 2 miles west of Stockbridge (298–5530). Year round, dawn till dusk. Annual antiques show, July. **Framingham.** *Garden in the Woods,* Hemenway Rd. (237–4924); open Apr 1 to Oct. 31. Wildlife sanctuary with self-guided trails. Closed Sun. **Weston.** *Case Estate,* 135 Wellesley St. (524–1718). Open all year, managed by Arnold Arboretum. 110 acres of woodland, cultivated trees, and flowers.

SUMMER SPORTS. Golf. Massachusetts has many fine courses, including the Kittansett Club, Marion (748 –1250); Salem Country Club, Peabody (532–2540); Trull Brook Golf Club, Tewksbury (851–6731); and Taconic Golf Club, Williamstown (458–3997). Golf is especially popular on the Cape; see Cape Cod and Islands Practical Information section for specific club listings.

Boating. Charter, party boats available at all major ports. Larger lakes and ponds have launching ramps; boats or outboards may be rented. Charles River is dotted with sailboats in summer, as are the waters of Gloucester, Marblehead and Cape Cod. Canoeing is popular on the Charles, Concord, and Ipswich Rivers. Several local firms offer rentals; show up early to assure a canoe.

Fishing. Excellent fresh water fishing in many lakes and streams, stocked by Division of Fish and Game. Trout fishing particularly good in Berkshires. Saltwater fishing popular along coast (see also Cape Cod Sports section).

Water skiing. The best lake for water skiing in the state is Lake Chargoggagaugmanchaugagoggchaubunagungamaugg. It's a 1,400-acre lake with a shoreline as long as its name. Webster (exit 10 on Mass. Tpke., then Rte. 12).

Swimming and sunning. Pools and freshwater lakes and ponds throughout the state; good beaches at Wollaston, Nantasket and on the North Shore at Revere, Marblehead, Lynn, Swampscott, Gloucester, Plum Island, and Salisbury. Greenfield has a 1,400-ft. outdoor swimming pool on Green River.

WINTER SPORTS. Skiing. Novice-expert skiers can try *Brodie Mt.,* New Ashford (443–4752); with a 1,250-ft. drop and 12 trails; *Berkshire East,* Charlemont (339–6617) with a 1,150-ft. drop and 12 trails; *Jiminy Peak,* Hancock (738–5500) with a 1,130-ft. drop and 20 trails; *Catamount,* S. Egremont (528–1262) with a 1,000-ft. drop and 7 trails. Areas with shorter drops are: *Butternut Basin,* Great Barrington (528–2000) with a 975-ft. drop and 10 trails; *Mt. Tom,* S. Holyoke (536–0416) with a 840-ft. drop and 3 trails; *Bousquet,* Pittsfield (442–8316) with a 750-ft. drop and 10 trails and *Otis Ridge,*

Otis (269–4444), with a 360-ft. drop and 3 trails. The novice-intermediate skier should look into *Berkshire Snow Basin,* W. Cummington (634–8808) with a 550-ft. drop and 4 trails.

Cross-country skiing has become immensely popular in Massachusetts and may be enjoyed wherever trails or open terrain are available. *Northfield Mtn. Touring Center,* Northfield St., Northfield (659–3713), has the state's most extensive trail network (25 miles).

Snowmobiling trails can be found at Ashfield, Lancaster, Lee, Lenox Dale, N. Brookfield, Northampton, Otis, Pittsfield, Savoy, Shelburne Falls, Williamstown and Winchendon.

 **CHILDRENS ACTIVITIES.** For the young set, there are summer **amusement parks** at *Salisbury Beach,* Salisbury; *Mountain Park,* Holyoke (534–5656); *Riverside Park,* Agawam (786–9300); and *Whalom Park,* near Fitchburg. *Edaville Railroad,* S. Carver (866–4526), features a train chugging through Cranberryland. Daily in summer; after Labor Day, wknds only. Closed Jan. through mid-June. Chicken barbecue restaurant and picnic grounds on premises. *Children's Museum and Museum Outdoors,* Dartmouth (993–3361) has antique doll and toy exhibits, live animals, hiking trails, educational games. *A&D Toy Train Village and Railway Museum,* Middleborough (947–5303) has 33 operating layouts.

Zoos: *Franklin Park Zoo,* Blue Hill Ave., Dorchester (442–0991) is open all year; free. Hundreds of animals and an excellent aviary on more than 50 acres. Children may pet animals in special area. Picnic grounds on premises. *Forest Park,* Springfield (787–6440) has an interesting zoo; picnic grounds. *Stone Memorial Zoo,* Stoneham (442–0991), has Siberian tigers, good aviary. *Buttonwood Park Zoo,* Rockdale Ave., New Bedford (no phone). Open Apr 17 to Labor Day.

Old Sturbridge Village, U.S. 20 and State 15 (347–3362) is a re-created 18th-century farming village. Children will see craftsmen making horseshoes, dipping candles, baking bread. In winter there are sleigh rides. Guided summer tours Mon. through Fri. Restaurant on the premises. Closed Christmas Day and New Year's Day. *Dinosaur Land* is in S. Hadley (off Amherst St.) (467–9566). The museum exhibits assorted dinosaur prints. Children should also visit *Plimouth Plantation* in Plymouth and *Mayflower II.* Apr. through Nov. Children will also enjoy going along on one of the increasing number of *whale watch* cruises being offered in Massachusetts. In addition to the Provincetown-based service listed in "Practical Information for Cape Cod," the following firms offer whale watch cruises: *Gloucester Sightseeing Cruises,* 12 Clarendon Street, Gloucester, 283–5110; and *Captain's Fishing Parties,* Plum Island Point, Newburyport, 465–7733.

 HISTORIC SITES AND HOMES. No place in America has preserved its historic resources more carefully than Massachusetts. It certainly seems that you don't have to drive far before you stumble upon a historic district, a restored home or even a plaque commemorating one of the great moments in American History. The following is a listing of many—but by no means all of—the state's historic treasures.

SOUTH SHORE

QUINCY. The *Adams National Historic Site,* 135 Adams St. (773–1177), was given to the nation by the descendants of John Adams. Original furnishings. Open mid-Apr. to mid-Nov.

PLYMOUTH. *Plymouth Rock* and exact replica of *Mayflower* at waterfront. Ship closed in winter.

Plimouth Plantation, Rte. 3A (746–1622), is a replica of the Pilgrim village. Tours conducted by guides and hostesses in costume. Twelve houses, an Algonquin Indian Campsite, and gardens are completed. More houses are planned. Open July, Closed winter. Many early homes in vicinity of Plymouth Rock open to public.

CONCORD/LEXINGTON AREA

ARLINGTON/LEXINGTON. *Jason Russell House.* Cor. Mass. Ave. and Jason St., Arlington. No phone. Apr. to Oct., Tues. through Sat. Bullet holes mark site of revolutionary skirmish.

Buckman Tavern. 1 Bedford St., Lexington (861–0928). Open daily mid-Apr. to Oct. Minutemen gathered here April 19, 1775.

Hancock Clark House. 36 Hancock St., Lexington (862–5598). Open daily mid-Apr. to Oct. This is where Paul Revere warned John Hancock of the approach of the British before the Battle of Lexington.

CONCORD. The *Minute Man National Historical Park,* Liberty St. (369–6993), commemorates the first skirmish of the Revolution. The Visitor Center, Monument St., is open daily. Audio visual program. The exhibit room at Lincoln is open daily June through Aug. Closed wknds. rest of year. *Fisk Hill Information Station* and picnic area is on Rte 2A. Open Apr. through Nov.

Emerson House. Rte. 2A, opposite Antiquarian Society (369–2236). This was R.W. Emerson's house in his later years; his books, notes, and furnishings are here. Open mid-Apr.–Oct.; closed Sun. and Mon.

Old Manse. Monument St., Concord (369–6944). (Minuteman National Historic Park.) Open daily mid-Apr. to Columbus Day. 18th-century house where Nathaniel Hawthorne lived.

WAYLAND. *Walden Pond.* Rte. 126 nr. Rte. 2. State reservation offers swimming, fishing, picnicking; walk to site of Thoreau's cabin.

NORTH SHORE AND MERRIMACK VALLEY

BEVERLY. *Balch House.* 448 Cabot St. (922–7076). Open Memorial Day to Oct. 15, Wed. through Sat. 1638 house is one of the oldest in New England.

GLOUCESTER. *Fisherman statue.* Rte. 127, Gloucester. Commemorates over three centuries of Gloucestermen who went "down to the sea in ships."

IPSWICH. *Whipple House.* South Village Green, Ipswich. No phone. Open Apr. to Nov., Tues. through Sun. A fine example of a "First Period" house (1640). Exquisitely restored and furnished with antiques.

LOWELL. The *Lowell National Historical Park,* (459–1000), includes mill buildings, old canals and locks; offers architectural and ethnic heritage tours. Trains from Boston; shuttle to Visitors' Center at corner of Market and Dalton streets.

MAGNOLIA. *Norman's Woe Rock.* Hesperus Ave., Magnolia. Immortalized in Longfellow's poem "Wreck of the Hesperus."

MARBLEHEAD. *Abbott Hall.* Washington St., Marblehead (631–0528). Open Mon. to Fri.; wknds in summer. Marblehead's Town Hall houses famous painting, "Spirit of '76."

PIGEON COVE. *Paper House.* 52 Pigeon Hill St., Rockport (546–2629). Open daily July and Aug.; by appt. rest of year. Sixty-year-old house built of over 100,000 newspapers.

SALEM. *The Salem Maritime National Historic Site,* 178 Derby St. (744–4323), includes a visitor center in the Custom House on Derby St., opp. the wharf, shipping center of Salem from 1760 to 1860. Open daily. Scale House and Bonded Warehouse are open year round. Free. *Derby House,* restored and furnished, is open year round.

Jonathan Corwin House. Essex St. (744–0180). Open daily Mar. 1 to Nov. 31. Restored home of witch trials judge.

SAUGUS. On the grounds of the *Saugus Iron Works National Historic Site* on Central St. (233–0050), are restorations of an ironmaster's house, blast furnace, forge slitting mill. There is also a museum. Grounds open all yr.; tours conducted daily, Apr. to Oct.

SPRINGFIELD AND PIONEER VALLEY

AMHERST. *Emily Dickinson's Home.* 280 Main St. (542–2321). Tours by appt. Birthplace and lifelong residence of poet. Owned by Amherst College, which arranges tours.

DEERFIELD. Site of the great Indian Massacres of 1675, 1704. Six Colonial homes are open, including *Frary House,* dating back to 1689, museums, the old graveyard. For information, call 774–5581. May to Nov.

Memorial Hall. Main St., Hatfield (773–8929). Houses colonial charter granted by William and Mary. Open daily May to Oct.

Indian House. Main St. (772–0845). Open May 1 to Nov. 1, closed Tues. Reproductions of building which survived famous 1704 Indian raid.

NORTHAMPTON. *Calvin Coolidge House.* 21 Massasoit St., Northampton. Not open to public.

Forbes Library. 20 West St. (584–8550). Closed July 4, Christmas, Thanksgiving. Romanesque bldg. houses Coolidge Room.

Cornet Jos. Parsons House. 58 Bridge St., Northampton (584–6011). Open Wed., Fri., Sun. all yr., 2–4:30 P.M. Oldest house in city, built 1658.

PITTSFIELD. *Berkshire Athanaeum.* Park Sq. (442–1559). Open year round, closed sun. and hols. Houses public library and Melville Memorial Room.

Arrowhead. 780 Holmes Rd. (442–1793). Open daily June 1 to Oct. 31; rest of year by appt. Melville lived here from 1850–1863.

SHELBURNE FALLS. *Bridge of Flowers.* 51 Bridge St. (625–9502). Open daily; floodlit until 10:30 P.M. in summer.

WORCESTER AND CENTRAL MASSACHUSETTS

FALL RIVER. *USS Massachusetts.* Battleship Cove (678–1100). Surviving battlewagon of WW II, 16-inch guns and all. Open daily except major hols.

THE BERKSHIRES

LENOX. *Pleaseant Valley Wildlife Sanctuary.* 472 W. Mountain Rd. (637–0320). Open daily; museum open wknds. only spring and fall, museum closed winter. 700-acre Mass. Audubon Society preserve; live exhibits in museum.

SAVOY AREA. *Susan B. Anthony House* (private). East Rd., 1½ miles off Hoosac St., Adams.

William Cullen Bryant Home. Rte. 112, Cummington (634–2192). Open mid-June to mid-Oct., Fri., Sat., Sun, hol. afternoons. Birthplace and longtime home of famous poet and editor.

STOCKBRIDGE. *Mission House.* Sergeant St. (298–3383). Open Memorial Day to mid-Oct., Tues. through Sun.

MUSEUMS AND GALLERIES. As the site of the country's first humble beginnings when America was mostly uncharted land, then one of the leaders of the industrial age, there is a wealth of history to be told and culture to be experienced in the museums and galleries that dot the state.

BOSTON SUBURBS, SOUTH SHORE, AND NEW BEDFORD

MILTON. *Museum of the China Trade,* 215 Adams St. (696–1815). Sea captain's home exhibiting orientalia imported in days of clipper ships. Closed Sun., Mon., holidays.

NEW BEDFORD. *Whaling Museum,* 18 Johnny Cake Hill (997–0046). June through Sept. *Glass Museum,* 50 N. 2nd St. (994–0115). Displays of glass from the days when this industry flourished in New Bedford. Closed Mon. and Tues. Oct. through May; open 7 days in summer.

WALTHAM. *Waltham Museum.* 194 Charles St. (893–8017). Bicycles, steam engine, Waltham memorabilia, in home of first employee of Waltham Watch Co. Open Sun.; wkdays by group appt.

CONCORD/LEXINGTON AREA

CONCORD. *Concord Antiquarian Museum,* 200 Lexington Rd. (369–9609). Period rooms, Emerson and Thoreau artifacts.

LEXINGTON. *Museum of Our National Heritage,* 33 Marrett Rd. (861–6560). Galleries of exhibits chronicle U.S. history and social development, also history of Freemasonry. Library, auditorium; films daily. *De Cordova Museum,* Sandy Pond Rd. (259–8355). Contemporary art; emphasis on New England artists. Music, theater, dance outdoors in summer.

NORTH SHORE AND MERRIMACK VALLEY

ANDOVER. *Addison Gallery of American Art,* Chapel St. (475–3403). Works of American artists, glassware, sculpture, ship models. Daily.

GLOUCESTER. *Beauport.* Eastern Point Blvd. (283–0800). Early American furniture and decorative arts. Mon. through Fri., May 15 to Oct. 31.
Gloucester Fishermen's Museum. Porter and Rogers Sts. (283–1940). Chronicles Gloucester's main industry for 350 years.

MAGNOLIA. *Hammond Museum,* 80 Hesperus Ave. (283–2080). Castle-styled home with art and historic exhibits; famed for one of world's largest pipe organs; concerts in summer.

NORTH ANDOVER. *Merrimack Valley Textile Museum,* 800 Mass. Ave. (686–0191). Old tools, photos, documents show growth of U.S. textile industry. Library. Spec. demonstrations Sun.

SALEM. *Salem Witch Museum,* 19½ Washington Sq., N. Salem (744–1692) with recreations of witch trials. Closed winter.
Witch House (Jonathan Corwin House) (1642), 310½ Essex St. (744–0180) is the house where the Salem witches were examined. Closed winter.

House of the Seven Gables, 54 Turner St. (744–0991) built 1668; made famous in Hawthorne novel. Also on grounds are Hawthorne's birthplace and other 17th-century dwellings. Closed Thanksgiving, Christmas, New Year's Day.

Peabody Maritime Museum, East India Sq. (745–9500). Natural history exhibits, artifacts from clipper trade, orientalia. Closed Thanksg., Christmas, New Year's Day.

Essex Institute, 132 Essex St. (744–3390). Restored homes and museum. Features Pingree House (1804), John Ward House (1684), Pierce-Nichols House (1782), Crowninshield-Bentley House (1727), Assembly House (1782). Also see reproduction of 1630 village at *Forest Park.*

WORCESTER AND CENTRAL MASSACHUSETTS

FALL RIVER. *Marine Museum.* 70 Water St. (674–3533). Open daily year round. Ship models and steamboat memorabilia.

STURBRIDGE. *Old Sturbridge Village* (347–3362). 36 old houses surround early 19th-century green on 200-acre site. Costumed guides explain exhibits. It is one of the best period restorations in the country, and should not be missed. One of its prime attractions is its staff of working artisans, who demonstrate how crafts such as blacksmithing and weaving were practiced in pre-industrial America.

WORCESTER. *Worcester Art Museum,* 55 Salisbury St. (799–4406). Closed Mon.; free Wed.

Worcester Historical Museum. 39 Salisbury St. (753–8278). Closed Sun. and Mon.

Worcester Science Center, Harrington Way (791–9211). Hands-on museum covers astronomy, ecology, animal, and earth sciences; small zoo features polar bears; Omnisphere planetarium. Great for kids. Open daily Apr. 15–Labor Day; closed Mon. and Tues. rest of year.

American Antiquarian Society, 185 Salisbury St. (755–5221). Isaiah Thomas printing press, colonial history. Mon. through Fri. *Worcester Science Center.* 222 Harrington Way (791–9211). Open daily.

SPRINGFIELD AND PIONEER VALLEY

HOLYOKE. *Dwight Memorial Art Museum.* Mount Holyoke College campus, South Hadley (538–2000). Hours vary with academic year. Small but interesting art collection; Mt. Holyoke is nations' oldest college for women.

SPRINGFIELD. *George Walter Vincent Smith Museum.* Museum Quadrangle (733–4214). Oriental rugs and decorative arts, 19th-century American art, period rooms. Closed Mon.

Springfield Science Museum. Museum Quadrangle (732–4317). Fresh water aquarium, ethnology, mounted animals, planetarium. Closed Mon.

Museum of Fine Arts. Museum Quadrangle (732–6092). European, Asian, American art. Closed Mon.

Springfield Armory Museum, Armory Sq. (734–6477). Features examples of every weapon made at famous armory. Open daily, closed major hols.

Connecticut Valley Historical Museum. 194 State St. (732–3080). Open Tues. through Sun. afternoons all year; closed holidays. Decorative arts; local business history.

WEST SPRINGFIELD. *Storrowton Village,* 1305 Memorial Ave. (736–0632). Authentic 200-year-old buildings in village setting.

BERKSHIRES

DALTON. *Crane Museum.* Rte. 9, 5 miles east of Pittsfield (685–2600). June 1–Sept.30: Mon.-Fri. afternoons. Evolution of American papermaking.

HANCOCK. *Hancock Shaker Village.* Rtes. 20 and 41 (443–0188). Historic settlement of Shaker community, with restored buildings. Open daily June to Oct. 31.

LEE. *Tyringham Art Galleries* (Gingerbread House, home and studio of late sculptor Henry Hudson Kitson). Tyringham Rd. (243–3260). Primitive art, painting, etchings. Daily.

PITTSFIELD. *Berkshire Museum.* 39 South St. (443–7171). Open daily July and Aug.; closed Mon. rest of year. Closed holidays. Excellent mineral collection; historical artifacts; Hudson River School and other paintings.

ROWE. *Historical Society Museum.* Zoar Rd. (339–4238). July 4-Columbus Day, Sat.-Sun. afternoons. Revolutionary and Civil War artifacts.

STOCKBRIDGE. *Chesterwood,* Rte. 183 (298–3579). Studio of Daniel Chester French, sculptor of "The Minute Man of Concord," at Concord, and Lincoln Statue, Washington, D.C. Plaster casts. Daily in summer; wknds, Labor Day-Oct. 15.
Norman Rockwell Museum at Stockbridge. Main St. (298–3822). Extensive collection of Norman Rockwell paintings. Closed Tues.

WILLIAMSTOWN. *Sterling and Francine Clark Art Institute,* South St. (458–8109). Impressive marble building. Renoirs, Sargents, Corots and many other masterpieces. Rare treasures exhibited also. Free. Closed Mon.; Feb. *Williams College Art Museum.* Williams Campus (597–2429). Open Mon. through Sat. all year. American, African, Renaissance and Baroque art in new gallery.

 **MUSIC AND DANCE.** Lenox: *Berkshire Festival,* Tanglewood. Nine-week festival begins June 30. Performances in Music Shed, Fri., Sat., Sun. Admission to open rehearsal, Sat. morning. Ticket information 637–1600. *Berkshire Music Barn* features folksingers and jazz groups from early July through early Sept. (637–0919).
Lee. *Jacob's Pillow Dance Festival,* Ted Shawn Theater (243–0745) Ballet, modern, ethnic dance. July, Aug.
Lincoln. Concerts are held in summer at the *de Cordova Museum,* Trapelo Rd. (255–8355).
Pittsfield. *South Mountain Concerts,* South St. Rtes. 7 and 20 (443–6517). Chamber music, opera, young people's concerts. Sun., July, Aug.; Sat., Sept., Oct.
Concord, Lexington. *The "Spirit of '76"* is revived with fife and drum competitions on Patriot's Day, Mon. closest to Apr. 19.
Ipswich. *Castle Hill Concerts,* July, Aug., Fri. and Sat., at Castle Hill estate (356–4070).
Weymouth. *Weymana,* large club features big bands (337–4700).
Northampton. *Iron Horse Coffeehouse,* 20 Center St. (584–0610) features top-notch folk and light jazz acts.
Worcester. *Mechanics Hall,* 321 Main St. (752–5608). Concerts are also held at Worcester's new *Centrum Civic Center* located at Foster and Commercial Sts.
Also, check newspaper listings for musical performances at Massachusetts' many colleges and universities.

STAGE AND REVUES. There are excellent summer theaters throughout the state. These include *North Shore Music Theatre*, Beverly (922–8500); *Loeb Drama Center*, 64 Brattle St., Cambridge (547–8300); *South Shore Music Circus*, Cohasset (383–1400); *High Tor Summer Theater*, Fitchburg (342 –6592); *Gateway Players*, Southbridge (764–4531); *Brandeis Theatre*, Waltham (647–2569); *Storrowtown Music Fair*, Eastern States Fairgrounds, W. Springfield (781–2340); *Adams Memorial Theater* on Williams College campus, Williamstown, houses college productions in winter, Williamstown Theater Festival in summer (597–2425); and *Barton Square Playhouse*, Salem (744–0114). *The Berkshire Theatre Festival* in Lenox has a 9-week season beginning in late June. *Mechanics Hall*, Worcester, hosts plays and other events. Don't forget to check offerings of the many excellent college drama groups during the school year.

SHOPPING. Danvers: *Deerskin Trading Post*, U.S. 1 (774–3816). Deerskin moccasins, gloves, jackets, etc. **Beverly:** *Johnny Appleseed's*, Rte. 1A (922–2040). Everything from food delicacies to hunting equipment (building constructed 1687). **Great Barrington:** *Jenifer House* (528–1500). Tableware, linens, colonial furniture, clothing. **Rockport:** *Bearskin Neck* offers a variety of craft shops, most notably *The Pewter Shop* (546–2105), and *London Venturers Co.* (546–7161). **Wareham:** *Grey Oaks Gift Shop* (295–0380), offers fine reproductions of early Massachusetts glassware.

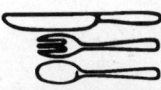

DINING OUT. Regional foods are Cape scallops, Ipswich clams, Cotuit oysters, native lobster, scrod (baby codfish), codfish, halibut, haddock, flounder. Traditional dishes include fish cakes, brown bread, Boston baked beans (on Saturday night) and New England boiled dinner (corned beef simmered with cabbage, potatoes, turnips and onions). Baked Indian pudding is a favorite dessert. In summer, it's blueberry pie made with native berries. In addition, international dishes of considerable sophistication are increasingly available even outside major metropolitan areas.

Most restaurants accept credit cards, however it is wise to call ahead to double check. Reservations are frequently a must—particularly during the high seasons.

The cost of a semi-à la carte dinner is the basis of our price ranges. *Expensive*, $22 and up; *Moderate*, $14–$22; *Inexpensive*, under $14.

SOUTH SHORE

COHASSET. Golden Rooster. *Moderate.* 78 Border St., N. Scituate (545–1330). Prime ribs, baked stuffed lobster. Children's portions.

Hugo's Lighthouse. *Moderate.* 44 Border St. (383–1700). Ocean-fresh seafoods, steaks, chops. Cocktails.

PLYMOUTH. Inn For All Seasons. *Moderate.* 97 Warren Ave. (746–8823). Victorian mansion features filet mignon Neptune, veal Oscar. Dance band. Closed Mon.

Mayflower Seafood. *Moderate.* Town Wharf (746–1704). New England menu and seafood. Take-out service. Pleasant nautical atmosphere. Cocktails. Children's portions.

Bert's. *Inexpensive.* Warren Ave. (746–3422). Seafood restaurant. Bar, entertainment. Overlooking bay.

CONCORD-LEXINGTON AREA

ACTON. Folsom's. *Moderate.* 77 Great Rd. (263–3162). Specializes in fresh seafood; fish market on premises.

Chez Claude. *Moderate.* 5 Strawberry Hill Rd. (263–3325). Small, pleasant restaurant serving French cuisine. Lunch Wed.-Fri. Closed Sun.

ANDOVER. Andover Inn. *Moderate.* On Andover Academy campus (475–5903). Relaxed atmosphere, good service. Rijsttafel—the Dutch Indonesian buffet—is a Sunday tradition.

Backstreet. *Moderate.* 19 Essex St. (475–4411). Veal Oscar; French onion soup; fresh vegetables. Good wine list. Sunday jazz brunch, 11 A.M. to 3 P.M.

Bishop's. *Moderate.* 99 Hampshire St., Lawrence (683–7143). Generous helpings of Middle Eastern food—hummus, rice pilafs, kebabs.

Thompson's. *Moderate.* Wilson's Corner, 435 Andover St., N. Andover (686–4309). Seafood, steak, and to top everything off, light foamy chiffon pies. Opp. Merrimack Coll.

CONCORD AREA. Colonial Inn. *Moderate.* Concord Green (369–9200). Traditional New England fare, tap room, antiques.

Different Drummer. *Moderate.* 86 Thoreau St. (369–8700). Veal marsala, filet of sole. Sunday brunch.

Lincoln Crossing. *Moderate.* Lincoln Rd. (259–9886). Cheery little restaurant in a village setting; American and continental menu.

GLOUCESTER. White Rainbow. *Expensive.* 65 Main St. (281–0017). In a registered landmark bldg. Fixed price dinner only. Bar, entertainment wknds. Menu changes, but fresh vegetables, fine soups and pâtés, and imaginative entrees are a standby.

Captain Courageous. *Moderate.* 25 Rogers St. (283–0007). Popular locally. New England specialties, plus steak, prime ribs. Piano music nightly in Captain's Lounge. Sunday buffets in late fall and winter.

Easterly. *Moderate.* 87 Atlantic Rd. (283–0140). Dover sole meuniere, veal scallopine Marsala. Overlooks ocean. Lounge, entertainment in summer. Closed Nov. 1 to early Apr.

Gloucester House. *Moderate.* Rte. 127 (283–1812). At Seven Seas Wharf, overlooking harbor. Excellent seafood. Bar. Children's portions. Dancing in summer.

The Rudder. *Moderate.* 73 Rocky Neck Ave. (283–7967). Steaks, roast beef, plus delicious baked clams farcis, filet of sole hollandaise. Children's portions. Closed Mon., Tues., and from Nov. to mid-May.

IPSWICH. The Apple Orchard. *Moderate.* 24 Essex Rd. (Rte. 133) (356–5969). Cozy spot with handmade quilts on the walls. Menu features northern Italian pasta, veal specialties. Closed Mon. in winter.

LOWELL. A.G. Pollard and Sons. *Inexpensive.* Middle St. (459–4632). Steaks, seafood, burgers, specials. Good soup and salad bar. Entertainment in adjoining lounge.

NEWBURYPORT. Scandia. *Expensive.* 25 State St. (462–6271). Small, intimate restaurant with a seasonally changing menu of American, French, and Northern Italian dishes. The seafood is always good, *especially* the chowder. **10 Center St.** *Expensive.* (462–6652). A crackling fire in winter, patio dining in summer. Home baking. Dinner specialties change with the season.

The Grog. *Inexpensive.* 13 Middle St. (465–8008). Two floors of dining, two bars, and rock bands in the basement. Menu includes burgers, prime rib, daily seafood specials, and an assortment of Mexican dishes.

ROCKPORT. Blacksmith Shop. *Moderate.* 23 Mt. Pleasant St. (546–6301). Unusual Greek bread and Greek salad a specialty. Charming restaurant overlooks harbor. Children's portions. Open mid-May to mid-Oct.

Old Farm Inn. *Moderate.* 291 Granite St., Pigeon Cove (546–3237). Roast duck, seafood specialties in family-run inn. Children's portions. Open Mar. to Nov. Closed Mon.

Oleana-by-the Sea. *Moderate.* 27 Main St. (546–2049). Scandinavian-American specialties. Smorgasbord. Open mid-Jan. to mid-Dec. Closed Mon.

Peg Leg. *Moderate.* 18 Beach St. (546–3038). Lobster, seafood, steak, roast beef served in greenhouse overlooking ocean. Closed mid-Nov to Mar. Children's portions.

SALEM. Chase House. *Expensive.* Pickering Wharf (744–0000). 100-year-old restaurant. Mako shark, halibut, swordfish, haddock creole, steak. Entertainment nightly. Cozy traditional atmosphere.

Lyceum. *Expensive.* 43 Church St. (745–7665). Black Bean soup, veal Oscar, duckling, good variety of local seafood. Excellent dessert selection.

Folsom's. *Moderate.* 7 Dodge St. (745–1230). Fine selection of fresh fish dishes.

SUDBURY. Longfellow's Wayside Inn. *Moderate.* Wayside Inn Rd., off Rte. 20 (443–8846). New England menu in beautifully restored historic inn. Sun. buffet. Children's portions.Seafood market on premises.

SWAMPSCOTT. General Glover House. *Moderate.* Salem St. (595–5151). Home of Gen. John Glover, father of U.S. Navy. Steaks, roast beef. Cocktails.

Hawthorne-by-the-Sea. *Moderate.* 153 Humphrey St. (595–5735). Waterfront restaurant featuring lobster stuffed with lobster.

WORCESTER AND CENTRAL MASSACHUSETTS

FRAMINGHAM. Ken's Steak House. *Moderate.* 95 Worcester Rd. (235–5414). Replica of Normandy farmhouse. Open hearth for cooking steak and lobster. Own pecan pie. Cocktails.

STURBRIDGE. Publick House. *Moderate.* Rte. 131 (347–3313). Colonial inn specializing in delicious lobster pie, Cornish hen. Bar. Bake shop on premises.

The Whistling Swan. *Moderate.* 502 Main St. (347–2321). Chef-owned, featuring American and continental cuisine. Entertainment Fri. and Sat. eve. Closed Mon.

Rom's. *Inexpensive.* Rte. 131 (347–3349). A popular Italian spot. Smorgasbord served Wednesday eve.

WORCESTER. Garden Court. *Moderate.* Sheraton Lincoln Inn, 500 Lincoln St. (852–4000). Lots of greenery, and not just in your salad. Prime rib, seafood, chateaubriand. Dancing in lounge Tues.–Sat.

Legal Seafoods. *Moderate.* 1 Exchange St. (792–1600). Boston's popular seafood spot moves west; this new branch keeps up the standards of fresh fish and shellfish in an astonishing variety.

SPRINGFIELD AND PIONEER VALLEY

AMHERST. Lord Jeffrey. *Moderate.* On the Green (253–2576). Colonial atmosphere. Baked stuffed shrimp, variety of New England dishes.

DEERFIELD. Jack McCarthy's Gables Restaurant. *Moderate.* Rtes. 5 and 10 (665–4643). Steaks, seafood. Bar. Dancing Wed. through Sat.

HOLYOKE. Yankee Pedlar Inn. *Moderate.* Exit 16, I–91 (532–9494). Seasonal seafood specialties, oyster bar. Wine cellar.

NORTHAMPTON. Beardsley's. *Expensive.* 140 Main St. (586–2699). Splendid service in an intimate French cafe setting. Steak, duckling, wonderful desserts. A fine spot for Sunday brunch.

Wiggins Tavern. *Moderate.* 36 King St. (586–5000). New England atmosphere prevails in century-old landmark. Candlelight dinner. Varied menu. Cocktails.

Sze's. *Inexpensive.* 50 Main St. (586–5708). Mandarin and Szechuan menu; also takeout. Sunday brunch buffet, 11:30 A.M.–3 P.M.

SPRINGFIELD. Chestnut Tree. *Expensive.* Chestnut and Mattoon sts. (736–3637). New American cuisine succeeds at this popular spot. Salmon terrine, escargot in puff pastry with walnuts, pheasant with pears and cassis, haddock with tomatoes and orange, great desserts. Piano on weekends.

The Student Prince and Fort. *Moderate.* 8 Fort St. (734–7475). German food; Oktoberfest and Mai Wine festivals. Accordion sing-along Sat. eve. Seasonal menus; game festival in Feb.

BERKSHIRES

GREAT BARRINGTON AREA. Egremont Inn. *Expensive.* Sheffield Rd., S. Egremont (528–2111). Supreme of salmon, chicken sautéed with tarragon, lemon sole, steak, veal, trout.

Windflower. *Expensive.* Rt. 23 (528–2720). Dinner by reservation only for non-guests. No printed menu; 3 selections per night, always changing. Veal and chicken dishes especially good.

20 Railroad Street. *Inexpensive.* (528–9345). Good burgers, stew, quiche, daily specials in Victorian saloon atmosphere.

LEE. Cork 'n Hearth. *Moderate.* Rte. 20 (243–0535). Italian pasta specialties, plus steak, seafood. Open daily except Tues. for dinner only.

Morgan House. *Moderate.* 33 Main St. (243–0181). Lobster, lamb, homemade soups, breads and dessert. Cozy Colonial atmosphere. Cocktails. Closed Mon.

LENOX. Candlelight Inn. *Expensive.* Walker St. (637–1555). Steak and kidney pie, coquilles St. Jacques, veal Marengo.

Gateways Inn. *Expensive.* 71 Walker St. (637–2532). Continental specialities prepared by owner-chef. Shrimp stuffed with crabmeat, veal, and mushrooms, broiled scrod casino, beef Stroganoff.

Wheatleigh. *Expensive.* West Hearthstone Dr. (637–0610). The dining room of this luxurious inn is open to the public for breakfast and dinner. Wheatleigh was a millionaire's turn-of-the-century summer "cottage"; there are 33 opulent rooms behind the Mediterranean facade.

Lenox House. *Moderate.* Pittsfield-Lenox Rd. (637–1341). Scampi, roast beef. Homemade relishes, rolls, pies. Cocktails. Children's portions.

The Restaurant. *Moderate.* 15 Franklin St. (637–9894). Cantonese duckling, marinated beef, shrimp.

PITTSFIELD. The Springs. *Expensive.* Rte. 7, New Ashford (458–3465). Veal Oscar, osso buco, tournedos Rossini, paella. Bar, dancing Sat.

Coach-Lite. *Moderate.* 148 S.W. Housatonic St. Rte. 20 (499–1523). Filet of sole Nantua, chicken Kiev, veal Marsala. Dining on wknds. Closed Mon.

Dakota. *Moderate.* Pittsfield-Lenox Rd. (499–7900). Steaks and other standbys done nicely in a rustic Western atmosphere.

STOCKBRIDGE. Red Lion Inn. *Expensive.* Main St. at Rte. 7 (298–5545). Continental menu, elegant atmosphere. Outside dining overlooking flower-filled courtyard. Bar. Entertainment.

Williamsville Inn. *Expensive.* Rte. 41, W. Stockbridge (274–6580). 18th-century farmhouse. Scampi provençale, breast of chicken stuffed with artichokes, mushrooms, and gruyère. Daily specials. Excellent desserts. Bar. Fine wine list. Brkfst. served to house guests.

WILLIAMSTOWN. Le Jardin. *Expensive.* 777 Cold Spring Rd. (458–8032). Poached salmon hollandaise, duckling with cherry sauce flambé. Pastries baked on premises. Brkft. in summer. Bar. Inexpensive accommodations available.

Country Restaurant. *Moderate.* 52 North St. at Rte. 7 (458–4000). Escalope de veau Oscar, clams à la marinara.

Mill on the Floss. *Moderate.* At the Carriage House Motel, 9 mi. S on U.S. 7 (458–9123). 18th-century house overlooking mill pond. Patio dining. Suggestions: sweetbreads aux capres, tournedos. Bar. 5 to 10. Closed Tues.

DRINKING LAWS. Drinks may be ordered until 1 A.M. (2 A.M. in some towns) daily; until midnight (1 A.M. in some towns) Sat. Serving hours Sun. are from 1 P.M. (11 A.M. in some towns) until 1 A.M. Package liquor sold until 11 P.M. in package stores; no sales Sun. Legal drinking age is 21. **Note:** Penalties for drunk driving are severe.

NEW HAMPSHIRE

A Playland Built on Granite

by
PAUL ROBBINS

Think of New Hampshire, and you think of mountains—the White Mountains, a series of impressive peaks topped by Mt. Washington, which, at 6,288 feet, is the highest mountain in northeastern America. A cog railway operates throughout the summer, carrying thousands of visitors to Mt. Washington's peak. Built in 1869, it was the first such railway of its kind.

New Hampshire is also the Granite State. Its people are as solid in their ideals, beliefs, and convictions as the granite formations underfoot.

For years, presidential hopefuls have used New Hampshire's primary elections as a proving ground for their public popularity. It is the nation's earliest primary, one that is jealously viewed by many other states. In national elections, Dixville Notch (about 15 voters) usually is the first in the country to send in its returns. In general, however, the citizens of New Hampshire are apt to be amused at the attention paid to their primary, and to be more concerned about local questions. It is not provincialism so much as practicality; they know they have considerable control over town affairs. The New England Town Meeting, an institution here, is probably the purest exercise of democracy still in existence.

While they certainly have cause to, the people of New Hampshire are not likely to boast. This reticence has caused the origins of several Granite Staters to be obscured in the pages of national and international history. The fourteenth President of the United States, Franklin Pierce, was from New Hampshire, as was Horace Greeley, founder of *The New York Tribune,* and the great orator, Daniel Webster. Joseph E. Worcester, compiler of the first American dictionary of the English language, was also from this state. Americans have a New Hampshire woman, Mrs. Sara Josepha Buell, to thank for making Thanksgiving Day into a national celebration; Mary Baker Eddy, founder of the Christian Science religion, was born here. And, of course, Christa McAuliffe, the first teacher chosen to go into space, was from here, too.

Millions of TV and movie viewers have watched Concord coaches bring the payroll and the new schoolmarm over the western plains. These wagons were used by thousands of migrating families in the early days of western expansion. And Oscar-winning *On Golden Pond* was filmed in the Granite State.

Besides being rather taciturn about their obvious assets, the people of New Hampshire have a reputation for being "firm" in their outlook. There is a local story of a little old lady who, surprised by a burglar, karate-kicked him into a stupor.

It's not that the people of New Hampshire are natural-born fighters; it's just that they never allow themselves to be backed into a corner. If pressed, they will definitely fight and fight well—whether verbally or physically. The state motto, as emblazoned on auto license plates: Live Free or Die.

None of this, however, was apparent at the founding of the colony. This rather polite stubbornness evolved slowly, just as the settlement of the state did.

Colonization

Many explorers traveled up and down the coast of northeastern America prior to actual colonization of the area. Among these were Martin Pring, Samuel de Champlain, and John Smith. But the first temporary settlement wasn't made until 1623. This was at Odiorne Point, at Rye, on the coast. The settlers arrived in April and set up a community mainly devoted to fishing and trading. A stone monument now marks the site of this first temporary community. The land is now privately owned, but it is open to visitors, who may roam the gardens and trails and see the oldest cemetery in the state. Here, too, is Falke Hill, an Indian well where fish was dried, and the creek site of the first grist mill in New Hampshire. There is no admission charge, and the Audubon Society conducts walks here from July to early September.

The Massachusetts Relationship

New Hampshire was slow to grow. In 1641, the population was about 1,000; by 1732 it had reached only 12,500. Harsh weather and attacking Indians were only partially to blame. Loosely worded and sometimes contradictory land grants were the real culprits. Few wanted to buy land and take the trouble to clear it, given the risk of someone else coming along with a conflicting claim.

In 1641, because of its small size, New Hampshire asked to be made part of Massachusetts. However, though it may have been small, in 1649 it voiced its rather strong opinion concerning some of its inhabitants: "Forasmuch as the wearing of long hair after the manner of ruffians and barbarous Indians has begun to invade New England . . . (we) do declare and manifest our dislike and detestation. . . ."

Indians were a constant worry, but conflicts occurred on a smaller scale than in the French and Indian wars. New Hampshire men, however, fought in such battles as the winning of Louisbourg in Nova Scotia. From 1754 to 1763, Rogers and his famous Rangers were constantly involved in Indian skirmishes. In addition to many other campaigns, they drove the St. Francis Indians back to Quebec.

In 1741, Benning Wentworth was appointed royal governor. He was popular at the beginning of his term, but by the time he had finished he had made a jigsaw puzzle of the land. Every time he granted tracts of land to anyone, he included a personally selected lot of 500 acres for himself. By the end of his term he had acquired 100,000 acres scattered about the region. His rambling mansion on Little Harbour Road in Portsmouth (where he married his servingmaid) is now state-owned and open to the public. A stand of lilac (now the state flower) grew beside a doorway there. In 1776, Wentworth was asked to resign by George III, and his nephew, John Wentworth, was appointed governor.

During the elder Wentworth's term, Eleazar Wheelock founded Dartmouth College at Hanover in 1769. He was helped by the governor in his fund-raising. The school was founded for the Indians but most did not remain enrolled. However, the college continued, on 500 acres of land provided by the ex-governor.

Although Governor John Wentworth was popular, and opposed such measures as the Stamp Act, it soon became clear that the people of New Hampshire wanted self-rule. In 1774, a riot broke out when an attempt was made to land a cargo of tea at Portsmouth, and in December of 1774, a force of locals captured a large store of munitions from the British at nearby Fort William and Mary, and distributed them to militia units in nine towns.

John Wentworth dropped out of the political scene in 1775 and a provincial congress drew up a temporary constitution for New Hampshire. Adopting this in January of 1776, New Hampshire became independent of Great Britain seven months before the rest of the colonies announced their similar intention! In November of 1776, New Hampshire's delegates to the Continental Congress signed the Declaration of Independence, and New Hampshire officially became part of the United States.

Three regiments of the state's militia were on the front line in the Battle of Bunker Hill, June, 1775, and throughout the Revolution New Hampshire maintained a strength in the Continental Army. In 1777, John Stark (later General) defeated the British at the Battle of Bennington in Vermont. The Redcoats were seeking supplies; had they been able to seize them, Burgoyne might well have won the crucial Battle of Saratoga.

Revolutionary Bustle

During the Revolution, Portsmouth bustled with maritime activity. More than 3,000 New Hampshire men took part in privateering, aiding in the defeat of the British at sea. From 1776 to 1781, the *Raleigh,*

America, and *Ranger* (made famous by John Paul Jones) were built at this seaport.

New Hampshire's many waterways afforded natural locations for mills; after the Revolution, manufacturing grew rapidly. Small textile and leather plants, foundries, and paper mills sprang up, until, by the 1850s, manufacturing was supporting more New Hampshirites than any other livelihood.

The first textile mill in the state was built at New Ipswich in 1804. By 1808, the state capital was located at Concord and it became apparent that New Hampshire was moving inland. By the mid-1800s, the Concord Coach was an integral part of America's western expansion.

Slavery was never a question for the people of New Hampshire. From the 1820s, anti-slavery societies had been active throughout the state. Loud protests went up from one end of the state to the other when Congress passed the Compromise of 1850. New Hampshirites considered the act favorable to slavery. In October of 1853, fourteen leading citizens with various political backgrounds met and organized a new anti-slavery political party, called the Republican Party; four years later, the new party elected its first governor, and in the Presidential election of 1860 a sizable majority of the state voted Republican. During the Civil War, New Hampshire sent 39,000 men to the front—more than 10 percent of its total population.

The early 1900s saw New Hampshire become a full-fledged industrial state, with its water power drawing many manufacturing firms. Over 20,000 men from New Hampshire marched off to World War I, while others helped make Portsmouth a highly important shipping center.

Following the war, a number of strikes slowed the textile industry to a virtual halt and eight years later the Depression struck. Wages dropped and unemployment soared. World War II brought an economic boom, but the decrease in employment following the war caused Governor Sherman Adams deep concern. He appointed an eight-man Industrial Development Committee in 1949. By 1966, the state's industrial growth showed that "on the basis of percentage employed in manufacturing," New Hampshire ranked second as the most industrial in the U.S.

The economy of New Hampshire, now the fastest-growing state in New England, rests first of all on manufacturing. Through the 1970s, southern New Hampshire became a magnet for companies seeking a rural setting and low taxes; the region drew upwards of a thousand companies, boosting the economy but severely taxing roads, sewer systems, and schools. As the 1980s pass their midpoint, the region is coming to grips with the effects of the booming growth.

At the same time, New Hampshire began to tap its tourism potential as major ski areas developed, most notably in the White Mountains. Cross-country skiing also became a major winter attraction; in the photogenic town of Jackson, the network of over 125 miles of cross-country ski trails threads it way past country inns right on the trail, providing easy access to the touring trails. Along the coast, New Hampshire's beaches are among New England's most popular, and its inland lakes are tops for boating.

A Four-season Wonderland

New Hampshire has long been a special place for winter sports. In 1872, a group of Norwegian-Americans founded the Nansen Ski Club in Berlin and built the first ski jump (1876) in the country. In 1909, the Dartmouth Outing Club was organized at Hanover. Colleges and communities throughout the U.S. have modeled their winter carnival celebrations on that established by the DOC.

In 1929, the first ski school in the country was established at Peckett's-on-Sugar Hill in Franconia. In 1938, a skimobile was built at Cranmore Mountain, North Conway, and a leading ski center was born. The same year, an aerial tramway, the first in the country, was built at Cannon Mountain in Franconia Notch; in 1980, the original tram was replaced by a modern, 80-passenger cable car.

Today, there are 23 major ski areas in the state and over 120 lifts, tows and trams. Most of these areas are open during the summer months as well, for visitors who wish to view the magnificent scenery. The major resorts—Waterville Valley, Loon Mountain, and Bretton Woods—have developed into four-season resorts with tennis and other warm weather activities in addition to the winter skiing. Other areas, such as the Alpine Slides at Attitash and Alpine Ridge, have expanded summer operations beyond just a scenic chair ride, too. The Balsams, a blue chip resort in Dixville Notch, went the other way: it built a ski area (1,000-foot vertical for alpine, 30 miles of XC trails) to go with its strong summer trade.

Lakes are as attractive to tourists as the mountains. The largest, Lake Winnipesaukee, called by the Indians "the smile of the Great Spirit," has hundreds of cottages along its shores and is said to have over 350 islands. It has been the site of boating events since 1852, when the first race betwen the crews of Harvard and Yale was held.

Tourism ranks second only to manufacturing as a revenue-producer. While many go, of course, to Mount Washington, the many charming towns, fine museums, art centers, summer theaters, and special events entice hundreds of thousands of visitors each year. To people living in congested population areas, New Hampshire is indeed a different world —peaceful, beautiful, a force for stability and steady social progress; invigorating in its climate, filled with educational, cultural, and recreational opportunities and with an economy that is constantly changing and expanding in the pioneering spirit that has prevailed for more than three centuries.

EXPLORING NEW HAMPSHIRE

One of the best ways to discover New Hampshire is to retrace the coastal routes of the earliest seafarers and settlers. While the state has only 18 miles of coastline, it is abundant in Americana.

After you see Portsmouth, which has been a center of shipbuilding and a haven for sailors since the early 1600s, you can head inland, as the early settlers did, southwest to Exeter and beyond.

The Seacoast Region

As you come into New Hampshire from Massachusetts in the south on I-95 or U.S. 1, turn east on State 286 for Seabrook Beach, where you should turn left onto State 1A. From here head north along the coast. If you are in the mood for a refreshing swim, try Seabrook Beach, Hampton Beach, or Great Boars Head, all of which are beautiful and all of which attract hundreds of thousands of visitors during the summer months.

If privacy is more to your liking, continue up the coast a bit farther to Little Boars Head, which has some beautiful summer mansions. The sea lies on your right, and there are several turnoffs where you can stop your car and watch lobster boats and freighters. From these turnoffs you can also see some islands off on the horizon. These are the Isles of Shoals. John Smith, an early explorer, saw them in 1614 and named them Smith's Isles. But fishermen renamed them after noting the shoaling or schooling of fish near their shores.

Farther along you will reach the magnificent summer resort of Wentworth-by-the-Sea. The hulking white haven is taking on a different character in the 1980s; Swiss investors announced plans to convert it into a conference center, but the plans have been slow to get beyond the drawing board. Plans for the elegant old resort are uncertain at this writing. Turn right on State 1B to circle several of the small islands that lie at the mouth of the Piscataqua River. This road will take you on to New Castle, one of the loveliest settlements in New Hampshire. On a side street in this town, a small historical marker commemorates the William & Mary Raids of December 14, 1774. In this action, several hundred men overpowered the small British garrison at Fort William & Mary (now Fort Constitution, New Castle) and removed quantities of military supplies. The raid, set off by Paul Revere's ride to Portsmouth on December 13, was among the first overt acts of the American Revolution. State 1B circles back into Portsmouth, one of the most historically interesting cities in the country. A good place to start your tour is at the restored settlement of Strawbery Banke. This historic reconstruction is a ten-acre section of Old Portsmouth where visitors will see 17th- and 18th-century homes, many on their original foundations, as well as crafts of this early maritime community. The site is open April 15 to November 15. Just across the river is Kittery, Maine.

In 1630, a band of some eighty settlers sponsored by Captain John Mason disembarked on the shores of the Piscataqua River. Finding the embankment covered with wild strawberries, they gave the settlement its original name of Strawbery Banke. Not until 1653 was it changed to Portsmouth.

By the year 1700, the settlement had grown into a prosperous and vigorous community. The fisheries of the Piscataqua employed many ships from the busy yards that had already supplied two warships for the Royal Navy. The ninety sawmills of the Piscataqua region were producing nine million feet of lumber a year and the forests of the region were providing Britain's shipyards with the finest masts and spars the world had ever seen.

The houses kept pace with the burgeoning population. Many displayed the owners' wealth through a lavish use of paneling, carving, and costly furniture. Homes, of modest size and few pretensions, in which craftsmen, mariners, and shopkeepers lived, crowded around the creek, later named Puddle Dock, at the center of Portsmouth's waterfront. The port city flourished on sea commerce for over two centuries, until the advent of the railroad. By 1900, Puddle Dock had gone to ruin and the port city was sadly deteriorated. In the 1930s, a National Park Service plan under the auspices of the WPA sought to preserve and restore many of these old houses. But in the early 1960s, the local Urban Renewal authority recommended that everything in the ten-acre area be demolished. Fortunately, a group of concerned citizens, reject-

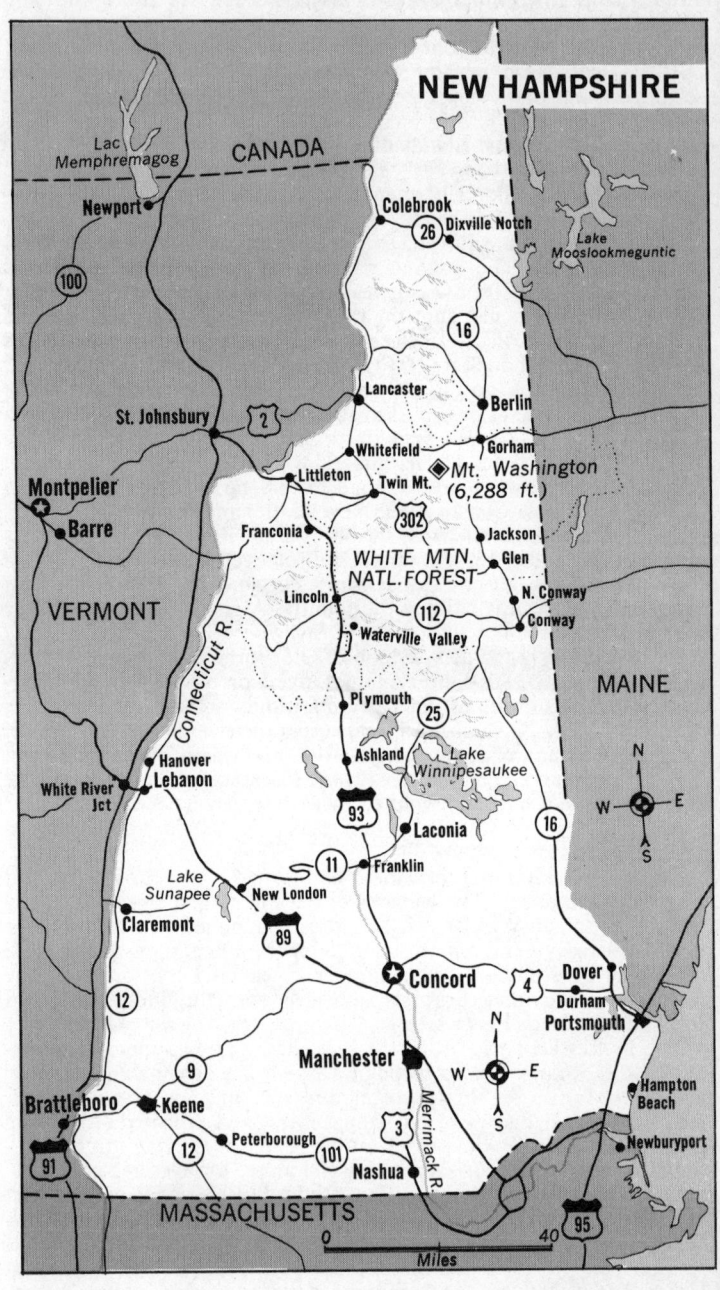

NEW HAMPSHIRE

CANADA

Lac Memphremagog

Newport

Colebrook

26 Dixville Notch

Lake Mooslookmeguntic

100

16

Lancaster

Berlin

St. Johnsbury

2

Whitefield

Gorham

Littleton

Twin Mt.

◆ Mt. Washington (6,288 ft.)

Montpelier

Barre

Franconia

302

Jackson

Glen

WHITE MTN. NATL. FOREST

VERMONT

Lincoln

N. Conway

112

Conway

Waterville Valley

MAINE

Connecticut R.

Plymouth

25

Hanover

Lebanon

Ashland

Lake Winnipesaukee

White River Jct

93

16

Laconia

11

Franklin

N

W   E

S

Lake Sunapee

New London

Claremont

89

Concord

4

Dover

12

Durham

Portsmouth

N

W   E

S

Manchester

Hampton Beach

9

Brattleboro

Keene

Merrimack R.

12

Peterborough

101

3

Newburyport

91

Nashua

95

MASSACHUSETTS

0   40

Miles

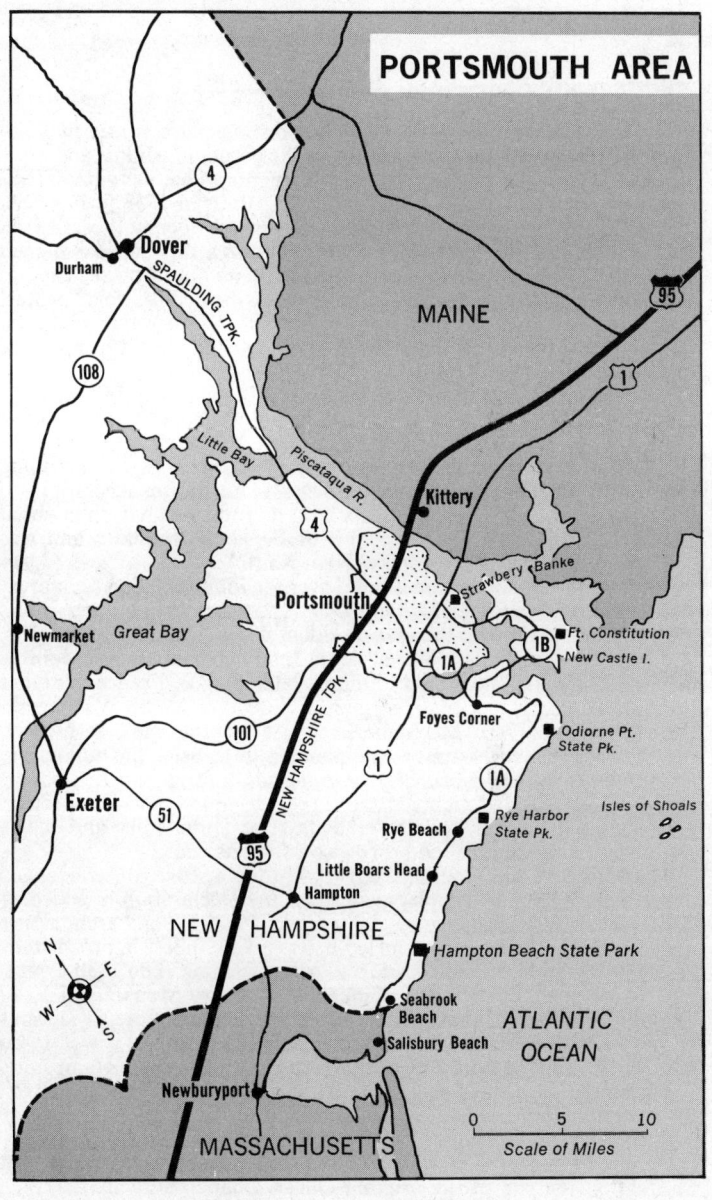

PORTSMOUTH AREA

ing this plan, proposed that urban renewal funds be used for historic preservation, thus Strawbery Banke was reborn.

Portsmouth . . . Beyond Strawbery Banke

Strawbery Banke is not the only interesting place to see in Portsmouth. The John Paul Jones House on the corner of Middle and State Streets contains a valuable collection of memorabilia, including furniture, portraits, china, silver, and costumes. Built in 1758, it has been owned since 1920 by the Portsmouth Historical Society; hostesses in period costumes give conducted tours. Although this house is named after John Paul Jones, he never owned it. It was built by sea captain and merchant Gregory Purcell, whose widow turned it into a "genteel boarding house" in order to support herself and her seven children. Captain Jones merely stayed here while supervising the outfitting of the *America.*

Perhaps the finest example in New England of an early 18th-century urban brick dwelling is the Warner House, 150 Daniel Street. Built in 1716, it is now a registered historic landmark. It has remarkable murals on the staircase walls, an early example of marble-izing in the dining room, and a number of exquisite pieces of furniture. According to historian Charles W. Brewster, "its lightning rod was put up in about 1762 under the personal inspection of Benjamin Franklin and was probably the first put up in New Hampshire."

Another fascinating house is the Governor John Langdon Memorial, 143 Pleasant Street, one of America's greatest Georgian houses. It was built by John Langdon, the first president of the U.S. Senate, in 1784, and was visited by George Washington, John Hancock, James Monroe, General Lafayette and Louis Philippe, later king of France. Another example of nearly perfect Georgian architecture is the Wentworth-Gardner House (1760), Mechanic Street. At one time one of its owners, the Metropolitan Museum of Art, planned to transfer the building to Central Park in New York City. The carving throughout the house is said to have required eighteen months to complete and is especially good along the upper and lower halls. The Dutch tiles and scenic wallpaper in the dining room are also of special note.

The Moffatt-Ladd House (1763), 154 Market Street, once belonged to General William Whipple, a signer of the Declaration of Independence. It is a treasure trove of 18th-century furniture and architecture with spacious, handsomely paneled halls and chambers, a broad staircase with magnificent balustrade and soffit paneling. The 1830 Counting House overlooks the Piscataqua River where Moffatt and Ladd cargoes once were loaded. The elegant gardens and the mysterious secret passage offer an intriguing insight into the life of a well-to-do mercantile family at the end of the 18th century in New Hampshire.

Portsmouth has many other interesting and beautiful houses. So pick up a brochure on the historic houses and interesting places and explore further.

Be sure to stop in at St. John's Church on Chapel Street. It was built in 1808 on the site of the original Queen Chapel, built in 1732. On display is a copy of the rare Vinegar Bible, one of four in existence in the U.S.

There are a great many things to do in Portsmouth besides seeing historic homes and churches. There are a summer theater, a waterfront, and a marvelous trip to the Isles of Shoals by boat. There's a story that prior to ship-to-shore communications, the Isles of Shoals boats would carry carrier pigeons. Once the boat had left Portsmouth, passengers were asked how many expected to eat at the restaurant at the Isles. The number of prospective diners was inscribed on a paper clipped to a pigeon's leg, and the bird would be dispatched to the restaurant.

When you decide to leave Portsmouth, take U.S. 4 to Durham, home of the University of New Hampshire. Stroll about the campus and visit the Paul Arts Center, which has changing exhibitions, concerts, and theater. On campus there are also horticultural exhibits, and the dairy bar has the famed University of New Hampshire ice cream to sample. It is in the former station of the Boston and Maine Railroad. The home of Major Gen. John Sullivan, a Revolutionary war hero, is found in Durham and is open to visitors. There are several fine old homes on Church Hill, at the lower end of the Main Street. The second floor of the Town Office Building contains a historical museum. In Dover, 5 miles north, is the Woodman Institute museum, 182 Central Avenue, open year round.

From Durham take State 108 south to Exeter, home of Phillips Exeter Academy, one of the most famous preparatory schools in the country. Exeter is a handsome, elm-shaped town with a rather belligerent past. Around 1734, British royal agents were here, commandeering prime trees for masts for the Royal Navy. No matter whose property they grew on, the best trees were cut down and shipped to England. Some Exeter men who didn't care for this dressed up as Indians and waylaid some of the tree-nabbing agents at a local tavern. The agents hurried to the river to escape, only to find their boat scuttled. There was nothing for them to do but make the long hike back to Portsmouth.

Exeter's War Memorial is the work of sculptor Daniel Chester French, who was born here. French is probably best known for his statue of our sixteenth president in the Lincoln Memorial in Washington, D.C.

From Exeter take State 111A to State 107, turn right onto 107 and then left (south) when you reach State 102, to Derry. The poet Robert Frost lived here for several years and his home is open to the public Mondays and Tuesdays from late June to Labor Day.

In nearby East Derry is the childhood home of our first astronaut, Alan Shepard Jr. By this time you have probably noticed that in New Hampshire the names of towns are not posted at the entrances of the towns proper. They are found at the legal town lines, which may be miles from the actual hub of the community. Just be patient; the town will come along soon.

The Merrimack Valley

From Derry, take State 28 south to its intersection with State 111, where you turn east toward Salem to Mystery Hill, which now bills itself as America's Stonehenge. At the least, the site is highly controversial. There have been many speculations over the stone structures here for the last 40 years. The early professional and amateur archeologists theorized that the structures might have been erected by a colonial farmer involved in smuggling, or perhaps they were made by a group of monks who left Ireland back in the 10th century to escape the Scandinavian invasions of their country. However, continuing research now dates these structures at around 2000 B.C., which would make them the oldest manmade construction in North America. In 1975 inscriptions on the stones were identified by Dr. Barry Fell, a linguistics professor at Harvard, as being in characters used only by the ancient Celts along the Iberian peninsula in pre-Christian times.

It has been determined that Mystery Hill was a system for determining the annual equinoxes and solstices, as well as other astronomical events. It is a fascinating place to see, whatever its history. Open May 1 to October 31, weekends in April and November.

From Mystery Hill take State 111 southwest to Benson's Wild Animal Farm. It's open from early April through January (weekends only after Labor Day) and will interest adults as well as children. New shipments of animals keep arriving for training and exhibition. The beautiful grounds and landscaped gardens are perfect for a picnic.

Continue on 111 southwest to Nashua. Primarily an industrial city, Nashua was originally a trading post to which Indians brought fur pelts from the north. The Arts and Science Center, 41 East Pearl Street, is open all year with exhibitions and classes for both adults and children.

Take State 101A west from Nashua and turn right (north when you come to 101). You'll soon reach Amherst (named for Lord Jeffrey Amherst), a lovely little village. President Franklin Pierce married Jane Appleton here in 1834, and George W. Kendall, who founded *The New Orleans Picayune,* was born here. Also born here was Horace Greeley, founder of *The New York Tribune.* After exploring Amherst, return to State 101 and continue north. A few miles farther, you will find a marker for Greeley, who made "Go West, Young Man!" a famous admonition.

Manchester

Just beyond Bedford is Manchester, New Hampshire's largest city. The Manchester Institute of Arts and Sciences, 148 Concord Street, has very interesting exhibits as well as classes in arts and crafts. The Currier Gallery of Art, 192 Orange Street, has an outstanding collection of American and European paintings, sculpture, New England furniture, silver, glass, etc. There are also special exhibits each month, and guided tours can be arranged by appointment. Here, too, is the Manchester Historic Association, 129 Amherst Street, where early documents, Indian relics, and old tools are displayed. At State Park, by the Merrimack River, is a memorial to General John Stark, a member of Roger's Rangers during the French and Indian Wars. He is remembered for the phrase "Live free or die," later adopted as the state's motto. The great Amoskeag Manufacturing Company, once the largest textile mill in the world, thrived here. During the Depression, however, the company filed for bankruptcy. A group of farsighted businessmen bought it, leasing or selling sections of the complex to new and smaller companies. In less than ten years more than 100 firms and their employees were established on the site of the lost company.

A nice stopover after Manchester is Candia. To reach it, take State 101 east out of Manchester to 101B, where you turn left, then right onto State 107A.

Originally Candia was known as Charming Fare. Sam Walter Foss used to live here; his name is little known, but many people may remember his poem that begins, "Let me live in my house by the side of the road." The Fitts Museum here has a nice collection of Americana and local memorabilia.

State 107A joins 107 at Deerfield. John Simpson set out from this town one day in June of 1775 for Bunker Hill, where he was credited with firing the first shot of the battle. When he returned home from the war as a major, he went back to farming and never applied for a pension. He explained, "My country is too poor to pay for pensions."

If you travel through this area in August or September, be sure to check the local papers for county fairs and festivals, which are great fun to attend.

Concord, Canterbury: Movers & Shakers

To reach Concord, head north on State 107, then turn west onto U.S. 202; presently you'll find yourself in the capital of New Hampshire. The State House, 107 North Main Street, was completed in 1819 and is notable for its architecture and landscaping. The military-minded, or anyone fascinated by flags, will want to visit the Hall of Flags, with battle flags of New Hampshire's troops from the 18th century to the present. The State House also has some excellent portraits and statues of Daniel Webster and other New Hampshire notables.

The New Hampshire Historical Society at 30 Park Street is open all year (closed weekends). Its permanent exhibits include four period rooms depicting New Hampshire domestic interiors from 1680 to 1720. Western movie fans will want to see the original Concord Coach. This large stagecoach carried many settlers westward. The Historical Society also has samples of New Hampshire furniture and some fine paintings.

Concord's First Church of Christ Scientist, on North State Street, is particularly noteworthy. It was established by Mary Baker Eddy, founder of the Christian Science movement. Mrs. Eddy, who lived for a long time in Concord, was born in nearby Bow, New Hampshire.

Concord is also the home of the main display center and salesroom of the League of New Hampshire Craftsmen. The shop is at 205 North Main Street. Although it is open all year, you should contact the director of the League for hours of the various shops and craft centers statewide (224–3375).

When you leave Concord, head north on I–93 to the Canterbury cutoff. Drive east, watching for a sign directing you to Canterbury Center and the Shaker Settlement. The village here was built by one of the last Shaker groups in the country. There is a most interesting museum of Shaker handicrafts and inventions, and this is one of just two villages where you may see one or more of the last living "sisters" of the sect; the other is the village of Sabbathday Lake, Maine. Canterbury, where the first of the 22 buildings was built in 1792, is open mid-May to mid-October, closed Sundays and Mondays.

Now head west until you reach U.S. 3, and drive north along the banks of the Merrimack River to Franklin. This town was named in honor of Benjamin Franklin, and was the birthplace of Daniel Webster. You can still visit the Webster family cabin, which has many relics and pieces of period furniture. Open Sundays only, July and August, plus the last week of August.

From Franklin take State 11 east to Tilton, and then 140 to Gilmanton. While the name of this town may mean nothing to you, it was the home for some years of Grace Metalious, and was reputedly the real-life original of now-not-so-scandalous *Peyton Place*. It's a charming, sleepy little town with a meeting house that was built in 1774. The

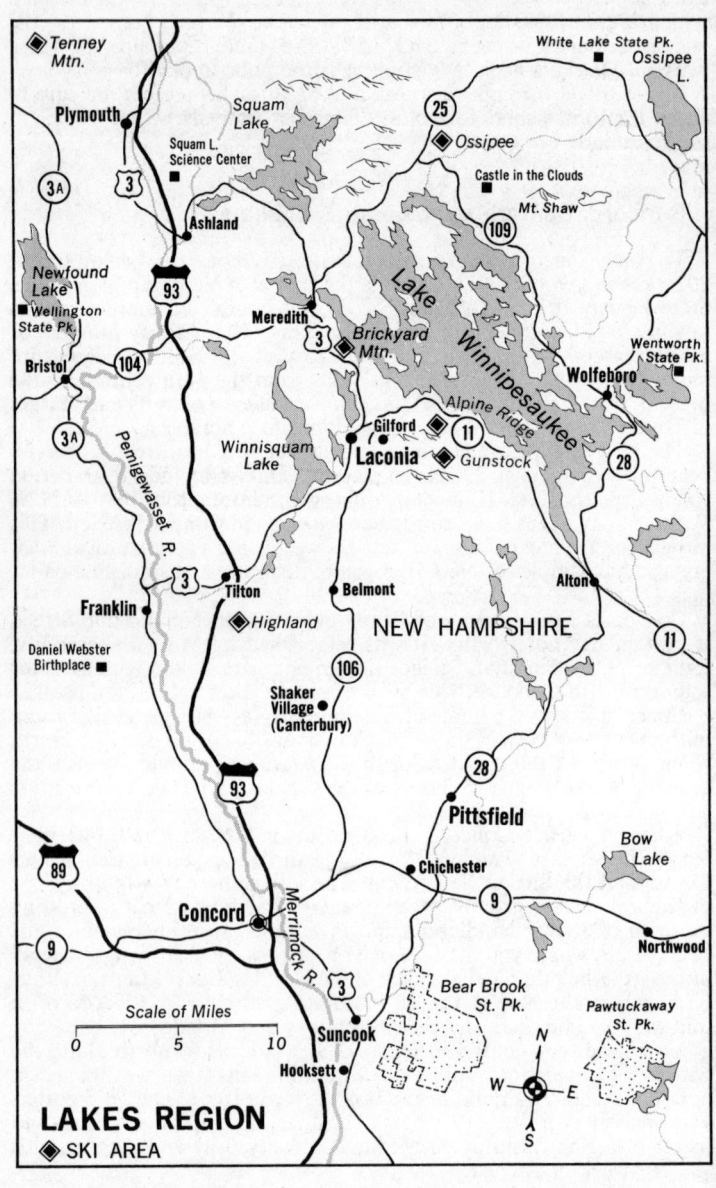

◈ Tenney Mtn.

White Lake State Pk. ■ Ossipee L.

Plymouth

Squam Lake

Squam L. Science Center ■

25

◈ Ossipee

Castle in the Clouds ■ Mt. Shaw

3A

3

109

Ashland

Newfound Lake

93

■ Wellington State Pk.

Meredith

3

◈ Brickyard Mtn.

Lake Winnipesaukee

Wentworth State Pk. ■

Bristol

104

Wolfeboro

3A

Winnisquam Lake

Gilford ●

Alpine Ridge

11

28

Pemigewasset R.

Laconia

◈ Gunstock

Tilton

● Belmont

Alton

Franklin

◈ Highland

NEW HAMPSHIRE

11

Daniel Webster Birthplace ■

106

Shaker Village (Canterbury) ●

93

28

89

Pittsfield

Bow Lake

9

● Chichester

Concord

Merrimack R.

9

Northwood ●

3

Bear Brook St. Pk.

Pawtuckaway St. Pk.

Scale of Miles

0   5   10

Suncook

N

Hooksett

W ✦ E

LAKES REGION

◈ SKI AREA

S

natives may be reticent about *Peyton Place,* but will be happy to show you Ralph Waldo Emerson's old school.

The Lakes Region, Water and Mountains

As you head north on Route 107 toward Laconia, you may want to sample some of the local nectar at White Mountain Vineyards (open all year, closed Sundays). Vineyard and winery tours available in summer; open weekends in spring and fall, by appointment in winter.

A couple of miles farther north is Laconia, the major community in the Lakes Region. There are several alpine ski areas, headed by county-run Gunstock, and some cross-country skiing available plus the annual sled dog championships in February, but this is primarily a warm weather resort area. Weirs Beach, just up the road, has a steady string of special events throughout the summer.

Winnipesaukee, as might be expected, has plenty of places to rent boats, go swimming, take cruises on the lake or just enjoy a beer or a meal at a lakeside table. There is also an Alpine Slide at Alpine Ridge in Gilford (open mid-May to Columbus Day; 293–4304) and the Wolfeboro Rail Road (659–4884).

At Holderness, the Squam Lakes Science Center on Route 3 has programs on ecology as well as exhibits. In addition to live animals, there is a sawmill, a sugar house, a blacksmith shop, and hiking trails.

From Center Harbor, continue northeast to Moultonborough. Just before Moultonborough, you'll come to the Castle in the Clouds, 6,000 acres of natural beauty. Here you can get magnificent views of Lake Winnipesaukee and the White Mountains. The magnificent mansion was built in 1910 by Thomas Gustavus Plant, an eccentric, unusually short millionaire. His idol was Napoleon, and portraits and other memorabilia of the Little Corsican adorn Plant's favorite rooms. The Castle is open daily from late June until mid-October and on weekends from early May to late June. There are also superb hiking trails for novice and expert alike, and in Moultonborough Corner, on Route 25 you'll come to the Old Country Store and Museum. While many will pass it by as a tourist trap, others will enjoy its wide selection of maple products, penny candy, and small gift items.

Continue south on 109 and you will come to Wolfeboro, on the shores of Lake Winnipesaukee. Boat trips from Wolfeboro cruise the lake. The Libby Museum of natural history, open late June through Labor Day (closed Mondays), has special art exhibits as well as exhibits of Indian artifacts. The Wolfeboro Rail Road offers steam- and diesel-powered train runs from mid-May through mid-October.

Continuing south, take State 28, at South Wolfeboro, to Alton. This entire area is a summer colony. At Alton, take State 11 south to Farmington. From Farmington, head north on State 153 to Union. In winter you can ski at Moose Mountain, a medium-size area.

From Union, head north on 16 to Whittier, named for poet John Greenleaf Whittier, who spend many summers here and wrote several poems about the region. Mount Whittier has a spectacular gondola lift that is open from the end of May to late October as well as during the ski season.

From Whittier turn north on State 113 to Tamworth. There is an excellent summer theater here called Barnstormers Theater. Open July to August, it offers a wide selection of drama and comedy, as well as an occasional musical, by a resident company. Continuing north on

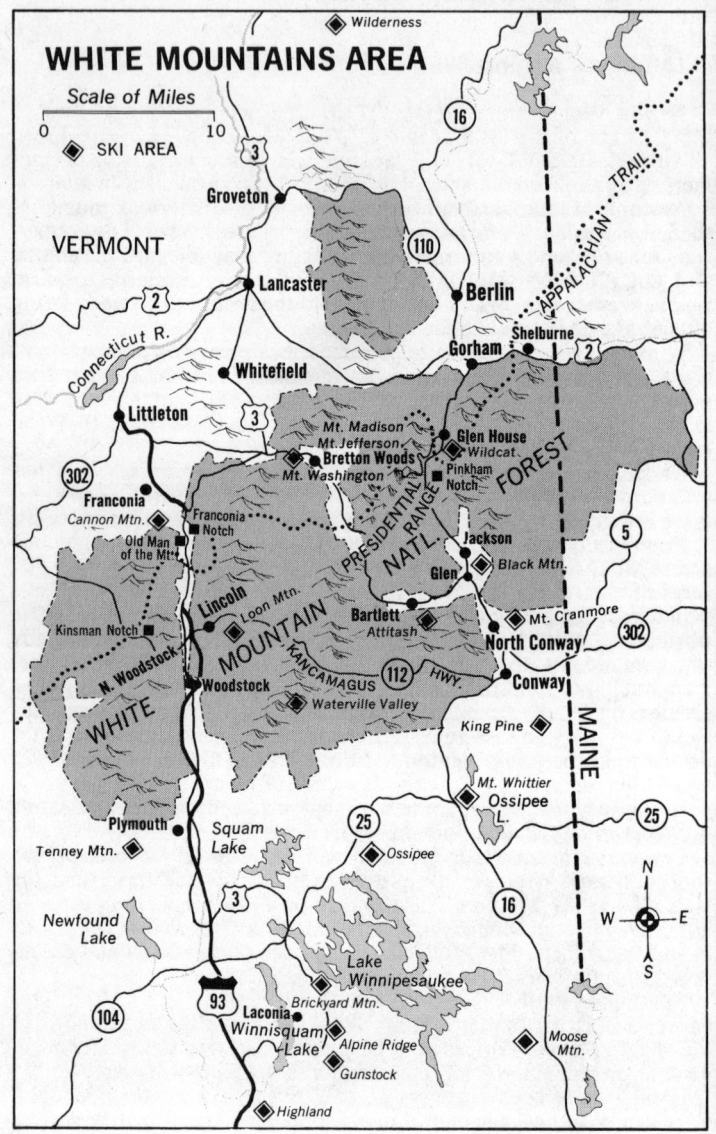

WHITE MOUNTAINS AREA

Scale of Miles

0   10

◆ SKI AREA

Wilderness

VERMONT

Groveton

Lancaster

Connecticut R.

Whitefield

Littleton

Berlin

Shelburne

Gorham

Franconia

Cannon Mtn.

Old Man of the Mtn.

Franconia Notch

Kinsman Notch

Mt. Madison
Mt. Jefferson
Bretton Woods
Mt. Washington

Glen House
Wildcat
Pinkham Notch

PRESIDENTIAL RANGE

NAT'L.

FOREST

Jackson

Glen

Black Mtn.

Lincoln

Loon Mtn.

MOUNTAIN

Bartlett
Attitash

Mt. Cranmore

North Conway

N. Woodstock

Woodstock

KANCAMAGUS HWY.

Waterville Valley

Conway

King Pine

WHITE

Plymouth

Tenney Mtn.

Squam Lake

Ossipee

Mt. Whittier
Ossipee L.

MAINE

Newfound Lake

Laconia

Winnisquam Lake

Brickyard Mtn.

Lake Winnipesaukee

Alpine Ridge

Gunstock

Highland

Moose Mtn.

N
W   E
S

113, you'll come to the Madison Boulder Wayside Area. This boulder is 83 feet long, 37 feet wide, and 23 feet high; geologists believe it was brought from farther north by a glacier flow. Some say it is the largest displaced boulder in America.

Mount Washington Valley/White Mountains Region

There are two covered bridges on 113 at Conway on the southern edge of the Mount Washington Valley with many more in the surrounding area. Farther north in North Conway, you'll find some of the most spectacular views of the White Mountains. North Conway is a true tourist town with a neon-lined "strip" (Route 16) and plenty of shops, restaurants, inns and motels . . . and views. Conway Scenic Railroad, which sends its puffer-belly engines down along the Saco River, chugs out of the bubbletop train depot weekends in May and early June, daily from mid-June to late October. There's a small train museum in the depot, too. Mount Cranmore became one of the cradles of alpine skiing when skimeister Hannes Schneider fled the Nazis as they hit Austria in the late-1930s. Schneider's so-called Arlberg instructional method was one of the sport's earliest and most popular teaching styles. Cranmore's Skimobile is like riding a golf cart to the top of the modest (1,500-ft. vertical) hill.

Just north of town on 16 is a breathtaking vista of the White Mountains; then continue to Glen. Storyland and Heritage New Hampshire are side-by-side on 16; take a right at the junction with U.S. 302. Storyland is geared to the kid in all of us, an immaculately clean collection of rides and storybook scenes with Cinderella's Castle and other fairy-tale settings. Next door is Heritage New Hampshire, a multi-media presentation set in a Colonial-style building. You start by boarding the 1634 sailing voyage which brought the first settlers from England, and you traipse through Granite State history, see an Indian settlement, meet Daniel Webster, and sit in on a town meeting. Well done. Both attractions are open through late October; Heritage opens on Memorial Day, Storyland on Father's Day.

A few miles north, hang a right at a covered bridge and make at least a short visit to picturesque Jackson; there are a couple of abandoned old resort hotels, but the rest of the village is tidy. The Christmas Farm Inn up the hill on 16B dates back to Revolutionary times, but it's thoroughly modern in comfort.

Continuing north on 16, you'll come to the Glen Ellis Falls Scenic Area and Wildcat Mountain (466–3326) with its gondola cable car (the first such enclosed car in America).

The Mount Washington Auto Road begins from Glen House. It's an eight-mile trip to the top of the 6,288-foot mountain, and after about four miles you pass the timberline. The road was first hacked out as a carriage road in 1861 and is considered by some to be the first manmade tourist attraction in this country. P.T. Barnum once called this trip "the second greatest show on earth."

The views from the top of the mountain are superb. Equally marvelous is the history of its discovery. In 1642, a man named Darby Field found the mountain and scaled it. Field, and two Indians who went with him, are the first known humans to climb the peak, but historians credit Giovanni Verrazano, for whom the Verrazano Bridge in New York City is named, with first sighting it in 1524. Sailing on the Maine coast, he noted in his log "high mountains within the land." Gerhardus

Mercator put it on his great map in 1569. Today, a multi-million dollar summit complex has replaced the ramshackle wooden summit building. There are also a television transmitter and a weather station where on April 12, 1934, the wind velocity reached an incredible 231 mph—the highest ever recorded in the United States. Bring a windbreaker or sweater with you since the weather changes quickly up here and, even if it's sunny when you start up in your car, by cog railroad, or in one of the specially designed "stages," it could be cloudy or even raining when you reach the top.

When you get back down to Route 16, head north. A right turn at Route 2 in Gorham and it's a mile or so to the spectacular Shelburne Birches, perhaps a half-mile of gorgeous white birch trees clustered on both sides of the road. Retreat to Route 16 and head north to Berlin—and they pronounce it BER-lin up here. There is a Russian Orthodox church with lovely onion domes, and just outside of town is Nansen Ski Jump, once the tallest jump in the country (171½ ft.). Berlin is also the home of "Big Bella," a mobile horn with an earsplitting hoot used to lead lost campers out of the surrounding woods.

The region farther north on State 16, towards Errol, begins to look like a backdrop for Santa Claus, for it is covered with spruce trees. Before going up to Errol you might want to pack lunch; there aren't many restaurants in this north country. But there are some fine spots to stop for views: for example, Dixville Notch and Colman State Park. At Dixville Notch you'll find more Alpine ruggedness than anywhere else in New Hampshire. At the far end of Dixville Notch you'll come to the Wilderness Ski Area, which is part of the Balsams resort, a modest ski area (a thousand-foot vertical drop) at a remote, well-kept Moorish-looking hotel in the middle of its own 15,000 areas. Way up near the roof of New Hampshire, the Balsams is a self-contained playpen with year-round activities.

A little farther north on 26, you'll come to the intersection with 145. Take it north to the Colebrook Fish Hatchery, an interesting spot to visit for adults and children alike.

New Hampshire's Wild West

Much of the area around Colebrook still resembles the frontier towns of the west. This was an area settled by hunters and fishermen. Today, north on State 145 at Pittsburg, you can still pan for gold at Indian Stream. The covered bridges at Happy Corner and River Road are the state's northernmost.

During the Revolution much of this area was claimed by both Canada and the United States. Finally, bored with being the object of this territorial tug-of-war, the inhabitants formed their own local government and in 1832 declared themselves the independent Republic of Indian Stream. However, three years later, after an altercation with Canadian authorities, the New Hampshire militia moved in and the republic was dissolved. In 1840, the area took the name of Pittsburg and soon after the Webster-Ashburton Treaty gave the region to New Hampshire, finally settling the dispute.

By now you are probably as far north as you want to go. The adventurous may travel onward through some of the most unspoiled land in the country up to the Canadian border, spending a few nights camping out in the Connecticut Lakes State Forest. This is where the Connecticut River begins.

Should you turn around and head south back to Colebrook, you'll come to the shrine of Our Lady of Grace (237–5511). Operated by the Oblate Fathers, it encompasses 35 acres of beautiful grounds. It is open for services Sunday afternoons, from May through October, and special group services can be requested.

About 30 miles south on State 3 is Lancaster, noteworthy for St. Paul's Episcopal Church and for a nearby house built in 1859, which has often been called the House of the Seven Gables (the "real" one is in Salem, Massachusetts), though if you count its gables carefully you will discover there are actually nine. Charles Farrar Browne, whose famous pen name was Artemus Ward, spent his early writing years here.

From Lancaster, continue south on 3 a few miles for spectacular views from a famous hilltop here. At Weeks State Park, a road will take you to the top of Mount Prospect. This 430-acre area was once the summer estate of John Wingate Weeks, who, as a member of Congress, worked successfully to establish the White Mountain National Forest.

If you want to spend a truly refreshing night (or a few) in the Whitefield area, return to State 3 and turn at the sign for Mountain View House. This charming hotel, with excellent dining facilities, has origins going back to 1865, when some stranded travelers from a stage-coach party were given a night's hospitality in a little farmhouse. The party stayed a few days, and enjoyed their hosts so much that they spent several weeks with them the following summer. It was then that William and Mary Jane Dodge decided to take in boarders. Since that time the farmhouse has expanded to 200 rooms, with golf, tennis, and a heated pool, as well as sumptuous rooms and dining facilities. The inn has a breathtaking view of the Presidential Range.

South at Whitefield, take State 116 east to Jefferson. North and south of Jefferson on intersecting State 2, you'll find several spots—most rather commercial—that might be of interest, especially if you have children in tow. Santa's Village is open mid-June to early October, and is the "home" of Santa Claus and animals in 25 different settings. Fallow deer and ducks meander freely around the grounds, eating from your hand, and kids can climb onto Santa's lap. There are also a magic castle, animal acts, and rides. Six Gun City, at the junction of Routes 2 and 15, is open mid-June to Labor Day, weekends into mid-October. They deputize kids to track down desperadoes, have a free stagecoach and pony rides, and a wagon museum.

The Waumbek Arts Center (586–4350), also in Jefferson, sets up housekeeping each summer on the grounds of the old Waumbek Inn, which folded in 1973 after 120 years in operation. The center conducts sculpture and crafts workshops from about the 4th of July to Labor Day. There also are musical productions and performances.

Down to Crawford Notch

From Jefferson, head south (right) on State 115A until you reach State 3 again. Turn left at 3 and again at Twin Mountain, taking U.S. 302 to Crawford Notch.

At Crawford Notch State Park you will be treated to some rugged scenery. South of the Silver Cascade is a sign marking the site of an eerie event that occurred in 1826 and was later recounted by Nathaniel Hawthorne in *Twice-Told Tales*. That year, there was a great landslide, which thundered into the valley just above the site of a house belonging to the Willey family. Hearing the roar of the slide, the entire family rushed out of the house to what they believed to be safer ground. Would-be rescuers were astonished to find the house still standing the following day. It seems the slide had been diverted into two streams by a huge boulder that stood just in back of the house. But the slide had flowed together farther on and the unfortunate family was crushed beneath the rubble.

If that kind of site isn't your cup of tea, perhaps the resort at Bretton Woods can provide some relaxation. The Mount Washington Hotel, open only in warm weather, dates back to the start of the century and at one point would see up to fifty trains arrive daily with guests—some came on their own private trains. The hotel, largest frame structure in New England, is the centerpiece for Bretton Woods resort, which includes condominiums, a golf course, plenty of tennis courts, riding stables, not to mention indoor and outdoor pools. In winter, there are alpine and cross-country trails. Bretton Woods was the site of the 1982 national cross-country ski championships, and a 50-kilometer cross-country ski marathon is held each March.

Mount Washington Cog Railroad

About a mile west of the resort on U.S. 302 is the turn for the cog railway. Safety precautions have been tightened since an accident in 1968 killed 8 and injured more than 50 passengers; the state keeps a close eye on the wooden tracks and trestles leading to the summit. For train buffs this is a must, and even the timid should enjoy the memorabilia at the bottom.

The story of this engineering feat, the first mountain-climbing cog railway in the world, is amazing. At the time the railroad was contemplated, scoffers suggested one might as well try to "build a railroad to the moon"; but in 1858, a model engine and cog railway was exhibited before the New Hampshire State Legislature, which, probably to its own surprise, granted a charter for this venture. Work began in April of 1866, and at the end of August the first demonstration was successfully given. After a great deal of engineering ingenuity and back-breaking labor, the track was laid to the top. Passenger service was inaugurated on July 4, 1869, and has continued to the present day, halting service for one year during World War I and for three years during World War II. The railway is 3½ miles long, most of it trestle-mounted; the steepest grade is called Jacob's Ladder. Arriving at the top, you may be surprised to see hikers who have trekked up along one of the many foot trails rising along the Presidential Range.

After descending, take the main highway (302) up to Littleton, continuing from there on State 18 to the Samuel C. Moore Power Station and Dam. This enormous hydroelectric station has a capacity of 190,000 kilowatts. Visitors are welcome at the plant and tours are given during the summer months.

Returning to Littleton, take 302 to Bethlehem. Here turn south again on 18. On this road west of Mount Agassiz, you'll find another stopoff for a breathtaking view of the White Mountains, as well as Vermont's Green Mountains. Continue south on 18 to Franconia. Robert Frost lived here for several years; as a summer resort the town attracted such figures as Washington Irving, Nathaniel Hawthorne, William Cullen Bryant, John Greenleaf Whittier, and Henry Wadsworth Longfellow. A powerboat regatta is held in Franconia in mid-September.

The first ski school in the United States was established in Franconia in 1929 by Sig Buchmayr, an Austrian ski expert, at Peckett's-on-Sugar Hill. Peckett's is long gone, burned down years ago, but a marker designates the site and Franconia remains rich in skiing. Cannon Mountain is a state-run ski area with some of the toughest (and most gentle) trails in the East; wind can be a problem in winter. While Cannon flourishes, locals shake their heads over the Mittersill resort. Started by an Austrian baron, the area was poorly sited; chalets that were built around the Mittersill Inn were sold, and the area has been floudering under different owners since the mid-1970s. Beyond Mittersill, State 18 joins 3. Turn south and you'll be in Franconia Notch State Park. There are many things to do and see here. For instance, you can take the Cannon Mountain Aerial Tramway which operates in summer as well as winter. The first such tramway in the U.S. when it was built in 1938, it was replaced in 1980 with an 80-passenger car which runs to an observation platform at the summit. There are also several footpaths ringing the summit.

The Old Man of the Mountain

From here you will see the "Old Man of the Mountain" (described by Hawthorne in "The Great Stone Face"). This profile rises above a steep precipice that plunges down toward the gorge. Geologists surmise it was formed over 200 million years ago. Farther along the notch is the Basin, a granite pothole 20 feet in diameter at the foot of a waterfall. Experts believe it was eroded in this manner some 25,000 years ago, while a glacier of the last Ice Age was melting. Here too is the Flume, a natural chasm 800 feet long. With walls 12 to 20 feet apart, rising 60 to 70 feet above you, it terminates at the 25-foot Avalanche Falls. There are bus rides and many footpaths within the notch area, and it is well worth a stopover for its stunning views and cool, tree-shaded walkways. Farther south on Route 3, there are two more family attractions, Fantasy Farm with a variety of rides and a chance to feed animals, and Clark's Trading Post with several delightful trained bears, an Americana Museum, and a steam train ride.

Off Route 3, the Kancamagus Highway, one of the most popular routes for autumn's parade of foliage followers, is just south of Clark's and leads to Loon Mountain, which, with Waterville Valley, about 10 miles south on Route 3, has become a major year-round resort. Both have extensive snowmaking, and alpine and cross-country skiing in winter. In summer, Waterville has more than a dozen tennis courts and a 9-hole golf course. The area around Loon—in Lincoln—has seen an astounding surge in condominium building, indicative of the area's growth in popularity; Loon has a year-round schedule of events, including a Scottish clans weekend in September.

At North Woodstock, turn west on State 112 to Lost River Reservation. You will discover Paradise Falls and an alpine garden in a natural setting. There is also a good mineral collection. Sponsored by Society for the Protection of New Hampshire Forests, it is an appealing place to visit for young and old alike.

From Lost River, head east on 112 about a mile down the hill to the junction with State 118 and turn right (south). Warren has the Morse Museum, open from Memorial Day to Labor Day. Here you'll find a collection of mounted animals and trophies from the African jungle, as well as a collection of curios from around the world. Stay on Routes

25 and 118 (which join north of Warren) to the Polar Caves in Plymouth, a series of glacial caves and a maple museum. Continue southeast on 25 to 3A, turning right (south) to Bristol (do not follow Route 3A straight ahead to Plymouth). As you head south, you skirt Newfound Lake. The fourth largest lake in New Hampshire, it is considered by some the most scenic, with majestic Mount Cardigan as a backdrop.

At Bristol, take State 104 southwest to Danbury and turn right on U.S. 4, leading to some rock-hound territory, with the Ruggles Mine, oldest mica mine in the U.S. (1803). Here are mine tunnels, pits, and specimens galore for the picking. The Ruggles Mine exhibit includes many regional specimens. Open late May to mid-October.

The Upper Valley: Dartmouth/Lake Sunapee Region

Stay west on 4 to Lebanon as you come into what local residents call the Upper Valley since this is part of the upper reaches of the Connecticut River. Turn right onto State 120 to Hanover, site of Dartmouth College and Hopkins Center, the cultural focus for the entire region. Dartmouth's campus is a pleasure to stroll through. Baker Memorial Library has famous Orozco murals. The library has a rare books division and a special collection donated by explorer and author Vilhajalmur Stefansson on Artic, Antarctic, and permafrost regions.

Dartmouth is the oldest educational institution in New Hampshire. It was chartered in 1769 under a grant from King George III. Besides its outstanding liberal arts program, it has high-quality professional schools of medicine, engineering, and business administration.

For the tourist, however, it is the Hopkins Center that is Dartmouth's greatest attraction. Open year round, it includes two theaters, a concert hall, four art galleries, films, exhibitions, and a sculpture court. There are practice rooms, studios for painting, designing, sculpture, ceramics, wood, metal-working, costume and scenery workshops, and rehearsal rooms. For a schedule, write to the Hopkins Center, Hanover NH 03755.

From Hanover, State 10 will take you south to West Lebanon and to State 12A South. After Plainfield, which is home to the Maxfield Parrish Museum, noted painter and cover artist for major magazines in the 1930s and '40s, watch for signs for the St. Gaudens National Historic Site in Cornish. In summer there are special art exhibits and Sunday concerts. The house and grounds are beautiful and the sculptor's studio is fascinating. He is especially noted for *The Puritan* and for the statue of Lincoln now found in Chicago's Lincoln Park. Another American notable from this area, whose home on 12A is denoted by a marker, was Salmon P. Chase, who served for a time as Lincoln's secretary of the treasury. Chase, a prominent figure in the defense of fugitive slaves, originated our national banking system, and his picture appears on the ten-thousand-dollar bill. (The bill's denomination has, however, prevented Chase's features from becoming as familiar as Abraham Lincoln's.) Continue south on 12A and on your right you'll see the Windsor-Cornish covered bridge, which crosses the Connecticut River to Windsor, Vermont. This covered bridge is 460 feet long, was built in 1866, and is the longest in the United States; it also is one of four in this immediate area.

South of here, turn left on State 103 to Claremont, a tired old mill town. The community got a boost in the late 1970s when the federal government designated its red brick mills as a national historic site, but help has been slow in coming to restore the riverside structures. Just south of Claremont, in Charlestown, a river community, is Old Fort No. 4, a re-creation of the original French & Indian War stockade. The fort went up in 1745 for defense against Indians. Backtracking into Claremont, continue on 103 to Newport. The highly photogenic Congregational Church here was bult in 1822 and has a Paul Revere bell. Newport was also the site of the Little Red Schoolhouse (since removed to Sudbury, Mass.).

In Newport, you can also tour the Newport Historic Museum. It is on the second floor of the District Court House on Court Square.

From Newport take State 11 to New London, a pretty hilltop town. The Colby-Sawyer College campus is a pleasant place to walk about, and King Ridge Ski Area (526–6966), a fine family ski area, holds lobster bakes and occasional concerts in summer.

From New London, return on 11 a mile or so to State 103A, taking this road south to Newbury. Where it joins 103, turn right. You'll find Mount Sunapee State Park, with four-passenger gondolas which go 2,700 feet up to the summit, where there are a cafeteria and observation platforms. Mount Sunapee also boasts a fabulous beach with bath houses if you happen to be touring during the summer.

Just beyond Sunapee State Park, west on 103, take the unmarked road to Goshen, then State 10 a very short distance to State 31. On 31, drive south to Washington, one of New Hampshire's most pristine towns, with a 1729 meeting house. In December of 1776, it took its name in honor of George Washington. Although it claims to have been the first to do so, in fact Washington, North Carolina, can claim that honor, for its name is documented as dating from October 1, 1776.

Continuing south and east on 31, you'll come to Hillsborough—the home of Franklin Pierce, the 14th President. The Homestead is just off the highway and is open to the public all summer.

Monadnocks Region

From Hillsborough, take U.S. 202 to Antrim; several miles beyond (past Bennington), take the unmarked road to Hancock. It's a very pretty town with a village green (naturally) and beside Norway Pond is a Congregational Church with a three-tiered steeple. The Paul Revere bell still calls the congregation to worship. The town was named, of course, for John Hancock. From Hancock, go east on an unmarked road to Greenfield. Just north of this community is the Crotched Mountain Rehabilitation Center. Hundreds of visitors come here every year to see this handsome, widely known center for training deaf, mute, and otherwise handicapped children and adults. Contact the Center for an appointment (547–3311).

From Greenfield continue south on State 31, turning west at Wilton on 101. At Miller State Park, you'll find a road to the summit of Pack Monadnock Mountain, with spectacular views from the 2,288-foot elevation. When the season is right (May), stop at the beautiful Curtis Dogwood Reservation at Lyndeborough just off 31 from Wilton.

Continue west on 101. Just before Peterborough, watch for signs to Sharon to the left on 123. South on this road, you'll find the Sharon Arts Center (924–7256). Its many exhibits of arts and crafts make it a favorite with visitors.

By now, you are in the heart of what has been called the Currier & Ives Corner of New Hampshire.

South of Sharon, turn left on 124 to New Ipswich. This was the site of New Hampshire's first textile mill. The Barrett House here is a Federal Period mansion with outstanding period furniture. Barrett House is open June to Columbus Day, except for Mondays, Wednesdays and Fridays.

From New Ipswich, retrace your route and drive north on 124 to Jaffrey. There are over 200 lakes in the Monadnock area, and Jaffrey's Woodbound Lake is a beauty. The Meeting House here is noteworthy not only for its age (1774) and its Revere bell, but also for its old burying ground. Among the headstones you'll find one marking the grave of an ex-slave named Amos Fortune. At the age of sixty, he bought his freedom and came to Jaffrey, where he gained fame as the area's best tanner. His gravestone reads: "Sacred to the memory of Amos Fortune, who was born free in Africa. A slave in America, he purchased liberty, professed Christianity, lived reputably and died hopefully Nov. 17 1801, At 91." At his death, Fortune left $100 to the church and $233.85 to the town for its public school. The Amos Fortune Forum, established in his memory, brings many outstanding speakers to the Jaffrey Meeting House.

Distinguished American writer Willa Cather is also buried here. While at the nearby MacDowell Colony one summer, she became so fond of the Meeting House and grounds she requested that this be her final resting place.

Peterborough and the MacDowell Colony

North from Jaffrey on U.S. 202 is Peterborough. This little town, home of the MacDowell Colony, is well known to creative people. After the death of composer Edward MacDowell, his wife and friends established this composers' and writers' refuge in his memory. Among those who came here were Edwin Arlington Robinson, Stephen Vincent Benet (*The Devil and Daniel Webster* may have been inspired here), Willa Cather, Elinor Wylie, William Rose Benet, Padraic Colum, Thornton Wilder, and many others. Here Wilder wrote *The Bridge at San Luis Rey,* and perhaps gathered background material for the classic *Our Town,* whose setting is a mythical New Hampshire hamlet. Peterborough still flourishes as a gathering place of aspiring and established creative talent.

Just beyond Peterborough, west on State 101, is Dublin. The town used to be the nucleus of a large summer colony attracting such figures as Mark Twain and Amy Lowell. It is also publishing headquarters for both *Yankee* magazine and *The Old Farmer's Almanac.* Just beyond the center of Dublin, take a right turn on an unnumbered road north to Harrisville and Nelson. Harrisville is a striking little mill town built almost entirely of red brick. A lovely church and vestry (the latter used for services in winter, as it is easier to heat) dominate the scene on serene Harrisville Pond.

Beyond, at Nelson, there is a well-preserved monument that reads: "Nelson will cherish in perpetual remembrance the memory of her heroic Sons who fell in the War of Great Rebellion for the Preservation of Liberty, and the Unity of the Republic. 1861–1865." The inscription is typical of what you will find on many Union soldier monuments; New England states, especially northern New England, viewed what we call the Civil War as "the War of Great Rebellion."

Beyond Nelson, turn south at State 9, which soon joins State 10, to Keene. It was here that John Dickson composed the first antislavery speech made in Congress (1835). Joyce Kilmer wrote his famous poem, "Trees," while summering here at Swanzey. The Wyman Tavern here, open to the public, is a fascinating period house and museum to visit. From Keene, return east on 9 to the intersection of State 63. Take 63 south to Hinsdale. Greyhounds run at Hinsdale Raceway from September through June, and then harness racing takes over for July and August.

From Hinsdale take Route 119 east to Fitzwilliam. Here, about mid-July, some 16 acres of rhododendron burst into glorious bloom at the Rhododendron State Park. The park is open from late June through Labor Day; a small admission fee is charged.

Some say Fitzwilliam is just about the most beautiful old American village. The Congregation Church here is magnificent with its four-story steeple, each deck surrounded by a carved balustrade. The Fitzwilliam Inn, another lovely building, is a charming spot to stop for refreshment after a day's drive.

From Fitzwilliam take State 119 east to Rindge and follow the sign for Cathedral of the Pines, a most remarkable memorial on Cathedral Road. Begun in 1945, this international shrine incorporates two national war memorials: the Altar of the Nation—recognized by Congress as a national memorial for all American war dead—and the Memorial Bell Tower, a national memorial specifically honoring women lost in war. Open from May to November, it has been visited by over seven million people. The Cathedral, high on a hilltop, has traditionally been a depository for stones brought by people from all over the world. Many of the stones have been incorporated in the Altar of Nations. While it is called a cathedral, no particular religion is espoused, nor will you find an actual church—the "cathedral" is the pine forest. It is a peaceful and inspiring place to visit.

 **SIGHTSEEING CHECKLIST.** New Hampshire is an interesting mix of things manmade and Mothermade, i.e., made by Mother Nature. The White Mountains, according to scientists, go back more than 350-million years—they were upwards of 200-million years old when the Rockies were "born." The Hopkins Center at Dartmouth College in Hanover, one of those manmade accomplishments, is just over 10 years old. The numbers hardly compare, between manmade and Mothermade, but there are significant things in both areas.

In any event, if you only have a limited time in New Hampshire, but want to see a couple of noteworthy (for whatever the reason) sites or sights, perhaps the following checklist will help you save time hunting.

Strawbery Banke. The first white settlers in New Hampshire dropped anchor, literally and figuratively, on the banks of the Piscataqua River more than 350 years ago. They had their water transportation link and they liked the wild strawberries which carpeted the banks of the river. In time, of course, they grew away from that area, but a determined historic restoration and preservation project has breathed new life into what used to be known as Puddle Dock. Not only are buildings saved, though; Strawbery Banke, the nonprofit project in Portsmouth, is also preserving crafts of that earlier period (Tel. 436–8010).

Shaker Village. There are just three communities of Shakers left and the one in Canterbury, just north of Concord, is perhaps the preeminent. When the sisters living in Canterbury, the last survivors of the religion which came to this country in the late 18th century, die, that's it; the religion will expire with them. Open spring through fall, the village offers guided tours of the community as well as special events (783–9822).

Mystery Hill/America's Stonehenge. Whether you're a believer or a skeptic, Mystery Hill in Salem is intriguing. The site, which is off I-93, bills itself as "America's Stonehenge." Researchers claim it was used by Celtic-Iberian people from Europe perhaps as early as 1,000 B.C. Fueling the controversy about Mystery Hill is the more recent bulldozing that has been done (893-8300).

Amoskeag Mills. Young America imported its industrial technology from England and the Merrimack River, which cuts through Manchester (and eventually through the Massachusetts cities of Lowell, Lawrence and Haverhill), was the major incubator for that trans-Atlantic genius. At one point, the mills on both sides of the river in Manchester formed the largest single such complex in the world. Many of those red brick structures have been torn down but an impressive collection still stand. Prowl the streets, or what's left of them, observe the architecture and think about what it must have been like in that womb-to-tomb industrial socialistic era when a child could be born in the company system, work for the company and finally die—all without ever leaving the area.

Mount Washington. The tallest peak in the Northeastern U.S., at 6,288 feet, is best seen from a distance. Perhaps the best viewing spot is near Bretton Woods resort, a long-range sweep that sets the peak in the middle of everything and has the peaks of the Presidential Range sliding off to either side. If you're really pressed for time but want to go to the summit, take one of the "stages" which shuttle up and down in specially engineered vehicles; you get a guided tour and better appreciation. If you're feeling energetic, perhaps a hike is in order—go to the Cog Railway terminal and then follow the Ammonoosuc Trail up the western flank to the summit. Make sure you've got someone with you, though, and that you've got an Appalachian Mountain Club guide (5 Joy Street, Boston 02108).

The Old Man, Lost River and the Flume. The White Mountains once were part of a vast inland sea; as glaciers came and receded millions of years ago, they carved the ridgelines. At one point, the Whites were majestic peaks; they still are in many ways, but not the jagged, sawtooth beauty that we still find in the Rockies. Still, these peaks contain their share of interesting sites and sights. The Appalachian Trail slices across the Whites as it runs between Maine and Georgia and there are countless hiking trails. High above Franconia Notch, the so-called Old Man of the Mountain keeps his eye on mankind; a unique outcropping of several rock formations, the hallowed profile is visible for only a few hundred feet from the valley below. A little south, the Flume, which probably should be renamed the Fluke, is another part of Franconia Notch State Park. It's like a gigantic mining sluice, an 800-foot chasm which you can walk via the specially constructed boardwalks along the walls. High up on Kinsman Notch above North Woodstock, Lost River offers a look at the glacial river beds. As the glaciers melted, their fast-moving water flows tore away at the mountainsides, tumbling boulders into the ravines. Visitors to Lost River can stick to the boardwalk and listen to special tape recordings explaining the dozen-plus stops or clamber down, over and around the rocks and through the dark shadows.

St. Gaudens and Parrish estates. The area around Plainfield and Cornish long has been known as an artists' colony. J.D. Salinger—or is it Holden Caulfield?—has lived there in reclusive fashion for years. Decades ago, though, Augustus St. Gaudens and Maxfield Parrish were among the more celebrated "locals." St. Gaudens was a sculptor of major fame at the end of the last century while Parrish was a well-known painter, thrust to fame and fortune by covers which he painted for *Life* and *Collier's*. Both of their estates are just off Route 12A; the St. Gaudens National Historic Site in Cornish open during the summer months with Sunday afternoon concerts (675-2175) while the owner of the Maxfield Parrish Museum, just up the road in Plainfield, became embroiled into a dispute with the community in 1985 and has closed the museum.

Hopkins Center. Performing arts centers normally hold little appeal for most people; they're glorified hangars—an acoustically engineered marvel, to be sure, but still a hangar. The Hop, though, is a bit different. A lovely perch on The Green at Dartmouth in Hanover, the center trots performing artists of all stripe through its myriad stages and theaters 12 months a year. There are also a couple of small galleries for various exhibits and they even hold some exhibits in the hallways. The Hopkins Center was augmented in 1985 by the addition of the Hood Museum with its many historical exhibits. And if you don't like the Hop or the Hood, walk out the front door and enjoy the campus setting and '40s look of Hanover's Main Street (646–2422).

Mountain rides. If you've got a hankering for a mountain ride, to grab those rolling views perhaps the aerial tram at Cannon Mountain in Franconia is the best. Moves fast, holds a gang of people and gets you to the top of the "notch." Nice walking paths up there, too. Or you might try the Alpine Slide, a different way of coming down, at either Attitash in Bartlett or Alpine Ridge, looking out across Lake Winnipesaukee in Gilford. Gondola rides are available at Loon Mountain in Lincoln and Wildcat in Jackson.

A country fair. Or is it county fair? In either case, the fair season takes hold in August and September with at least one a week until Columbus Day. If not a full-fledged county-country shindig, complete with horse-pulling contests and 4-H competitions to go with the entertainment, then there are countless one- or two-day special events. The New Hampshire Office of Vacation Travel, Concord, 03301, (271–2343) can fill you in on dates and places.

PRACTICAL INFORMATION FOR

NEW HAMPSHIRE

Note: Large sections in Practical Information have been organized by touring area for your convenience.

 **FACTS AND FIGURES.** The state takes its name from Hampshire County, England. Its nickname is Granite State. The purple lilac is the state flower; the white birch, the state tree; the purple finch, the state bird. "Live Free or Die" is the state motto, "Old New Hampshire" its song.

Irregularly tapering, New Hampshire is 168 miles from north to south, about 90 miles wide in the heavily settled southern part, about 15 miles wide where its northern tip projects into Quebec. Total area is 9,304 square miles, 44th among the 50 states; and the population is about 920,600, 42nd in the nation. Concord (properly pronounced, locally that is "Kawng-Kudd"), population 30,000, is the state capital, but Manchester, with 90,000, is the state's largest city. New Hampshire was the ninth of the original thirteen states to ratify the Constitution, on June 21, 1788; with this the Constitution came into force and the new nation of the United States of America was officially born.

There are two economic New Hampshires; the high-tech belt of the southern part of the state (which feeds off its proximity to Boston), and tourism–oriented central and northern New Hampshire. It is not generally recognized that on a per capita basis New Hampshire is actually one of the most heavily industrialized states in the country. However, 80% of the state's largest firms are absentee-owned. Dairying, poultry, apples, peaches, corn and maple syrup are the chief agricultural products. Famous Americans from New Hampshire include Daniel Webster, Robert Frost, Franklin Pierce (14th president of the U.S.), Horace Greeley, Mary Baker Eddy, and sculptors Daniel Chester French and Augustus Saint-Gaudens.

Handsome forests, New Hampshire's chief natural resource, cover 87% of the state. The mountains attract visitors throughout the year, but especially in the fall for hunting and foliage viewing, and in the winter for skiing. Lovely, historic Colonial towns are also among the state's attractions, and the coastal lowlands in the southeast provide superb beaches. Though the heavily developed seacoast fronts on the Atlantic ocean for only 18 miles, the southeastern seacoast region's bays and rivers give the state 131 miles of salt-water shoreline. Winters are cold and snowy, summers cool with pleasantly low humidity; fine weather lingers long into fall. Specifically, year-round average conditions are as follows:

NEW HAMPSHIRE

	Jan.	Feb.	Mar.	Apr.	May	Jun.
Average Temperature (F)	21	23	32	45	55	64
Average Temperature (C)	−6	−5	0	7	13	18
Days of Rain or Snow	11	10	11	11	12	10

	Jul.	Aug.	Sept.	Oct.	Nov.	Dec.
Average Temperature (F)	70	68	59	48	37	25
Average Temperature (C)	21	20	15	9	3	−4
Days of Rain or Snow	10	10	9	8	12	11

HOW TO GET THERE. By air. The principal airport is Grenier Field, Manchester (18 miles from Concord). Airline deregulation and then the 1981 traffic controllers strike have turned the state's airline picture upside down (deregulation had the greater impact). Airlines have been in and out of serving Manchester, Keene, Laconia and West Lebanon airports, but the service seems to have fallen to two smaller carriers, *Precision,* which serves all four airports, and *Command Airways,* which flies in and out of Lebanon. Check with your travel agent. There is *taxi service* from the airports to nearby towns.

By bus. *Greyhound* and *Trailways* have year-round service, with extra buses during the summer and ski seasons.

By car. From Massachusetts: I–93 from Medford MA, to Salem. U.S. 3 from Medford and Boston area to Nashua. I–95 from Mass. crosses N.H. Seacoast Region and the Piscataqua River and on to Kittery ME, and the Maine Tpke. U.S. 202 from Mass. to Jaffrey in the central part of New Hampshire. From Vermont: I–89 from White River Jct. VT, to West Lebanon. From St. Johnsbury, Rte. 2, then 18 to Littleton. From Connecticut: I–91 to Springfield MA then U.S. 202 up to Keene. From Maine: I–95 from Kittery into Portsmouth. Rte. 2 from Bangor to Gorham. U.S. 11 and 202 from Sanford ME, to Rochester. U.S. 302 from Portland to Center Conway. From Rhode Island: I–95 to Boston, then I–93 to Manchester. From New York: I–87 (New York Thruway) to Albany, then Rtes. 7 and 9 through Brattleboro to Keene. From Quebec, Canada: Canadian Rte. 10 from Montreal, then 55 which connects with I–91 & Rte. 5 in Vermont, to St. Johnsbury; then Rtes. 2 and 18 to Littleton.

TELEPHONES. The area code for all of New Hampshire is 603. Information (known as directory assistance) is 1–555–1212 for all in-state calls. When direct-dialing a long distance number, you must dial "1" (one) *before* you dial the area code and number. An operator will assist you on all person-to-person, credit card and collect calls if you dial "0" (zero) first. Pay telephones are usually 10 cents.

HOTELS AND MOTELS. As New Hampshire's tourism business has grown in recent years, particularly in the last decade, so has its lodging base. Accommodations range from modern, slopeside condos to modest cottages or guest houses. Keep two things in mind: package plans (to cover meals and length of stay) usually are available, especially during ski season, and you'll find rates lower along the seacoast in winter (when, obviously, they're higher in the mountains). Rates based on double occupancy in season: *Deluxe,* $75 and up; *Expensive,* $50–$75; *Moderate,* $30–$50; *Inexpensive,* $30 and under.

HANOVER-LAKE SUNAPEE REGION

ANDOVER. **Andover Meadow Inn.** *Moderate.* Rte. 11 (735–5224). Nothing pretentious, just comfortable. Outdoor pool. TV.

CLAREMONT. Stone Eagle Motel. *Inexpensive-Moderate.* Rtes. 11 and 103 (between Claremont and Newport) (542–2511). Nice hilltop site, handy to attractions, shopping, but away from main traffic. Coffee Shop.

HANOVER. Hanover Inn. *Deluxe.* Main and Wheelock Sts. (643–4300). Dartmouth-run, two-centuries-old inn on a perfect spot: on The Green, next to Hopkins Center, at head of Main St. First-rate meals, comfortable rooms, Colonial decor lounge. Children's portions in dining room. Pets. Color TV (cable). Make reservations because this is a busy place.

Chieftain Motor Inn. *Moderate.* Rte. 10 (643–2550). Small, overlooks Connecticut River. Continental breakfast. Pool, boating, fishing. Color TV (cable).

LYME. Lyme Inn. *Expensive* (breakfast included). On the Village Common (795–2222). Ex-stagecoach stop (1809) between Montreal and Boston. Each room drips with atmosphere and antiques (many for sale). Some rooms have canopy beds, private bath. Fine, relaxed dining; dining room closed Tues. Inn closes for three weeks in Apr., Dec.

Loch Lyme Lodge & Cottages. *Moderate-Deluxe* (EP or MAP). On Post Pond (795–2141). Main lodge is a farmhouse built in 1784 and there are 26 cottages (including 13 housekeeping units) sprinkled around the grounds. B&B available. Pond swimming, canoeing, boating, fishing. Tennis, badminton, croquet, hiking. In winter, cross-country skiing, skating, ice fishing.

NEW LONDON. New London Inn. *Expensive.* Main Street (526–2791). Medium-sized, attractive inn that goes back to 1792. Two dining rooms.

Hide-Away Lodge. *Moderate-Expensive* (MAP). Twin Lake Villa Rd., off Route 11 (526–4861). Rooms in cottage and lodge, some without bath. Woodland setting. Gracious dining, lounge. Pets. Open mid-May to late Oct.

Lamplighter Motor Inn. *Moderate.* Route 11 (526–6484). Four kitchenettes. Pets. TV.

NEWPORT. Hilltop Motel. *Moderate.* Routes 11 and 103 (863–3456). Italian restaurant. Pool. Color TV.

Newport Motel. *Moderate.* Routes 11 and 103 (863–1440). Small with play area, pool, rec rm. Pets. Color TV (cable).

PLAINFIELD. Home Hill Country Inn. *Deluxe.* River Rd., off Rte. 12-A. Restored ex-mansion with only six rooms. Superb French restaurant; light sauces. Sinful desserts. Closed Sun. and Mon.

WEST LEBANON. Sheraton North Country Inn. *Expensive-Deluxe.* Airport Rd., just off Rte. 12–A. Restaurant and lounge well-known for nightly live entertainment. Color TV (cable). Indoor pool.

Sunset Motel. *Inexpensive-Moderate.* Rte. 10 (298–8721). Quiet, clean spot to hang your hat. Riverside locale. Color TV (cable).

WHITE MOUNTAINS REGION

BARTLETT. Attitash Mountain Village. *Moderate-Deluxe.* Rte. 302, across from Attitash Ski Area (374–2386). Condos and motel-style rooms. Kitchenettes and fireplaces. Beach and swimming, Alpine Slide, tennis, water slide. Alpine and cross-country skiing in winter plus skating. Color TV (cable).

Sky Valley Motel & Chalets. *Moderate-Expensive.* Rte. 302 (374–2322). Apartments, chalets and cottages—some with fireplaces—spread over 35 acres. Pool. Kids' play area. TV.

BERLIN. Traveler Motel. *Moderate.* 25 Pleasant St. (752–2500). Neat, clean rooms. Pets. Color TV (cable).

BETHLEHEM. Wayside Inn & Motel. *Moderate.* Rte. 302 at Pierce Bridge (869–3364). Combination inn and modern motel overlooking the Ammonoosuc River. Private beach, tennis. Pets. Chef-owned, excellent restaurant. Snowmobile trails. Closed May and Nov.

BRETTON WOODS. Mt. Washington Hotel. *Expensive-Deluxe.* Rte. 302 at the foot of the Presidential Range (278–1000). Spectacular setting on a clear day; when it rains, there are things to do but it's just another big room factory. Grand Dame (1904) of New England's once-elegant summer hostelries. Open only in summer, but what a playpen—tennis, golf, horses, fishing, indoor and outdoor pools or just plop down in a wicker chair on that wide porch and look at Mt. Washington. Fine food, lively entertainment nightly. Big on groups May and June, Sept. and Oct. but no groups July and Aug.

Lodge at Bretton Woods. *Moderate.* Rte. 302, across the street from the big place (278–1000) (same switchboard). Newly rebuilt after 1981 fire. Standard motel but the only thing open in these parts (other than BW's condos) in winter. Indoor pool, good steaks in restaurant. Color TV.

CAMPTON. King's Grant-Inn. *Moderate–Expensive.* Exit 27 off I–93 (536–3520). One time Holiday Inn. Restaurant, lounge. Indoor pool, sauna. Color TV (cable).

Scandinavi-Inn. *Moderate-Expensive.* Exit 28 off I–93 (726–3737). Fine lodging and dining. Plenty-big rooms, family rooms with a loft. Heated pool, sauna, tennis.

CHOCORUA. Stafford's in the Field. *Deluxe* (MAP). Rte. 113, off Rte. 16 (323–7766). A 200-yr.-old inn with sensational dining. Reservations a must. Tennis, hiking. Dining room closed Mon. and Tues. to the public. Inn closed Apr. and May, Nov. to mid-Dec.

COLEBROOK. Sportsman's Lodge & Cottages. *Inexpensive-Expensive* (EP or AP). On Big Diamond Lake (237–5211). Lodge rooms or stove-heated cottage units. Beach, swimming, boating, fishing. Hunting, cross-country skiing, snowmobiling. Pets.

CONWAY. Darby Field Inn. *Deluxe* (MAP). Bald Hill Rd., off Rte. 16 (447–2181). Just 11 rooms but what a view of the Mt. Washington Valley! Exquisite candlelight dining, bar. Pool. Cross-country skiing. TV room.

DIXVILLE NOTCH. The Balsams. *Deluxe* (MAP). Off Rte. 26 (255–3400). Spectacular, secluded setting in its own 15,000-acre site just north of the beaten path. Self-contained resort with everything in summer, alpine and cross-country skiing in winter. Family-style, sit-down dinners, superb cuisine. Golf, tennis, swimming, hiking, fishing. TV room. Pets.

EATON CENTER. Rockhouse Mt. Farm Inn. *Moderate.* (447–2880) Delightful, 350-acre working-farm-inn. Saddle horses, farm animals, tennis, golf plus; beach, sailing, boating. Renowned for home-cooked meals. Open June to Oct.

FRANCONIA (Cannon Mtn.) (See also Sugar Hill). **Lovett's Inn.** *Deluxe* (MAP). Rte. 18 (823–7761). Mix of inn rooms and cottages; 9 kitchenettes; some with fireplaces. Pool. TV room. Colonial inn (1784). Good meals and lineup of innovative desserts. Bar. Open July 1 to mid-Oct., Christmas to Apr. 1.

Hillwinds Inn. *Moderate.* Rte. 18 (823–5551). Rooms in old inn and newer motel. Fine steakhouse, very active bar during ski season. Pool, sauna. TV.

Horse & Hound Inn. *Moderate-Expensive.* Off Rte. 18 (823–5501). "Children discouraged" is the way they let you know this is a quiet, adults-only spot with the emphasis on gentility, superb Continental cuisine, a deep, deep wine cellar and escape. Seven comfy rooms. Open May to Oct., weekends in winter.

Franconia Inn. *Moderate.* Rte. 116 (823–5542). Rustic inn with French cuisine. Mini-resort—tennis, horses, hiking, fishing in summer (with golf nearby), alpine (nearby) and cross-country skiing (on-site) in winter. Bar. Open Memorial Day to Columbus Day, mid-Dec. to mid-March.

Gale River Motel. *Moderate-Deluxe.* Rte. 18 (823–5655). Motel or 3 housekeeping units. Heated pool, picnic area, grills. Pets. Color TV.

Raynor's Motor Lodge. *Moderate.* Jct. Rtes. 18 and 142. Motel rooms and 2 kitchenettes. Heated pool. In-room coffee. Color TV.

Red Apple Inn. *Moderate* Rte. 302 (383–9680). Inconspicuous, homey. Outdoor pool, game room. Color TV (cable). Pets.

GLEN. Bernerhof. *Moderate-Deluxe* (EP or AP). Rte. 302 (383–4414). Terrific restaurant, lounge. Heated pool, tennis, sauna. Kids play area, laundry. Color TV.

Red Apple Inn. *Moderate.* Rte. 302 (383–9680). Homey feeling to small motel-inn. Breakfast available. Pool. Color TV (cable).

Storybook Motor Inn. *Moderate.* Jct. Rtes. 302 and 16 (383–6800). Motel units to go with Colonial era inn. Leafy setting. Heated pool, sauna, playground. Tennis. Laundry. Color TV.

GORHAM (See also Shelburne). **Brabo's Motor Lodge.** *Moderate.* Upper Main St. (466–2112). Pool. Pets. Cable TV.

Gorham Motor Inn. *Moderate.* 324 Main St. (466–3381). Pleasant rooms in attractive layout. Restaurant, bar. Heated pool. Color TV (cable).

INTERVALE. Holiday Inn. *Deluxe* (MAP). Rte. 16–A (356–9772). No, not *that* kind of Holiday Inn; just 13 rooms in a 19th-century inn. Home-cooked meals and peaceful setting. Skating rink and lighted cross-country ski trails.

New England Inn. *Expensive-Deluxe* (MAP). Rte. 16–A (356–5541). Country inn (1809) with 9 cottages with fireplaces. Pool, tennis. Cross-country ski trails. Fine dining, lounge.

JACKSON (Wildcat Mtn.) **Christmas Farm Inn.** *Deluxe* (MAP). Rte. 16–B (383–4313). An unforgettable place, from its sugarhouse unit to its true, family feeling. Excellent dining, peewee bar and welcome parties Sun. nights in winter. Pool, game room. Yesterday setting (1778) with 20th-century services. On Jackson's cross-country ski trail network.

Inn at Thorn Hill. *Deluxe* (MAP). Thorn Hill Rd. (383–4242). Up on a knoll, overlooking Jackson village and Mt. Washington. Candlelight dining, fireplaced living room. Pool. Cross-country skiing. Closed May and 3 weeks in Dec.

Wentworth Resort Hotel. *Expensive.* (MAP avail.) Gracious, nicely restored hotel. Revived under new owners. Tennis, golf. Outdoor pool. Part of town's cross-country ski system. Color TV (cable).

Eagle Mountain House. *Moderate-Expensive.* Rte. 16–B, across the meadow from Christmas Farm Inn (383–4347). Century-old hotel which has lost the elegance, but retains the friendliness and service. Fine dining room, weekend entertainment in lounge. 9-hole golf, tennis, pool and in winter there's cross-country skiing, skating, tobogganning.

Covered Bridge Motel. *Moderate.* Rte. 16. Nothing fancy but a fine spot, handy to plenty of things. Pool, tennis.

Whitney's Village Inn. *Moderate.* Rte. 16–B (383–6886). Way back up at the bend of the road, at the foot of Black Mtn. Ski Area, but well worth the effort to get there. Rooms draped over main inn, apartment units and a couple of chalets. Peace, seclusion in summer, alpine and cross-country skiing plus skating, tobogganing, sleigh rides in winter. Delightful.

JEFFERSON. Evergreen Motel. *Moderate.* Rte. 2 near Santa's Village (586–4449). Dozen campsites with electricity, sewer, water plus motel. Restaurant. Color TV. Open June 1 to Oct. 15.

Skywood Manor Inn & Motel. *Inexpensive-Moderate.* Rte. 2 (586–4491). Spacious grounds, lawn games, picnic tables. Fishing in brook or natural pond. Pets. Open May 15 to Oct. 15.

LANCASTER. Mary Elizabeth Motor Inn, Motel & Cottages. *Inexpensive-Moderate.* Rte. 3 (788–4621). Cottages and kitchenettes. Pets. Cable TV.

LINCOLN/NORTH WOODSTOCK (Loon Mtn). **Jack O'Lantern Resort.** *Deluxe* (MAP). Rte. 3 (745–8121). Restful site on Pemigewasset River with golf, tennis, heated pool, rec room. Restaurant, bar. Color TV (cable).

Beacon Motel. *Moderate-Expensive.* Rte. 3 (745–8118). Motel rooms or cottages. 2 restaurants, lounge. Indoor and 2 heated, outdoor pools, sauna, indoor tennis. Color TV (cable).

Drummer Boy Motor Inn. *Moderate.* Rte. 3 (745–2480). Motel units and 11 kitchenettes, 3 cottages. Heated pool, play area. Color TV (cable).

Indian Head Motel Resort. *Moderate-Deluxe.* Rte. 3 (745–8181). Motel rooms and cottages. Fine restaurant, lounge. Indoor and heated outdoor pool, sauna, tennis. Cross-country skiing. Color TV (cable).

Inn at Loon Mountain. *Moderate.* Kancamagus Hwy., right at Loon Mountain Ski Area (745–8111). Excellent dining room, bar. Tennis, swimming, play area in summer, alpine and cross-country skiing in winter.

Kancamagus Motor Lodge. *Moderate.* Kancamagus Hwy. (745–3365). Quiet dining room, bar. Unheralded—clean, cozy and in the right spot. In-room steam baths. Color cable TV.

Parker's Motel. *Moderate.* Rte. 3 (745–8341). Nice grounds, next to Franconia State Park. Pool. TV. Open mid-May to Oct. 31.

Woodward's Motor Inn. *Moderate.* Rte. 3 (745–8141). Steakhouse restaurant, lounge with entertainment. Heated pool, tennis. Color TV (cable). Open Christmas to Apr. 1, mid-May to mid-Oct.

Maple Lodge Motel. *Inexpensive-Moderate.* Rte. 3, Main St. in North Woodstock (745–2416). Nothing flashy, just friendly. Cable TV.

Mt. Liberty Motel & Cabins. *Inexpensive.* Off Rte. 3, on Pemigewasset River (745–2288). Motel and 7 kitchenettes. Heated pool. Pets. Cable TV. Open mid-May to Columbus Day.

Red Doors Motel. *Inexpensive-Moderate.* Rte. 3 (745–2267). In-room coffee. Heated pool. Color TV (cable).

LITTLETON. Beal House Inn. *Inexpensive-Moderate.* Rtes. 302 and 18 (444–2661). Home (1833) dripping with antiques. Breakfast served. Antiques shop.

Continental 93 Motor Inn. *Inexpensive-Moderate.* Rte. 18, Exit 42 off I–93 (444–5366). Dining room and lounge. Private fish pond (skating in winter). Pets. Indoor and outdoor pools, sauna. Color TV (cable).

NORTH CONWAY (Mt. Cranmore) **Fox Ridge Resort.** *Expensive-Deluxe.* Rte. 16 (356–3151). Modern resort on a 300-acre hilltop perch. Fine dining, lounge. Indoor and heated outdoor pools, whirlpool, sauna, tennis. Color TV (cable).

Red Jacket Motor Inn. *Expensive-Deluxe.* Rte. 16 (356–5411). Modern, if miniature, resort complex set along a hillside. 20-plus acres with great views. Fine restaurant, saloon and a dozen kitchenettes. Indoor and heated outdoor pools, whirlpool, sauna, tennis. Game room, play area. Color TV (cable).

Stonehurst. *Expensive-Deluxe.* Rte. 16 (356–3113). "Upstairs, Downstairs" setting. Place drips of old money, the faded elegance and class of a century or so ago. Converted mansion, complete with fireplaces, oak decor, tree-filled site. Outstanding food, lounge. Pool, tennis, shuffleboard. Cable TV.

Wildflowers Guest House. *Moderate.* Rte. 16 (356–2224). Just north of town, a century-old home. Breakfast available. Only 6 rooms.

Eastern Slope Inn. *Moderate-Expensive* (EP or MAP). Rte. 16, center of town (356–6321). Restaurant, bar. Heated pool, tennis. Color TV.

Green Granite Motel & Apartments. *Moderate-Expensive.* Jct. Rtes. 16 and 302 (356–3960). South of town, across from shopping mall. Dining room and free morning coffee; 6 kitchenettes. Pool. Cable TV.

School House Motel. *Moderate.* Rte. 16, down on "Motel Row" (356–6829). Nothing fancy, just nice and clean, handy to everywhere. Color TV (cable).

Scottish Lion. *Moderate.* Rte. 16 (356–6381). Pintsize pearl, storybook tale of urban couple who made dream work up-country. Homey. Just 11 rooms, one of New England's first bed & breakfast spots; get a table on the porch. Small pub-like lounge, shop with Scottish imports.

White Trellis Motel. *Moderate.* Rte. 16 (356–2492). Just a nice place with fine views of the Presidential Range. Handy to everything. Cable TV.

Wildflowers Guest House. *Moderate.* Rte. 16 (356–2224). Just north of town, a century old home. Breakfast available. Only 6 rooms.

PITTSBURG. The Glen. *Moderate-Expensive.* Rte. 3 on First Connecticut Lake at the top of New Hampshire (538–6500). Rooms in lodge (1900) or lakefront cabins. Beach, swimming, fishing. Pets. Open May 15 to Oct. 15.

Timberland Camps. *Moderate.* Rte. 3 (538–6613). Seven housekeeping units. Tackle shop, boat rental. Open late Apr. to late Nov.

PLYMOUTH. Deep River Inn. *Moderate.* Highland St. on the Baker River (536–2155). Fine views of mountains. Pool. Cable TV.

Pilgrim Motel. *Moderate.* Rte. 3 (536–1319). Clean and cozy. Cable TV.

Red Sleigh Motor Court. *Moderate.* Rte. 3 on Pemigewasset River. 1 and 2-bedroom cottages, some kitchenettes. Pool, game area outside, TV.

Knoll Motel. *Inexpensive-Moderate.* Rte. 3 (536–1245). Motel or cottage rooms. Pool. Pets. Cable TV.

SHELBURNE (See also Gorham). **Shelburne Birches Motor Inn.** *Moderate.* Rte. 2 (466–3941). Motel rooms, 8 kitchenettes. Pool, cross-country skiing, snowmobiling. Color TV (cable).

Town & Country Motor Inn. *Moderate.* Rte. 2 (466–3315). Fine spot on well-traveled road. Restaurant, lounge. Indoor pool. Pets. Color TV (cable).

SNOWVILLE. Snowvillage Inn. *Deluxe* (MAP). Off Rte. 153, near Conway (447–2818). Pleasant country inn (14 rooms). Four-seasons despite name. Tennis, swimming, hiking in summer, cross-country touring center at the inn and King Pine Ski Area just around the corner in winter. Sauna. Pets.

SUGAR HILL (See also Franconia). **Sunset Hill House.** *Deluxe* (MAP). Refurbished throwback to days of moneyed travelers. Superb meals, cozy lounge, occasional nightly entertainment in winter. Golf and tennis in summer, 75 miles of cross-country ski trails.

The Homestead. *Expensive.* Main St. (823–5564). Historic inn built in 1802 by one of town's first settlers. Like going to your grandmother's. Ultra-homey, folksy atmosphere and hearty, heaping, home-cooked meals. Some rooms without bath. Chalet available. Closed Nov. and Apr. to late May.

Sugar Hill Inn. *Expensive-Deluxe* (MAP). Colonial style inn (1748). Antiques and stenciled walls, floors that creak. Excellent dining, but you have to shoehorn into the bar, it's so small. Closed Apr. and Nov.

TWIN MOUNTAIN. Paquette's Motor Inn. *Moderate.* Rte. 3 (846–5562). Hearty fare in dining room; lounge. Pool. Snowmobiling. Closed Nov.

Twin View Cottages. *Moderate.* Rte. 302, near jct. with Rte. 3 (846–5501). Chalet-type motel, fireplace in lobby. 2 kitchenettes. Pool.

Carroll Motel & Cottages. *Inexpensive.* Jct. Rtes. 302 and 3 (846–5553). Cottages, kitchenettes and motel rooms. Heated outdoor pool. Play area, picnic grills. Free in-room coffee.

WATERVILLE VALLEY. Snowy Owl Inn. *Deluxe.* Village Center (236–8366). Perhaps nicest, luxury lodge in Ski Country because of tasteful decor. Continental breakfast available. Outdoor pool (heated), whirlpool, sauna. Game room, huge stone fireplace; free cocoa, coffee, tea after skiing. Color TV (cable).

Along with the Snowy Owl, other Inns of Waterville Valley are the **Silver Squirrel** and **Landmarc Lodge,** also in the village core. Accommodations are *Expensive-Deluxe* in each case. Indoor pool, whirlpool, sauna, fireplace, game room in each inn plus color TV in Silver Squirrel. Again, no dining room but Continental breakfast available each place.

Valley Inn & Tavern. *Deluxe.* Village center (236–8336). Lone inn which is not part of Inns of Waterville Valley lodging group. Rustic, cozy fireplace. Fine dining, lounge. Indoor/outdoor pool, sauna, platform tennis, game room.

Waterville Valley condos. *Expensive-Deluxe.* Village core (236–8211). Three modern condo complexes are part of lodging pool. Small health center at Tripyramid condos.

WHITEFIELD. Mountain View House. *Deluxe.* (MAP) Mtn. View Rd. off Rte. 3 (837–2511). A page from the past with fine service, elegant food, moneyed setting. Heated outdoor pool, tennis, golf. Open mid-May to mid-Oct.

Spaulding Inn Club. *Deluxe.* Mtn. View Rd. off Rte. 3. Another handsome throwback: gracious 19th-century inn and deluxe cottages with golf, tennis, pool and 400 magnificent acres in the middle of the White Mtns. Superb dining, wine cellar. Open June to mid-Oct.

Lakeside Farm Inn & Cottages. *Moderate.* Rte. 116, Burns Lake (837–2741). Old homestead plus 3 kitchenettes. Comfy, country, casual. Beach, swimming, fishing. Pets.

Mirror Lake Motel & Cottages. *Moderate.* Rte. 3 (837–2544). Name says it all: motel and cottages on Mirror Lake. Beach, swimming, fishing, boating. Shuffleboard. Color TV (cable) in motel units. Open May to Oct.

Playhouse Inn. *Moderate.* Rte. 302 (837–2527). Pleasant restaurant, lounge. Heated outdoor pool. Next to summer theatre. Open mid-May to mid-Oct.

WOODSVILLE. White Mountain Profile Motel. *Inexpensive.* Jct. Rtes. 10 and 302. Comfortable motel with outdoor pool. Shuffleboard. Color TV.

LAKES REGION

ALTON/ALTON BAY. Bay-side Motel. *Moderate.* On Alton Bay (875–5005). Some kitchenettes and family units. Beach, boating, fishing.

King Birch Motor Lodge. *Moderate.* Rte. 11–D, Alton Bay (875–2222). Lakefront, cottages. Beach, boating, canoeing, fishing. Picnics. TV.

Riverview Motel. *Inexpensive.* Rtes. 11 and 28, Alton (875–5001). Picturesque setting on small river, 5 kitchenettes. Color TV.

ASHLAND. Little Holland Court. *Moderate.* Rtes. 3 and 175 (968–4434). Cottages on Little Squam Lake. Private beach, fishing, boating, canoeing. Play area includes horseshoes, volleyball, table tennis.

EAST MADISON. Purity Spring Resort. *Expensive* (AP). Rte. 153 (367–8897). Full-service resort on private lake. Beach, boating, canoeing. Tennis, shuffleboard, lawn games. King Pine Ski Area next door and snowmobile trails. Closed Apr. and May, late Oct. to late Nov.

GILFORD (See also Laconia, Weirs Beach). **Saunders Bay Motel & Cottages.** *Expensive.* Rte. 11–B, on Lake Winnipesaukee (293–7871). Housekeeping and efficiencies. Power and sail boating. Beach, playground, pool. TV. Open Apr. to mid-Sept.

Silver Sands. *Moderate.* Rte. 11–B, on the lake (293–4481). Lakefront site, private beach, boating. Kitchenettes. Heated pool. Open Apr. to mid-Oct.

HOLDERNESS. Squam Lakes Resort. *Deluxe* (MAP.) Rte. 3 (968–3348). Comfortable and attractive, excellent food. Tennis, pool, putting green, lake swimming and boating. Color TV.

Boulders. *Moderate.* Rte. 3 overlooking Little Squam Lake (968–3600). Beach, swimming. TV.

Normandie Farms Inn. *Moderate.* Rte. 3 (968–3012). Emphasis in this 10-room inn is on antiques. Restaurant, lounge, antique shop. Open June to Oct.

White Oak Motel & Cottages. *Moderate.* Rte. 3 on Squam Lake (968–3673). Scenic setting, pleasant grounds. 14 kitchenettes, snack bar, heated pool, beach, fishing. Open May to Oct.

LACONIA (See also Gilford, Weirs Beach). **Margate Resort.** *Expensive-Deluxe.* Rte. 3 on Lake Winnipesaukee (524–5210). First-rate hotel with modern rooms, fine restaurant and lively lounge. 300-ft. beach, tennis, indoor and heated outdoor pools, whirlpool and sauna. Color TV (cable).

Christmas Island Resort. *Moderate-Expensive.* Rte. 3 on Lake Winnipesaukee (366–4378). Motel and housekeeping units. Rest. and lounge with nightly entertainment. Beach & indoor pool, boating, cross-country skiing. Color TV (cable).

Lord Hampshire Resort. *Moderate-Expensive.* Rte. 3, on Lake Winnipesaukee. 500-ft. beach, boating, fishing. Housekeeping and motel units. TV in cottages, color TV in motel rooms.

Shalimar Resort Motel. *Moderate-Expensive.* Rte. 3 (524–1984). Restaurant, bar. Indoor pool, whirlpool, sauna, exercise room.

Sheraton-Laconia Inn. *Moderate-Expensive.* Rte. 3 (524–8000). Restaurant, bar. Indoor pool, steam room. Color TV (cable). Pets.

The Anchorage. *Moderate.* Rte. 3 on Lake Winnisquam (524–3248). Housekeeping on wooded, 32-acre estate. 3 beaches, play area, boating, canoeing, boardsailing. Open mid-May to mid-Oct.

MEREDITH. Olmec Motor Lodge. *Moderate.* Pleasant St., off Rte. 25 (279–8584). Nine units, tucked away on Meredith Bay. Swimming, boating. TV.

MOULTONBOROUGH. Kona Mansion Inn. *Deluxe* (MAP). Moultonborough Neck Rd. (253–4900). On Lake Winnipesaukee, a throwback to the old, elegant days. Par-3 golf and tennis to go with swimming. Restaurant and lounge. TV.

Olde Orchard Inn. *Moderate-Expensive.* Rte. 109, off Rte. 25 (476–5004). Five rooms. Cross-country skiing from front door. Breakfast included. Closed April, Nov.

Matterhorn Motor Lodge. *Moderate.* Rte. 25 and Moultonborough Neck Rd. (253–4314). Snowmobile trail, heated pool. Color TV (cable).

Rob Roy Motor Lodge. *Moderate.* Rte. 25 (476–5571). In-room whirlpool, steam bath. 75 miles of snowmobile trails. TV. Fine seafood restaurant next door.

SILVER LAKE. Silver Lake Motor Lodge. *Inexpensive-Moderate.* Rtes. 41 and 113 S. (367–4786). Motel and 4 efficiencies on lake. Private beach, free boats, fishing, game room.

TILTON. Waylander Motel. Rte. 3, at Exit 20 off I-93 (286–4430). Motel & cottage units. Outdoor pool. Color TV (cable).

WEIRS BEACH. Brickyard Mountain Resort. *Expensive-Deluxe.* Rte. 3, overlooking the lake (366–4316). Hotel-motel plus timesharing condos. Restaurant and lounge. Pintsize ski area, indoor and outdoor pools, tennis, saunas and beach. Color TV (cable).

Look-off Rock Motel & Cottages. *Moderate-Expensive.* Scenic Rd., off Rte. 3 (366–4433). Swimming, 6 kitchenettes. TV. Open May to Oct. 15.

Green Arrow Motel & Cottages. *Moderate.* 381 Lakeside Ave. (366–4604). Motel units and 25 kitchenettes. Beach. Color TV (cable). Open mid-May to mid-Oct.

Lakeside Hotel & Motel. *Moderate.* Lakeside Ave. (366–4662). Family hotel with cottage and efficiencies. Private beach, rec room. TV. Open May to Oct.

Weathervane Lodge & Cottages. *Moderate.* Rte. 3, on the lake (366–5504). 8 kitchenettes. Private beach, boating, table tennis, picnic tables. Color TV. Open late May to Columbus Day.

WOLFEBORO. Pick Point Lodge & Cottages. *Deluxe.* Tuftonboro Neck, on Lake Winnipesaukee (569–1338). Lovely, 75-acre, wooded surroundings and wildlife sanctuary. Lodge and 10 efficiencies. Half-mile beach and shoreline, boats, fishing, tennis, putting green. Game room. TV. Open late May to late Oct.

Lake Motel. *Expensive.* So. Main St., on the lake (569–1100). Private beach, boats, fishing. Color TV. Tennis. 5 kitchenettes. Open May 15 to Oct. 15.

Lakeview Inn and Motor Lodge. *Moderate.* 120 N. Main St. (569–1335). Luxurious rooms with scenic view; 4 kitchenettes. Colonial atmosphere, large grounds. Restaurant and bar. Coffee-maker in rooms. Color TV. Cross-country skiing.

Piping Rock Cottages & Motel. *Moderate.* No. Main St., (569–1915). Handsome lakefront setting, private beach. Cottages and 19 kitchenettes, some with fireplace. Swimming, sailing, boating, fishing. Cross-country skiing. TV.

MERRIMACK VALLEY

BEDFORD (See also Manchester). **Sheraton-Wayfarer Motor Inn.** *Expensive-Deluxe.* Jct. Rte. 3 and 101 (622–3766). Excellent dining room, lively bar. Landscaped grounds, including small covered bridge; definitely not your basic chain hotel-motel. Indoor and outdoor pools, sauna, even a waterfall. Pets. Color TV (cable).

BOSCAWEN. Daniel Webster Motor Lodge. *Moderate.* Rtes. 3 and 4 (796–2136). Daniel Webster Homestead, peaceful setting. Motel and 5 efficiencies. Coffee-maker in each room. Pool. Pets. Color TV (cable).

Shady Pines Motel. *Inexpensive.* Rte. 3 (796–2358). TV. Open May to Oct.

CONCORD. Brick Tower Motor Inn. *Moderate-Expensive.* Exit 12–S, off I–93 (224–9565). Modern, clean rooms. Pool and sauna. Restaurant and liquor license (no bar). Pets. Color TV (cable).

Concord Coach Motor Inn. *Moderate.* 406 S. Main St. (224–2511). Colonial motif. Kids' area, heated pool, Color TV (cable).

New Hampshire Highway Hotel. *Moderate.* Exit 14, off I–93 at Rte. 9 (225–6687). Colonial decor, traditional political center (just a few blocks from State House). Restaurant, bar. Heated pool. Beauty salon. Color TV (cable).

HENNIKER. Colby Hill Inn. *Moderate.* W. Main St. (428–3281). Comfortable, oldfashioned inn (1800). Fine dining; (Tues.–Sun.). Bar. Pool. TV.

Henniker Motel. *Moderate.* At Pat's Peak, off Rte. 114 (428–3536). Heated indoor pool, whirlpool. Color TV (cable).

MANCHESTER. Holiday Inn. *Expensive.* Rte. 3 at Amoskeag Bridge (669–2660). Restaurant, bar, coffee shop, in-room coffee. Pool, racquetball. Color TV (cable).

Howard Johnson's. *Expensive.* Queen City Ave., Exit 4 off I–293 (668–2600). Lounge and 24-hour restaurant. Indoor pool, sauna. Pets. Color TV.

Queen City Motor Inn. *Moderate.* 140 Queen City Ave., Exit 4 off I-293 (622–6444). Efficiencies and motel units. Outdoor pool. Color TV.

MERRIMACK. Hilton at Merrimack. *Deluxe.* Exit 8 off Rte. 3 (Everett Tpk.) (424–6181). Excellent dining to go with tranquil, wooded site. Lounge. Indoor pool, sauna. Pets. Color TV (cable).

NASHUA. Sheraton-Tara Hotel. *Deluxe.* Exit 1 off Rte. 3 (Everett Tpk.) (888–9970). Restaurant and 2 bars. Indoor and outdoor pools, whirlpool, saunas, steam bath, complete health club facilities. Tennis, racquetball. Pets. Color TV (cable).

Hannah Dustin Motel. *Inexpensive.* 172 Daniel Webster Hwy., Exit 1 off Rte. 3 (888–2315). Family units and 6 kitchenettes. Pool. Color TV.

SALEM. Fireside Inn. *Moderate.* Rte. 28, Exit 1 off I–93 (893–3584). Some kitchenettes. Pool. Color TV.

Salem Inn. *Moderate.* Exit 2 off I–93. Restaurant, lounge. Pool. Pets. TV.

MONADNOCKS REGION

FITZWILLIAM. Fitzwilliam Inn. *Moderate.* Jct. of Rtes. 12 and 119 (585–9000). Goes back to 1796 as an old stage stop. Right on the Village Green. Early American atmosphere and excellent dining. Oldtime travelers, though, didn't have benefit of the inn's pool or sauna. TV.

FRANCESTOWN. Tory Pines Resort. *Moderate-Expensive.* Rte. 47 (588–6352). Good lunch spot, fine dinners, lounge. Golf, tennis, pool. Converted barn into elegant rooms. Skating and 25 miles of cross-country ski trails.

Inn at Crotched Mountain. *Moderate.* Mountain Rd. (588–6840). Dining room, lounge; dining room closed Sun. and Mon. nights. Outdoor pool, tennis. Cross-country skiing. Pets.

HANCOCK. John Hancock Inn. *Moderate.* Main St. (525–3318). Closing out second century (since 1789) of hospitality; state's oldest operating inn. Fine dining by candlelight; lounge.

JAFFREY. Woodbound Inn. *Deluxe* (AP). Woodbound Rd. (532–8341). Multiple-day visits only in July and Aug.; one or two-day stays okay in other seasons. Excellent dining. Small alpine ski hill on grounds, 18 miles of cross-country ski trails. Beach, swimming in Contoocook Lake. Par-3 golf, tennis.

KEENE. Coach House Motel. *Moderate.* Rte. 12–S (352–4208). Cabins and cottages, located on mill pond. Heated pool. Pets. Cable TV.

Valley Green Motel. *Moderate-Expensive.* 379 West St. (352–7350). Miniature golf, shuffleboard. Heated outdoor pool. Color TV (cable).

Winding Brook Lodge. *Moderate.* Park Ave. (352–3111). Restaurant, lounge. Pool. Pets. Color TV (cable).

Yankee Traveler Motel. *Inexpensive.* Rte. 12, outside of town. Nice rooms in country setting.

PETERBOROUGH. Salzburg Inn & Restaurant. *Moderate.* Steele Rd. (924–3808). Motel or inn rooms. Hearty restaurant fare; Wed. night buffet. Lounge. Pool. Pets. TV.

TROY. Inn at East Hill Farm. *Moderate-Deluxe* (MAP). Mountain Rd. (242–6495). Farm setting for modest resort that includes hefty family-style meals, beach with swimming, hiking, water skiing, horseback riding, kids' programs. In winter, rope tow for alpine skiing, cross-country skiing.

SEACOAST REGION

DURHAM. New England Center. *Expensive.* Strafford Ave. (862–2810). Gorgeous setting on-campus. Restaurant, lounge. Color TV (cable).

EXETER. Exeter Inn. *Moderate-Expensive.* 90 Front St. Georgian setting with comfortable rooms. Excellent dining, bar. Pets. Color TV.

HAMPTON/HAMPTON BEACH. Atlantic Motel. *Moderate-Expensive.* 393 Ocean Blvd. (926–3292). Heated pool to go with the ocean. Color TV.

Drop Anchor Motel. *Moderate-Expensive.* 581 Ocean Blvd. (926–2769). Kitchenettes. Pool, playground.

Seascape Motel. *Moderate-Expensive.* 955 Ocean Blvd. at North Beach (926–9153). Color TV.

Sheraton Inn. *Moderate-Expensive.* Rte. 1 at 101–C (926–8911). Early American furnishing in modern motel units. Superb restaurant, lounge. Five mins. to Hampton Beach.

Ashworth by the Sea. *Inexpensive-Expensive.* 295 Ocean Blvd., Rte. 1–A and 51 (926–6762). Oceanfront property with heated indoor-outdoor pool to go with the beach and ocean. Fine seafood restaurant, lounge.

PORTSMOUTH. Anchorage Motor Inn. *Expensive.* On the Portsmouth Traffic Circle (431–8111). Indoor pool, sauna. Pets. Color TV (cable).

Inn at Christian Shore. *Moderate.* 335 Maplewood Ave. (431–6770). Federal Era home (1800) with period furnishings. Full course breakfast included. Pets. Color TV (cable).

The Inn at Newington. *Moderate.* Rtes. 4 and 16 (431–0777). Small, quiet place with guest kitchen available. Continental breakfast. Pets welcome.

Martin Hill Inn. *Moderate.* 404 Islington St. (426–2287). Another 19th-century pearl with antiques in all six guest rooms and full course breakfast included.

RYE/RYE BEACH. Hoyt's Lodges. *Moderate-Expensive.* 891 Ocean Blvd. (436–5350). Oceanfront cottages with pine paneling; all are kitchenettes. Cable TV. Open Memorial Day to Columbus Day.

Rye Beach Motel & Cottages. *Moderate-Expensive.* Old Beach and Locke roads. Housekeeping units and motel rooms. Beach. Color TV. Open May to Oct.

 **BED AND BREAKFAST.** The bed & breakfast concept, so popular in Europe—in which you get breakfast included in the room rate—is catching on in the United States. It usually means less-than-luxury accommodations—comfortable but not costly . . . with breakfast the next morning.

For more information about B&B places in New Hampshire, three possible sources: *American Bed & Breakfast,* Box 983F, St. Albans VT 05478 (802–524–4731); *New England Bed & Breakfast* 1045 Center St., Newton Center MA 02159 (617–498–9819); and *Pineapple Hospitality,* 384 Rodney French Blvd., New Bedford MA 02744 (617–997–9952).

In New Hampshire, B&B arrangements are available at:

Bath. *Green Pastures Farm* (747–2802). Off-track cross-country skiing, snowmobiling, hiking. One double, one single room.

Fitzwilliam. *Fern Hill.* (685–6672). Rural Colonial home; one twin-bedded room with private bath. Cross-country skiing.

Hanover. *Trescott Wayside.* (642–5798). Another country place. One twin-bedded room with bath; one single room. No smoking, please.

HOW TO GET AROUND. By car. The state has 203 miles of expressways and many excellent secondary roads. The main north-south arteries are I–93 and the Everett Tpk. (U.S. Rte. 3), each of which starts near Boston; Rte. 3 ends in Twin Mountain, I–93 runs to Littleton. I–89 runs east-west, connecting Concord with West Lebanon and the Vermont state line. Other good roads through the Granite State are: U.S. 302, 4, 202, 3, and 2; State routes 16, 25, 26, 28, 11, 103, 10, 101, 111, 114 and 110. Rte. 112, a part of the 34½-mile-long Kancamagus Hwy., winds its way through the White Mountain National Forest between Conway and Lincoln, a very scenic drive. From the seacoast to the northern slopes adjoining Canada and down along the western boundary edging Vermont, New Hampshire offers a wide variety of exciting drives.

Rte. I–89 in Springfield, I–93 in Littleton, Bethlehem, and sections of it at Windham and Sanborton, and I–89 in Hopkinton have been judged among America's most beautiful highways.

Car rentals. Major national chains have car rentals at all airports and population centers. Check local Yellow Pages.

TOURIST INFORMATION SERVICES. Maps, recreational calendars and many pamphlets for special activities are distributed by the *New Hampshire Office of Vacation Travel* (OVT), Box 856, Concord NH 03301 (271–2343). The OVT is the basic resource for virtually all printed tourist material in the Granite State, certainly for all major sites and sights, including seasonal vacation guides (summer and winter editions) as well as the annual camping guide. The state *Division of Parks,* 6 Loudon Rd., Concord 03301 (271–3556) produces a folder on wayside picnic areas and the state map contains a listing of state parks; the map is available from the OVT. For information on the White Mountain National Forest, contact the regional office, Box 638, Laconia NH 03246 (524–6450). The state's regional tourist associations have all but disappeared in the last year or two, but free literature is still available by contacting: *Seacoast Council on Tourism,* Box 4669, Portsmouth, NH 03801; *Monadnock Region Association,* Box 269, Peterborough, NH 03458; *Lakes Region Association,* Box 300, Wolfeboro NH 03894 (569–1117); *White Mountains News Bureau,* Box 176F, North Woodstock NH 03262 (745–8720). Information and assistance also are available from the following: *Greater Keene Chamber of Commerce,* 12 Gilbo Ave., Keene 03431 (352–1303) for southwestern N.H.; *Greater Portsmouth Chamber of Commerce,* Market St. Ext., Portsmouth 03801 (436–1118) for the seacoast area; *Mt. Washington Valley Chamber of Commerce,* Box 385, North Conway NH 03860 (356–3171); and the *N.H. Campground Owners' Association,* 30 Bonny St., Nashua 03062 (880–1471).

Turnpike information booths are situated at the Dover, Merrimack, and Rochester toll plazas. Year-round information services are available at safety rest areas at Canterbury-Northfield, Rte. I–93; Sutton, Rte. I–89; Sanbornton-Boulder, Rte. I–93; Lebanon, Rte. 120; North Conway, Rte. 16; Springfield, Rte. I–89; Salem, Rte. I–93; Seabrook, Rte. I–95; Nashua, Everett Turnpike. Tourist booths are open on various highways during the summer months.

For information about the operating and equipping of motor boats on inland waters, write to the New Hampshire *Dept. of Safety,* Division of Safety Services, Concord NH 03301, and to the Bureau of Off-Highway Vehicles, Box 856, Concord, for those planning to use snow traveling vehicles, for their book *Snow Travelling Vehicle Law.*

Saltwater boating enthusiasts should write to New Hampshire *State Port Authority,* P.O. Box 506, 555 Market St., Portsmouth NH 03801 to obtain information concerning regulations and facilities.

For information on saltwater fishing on the New Hampshire coastline, write the *Seacoast Council on Tourism,* address above.

SEASONAL EVENTS. February: Dartmouth College Winter Carnival in Hanover; Annual Sled Dog Championships in Laconia.

March: Cross-country ski marathon at Bretton Woods Resort (held irregularly from Jan. through March; contact Bretton Woods, 278–1000).

April: Antique Fair in Lebanon (early Apr.); Antique Fair in Amherst from late Apr. to Oct.

July: (early July) Antique Fairs in New Castle and New London; (late July) Antique Fair in Alton; Stratham Country Fair; Harness racing at Hinsdale from July through Aug.

August: (early Aug.) Cheshire Fair at Keene; North Haverhill Fair; (mid Aug.) Canaan Agricultural Fair; Vermont-New Hampshire high school all-star football game, followed the next day by a 10 km. road race in Hanover; (mid-Aug.) Cornish Fair; Belknap County 4-H Fair at Laconia; Plymouth State Fair.

September: (early Sept.) Lancaster Fair; Hopkinton Fair; Hillsboro County Fair at New Boston; mud football world championship in North Conway; (mid Sept.) power boat regatta at Moore Dam in Littleton; runners marathon in Hanover; (late Sept.) Rochester Fair; Greyhound racing at Hinsdale from Sept. through June; Deerfield Fair from late Sept. to early Oct.

October: Antique Fair at Hopkinton in early Oct.; Sandwich Fair in early Oct.; Antique Fair in Concord in mid Oct.

FALL FOLIAGE. Autumn is one of the most spectacular—and crowded—times in New Hampshire. The changing colors of the leaves attract hundreds of thousands annually. The foliage begins to turn after Labor Day in the northernmost sections of the Granite State and moves south, depending on the weather; the combination of warm days and cool nights helps produce the best color. If the weather is poor, i.e., always warm or drizzly or cool, the color is muted. Since the weekends are generally jam packed—especially Rte. 16 through the Mt. Washington Valley and Rte. 3 as it snakes its way through Franconia Notch, the best advice is to visit midweek, if possible. And make lodging reservations in advance; don't figure you'll "just find a place." The highway work through the Notch into 1987 will not ease things, either, although the widened roadway should make things more enjoyable. The interstate highways provide the best viewing spots but getting off the interstates, such as taking Rte. 112 from North Woodstock through Kinsman Notch and out toward Woodsville, then circling back over Route 302 into Littleton or Franconia, is equally enjoyable. Or take Rte. 11 west from I–89 at New London, on to Claremont, then north on Rte. 12–A, along the Connecticut River to the Hanover-West Lebanon area.

TOURS. By boat: A way to relax while touring is to take one of the many boat cruises on Lake Winnipesaukee or Lake Sunapee. If ocean voyages are more to your liking, try the cruise to the Isles of Shoals from Portsmouth.

On Lake Winnipesaukee, the M.V. *Mt. Washington* departs from Weirs Beach and stops at Center Harbor, Wolfeboro and Alton Bay. Open Memorial Day to Oct. 15. 3 trips daily in summer from Weirs Beach, 2 trips daily from Wolfeboro and Alton Bay, both stopping at Center Harbor. Leaving from Meredith and Weirs Beach several times daily the *Sophie C.* and *Doris E.* tour Lake Winnipesaukee. U.S. mail trips on *Sophie C.* depart from Weirs Beach at 1 P.M. mid-June–mid-Sept., with extra cruises at 11 A.M. and 3:00 P.M. July 1 to Labor Day. Stops at some islands rarely seen by tourists.

Two boats cruise Lake Sunapee: the M.V. *Mt. Sunapee II* and the M.V *Kearsarge;* each leaves daily from Sunapee Harbor, off Rte. 11, from late May to early Sept. M.V *Mt. Sunapee II* offers twice-daily cruises of the lake during the day while the *Kearsarge* has two dinner cruises (buffet dining) daily (or nightly). Phones: *Sunapee II,* 763–4030; *Kearsarge,* 763–5477.

To Isles of Shoals: Viking Cruises (431–5500) handles daily narrated cruises around Isles of Shoals departing from Market St. dock in Portsmouth. Daily cruises from mid-June to Labor Day. Dinner cruise featuring lobster is also available. Reservations required for all cruises.

Atlantic Fleet fishing parties depart from Rye Harbor. Open May to Oct. for fishing trips all or half days and night fishing mid-June to mid-Sept.

By train: *Conway Scenic Railroad* operates daily from early May (weekends until early June) through late Oct. One-hour rides leave Russian-looking depot in North Conway as steam train chugs down along Saco River. *Wolfeboro Rail Road* provides 24-mile roundtrip late-May to mid-Oct. daily. Boardings at three stations—Wolfeboro, Wakefield, Sanbornville. Phones: Conway Scenic RR, 356–5251; Wolfeboro RR, 569–4884.

SPECIAL-INTEREST TOURS. Popular touring seasons are spring, when flowering shrubs and unfolding leaves bring subtle pastel tones to the landscape; and autumn, when brilliant autumnal foliage spreads a mosaic of color over the land.

The Kancamagus Highway is the loftiest mountain highway in the East— 34½ miles, through the *White Mountain National Forest* between Lincoln and Conway, of unspoiled, spectacular views, picnic areas, and campsites.

Blossoms and foliage: Eight different tours on secondary roads in the White Mountains are listed and mapped in a brochure entitled *Shunpike Fall Foliage Tours in New Hampshire's White Mountain Region.* These trips would be interesting at other seasons, too. Contact New Hampshire Office of Vacation Travel, Box 856, Concord 03301.

A special group called "Leaf Watchers" goes into action each fall to observe the progress of leaf color in all regions of the state. The information is then given to a Foliage Reporting Headquarters at the Office of Vacation Travel in Concord. They, in turn, send out reports once a week for four weeks just prior to and also during the fall foliage season. The most brilliant leaf color usually begins by the third week in Sept. and spreads south, reaching a peak in southern areas by Columbus Day.

Also suggested are: *Curtis Dogwood Reservation* in Lyndeborough, off Rte. 31 from Wilton. Apple Blossom tour in May. *Rhododendron State Park* in Fitzwilliam is open late June to Labor Day. Maximum blossoms about July 1 to 15.

Historic tours of the New Castle-Portsmouth area, based on scholarly research and presented in sprightly fashion, are offered by *Insight Tours,* Box 61, New Castle 03854.

Covered Bridges: Also popular are the 64 covered bridges in N.H. Many travelers enjoy planning their route so that they get to see them all (and see a great deal of New Hampshire in the process). A few of these wooden structures are known as "kissing bridges;" they were romantic stopping places for a horse and buggy. Locations are pinpointed on the official state highway map and in the OVT's annual Guide to Events and Attractions.

Polar Caves on Rte. 25, 4 miles west of Plymouth and I–93. Open daily mid-May through mid-Oct. Guided 1-mile walk through natural gorge. **Lost River Reservation,** Rte. 112, Kinsman Notch, N. Woodstock, (745–8031). Guided tours through glacial gorge. Open mid-May through mid-Oct.

The Flume at Franconia Notch on U.S. 3 is open from end of May through mid-Oct. **Ruggles Mine,** Rte. 4 in Grafton (523–4275), is open daily mid-June through mid-Oct. Weekends end of May through mid-June.

The Colebrook Fish Hatchery, Colebrook, is open to visitors daily.

Scenic rides: Major ski areas such as Cannon, Sunapee, Waterville Valley, Wildcat, Loon, and Mt. Cranmore offer scenic chairlift or gondola rides. For a little more zip, perhaps the Alpine Slides at Attitash and Alpine Ridge, in which you control your own speed as you ride a specially engineered sled downhill, are what you're seeking. They're operating mid-June to mid-Oct.

Water slides: There are water rides are Attitash Ski Area (Bartlett), Weirs Beach and Lancaster. Bring your bathing suit and "rent" the slide for as many rides down the watery trough as you can squeeze into a specified time period.

Up Mt. Washington: The *Mt. Washington Cog Railway* is open from end of May through mid-Oct. Daily trains from end of June to Sept. 9. Trains run weather permitting. Base station on paved road from U.S. 302 in Bretton Woods. The *Mt. Washington auto road,* Rte. 16, Pinkham Notch, is open mid-May to early Nov. While it is an excellent road, it should be undertaken only by thoroughly experienced drivers with cars in top condition, and it is not for acrophobes. Rides are available for those not wishing to drive.

 **NATIONAL PARKS AND FORESTS.** *The White Mountain National Forest* was established in May 1918, and contains some 724,000 acres of fabulous scenery, hiking, camping sites, and some top winter sports areas. About 678,000 acres of the forest are in north-central New Hampshire; the rest are in western Maine. To reach the White Mountain National Forest, you can take some of the most scenic highways in the country. Among the most popular are: Franconia Notch Highway (U.S. 3), which runs north-south; Crawford Notch Highway (U.S. 302), east-west; Pinkham Notch Highway (State 16), north-south through the Mt. Washington Valley. One of the most spectacular drives is along the Kancamagus Highway. From Conway, this 34-mile forest highway follows the Swift River to Passaconaway Valley. From here, it climbs high up the flank of Mt. Kancamagus, crosses the nearly 3,000-ft.-high pass, and winds down the Hancock branch and east branch of the Pemigewasset River to Lincoln. Previously closed at night in winter, the "Kanc" is open all day, all year thanks to state road crews' constant plowing in winter. Marvelous views of towering mountain peaks and clear, cool mountain streams make this picturesque highway a prime attraction of the White Mountains area.

The National Forest has 19 camp areas, numerous lakes and ponds, and miles upon miles of fishable streams. The entire forest is open for fishing and hunting during the state's open seasons. Facilities at the *White Mountain National Forest Campgrounds* consist of family units including an individual parking spur, tent pad, table, and fire grates. No special facilities are provided for trailers, but they may be used at most areas. Sites are available on a first come, first served basis, and no reservations are accepted. Nominal fees are charged at most campgrounds and the length of stay may be limited to 14 days. Dogs are permitted only on leash. *Dolly Copp, Campton, Jigger Johnson, Sugarloaf I,* and *Russel Pond* are usually open late May to Oct. Most other areas may be used at any time during the year, but are not maintained from late Oct. to early May.

Permits are required for all campfires in undeveloped sites in the *White Mountain National Forest,* but not if you're planning to cook on a portable stove. At improved roadside campgrounds and picnic areas where there are fireplaces, no permit is required. Permits may be obtained in person or by mail from the Forest Supervisor's Office, 719 North Main St., Laconia NH 03246 (524–6450), or from the District Ranger offices: Trudeau Road, Bethlehem, NH 03574 (869–2626); Kancamagus Highway, Conway NH 03818 (447–5448); 80 Glen Road, Gorham NH 03581 (466–2713); 127 Highland St., Plymouth NH 03264 (536–1310); or just over the state line on Bridge St., Bethel ME 04217 (207–824–2134). In addition, the Plymouth (NH) Fire Department, 42 Highland St. (436–1252), issues fire permits 24 hours if you were unable to get one elsewhere or require one after the ranger offices close.

STATE PARKS AND BEACHES. New Hampshire's 34 state parks and one state beach have some of the most beautiful natural sites in the East. Among the most popular is *Crawford Notch State Park* (846–5404) with superb views of Crawford Notch, Mt. Washington and the Presidential Range (U.S. 302). The Cog Railway is also at Crawford Notch.

There is more scenic wonder at *Mt. Sunapee State Park* (763–2356), at Newbury, with its 125 acres of ski slopes and trails, gondola lift, and a well-developed beach.

Franconia Notch (823–5563), at Franconia and Lincoln, is a deep valley of 6,552 acres between towering Franconia and Kinsman Mountain ranges. Some of the scenic highlights of this area are: the Flume Gorge, an 800-ft. natural chasm; Cannon Mt. Tramway, Echo Lake, and the Old Man of the Mountains rock profile.

At *Rhododendron State Park* (in Fitzwilliam) (532–8862), some 16 acres of rhododendron shrubs open their pink heaps of blossom in mid-July.

White Lake State Park at Tamworth (323–7350) and *Monadnock State Park* at Jaffrey (532–8862) are among the 12 parks with public campgrounds for tenting and many trails for hiking—especially suitable for families and young campers.

Ocean bathing is a featured attraction at *Wallis Sands* (at Rye), which has a large bath house. A short drive away is *Hampton State Beach* with two miles of sandy beach along the Atlantic Ocean and a modern recreational complex.

Bear Brook State Park, Allenstown (485–9874), includes an *Audubon Nature Center* (485–3782), which usually opens the last week in June.

Some state parks are open through the fall foliage season when the warm Indian summer days draw thousands into the outdoors for camping. Major ski areas are operated by the New Hampshire Division of Parks at Franconia's *Cannon Mountain* and at *Mt. Sunapee State Park.* Free information is sent on request by the New Hampshire OVT, Box 856, Concord NH 03301 or the Division of Parks, 6 Loudon St., Concord NH 03301.

CAMPING. Campsites are available in the state parks, the White Mt. Nat. Forest, and in privately owned campgrounds. For a complete listing write to the NH Campground Owners Assn., 30 Bonny St., Nashua NH 03062, for the *New Hamsphire Camping Guide,* which also contains the regulations covering each type of site.

SUMMER SPORTS. Water Sports: The seacoast region offers excellent beaches for saltwater bathing. *Hampton Beach,* with a broad, sandy beach, is a very popular resort area. *Little Boars Head* in North Hampton and Rye provides tourists with swimming from supervised beaches and picnic area.

The Monadnock Region is dotted with numerous waterways just made for summer water sports.

In the Lakes Region, which covers the central part of the state, there are eight major lakes: *Winnipesaukee, Squam, Winnisquam, Sunapee, Newfound, Ossipee, Mascoma* and *Wentworth. Weirs Beach,* a boating center on the western side of Lake Winnipesaukee, offers a wide range of summer activities. There are speed boat rides, water skiing, boat races and swimming races.

Wolfeboro is another resort area of Lake Winnipesaukee. *Brewster Beach,* a supervised town beach, is a natural attraction for the swimmer. Boat launching facilities are nearby.

The town of *Sunapee* is the gateway to the lake of the same name. Boating and swimming are the main attractions. Water skiing and water ski shows are put on during the summer season.

Fishing: More than 1,300 lakes and ponds and 1,500 miles of streams in New Hampshire furnish a variety of fishing for beginner or expert. Brook (native), brown, and rainbow trout; landlocked salmon; lake trout; bass; pickerel; whitefish; white and yellow perch; and many other species offer sport in season from "ice out" time in April until autumn. Licenses are required for freshwater fishing, except for nonresident minors; write to the N.H. Fish & Game Dept., 34 Bridge St., Concord 03301. New Hampshire's seacoast offers further opportunities to the angler, either as a steady diet or as a change of pace. Favorite rod-and-reel fish include tuna, striped bass, mackerel, harbor pollock, and the larger sea pollock. There are also cod, haddock, cusk, hake and other species. The coho salmon has been introduced, and flounder is abundant in the harbors and rivers. Cunner is taken either off rocks and piers or from boats. No license is required for saltwater fishing except for smelt in Great Bay, oysters, and clams (consult *Seacoast Region Association,* Box 476, Exeter, 03833).

Boating: The tremendous popularity of motorboating in New Hampshire is evidenced by the registration of 40,585 boats and outboard motors in 1980 for operation on the state's hundreds of lakes, ponds, and rivers. Most of the spots offer launching facilities for those who trailer their boats. Boating in the Seacoast-Southern Region can be either on the ocean or on the hundreds of lakes, ponds and rivers in the area. *Great* and *Little Ponds,* which are large saltwater ponds to the west of Portsmouth, offer excellent boating facilities. There are launching sites and piers available to the public on the *Piscataqua River* at Dover. On the *Hampton River,* at Hampton, boat rentals, anchorage as well as piers, motor rentals and charter boats are available. *New Castle* has public anchorage; *Portsmouth* offer boat rentals, charter boats and public piers. *Rye* boasts boat rentals and launching areas at Rye Harbor. *Seabrook Beach* also has boat rentals and launching areas for the public.

Freshwater lakes and ponds in the Seacoast Region, for the most part, have boats to rent and public launching area. Speedboat rides can be enjoyed at *Lake Massabesic* in Manchester and on *Lake Canobie* in Salem.

The Lakes Region is one of the major inland boating areas in the Northeast. There are many boat yards and supply areas located at points on *Lake Winnipesaukee, Sunapee, Squam, Winnisquam* and *Newfound.*

The largest lake in the Granite State, *Lake Winnipesaukee,* offers boat and motor rentals, launch areas and public piers at *Alton Bay, Center Harbor, Glendale, Weirs Beach, Lakeport, Meredith, Moultonborough* and *Wolfeboro.* Charter boats can be obtained at *Alton Bay, Lakeport, Weirs Beach, Wolfeboro* and *Meredith.*

Lake Sunapee, Burkehaven, George's Mills, Mt. Sunapee and *Blodgett's Landing* at Sunapee have motor and boat rentals, as well as piers and public launch sites.

Ashland and *Holderness,* on *Squam Lake,* provide motor and boat rentals, public piers and launching areas. *Lake Winnisquam* and *Newfound Lake* also have boats to rent, piers and launch sites. At *Bristol* and *Hebron* on *Newfound Lake,* motors are also for hire. *Lake Ossipee* offers boat rentals and launch areas only.

Other lakes and ponds in the region offer the visitor boats to rent and a place to launch their own boat. Navigational charts, recommended for safety, are available for all large lakes.

Speedboat rides are available on *Lake Winnipesaukee* at *Alton Bay, Lakeport, Meredith,* and *Weirs Beach. George's Mills* and *Sunapee* are where you'll find speedboat rides on *Lake Sunapee. Newfound Lake,* at the southern end, also has speedboat rides available.

Sailing is also a favorite activity and boats may be rented at *Lakes Winnipesaukee, Sunapee* and *Newfound.*

There are small boat harbors at *Portsmouth, Rye,* and *Hampton* (each has a harbormaster). Boating is also enjoyed on *Great* and *Little Bays,* New Hampshire's unusual inland tidewater area (which also has a harbormaster). Power boats operating in the state's tidal waters are registered by the U.S. Coast Guard and numbered according to their federal system. Boats which operate on both tidal and inland waters must carry both registrations.

Hiking: For novice and expert hikers there is a vast network of marked trails throughout the state. The best, perhaps, can be found in the *White Mountain National Forest.* Those wishing complete information should read the *White Mountain Guide*—a booklet which can be purchased from the Appalachian Mountain Club, 5 Joy St., Boston, 02108. A free folder, "AMC Huts System," is also issued by the club to describe the system of shelters located a day's hike apart where sleeping quarters and meals are provided. Since 1888, New Hampshire has pioneered in the hut system to accommodate the thousands of hikers who wend their way through the high country. For the physically fit and hardy, this is a superb way to enjoy the New Hampshire landscape. Recommended: *Fifty Hikes in New Hampshire's White Mountains* (NH Publishing, Somersworth, NH 03878).

Horseback Riding: For riding enthusiasts New Hampshire offers several places around the state where one can rent a horse and go riding. At *Four Seasons Lodge* in Sunapee; *Highlawn Farm* in Warner; *Thousand Acre Farm* in Franklin; the *Circle K* in Laconia; in Wolfeboro at *Allen "A" Ranch; The Whippoorwill Stables* in Amherst; *Deerfield Riding Academy* in Deerfield, where instruction is also available; *Warrior Ranch* in Windham; in Chesterfield the *Dude Ranch; Silver Ranch* in Jaffrey; at *Waterville Valley resort;* Rockhouse Mt. Farm in Conway, and *Castle in the Clouds,* Moultonboro.

Tennis: Special tennis programs, some including pro instruction, are offered at a number of resorts. The *White Mountain Tennis Association,* Box 517A, Lincoln 03251, will supply information on programs in that area.

Golf: There are 75 golf courses in N.H., including *Province Lake Country Club,* Province Lake, a lakeside course; *Wentworth by the Sea,* Newcastle, designed by Geoffrey Cornish (the resort was closed at presstime, however), three holes play over the ocean. *Lake Sunapee C.C.,* New London, with rolling terrain; *Sunset Hill Golf Club,* Sugar Hill, beautiful setting; *Jack O'Lantern Resort,* Woodstock, flat, valley course along river; *Mt. Washington Hotel & CC.,* Bretton Woods, a Donald Ross layout with frequent slopes; *Mountain View Golf Club,* Whitefield, a slightly hilly course and one of the best resorts in New England; *The Balsams Hotel C.C.,* Dixville Notch, a famous Donald Ross course with mountaintop 18. Also, *Tory Pines,* Francestown, has an 18-hole Hall of Fame course re-creating top holes around the world.

For a list of courses open spring to autumn write the N.H. OVT, Box 856, Concord 03301.

Hunting: Deer, bear, grouse, duck, woodcock, pheasant, snowshoe hares, cottontail rabbits, squirrel, coon, fox, and wildcat are among the species commonly hunted in New Hampshire. There are special seasons and licenses for hunting deer with bow and arrow and with muzzle-loading firearms.

For information on resident licenses, open seasons and bag limits write to the N.H. Fish & Game Dept., 34 Bridge St., Concord 03301.

All persons over 16 are required to have a license to hunt and fish in the state. Non-resident minors need a license to hunt but not to fish.

WINTER SPORTS. Downhill skiing: There are now some two dozen major ski areas with almost 125 lifts, tows and trams. The alpine ski season, reinforced by extensive snowmaking systems at New Hampshire's major alpine areas, will run from late Nov. (usually by Thanksgiving) until late April. The most challenging skiing is perhaps at *Tuckerman Ravine* on the eastern flank of Mt. Washington, but that's an undeveloped area and the U.S. Forest Service bars would-be skiers until the avalanche danger is past (usually by late Apr.).

Other noted ski areas are *Cannon Mt.,* Franconia; *Wildcat Mt.,* Jackson; *Waterville Valley, Loon Mt.,* Lincoln; *Mount Cranmore,* N. Conway; *Attitash,* Bartlett; *Gunstock,* Gilford; *Bretton Woods; Wilderness at the Balsams,* Dixville Notch; *Mount Sunapee,* Newbury. Areas with shorter drops are: *Crotched Mt.,* Francestown; *Pat's Peak,* Henniker; *Dartmouth Skiway,* Lyme; *Alpine Ridge,* Gilford; *Highland,* Northfield; *Tenney Mt.,* Plymouth; *Ragged Mt.,* Danbury; *Mt. Whittier,* Ossippee; *Black Mt.,* Jackson; *Moose Mt.,* Brookfield; *King Pine,* E. Madison; *Whaleback,* Lebanon; and *King Ridge,* New London.

Cross-country skiing is becoming increasingly popular. Jackson has 125 miles of cross-country trails lacing the valley town, and North Conway has perhaps 50 miles. Waterville Valley adds 35 miles; Bretton Woods has 50 miles; Gunstock adds 10; *Franconia Inn* has 40 miles and *Sunset Hill House,* in Sugar Hill has 45 miles. There are over 20 cross-country touring centers throughout the state.

Snowmobiling: N.H. leases thousands of acres of land with groomed trails for free snowmobiling. A map is available from the state Highway Vehicle Dept. Visitors who plan to use snow-traveling vehicles should contact the Bureau of Off-Highway Vehicles, P.O. Box 856, Concord 03301, for a free guidebook and any further information desired. Vehicles are required to be registered; the fee is $17 for nonresidents; reciprocity is granted only with the states of Vermont and Maine and the province of Quebec. Other off-road or multi-terrain vehicles not used on snow, such as trail bikes, minibikes and ATVs, may not be used on state park lands or certain trails in the White Mountain National Forest. Check with WMNF District Ranger Offices to find which trails can be used. They are prohibited from all campgrounds including privately operated ones, and may not be used on private land except with the owner's permission. This is a great way to tour, but it is important to follow regulations.

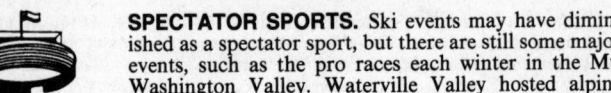

SPECTATOR SPORTS. Ski events may have diminished as a spectator sport, but there are still some major events, such as the pro races each winter in the Mt. Washington Valley. Waterville Valley hosted alpine World Cup races in 1980, then again from 1982–86 and was to hold another in December '86. Bretton Woods hosted the '82 national cross-country ski championships and holds a 50-km. cross-country race each winter. Major ski jumping meets at Gunstock (Gilford) and Nansen Jump (Berlin) depend each Feb. on the weather. Dartmouth's Winter Carnival is in Feb.; the ice sculpturing is nationally famous. The *Sled Dog Derby* in Laconia is a 60-mile trek over three days in the latter part of Feb. Sled dog races are held in *Lincoln, Tamworth, Meredeth, Pittsfield* and *Manchester.* The *Lancaster* snowmobile races are held every year in Feb.

Flames leveled Rockingham race track in Salem in 1980, but it reopened in 1984 with thoroughbred races in summer; Hinsdale Raceway in Hinsdale offers harness races in July and Aug. There also are some pari-mutuel races at county fairs in late Aug. or Sept. Greyhound racing goes on year round at Seabrook and Sept. to June at Hinsdale.

North Conway lost the Volvo tennis tourney but still has the alleged world championship of mud football in early Sept.; the annual *Shrine Maple Sugar Bowl* in mid-Aug. at Dartmouth pits VT and NH high school footballers and also includes a 10-km. road race the next day.

CHILDREN'S ACTIVITIES. There are attractions and fun places for children from the beaches through the White Mountains. Perhaps the greatest concentration is in the White Mountains region, but there are fun places throughout the state.

Captain Blastoff's Fun City, Rte. 3A, at the base of Newfound Lake, Bristol, is open daily from Memorial Day to Labor Day; mid-May to Memorial Day and Labor Day to mid-Oct. just weekends. Adm. free, but there is a charge for rides and golf. *The Lockhaven Schoolhouse Museum* at Enfield (632–7746) is open Sun. 2 to 5, from June through early Oct. The school is over 100 years old and has old school registers from 1858 on. Free.

Lost River on Rte. 112, 3 miles west of North Woodstock and I–93 (745–8031), open mid-May to mid-Oct., has guided tours along a boardwalk and fallen boulders in a glacial gorge. Nature garden, small museum and displays.

Six Gun City, at the intersection of Rtes. 2 and 15, in Jefferson, is open mid-June to mid-Oct., weekends only after Labor Day. Authentic rides, skits, free pony rides and stagecoach rides. *Wagon Museum,* too (586–4592).

Santa's Village, also in Jefferson (586–4445), open from mid-June through Oct., provides a chance to see Santa early, pet free-roaming deer and ducks, and take a few rides.

Benson's Wild Animal Farm in Hudson, Rte. 111 east of Nashua (882–2481), is open daily mid-Apr. through Oct. Animal farm, amusements, beautiful gardens.

Mt. Washington Cog Railway, Bretton Woods (846–5404), is open late May to mid-Oct., weekends to mid-June. All rides weather permitting. Children under 6 travel free.

The Friendly Farm, Rte. 101, Dublin (563–8444), has farm animals and their young. Open May to mid-Oct. After Labor Day, weekends only.

In Glen: At Jct. of Rtes. 16 and 302 (383–4293), *Story Land* is open mid-June through mid-Oct. Fairy-tale setting, kids' rides, very clean.

Heritage New Hampshire, Rte. 16, just north of jct. Rte. 302 (383–9776). Next to Storyland, another treat. Multi-media look at the state's 3½ centuries of history. Open late-May to late-Oct.

Canobie Lake Park, just off I–93, Rte. 28 in Salem (893–3506), has numerous amusements on 50-acre area. Open weekends Easter to Memorial Day, then daily to Labor Day.

Clarks Trading Post, Rte. 3, Lincoln (745–8913), has bear shows, locomotive rides, museums. Open July to Labor Day. Entertainment during July and Aug. but only on weekends May to June and Sept. to Oct.

Children's Museum, Meeting House Hill, Portsmouth (436–3853). Part of Strawbery Banke complex; hands-on experiences for kids with look at American life as well as other cultures.

 **HISTORIC SITES AND HOMES.** Since its creation in 1955 by the state legislature, the State Historical Commission has set up markers throughout New Hampshire at places of historical interest. The 115 markers are described in a booklet of the State Historical Commission and are identified on the New Hampshire Tourist Map obtainable from the NH Division of Economic Development, State House Annex, Concord. In 1973 both Dover and Portsmouth celebrated their 350th anniversary with extensive restoration of many of the towns' Colonial homes. Most places are open to tourists only during the summer, but check locally.

SEACOAST REGION

DERRY. *Robert Frost's Home,* Rte. 28, south of town. The famed poet's home 1900–09. Open 9 to 5 P.M. daily except Mon. and Tues., late June to Labor Day.

DOVER. *Woodman Institute,* 182 Central Ave. (742–1038). Open 2 to 5 P.M. daily except Mon., March 1 to mid-Jan. Free. Natural history and military museum; bird, animal, Indian exhibits plus 17th-century Dame Garrison House.

DURHAM. *Major General John Sullivan House,* Rte. 108. Home of Revolutionary War general; set back off the road with a small marker designating it but used as private residence. Not open to public.

EXETER. *War Memorial,* Gale Park on Front St. Created in 1920 by sculptor Daniel Chester French, who is better known for doing the Lincoln Memorial and the Minute Man at Concord (Mass.) Bridge.

NEW CASTLE. *Fort Constitution,* off Rte. 1–B, on point of land overlooking Piscataqua River emptying into Atlantic Ocean. Fort originally built in 1635; current structure went up in 1808. On Dec. 14–15, 1774, colonists—alerted by Paul Revere—removed gunpowder and cannon . . . four months before Lexington and Concord. Open daily 9 to 5 P.M. mid-June to Labor Day, weekends rest of year.

PORTSMOUTH. *Strawbery Banke,* Marcy St., off Rte. 1 (436–8010). This is a multi-million dollar historic restoration of the section of Portsmouth that was once the colony's capital. The entire area is a model of early architectural styles—especially Georgian—and should not be missed. Open daily 9:30 to 5 P.M. mid-Apr. to mid-Nov., by appointment in winter.

John Paul Jones House, corner of Middle and State Sts. (436–8420). Built in 1760, the house was home to Jones twice while he waited to take command of ships under construction nearby. Open June 1 to Columbus Day except Sun., 10 to 5 P.M.

Warner House, 150 Daniel St. Built in 1716 of stones used as ballast in sailing ship. Early Georgian architecture, well-preserved. Open mid-May to Columbus Day, 10 to 5 P.M.; 2 to 5 P.M. on Sun.

Governor John Langdon Memorial, 143 Pleasant St. (431–1800). Another Georgian beauty, home was erected in 1784 by ex-governor who also was first president of U.S. Senate, John Langdon. George Washington, visiting in 1789, called it the "handsomest house in Portsmouth." Open daily, June 1 to Columbus Day, 10 to 5 P.M.

Wentworth-Gardner House, 140 Mechanic St. Nearly perfect example of Georgian style (1760), overlooks the river. Open Memorial Day to Columbus Day, 10 to 5 P.M., except noon to 5 P.M. on Sun.

Moffatt-Ladd House, 154 Market St. (436–8221). Yet another Georgian gem (1763), neatly set behind white fence. Great stair hall, formal gardens and period furniture. Open mid-May to Columbus Day, 10 to 5 P.M.

St. John's Church, Chapel St. Great Fire of 1806 destroyed the Queen's Chapel and St. John's went up to replace it. George Washington visited here and Paul Revere recast the bell in 1807 when the church was completed.

MERRIMACK VALLEY

CANTERBURY. *Shaker Village,* off Rte. 106 (783–9977). Open from mid-May to mid-Oct. Guided tours. Open Tues. to Sat., and holidays, 10 to 5:30 P.M. One of villages formed in late 18th century; one of only two with several Shaker "sisters" still residing in it. Meeting House dates to 1792; other buildings on tour include schoolhouse, so-called Dwelling House, carriage house.

CONCORD. *State House,* 107 North Main St. (271–2154). Completed in 1819 of granite quarried in Concord area. No building in city may be taller than four stories, so the capitol's golden dome is visible from all directions. Visitors Center open all year, Mon. to Fri., 8 to 4:30 P.M.

First Church of Christ Scientist, North State St. Born in nearby Bow, Mary Baker Eddy was living here (1892–1908) when she reorganized the Christian Scientist Church, establishing Boston as the Mother Church. Historic site but not for sightseeing.

FRANKLIN. *Webster Family Cabin,* Rte. 127 between Salisbury and Franklin. Two-room childhood home of Daniel Webster. Built in 1780 and contains mementoes, papers, etc. Open daily mid-June to Labor Day.

MANCHESTER. *Gen. John Stark House,* 2000 Elm St. Open mid-May to mid-Oct., Wed. and Sun. only. Built in 1736; hero of Battle of Bennington grew up in this house, which was moved in 1970 to make way for bridge over the Merrimack River. Period furnishings, etc.

NORTH SALEM. *America's Stonehenge* (Mystery Hill), off Rte. 111 (893–8300). Previously known as Mystery Hill. Open May 1 to Oct. 31, 9:30 to 5 P.M. in summer, 10 to 4 P.M. at other times. Controversial site which claims to be 4,000-year-old astronomical complex built by Celts who came here from Europe's Iberian Peninsula.

WHITE MOUNTAINS REGION

COLEBROOK. *Our Lady of Grace Shrine,* Rte. 3 (237–5511). Open early May to Columbus Day. Operated by Oblate Fathers on 25-acre site. Chapel and many lifesize monuments.

DANBURY. *Ruggles Mine,* off Rte. 4 on Isinglass Mountain (523–4275). The nation's oldest mica, feldspar, beryl mine; mineral collecting is permitted. You have to be "into" minerals, otherwise, it's an open pit and a couple of boring tunnels. Open weekends mid-May to mid-June, daily from then until Columbus Day; 9 to 6 P.M. in summer, 9 to 5 P.M.

FRANCONIA. *Old Man of the Mountain,* Rte. 3 at Cannon Mountain (823–5563). Tramway to the top of this unique outcropping of rock that overlooks Franconia Notch. Profile is visible for only a short distance from below; scientists say it's made up from five different pieces of rock. Open Memorial Day to Columbus Day, 9 to 5 P.M. in July and Aug., 9 to 4:30 P.M. at other times.

The Flume, off Rte. 3 just below Franconia Notch (823–5563). Amazing 800-ft. chasm, like a miner's sluice, created by geothermal pressure belowground millions of years ago. Cooling on summer days because of tree-lined boardwalk or forest paths. Same hours as Old Man.

GORHAM. *Mt. Washington Auto Road,* Rte. 16 (466–3988). Climb eight-mile road to the summit of the tallest peak in northeastern U.S. by your own car or specially engineered "stage" vans. Museum and observatory at the summit. Open mid-May to late Oct., weather permitting; private cars 7 to 6 P.M., stages 8:30 to 4:30 P.M.

NORTH WOODSTOCK. *Lost River,* Rte. 112 at Kinsman Notch (745–8031). Boardwalk leads you three-quarters of a mile as you follow the stream-like "river" through relaxing, tree-lined boulder field. Fantastic for kids who like to crawl over, around huge rocks. Open mid-May to Columbus Day, 9 to 6 P.M. in June, July and Aug., 9 to 5:30 P.M. at other times.

PLYMOUTH. *Polar Caves,* Rte. 25 (536–1888). Boardwalk takes you through glacial caves formed when boulders fell from Mount Haycock as glaciers receded millions of years ago. Open daily 9 to 5 P.M. late May to Columbus Day.

HANOVER/LAKE SUNAPEE REGION

CHARLESTOWN. *Old Fort No. 4,* Rte. 12 (826–5094). Open mid-June to Labor Day, weekends to Columbus Day, 10 to 5 P.M. daily in summer, 11 to 5 P.M. on autumn weekends. Reconstruction of French & Indian War stockade built on site in 1744. Was northernmost and westernmost settlement at the time. Costumed guides and a 25-minute audio-visual program.

CLAREMONT. *Claremont Historical Society Museum,* Mulberry St. (543–1400). Open Thurs., 2–4 and 7–9 P.M., June to Sept. The city in a nutshell, from the original property map—on a goatskin—to countless other artifacts from Claremont's history.

CORNISH. *St. Gaudens National Historic Site,* Rte. 12–A (675–2175). Open mid-May to Oct. 31, 8 A.M. to 5 P.M. One-time estate of sculptor Augustus St. Gaudens, displays his works plus changing art exhibits. Sun. concerts in summer.

HILLSBOROUGH. *Franklin Pierce Homestead,* Rte. 31, west of village (271–2669). Not to be confused with Pierce Manse just north of Concord. Home of state's lone occupant of the White House, period pieces and restoration help recreate the period of 1804–1839. Open late June to Labor Day except Mon., 9 to 5 P.M.

MONADNOCKS REGION

KEENE. *Wyman Tavern,* 339 Main St. (352–1147). Open Tues. and Thurs., 1 to 4 P.M. Built in 1762 at tavern, served as meeting site in 1770 of first gathering of Dartmouth College trustees and in 1775 local "rebels" set out from here to join other colonists at Lexington.

NEW IPSWICH. *Barrett House,* Main St., off Rte. 124 (227–3956). Open Tues., Thurs. and weekends June 1 to Columbus Day, noon to 5 P.M. Headquarters for Society for Preservation of New England Antiquities, so you know it's in tip-top shape. Three-story, Federal Period (1800) building, maintained beautifully.

RINDGE. *Cathedral of the Pines,* Cathedral Rd. (899–3300). Open daily May 1 to Oct. 31, 9 to 5 in summer, 9 to 4 P.M. at other times. Religious and military or patriotic services at this non-denominational outdoor site built by a couple whose son was killed in World War II. Gorgeous hillside site.

LAKES REGION

MOULTONBOROUGH AREA. *Castle in the Clouds,* Rte. 171 (476–2352). Open weekends May 1 to late June, then daily 9 to 5 P.M. until Columbus Day. Onetime estate of eccentric millionaire; spectacular setting as part of 6,000-acre layout; sensational views, especially in foliage season, of woodlands at Lake Winnipesaukee from this hilltop perch. Cost $7 million when built in 1907.

 MUSEUMS AND GALLERIES. Throughout New Hampshire, you will find extensive examples of American and European art of the last three centuries, all well-housed and fascinating to visit.

SEACOAST REGION

DURHAM. *Paul Creative Arts Center* at the University of New Hampshire (862–3712). Two small galleries (the *Scudder* and the *Carter*) and a theater in a modest building that also houses several academic departments. Galleries open during school year but check for seasonal hours.

Historical Museum, 2nd floor of Town Office Building, Rte. 108 (868–5560). Open Tues. to Sat., 1 to 4 P.M. in July and Aug., by appointment at other times. Operated by Durham Historic Association; building was built in 1825. Extensive costume collection, plenty of local memorabilia.

HAMPTON. *Tuck Memorial Museum* (Hampton Historical Society), Meeting House Green, 40 Park Ave. Open July and Aug., Mon. to Fri., 10 to 4 P.M. One-room schoolhouse and a trolley collection to go with "Made in Hampton" items, among other things.

MERRIMACK VALLEY

CANDIA. *Fitts Museum,* Rte. 101–B (483–8527). Open to visitors in July and Aug., only on Sat., 2 to 5 P.M.; by appointment at other times. Building (1800) was given to town in 1901 by Fitts family, local residents. Museum contains Candia-oriented artifacts, documents, etc.

CONCORD. *The New Hampshire Historical Society Library and Museum,* 30 Park St. (225–3381). A library, museum and education center (there are classes and lectures all year-round). Permanent exhibits include four period rooms showing New England domestic interiors, 1680–1720. Free.

Conservation Center of the Society for the Protection of New Hampshire Forests, 54 Portsmouth St. (224–9945). Open all year, 8 to 5 P.M., Mon. to Fri. (8 to 4:30 P.M. in summer). Educational center concerning passive solar energy. Free.

MANCHESTER. *New Hampshire Art Association,* 24 W. Bridge St. (622–0527). Changing exhibit of fine arts by New Hampshire artists in all media.

Currier Gallery of Art, 192 Orange St. (669–6144). Open all year except Mon. and holidays, 10 to 4 P.M. (2 to 5 P.M. Sun.). Quality, not quantity. Small museum with fine collection of paintings (U.S. and European) and decorative arts. Silver, glass, sculpture.

Manchester Historic Association Museum, 129 Amherst St. (622–7531). Open year round, 11 to 4 P.M., except Sun. and Mon. and Tues. following Mon. holidays. Library and museum with the focus on the Queen City and its mills-dominated history. Free.

Manchester Institute of Arts and Sciences, 148 Concord St. (623–0313). Open Mon. to Sat., 10 to 5 P.M., all year. Gallery and gift shop in addition to fine and performing arts classes. Accent on regional artists in the gallery.

NASHUA. *Arts and Science Center,* 14 Court St. (883–1506). Open year round; children's museum open Mon. to Fri., 1 to 4:30 P.M., Sat. 10 to 4:30 P.M.; science center open 9 A.M. to 9:30 P.M. Mon. to Thurs., Fri. and Sat. 9 to 5 P.M. Kids' museum plus full-scale science center with 80-plus classes, from crafts to computers.

WHITE MOUNTAINS

NORTH CONWAY. *Conway Scenic Railroad Museum,* at village train depot off Rte. 16 (356–5251). Pintsize collection of rail memorabilia to go with daily train rides from Dr. Zhivago-like, bubbletop train station. Open daily mid-June to late Oct.

WARREN. *Morse Museum,* Rte. 25–C (764–9407). Contains a collection of mounted trophies from the African jungles as well as artifacts, military souvenirs, and curios from Africa and the Orient. Open Memorial Day to Labor Day, 9 to 5 P.M. Free.

HANOVER/LAKE SUNAPEE REGION

CANAAN. *Canaan Historical Museum,* Canaan St., off Rte. 4 (523–4501). Open from late June to late Aug., weekends only, 2 to 4 P.M. The building goes back to 1839, the artifacts well before that: Indian relics, Americana.

CORNISH. *St. Gaudens National Historic Site,* Rte 12–A (675–2175). Open daily mid-May to Oct. 31, 8 to 5 P.M. Displays the works of this famous sculptor as well as changing art exhibits and Sun. concerts in summer.

ENFIELD. *LaSalette Shrine and Shaker Visitor Center,* Rte. 4–A (632–4301). Recreation of famed French shrine; built on site of former Shaker Village on Mascoma Lake.

HANOVER. *Hopkins Center,* Dartmouth College (646–2422). Described by one newspaper as "the culture palace on the frontier," it offers fine and performing arts year-round plus four galleries in the heart of the Dartmouth campus. Orozco frescos at Baker Memorial Library are featured.
Hood Museum, Dartmouth College (646–2808). Newest addition to the cultural complex. Open year-round.

NEWPORT. *Newport Historic Museum,* District Court House (2nd floor), Court Sq. (863–2079). Open Wed., 10 to 3 P.M., late June to Labor Day. Local historical materials, genealogical assistance.

PLAINFIELD. *Maxfield Parrish Museum,* off Rte. 12–A (675–5647). Open daily, Tues. to Sat., 11 to 4 P.M., year round. Famed muralist's 50-acre estate; rustic, handsome grounds with museum containing many of his works. Fire destroyed home and studio in 1979 but they have been rebuilt.

MONADNOCKS REGION

KEENE. *Colony House Museum,* 104 West St. (357–0889). Open May 1 to late Oct. except Mon., 10–4:30 P.M. Built in 1819 by Keene's first mayor, Horatio Colony. Fine collection of glass, pottery and china from the area's makers.

PETERBOROUGH. *Peterborough Historical Society,* Grove St. (924–3235). Open to visitors year round, Mon. to Wed., 10 to 4 P.M.; tours in summer, 2 to 4 P.M., Mon. to Fri. Three buildings containing a wealth of toys, dolls, furnishings, occasional special exhibits.

SHARON. *Sharon Arts Center.* Rte. 123, south of Peterborough (924–7256). Open May 1 until Christmas, 10 to 5 P.M. Mon. to Sat., 1 to 5 P.M. Sun. Offers classes in several different crafts all year but also showcases 300-plus New Hampshire artists and artisans. Exhibits, films, lectures. Free.

LAKES REGION

HOLDERNESS. *Squam Lakes Science Center,* Rte. 3 (968–7194). Open year round, Mon. to Sat. July and Aug., Mon. to Fri. rest of year, 9 to 5 P.M. Neither fish nor fowl—not strictly a natural science museum but there are plenty of animal and birds exhibits, and not just a science show, either. Well worth the stop.

WOLFEBORO. *Libby Museum,* Rte. 109 W (569–3900). Open Memorial Day to Labor Day, 10 to 4 P.M., except Mon. Natural history museum, from archeology to stamps, Indian artifacts to newspapers.

Clark House, Home of the Wolfeboro Historical Society, So. Main St. (569–4779). Open during July and Aug. except Sun. and weekends in autumn, 9 to 4:30 P.M. Like walking into an 18th-century New England farmhouse. All sorts of farming and lifestyle artifacts plus a scale model of a mansion built in mid-1700s by John Wentworth, the last royal governor, on the shores of nearby Lake Wentworth, thus creating what was believed to be the first vacation home in the then-colonies.

MUSIC. *Hopkins Center,* Dartmouth College, Hanover. Superb array of performers and orchestras here all year. Since 1963 the Congregation of the Arts has sponsored performances in the *Spaulding Auditorium.* Both symphony and chamber music offered. Contact Hopkins Center, Hanover 03755 (646–2422) for details. *Monadnock Music Summer Concert Series,* mid-July to the end of Aug.; concerts in 15 towns of the Monadnock region. Write P.O. Box 225, Peterborough 03458, for schedule. *New Hampshire Music Festival,* Tues. through Fri. nights, early July to mid-Aug., with sites revolving each night. Pops concerts at various locations during season. For information, N.H. Music Festival, Center Harbor, N.H. 03226 (253–4331).

THEATER. *Theatre by the Sea,* Portsmouth presents classical and modern plays at the Prescott Park Arts Festival, early July to late Aug., and in winter at a converted warehouse on Barre St. Year-round student theaters at Dartmouth's *Hopkins Center* in Hanover and at the Univ. of New Hampshire, Durham. Excellent summer theaters include *The Old Homestead,* Swanzey Center; *The Barnstormers,* Tamworth; *Hampton Playhouse,* Hampton; *Keene Summer Music Theater,* Keene State College, Keene; *Barn Playhouse,* New London; *Peterborough Players,* Peterborough; *American Stage Festival,* June 17 to Aug. 30, Milford; *Anselmian Summer Theater,* Manchester; *Weathervane Theater,* Whitefield.

SHOPPING. *Antiques* dealers abound; for a list of members of the N.H. Antique Dealers Association send a stamped, self-addressed legal-size envelope to the secretary, Ralph F. Reed, P.O. Box 904, Wolfeboro 03894.

Maple syrup and sugar are available at most gift shops. You'll probably save a couple of bucks if you buy at a farm where there's a "Maple Syrup" sign hanging; they don't have the overhead, so their prices are lower. Popular *souvenirs* are pillows stuffed with fragrant fir balsam; items made from birch bark.

League of New Hampshire Craftsmen centers are open year-round in Concord, Exeter, Hanover, Nashua, and Conway. Shops in Sharon, Wolfeboro, Meredith, Sandwich and Franconia, usually open May to Dec.

Factory outlets: Buying directly from the factory, via outlet stores, is one way to help pinch pennies by eliminating the middle-man. The *Factory Outlet Shop-*

ping Guide, New England States, Box 256 N, Oradell, New Jersey 07649, will provide a recap (at nominal fee) of top outlets in New Hampshire. But more outlets open all the time, so don't be surprised to find one or more along your route which might not be listed in the guide. The North Conway and Manchester areas are two major areas for outlets; others include Laconia, Claremont, Concord and even spots such as Guild, Plaistow and West Lebanon.

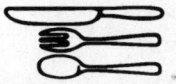 **DINING OUT.** The clear mountain air or prowling the seacoast can make a traveler hungrier than usual. Fortunately, New Hampshire can provide tasty food aplenty, not only traditional New England chowders and other fare but a wide range of international cuisines as well. Beef and fowl, seafood and freshwater fish, all are tastefully complemented by homemade soups, breads and pastries. The growth of the tourism industry has meant a similar increase in the number of up-scale restaurants; at the same time, there are still plenty of down-home eateries throughout the Granite State. Per-person price range used are: *Expensive,* $25 and up; *Moderate,* $10–$25; *Inexpensive,* $10 and under.

HANOVER/LAKE SUNAPEE REGION

CHARLESTOWN. Indian Shutters Inn. *Moderate.* Rte. 12 (826–4445). Lovely old (1791) country inn. Varied menu. Homemade soups.

CLAREMONT. Annie McCassar's. *Moderate-Expensive.* Pleasant St. (542–9289). Greenhouse setting. Good steaks, even better veal.
   Royal Dragon. *Inexpensive-Moderate.* Rte. 11 (543–1211). Everything your Oriental-loving palate could want. Go for the BBQ spare ribs and chicken with cashews.

HANOVER. Jesse's. *Expensive.* Rte. 120 (643–4111). Steak and seafood in an oversized log cabin. Recommended: Steak Teriyaki.
   Bentley's. *Moderate-Expensive.* 11 S. Main St (643–4075). "Sister" to the Bentley's in Woodstock, Vt., and just as delectable. Good lunches, great dinners.
   Molly's Balloon. *Moderate-Expensive.* 43 S. Main St. (643–2570). Hanging plants. Good quiches.
   Peter Christian's. *Moderate.* 39 S. Main St. (643–2345). Wooden booths and tables set the mood: relaxed. Great soups, hefty sandwiches and quiches. Homemade desserts, too.
   5 Olde Nugget Alley. *Moderate.* 5 Olde Nugget Alley (643–5081). Soups, salads and sandwiches for lunch or late in the day. Immense burgers.

LEBANON. Lander's Restaurant. *Moderate.* Rte. 120 (448–1243). Heavy local favorite. Nice job with fish. Closed Mon.
   Owl's Nest. *Moderate.* 213 Mechanic St. (448–2074). Wooden decor with Tiffany lamps. Immense salad bar. Good prime rib.

LYME. D'Artagnan's. *Expensive.* 13 Dartmouth Clg. Hwy. (795–2137). "Rural French" cuisine with the emphasis on lightness. Reservations recommended. Fixed-price, 5-course meal, or à la carte selections. Closed Mon. and Tues.

NEW LONDON. Peter Christian's Tavern. *Moderate.* Main St. (526–4042). Not quite as crammed as the Hanover version (see above). Fine soups or stew, sandwiches and desserts.
   Gray House Restaurant. *Moderate.* Rte. 11 (526–6603). Fine seafood in midst of the mountains.

WARNER. Hicks' Red Horse Tavern. *Moderate.* Main St. (456–2400). Great atmosphere (Victorian home). Casual. Grilled salmon steaks are first rate.

WEST LEBANON. China Lite. *Moderate-Expensive.* Colonial Plaza on Rte. 12–A (298–8222). Polynesian and Cantonese menu. Mounds of food. Excellent, big ribs.

MERRIMACK VALLEY REGION

BEDFORD. Four Seasons Restaurant. *Expensive.* At the Sheraton-Wayfarer, Jct. Rtes. 3 and 101 (622–3766). Relaxing, intimate setting. Excellent lobster, steak. Outdoor dining in season. Children's portions.

CONCORD. B. Mae Denny's (City Edition). *Moderate-Expensive.* Depot St. (225–3536). You'll have no beef with their steaks or seafood. Homemade breads and pastries top it off. Sunday brunch notable.
  Callahan's. *Moderate.* Eagle Sq. (228–1648). Located in old stone warehouse, part of nifty recycling project. Excellent meat and potatoes spot.
  Thursdays. *Moderate.* 6 Pleasant St. (224–2626). Homemade crepes, quiches & desserts. Super dill dressing.
  Tio Juan's. *Moderate.* Bicentennial Sq. (224–2821). Former police station with renovated cells. Mexican menu for this lockup.

MANCHESTER. The Chateau. *Moderate.* 201 Hanover St. (627–2677). Luncheon specials and occasional nightly buffets.
  The Millyard. *Moderate.* 333 No. Turner St. (668–5584). Steak, prime ribs, seafood, surf 'n turf. Heavy on sirloin. Recycled factory building.

MERRIMACK. Country Gourmet at Riddle's Tavern. *Moderate-Expensive.* Rte. 3 (424–2755). International menu with French cuisine as well as dishes from the Orient, the Mediterranean.
  Levi Lowell's. *Moderate–Expensive.* Dan'l Webster Hwy. (429–0885). International cuisine. Suggested: Sea bass in parchment envelope.

NASHUA. Chart House. *Moderate-Expensive.* Nashua Dr. (882–4433). Housed in 1919 hydroelectric plant overlooking a waterfall on Nashua River. Seafood and prime rib are specialties. Children's menu.
  Green Ridge Turkey Farm. *Moderate-Expensive.* Rte. 3 (888–7020). Turkey is No. 1 here but they also have beef, seafood. Children's menu.

LAKES REGION

ALTON/ALTON BAY. William Tell Restaurant. *Moderate-Expensive.* Rte. 11, West Alton (293–8803). Swiss cuisine, notably the veal.

ASHLAND. The Common Man. *Moderate.* Main St. (968–7030). Good enough for the locals to stop in here. Hearty portions of seafood, veal.

GILFORD (See also Laconia, Weirs Beach). **B. Mae Denny's.** *Moderate-Expensive.* Jct. Rtes. 11 and 11–B (293–4351). Superb steakhouse (owned by same folks who run Red Parka Pub in Glen—see White Mtns. Section). Fresh fish and homemade soups, breads, desserts. Victorian decor.
  Mountain Air Resort. *Moderate.* Rte. 11-A (293–2021). Mountains at your back, lake in front of you. Excellent continental dining.

HOLDERNESS. Café Normandie. *Moderate-Expensive.* Rte. 3 (Normandie Farms Inn) (968–3012). French cuisine.

LACONIA (See also Gilford, Weirs Beach). **St. Pierre's.** *Moderate-Expensive.* Church St. (524–3275). Seafood is the specialty, from breaded haddock to shrimp scampi, Seafood Rockefeller to a surf 'n turf.

Summerfield's. *Moderate-Expensive.* 1106 Union Ave. (524–3111). Recycled 1870 barn but it's Park Ave. style with Tiffany lamps, superb food. Recommended: Baby back ribs or stuffed lobster (broiled).

Hector's. *Moderate.* Beacon St. W. (524–1009). Good steaks, seafood.

Hickory Stick Farm. *Moderate.* 2 miles off Jct. Rtes. 3 and 11 (524–3333). Country-style roast duckling of this converted farmhouse. Children's portions. Open Memorial Day to Columbus Day.

MEREDITH. **Hart's Turkey Farm.** *Moderate-Expensive.* Jct. Rtes. 3 and 104 (279–6212). Family-style dinners, varied menu from turkey to beef or seafood. Children's portions. Weekends-only in winter.

Mame's. *Moderate.* Jct. Rtes. 3 and 25 (279–4631). 200-yr.-old home sets stage for fine lunches, sumptuous dinners. Daily specials.

Mill Works. *Moderate.* Rte. 3 (279–4116). Recycled mill building. Go for the prime rib.

Jade Island. *Inexpensive-Moderate.* Rte. 3 (279–8184). A change of pace from steak and seafood; offerings include Chinese, Cantonese, Polynesian. Takeouts.

OSSIPEE. **Sunny Villa.** *Moderate-Expensive.* Rte. 16 (539–2252). Typical northeast fare for over 50 years. Excellent homemade soups, desserts. Kids' portions.

WEIRS BEACH (See also Gilford, Laconia). **Brickyard Mountain Resort.** *Expensive.* Rte. 3 (366–4316). Restaurant and active lounge. Steaks and seafood.

Pancakes Plus. *Inexpensive-Moderate.* Rte. 3 (366–7322). One of two outlets in Lakes Region; other is Rte. 11 in Gilford, across from Lakes Shopping Center (four others in N.H.). Pancakes and blintzes with some heftier meals, too, beyond only breakfast fare.

WOLFEBORO. **Wolfeboro Inn.** *Expensive.* Rte. 109 (569–3016). Colonial atmosphere, regional menu. Home-baked treats. Children's portions. Closed Mon.

Weary Traveler Restaurant. *Moderate.* Rte. 109, Melvin Village (544–8681). If the name didn't get you, the home-cooked dinners would. Fine soups.

MONADNOCKS REGION

BROOKLINE. **Riverside.** *Moderate.* Rte. 13 (673–4698). Fresh fish and seafood are the specialties.

FRANCESTOWN. **Grandmother's House. Tory Pines Resort.** *Moderate-Expensive.* (588–6352). Amazing setting, a 200-year-old inn and a recycled dairy barn. Have a beer by a fireplace or relax over a nicely done steak.

Moderate. At foot of Crotched Mtn. Ski Area (588–2355). Far-reaching menu but you can't go wrong with the schnitzel; in season, rhubarb pie.

HANCOCK. **John Hancock Inn.** *Moderate-Expensive.* Main St. (525–3318). Wide variety of entrees, fish and meats. Prime ribs are the locals' choice.

KEENE. **Black Lantern.** *Moderate.* Rte. 12, south of city (357–1064). One of the best values anywhere. Buffets are a big favorite. Fried chicken rates a mention. Closed Mon.

Henry David's. *Moderate.* 81 Main St. (352–0608). Spinoff of Thoreau's name, then Walden-ish decor with greenhouse design, skylights. Fine soups.

Guerriero's. *Moderate.* Colony Mill Marketplace (357–4353). Fresh pasta.

MARLBOROUGH. **Suffolk House.** *Moderate.* Rte. 101 (876–4424). Fine seafood in a streamside setting. Rave-rated breads and soups.

PETERBOROUGH. Ridan Restaurant. *Moderate.* Rte. 202–N (924–7008). Family fare. Italian meals plus steaks, seafood.

    Salzburg Inn. *Moderate.* Steele Rd. (924–3808). Traditional New England and Austrian cuisine. Schnitzel noteworthy. Wed. night buffet, too.

SEACOAST REGION

DOVER. Newick's Lobster House. *Moderate.* Rtes. 4 and 16 (742–3205). Your basic seafood restaurant. Closed Mon. and Tues.

    Firehouse One. *Moderate.* One Orchard St. (749–3636). Recycled fire station. Hearty American fare.

EXETER. Exter Inn. *Expensive.* 90 Front St. (772–5901). Specialties are seafood and steak. Good luncheon stop.

HAMPTON/HAMPTON BEACH. Ashworth's by the Sea. *Moderate-Expensive.* 295 Ocean Blvd., Hampton Beach (926–6762). Plenty of seafood, especially lobster and clams. Light entertainment nightly. 3 restaurants.

    Galley Hatch. *Moderate-Expensive.* Rte. 1 (926–6152). Emphasis is on seafood but they can rustle up a mean steak, too. Homemade soups and pastries.

    Lamie's Tavern. *Moderate-Expensive.* At the Sheraton, Rte. 1 (926–8911). Definitely standard motel fare; Dunfey Family made its name in restaurants—starting in Hampton—before pushing into lodging. Seafood and traditional northeast dining are specialties. Kids' portions, too.

    McGovern's Boar's Head. *Moderate.* Great Boar's Head, off Ocean Blvd. (926–3911). Continental cuisine but they don't forget the seafood. Fine veal.

NEWMARKET. Johanna's. *Inexpensive-Moderate.* 118 Main St. (659–5151). It's a diner but no one told the chef, who thinks it's the Ritz. Whoever heard of fettucine alfredo in a diner?

PORTSMOUTH. Blue Strawbery. *Expensive.* 29 Ceres St. (431–6420). Gourmet dining in the port city. Relax and enjoy. Small restaurant and popular so be sure to make advanced reservations.

    Anthony's Aldente. *Moderate-Expensive.* 65 Penhallow St. (436–2527). Base of the old Customs house. Fresh pasta, other Italian dishes.

    The Oar House. *Moderate-Expensive.* 55 Ceres St. (436–4025). Chow down on traditional fare in an 18th-century warehouse on the waterfront. Steak and seafood.

    Pier II. *Moderate-Expensive.* State St. (426–0669). Next to Memorial Bridge, overlooking the harbor. Seafood and steaks, chops and chicken.

    Ken's Kitchen. *Inexpensive.* 54 Birdge St. (436–9815). That open-all-night place every resort needs. Takeouts and hearty breakfasts.

RYE/RYE BEACH. Harbormaster. *Moderate.* Rte. 1-A, Rye. Good chowder, excellent preparation.

    Pirate's Cove. *Moderate.* Rte. 1-A, Rye (436–8733). Pirates decor. (Pieces of ate?) Fine seafood.

WHITE MOUNTAINS REGION

BARTLETT. W.W. Doolittle's. *Moderate.* Rte. 302 across from Attitash Ski Area (374–6055). Upstairs lounge and Downstairs dining. Lunch and dinner; good chicken cacciatore and seafood.

    Mad Hatter. *Inexpensive-Moderate* Rte. 302 (374–6667). Pasta and pizza place. Penny-pincher paradise.

BRETTON WOODS. Darby's Tavern. *Moderate.* Rte. 302 in Lodge at Bretton Woods (278–1500). Steakhouse and seafood fare. Fine omelettes at breakfast. Subdued decor.

Fabyan's Station. *Moderate.* Rte. 302 (846–2222). Recycled rail depot and you're likely to have a train rumble by sometime at dinner. Good range of seafood and meat dishes.

CONWAY. Darby Field Inn. *Moderate-Expensive.* Bald Hill Rd., off Rte. 16 (447–2181). Valley views are mouth-watering, the menu and cooking finish you off. Candlelight dinner and daily specials. Recommended: lamb chops.

DIXVILLE NOTCH. The Balsams Resort. *Deluxe* (MAP). Off Rte. 36 (255–3400). New Hampshire's only four-star resort, so don't worry about what you pick at mealtime. Resort facilities keep people busy but the cooking keeps 'em coming back. Strong on beef and fresh fish.

FRANCONIA (See also Sugar Hill) (Cannon Mtn.). **Horse & Hound Inn.** *Expensive-Deluxe.* Off Rte. 18 (823–5501). A little off the beaten path but worth the effort. Excellent Continental meals, delightful, restful chamber music in the background. Award-winning meals heightened by wide selection of wine.

Franconia Inn. *Expensive.* Rte. 116 (823–5542). Rustic greenhouse appeal to decor. Continental dining, excellent veal. Great desserts.

Lovett's Inn. *Expensive.* Rte. 18 (823–7761). Gracious and delectable dining. You may want to skip dinner and get right at the desserts, such as The Velvet Hammer (Tia Maria, scotch and coffee ice cream) and Aspen Crud (rum and vanilla ice cream, frozen). Open for breakfast and dinner when the inn operates (see hotels). Bar. Children's portions. Jacket and tie, please, for the men at dinner. Reservations required if not staying at the inn.

GLEN. Bernerhof Inn. *Expensive.* Rte. 302 (383–4414). Chef-owned. Superb continental dining in turn-of-century inn. Swiss bar and European feel to everything. Specialties: fondue, escargots, schnitzel. Children's portions.

Papa Mike's. *Moderate.* Rte. 302 (383–6105). Mexican fare. Change of pace.

Red Parka Pub. *Moderate.* Rte. 302 (383–4344). "Action central" for locals; lively entertainment, excellent food. Free seconds on spare ribs.

INTERVALE. Anna Martin's at the N.E. Inn. *Moderate-Expensive.* Rte. 16–A (356–5541). Creative cuisine with popovers on the side. "Enjoyable" is an understatement. Try the Chicken Elizabeth: chicken stuffed with Alaskan king crab and lobster, served in a pastry.

JACKSON. Wentworth Resort Hotel. *Expensive.* Rte. 16-B (383–4245). Easy elegance in resurrected full-scale resort. Superb continental dining. Scallops recommended.

Christmas Farm Inn. *Moderate-Expensive.* Rte. 16–B (383–4413). Homemade soups, varied menu. Excellent prime rib. Delightful desserts.

Garden Spot at Whitney's Inn. *Moderate-Expensive.* Rte. 16–B (383–6886). Relaxed refinement. Fresh fish special daily but don't overlook the veal.

Wildcat Tavern. *Moderate.* Rte. 16–A in village (383–4245). Colonial motif, homemade entrees, sinful desserts. Entertainment on weekends in ski season.

LINCOLN/NORTH WOODSTOCK (Loon Mtn.). **D.G. Wagoner's.** *Moderate-Expensive.* At Village at Loon Mtn. (745–2278). Multi-level dining room, sunken bar. Wide selection of entrees, but start with mussels or escargots. Homemade desserts.

Chalet Restaurant. *Moderate.* Main St., North Woodstock (745–2256). Known locally for lobsters. Daily specials.

Dad's Restaurant at Beacon Motel. *Moderate.* Rte. 3 (745–8511). Hearty fare. Lunches served only in summer. Chicken is notable.

Terrace Restaurant. *Moderate.* At Kancamagus Motor Lodge (745–3365). Relaxed environment, fine steaks.

Woodward's Open Hearth. *Moderate.* At Woodward's Motor Inn (745–8141). Fine steakhouse, but emphasis also on baked stuffed shrimp.

Truants Taverne. *Inexpensive.* Jct. Rtes. 3 and 12, North Woodstock (745–2239). How do they make a nickel at these prices? Rustic schoolhouse decor; check the old pull-down maps on the wall. Outstanding sandwiches (the valedictorian: roastbeef, bacon, tomato, smothered in melted provolone cheese and served open-faced) with one chicken and one fish on the menu, too.

LITTLETON. Clam Shell. *Moderate.* Rte. 302, Exit 42 off I–93 (444–5366). Not much doubt about this one: seafood, especially clams. Sun. brunch.

The Coffee Pot. *Inexpensive.* Main St. (444–5722). Basically breakfast and lunch spot. Good sandwiches.

NORTH CONWAY. Stonehurst. *Expensive.* Rte. 16 (356–3113). Superb dining in superb setting; recycled mansion that oozes class. Perhaps the finest dining spot in New Hampshire. One pick? Beef Wellington.

Merlino's Steak House. *Moderate-Expensive.* Rte. 16 (356–9705). Family dining with Italian and beef dishes front and center. Children's portions.

Snug Harbor. *Moderate-Expensive.* Rte. 16, "a few fathoms north" of village (356–3000). Fresh seafood specialties, fine chowder. Closed Tues.

Barnaby's. *Moderate.* Rte. 16 (356–5781). Excellent steakhouse but don't overlook the veal. Rustic, candlelight dinner in a wooden booth. Different, but so is the cuisine. Live entertainment, too.

Horsefeathers. *Moderate.* Main St. in the village (356–2687). Lively, fun place with cheap eats. Rowdy steakhouse atmosphere. Food for thought: Beefsteak Black Jack—chopped sirloin, Bermuda onion, peppercorns, flame-broiled in Jack Daniel's. Packed at lunch.

Pancakes Plus. *Moderate.* Rte. 16 (356–2931). Name pretty much sums it up: outrageous blueberry pancakes. Large-sized omelettes.

Scottish Lion. *Moderate.* Rte. 16, just north of village (356–6381). Traditional Scottish lineup—hearty soups and breads, beef and lamb, among others. Sunday brunch. Black Watch carries 30–plus brands of Scotch.

PLYMOUTH. Candlelite Traveler. *Moderate.* Rte. 3 (536–2330). Motel restaurant specializing in northeast food, e.g., chicken pie, Yankee pot roast, homemade pastries, soups, breads. Children's portions.

Green Parrot. *Moderate* 51 S. Main St. (536–4717). Mexican food but don't ignore the ham and cheese croissant melt.

Suzanne's Kitchen. *Inexpensive.* 56 S. Main St. (536–3304). Fine soups, good spaghetti pie. Poetry Thurs. nites and live music Sun. nites.

SUGAR HILL. (See also Franconia). **Polly's Pancake Parlor.** *Inexpensive.* Rte. 117 (823–5937). Positively palate-pleasing! Great views and greater griddle cakes. French toast, too. Fine soups and muffins. Open summer and fall.

Sunset Hill House. *Expensive.* Off Rte. 117 (823–5522). Excellent dining but it's the desserts which help set this inn apart.

WATERVILLE VALLEY. Valley Inn. *Expensive.* Village core (236–8336). Quiet, rustic elegance. Excellent shrimp. Second pick: gingered beef tips.

O'Keefe's. *Moderate-Expensive.* Village core (236–8331). Nightly specials. Seafood and stick-to-your-ribs steaks. Children's portions. **William Tell Restaurant.** *Moderate-Expensive.* Rte. 49, Thornton (726–3618). Swiss cuisine with heavy emphasis on meats. Try the rack of lamb.

Alpine Pizza. *Inexpensive.* At Cross-Country Touring Center (236–4173). Just what the valley needed: cheap eats. Plenty of cheese on pizzas.

 **DRINKING LAWS.** Liquor is sold in stores operated by the State Liquor Commission. These stores are generally open from 10:00 to 5:30, Mon. through Sat. (later on Fri.), except legal holidays, Sun., and election days. Beer, ale, and wine may be sold for off-premises consumption by grocers and druggists having proper permits; individual glass sale of liquor, beer, or wine

is permitted at licensed hotels, restaurants, and clubs. Most golf club bars and cocktail lounges are closed until noon on Sun. Legal drinking age is 21.

NIGHT LIFE AND BARS. The after-dark scene in New Hampshire is not quite reclusive, nor is it gay Pa-ree. There are a few places to dance, a few more to enjoy live entertainment and even more where you can simply swill beer and ponder the imponderables. Resort areas, as might be expected, tend to have the largest assortment of saloons and nightspots. Today's version of a nightclub often winds up as sort of a British pub done in barnboard with a rock and roll or country group at the mike. Bars in hotels or motor inns may be toned down in decor and you usually can be sure of finding lighted bug candles on the dimly lit tables. Among some of the top spots in New Hampshire: **Merrimack Valley region**—Concord: *Thums,* 6 Pleasant St. under Thursday's restaurant (224–2626) (intimate, mellow, rock); *Red Blazer,* 72 Manchester St. (224–7779) (young, singles, rock). **Monadnocks**—Peterborough: *The Folkway,* 85 Grove St. (924–7484) (gentle, folk music with occasional foreign acts). **Dartmouth-Lake Sunapee Region**—West Lebanon: *Sheraton North Country Inn,* Airport Rd. off Rte. 12–A (298–5906) (top lounge in the region); Hanover: *Peter Christian's Tavern,* 39 South Main St. (643–2345) (it's what you make it—great spot to nurse a beer or a coffee). **Lakes Region**—Alton Bay: *William Tell Restaurant,* Rtc. 11, West Alton (293–8803) (excellent atmosphere, shhhhh); Laconia: *Christmas Island Resort,* Rte. 3 on Lake Winnipesaukee (366–4378) (usually something happening here); *Margate Resort,* Rte. 3 on the lake (524–5210) (generally conceded to *the* local spot for action). **Seacoast**—Hampton Beach: *Hampton Beach Casino,* on the ocean (926–4541) (perhaps the only "real" nightclub in the state with drinks at your table, listen to the headline performers, etc.); Portsmouth: *The Metro,* 20 High St. (436–0521) (a little jazz, among other things); *Luka's,* 172 Hanover St. (431–5795) (soft rock, jazz and plenty of room to dance). **White Mountains**—Franconia: *Hillwinds,* Rte. 18 (823–5551) (jumpingest place around, especially during ski season); Glen: *Red Parka Pub,* Rte. 302 (383–4344) (active crowd, hellacious fun); Lincoln: *The Barn at Loon Mountain,* Kancamagus Highway (745–8111) (especially in ski season); North Conway: *Horsefeathers,* Rte. 16 (356–2687) (good eats, good drinks, good chitchat; be prepared to stand).

RHODE ISLAND

America's Smallest Bundle of Surprises

by
MONIQUE PANAGGIO

Monique Panaggio has been a public relations executive for many years and has written articles for numerous newspapers, magazines and other publications. She is currently public relations director of The Preservation Society of Newport County and an associate member of the Society of American Travel Writers.

"Whereas Mr. Roger Williams, one of the elders of the church of Salem, hath broached and divulged new and dangerous opinions against the authority of magistrates; hath also writ letters of defamation, both of magistrates and churches here . . . it is therefore ordered that the said Mr. Williams shall depart out of this jurisdiction . . . not to return any more without license from the Court."

This order of banishment, issued in October, 1635, by the Puritan leaders of the Massachusetts Bay Colony, was one of the foundation stones of the State of Rhode Island. Roger Williams did depart. Unshaken in his strong convictions about religious liberty, and accompanied by a few followers, Williams fled Salem for the relatively unknown territory to the south. The following spring, a canoe bearing Williams and his party floated down the Seekonk River, rounded Fox

Point and arrived at the confluence of the Woonasquatucket and Moshassuck rivers where Williams decided to found his settlement. He named the place Providence, "having sense of God's merciful providence unto me," and set in motion the formation of a new colony in the New World.

Thus the founding of the first settlement on the shores of Narragansett Bay was a curious and ironic echo of the Puritans' own experience. As dissenters, they had migrated to the New World in search of religious freedom, only to deny it to dissenters in their midst.

Williams and the other settlers who followed gradually acquired spacious tracts of land from the local Indians, chief among which were the Narragansetts. Indeed, many place-names in modern Rhode Island are a direct legacy from the Indian tongue. The city of Pawtucket, for example, takes its name from the Indian term for "waterfall place." Woonsocket, Apponaug, Pettaquamscutt, Conanicut, Narragansett—all these names and more add flavor to the Rhode Island of today and are an important link with its past.

After Providence, Portsmouth and Newport were the next Rhode Island towns to be founded. The new settlers bought from the Indians the largest island in Narragansett Bay. On the northern end of the island, then called Aquidneck, Portsmouth was established in 1638. A year later, Newport was founded at the island's southern end. In 1644 Aquidneck itself was renamed the Isle of Rhodes, or Rhode Island, marking the first official use of that name in the growing colony. The fourth of the original settlements, Warwick, was founded on the mainland south of Providence in 1642.

(Portsmouth was founded by Anne Hutchinson, also banished from Boston for her religious convictions. She was the first woman in the country to establish a town.)

Religious Freedom for All

The four towns sent Roger Williams to England in 1643, for the purpose of obtaining the colony's first charter. This was superseded in 1663 by a royal charter from Charles II, which guaranteed full religious freedom to the colony, an important step in largely intolerant New England. The charter served as a basis for Rhode Island's government until 1843, a span of 180 years.

In the 18th century, a transition from agricultural activities to commerce saw the colony experience a rapid growth in wealth and prosperity. It became part of the famous triangular trade, in which ships hauled rum from New England to Africa, slaves were transported from Africa to the West Indies, and molasses was shipped from the West Indies to New England for the profitable manufacture of rum.

Rhode Island's history after the middle of the 17th century is mainly concerned with military and naval affairs. In the Great Swamp Fight of King Philip's War (1675–76), the winter camp of the Narragansett Indians, near South Kingstown, was destroyed by troops from the New England colonies.

The Great Swamp is still one of Rhode Island's more unusual areas. This 3,000-acre morass, now a wildlife reservation, offers nature lovers a chance to observe plants and animals in an environment virtually untouched by man.

In the winter of 1675, the Great Swamp was the scene of a bloody and decisive battle between the Indians and the growing number of settlers in the colony. The battle in the swamp was the major engagement of King Philip's War. Philip, son of Massasoit, was the leader of the Wampanoag tribe and feared the growing strength of white settlers. Long-simmering resentments had led the Wampanoags, along with the Nipmucks, to open hostilities against the settlers. They were joined, in turn, by the more powerful Narragansetts, and a full-fledged Indian uprising began. The Indians took refuge in the swamp, believing themselves secure, but the Colonial troops took them by surprise and virtually ended their effectiveness as a fighting force.

Today, a road leads into the swamp to the battle site, and a granite shaft marks the place where the Indian fortifications are believed to have stood. There are several picnic groves near the swamp's borders. To the north, within easy driving distance, is Smith's Castle, a trading post burned by the Indians after the great battle. Rebuilt in the 1680's, it is the oldest structure in southern Rhode Island and is the only existing house in the state known to have been visited by Roger Williams.

On May 4, 1776, a year after British troops clashed with the Minutemen at Lexington and Concord, Rhode Island declared its independence from the British Crown. It was an act fully in keeping with the same motivations that moved Roger Williams. Rhode Island acted two months before the Declaration of Independence was approved by the Continental Congress in Philadelphia, giving it claim to the title of the first free republic in the New World. After the Revolution, however, Rhode Island was plagued by severe economic strains. The state opposed the idea of a strong central government because of its fear of heavy taxation and further interference with trade. As a result, Rhode Island did not send delegates to the Constitutional Convention in 1787, nor did it ratify the Constitution until economic pressures forced it to act in 1790. Thus, although Rhode Island was the first of the 13 colonies to declare its independence, it was the last of the 13 to ratify the Constitution—and then by only two votes.

Few Revolutionary War battles were fought in Rhode Island, but the war left its mark upon the economy of the state and reduced one of its major cities to ruins. Newport had prospered during the years preceding the Revolution, reaching a peak of commercial splendor during the period 1740–75. The city's fine harbor brought in great quantities of shipping, and wealth began to transform the town into one of the showplaces of New England. Only Boston and Philadelphia topped Newport as a trade center. Then, as now, the city's climate and seaside location attracted numbers of wealthy summer visitors. Impressive homes were built, trees lined the avenues of the town, and a gay social life enlivened the hard-headed business atmosphere. Then, in December of 1776, a British fleet landed 9,000 troops in Newport, and the town remained in British hands until 1779.

Newport's Gilded Age

Newport under the occupation was bleak, but the British left it in still worse shape. Many homes and wharves were burned, trees were cut down, and properties were ransacked and destroyed. Many residents had fled during the war. Afterwards, the tide of commerce turned toward New York, and the town did not recover for some time. By the 1850's, Newport's role as a summer retreat for the well-to-do was becoming reestablished. The town's social life really began to regain some of its pre-Revolutionary glitter after the Civil War, when wealthy Northerners took a shine to the place.

Newport's gilded age, from the 1890's to the eve of the First World War, saw the art of entertainment rise to fantastically expensive heights. Among the hostesses of that Newport era was Mrs. Pembroke Jones, who, it was said, set aside no less than $300,000 for entertainment purposes at the beginning of every season. The names of millionaires—Astor, Belmont, Vanderbilt—became synonymous with Newport society, and Newport society, with a capital S, was promoted untiringly by its chief spokesmen and drumbeaters, Ward McAllister and Harry Lehr. Supposedly, the designation for members of Society's Blue Book—The Four Hundred—was arrived at by Mrs. William Astor and Ward McAllister. Her Newport ballroom could accommodate only 400 guests. That summer, only the elite made the grade and took title to the label.

After World War I, different money came to Newport, some of it to depart when the stock market dissolved in 1929. The age of huge dinner parties and cotillions continued in less lavish style. Some of the baroque summer villas and chateaus that lined the shore—"cottages" they were called—closed down or were otherwise dispensed with. There is still wealth and society in Newport, although it is more discreet. Taxes and World War II reduced lavish living, but Society still flourishes—and there are mansions occupied by Doris Duke, John R. Drexel III and Mrs. Harvey S. Firestone, Jr., among others. Much of Newport's social, economic, political and religious history can be seen in its architecture. The diverse churches along with the Touro Synagogue, a National Historic Site, underscore the religious toleration of earlier days. The period when Newport was one of the most important cultural centers on the seacoast is relived at the Redwood Library. And the remaining millionaires' "cottages" are revealing clues to the nature of the town's Gilded Age.

Newport's economy is strongly linked to the expenditures of the United States Navy. The Naval Education and Training Center with several commands, along with the Naval War College and the Naval Underwater Systems Center, keep the Navy presence in evidence. As a major boating center, Newport continues to play host to numerous national and international yachting competition.

The New Immigrants

While Newport's fortunes limped along for many years after the Revolutionary War, the rest of Rhode Island began to change. Agriculture and shipping shrank in importance as the state became more and more industrialized. Successive waves of immigration brought French-Canadians, Portuguese, Irish and Italians to Rhode Island's cities. The importance of Rhode Island's seagoing commerce during the 18th century can be inferred from a single voyage of the ship *John Jay* in 1794. That vessel sailed from Providence with a $34,000 cargo of iron, rum, gin, pork, candles, and tobacco, and returned from Bombay carrying $250,000 worth of tea.

However, four years before the voyage of the *John Jay,* an English mechanic had arrived in Pawtucket with a secret that was to add an important new ingredient to the state's economy. The mechanic, Samuel Slater, brought with him details of the power spinning-frame, called the Arkwright process, and established himself in the textile business in Pawtucket. Textiles soon became a major factor in the growing industrialization of Rhode Island, and many of the new immigrants went to work at the looms. One of Slater's early mills, now a museum, still stands beside the Blackstone River in Pawtucket.

Growing urbanization has created new problems. The state's population shifted from about 20 percent urban in 1800 to nearly 90 percent urban in 1900. Because Rhode Island had poor urban representation in the legislature and no suffrage for non-landed citizens, Thomas Wilson Dorr led an armed revolt in the 19th century. Dorr's Rebellion led to the adoption of a new state constitution, the Freeman's Constitution, in 1842. This gave voting rights to all adult males of American birth who owned real property valued at $134, or who paid an annual tax of at least $1.

The state's industrialization continued to expand after the Civil War. In 1880, Rhode Island was first among the jewelry-producing states of the nation. By 1890, Providence was the second most important woolen-manufacturing city. After World War I, however, a marked change occurred in the state's industrial pattern. When many textile factories were moved to the southern states in the 1920's, Rhode Island's textile industry underwent a severe decline. Forced to diversify its manufacturing activities, the state placed more emphasis upon the manufacture of machinery, machine tools, and metal products.

The metal trades—primary and fabricated metals, machinery and electrical equipment—now represent the state's most important industrial group. Electronics and hi-tech companies are among the state's fastest growing industries. The state has emphasized the importance of tourism, and through the Tourist Promotion Division of the state's Department of Economic Development has seen the income of America's First Vacationland increase in 25 years from $18 million to about $550 million annually by current estimates.

Rhode Island may be the smallest state, and the second most densely populated, but its natural recreational assets are varied and surprisingly unexploited. More than 60 percent of the state still consists of wooded and farmland areas. There are beaches and parks, fishing ports, harbors, historic homes and monuments, and pleasant rolling countryside. The climate, influenced by the Gulf Stream and Narragansett Bay, averages about 72 degrees in July and 50 degrees on a year-round basis.

Rhode Islanders also take pride in their state's educational history and facilities. In 1640, Robert Lenthal founded the first public school in the colonies in Rhode Island. Henry Barnard, in 1844, established the Rhode Island Institute of Instruction, the oldest association of its kind, in this country. And "the patron saint of the nation's public school system," Horace Mann, was educated at Brown University, founded in 1764 and the state's oldest institution of higher learning. Brown is a major research center and ranks among the nation's top 25 graduate schools. M.D. degrees are awarded by the division of biology and medicine.

Politically, Rhode Island's voting pattern has been far from consistent over the years. At first, the state tended to lean toward conservatism in presidential elections. Then, in 1928, Alfred E. Smith carried the state for the Democratic Party. Rhode Island stayed with the Democratic nominee in every election until it went for Eisenhower in 1952 and 1956. Democrats have held the Rhode Island gubernatorial seat continuously since 1941 except for 1959–1961 and 1963–1969. The Republicans won the governor's office in 1985.

The political machinery of Rhode Island is, of course, in its capital. Providence is a curious mixture of many elements. There is history to be found during a walking tour of the older sections of the city, and its varied cultural heritage provides touches of cosmopolitan flavor. Providence is also an important deep-water port (the fourth largest in New England in tonnage handled), an industrial complex, a legislative seat, and an educational center. Its schools include Brown University, Providence College, the Rhode Island College of Education, the Rhode Island School of Design, Johnson & Wales College, and New England Institute of Technology.

One of the major landmarks in Providence is the State House, home of the Senate and House of Representatives. Completed in 1904, the State House boasts having the second largest unsupported marble dome in the world. Numerous older buildings, some in acute disrepair, have survived the ravages of time and progress in Providence, but the city has seen several of its downtown buildings restored and, in at least one instance, a former motion picture theater converted to needed office space. Two office towers were erected during the 1970's and by 1985 two additional skyscrapers changed the skyline. The city, like the state, is beginning to plan more determinedly for the future and in doing so has preserved much of its early architecture.

EXPLORING RHODE ISLAND

The Providence Area

Your tour of Rhode Island should begin with a comprehensive exploration of Providence, the state's capital. You may obtain useful information from the Greater Providence Convention & Visitors Bureau (10 Dorrance Street) and the state's Tourist Promotion Division (7 Jackson Walkway). The new Roger Williams National Memorial maintains a visitor center. Also consult automobile club offices.

The presence of the city's founder makes itself felt through a bust of Roger Williams situated over the main entrance to Providence City Hall. Across the street is the civic center, J.F. Kennedy Plaza, reportedly the first, and one of the finest, central squares of its kind in the nation. Highlighting the square's many structures is the Fleet National Bank Building, 420 feet high, which is capped by a huge lantern that can be seen at night from a distance of 40 miles. Other towers include 40 Westminster Street, 301 feet (1971) and Hospital Trust Tower, 408 feet (1973).

The square, including City Hall Park, boasts several monuments that commemorate Rhode Island's participation in the nation's wars. A mounted figure of General Ambrose E. Burnside, Civil War commander, later governor of Rhode Island and U.S. Senator, stands at the east end. Just west of here is *The Scout,* in memory of Major H.H. Young, chief of scouts to General Phil Sheridan. Other attractions in the square include a monument paying tribute to Civil War soldiers and sailors, and a Spanish War memorial, *The Hiker.*

From J.F.K. Plaza, drive east, passing the Federal Building, into Memorial Square. Bear left by the World War I Memorial, a 115-foot granite shaft topped by an heroic figure symbolizing peace, turn right on Waterman Street, then left on North Main Street. Here, you can see the First Baptist Meeting House. It is the oldest church of any denomination in the state and was the first Baptist church in America, founded by Roger Williams in 1638. Its beautiful interior is preserved in Colonial form, including a crystal chandelier which was first lighted in 1792. The structure was built for a dual purpose: "for the public worship of Almighty God; and also for holding Commencement in." Today, the church still serves both functions. If you desire a conducted tour, you can reach the office by the Waterman Street entrance.

Just left of the First Baptist Meeting House, at 11 Thomas Street, is the Providence Art Club. Inside the building, which was erected in 1793, are headquarters of the Providence Water Color Club. Its galleries host local art exhibitions, which are changed frequently. Adjacent to the art club, at 9 Thomas Street, is the Deacon Edward Taylor House, built about 1790 by a deacon of the First Congregational Church. Next, at number 7, is the Fleur de Lys Building, a studio building erected in 1886 by Sidney R. Burleigh, who was called dean of Rhode Island artists until his death in 1929. Its half-timbered design is of the 17th-century Norman and Breton style. Of particular interest are the ornate decorations in the wood and stucco.

Opposite the church, on Waterman Street, are some of the buildings of the Rhode Island School of Design. Founded in 1877, it is known as one of the finest schools of design in the country. At the corner of Waterman and North Main Streets is the East Side bus tunnel. The entrance, which is marked by a bronze plaque, was the site of the first Town Meeting House of Providence, where, from 1644 to 1647, Roger Williams often presided over the freemen.

Continuing north on North Main Street, you will see the Joseph Russell House at number 118. An ambitious Providence merchant, Russell traded with the Far East, building the house in 1772. It has been raised to allow room for stores on the ground floor. Almost across the street is Meeting Street and Shakespeare's Head where the Rhode Island Federation of Garden Clubs maintains a Colonial garden. The square wooden house, built in 1763, was once adorned by a sign of Shakespeare's head. This was the residence of John Carter, at one time an apprentice of Benjamin Franklin. When Franklin, as Postmaster General, appointed Carter postmaster of Providence, the house became the post office. It was also used as a bookstore and popular meeting place. Supposedly, the house later served as a station of the "underground railroad" for runaway slaves.

On the opposite side of Meeting Street is the Brick School House (1769), which was used as both a school and a place for town meetings. This building was also the first used by Brown. Today it is headquarters for the Providence Preservation Society. In 1800, it became one of the four first free public schools, and just before the Civil War, the building was a school for blacks. At the next block on North Main Street is the Old State House, meeting place of the General Assembly from 1762 until 1900. Today, it serves as the headquarters for the Historic Preservation Commission of Rhode Island. A little farther up North Main Street, on the left-hand side, you can see the Roger Williams Spring, which is enshrined in the Roger Williams National Memorial. By a Proprietors' Grant in 1721, "liberty is reserved for the inhabitants to fetch water at this spring forever." A house across the street, at the corner of Howland Street, bears a tablet stating that "a few rods east of this spot stood the house of Roger Williams, founder of Providence, 1636."

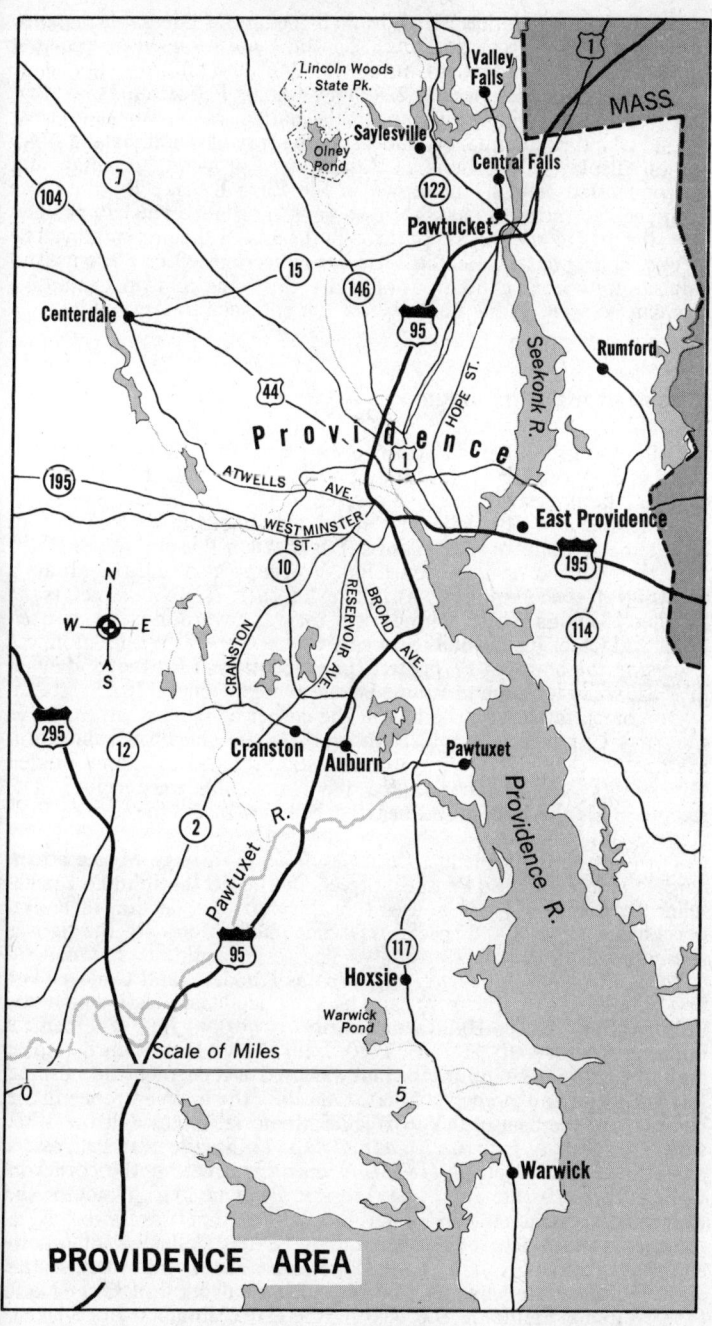

PROVIDENCE AREA

Benefit Street parallels North Main Street and is lined with restored 18th- and 19th-century buildings. Continue south on this street, past the rear of the First Baptist Church. The Museum of Art of the Rhode Island School of Design is at 224. This adjoins Pendleton House, the first "American Wing" museum in the nation. Here, works of great Rhode Island cabinetmakers and a superb array of Rhode Island silver are on display. Collections of American, European, Oriental, and aboriginal arts, which are shown in the Eliza Radeke Building, are arranged, for the most part, in chronological order so you can proceed from the arts of ancient Egypt through the arts of the present day. The second floor houses splendid Oriental collections. Study rooms and galleries for special exhibitions of prints, drawings, and the decorative arts can be seen on the floors below the entrance to the building.

Love in the Athenaeum

Follow south on Benefit Street to the corner of College Street. Here you find one of the nation's oldest libraries, the Providence Athenaeum (1753). The present edifice was erected in 1838 in the Greek Revival style. It houses a vast collection of valuable books in shelved alcoves off the main room. In these alcoves Edgar Allan Poe and Sarah Helen Whitman carried on their courtship. You may also find the library's paintings of special interest. At the next corner, Hopkins Street, is the Stephen Hopkins House, whose occupant was governor of the state ten times and Chief Justice of its Supreme Court. General Washington was a guest in the house in 1776, after the evacuation of Boston, and again in 1781, when he came to Rhode Island to meet General Rochambeau.

One block farther on the left, at the corner of Benevolent Street, is the First Unitarian Church. Built in 1816, the church is a beautiful example of early 19th-century ecclesiastic architecture. John Holden Greene, its designer, considered the church his masterpiece. The steeple holds the largest and heaviest bell cast in the foundry of Paul Revere and Son.

Turn left on Benevolent Street and left again through Megee Street, across George and into Prospect Street. On the left the John D. Rockefeller Jr. Library (1964) houses the university's collection of books, periodicals, general and special reference publications. On the right is the campus of Brown University. The seventh oldest of American colleges, Brown was chartered in 1764 as Rhode Island College. The first building, facing the front campus, is Rhode Island Hall, which was built in 1840. Slater Hall, a dormitory, is next in line. The central building is University Hall. In 1770, John Brown laid its cornerstone, and during the Revolution, the hall was used as a barrack and hospital for American and French soldiers. Guarding the main entrance to the campus are the beautiful Van Wickle Memorial Gates. On the other side of University Hall are Manning Hall (1835), a lecture hall, and a dormitory, Hope College (1822). Across the street, at the corner of College Street, is the John Hay Library. Built in 1910, it houses the university's special collections and the Physical Sciences Library. Collections of particular interest include the Harris Collection of American Poetry and Plays, the Rider Collection of books and manuscripts about Rhode Island history, the McLellan Collection of Lincolniana (11,000 items, including 800 bearing the Great Emancipator's signature) and the Webster Knight stamp collection, containing U.S. stamps in blocks of four, uncancelled—one of the best of its kind in the country.

Proceed on Prospect Street until coming to the corner of Meeting Street, where stands the First Church of Christ, Scientist. The church's lofty green dome, completed in 1913, is a prominent feature of Providence's skyline. This hill, which is one of the highest spots in the city, was used for a beacon in 1667 to warn of Indian attack, and again in 1775, to give warning of British approach. Turn left on Meeting and right on Congdon Street. Here, at Prospect Terrace, you can obtain a panoramic view of the city. Established in the mid-1800's, the park is the site of the Roger Williams Memorial Monument, where the ashes of Rhode Island's founder were deposited when the monument was dedicated in 1939.

From Congdon Street, turn right on Bowen Street and then right again on Thayer Street. Follow Thayer past the east side of Brown's campus until taking a right on George Street. Near the George Street gate to the university is John Carter Brown Library. This building of neo-classic design houses a collection of Americana, one of the very best in the world. John Carter Brown, grandson of John Carter, the printer, started this assemblage of printed books, surveying the literature of this hemisphere until the 19th century. Today, the collection numbers more than 40,000 rare books and 15,000 reference works. The library's main reading room is constructed and furnished as a gentleman's library.

Across the street is The Wriston Quadrangle, encompassing the better part of two city blocks. In the largest single expansion program ever undertaken by the university, the quadrangle was added to Brown in 1951. It consists of ten buildings, including the Refectory, Rhode Island's largest college dining hall, seating 1,800 students. After turning left on Brown Street, stop to view the Annmary Brown Memorial, a block down on the left. This building of simple classical style, which boasts two wrought bronze doors, houses that part of the university devoted to incunabula and Renaissance studies. Bibliophiles will be fascinated by the collection of literature from the end of the 15th century. The memorial also has a collection of portraits, paintings, family heirlooms, and Civil War relics. Open for research only.

Four Early Mansions

Continue to the end of Brown Street, where, within a block of the spot, stand four mansions dating from the early days of the Republic. On the left, at 66 Power Street, is the Thomas Poynton Ives House (private). Ives, for whom the house was built in 1806, was supposedly foremost among the citizens of Providence of his day. Turn right on Power Street, where, at number 52, stands the John Brown House. Built in 1786, and one of the finest examples of Georgian design architecture, this house is presently the headquarters of the Rhode Island Historical Society. John Quincy Adams wrote of the house in 1789: "We only saw the outside of it, which is the most magnificent and elegant private mansion that I have ever seen on this continent." The house exhibits some outstanding examples of furniture made by the Townsend-Goddard craftsmen of Newport in the 18th century. There is a small museum in the rear. The carriage-house display features the oldest American-made vehicle in the nation. Several architectural features set the house apart: four chimneys, rather than two; a slight projection, crowned by a pediment, in the center of the facade, with the open entrance porch set in the projection; and the Palladian window over the entrance. The Society now owns the Aldrich House (residence of late Vice President Nelson Rockefeller's uncle, U.S. Senator Nelson Aldrich), which houses the Museum of Rhode Island History.

Just around the corner to the left, at 357 Benefit Street, you can see the Joseph Nightingale House (private), one of the largest frame Colonial houses in existence. In this house, built around 1792, John Carter Brown assembled his famed collection of Americana. Follow Benefit Street for a block and turn left on Williams Street. At number 66 can be seen the fourth of this noted group of mansions, the Edward Carrington House (private). The structure is of early Republican design, although its porch belongs to a later period. Erected in 1812, it once housed many elegant Colonial furnishings and some valuable Chinese work collected by Carrington, a shipping merchant, through his trade with the Orient.

Return to Benefit Street, turn left, and follow it past Arnold Street. On the right is the Tillinghast Burial Ground, named for Pardon Tillinghast, who came to Providence in 1643. In 1680, he built the first wharf on what later became a flourishing waterfront. In 1700, as a Baptist minister, he built the first church, at his own expense, "in the shape of a haycap, with a fireplace in the middle, the smoke escaping from a hole in the roof." He died in 1718 and is buried, with his family, on this land, his private burial ground.

Turn right on Transit Street and be sure to notice, at number 53, the old Lightning Splitter House. Its sharply-pitched gables suggest the steep roofs of medieval houses. Turn right onto South Main Street, where, on the left at number 403, stands the Dolphin House. A sailing captain, Joseph Tillinghast, built the house about 1770. Its name is thought to stem from the building's use as a tavern for sailors during the days of the China trade.

The farther corner of Planet Street is the site of Sabin Tavern. Built about 1763, the building served as the Providence depot for the first stagecoach line to Boston. A tablet on a slab monument indicates: " . . . upon this corner stood the Sabin Tavern in which on the evening of June 9th, 1772, the party met and organized to destroy H.B.M. Schooner *Gaspee*, in the destruction of which was shed the first blood in the American Revolution." Nearby at 231 is the Bayard Ewing Building, the school of architecture of the Rhode Island School of Design. This structure is a superb example of local commercial architecture of the 1840's. Recently restored, an exhibition center is open to visitors. At 50 South Main Street is the Joseph Brown House, designed and built in 1774 by Joseph Brown, one of four brothers whose efforts were largely responsible for the city's commercial progress. It is reported that in the rear of the house, where there used to be a huge pear tree, "George Washington once sat and regaled himself with the luscious fruit." Follow South Main Street past Hopkins Street to the Providence County Court House (1933). It is the largest Georgian style example of architecture in the nation. Built on the side of a hill, it has eight stories in front, six in the rear.

Across the street is the historic heart of the city, Market Square. As a market place in the Colonial days, the square was a spot for political as well as commercial activities. Here, you can see the "world's widest bridge." Crawford Street Bridge is 1,147 feet wide, covering the Providence River from Crawford Street to the rear of the parcel post building at Exchange Street and Memorial Square. The central feature of the square is the Market House, which was completed in 1774. The lower floor served as a market. The second story was used as a banquet hall, barracks for French soldiers, and office of Samuel Bridgham, first mayor of the city. The third floor served as Masonic quarters. A tablet on the buildings marks the height of water reached in the great gale of 1815, when ships were thrown over the square. This mark was blurred when the 1938 hurricane forced tidal flood waters to an even higher level.

From Market Square, follow north on North Main Street, turn left on Steeple Street, keeping the tall World War I monument on your left. The third right is Westminster Street, one of the chief business and shopping streets of the city. But you cannot drive on it—Providence's new half-million-dollar Mall has transformed Westminster Street from a narrow, congested, uninspiring thoroughfare into a pleasant and colorful shoppers' walkway 950 feet long. Stretching from Dorrance Street to Snow Street, the pedestrians-only mall includes a cross spur along two parts of Union Street. The Mall is tied to the city's other two major shopping streets, Washington and Weybosset, where the Mall has been continued, and to main bus lines. As you first enter Westminster Street, you will see Turk's Head, which is the name given to the fork at Westminster and Weybosset streets. About 1750, a huge wood carving, originally a ship's figurehead, was mounted over the facade of Jacob Whitman's house. Today, an office building occupies this site, but a Turk's Head still appears in the belt course ornamentation of the present structure.

A Greek Revival Arcade

Continue on Westminster Street, where, on the left, is The Arcade. Built in 1827, this building, which closely resembles a Greek temple, was a 19th-century five-and-ten-cent store. It was a shopper's paradise and a show place of the town. The Arcade is the last of the temple-like structures built in America during the Greek Revival period. Its columns, each weighing 12 tons, are said to be some of the largest monoliths in the country. Extensively restored in 1980, it now houses scores of boutiques, specialty shops and restaurants. Beyond Dorrance Street, where the Mall begins, is the center of the shopping district. Included among the many shops and stores is Gladding's, which claims to be the oldest department store in America. The store is now operated by Johnson & Wales College in connection with their Fashion and Merchandising School.

A few blocks farther on the left, on the corner of Mathewson Street, is Grace Church (Episcopal). This brownstone Victorian Gothic building, consecrated in 1846, houses chimes that ring the quarter hours as well as an occasional melody throughout the city. From here, continue on Westminster Mall and turn right on Empire. At the next corner, Washington Street, is the Providence Public Library, an Italian Renaissance edifice completed in 1900. This central library and its branches boast 600,000 volumes and many notable collections. From Empire Street, turn right on Fountain Street and proceed past the *Providence Journal* Building. Bear left at the end of the street, pass the railroad station, and go through the underpass. Turn right at the next corner and bear left at the Pershing Square rotary onto Stillman Street.

The Marble-Domed Capital

You are now facing the State Capital, considered one of the most beautiful in the nation. Made of white Georgia marble, the building is capped by the second largest among four famed unsupported marble domes in the world, the largest being the top of St. Peter's in Rome. The dome is particularly attractive at night, when it is illuminated by floodlights. The best approach is across the 14-acre lawn and up the terraced steps. Bronze statues of General Nathanael Greene and Commodore Oliver Hazard Perry guard the entrance. But, before entering the building, you might want to know about the statue on top of the dome. The figure watching over the liberties of the state from a height of 235 feet is a symbolic statue, *The Independent Man.*

The statue is of classic-heroic style and depicts a man, clothed only in a lion's skin, holding a spear in his extended right hand while his left hand rests on an anchor, the emblem of Rhode Island since 1647. The bronze figure is about 11 feet high and weighs around 850 pounds. In the great state reception room hang portraits of Washington, General Greene, and Commodore Perry. The governor's office and the halls display portraits of nearly every governor from Colonial days to the present. Historical relics, battle flags, and other memorials can be seen at the building's many entrances. The most valuable historical relic, presently enshrined in the office of the Secretary of State, is the original parchment charter granted by King Charles II, July 8, 1663.

Across from the Capital, on Smith Street, is the State Office Building. To finish your route of Providence, however, turn left on Francis Street and follow it under the Union Station to Kennedy Plaza, near the City Hall. The new Capital Center Project will transform much of this section of Providence within a few years. Union Station will be replaced by a more functional building nearer the State House. The present railroad station is scheduled to become a convention center and the railroad tracks which now divide that part of Providence will be relocated. Another change occurred late in 1982 when Davol Square, a shopping mall-arcade, was created out of an antiquated rubber factory complex.

From Providence, take Interstate 195 east to State 114, which will lead you south to Barrington, a distinguished suburban community. This town boasts the prestigious Rhode Island Country Club, which has hosted two U.S. Women's Amateur Golf Championships. Many estates are nearby, particularly at Nayatt Point and Rumstick Point on Narragansett Bay.

Resume your trip on State 114 south through historic Warren, along antique-shop lined Water Street, pass Blount Marine shipbuilding yard to 114. Soon after entering Bristol you will see Colt State Park, a complete recreational area with bridle paths, two mile drive along Narragansett Bay, an outdoor chapel, and Coggeshall Farm, a working 18th-century farm and garden.

One of the state's most historic towns, Bristol was an important seaport for trading vessels for 150 years. Bristol's harbor today serves mostly pleasure craft. The Reynolds House (private), at 956 Hope Street, was used as headquarters by Lafayette in 1778. Mount Hope Farm, which is reached via Metacom Avenue, is where King Philip and his tribe made their home. Here is the Haffenreffer Museum of Anthropology featuring ethnographical objects from Africa, Asia, the

Pacific and of numerous American Indian tribes. It is a Brown University property. The Bristol Art Museum has several changing art exhibits and the historic coach of James DeWolf.

The Newport Area

Continue on State 114 out of Bristol, and continue on across Mount Hope Bridge to Portsmouth. This town, first settled in 1638, embraces the northern portion of the island named "Rhode Island." Butts Hill Fort, off Sprague Street, is the site of the only major land battle in the state during the Revolutionary War. At junction of 114 and 24 is a memorial to the Rhode Island Black Regiment, the first organized unit of its kind in the Continental Army. It fought bravely at the Battle of Rhode Island (1778). Founder's Brook, located off Boyd's Lane, is where the first settlers from Boston landed in 1638. Another attraction you may find interesting is Portsmouth Abbey on Cory's Lane, a Benedictine monastery and preparatory school. This church of contemporary style houses a wire sculpture by Richard Lippold. Green Animals, just down the lane, a unique topiary garden, is open daily from May 1 to September 30 and weekends in October.

Take a left at Union Street traffic light to State 138, follow to Middletown, the central town on the island. Off Purgatory Road, be sure not to miss Purgatory, which is a huge cleft in the rocks. On Hanging Rock Road, a continuation of Purgatory Road, you can view the unusual "hanging rocks." Whitehall, a house built in 1729 by Dean George Berkeley, noted English philosopher and bishop, lays claim to being a shrine of American culture. The quaint, hipped-roof house contains an original fireplace, a small garden, and many furnishings of the 18th century. Near the Portsmouth border on State 114, is the Overing House. Here, British General Prescott was captured in a daring raid on July 9, 1777. Adjoining is Prescott Farm and its working wind grist mill, open to visitors. Continue on 114 south to Broadway, which will lead you to Newport.

Newport's Elegant Mansions

Colonial Newport, one of the state's nine cities, is probably best known for its magnificent "museum mansions." What is a "museum mansion"? It can best be defined as a former private home which, because of its historic value and architectural significance, has been preserved for current and future generations, and which is open to the public on a regular or semi-regular basis. Each one is a living record of a fabulous period in the history of the United States.

"The Breakers," on Ochre Point Avenue, is considered the most stunning summer residence in Newport. Originally designed for Cornelius Vanderbilt, it is a grandiose monument to a fabulous age. Its 70 rooms contain massive fireplaces, giant crystal chandeliers, mirrored walls, mosaic floors, a stained glass skylight, paintings, frescoes, carvings, tapestries, and furnishings that required the skills of two continents. In general, the design follows that of 16th-century northern palaces of Genoa and Turin. The house measures approximately 250 feet by 150 feet and its rooms are distributed among four floors, arranged symmetrically around a center hall. The first, or main, floor contains the formal rooms, and the second and third floors are devoted to sleeping apartments. Built for entertaining, the house shows off to

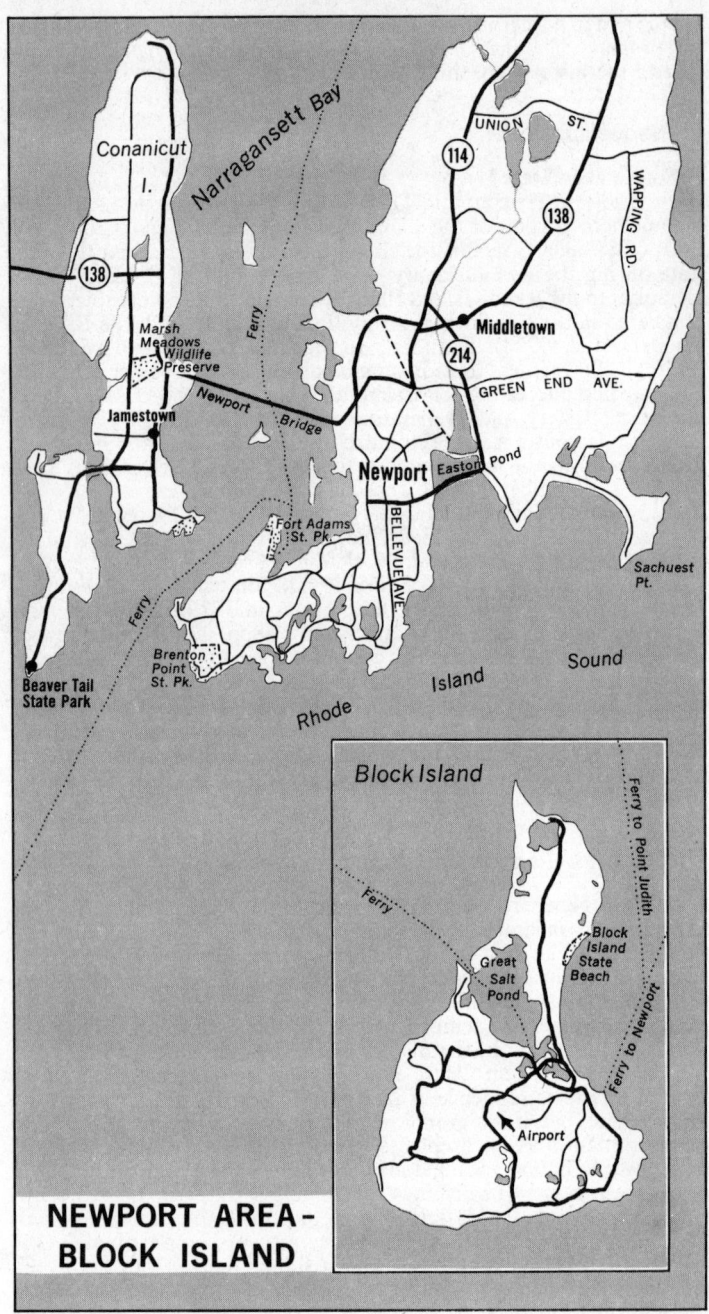

Narragansett Bay

Conanicut I.

UNION ST.

114

138

WAPPING RD.

138

Marsh Meadows Wildlife Preserve

Middletown

214

Jamestown

Newport Bridge

GREEN END AVE.

Newport

Easton Pond

Fort Adams St. Pk.

BELLEVUE AVE.

Sachuest Pt.

Ferry

Beaver Tail State Park

Brenton Point St. Pk.

Rhode Island Sound

Block Island

Ferry to Point Judith

Ferry

Great Salt Pond

Block Island State Beach

Ferry to Newport

Airport

NEWPORT AREA - BLOCK ISLAND

its best advantage at night when illuminated by glittering chandeliers suspended from the high ceilings.

One of the most beautiful Bellevue Avenue estates open to the public is "The Elms," home of the late E.J. Berwind, Philadelphia coal magnate. Designed by the famous architect Horace Trumbauer, the estate was largely modeled after the Château d'Asnières, near Paris. The rooms on the first floor reflect the elegance of the mansions built in Newport at the turn of the century. The main hall boasts 18th-century paintings from the Palazzo Cornaro in Venice. You can see the opulence of the era in the Venetian-style dining room with its unusual furnishings, the breakfast room with large black and gold lacquer Chinese panels of the K'anghsi period (1662–1722), and the ballroom with a crystal chandelier. The mansion is completely furnished with museum pieces, some of which are part of the original furnishings. "The Elms" features bronze and marble statues, playing fountains, gazebos, sprawling green lawns with trees and hedges trimmed in the French manner, and beautiful, formal, sunken French gardens. You may also enjoy viewing a rare collection of trees and shrubs from all over the world, all properly labeled.

Bellevue Avenue also boasts the "Marble House," which is often referred to as the "Sumptuous Palace by the Sea." Completed in 1892 for William K. Vanderbilt, the house was designed by Richard Morris Hunt, who also designed The Breakers. The Marble House takes its name from the many kinds of marble used in its construction and decoration. Many features of the Grand and Petit Trianon at Versailles are incorporated in the architecture and decor of this mansion. The wrought ironwork of the gates and driveways is modeled after the ironwork at Versailles and is repeated in the entrance doors, staircase, and balcony railing of the central hall. The yellow marble in the hall comes from Siena, Italy, and the formal walls of the dining room are made of deep pink Numidian marble.

You can easily distinguish the Marble House's Gothic Room from the rest of the mansion, which is characterized by its 17th- and 18th-century French style. The mantelpiece of Gothic figures was modeled in plaster by sculptors in Italy. Unquestionably, the most elaborate of the rooms is the ballroom, which is known as the "Gold Room" because of its extensive gold ornamentation. Candelabra in the form of bronze figures flank the stunning marble mantelpiece, in the center of which is a French clock, contrived to indicate the various times all over the world. Many emblems can be seen throughout the mansion, but particularly in the Gold Room, where you can see the face of *le Roi Soleil,* the Sun King, Louis XIV. Stories from Greek mythology are depicted on four gold bas-reliefs on each side of the fireplace and on the opposite wall. The Marble House is completely furnished with the original pieces placed in the house when it was built. Added to the tour are the recently restored kitchen and the Chinese Teahouse on the grounds of the mansion overlooking Cliff Walk and the Atlantic Ocean.

Chateau-sur-Mer, on Bellevue Ave., will take you back to Victorian high society life. It has a mirrored ballroom, magnificent woodwork, children's playroom, and beautiful trees. Rosecliff, also on Bellevue Avenue, overlooks Cliff Walk. The Grand Trianon, at Versailles, was its inspiration. A romantic, heart-shaped staircase, grand ballroom, Louis XV and XVI furnishings, the formal garden and sculptures are highlights of this 40-room mansion.

Another recommended visit is "Belcourt Castle," also on Bellevue Avenue, which was built by a descendant of Commodore Matthew

Calbraith Perry, Oliver Hazard Perry Belmont. In 1891, Richard Morris Hunt designed the 52-room mansion, completed in 1894 at an estimated cost of three million dollars. Purchased in the 1950s by the Harold B. Tinney family for use as both a residence and a private museum, Belcourt Castle, with its King Louis XIII architecture, is enhanced by the Tinney collection of antiques and art treasures from 29 countries of the world. Within the castle, you can see what is considered the largest private collection of stained glass on earth. Included in the array are representative windows from throughout France, Germany, and America. European craftsmen were brought in to complete the magnificent wood carvings for which the estate is also noted. The Grand Stair is an authentic reproduction of the Francis I stair housed in the Musée de Cluny in Paris.

Return to Bellevue Avenue and, at the corner of Bowery Street, stands Kingscote, a charming cottage built in 1839 by Richard Upjohn for George Noble Jones of Savannah, Georgia. It was acquired in 1864 by William Henry King when it received its present name. The McKim, Mead & White dining room was added in 1881, when, it is said, cork was first used as a decorative ceiling and for acoustical purposes.

Continue north to the Newport Casino, the nation's first recreation complex designed by architect Stanford White, near the corner of Memorial Boulevard. Designed in 1880, it houses the International Tennis Hall of Fame. The museum comprises two floors, a "Hall of Fame" grass tennis court and a restored royal court, one of the few in the nation. Each year, thousands of people visit this shrine of American tennis.

Turn right on Memorial Boulevard to reach Cliff Walk. Starting at Easton's Beach, it skirts the cliffs along the ocean for three miles, in front of the mansion museums, and ends at Bailey's Beach at Bellevue Avenue. At the north end of the long avenue you will come to the Newport Art Museum, which holds frequent exhibitions of paintings, and the Redwood Library, National Historic Landmark. Designed by Peter Harrison in 1748, the library has the oldest reading room in continuous use in the country, and an outstanding collection of American paintings. Across the street is the Old Stone Mill, concerning which much time and effort have been spent to determine its origin. Some maintain that the mill was built by Benedict Arnold while he was governor of the colony. But the most popular theory is that this "mystery tower" was erected by Norsemen seven centuries ago.

A block away, at the corner of Church and Spring Streets, is Trinity Church, which has been called a supreme and matchless reminder of Colonial America. Built in 1726, the church is said to be more perfectly preserved than any other major wooden structure of early Colonial days. The three-tier wine-glass pulpit is the only one left in America. You can see many treasures that add to Trinity's fame, such as the simple table which serves as the altar, first used by a visiting missionary in 1698. The Kay Memorial Baptismal Bowl, hammered out of a single sheet of silver, is possibly the finest piece of silverware in the country. Since 1734, Trinity's babies have been baptized from this font. The bell in the Tower Room is dated 1702, and is thought to be the first church bell heard in New England. Another priceless relic is the original casework of Bishop Berkeley, with its royal crown and bishop's mitres. You can see the George Washington pew and the grave and memorial tablet of Admiral D'Arsac de Ternay, which are reminders of Newport's crucial part in the struggle for independence. The black and gold altarpiece has been in place since 1733, although the British Royal Arms which surmounted it was destroyed by a mob after the British troops evacuated Newport. This was the only damage sustained by the church during the Revolutionary War. Trinity Church is closed until 1988 for extensive restoration.

Follow north on Spring Street to Washington Square, where, within short walking distance of the area, many more historic landmarks should be seen. The Newport Historical Society occupies a group of buildings, all connected, at 82 Touro Street. One of these is a Colonial church, built in 1729, the oldest Seventh Day Baptist Church in America. Downstairs, to the right of the front entrance, you can visit the Marine Museum, which displays objects relating to the Navy and its history in Newport, pictures illustrating the life of the Naval Academy when it was located at Newport during the Civil War, and models and pictures depicting the Merchant Marine. Also on display are rare Townsend and Goddard furniture, china, Rhode Island silver, miniatures, silhouettes, clocks, portraits, and paintings. The Society's library is strong in regional genealogical reference books and materials and has on file hundreds of documentary photographs.

America's Oldest Synagogue

Next door to the Newport Historical Society stands Touro Synagogue, a National Historic Site. A symbol of religious liberty since 1763, this is the oldest synagogue building in America. When Peter Harrison designed Touro Synagogue (often called his masterpiece), he used the Georgian style, but modified it to accommodate the Sephardic ritual. As was the custom of Sephardic Jews, the synagogue was inconspicuously located on a quiet street. It stands diagonally on its small plot so that worshippers standing in prayer before the Holy Ark face eastward toward Jerusalem. This symbolic placement gives an air of individuality to the building and subtly insulates it from its surroundings.

The plain brick exterior gives no idea of the richness you can find within the building. Twelve Ionic columns, representing the tribes of ancient Israel, support a gallery. Above these rise twelve Corinthian columns supporting the dome ceiling. Five huge brass candelabra, dating back to the 15th century, hang from the ceiling. The Holy Ark, at the east end of the room, contains the Scrolls of the Law, or Torah. Handlettered with special ink by scribes of great skill, these scrolls are the most sacred of Jewish objects. On them are recorded the Five Books of Moses, the source of Jewish faith. The scrolls are mounted on wood rollers, two of which are decorated with exquisite silver belltops. Above the Ark, you can see a representation of the Ten Commandments in Hebrew, painted by the Newport artist Benjamin Howland.

The Old Colony House (1739), on Washington Square, is one of the early government buildings of America. The house was the scene of inaugurations of governors for 150 years, and from its handsome second floor balcony the acceptance of the Declaration of Independence by Rhode Island was proclaimed.

The Vernon House, at 46 Clarke Street (private), is the well-preserved building which served as General Rochambeau's headquarters during the American Revolution. Built in 1758, the house is noted for its interior paneling and its curious 18th-century Chinese wall decorations.

The Wanton-Lyman-Hazard House (1675), at 17 Broadway, is the oldest house in Newport and one of the finest Jacobean houses in New England. Of special interest is the small Colonial garden in the rear of this National Historic Landmark. A block away, at the corner of Farewell and Marlborough Streets, stands the White Horse Tavern, oldest tavern in the country. Erected in 1673, the building is restored as a Colonial tavern. Also on Marlborough Street is the nation's oldest Great Friends Meeting House. Built in 1699 on the site of an earlier meeting place, it is open June to Labor Day.

An outstanding example of Newport's pre-Revolutionary Golden Age is the Hunter House, on Washington Street. It was built in 1748 by Jonathan Nichols, Jr., a prosperous merchant of the period. During the hundred years from 1750 to 1850, the house was occupied successively by Nichols, Colonel Joseph Wanton, and William Hunter, a graduate of Brown University, United States Senator from Rhode Island, and Minister to Brazil. Now, fully restored to its 18th-century appearance, the Hunter House ranks among the nation's ten best specimens of Colonial residential architecture. It has five rooms fully paneled from floor to ceiling, a rare feature that should not be missed. You can see fine examples of the cabinet-making skills of the Townsend and Goddard families of Newport. Silver, paintings, and furniture can also be seen in their appropriate settings. The last recommended stop before leaving Newport, at Washington Square, on the corner of Long Wharf and Thames Street, is the Brick Market. A National Historic Landmark, it was built in 1762 by Peter Harrison.

Take the Newport Bridge to Jamestown, on Conanicut Island. This entire island is devoted to recreation during the summer months. Some of the houses that escaped the British torch in 1775 can still be seen. Sportsmen will enjoy the facilities offered by the town, including swimming and fishing. Beavertail Lighthouse is where the original lighthouse was built in 1749, the third light established in America. The present tower, made of granite, was erected in 1856. Enjoy a spectacular view of the Atlantic coast from here. For more good views, drive north on Ocean Avenue (East Shore Road) from Jamestown. You may be interested in the Old Windmill, erected in 1787. Located about a mile and a half from Jamestown, on North Road, the windmill has been restored to working condition. The Fire Museum on Narragansett Avenue displays a horse-drawn fire pumper and antique fire-fighting equipment. Just a couple of doors away is the Jamestown Historical Society. Back at the corner of Narragansett Avenue and North Road is the Old Burying Ground, which dates back to 1656.

Narragansett

Take Eldred Avenue over the Jamestown Bridge. Follow State 138 onto Highway Alternate (Scenic 1A) to reach Narragansett Pier, which was referred to by the *New York Times* as " . . . without a doubt, one of the finest beaches in the world." This narrow strip of seacoast on Rhode Island Sound has been a well-known resort for years. Narragansett's crescent beaches are lined with luxurious summer residences and modest seashore cottages. "The Towers," designed and built in 1882 by Charles McKim, is a landmark of the Pier. Fishing is a chief recreational facility, as Narragansett boasts of being "world tuna headquarters." You can surf-cast, fish from shore, sail on any of dozens of boats with experienced skippers, or rent a skiff and motor. In addition to fishing, swimming, and boating, Narragansett offers a variety of vacation activities. Sprague Park has facilities for tennis, baseball, softball, practice golf, and horseshoes. The summer school of the University of Rhode Island features art shows, concerts, and cultural programs. Follow Ocean Road past Scarborough State Beach to Point Judith.

Of special interest here is the Point Judith Lighthouse, an important beacon known to coastal mariners. The original lighthouse, a wooden structure built in 1806, was demolished in the great gale of September, 1815. Standing today on the same spot is an octagonal stone structure, erected in 1816. During the Revolution, a coast guard and tower beacon were maintained at the point. At the entrance of Point Judith Pond, known as "The Breachway," are the fishing villages of Galilee and Jerusalem. Commercial fishermen, lobstermen, and draggers ship their catches from these points, and the bulkheads are thronged with pleasure craft and charter boats. From the docks at the State Pier in Galilee, take the ferry to Block Island.

Block Island

About nine miles south of the mainland, Block Island is a summer resort and fishing center. Visitors spend many pleasant hours on Block Island State Beach or at the resorts where privately owned beaches are at the disposal of guests. Skin-divers and surf-fishermen feel at home here, where world records for fish are common. Deep-sea fishing is the primary interest. The waters off Block Island are plentiful with school tuna, bluefish, cod, striped bass, and flounder. Offshore are giant bluefin tuna, sword and marlin. At the southeastern section of the island are Mohegan Bluffs, spectacular cliffs of clay, which bear a strong resemblance to the chalk cliffs of Dover, England, rising about 200 feet above sea level and stretching along the seacoast for about five miles. The bluffs are so named because in many places, they seem to resemble profiles of Indians.

Whittier's poem "The Palatine Light" commemorates the Palatine Graves area near Dickens Point, where the crew of an ill-fated Dutch ship lie buried. In 1661, the settlers of Dickens Point arrived at Cow Cove; the well-known Settler's Rock is inscribed with their names. Beacon Hill Road, where you will be over 200 feet above sea level, offers a superb view of the sea.

A man-made harbor, New Harbor, graces the western shore of the island; it was constructed by connecting the Atlantic with the Great Salt Pond by means of digging a channel across the separating finger of land, no small task considering the tools available. A ferry from New London docks at New Harbor. Old Harbor, on the other side of the island, is also the name applied to the principal village. A small fishing fleet, pleasure craft and ferries from Galilee, Providence and Newport dock here.

The South County Area

After taking the ferry back to Point Judith, follow State 108 to the outskirts of Wakefield. In Peace Dale, just north of Wakefield, is the Museum of Primitive Culture. Here, you can see a collection of American Indian, South Seas, African, and other primitive weapons and tools. In the village center is "The Weaver," the work of sculptor Daniel Chester French. From Wakefield, take U.S. 1 south to Matu-

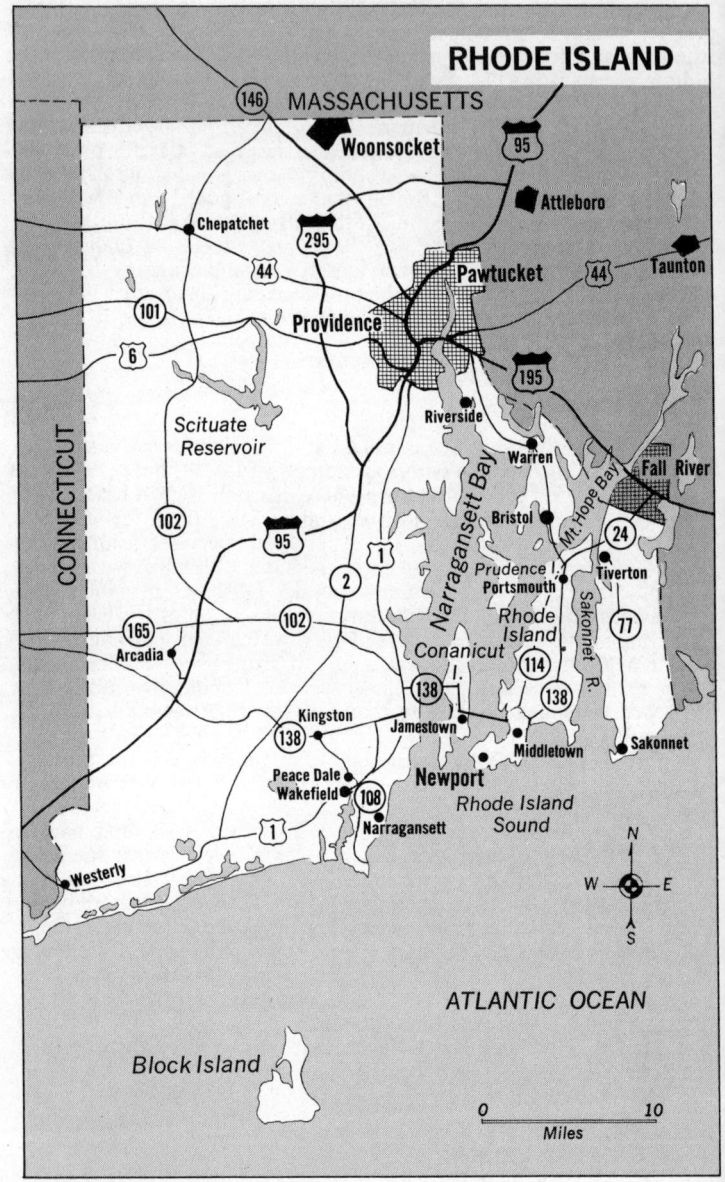

RHODE ISLAND

MASSACHUSETTS

Woonsocket

Attleboro

Chepatchet

Taunton

Pawtucket

Providence

Riverside

Scituate
Reservoir

Warren

Fall River

CONNECTICUT

Bristol

Prudence I.

Tiverton

Portsmouth

Rhode
Island

Arcadia

Conanicut
I.

Kingston

Jamestown

Sakonnet

Peace Dale
Wakefield

Middletown

Newport

Narragansett

Rhode Island
Sound

Westerly

N
W   E
S

ATLANTIC OCEAN

Block Island

0   10
Miles

nuck Beach Road, to Browning Beach Road, to Moonstone Beach Road, to Matunuck School Road. The last road, which goes back to U.S. 1, leads you to Charlestown. This drive affords splendid views along the shore, where there are many opportunities to swim and fish. Charlestown includes the summer resorts of Charlestown Beach and Quonochontaug. The Royal Indian Burial Ground, Narrow Lane, off U.S. 1, is the resting place of Narragansett sachems. On the shore of Ninigret Pond, south of Charlestown, you may visit Fort Neck Lot. At an old fort built by early Dutch traders. Captain John Smith and his men camped here in 1637. Kimball Bird Sanctuary on the shore of Watchaug Pond is reached via U.S. 1 (westbound) via paved road at Windswept Farm, to first paved left road and follow to bottom of hill; at the T, turn left on dirt road to parking area. The General Stanton Monument, farther west of the sanctuary on U.S. 1, was built in memory of Joseph Stanton, native of Charlestown who served in the French and Indian War as well as the Revolution.

From the Stanton Monument, follow U.S. 1 onto Scenic 1A. Turn left at Old Shore Road to reach Weekapaug, where you can start a pleasant drive along the shore on Atlantic Avenue. A highlight of this route is Misquamicut State Beach, unquestionably one of the finest in the state. There are privately-operated amusement concessions including an exquisite merry-go-round and a water slide. Return to Shore Road and proceed west to Avondale, where you can take Watch Hill Road to Watch Hill, a popular resort with a fine ocean beach. The Flying Horse Carousel, a merry-go-round well over 100 years old, still makes the rounds day after day. On Bay Street, you can see Ninigret Statue, commissioned in Paris in memory of the chief of Rhode Island's Niantic Indians. A live Indian from Buffalo Bill's Wild West Show, in Paris at the time, was the model. Surf-bathing and fishing are popular at Watch Hill, and boats are available. Return to Avondale and follow Scenic 1A to Westerly, logically enough the most westerly town in the state, in what was the territory of Misquamicut prior to 1669. Before the War of 1812, Oliver Hazard Perry built gunboats here for the government. Westerly granite is known the world over and has been quarried as early as 1846.

From Westerly, take State 91 to the outskirts of Kenyon. Turn left onto State 2 and follow it until coming to the entrance to Rhode Island's primitive Great Swamp, a 2,600-acre marsh carved by a glacier some 100 centuries ago. You can see an infinite number of harmless creatures walk, crawl, swim, glide, and fly amid vegetation of all types. The Great Swamp became a part of Colonial history on a frigid day in 1675, when its waters turned to ice.

In that year, two Indian tribes, the Wampanoags and Nipmucks, were fighting desperately to win back their land from the British. The settlers were not faring well in the war, and as a result, they became increasingly wary of the nearby neutral, but powerful, Narragansett Indians. When the Narragansetts joined in the fight, the New England Federation sent a thousand men to battle the tribe. The army assembled at Smith's Castle, a Wickford trading post and blockhouse. When the men set out to attack the Indian village in the Great Swamp, on December 19, the Narragansetts were confident that the waters surrounding them would slow any aggression. But the swamp had frozen solid. The army found an opening in the Indians' strong defense, fired the wigwams, and the battle turned into a massacre. The site of this encounter is marked by a granite shaft in the small clearing where wigwams and fortifications are believed to have stood.

From the Great Swamp, follow Liberty Lane, then State 138 to Kingston, a small village dating from 1700. One of the town's many historic buildings is the Helme House, on Kingston Road. Erected in 1802, different shows of the South County Art Association are displayed here weekly. Kingston is also the home of the University of Rhode Island, established in 1892. You may have a guided tour of the school's grounds and other points of interest in the village by students during summer session. Old Kingston Court House (1775), on Kingston Hill, was the meeting place of the General Assembly from 1776 to 1854 and was used as a court from 1776 until 1900. The old Washington County Jail now houses the Pettaquamscutt Historical Society. Continue on State 138 to the junction of U.S. 1. Nearby, west of Pettaquamscutt Road, lies Pettaquamscutt Rock, where the white settlers and Indians signed deeds.

Follow north U.S. 1 to Saunderstown until turning right on Gilbert Stuart Road. Here, you can see the Gilbert Stuart Birthplace, which dates from 1751. Stuart, the best known of Colonial artists and one of America's foremost portrait painters (especially for his series on George Washington), was born in 1755. A water wheel powers a mortar and pestle which once made snuff. Not far from here on Scenic 1A is Silas Casey Farm, a New England farmhouse and out-building, built around 1750. North on scenic 1-A leads you to Wickford.

Main Street in Wickford Village contains an outstanding collection of houses dating from the late 18th and early 19th centuries. Some say that the village boasts the largest concentration of such houses in the country. One structure on Main Street that should not be missed is Old Narragansett Church, erected in 1707, the oldest Episcopal Church building in use north of Williamsburg. It is one of four original Colonial parishes in Rhode Island and features Queen Anne communion silver service, box pews, a wine-glass pulpit, and a slave gallery. On West Main Street, you can view Firemen's Memorial, home of the North Kingstown Veteran Firemen's Association. It displays a restored, hand-pumped fire engine, built in 1875, as well as other antiquated fire-fighting equipment. A key to the building is available at the nearby Public Safety Building, 8150 Post Road.

An outstanding example of a late 18th-century house is the Immanuel Case House (private), 64 Main Street. This rectangular two-and-a-half-story dwelling has two large brick chimneys rising from the ridge of the gable roof. On Pleasant Street is the John Updike House (1745) (private), one of the largest and better furnished homes of old Wickford. Poplar Point, about a half mile east of the Town Hall, is where a company of American soldiers, the Newtown Rangers, was captured during the Revolution. In 1777, British soldiers attempting to make a landing were forced back. The old lighthouse is now used as a private home. The American Legion Hall on West Main Street, a one-story frame building constructed in 1807, was originally the Old Town Hall.

Nearby is Smith's Castle, erected about 1687, 1 mile north of Wickford. Originally erected in 1677 as a trading house by Richard Smith, it was used as a rendezvous for troops who fought in the Great Swamp Fight. The building, which features an 18th-century garden, is believed to be the only house standing in which Roger Williams preached. From here, follow Stony Lane to South County Museum, Route 2, North Kingstown. The museum houses a collection of articles from early New England life and industry, including tools, farming implements, vehicles, appliances, and mechanical devices. Return to US 1, turn left and follow it to Quonset Point, where signs will direct you to the former

Quonset Point Naval Air Station, birthplace of the Navy's Quonset Hut and the "Seabees," a small force of which now remains here.

Continue on US 1 to reach East Greenwich, one of Rhode Island's most attractive residential communities. Of the town's many Colonial buildings, the General James M. Varnum House (1773) recalls the Revolutionary War. The interior is accented by memorabilia from the Revolutionary era and boasts rare paneling and wallpaper. Washington, Lafayette, and Rochambeau are among those who were entertained here. Kent County Court House, at the corner of Main and Court Streets, was erected in 1750 and enlarged in 1805. The Rhode Island Constitution was framed here in 1842, following Dorr's Rebellion. The Independent Company of Kentish Guards, chartered in 1774, was joined by Nathanael Greene, who became the second-in-command of Revolutionary Army troops under Washington. Greene's birthplace (private), built in 1684, can be reached via Forge Road. Varnum Memorial Armory's Military and Naval Museum can be seen at the corner of Division and Main Streets. Erected in 1913, the building contains a collection of objects pertaining to all of the nation's wars. In the northern outskirts of East Greenwich, near Greenwich Cove, you may visit Goddard Memorial State Park. Featured attractions include recreational facilities and a beach and golf course.

From the park, follow U.S. 1 to Apponaug and turn left onto State 117, which will lead you to Anthony. This mill village is the site of the Nathanael Greene Homestead, at 48 Taft Street. Built in 1770, the 14-room house has been restored as a patriotic shrine in Greene's memory. Return east on State 117 and pass through Apponaug to Warwick. Rocky Point, reached via 117 and Rocky Point Road, is a pleasant shore resort famous for its seafood dinners. Warwick Neck Lighthouse can be seen following Warwick Neck Avenue from 117. There is salt-water bathing at Oakland Beach, at the end of Oakland Beach Avenue.

Blackstone Valley Area

This tour, so far, has focused primarily on the shoreline areas of Rhode Island, along Block Island Sound, Narragansett Bay, and Rhode Island Sound, which are the best-known parts of the state. As a result, these areas are usually the only places visited by vacationers. This is unfortunate because some of the state's most attractive sections are to the north and northwest—miles from the busy, salt-water shores.

Just north of Providence is Pawtucket, known as "the birthplace of America's cotton industry." Here, in 1790, Samuel Slater started North America's first successful cotton manufacturing plant operated by waterpower. You can see the Slater Mill Historic Site, Roosevelt Avenue, with its 1793 Slater Mill and recently restored Wilkinson Mill, 1810, and the Sylvanus Brown House, 1758. The mill has been restored to its mid-19th-century appearance. Maintained as museums, Slater and Wilkinson Mills represent pioneer textile production and textile machinery manufacturing in New England and the beginning of the American factory system. Demonstrations of hand spinning, weaving, and operation of early textile machines highlights a visit.

Pawtucket also boasts the Daggett House, originally built in 1695, which can be seen in Slater Park. This example of early Americana is completely furnished with outstanding antiques, including rare articles used by Samuel Slater. Nearby is Lincoln Downs Greyhound Racing

Park, Route 246, Lincoln. It provides exciting pari-mutuel betting during its meets. Another point of interest may be the Eleazer Arnold House, 449 Great Road, near entrance to Lincoln Woods, which once served as a tavern and a court, built in 1687.

From Pawtucket, follow Highway 114 to the northeastern corner of Rhode Island to Cumberland. Here music-lovers can enjoy outdoor summer Sunday festivals, at Diamond Hill State Park. This area also provides some fine skiing during the winter months.

A few miles west of Diamond Hill is Woonsocket, where there are an unusual number of good community parks, with picnic and recreational accessories. You may take particular interest in Cold Spring Park, 25 acres along the Blackstone River, off Harris Street. Globe Park, at the south edge of town, has special facilities for children. The World War II Memorial Park, near downtown, has a beach and is the site of the city's mid-October "Autumn-fest." The falls of the Blackstone River, in the center of the city, are scenic, and holes in the river bed can be seen from Globe Bridge. One may view the multi-million-dollar Globe Dam, a hurricane and flood barrier control erected after the damaging flood "Diane," 1955. Recently "Thundermist Hydro," Woonsocket's municipally owned hydroelectric project, went into operation and was expected to generate electricity for 10 months a year. For a good view of northern Rhode Island, go to the top of Woonsocket Hill. The 588-foot hill is reached via 146A (Park Square, Woonsocket). Just beyond cemetery on left a sign indicates road to the hill. At 22 Hamilton Avenue, you can see St. James Church (Episcopal), which was the first organized church in the city. Parts of the present structure date from 1883. St. Jean de Baptiste Society, 1 Social Street, houses one of the most complete French libraries in New England, specializing in French history and culture.

The northwestern corner of Rhode Island (reached via Highways 146A, 102, through Harrisville and Pascoag, and Highway 100) is one of the most charming sections of the state. This corner, bounded on the north by Massachusetts, on the west by Connecticut, and on the southeast by a rough line drawn from Diamond Hill State Park to Arcadia State Park, is a land of lakes, streams, state parks, forests, family campgrounds, and farmlands. Pulaski Memorial State Forest, just west of Pascoag, has many scenic trails as well as fine facilities for swimming, camping, and sunbathing.

From Pulaski State Forest, take US 44 to Chepachet, where Thomas W. Dorr, leader of Dorr's Rebellion in 1840–1842, made his last stand on June 26, 1842. Out of his activities came the present Rhode Island constitution giving universal suffrage. Under the old constitution, only land owners and certain other privileged persons were entitled to vote.

Follow Highway 102 to Highway 12, which can start you on a fine scenic tour around Scituate Reservoir. From here, Highways 116, 117, via 33, to 3 will lead you to Arcadia Management Area, an ideal spot for leisurely drives. Arcadia State Park has attractive facilities for swimming and beach fun. Another popular bathing beach is Beach Pond, on the western edge of the forest. This is reached via Rte 165.

 **SIGHTSEEING CHECKLIST.** The following attractions, sites, or events are the *"musts"* of Rhode Island. *In the Newport area.* **The Breakers,** Ochre Point Avenue (847–1000) is the most magnificent of all Newport mansions, built in 1895 for Cornelius Vanderbilt. Open daily April 1 to October 31, 10 A.M. to 5 P.M. From July 1 to mid-September open until 7 P.M. on Tuesdays,

Wednesdays, Thursdays and Sundays. Inquire about the Preservation Society combination tickets at any one of the Society's mansions.

More mansions can be seen along Bellevue Avenue and the Ocean Drive with wonderful vistas of the coastline and the Atlantic Ocean.

The Wharves hugging Newport Harbor are filled with unusual shops and attractive restaurants. Wear your walking shoes and enjoy the beautiful sights of hundreds of expensive sailboats, especially in the summer months.

The Point and **Hill** sections of Newport are filled with restored Colonial and Victorian houses on quaint narrow streets. These private homes are especially pretty in the spring with their attractive small gardens. Many Colonial buildings are open to the public and the best are Trinity Church, Touro Synagogue, Colony House and Redwood Library.

Nearby in Portsmouth are the **Green Animals Topiary Gardens,** Cory's Lane, off Route 114. They are open May 1 through September and weekends in October, 10 A.M. to 5 P.M.

In the Providence area. **Benefit Street,** known as "The Mile of History" has dozens of houses dating back to the 18th century that have been restored during the 1960's and 70's. Walking tours of this area, known to Washington, Lafayette and scores of distinguished Providence visitors, may be arranged with the Providence Preservation Society, 24 Meeting Street (831–7440).

Slater Mill Historic Site, Roosevelt Avenue, Pawtucket (725–8638) is the birthplace of American know-how of mass production. Here in 1790 Samuel Slater established his cotton mill, replaced the present structure, 1793. Open year round.

In the southwest corner of Rhode Island. **Watch Hill,** a summer resort dating from the 1850s. This exclusive enclave in the town of Westerly borders the Atlantic Ocean and is noted for its elegant summer mansions built on a less lavish scale than those in Newport. The famous "flying horses" carousel continues to attract the young set during the summer months who thrill to ride on the nation's oldest merry-go-round. It was made in Germany around 1850 and has been in use at this resort since the 1870s.

PRACTICAL INFORMATION FOR RHODE ISLAND

Note: Large sections in Practical Information have been organized by touring areas for your convenience.

 **RHODE ISLAND FACTS & FIGURES.** The state is named for the Isle of Rhodes in the Mediterranean. Its nickname is *Little Rhody;* in recent years it has been called the *Ocean State.* The violet is the state flower, the maple, the state tree, the Rhode Island red, the state bird. "Hope" is the state motto. "Rhode Island" is the state song. Famous Rhode Islanders include Commodore Matthew Perry, Gilbert Stuart, George M. Cohan, Nelson Eddy and David Hartman.

Providence, with a population of about 140,000, is the state capital and largest city. No more than 50 miles from north to south and 40 miles from east to west, deeply indented by Narragansett Bay, Rhode Island's five counties have a total area of 1,214 square miles, making it the smallest of the 50 states. The population is about 950,000, 40th in the nation, and second only to New Jersey in density per square mile.

The sea is the dominating factor in this tiny north Atlantic state. Although the state has only 40 miles of coast facing onto open ocean, it has over 400 miles of shoreline touched somewhere by tidewater. In Colonial days, Rhode Island was a leading seafaring province. Today shipbuilding continues. The Atlantic beaches attract thousands of visitors to the coastal resorts (including the prestigious and elegant Newport). Textiles, which flourished in the 19th century, have seriously declined but remain an important industry. Shipbuilding has made a comeback: Pearson Yachts, Portsmouth; Blount Marine Company, Warren;

Derektor Shipyard, Middletown, among others, are flourishing. Rhode Island contains many charming old towns, sleepy mementoes of the state's Colonial past. Inland, the state is a land of rolling hills and small lakes.

The climate is cold in the winter, warm in summer. The weather is extremely variable, and marked by occasional gales and high tides. Specifically, year-round average conditions are as follows:

	Jan.	Feb.	Mar.	Apr.	May	Jun.
Average Temperature (F)	28	30	37	46	57	66
Average Temperature (C)	−2	−1	3	8	14	19
Days of Rain or Snow	11	10	11	11	11	10

	Jul.	Aug.	Sept.	Oct.	Nov.	Dec.
Average Temperature (F)	72	70	63	54	43	32
Average Temperature (C)	22	21	17	12	6	0
Days of Rain or Snow	9	10	8	8	12	12

TELEPHONES. The area code for all Rhode Island is 401. Pay telephone costs 15¢. Dial "O" for the operator if you need police, or ambulance or to report a fire.

HOW TO GET THERE. By air. Theodore Francis Green State Airport, 9 miles south of Providence by direct Interstate 95; served by *USAir, Eastern, United, Mall, Empire, Piedmont, Pilgrim, American, Ransome,* and several small local airlines. Flight time from New York is about 45 min. Limousine from airport to downtown Providence (20 min. drive) is about $5.75. Air charter and scheduled services to other Rhode Island points from TFG: Shuttle to Newport (Cozy Cabs Company), 5 trips daily; other times by reservation (846–2500). Trip is about 40 min. and costs $11. *New England Airlines* has regular service from Westerly State Airport to Block Island State Airport; *Sakonnet Air Charter,* Middletown (for service to and from Newport).

By rail. Providence is served by *Amtrak.* From New York, train trip is about 4 hours; 1 hour from Boston.

By bus. *Greyhound* (751–8800); and *Bonanza* (751–8800, also); *R. I. Public Transit Authority* (781–9400, Providence, or 1–800–662–5088) provides service to many points and furnishes a free loop service for central Newport during the summer.

By car. From New York the quickest route to Providence is via the New England Thruway (I–95). For the Narragansett seashore, take exit at Connecticut Rte. 2 to Conn. and R.I. 78 (Westerly Bypass) to U.S. 1 and Scenic 1A north. Signs mark the way to Jamestown and Newport Bridges.

By ferry. From New London, CT and from Providence and Newport RI, to Block Island the ferry operates mid-June to about 10 days after Labor Day. Ferries operate year round from Galilee to Block Island. Written reservations necessary for car transport, accompanied by $10 deposit for each way. For schedule write: *Interstate and Nelseco Navigation,* Box 482, New London CT 06032. The company maintains a summer schedule from India Street, Providence, to Prudence Island, Newport, and Block Island; 203–442–7891. *The Prudence Island Navigation Company* provides daily service from Bristol to Prudence Island; 401–245–7411. *Oldport Marine* has service from Bend Boat Basin, Portsmouth (off Rte. 114), Thurs.–Sun. and Mon. holidays in season, Sat–Sun and Mon. holidays mid-May to late June and early Sept. to mid-October, to Bay Island Park, Prudence Island (401–847–9109).

HOTELS AND MOTELS. Accommodations range from family-style cottages to luxurious seaside resorts. Price ranges are based on double occupancy, peak season (summer), EP. Listings are in order of price ranges: *Deluxe:* $100 and up; *Expensive:* $60 to $100; *Moderate:* $45–$60; *Inexpensive:*

up to $40. Newport and Narragansett areas have numerous Bed and Breakfast establishments; prices range from $45 to $75. For B&B information write Bed & Breakfast of Rhode Island, Box 312, Barrington, RI 02806.

BLOCK ISLAND

1661 House and **Manisses Hotel** (466–2421). *Expensive.* Near Old Harbor. Under same management. The Manisses has been restored to its 1876 appearance. Breakfast at 1661, lunch and dinner at Manisses, which serves continental style cuisine on its open deck. Room rates for both range from $65 to $135. Rooms at the 1661 guest house are available year-round.

Ballard's Inn. *Moderate.* Water St. (466–2231). Dining room and bar are popular. Open Mid-April to Oct.

Island Towne House Motel. *Moderate.* Chapel St. (466–5567). The island's first motor hotel is convenient to Old Harbor. Restaurant and cocktail lounge.

Spring House. *Moderate.* Spring St. (466–2633). Long porch, rocking-chair hotel with ocean vista. Free transportation, restaurant, bar. Room rate includes breakfast and dinner. Open May to mid-September.

Surf Hotel. *Moderate.* On Old Harbor (466–2241). A fine hotel for the whole family. Homelike atmosphere and good home cooking. Private beach. Central location. Open May 1 to Oct. 31.

Narragansett Inn. *Inexpensive.* Ocean Rd. (466–2626). Airy, pleasant hotel and annex overlooking New Harbor. Free transportation, restaurant, bar. Room rate includes breakfast and dinner. May to mid-September.

The National Hotel and Conference Center. *Expensive* (466–5577 or 1–800–225–2449). Dining room serves three meals daily. Recently restored Victorian structure. Open year round.

Seacrest Inn. *Moderate-Expensive.* High St. (466–2882). A restored inn with the charm of the 19th century.

COVENTRY. Congress Motor Inn. *Moderate.* Rte. 3 at I–95, Exit 3 (397–3381). Perched on a hill in rolling wooded area. Restaurant, bar. Outdoor pool.

CRANSTON. Hillside Motor Lodge. *Inexpensive.* Rte. 2 (New London Ave.) (942–4200). 10 minutes from center of Providence via nearby connecting I–95.

PROVIDENCE. Marriott Inn. *Deluxe.* Charles and Orms St. (272–2400). An in-town resort with connecting outdoor-indoor pool, sauna, whirlpool bath, children's play area. Pets. Restaurant and adjoining bar and entertainment area.

Biltmore Plaza Hotel. *Expensive.* Dorrance St., Kennedy Plaza (421–0700). One of the state's largest hotels, conveniently located in center city near banking district, rail and bus stations. $9 million dollar renovation makes this one of southern New England's finest hotels.

Holiday Inn. *Moderate.* 21 Atwells Ave. I–95, Exit 21 (831–3900). Large downtown hotel opposite Providence Civic Center. The Garden Dining Room serves meals and The Cellar Lounge is a popular bar. Heated indoor pool. Pets.

Wayland Manor. *Moderate.* 500 Angell St. (751–7700). Cheswick's is a good dining room for lunch and dinner. Bar. Located near good shops and attractive residential section.

New Yorker Motor Lodge. *Inexpensive.* 400 Newport Ave., East Providence (434–8000). Lounge. Breakfast only.

WARWICK. Sheraton Airport Inn. *Expensive.* 1850 Post Rd., U.S. 1 (739–3000). Conveniently located near Theodore Francis Green State Airport. Indoor pool, sauna baths and a game room. Restaurant. Bar.

Carlton House Motor Inn. *Moderate.* 2082 Post Rd., U.S. 1. Annex of Rhode Island Inn.

Howard Johnson's Motor Lodge. *Moderate.* 20 Jefferson Blvd., off I–95 (467–9800). Restaurant. Bar and lounge. Entertainment weekends. Planned tours.

Rhode Island Inn. *Moderate.* 2081 Post Rd., U.S. 1 (739–0600). Across highway from Theodore Francis Green State Airport. Restaurant. Pool. Pets. Operated by Johnson & Wales College.

Susse Chalet. *Inexpensive.* Jefferson Boulevard at I–95, Exit 15, (800–258–1980). New in 1984. Featuring Super Rooms.

NEWPORT AREA

JAMESTOWN. Jamestown Shores Motel. *Moderate.* Eldred Avenue, (423–0023).

NEWPORT. The Inn at Castle Hill. *Deluxe.* Ocean Dr. (849–3800). A former mansion situated at the ocean. Restaurant serves lunch and dinner. Cocktails. Tennis. Entertainment weekends.

Oceancliff Hotel Resort. *Deluxe.* Ocean Dr. (847–7777). This oceanside hotel was once a mansion built to resemble an Irish castle. Dining room and lounge entertainment. Commanding view of Atlantic Ocean and entrance to Newport harbor.

Sheraton Islander Inn. *Deluxe.* Goat Island (849–2600). A resort facility with restaurant, coffee shop, pub. Indoor and outdoor swimming pools, tennis courts, sauna baths, game room, children's play area, 9-hole putting green, shuffleboard, horseshoes; adjoins an indoor tennis court facility. Entertainment nightly. Pets. Marina.

Treadway Inn and Marina. *Deluxe.* Americas Cup Ave. (847–9000). Located in center of Newport's historic wharf district. Restaurant, bar/lounge. Sauna, indoor pool. Pleasure boat rentals and harbor tour boat. Entertainment nightly.

The Harborside Inn. *Expensive.* Christie's Landing (846–6600). New guest house in the heart of downtown Newport.

The Inn on the Harbor. *Expensive.* 359 Thames St. (849–3171). Opened Sept. 1982. A luxury time-sharing facility with transient accommodation.

The InnTowne. *Expensive.* 6 Mary St. Corner of Thames and Mary Sts. (846–9200). Rooms are handsomely furnished.

Howard Johnson's Motor Lodge. *Expensive–Moderate.* 351 West Main Rd., Middletown (849–2000). On immediate outskirts of Newport. 24-hour restaurant service. Indoor pool, sauna, tennis. Pets.

Hotel Viking and Motor Inn. *Expensive.* One Bellevue Ave. (847–3300). Centrally located and ideal for walking tours of Colonial and historic Newport. Restaurant, lounge. Indoor pool, sauna. Entertainment.

The Newport area is not all deluxe and expensive accommodations. Numerous motels have excellent accommodations and include the **Harbor Base Motel** (747–2600) overlooking Navy ship piers and convenient to the Naval Station, Newport; **Cliff Walk Manor,** (847–1300), Memorial Boulevard, on Cliff Walk overlooking Easton Beach; and the **Sea View Motel,** Aquidneck Ave., (847–0110) with a beautiful vista of Easton Pond and Beach, Middletown, as well as **Budget Motor Inn,** (849–4700), **Gateway Motel,** (847–2735), **Easton's Inn** (846–0310) **Pine Motel,** (847–3204).If you like cabins, try the **Floradale Motor Court.** All in Newport or Middletown. Also Guest House Association of Newport, Box 981, Newport (849–7645).

PORTSMOUTH. Ramada Inn. *Expensive.* 144 Anthony Rd. (683–3600). Restaurant, bar. Indoor pool, sauna. Short walk from 18-hole public golf course. Entertainment.

TIVERTON. Stone Bridge Inn. *Inexpensive.* 1 Lawton Ave. Jct Rtes. 138 & 177 (624–6601). Overlooking the Sakonnet Passage, it has a few accommodations, and is open all year round. Restaurant, bar.

SOUTH COUNTY AREA

CHARLESTOWN. The Willows Resort Motel & Restaurant. *Moderate.* On U.S. 1 (Post Rd.) (364–7727). Open late May to Oct. Restaurant, bar. All sports facilities nearby and shuttle service to beaches only a mile away. Private landing strip, boat dock and launching facility. Tennis courts.

Sea View Motor Court. *Inexpensive.* Old Post Road off U.S. 1 (364–6212). Family-style motel. Electric-heated units; kitchens and cribs. Open May 30 to Oct.

NARRAGANSETT. Durfee's at the Pier. *Expensive.* Narragansett Pier Village, off Beach Street (783–6767 or 1–800–THE PIER). A contemporary building dominating recent redevelopment of this historic resort. Spacious restaurant with views of village and ocean.

Dutch Inn. *Expensive.* Great Island Rd., Galilee (789–9341). Rhode Island's famous commercial and charter fishing boat port's principal visitor facility. Tennis courts, indoor tropical-motif pool. Restaurant, bar-lounge. Entertainment. Thurs. through Sun. Near beaches and bird sanctuary.

The Chamber of Commerce, The Towers, Narragansett (783–7121) has a list of bed-and-breakfast guest houses

NORTH KINGSTOWN. Cove Motel. *Moderate.* 7835 Post Rd., U.S. 1 (294–4888). A mini-resort with outdoor pool, shuffleboard. Dining room. No pets. Near several outstanding historic attractions.

Bob Bean Motel. *Inexpensive.* 600 Boston Neck Rd., Scenic 1A (294–2411). A comfortable motel near beaches, scenic and historic attractions.

Kingstown Motel. *Inexpensive.* 6530 Post Rd., U.S. 1 (884–1160). A convenient facility near historic Wickford village, ocean beaches and scenic attractions.

SOUTH KINGSTOWN. Holiday Inn South Kingstown/Newport. *Expensive.* Tower Hill Rd., near Rtes. U.S. 1 and 138 (789–1051). Located near beaches, fishing and scenic attractions. Convenient to University of Rhode Island. Restaurant. Bar. Game room. Entertainment nightly except Sun.

Coachman Motor Inn. *Moderate.* At U.S. 1 and State 138 (783–2516). Near beaches, historic attractions, University of Rhode Island. Dinner only. Bar.

Larchwood Inn. *Inexpensive.* 176 Main St., Wakefield (783–5454). A comfortable and attractive inn that was once a country mansion. Beautiful grounds. Entertainment weekends. Tastefully appointed dining room serving varied menu. Bar-lounge.

WESTERLY. Ocean House. *Expensive.* Bluff Ave. (348–8161). One of the hotels that gave prestige to Watch Hill. Excellent food and beverages. Atop bluff with commanding view of Block Island and Long Island Sounds. Private ocean beach. MAP. Summer season only.

Weekapaug Inn. *Expensive.* Take Old Shore Rd. off U.S. 1 at Dunn Corner to Weekapaug Rd., Westerly (322–0301). Attractive resort on the ocean and overlooking Quonochontaug salt pond. Outstanding cuisine. Water-oriented sports, use of private ocean beach. Summer season only. AP.

Blue Star Motel. *Moderate.* 110 Post Rd. (U.S. 1) (596–2891). Convenient and pleasant place to stay. Pool. Near ocean beaches and opportunities to drive to numerous woodland state parks. Outdoor pool. Off season rates. Near restaurants.

Pine Lodge Motel. *Moderate.* Post Rd. (U.S. 1) (322–0333). Near ocean beaches and restaurants. Heated cottages, and a few family units with kitchens.

Pony Barn Motel. *Moderate.* Shore Rd. Scenic 1A (348–8216). A small motel, complete with play area and picnic grounds. Pool. Pets. Open year round.

S & S Motor Lodge. *Moderate.* 171 Post Rd. (U.S. 1) (322–0304). Near ocean beaches and several excellent nearby restaurants.

Shelter Harbor Inn. *Moderate.* Post Road (U.S. 1) (322–8883). 18th-century restored farmhouse and renovated barn, where "bed and breakfast" are included in the rates.

Traveltel. *Inexpensive.* Post Rd. (U.S. 1) (596–7475). This two-level motel has all the comforts for the budget-conscious traveler. Open May through Oct.

The Westerly area has numerous hotels and motels. Some are right on the Atlantic Ocean such as the **Pleasant View House**, (348–8200), **Sandpiper**

Motor Lodge, (783–2063), and the **Andrea Hotel,** (348–8788) at Misquamicut. **Narrangansett Inn** (348–8912) provides excellent vista of yacht-filled Watch Hill harbor. Chamber of Commerce, 159 Main St., Westerly (596–7761).

BLACKSTONE VALLEY

LINCOLN. Clover Leaf Motel. *Inexpensive.* George Washington Highway, Jcts. Rtes 146 and 116 (333–0087). Open year round.

PAWTUCKET. Howard Johnson's Motor Lodge. *Moderate.* 2 George St., off I–95 (723–6700). An attractive facility within minutes of business centers of Pawtucket and Providence and to area attractions. Restaurant. Bar. Indoor pool. Sauna.

WOONSOCKET. Woonsocket Motor Inn. *Inexpensive.* 333 Clinton St. (762–1224). A comfortable all-year in-town motel. Water beds. Adjoins El Dorado Restaurant.

 **HOW TO GET AROUND. By air.** Scheduled shuttle and charter flights from Providence, Westerly, Newport and Block Island. *New England Airlines* has scheduled service to Block Island from Westerly. *Yankee Airways,* Westerly State Airport, has charter service only, but covers Long Island, and other areas, including Block Island.

By bus. There is local bus service throughout the state. For routing and fare information contact: *R. I. Public Transit Authority,* 1 Sabin St., Providence (781–9400). They provide most of the bus service in the state. *ABC Bus Lines,* 375 Promenade St., Providence (353–2100). Providence to Worcester and local service to Boston. *Brander Bus Lines Inc.,* 24 Vernon Ave., Bristol (253–5799). Providence local service to Taunton, MA.

By car. I–95 goes diagonally from the Conn. state line through *Providence* to the Mass. border. From Mass., U.S. 6 goes west through *Providence* to the Conn. State Line. State 1A is the scenic highway; I–295 is a beltway from I–95 (Attleboro, Mass.) which connects with I–95 in Warwick (via Cumberland, Lincoln, Smithfield, Johnston and Cranston). U.S. 1 from Westerly to Providence is known as the *Heritage Trail.*

Car rental. *Avis:* Newport; Providence; Airport, Warwick. *Budget:* Providence; Airport, Warwick. *Dollar,* 717 Park Avenue, Cranston. *Econo-car:* Warwick (opp. Airport). *Hertz:* Newport; Providence; Airport, Warwick. *National:* Cranston; Airport, Warwick; Providence; Westerly, Watch Hill. *Thrifty:* Warwick (opp. Airport); Providence; Westerly.

By ferry. Daily service from Galilee to Block Island and Bristol-Prudence Island; from Providence-Block Island, via Newport, also from New London, Conn. to Block Island, mid-June until after Labor Day. Daily service to Prudence Island from Bristol. Summer service to Prudence Island from Providence, Portsmouth. For more information: see Prudence Island Navigation Co. (245–7411), Oldport Marine (847–9109). Interstate Navigation Company has daily year-round service to Block Island from Galilee, call 203–442–7891.

 **TOURIST INFORMATION SERVICES.** The *Rhode Island Department of Economic Development's* Tourist Promotion Division, 7 Jackson Walkway, Providence RI 02903 (277–2601) leaves no stone unturned when the subject is tourism. An extremely efficient organization, the council supplies reams of literature. Greater Providence Convention and Visitors Bureau, 10 Dorrance St., Providence (274–1636). The *Guide to Rhode Island* lists what to see, where to stay, what to do, a calendar of events, etc. Rhode Island's Heritage Month (May) activities are listed by the *Heritage Month Desk* of the Rhode Island Dept. of Economic Development. Information, licenses and permits for State Parks and streams stocked for fishing may be obtained from the *Division of Parks and Recreation,* Dept. of Environmental Management, 83 Park St.,

Providence RI 02903. Just about every town has its own chamber of commerce, including the *Block Island Chamber of Commerce* on Block Island, for specific vacation information. The *Preservation Society of Newport County,* 118 Mill St., Newport RI 02840 (847–1000), is very cooperative also and supplies informative literature. During season, several daily newspapers publish special sections featuring tourist and visitor information.

There are tourist and visitor information centers at Charlestown, Hopkinton, Theodore Francis Green State Airport-Warwick, Lincoln, Newport, Narragansett, Westerly. *Roger Williams National Memorial,* Providence, has a visitor's welcome center. The Greater Providence Convention & Visitors Bureau has hotel and dining information.

 **SEASONAL EVENTS.** There is a great deal going on in Rhode Island. From May to Oct. there are numerous fishing tournaments out of several ports. County fairs occur from June through the middle of Sept. Newport has a steady stream of yachting events. Antiques take center stage from spring through autumn throughout the state, with extraordinary flea markets attracting throngs. For more detailed information on events in Rhode Island, contact the Rhode Island Dept. of Economic Development, Tourist Promotion Division, 7 Jackson Walkway, Providence 02903 (277–2601).

May. One of the most important events is *Rhode Island Heritage Month,* an annual celebration commemorating the state's declaration of independence from Great Britain on May 4, 1776. *Greyholme Horse Show,* East Greenwich.

June. *Newport Motor Car Festival* is held in mid-June in Newport. *Block Island Week Sailing Regatta* is held the last full week in June on odd-numbered years. Block Island's *Cruising Week* is held on even-numbered years. Among other beauty pageants, *Miss Rhode Island* and *Little Miss Rhode Island* are held this month.

July. *Fourth of July* parades are held in Bristol, Chepachet and Arnold Mills. The *Narragansett Auto Fair* is held in Narragansett at the end of July. The *Providence County Kennel Club Dog Show* is one of the largest in the East. One of the big horse shows takes place at the Rocky Hill Fairgrounds, State 2, East Greenwich, in late July.

August. A *Victory Day Parade* is held on the second Mon. of Aug. in Providence.

September. Galilee is the scene of many fishing tournaments but the biggest is the *Rhode Island Tuna Tournament* over Labor Day weekend. The *Annual International Jumping Derby,* one of the state's big equestrian events, is held in Portsmouth.

October. Annual *Rhode Island Jonnycake Festival,* Usquepaug Village, off Route 138, Richmond. Celebrations at a century-old corn meal grinding grist mill honor the famous "journey cake."

 **TOURS.** *Viking Tours* 182 Thames St., Newport (847–6921), feature a 22-mile guided tour of historic Newport. At least 150 points of interest are pointed out, such as the famous Newport mansions, the Touro Synagogue, Wanton-Lyman-Hazard House, Naval War College, the Old Colony House, Hunter House, Trinity Church, the Old Stone Mill, Redwood Library, Newport Casino, Pirate Point, Hammersmith Farm (President John F. Kennedy's "summer White House"), etc. The trip includes the 10-mile Ocean Drive. Then you have your choice of a trip through one of these fabulous mansions: The Breakers, The Elms, Rosecliff or Marble House. The operator also conducts a harbor tour aboard two vessels reminiscent of the old overnight steamboats to New York. It is a one-hour narrated tour of Newport's waterfront, estates that face the harbor and along Jamestown's shore. Bus tours, of which there are two options, operate daily April 1 through October 31 from the Chamber of Commerce with stops at principal hotels. From Nov. through Mar., there are two tours each Sat. at 9:30 A.M. and 1:30 P.M. from C of C. The harbor tour leaves Goat Island daily May 1 through Oct. 31; first trip 11:30 A.M. Special arrange-

ments are made for groups and parties, or for walking tours. Tickets and information: 182 Thames St.

United Tours, Newport Gateway, tickets and information at railroad station (849–8005). Boyertown Trolley Cars are used over a 25-mile route of historic and scenic Newport. Tours leave hourly, 9:30 A.M. to 3:30 P.M., mid-April through mid-October. Tours arranged during off-season; special rates for groups, parties, and tours. Regular tours $6, children under 18 free. The company's Red Route covers historic center and mansion area; adults $4, children under 18 free. United Tours-Providence includes Federal Hill, historic East Side, etc., hourly from Marriott Hotel beginning 9:30 A.M. through 1:30 P.M., year round, except Mondays. Information: 467–8844.

Harbor Tours, Sayer's Wharf, provides narrated harbor tours with frequent trips hourly beginning at 9:30 A.M. with a sunset cruise at 7, mid-June to Labor Day; mid-May to mid-June, one tour daily and two on Sat. and Sun.; same schedule after Labor Day until late Oct. (847–9109).

Old Colony & Newport Railroad, Newport Gateway at Americas Cup Ave. at Bridge St. (849–5530), has an 8-mile scenic shore railroad ride from Newport to Melville (Portsmouth) by U.S. Navy piers and yacht basins.

You can ride a British double-deck bus for a tour of Narragansett, or ride in one of *Wright's British Taxi Service* vehicles (London taxicabs). For information call 783–0555.

SPECIAL-INTEREST TOURS. *University of Rhode Island,* Kingston (792–1000). Guided tours of university grounds and other points of interest in the village provided by students during summer session. The *Historic Textiles Collection,* Quinn Hall, is one of the treasures of the college and may be seen during university hours.

Blithewold, Ferry Rd., Bristol (253–8714). A Heritage Foundation of Rhode Island property, its acres of gardens were designed by John De Wolf (Prospect Park, Brooklyn) and features tallest (80–ft.) Sequoia tree east of Rockies. Open May to Oct., except Mon. and holidays.

State Trout Hatchery, 1106 Post Rd., Perryville (783–5358). Group tours should be arranged two days in advance. Open daily year round.

Old Narragansett Church (1707), Wickford (294–9331 or 294–4357). Oldest Episcopal church in use in the area. Open July and Aug., Fri. and Sat.

Prescott Farm, 2009 West Main Rd., Middletown (847–6230) is a group of restored buildings that features an operating windmill (1812) whose ground cornmeal is sold at the nearby Country Store (1715), which was once a ferrymaster's house. The General Prescott Guardhouse (1730) has a museum of furniture. British General Richard Prescott was captured at the neighboring Nichols-Overing House on July 9, 1777 by Rhode Islanders in the most daring raid of the Revolutionary War. Admission charge.

Providence Walking Tours are free architectural theme-tours by Providence Preservation Society, 24 Meeting St. (831–7440).

Harbor Tours: Great Salt Pond (Narragansett-South Kingstown) aboard M/V *Southland,* leaves from State Pier, Galilee (783–2954), during season for tour of Great Salt Pond and famous Point Judith; also ferry service between Galilee and Jerusalem. Newport Harbor tours, from The Mooring dock, Sayer's Wharf (849–2111).

Sakonnet Vineyards, West Main Rd., Little Compton (635–4356). Rhode Island's first winery, whose wines have already gained recognition. Retail sales at winery. Open June to Oct., Wed. and Sat. Tours by appointment.

Prudence Island Vineyards, a mile from Homestead Landing (via ferry from Bristol); tours by appointment (683–2452).

H. P. Lovecraft Tours of Providence's historic east side associated with this writer of supernatural tales. By appointment (351–9272).

Ranger/naturalist tours at *Beaver Tail State Park,* Jamestown, and other Bay islands and parks (for information: Division of Parks & Recreation, 83 Park St., Providence RI 02903) (277–2632).

Stumpf Balloon Tours. P.O. Box 1143, Providence, RI 02901 (726–3671). Trips from 1 to 1½ hours, $125 per person; four people per trip.

The Balloon Company, 86 Mail Coach Road, Portsmouth, RI 02840 (846–4074). Hot air balloon tours of Newport area.

The Guide to Rhode Island, free from the Tourist Promotion Division, 7 Jackson Walkway, Providence, RI 02903, lists special tours.

CRUISES. *M/V Bay Queen,* has a party/cruise, featuring exploratory stops at some Narragansett Bay islands, sails from Warren. Details from Rentacruise, Inc., 461 Water St., (Box 368), Warren RI 02885 (245–1350).

Windjammer Cruises: The Schooner *Bill of Rights,* a 125-ft. long replica of an 1850's topsail schooner, cruises from Fort Adams, Newport, to several southeastern New England ports of call. Weekend cruises, May to mid-June and mid-September through Oct. Week-long cruises, July to mid-Sept. Capt. Joseph M. Davis, Jr., 110 Wilcox St., Pawtucket RI 02860 (724–7612).

STATE PARKS. Little Rhody has big ideas in the recreation field—about 12,000 acres in 92 areas including beaches for state parks and forests. Facilities are excellent, including toilets, fireplaces, picnic tables, and drinking water in the majority of the state parks listed here. *Arcadia Management Area (Arcadia State Forest* is alongside) in Exeter has 25 tent sites, 130 picnic tables, 79 fireplaces; also good for swimming and fishing. *Beach Pond State Park,* Exeter (State 165), offers swimming, fishing and camping on about 3,000 acres. 60 picnic tables and 60 fireplaces. *Burlingame State Park,* off U.S. 1 near Charlestown. About 755 campsites are available. Swimming, boating, fishing in Watchaug Pond. *Kimball Bird Sanctuary* nearby.

Goddard Memorial State Park, about a mile from East Greenwich, is a favorite with families. Summer and winter sports. More than 300 picnic tables, over 300 portable stove slabs and fireplaces. *Lincoln Woods State Park,* only 5 miles from Providence, offers huge Olney Pond for summer water sports and winter skating; 10 miles of bridle paths; sports field. *Pulaski Memorial State Park* is off U.S. 44 in Glocester. Swimming, fishing and ice skating. Picnic tables, fireplaces. *George Washington Camping Area,* also in Glocester, U.S. 44, offers 40 tent and trailer sites and several miles of hiking trails.

Fort Adams State Park, Newport, believed to be the second largest seacoast fortification built in the United States, was begun in 1824 and essentially completed in 1857. Park and fort command an outstanding view of Newport Harbor, lower Narragansett Bay and channel to Atlantic Ocean. The park is open daily. Militia musters and patriotic pageants take place from time to time.

Colt State Park, Bristol, off Route 114, features a drive along upper Narragansett Bay. Formerly the estate of the Colt family, the park has fields, picnic areas, and a non-denominational chapel in a beautiful grove.

For general information regarding state-operated parks, picnic groves, management areas, fireplace permits, etc., contact the Division of Parks and Recreation, 83 Park St., Providence, RI 02903 (401) 277–2632.

CAMPING. The largest camping facilities are at *Burlingame State Park,* near Westerly, via U.S. 1, with more than 755 campsites; tents and trailers are permitted. Season begins Apr. 1, and ends Oct. 31. Permits are issued by the Division of Parks and Recreation, 83 Park St., Providence 02903. (277–2632). *Fishermen's Memorial State Park,* a "deluxe" family campground, now accepts reservations through State's Division of Parks & Recreation. *George Washington Management Area* in Glocester offers 40 tent and trailer sites. *Beach Pond State Park* in the Exeter-West Greenwich area, via State 165, has 18 overnight cabins. *Arcadia State Park* in Exeter offers 25 tent and 39 trailer sites.

Rhode Island has 38 state, municipal and privately-operated family campgrounds, most in wooded areas near fresh water fishing and boating, some at or near ocean beaches. Free booklet from: Tourist Promotion Division, Dept. of Economic Development, 7 Jackson Walkway, Providence RI 02903.

TRAILER TIPS. Visitors do not need a permit for a legal-size trailer 50 ft. in length, not exceeding 12 ft. in width. There are some trailer parks throughout the state where rental is on a permanent basis.

ZOOS. *Roger Williams Park Zoo* allows children to pet animals in special area. Zoo animals, just for watching, are at their best during feeding time. The *Enchanted Forest,* Rte. 3, Hopkinton, fairyland theme park; petting zoo, trails rides, ages 3 to 11; weekends: May to mid-June, and after Labor Day, Sun. through Sept., daily in season. *Slater Park,* Pawtucket, has a good zoo for city its size. Park has picnic area and tennis courts.

GARDENS. Formal sunken garden at *The Elms* in Newport, open May 1 to October 31, Sat. The Elms is modeled after the Chateau d'Asnieres near Paris, France.

Arabesque parterre at *The Breakers,* open May 1 to Oct. 31.

Rose garden at *Rosecliff,* open May 1 to October 31. Hammersmith Farm, Newport, May 1 to Oct. 31.

Wanton-Lyman-Hazard House, the oldest house in Newport, has a small Colonial garden.

In Portsmouth, *Green Animals,* famous topiary garden, Cory's Lane. Open May 1 to Sept. 30, weekends in Oct. *Roger Williams Park,* Providence. Textile garden, *Slater Mill,* Pawtucket. Colonial garden at *Smith's Castle,* Wickford. Colonial garden, Whitehall, Middletown.

Blithewold Gardens & Arboretum, Ferry Rd, Bristol (253–8714). *Shakespeare's Head* (1763), 21 Meeting St. Providence. Erected by John Carter, first postmaster and publisher of the first newspaper in Providence. Only Colonial garden is open to visitors and is maintained by R. I. Federation of Garden Clubs. A private club is also housed here.

SUMMER SPORTS. Swimming: You are never very far from a good beach in Rhode Island. The beach at Narragansett Pier is excellent, located on Rte. 1A about 5 miles north of Point Judith Lighthouse. About 2 miles north of that lighthouse is Scarborough State Beach. Between Pt. Judith and the Connecticut line are miles and miles of excellent beaches with such names as Roger W. Wheeler State Beach, Moonstone, Misquamicut and Watch Hill. Almost any road to the shore leads to the sand and sea. Many state parks have swimming facilities.

State beaches include Block Island State Beach, Block Island; East Matunuck State Beach, South Kingstown; Misquamicut State Beach, Westerly; Capt. R. Wheeler State Beach, Narragansett; Scarborough State Beach, Narragansett.

Fishing: Fishing is excellent in the state, from *surf-casting* (no license) to inland streams and lakes (license required). Many fishing tournaments are sponsored for tourists during the summer in most of the seaside towns. The Rhode Island Tuna Tournament is held annually Labor Day weekend and the prestigious U.S. Atlantic Tuna Tournament based mid-Sept. on Block Island. Charter boats are available for *big game fish.* "Boating in Rhode Island" lists charter and party boats, free from Tourist Promotion Division, Dept. of Economic Development, 7 Jackson Walkway, Providence RI 02903 (277–2601). Outboard and sailboat rentals, bait and tackle: Ocean House Marina, Ocean House Rd, Charlestown (364–6040).

Golf: There are 49 golf courses; half open to public play and many private golf courses are open to guests of various hotels and motels.

Tennis: There are private and public courts (grass and cement) throughout the state and about a dozen indoor tennis courts. One of the very few royal courts in existence is at the Newport Casino Tennis Hall of Fame.

Skeet and Trap: Open tournament shoots are held at Wallum Lake Rod & Gun Club, Harrisville; Tiverton Rod & Gun Club, Tiverton, and other gun clubs.

Hang Gliding: Permitted at Diamond Hill State Park, Cumberland.

Biking: Rhode Island's country roads are ideal. The Tourist Promotion Division, 7 Jackson Walkway, Providence, RI 02903, can furnish maps for biking the Metropolitan Providence area. Bicyclists are required to obey the rules of the road.

WINTER SPORTS. Skiing: Novice and intermediate skiing at Yawgoo Valley Ski Area, off Rte. 2, Exeter.

Cross-country skiing may be enjoyed at the Norman Bird Sanctuary, 583 Third Beach Rd., Middletown, and Pulaski Memorial State Park, Burrillville.

Snowmobiling: Colt State Park, Bristol; Pulaski Memorial State Park, Burrillville; Burlingame State Park, Charlestown; Arcadia Management Area and Beach Pond State Park, Exeter; Lincoln Woods State Park, Lincoln; Stepping Stone Ranch, Escoheag.

Hunting: Hunting in Rhode Island requires a license. Seasons vary and game includes rabbits, deer, squirrel, etc.

Hiking: Although Rhode Island is the nation's smallest state and densely populated, 60% of it is woodland and beaches, making it ideal for hiking. The *Hikers Club of Rhode Island; All-State Hikers* and *Yankee Trailers Hiking Club* rendezvous at different places for shore and beach or woodland hikes, year round except summer. These groups welcome visitors. For details concerning their Sunday programs consult the "What's Going On" column of the *Providence Journal-Bulletin* on Sat., or the "Weekend" section on Fri.

SPECTATOR SPORTS. Golf: A popular spectator event is the *Northeast Amateur Golf Tournament,* held annually during the last week in June. Information can be obtained from the *Providence Journal-Bulletin. Golf Digest* sponsors an annual tournament at the Newport Country Club where the first tourneys in the U.S. were held in 1894.

Intercollegiate sports. *Brown University,* the *University of Rhode Island, Providence College* and others provide *intercollegiate football, basketball* and *hockey* during winter months against other major collegiate teams.

Greyhound racing is at Lincoln Downs Greyhound Park, Lincoln, Rte. 246.

Jai Alai: Newport Jai Alai Fronton, Admiral Kalbfus Rd.; pari-mutuel wagering; nightly from spring to autumn, two matinees weekly. Closed Sun.

Football: The *New England Patriots* uses Bryant College, Smithfield, for summer practice.

Baseball: Pawtucket Red Sox (farm team for Boston Red Sox) of International League; home games, McCoy Stadium, Pawtucket (724–7303).

Yacht-watching has been developed to a fine point in the Newport area, especially during the *Biennial June Newport to Bermuda Yacht Race* and *Biennial Annapolis to Newport Yacht Race.* Also, *Block Island Race* late June. The *Newport Yachting Center* in and out of water boat shows, May to Oct.

CHILDREN'S ACTIVITIES. Amusement Parks: *Rocky Point Park,* Warwick, has rides, games, amusements, huge saltwater pool (night-lighting). Free parking. RIPTA buses from downtown Providence. *Roger Williams Park,* Providence, features merry-go-round, paddle boat rides, and newly designed zoo. Other areas with amusements are: *Easton's Beach,* Newport; *Watch Hill Beach,* Watch Hill; *Lake Mishnock,* West Greenwich; *Oakland Beach,* Warwick; *Slater Park,* Pawtucket.

Children's Playhouse at The Breakers, Newport, once belonged to Vanderbilt children. Hostess. Open daily Apr. to Oct. 31.

The Children's Museum, 58 Walcott St., Pawtucket. The state's first museum for youngsters up to 12 years of age is in an 1840 Victorian house.

Toy Museum at Green Animals, off Route 114, Portsmouth. Open daily May 1 to Sept. 30 and weekends in Oct., 10 A.M.-5 P.M.

Smith's Castle, 1 mile north of Wickford; narrative tour of this 1678 house. Open Apr. 15 to Oct. 15, daily except Thurs.; Oct. 15 to April 15, weekends.

Enchanted Forest, Rte. 3, Hopkinton, reached via I—95, exits 2 or 3; theme park especially planned for pre-teenagers.

Tomaquag Valley Indian Memorial Museum, Summit Rd., Arcadia, is regarded as an Indian cultural center and trading post. Open year round.

 **HISTORIC SITES AND HOMES.** Recorded history began for Rhode Island back in 1636 when Roger Williams stepped ashore from his canoe in what is now known as Providence. Throughout Rhode Island, you'll be able to visit homes and hallowed sites that have been restored and preserved.

PROVIDENCE AREA

ANTHONY. *General Nathanael Greene Homestead* (1770), Taft St. (821–8630). Home of Washington's second-in-command. Now maintained as a patriotic shrine. Open Wed., Sat. and Sun. and by appointment. Closed Dec. through Feb. Features furniture of the period.

BRISTOL. *Reynolds House,* 956 Hope St. dating from 1698, was used by General Lafayette as his headquarters in 1778. Privately owned.

Mount Hope Farm, off Metacom Ave. 253–8388. What remains of the property belongs to the Haffenreffer Museum of Anthropology. Open June to Labor Day, Tues.–Sun., 1:00 P.M. to 5:00 P.M.

CRANSTON. *Governor Sprague Mansion,* 1353 Cranston St. (944–9226). Open July and Aug, Sun., 2 to 4 P.M. Furnishings of the period and artifacts of the Sprague family. Home of two Rhode Island governors.

EAST GREENWICH. *General James Mitchell Varnum House,* 57 Peirce St. 884–4622. Open June to Sept., Tuesday–Saturday, 1–4 P.M., and by appointment. A fine mansion with magnificent paneling, Colonial garden, Victorian room of children's toys.

EAST PROVIDENCE. *Lloof Carousel,* Merry-go-round made by master carver Charles Lloof, considered best in U.S. From East Providence or Providence, follow Veterans Memorial Parkway and signs to Riverside.

PROVIDENCE. *Roger Williams Rock,* in area bounded by Power, Williams and Gano Sts. A monument near the spot Roger Williams landed in 1636.

First Baptist Meeting House, 75 North Main St. (751–2266). A landmark of old Providence was founded by Roger Williams in 1638. The church office, on the Waterman St. entrance, welcomes visitors. Open April–October, Mon. to Fri., 10–3; Sat., 10–12; Sunday tours at noon.

Roger Williams Memorial, Prospect Terrace. Panoramic view of Providence. Contemporary statue of Williams who is buried nearby.

Roger Williams National Memorial Park, North Main St. at Canal St., (528–4881). A project of the National Parks System. Here may be seen Roger Williams Spring, site of the original Providence settlement. Visitor reception center open Monday to Friday. Across the street, on the corner of Howland St., a plaque proclaims that Roger Williams lived here in 1636.

Governor Stephen Hopkins House, Corner of Benefit and Hopkins Sts. Opposite the Court House. Open for visitors. Hopkins was a signer of the Declaration of Independence. House built 1707, with addition constructed in 1743. Information: 751–1758.

John Brown House, 52 Power St. (331–8575). Headquarters of the Rhode Island Historical Society. George Washington was entertained here. Closed holidays. Described by John Quincy Adams as "the most magnificent and elegant mansion" that he'd ever seen on this continent.

The Old State House, 150 Benefit St. (277–2678). Built in 1762. Open week-days. Site where Rhode Island General Assembly renounced allegience to King George III on May 4, 1776. Currently houses offices of the Rhode Island Historic Presentation Commission and the Heritage Commission of Rhode Island.

State House, Smith St. (277–2357). This "new" state house dominates the city. Built of white Georgia marble, it boasts the second largest of the four unsupported marble domes in the world. Inside is a prize relic: the original parchment charter granted by King Charles II in 1663. The famous full-length portrait of George Washington by Gilbert Stuart hangs in the reception room. Visitors welcome.

Providence City Hall, Kennedy Plaza (4231–7740). Designed in the manner of The Louvre and Tuileries in Paris.

Joseph Russell House, 116 North Main St. This is a three-story brick building that was raised and had stores built under it.

Brick School House, 24 Meeting St. (831–7440). One of first public schools in Providence. Headquarters of Providence Preservation Society.

Providence Athenaeum, 251 Benefit St. (421–6970). One of America's oldest libraries and cultural centers. Edgar Allan Poe courted Sarah Helen Whitman here. Rare book wing.

Annmary Brown Memorial, 21 Brown St. (863–2429). Exhibit of early print-ing and European and American painting.

Thomas Poynton Ives House, 66 Power St. Built 1911. Large and handsome mansion of the Georgian Colonial style. Private home.

Joseph Nightingale House, 357 Benefit St. Built 1792. Private home.

Edward Carrington House, 66 Williams St. A three-story brick building of Early Republican design built in 1813. Private home.

Old Lightning Splitter House, Transit St. So-called because of the very steep pitch of the gables, not unlike the steep roofs of medieval architecture. Private home.

Dolphin House, 403 South Main St. Built by a sailing captain about 1770.

Old Market House, Market Square, built 1773, site of the Providence Tea Party in 1775. Now part of the Rhode Island School of Design complex.

NEWPORT AREA

NEWPORT. *Touro Synagogue,* 72 Touro St. (847–4794). The oldest syna-gogue in America. Built in 1763 by America's first architect, Peter Harrison, it is considered a colonial masterpiece. Open late June to Labor Day, Mon. to Fri., 10 A.M. to 5 P.M.; Sun., 10 A.M. to 6 P.M. Other times, Sun., 2–4 P.M. and by appointment.

Brick Market, Washington Sq. Designed by Peter Harrison in 1762. Now a gift shop, it was previously used as a theater and City Hall.

The Great Quaker Meeting House, Marlborough and Farewell St. (846–0813). Built in 1699. Open daily, June to Labor Day. A superb example of early Colonial architecture.

Wanton-Lyman-Hazard House, 17 Broadway (846–0813). Restored and fur-nished by the Newport Historical Society. Open daily from June to Labor Day. This is the oldest house in Newport, dating back to 1675, and is also a national historic landmark.

Newport Historical Society, 82 Touro St. (846–0813). Fine collection of Colonial and early American books, manuscripts, toys and dolls, furniture, silver, china, and costumes.

Seventh Day Baptist Meeting House, Attached to the Newport Historical Society on Touro St. (846–0813). America's oldest Seventh Day Baptist Church, built in 1729.

Trinity Church, Spring and Church Sts. (846–0660). One of the finest struc-tures of its type in America, features a three-tiered pulpit. Open daily in sum-mer, other times by appointment.

Redwood Library, Bellevue Ave. (847–0292). Another national historic land-mark. Designed by Peter Harrison, it is considered the oldest library room in continuous use in the U. S. The collection of American paintings is exceptional. Open weekdays 9:30 A.M. to 5:30 P.M.

Old Colony House, Washington Sq. (846–2980). National historic landmark dating back to 1739. Free admission. Second oldest capital building in nation. Features full-length portrait of George Washington by Gilbert Stuart.

Old Stone Mill, Touro Park. This is a mystery site as well as a conversation piece. No one really knows whether it was built by the Norsemen seven centuries ago or by the colonists sometime prior to 1665. Whatever, it is one of the nation's first tourist "curiosities."

Vernon House, 46 Clarke St. Built in 1748, home of William Vernon, Secretary of the Continental Navy, and headquarters of French General de Rochambeau (1780–81). Private home.

White Horse Tavern, corner Farewell and Marlborough Sts. Built in 1673. Oldest tavern building in America. Now a restaurant open for lunch and dinner.

Hunter House, 54 Washington St. (847–1000). A National Historic Landmark built in 1748. One of the ten best examples of American Colonial architecture in America. Furnished with outstanding Rhode Island and famous Townsend and Goddard furniture. Completely restored by The Preservation Society of Newport County. Open to the public daily May 1 to October 31, the first two weekends in November, and by appointment the rest of the year except in Apr. when it is open on weekends.

PORTSMOUTH. *Butts Hill Fort,* reached via Sprague St. Site of Rhode Island's only major Revolutionary War land battle, August 29, 1778. Old redoubts still discernable and marker tells of the battle in which Generals Lafayette, Hancock, Greene and Sullivan participated.

Portsmouth Abbey. Cory's Lane (683–2000). Benedictine monastery and preparatory school. Outstanding church in contemporary style designed by Pietro Belluschi. Noteworthy interior feature is wire sculpture by Richard Lippold.

Overing House, 2009 West Main Rd. in Portsmouth at Middletown line (can be viewed from Prescott Farm). Private home.

Prescott Farm, 2009 West Main Rd. Portsmouth at Middletown line (847–2071). Restored Colonial farm buildings featuring operating windmill.

TIVERTON. *Chase-Cory House,* Main Rd., Tiverton Four Corners. Open Sun. May to Labor Day. A gambrel-roofed building which has period furniture and changing exhibits.

SOUTH COUNTY AREA

ARCADIA. *Tomaquag Valley Indian Memorial,* Summit Rd. (539–7213 or 539–7795). Open daily, 1 to 4, except Christmas and Feb. Indian cultural center and trading post.

CHARLESTOWN. *Indian Church,* off Rte. 2. Services 11 A.M., Palm Sunday to October. Granite structure built by local Indians in 1859.

KINGSTON. *Old Kingstown Court House,* 1329 Kingstown Rd., South Kingston (783–8254). Built in 1775 as the King's county court house. Used by the state's General Assemby as a state house from 1776 to 1854. It is now the Kingston Free Library building.

Washington County Jail, 1348 Kingstown Rd., South Kingston (783–1328). Pettaquamscutt Historical Society headquarters. Old jail cells and period rooms.

Watson House, Univ. of Rhode Island campus. Open during college sessions or by appointment. Call 792–1000 for general campus information and 792–2200 for events of public interest. A typical two-story Colonial farmhouse furnished in the period 1790–1840.

SAUNDERSTOWN. *Gilbert Stuart Birthplace,* Gilbert Stuart Rd. (294–3001). Built in 1751. Open daily except Friday; closed Nov. through Feb. A rural 18th-century house, which combined a snuff mill operation. Birthplace of America's foremost painter of George Washington portraits.

Silas Casey Farm, on Scenic 1A (227–3956). Built around 1750. Open to visitors. Large 18th-century farmhouse with furniture and family memorabilia. The farm continues to operate.

Smith's Castle, 1 mile north of Wickford on U.S. 1 in North Kingstown (294–3521). Only house still standing that has connections with state's founder, Roger Williams. Open daily, except Thurs. mid-Apr. to Oct., 10 A.M. to 5 P.M. except Thurs.; Sun. 1 to 5 P.M. Also a collection of antique dolls and a Colonial garden.

WESTERLY. *Babcock-Smith House,* 124 Granite St. (596–4424). Open May to June and Sept. to Oct., Sun. 2 to 5 P.M.; July and Aug., Wed. and Sun., 2 to 5 and by appointment. A Georgian-style house (1732) where Benjamin Franklin often visited. He appointed Dr. Joshua Babcock to establish the town's first post office here.

WICKFORD. *Old Narragansett Church,* (1707) off Brown St. via a walkway. (294–9331 or 294–4357). Oldest Episcopal church building standing north of Virginia. Gilbert Stuart, noted Colonial portraitist was baptized here.

Firemen's Memorial, West Main St. Veteran Firemen's Association exhibits 1874 restored hand pumper fire engine and other firefighting memorabilia. Key available at Public Safety Building, 8150 Post Rd.

BLACKSTONE VALLEY AREA

LINCOLN. *Eleazer Arnold House,* Saylesville Village on the Great Rd. Built in 1687. It is an outstanding example of the huge "stone-ender" house. Not shown to visitors.

PAWTUCKET. *Daggett House.* Slater Park (434–8195). Built in 1685. Open Sun., July and Aug. Other times by appointment. Boasts china used by Gen. and Mrs. Nathanael Greene.

Slater Mill Historic Site, Roosevelt Ave. (725–8638). Closed Jan. and Feb. Regarded as the "birthplace of American Industrial know-how," the complex is composed of the Slater Mill (1793), the nation's first successful textile mill; the Wilkinson Mill (1810), the first factory to make machinery; and the Sylvanus Brown House (1758), typical of a house owned by a mill foreman or a skilled laborer.

Wilkinson Mill, Roosevelt Ave. (725–8638). A part of the Slater Mill Historic Site. Built in 1810. This was the first factory in America to manufacture machinery. It features a 16-ton water wheel that turns the machinery.

Sylvanus Brown House, Roosevelt Ave. (725–8638). Built in 1758. It is an example of an early skilled-worker's home.

 **INDIANS.** Rhode Island was the home of the *Narragansett Indians* in the 17th century. Canonicus, the Narragansett chief, sold Roger Williams the land on which he settled. The Narragansetts became allies of the colonists in the Pequot War, 1637. However, the Indian power in southern New England was destroyed in 1675 after King Philip's War. Their fort was attacked in Kingston (the Great Swamp Fight). The survivors migrated, some settling among the *Niantic Indians* near Charlestown.

The visitor will get a good look at—and even a taste of—Indian lore at the *Tomaquag Indian Memorial Museum* in the village of Arcadia, on Summit Road in the township of Exeter. The *Rhode Island Indian Heritage Dinner* is held there in early May. In mid-July the *Green Bean Thanksgiving Ceremony and Clambake* is another Tomaquag event.

NEWPORT MANSIONS. The Newport Mansions, owned and opened to the public by The Preservation Society of Newport County, are the State of Rhode Island's largest historic attractions. They include *The Breakers,* Ochre Point Ave. Open daily, Apr. 1 to Oct. 31, and the first two weekends in Nov. 10 A.M.–5 P.M. It is the largest and most magnificent of all Newport mansions built in 1895 for Cornelius Vanderbilt. Designed by Richard Morris Hunt, it contains all its original furnishings.

Chateau-sur-Mer, Bellevue Ave. Open daily May 1 to Oct. 31, 10 A.M.–5 P.M.; and weekends Nov. to Apr., 10 A.M.–4 P.M. One of the finest examples of lavish Victorian architecture in America, it was built in 1852 for William S. Wetmore made his fortune in the China Trade. A Chinese "moongate" is part of the south wall.

The Elms, Bellevue Ave. Open daily Apr. 1 to Oct. 31, 10 A.M.–5 P.M.; Nov. to Apr., weekends, 10 A.M.–4 P.M. Built in 1901 as a summer residence for Edward J. Berwind, the Pennsylvania coal magnate. It was modeled after the Chateau d'Asnieres near Paris and has lovely grounds including a sunken French garden, marble gazebos and statuary.

Marble House, Bellevue Ave. Open daily Apr. 1 to Oct. 31, 10 A.M.–5 P.M.; Nov. to Apr., weekends, 10 A.M.–4 P.M. It was built in 1892 by Richard Morris Hunt for William K. Vanderbilt. One of the most sumptuous of Newport's "cottages," it has its original furnishings. The restored kitchen in the basement and the restored Chinese Teahouse on the grounds, overlooking the Cliff Walk and the Atlantic Ocean, are two new additions to the tour. The Harold S. Vanderbilt Memorial Room features yachting memorabilia and trophies won by Mr. Vanderbilt, one of America's outstanding amateur skippers who defended The Americas Cup three times.

Rosecliff, Bellevue Ave. Open daily, Apr. 1 to Oct. 31, and the first two weekends in Nov., 10 A.M.–5 P.M. Designed by McKim, Mead & White, it was built in 1902 for Mrs. Hermann Oelrichs whose father, James Fair, was one of the discoverers of the Comstock Lode. It features the largest ballroom in Newport and was modeled after the Grand Trianon at Versailles. It has been the scene of major motion pictures such as "The Great Gatsby" and "The Betsy."

Kingscote, Bellevue Ave. Open daily May 1 to Oct. 31, 10 A.M.–5 P.M.; weekends in Apr. and early Nov. This charming Victorian cottage was built by Richard Upjohn in 1839 for George Noble Jones of Georgia. Considered the nation's first "summer cottage", it has a beautiful McKim, Mead & White dining room featuring Tiffany lighting fixtures and a glass wall.

Hunter House, 54 Washington St. Open daily May 1 to Oct. 31, 10 A.M.–5 P.M.; weekends in Apr. and early Nov. and by appointment the rest of the year by calling 747–7516. Built in 1748, it is one of the 10 best examples of American Colonial residential architecture. It features Rhode Island and famous Townsend and Goddard furniture and was the reason for the formation of the Preservation Society in 1945.

Green Animals, Cory's Lane, off Route 114, Portsmouth. Open daily, May 1 to Oct. 31, and the first two weekends in Nov. 10 A.M.–5 P.M., is one of the properties on the Preservation Society combination ticket. This beautiful topiary garden is considered one of the best in the country. There are 100 sculptured trees and shrubs, formal flower beds, fruit and vegetable gardens, and a plant and gift shop. A small Victorian toy museum is located in three rooms on the first floor of the main house.

Four of the above houses are open in the evening until 8 P.M. from July 1 to mid-Sept. They are: Mon. at Rosecliff; Tues., Wed., Thurs. and Sun. at The Breakers; Fri., Marble House; and Sat., The Elms.

If you plan to visit more than one mansion, the Newport Preservation Society sells combination tickets to all above houses at substantial savings and these may be purchased at any one of the houses. Information on these houses can be obtained from the Society, 118 Mill St., Newport RI 02840 (847–1000).

Other mansions are *Belcourt Castle,* Bellevue Ave. Open daily (except Thanksgiving) Apr. 1 to Nov. 30. Built in 1882, it was the home of Oliver Hazard Perry Belmont, older son of August Belmont, financier and sportsman. *Hammersmith Farm,* Ridge Rd. Open daily Apr. to Oct.; weekends in March and Nov. Built in 1889 for John W. Auchincloss of New York, it was the summer home of Jacqueline Bouvier, who later married Senator John F. Kennedy. President and Mrs. Kennedy later used the mansion as their "summer White House." *Beechwood,* Bellevue Ave. Open daily. Built in 1852 for Daniel Parish of New York. It was later owned by Mrs. William Astor. *Ochre Court,* Ochre Point Ave. Open daily. Now Salve Regina College, it was built in 1891 for Ogden Goelet. Visitors are welcome.

 MUSEUMS AND GALLERIES. For such a small state, Rhode Island has a wealth of excellent museums and galleries, many of which recreate the state's history in carefully restored houses. Rhode Island's small size is a boon because museums spread among the different towns are easily accessible.

PROVIDENCE AREA

BRISTOL. *Herreshoff Marine Museum,* 18 Burnside St. (253–6660). Open Wednesdays and Sundays, May to October. Exhibits models and other material pertaining to the golden age of yachting.

Haffenreffer Museum of Anthropology of Brown University, off Rte. 136 (Metacom Ave.) (253–8388). Open daily June 1 to Aug. 31, 1 to 5 P.M. and Sept. to Nov. and Apr. to May, Sat. and Sun., 1 to 5 P.M. Exhibits American Indian, Eskimo and South American aboriginal art objects.

Bristol Art Museum, Wardwell St. (253–8800). Open June to late Sept. daily. Changing exhibits. Features James DeWolf's 1817 coach.

EAST GREENWICH. *Varnum Military and Naval Museum,* corner of Main and Division Sts. (884–4110). Open by appointment. Contains a general collection of objects pertaining to all wars of the U. S.

PROVIDENCE. *Rhode Island Heritage Hall of Fame,* Providence Civic Center, La Salle Sq. Annual investiture adds to the growing gallery of portraits and photographs of famous native or adopted Rhode Islanders and includes Broadway playwright, producer, songwriter, director and actor George M. Cohan, singer Nelson Eddy, baseball great Napoleon Lajoie and television personality David Hartman. Visitors welcome whenever no special events are scheduled. Advance telephone notice required; (331–0700).

Providence Art Club, 11 Thomas St. (331–1114). Closed Sat. and Sun. July and Aug. Changing exhibits.

Pendleton House, 224 Benefit St. (331–3511), part of the Museum of Art of the R. I. School of Design.

Museum of Rhode Island History (Aldrich House), 110 Benevolent St. (421–6567). Former home of Ambassador Winthrop W. Aldrich.

Bayard Ewing Building, 231 South Main St. (331–3511). Part of the R. I. School of Design and used for architectural studies. Built in 1840's.

Museum of Art (Rhode Island School of Design), 224 Benefit St. (331–6363 or 331–3511). One of the nation's finest small museums. 19th-century French art, classical Greek, Roman and Etruscan art; medieval and Renaissance art; European decorative arts and oriental art; 19th- and 20th-century American painting, modern Latin American art, contemporary art and major holdings in graphics, costumes and textiles. Pendleton House, adjoining the museum, houses a collection of 18th-century English and American furniture, silver, china and paintings.

Rhode Island Black Heritage Society, 1 Hilton St. (751–3490). Features changing exhibits of black history and culture. Open Mon. to Fri.

WARWICK. *Warwick Museum,* 3259 Post Rd. (737–0010). Now housed in the former Kentish Artillery Armory (R.I. militia). Open year round. Tues. to Fri.

NEWPORT AREA

JAMESTOWN. *Fire Department Memorial Building,* 44 Narragansett Ave. (423–0062). Open daily except Sun. and Mon. Features a horse-drawn 1885 steam engine and other antique firefighting equipment.

Jamestown Museum, Narragansett Ave., North (423–0784). Open Tues. to Sat., mid-June to early Sept. Its main exhibit relates to the ferries that operated between Newport and Jamestown.

NEWPORT. *International Lawn Tennis Hall of Fame,* 194 Bellevue Ave. (846–4567). Open year round. History of tennis shown in dioramas and tennis memorabilia.

Newport Automobile Museum, One Casino Terrace (846–6688). The largest collection of automobiles in New England.

Newport Art Museum, 76 Bellevue Ave. (847–0179). Open weekdays, Sun. and holidays. Changing exhibits.

Naval War College Museum, Naval Education & Training Center (849–4473). Opened 1978. Graphic displays of background and students (Nimitz, Spruance, etc.) of world's first naval war college. Open to the public weekdays 9 A.M. to 4 P.M., except holidays, June to Aug., Sat. and Sun. afternoons; Sept., Sat. afternoons, noon to 4 P.M. Sentry at Gate 1, Training Station Rd. issues pass to visit museum.

Marine Museum, in Newport Historical Society, 82 Touro St. (846–0813) Collection of ship and yacht models and other memorabilia of Newport's maritime past.

SOUTH COUNTY AREA

KINGSTON. *Fine Art Center Galleries,* Univ. of Rhode Island campus. Features students' works.

South County Art Association (Helme House), 1319 Kingstown Rd. (783–2195). Open daily except Mon. and holidays. Closed for one week between exhibits. Changing exhibits.

PEACE DALE. *Museum of Primitive Culture,* 604 Kingstown Rd. next to Post Office (783–5711). Open Mon. to Fri., 10 A.M. to noon, and by appointment. American Indian, South Seas, African and other areas weapons, tool, etc.

BLACKSTONE VALLEY AREA

PAWTUCKET. *The Children's Museum,* 58 Walcott St. (726–2590). A "hands on" experience for youngsters.

Rhode Island Water Color Society, Slater Park Boathouse (726–1876). Graphics show, members shows and changing exhibits.

 **MUSIC.** The state has one philharmonic orchestra, the *Rhode Island Philharmonic.* Programs are announced in advance. There are concerts by the *Brown University Music Department Orchestra;* also by professors and students at the University of Rhode Island. The *Peloquin Chorale* has appeared on national television. They perform regularly at the Cathedral of SS Peter and Paul, downtown Providence. Also: *Music Mansion,* 88 Meeting St., Providence, free concerts; *Newport Cultural Foundation,* Newport; *Trinity Church Concerts,* Newport, off-season.

Concerts are presented by the *Rhode Island College Orchestra and Chorus,* Providence. University of Rhode Island, Kingston, has shows by the *U. R. I. Dance Company. Community Chorus of Westerly* gives several concerts.

Bach's *Mass in B-Minor* is presented annually on a May date by the Rhode Island Civic Chorale and Orchestra.

A calendar of musical and cultural events is free from the Tourist Promotion Division, Dept. of Economic Development, One Weybosset Hill, Providence RI 02903 (277–2601).

For summer performances: Brown University Summer Theatre, Providence, mid-June to mid-August. *Music Festival,* Cumberland, at Diamond Hill State Park, concerts Sun. July and Aug. *Warwick Musical Theatre,* Warwick. Late June to Sept. *Lafayette Band Concerts,* North Kingstown.

THEATER. The *Sock & Buskin Players of Brown University,* Providence (863–1000) perform for a full season series Oct. through May. *Trinity Square Repertory Company,* internationally acclaimed, 1981 Tony Award winner, has a winter schedule. In summer, presentations are by the "Summer Rep" company, with all performances at the Lederer Theatre, 201 Washington St., Providence (351–4242). *Theatre-by-the-Sea,* Browning Beach Rd., Matunuck, South Kingstown (789–1094) June to Sept. *Warwick Musical Theatre,* Quaker Ln. Warwick (821–7300) presents summer shows with leading Hollywood, Broadway, and TV stars. Also: *The Incredible Far Off Broadway Theatre,* Newport (847–1996). *Colonial Theatre,* 3 Granite St., Westerly, (596–0810); *Second Story Theatre,* cor. Hope and John sts., Providence (421–5593).

The Providence Performing Arts Center, 220 Weybosset St., Providence (421–9075) one of the last of the lavish motion picture-stage theaters, has been restored and offers Broadway shows, stars in concert, and variety programs.

Other theatrical groups of note: *The Players,* Barker Playhouse, 400 Benefit St., Providence (421–2855); *Blackfriars Theatre* of Providence College; *Newport Playhouse,* 104 Connell Highway; *Brown University Summer Theatre,* Providence (863–2838); *University of Rhode Island Theatre Department,* Fine Arts Center, Kingston (792–1000); *Rhode Island Feminist Theatre* (273–8654); *Rhode Island Shakespeare Theatre,* Webster St., Newport (849–7892); *Rhode Island College, Roberts Hall Theatre,* 600 Mt. Pleasant Ave., Providence (456–8000); *City Nights Dinner Theatre,* 27 Exchange St., Pawtucket (723–6060); *Bright Lights Theatre Company,* St. John's Cathedral, 275 No. Main St., Providence (728–5926); *Cabot Street Playhouse,* 15 Cabot St., Providence (272–5766); *Academy Players,* Civic Center, East Greenwich (884–2467).

There are a score of local thespian organizations that present Broadway and Hollywood or orginial presentations in professional style. Among them are the *Newport Players Guild* and the *Swanhurst Theatre Workshop,* Newport; *Barrington Players,* Barrington; *Community Players* of Pawtucket; *Theatre Works, Inc.,* Woonsocket; *Theatre Workshop,* Westerly; *Scitamard Players,* Providence; *Coventry Players, Warren Community Players,* Providence.

The *Providence Civic Center,* LaSalle Sq., Providence, hosts ice show, professional sports, personal appearances by celebrities, circus, horse shows, antique shows and other spectaculars.

The Westerly Center for the Arts, 119 High St. (596–2854) has become a strong cultural influence in southern Rhode Island and nearby Connecticut; features pageants, concerts, etc.

SHOPPING. Department stores, which once flourished in downtown Providence, have moved to the adjoining Midland and Warwick Malls, Warwick, about 10 miles from city center. Downtown, however, retains its specialty shops such as *Tilden-Thurber,* 292 Westminster Mall, jewelers; *T.W. Rounds & Co.,* 35 Dorrance St., gifts, luggage, etc; and *The Arcade,* 130 Westminster St., America's oldest shopping center (1828), has exquisite and exciting shops and restaurants. *Mayan Shop I,* 33 Bay St., Watch Hill, unusual women's apparel. In East Greenwich, *Country Clothes,* Main St., features top fashions and sportswear. Others: *Wilson's,* 35 Brown St., Wickford. *India Imports of R.I.,* 121 Union St., Providence. *Mekong Market,* 316 Broad St., which accommodates the growing Indo-Chinese population of the area. *The Talbots,* 162 Bellevue Ave., Newport and Davol Square, Providence, well-known women's shops. There are numerous mill outlets in the state; free list available from Tourist Promotion Division, 7 Jackson Walkway, Providence.

The *Art Shanty* of Wickford, Inc., 7 Main St., Wickford, is one of several fine gift shops in village. *The Cranston Mercantile,* 1390 Cranston St., Cranston, features Cranston prints and gifts in a former meeting house built for textile mill workers. There are over a dozen antique dealers in Washington County. In Newport about the same number can be found on Franklin, Spring and lower Thames Sts. *The Blackstone Valley Factory Outlet Association,* 42 Park Place, Pawtucket, RI 02862, offers a free folder with maps of 14 outlets.

For the bibliophile there are several bookstores throughout the state. The *Current Company,* 12 Howe St., Bristol, offers rare books, prints and graphics. *Fortunate Finds Shop,* 14 West Natick Rd., Warwick, holds a weeklong outdoor sale annually in Sept. which attracts thousands from several states. Other book stores: *Simister's,* 99 Brown St., North Kingstown; *Book & Tackle,* Bay St., Watch Hill; and in Newport, *Armchair Sailor,* Lee's Wharf; *Corner Book Shop,* 418 Spring St.; *Chase & Chase,* 202 Thames St.; and *Book Bay,* Brick Market Place. Libraries such as *Redwood Library,* Newport, and the *Newport Public Library* offer discards sales. The latter is held annually early in Dec. Highlight in Oct. is the annual book sale sponsored by the *American Association of University Women,* 10 Mayflower St., Providence RI.

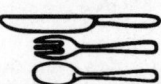

DINING OUT. After three centuries, the oldest food tradition along the rockbound New England coast is the clambake. The Indians taught the early settlers how to cook green corn, clams, and fish covered in seaweed over white-hot stones. Now, bakemasters have their own method of arranging firewood in a shallow pit over layers of big stones gathered along the shore. The stones are heated until only embers of the wood remain, then the ash is raked away and the stones covered with seaweed, which makes the steam that flavors the ingredients then added for the bake—lobster, fish, fresh corn, sausage, sweet potatoes—usually in mesh trays, and each layer of trays covered with more seaweed. Tarpaulins then cover the bake. Clambakes are held by many organizations throughout the state. Many are open to the public. Check the *East Warren Rod & Gun Club,* Long Lane, Warren (245–5763) on summer Sunday when church, firefighters and other local groups often sponsor Rhode Island clambakes to which tickets are sold. The *Moosup Valley Grange,* Moosup Valley Rd., Foster, has staged one every Labor Day for over half a century, and the public is welcome.

For more than a century Rhode Islanders have enjoyed May Day Breakfasts, an English tradition brought to Cranston, RI in 1867. These are held by churches, granges, service clubs, fraternal groups, historical societies, etc. to raise funds for non-profit organizations such as cultural groups and church projects. Meals are bounteous and reasonable. The breakfasts are held from about the third week in Apr. until mid-May and feature, at many places, Rhode Island Jonnycakes, native sausages, homemade baked beans, breads, pies, etc. Adults can satisfy themselves for around $4, children usually half-price. For a list of these breakfasts, available Apr. 1 each year, write to May Breakfasts, Department of Economic Development, 7 Jackson Walkway, Providence RI 02903.

Price ranges for the restaurants listed below are as follows: *Expensive,* $18 and up; *Moderate,* $10–$18; *Inexpensive,* $10 or under. These prices are *per person without* tips and taxes, and do *not* include wine or drinks. Of course, many restaurants have à la carte dishes, which will increase your check.

BLOCK ISLAND. Ballard's Inn. *Moderate.* Old Harbor (466–2231). Large dining hall and outdoor terrace overlooking beach and ocean. A fun place with nightly entertainment. May to Oct., while you enjoy Block Island swordfish, lobster, shellfish, or good roasts of beef.

Narragansett Inn, Ocean Rd. (466–2626); **Spring House,** Spring St. (466–2623); **Dead Eye Dick's,** Ocean Rd. (466–2654); **Barone's,** Water St. (466–2605); **Harborside Inn,** Water St. (466–5504); are noted for Block Island swordfish, full course meals and water views. All are *moderate.*

Manisees Hotel. *Moderate.* Spring St. (466–2836). Built in 1876, restored in 1981 to its Victorian splendor. Many vegetables served are grown in own garden. Good selection of wines.

Smuggler's Cove, Finn's, 1661 Sandwich Shop, and **Champlin's Pier** for snacks. *All moderate.*

High View Hotel. *Moderate.* Connecticut Ave. (466–5912). Good food in a cheery, bright dining room. Lounge/bar with entertainment. May–Sept.

The Cat and the Fiddle. *Inexpensive.* Corn Neck Rd. Open daily year round.

PROVIDENCE AREA

BRISTOL. The Lobster Pot. *Moderate.* 119 Hope St. (253–9100). Lots of lobsters are boiled in the pot here. Try their chowder. Bar. Children's portions. Walls are adorned with transoms of yachts that defended the Americas Cup, several of which were built nearby at former Herreshoff Manufacturing Co. Open year round.

Eliza's. *Moderate.* State St. (253–2777). This waterfront view restaurant rates high for lovers of seafood (try sole Veneto) and pastries. Midweek specials are bargains. Dinner only.

S.S.Dion, *Moderate.* 520 Thames St. (253–2884). Good traditional fare. Diners view Bristol Yacht Club across harbor. Open deck in summer.

CRANSTON. Coffee's Cafe and Restaurant. *Inexpensive.* 357 Dyer Ave. (942–9751). Italian. Whether you order the white clam sauce or the red clam sauce, you'll proclaim it delicious. Big portions at budget prices. Open daily except Thanksgiving and Christmas.

EAST GREENWICH. Harbourside Lobstermania. *Expensive.* Water St. (884–6363). Outstanding seafood selection; outdoor dining porch; one of several restaurants along rejuvenated harborfront.

The Warehouse Tavern. *Inexpensive.* King St. (884–4433) and Twenty Water St. (885–3700) are among waterfront restaurants now flourishing in the Greenwich Cove area.

PROVIDENCE. L'Apogée. *Expensive.* Atop Biltmore Plaza Hotel (421–0700). Excellent cuisine, superb service. Commanding view of downtown Providence and State Capitol. Sun. brunch (à la carte) runs from pheasant pâté to hangtown fry.

Camille's Roman Garden. *Expensive.* 71 Bradford St. (751–4812). Serving excellent Italian dishes since 1914 in well appointed dining room of an old mansion. Small alcoves fringe main dining room. Outstanding selection of Italian and French wines. Open year round. Reservations requested. Closed Sun.

Capriccio. *Expensive.* 2 Pine St. (421–1320). Continental cuisine in attractive setting; comfortable bar-lounge. Open daily except Sun. and Christmas Eve and Day. Reservations suggested.

Bean Sprouts Oriental Café. *Moderate.* Davol Square (861–0097). Specializes in Oriental Sunday brunch.

The Chalet. *Moderate.* 1021 Mineral Spring Ave., North Providence (723–6084). Swiss chalet atmosphere in a restaurant that prides itself on Neapolitan style dishes. Bar is popular. Open year round except Sun.

The Forum. *Moderate.* 265 Atwells Ave. (273–5550). Another good restaurant in Providence's "Little Italy."

Hemenway's Sea Food Grill & Oyster Bar. *Moderate* One Old Stone Sq., South Main St. (351–8570). Many seafood specialties. Mahogany paneling with bright brass rails in a new building at the edge of downtown Providence.

Ming Garden. *Moderate.* 141 Westminster St. (751–1700). Cantonese food featuring savory chicken wings à la Ming Garden. Upstairs specializes in cuisine from the Szechuan/Hunan, Peking, Canton and Shanghai regions; dinner attire is required. Open daily except Thanksgiving.

Oki Japanese Steak House. *Moderate.* 1270 Mineral Spring Ave., North Providence (728–7970). In an atmosphere of Japanese decor, your chef prepares your selection tableside on his Teppanyaki table. Open daily. Closed Thanksgiving, Christmas and New Years Day.

The Rusty Scupper. *Moderate.* 530 N. Main St. (831–5120). Located in the Moshassuck Arcade, converted from a 19th-century textile mill, specializes in steak and fish. Try the kushiyaki (marinated sirloin and chicken brochette). Open year round.

Smith's Restaurant. *Moderate.* 1049 Atwell's Ave. (861–4937). Same menu for lunch and dinner. Primarily Italian cuisine (the Smith is from the blacksmith trade of the founding owner). If veal is your desire—it's served here in many ways. Open year round; closed Sun., Christmas and Thanksgiving.

Taj Mahal. *Moderate.* 230 Wickenden St. (331–2442). Rhode Island's first restaurant featuring exotic cuisine of India—spicy for the connoisseur, mild for the novice.

Winkler's Steak House. *Moderate.* 63 Washington St. (521–4626). Carrying on at its new location, this famous Rhode Island steak house serves a varied menu with a surprising accent on fish. Open daily except Sun. and holidays.

The Wokery. *Moderate.* 272 Thayer St. (331–5544). Over 75 main dishes on menu heavy with Cantonese selections. Open daily.

Blue Point Oyster Bar and Restaurant. *Moderate.* 99 North Main St. (272–6145). Raves for its oyster stew.

Abilheira's Family Restaurant. *Inexpensive.* 218 Warren Ave., East Providence (434–9674). Portuguese-style cooking. Try the pork with steamed little necks, or rabbit.

Ground Round. *Inexpensive.* 1303 N. Main St. (272–5525). A popular restaurant where steaks are cooked to order, with club steak and filet mignon topping the list. À la carte menu. Open daily.

Luke's Restaurant. *Inexpensive.* 59 Eddy St. (331–4265). Cantonese and Polynesian dishes and exotic drinks are the specialty in a relaxing island atmosphere.

Providence, where nation's dining wagons originated in the 1870's, has one that rolls up to the City Hall sidewalk each evening at six.

WARREN. Fore'n Aft. *Expensive.* 1070 Main St. (245–1900). This is an attractive restaurant with nautical decor and museum-type marine lithographs. New England style cooking, specializing in seafood, and good wine selection. Bar. Open daily for lunch and dinner.

Wharf Tavern. *Expensive.* Water St. (245–5043). In this Colonial rustic setting overlooking Warren harbor the emphasis in on lobster and fish. Bar. Open daily.

WARWICK. Plantations Room. *Moderate.* 2081 Post Rd. (738–0023). Operated by the Culinary Arts Institute of Johnson & Wales College, it prides itself on prime ribs and veal prepared in lemon butter.

Great House. *Moderate.* 2245 Post Rd. (U.S. 1) (739–8600). Near the state airport, this long-established restaurant is open daily. Noted for its Chinese-American specialties and New England-style dishes. Chinese/American decor. Cocktail lounge is in converted rail freight car. Dancing.

Rocky Point Park. *Inexpensive-Moderate.* Rocky Point (737–8000). Famous Rhode Island Shore Dinners in world's largest shore-dinner dining hall.

NEWPORT AREA

LITTLE COMPTON. Abraham Manchester Restaurant & Tavern. *Moderate.* Main Rd. at Junction Rts. 179 and 81 (635–2700). Nightly steak or rib menu includes all the beer you wish and same for home-baked Anadama bread. Entertainment weekends.

MIDDLETOWN. The Greenhouse Restaurant, 30 Wave Ave. (846–0911). Overlooks Newport Beach. Also **Aquidneck Pizza Restaurant,** 27 Aquidneck Ave. (849–3356) for family Greek and Italian dining.

NEWPORT. Christie's. *Expensive.* Christie's Landing (847–5400). A full course dinner or a refreshing lunch overlooking the restaurant's marina. Very popular with the yachting fraternity. A good bar with pictures of yachts that have defended or challenged for the America's Cup.

Frick's. *Expensive.* 673 Thames St. (846–5830). The Swiss-born chef does magic with fish, chicken, veal, and lamb. Very good soups.

La Petite Auberge. *Expensive.* 19 Charles St. (849–6669). Located in the ancestral home of Commodore Stephen Decatur, this lives up to its billing of superb French dining. Reservations a must.

Le Bistro. *Expensive.* Bowen's Wharf (849–7778). Provincial French cuisine.

The Pier. *Expensive.* West Howard St. at Williams & Manchester Shipyard (847–3645). Whether you order a seafood specialty, such as the clambake, or steak, you will be pleased. Both restaurant and bar are very popular and dinner reservations are necessary. Open for lunch and dinner daily; Sun. dinner from noon. You can dock your boat at its pier, or park near sleek yachts.

White Horse Tavern. *Expensive.* Corner of Marlborough and Farewell Sts. (849–3600). Continental cuisine served in Americas oldest original tavern, first licensed in 1680's, and used by colonial legislators. Open daily.

The Chart House Restaurant. *Moderate.* 22 Bowen's Wharf. (849–7555). Good seafood and beef dishes. Contemporary building whose walls have countless marine pictures, half models and full-rigged ship models. Open daily, dinners only. Sun. noon opening during summer.

The Mooring. *Moderate.* Sayer's Wharf (846–2260). Former New York Yacht Club Station No. 6. Steak, seafood, sandwiches, salads. Patio and deck with best view of harbor and luxury yachts. Newport waterfront heritage in pictures and prints. Open daily, lunch and dinner, year round.

SS Newport. *Moderate.* Waite's Wharf (846–1200). Floating restaurant, a former fishing trawler. Seafood, steaks, Italian dishes.

Mack's. *Inexpensive.* 117 Long Wharf. Good seafood and general fare at family prices.

Newport has many outstanding restaurants; a few that might be mentioned are **The Black Pearl,** Bannister's Wharf; **Clarke Cooke House,** Bannister's Wharf; **LaForge Casino,** 186 Bellevue Ave.; **Salas' Dining Room,** 343 Thames St., popular with the young; **La Gourmandise,** 136 Thames St., operated in the style of a European tea shop; **The Ark,** 348 Thames St., serves English dishes; and **Southern Cross,** 509 Thames St., features Australian cuisine. **Cappuccino's,** 92 William St. and nearby **Puerini's,** 24 Memorial Blvd. W., feature sandwiches and desserts, and Italian dishes, respectively.

NORTH KINGSTOWN. Red Rooster Tavern. *Moderate.* 7385 Post Road (295–8804). Combines continental and Yankee cuisine; good wine selection.

PORTSMOUTH. Pocasset Country Club. *Moderate.* Bristol Ferry Rd. (683–2266). American–style kitchen specializing in steak and fish.

The Seafare Inn. *Moderate.* 3352 E. Main Rd. (683–0577). A Victorian mansion featuring continental cuisine and seafood.

TIVERTON. The Coachmen. *Moderate.* Main Rd. at junctions of Rtes. 24 and 138 (624–8423). Dinners are served in attractive large dining room with view of Mt. Hope Bay. Try their Coquilles St. Jacques. Open daily year round.

Sunderland's. *Moderate.* 2753 Main Rd. (624–3991). This rambling farmhouse features country-style dining. Home cooking and baking. Bar-lounge. Open daily. Closed Mon., Christmas, and Jan. to Feb.

Evelyn's Nanaquaket Drive-in. *Inexpensive.* 2335 Main Road (624–3100). A "must" for lobster roll enthusiasts. Every one made to order. As Evelyn says: "If you're in a hurry, you're in the wrong place."

SOUTH COUNTY AREA

CHARLESTOWN. Nordic Lodge. *Expensive.* Off Route 2, Kenyon (783–4515). Follow signs through countryside. Outstanding Scandinavian cooking.

All the lobster you can eat buffet, under $25. Memorial Day through Labor Day: Tues-Fri., 5-10; Sat., 1-10; Sun., 1-5. Other times: Thurs.-Fri., 5-10; Sat., 1-10; Sun., 1-8. Closed Jan-March.

Old Wilcox Tavern. *Expensive.* U.S. 1 (322–8811). Open daily for dinners. Sun. afternoon buffet features steamship round of beef, ham and roast turkey.

Ninigret Landing Restaurant. *Moderate.* U.S. 1 (322–7686). American/Continental dishes.

Windswept Farm. *Moderate.* U.S. 1 (364–3333). Colonial cooking includes Ragout of Rabbit, Venison Pie, Mussels with sweet herbs. Closed Christmas.

NARRAGANSETT. Sweet Meadows Inn. *Moderate.* 20 Point Judith Road (783–7336). An old favorite, just reopened.

RICHMOND. Wood River Inn. *Moderate.* Junction of Rtes. 3 and 138, ½ mile west of I–95 (539–2862). The atmosphere of countryside Rhode Island complements its regional fare.

WESTERLY. Weekapaug Inn. *Expensive.* On the ocean a few miles southeast of Westerly (322–0301). Gourmet cuisine; no bar, but bring your own; reservations required. Open July 1 to Labor Day only.

Bogarts. *Moderate.* 55 Beach St. (596–7788). A new restaurant, tastefully decorated, with emphasis on fish; excellent wine selection.

Shelter Harbor Inn. *Moderate.* Post Road (U.S. 1). (322–8883). A few miles east of Westerly. New England fare; famous Rhode Island jonnycakes are featured. Open year round.

Swiss Chalet Restaurant. *Moderate.* Post Rd. (322–0314). Fresh seafood, Continental cuisine. Daily year round, lunch and dinner.

BLACKSTONE VALLEY AREA

WOONSOCKET. Ciro's. *Moderate.* 42 Cherry St. (762–9567). In a Tudor setting, enjoy a menu ranging from clams casino to frog legs. Good wine cellar. Entertainment Fri. and Sat.

El Dorado. *Moderate.* 401 Clinton St. (767–1961). Steak and fish specialties. Dinner only, closed Mon.

NIGHTLIFE AND BARS. Nightclubs. *Lupo's Heartbreak Hotel,* 377 Westminster St., Providence, features headline entertainers. *Cahoots* is a popular bar/lounge in the Providence Marriott; *Chasers* in the Providence Holiday Inn and *Goddard's* in the Biltmore Plaza are popular with all ages. For a night out on the town in Newport, stop in any of these: *The Tavern,* 3 Memorial Blvd.; *Rodger's Roost,* in The Sheraton-Islander; *The Candy Store* in the Clarke-Cooke House; *One Pelham East,* Thames St. and *Yesterday's* 28 Washington Square, both cater to a younger crowd. *The New Wreck II,* Atlantic Ave., Misquamicut, has good contemporary artists on weekends.

Bars. *Player's Corner Pub,* 194 Washington St.; *Capriccio,* 2 Pine St.; are popular Providence bars. *One Pelham East,* Thames St., Newport, is popular with young people.

DRINKING LAWS. You have to be 21 to order a drink or buy packaged liquor in local liquor stores. Legal hours, 6 A.M. to 1 A.M. Sun. from noon. No sales Christmas Day. Package stores are closed Sun. and certain holidays. In some areas drinking is permitted until 2 A.M. during season (June to September) and weekends Oct. to May.

VERMONT

The Green Mountain State

by
PAUL ROBBINS

Life winds down here; the pace is natural, unhurried. Vermont is a land apart from most areas of our country. Tourists come to Vermont for what they cannot find in places where natural beauty has been destroyed in the rush toward "progress." A floating bridge, dirt roads, forests, gentle mountains cloaked in green, rivers and streams, a cow looking up at a passing car, a fleetingly poised deer, fields of wildflowers, all this and more: the abundant richness of living naturally.

The people are special, too. The Vermont Yankee's zealous belief in independence has been proven over generations. Many years before the Civil War, Vermonters opposed slavery. Horace Greeley and Thaddeus Stevens were the state's most famous abolitionists. Today, when registering to vote, Vermonters recite the Freeman's Oath.

Vermonters live by the pulse of the earth. Winter purifies the land; even regions which have endured long periods of neglect are transformed by a cloak of snow.

March and April are months when outsiders are warned to stay clear of country dirt roads. Deep masses of mud clog the roads, making them virtually impassable at times.

411

This is also the time when sugaring is done and the horizon is smudged by smoke from the sugar houses. Maple syrup on griddle cakes is traditional; but it can be enjoyed other ways, including on snow with pickles! The first run tastes more delicious than any syrup ever bought. Vermont traditionally leads the U.S. in maple production.

Suddenly it is spring. The first robin appears; the first crocuses peek up from under the leftover snow. People smile greetings and talk of "laying in the garden."

Vermont lives outside in the summer. Days are rarely so hot that one need retreat to air-conditioned rooms. Crops grow. Friends meet at community barbecues, fiddling contests, horse shows. Hiking, camping, and boating are common pastimes.

County fairs, cider, and apple pies mean that autumn is here. Nature's last celebration, the turning leaves' raging color, makes an invigorating farewell to summer.

Vermont's beauty, contrasts, and variety are an invitation to travel the highways and back roads of the Green Mountain State. At the same time, a look back into the dynamic and colorful history of the region will help to explain the sense of tradition and solidity you feel in this small state.

In April 1973, the remains of a 3,000-year-old Indian culture were unearthed in Swanton, Vermont, during a building excavation. Swanton is located in the northwestern corner of the state, not far from the Canadian border—an area inhabited by Indian tribes from ancient to modern times.

In fact, digs along the shores of Lake Champlain and Otter Creek have turned up Indian fishing and hunting implements, artifacts, tools and pottery, dating in some cases as far back as 2000 B.C. Scholars have connected these object with the Old Algonkians (2000 B.C. to A.D. 1300). The Swanton findings have turned up evidence of a pre-woodland people called the Adenas, and there are those who assert that Paleo-Indian hunters roamed the forests of the Champlain Valley some 4,000 years ago.

Indian Trails

In more recent history, Vermont was the temporary home and hunting ground for the Iroquois, Algonkians, Mohicans, and Abnakis. It appears that Vermont was used primarily as a trail to cross from Massachusetts to New York. Some students of Indian history have suggested that Vermont was considered sacred land by Indians, which may explain the presence of ancient Indian burial grounds.

When Samuel de Champlain first laid eyes on the magnificent lake which would bear his name he was accompanied by Algonkians, who had promised to show him the great lake of the Iroquois. The Algonkian and Iroquois had been feuding nations for some years before Champlain's voyage down the lake in 1609.

When the Champlain party sighted Iroquois on the shore, a battle ensued, with the reluctant aid of Champlain's armed party. The Iroquois were angered by the Algonkian betrayal and by the French muskets that overpowered them. Iroquois hatred for the French began with that battle, and they pursued their enemy relentlessly for years along the Hudson and the St. Lawrence. The first white settlement in what is now Vermont was a French military outpost, Fort St. Anne, built in 1666 on the Isle La Motte, from which raids against the Iroquois were launched.

The Indian-French enmity lasted long enough for the British to make use of it in securing their ultimate victory against the French in 1759 on the Plains of Abraham in Quebec City.

To protect its settlements in northwestern Massachusetts, the English built Fort Dummer in 1724. The fort was built on land which had been bought in an auction by Sir William Dummer and Colonel William Brattle (the towns of Dummerston and Brattleboro bear their names).

Fort Dummer, Vermont's earliest English settlement, was probably the most easily established territory in Vermont. For the most part, the land which is now the Green Mountain State has a tug-of-war history. Tracts of land were granted in moments of caprice by kings, governors, and land speculators who did not even know the territory with which they were playing games of profit.

Naturally enough, land bestowed at a distance became the subject of fierce controversy on the spot. All of the area now known as Vermont was once part of the British province of New York, with the Connecticut River serving as the boundary with New Hampshire. New Hampshire's governor, however, began taking land as far west as Bennington. By 1764, these New Hampshire Grants comprised 131 townships.

In the same year, George III ruled the disputed territory to be New York's. With their lands under threat, the settlers under the New Hampshire Grants rallied in a loose-knit military group called the Green Mountain Boys. During 1770–1771, the band began acting to drive the Yorkers off the disputed lands.

A reward was posted for the militants' capture. Ethan Allen responded in kind by printing and circulating a poster calling for the capture and delivery of two Yorkers to the Catamount Tavern (a monument in Old Bennington now marks this site).

At length the territorial rivalry was eclipsed by the outbreak of the colonies' struggle for independence from the British. The Green Mountain Boys now played a vital role in the Revolution, capturing Ticonderoga and Crown Point and supplying Washington with a hundred British cannons.

Independent Vermont

After the signing of the Declaration, a convention in Windsor in 1777 declared Vermont an independent republic. The constitution adopted at Windsor was a historic achievement: it was the first in the nation to outlaw slavery and to establish universal manhood suffrage without property qualifications.

The Windsor convention almost broke up in disorder. The men of the new republic wanted to hasten to their families and homes lying in the path of "Gentleman Johnny." General John Burgoyne was rapidly approaching down Lake Champlain in a campaign to sever the Colonies. He took Ticonderoga and some of his troops fought with Seth Warner's Green Mountain Boys at Hubbardton; Burgoyne, heading for a thrust toward the Hudson, needed supplies badly. He heard that he could get them at Bennington, where there was only a small militia standing guard over the munitions.

Vermonters knew what the British General and troops had in mind, so they sent out an appeal for help to Massachusetts, Connecticut, and

New Hampshire. New Hampshire, particularly, responded most generously in ordering General John Stark out of retirement. He led a force of 1,000 men across the Molly Stark Trail (Vermont Route 9) to Bennington. Entering battle, Stark said, "There stand the redcoats. Today they are ours, or Molly Stark sleeps this night a widow." Led by Stark and Warner, the "people's militia" waged a remarkable defense against the skilled British and mercenaries. Finally defeated and deprived of his badly needed supplies, Burgoyne lost the subsequent Battle of Saratoga.

The Battle of Bennington (which actually was fought in Hoosick Falls, N.Y.) is a rare historic example of an improvised army defeating regular troops. Burgoyne, in a letter to England after the battle, wrote, "The Hampshire Grants in particular—a country unpeopled and almost unknown in the last war—now abounds with the most active and rebellious race on the continent, and hangs, like a gathering storm, on my left."

In 1791, fourteen years after expressing its wish for statehood, Vermont joined the Union. The original thirteen colonies delayed its admission, partly out of antagonism over Vermont's revolt from New York's authority. Some states felt that Vermont had not contributed enough during the Revolution.

George Washington believed Vermont might have to be subdued by arms. As late as 1782, Vermonters arrested and ejected a New York sheriff's posse for violating the Vermont border. Congress, urged on by influential New Yorkers, protested Vermont's action. Vermont refused to back down. Each disappointment only strengthened Vermont's growing independence and tenacity. Congress finally ceased to question Vermont's state sovereignty and approved statehood.

Vermont's development began even before statehood. A bridge was built at Bellows Falls, the first of any type (it is said) to be built across the Connecticut River, and the nation's first canal was started there in 1802. In 1785, the first marble quarry was opened in Dorset.

In 1805, Montpelier was established as the State Capital; by 1808, the *Vermont,* the world's second regularly operated commercial steamship, was proudly traversing Lake Champlain. By the time it entered the Union, Vermont's population had grown from 300 to 85,425 and by 1980, it finally had crept over a half-million.

Local Politics

A fierce independence still marks political activities. Vermonters have a history of resistance to any federally backed project they feel may bring increased federal control over state land. Citizens attend town meetings, and play an unusually direct part in the governing of their communities.

Responding to the voracious appetite of developers and land speculators, Vermont passed Act 250, a set of strict land use laws in 1970, leading the way for the rest of the nation, rather than waiting for dilatory federal action in the areas of environment and development.

The controversial Land Capability and Development Act (Act 250) grew out of the desire to protect Vermont's natural beauty. When he was inaugurated in 1973, Democratic Governor Thomas P. Salmon said, "Vermont is NOT for sale." Vermonters had been wanting to hear this for a long time.

Preserving the land and reviving old crafts are becoming increasingly popular in Vermont. Large groups of people looking for an alternative to the acquisitive, mass-produced way of life have come to Vermont, knowing that here is where they will have the chance to live as they desire—peacefully. Vermonters do not interfere with independent life-styles.

Some people believe Vermonters to be unfriendly, uninterested, and annoyingly taciturn. This isn't so. A Vermonter gives help and advice willingly *when asked;* otherwise; he assumes you can get along just fine. It has truly been said, "Vermonters will do nothing that you tell them to; most anything that you ask them to."

EXPLORING VERMONT

The Pownal Valley and Bennington

Located at the junction of U.S. 7 and Route 9, Bennington is the southwestern gateway to Vermont. If you approach Bennington from U.S. 7, you will first drive through the southernmost town in this part of the state, Pownal. The Pownal Valley is considered one of the most picturesque in the state. Vermont's only pari-mutuel race track, Green Mountain Race Track, where greyhounds race between March and November, is in Pownal.

In the apple orchards scattered over the Pownal-Bennington area, lovely scenic rides are offered in the fall as well as in spring when the trees are in blossom. There are times during the harvest when the orchards are opened to tourists and residents to pick their own apples.

North of the junction of Route 346 (which heads to New York) and U.S. 7 is Barber Pond Road, east of U.S. 7. Barber Pond Road is a typical Vermont dirt road which takes you up into the hills, past farms, fields, and streams. The road will eventually lead to Route 9, just east of the center of Bennington. Turn left on Route 9 (Main Street) and continue west approximately five miles to the Bennington Museum, located in Old Bennington.

This museum is one of the country's finest regional museums. It has a large collection of Old Bennington pottery, a very rare collection of American blown and pressed glass, the oldest Stars and Stripes in existence, rare documents, costumes, uniforms, and furnishings. On its property is the Grandma Moses Schoolhouse, moved here from Eagle Bridge, N.Y. Her furniture, paintings, and memorabilia complete the display.

Just up the hill and to your right, in beautiful, historic Old Bennington, is a 306-foot obelisk, the Bennington Battle Monument, commemorating the victory of the American forces. Visitors can take an elevator to the top of the monument.

South from the green where the monument stands is the lovely Old First Church, built in 1805 and designed by Lavius Fillmore, who was also the architect of the Middlebury Congregational Church. The churchyard has a number of interesting monuments, not the least of which is Robert Frost's gravesite with his famous inscription, "I had a lover's quarrel with life."

Bennington College is located here. It is a small, coeducational college which pioneered many progressive teaching methods now used by

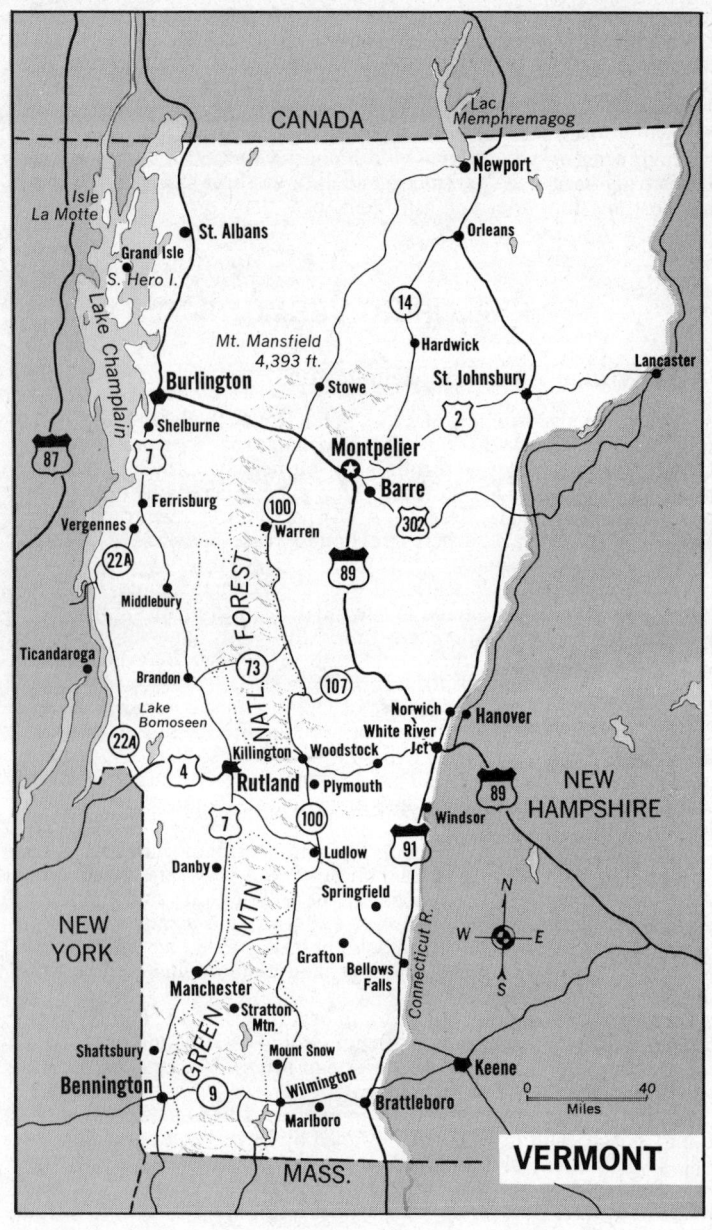

VERMONT

liberal universities. The college is a year-round center for music, art, dance, lectures, and movies—most of which are open to the public. Several famous sculptors, painters, and writers are in residence.

There are three covered bridges in the college area.

Nearby, Route 67A will take you into North Bennington, once called Sage City. Here is the Park-McCullough Mansion, a national historic site and now also a center of cultural and community events. In the summer there are craft demonstration weekends, barbecues, art exhibits, square dancing, and tours through the big house, once the home of Vermont's Governor John McCullough. In fall, winter and spring, visitors can see plays, movies, lectures, courses, a costume ball and many other events.

North Bennington is the home of the Sage City Symphony, organized in 1973 under the direction of composer-musician Louis Calabro. The symphony performs regularly.

The Annual Antiques and Classic Car Show is held in Bennington on the second weekend in September.

North on U.S. 7, you'll pass Harwood Hill Orchards as you drive into Shaftsbury. Vermont's first Baptist Church was built here in 1768; it is now the Shaftsbury Historical Society. Like the Old First Church, it is adjoined by an historic graveyard. Shaftsbury has been the home of many well-known artists and craftspeople. The Gerhard Gerlachs, noted bookbinders, reside here. The beautiful home of nine-term governor James Galusha was designed by Lavius Fillmore and architects consider its Palladian window to be the most beautiful in a private home. Shaftsbury still has quite a bit of open farmland, and on one of its many back roads, East Road, is the Peter Matteson Tavern Museum, an authentic 18th-century tavern with outbuildings containing a blacksmith area, basketmaking room, produce storage bins, etc. There is a considerable collection of 18th- and 19th-century tools and utensils. The tavern has a keeping room, taproom, living room, ballroom and two 18th-century bedrooms. It was at one time the summer residence of the earl and countess of Gosford.

Southern Vermont: Manchester, Mountains, Ski Country

On to Arlington, via Routes 7 and 313. The late Dorothy Canfield Fisher lived here; she is known for many novels and histories, some of them about Vermont. Norman Rockwell was another resident of Arlington; consequently, the town was used many times for covers of *The Saturday Evening Post*.

Continue north on U.S. 7 to Sunderland, where one of the Basketville stores is located (the other is across the state in Putney); both are well-known for their wicker, woodenware and gifts. Across the road is the entrance to the Skyline Drive, a steep, narrow toll road (closed in winter) which winds its way to the summit of Mount Equinox. You can see the Carthusian Monastery, built of Vermont granite and closed to the public. The views from this height are magnificent; for a closer look at the wildlife, follow one of the hiking trails that wind from the summit.

After your journey up the 3,816-foot mountain, continue north to Manchester, a famous southern Vermont town. U.S. 7 is lined with stately old trees and homes set back from the road, all neatly trimmed and most of them painted white. They are in sharp contrast to the once elegant and newly reopened Equinox hotel just up the street. Abe

Lincoln reportedly had reservations to stay there when he was assassinated; his son, Robert, once owned an estate, Hildene, at the other end of the street, and it is open from mid-May through late October.

One notable place to visit is the Orvis Company, one of America's largest producers of fishing equipment. The attractive Jelly Mill is nearby, featuring boutique items of all sorts, a gourmet section, and a coffee shop serving homemade foods.

Just north of the Equinox, West Road branches off and parallels U.S. 7. From West Road, you can reach the beautiful Southern Vermont Art Center; formerly an estate, the Art Center has fine views and a magnificent sculpture garden. Inside, paintings, woodcuts, and sculptures are exhibited. The center also has concerts and films, plus a summer school of art, dance, and drama.

Back on U.S. 7, you will come to a shopping area called Factory Point Square. Manchester bustles with commerce and there is a shop or gallery to suit every taste.

In Manchester U.S. 7 meets Route 30, which goes northwest-southeast. Going west eventually would lead you north to Rutland. But for now we will stay within the two southern counties.

If you bear left onto Route 30 you will head toward Dorset, where Vermont marble was first quarried.

Dorset's elegance is simpler and more quiet than Manchester's. The Dorset Inn is the town's center, on a handsome village green. The famous Dorset Playhouse, one of the oldest summer theaters in New England, is quartered here. Further on, on Route 30, is the J.K. Adams Company, which manufactures wooden items. The factory shop is open for retail sales.

Northwest of here on Route 315, is Rupert, whose few residents own large tracts of land. Here is the Merck Forest Foundation, a private preserve for environmental study. The Merck Forest is open most of the year for hiking, cross-country skiing or simply enjoying nature. Call 394–7836 for information.

Turning back to Manchester on Route 30, head north on U.S. 7. Within the limits of the shire is a group of unusual stores.

Farther north, you'll find the beautiful, peaceful Emerald Lake State Park, surrounded by 3,000-foot mountains and marble quarries, where camping, picnicking, boating, swimming, and fishing may be enjoyed. The lake has a strikingly vivid green hue.

Backtracking to the south, through Manchester and at the junction of U.S. 7 with Routes 11 and 30, go east on 11–30 to Bromley Ski Area, a fine family ski area in winter and home of the world's longest Alpine Slide in summer (Memorial Day through late October). Since Bromley faces south, it catches the warm sun for skiers; snowmaking protects 83 percent of the trails.

Proceeding east on 11, you will arrive in Peru, a lovely mountaintop village best known as the home of Bromley Ski Area and the first Alpine Slide in North America. North of Peru, on a partially paved road, is North Landgrove, another small community. Samuel Ogden, its most famous resident, bought a number of abandoned houses here, restored them, and created a community of friends. Ogden is well known among organic gardeners.

Circle Landgrove and head south to Route 100, toward Londonderry, which is on Route 11, and South Londonderry, on 100. Magic Mountain Ski area is in Londonderry as well as scenic Lowell Lakes, and mountains where several inns are located.

Route 100 runs into Route 30; go west just over two miles to the entry to Stratton Mountain, one of the first four-season resorts in the East. In winter, its trails have hosted World Cup and pro races; by summer, the activities continue with a golf academy, tennis school and the Volvo International Tennis Tournament in early August. Summer winds down with the annual month-long Stratton Arts Festival from mid-September to mid-October. The festival includes craft demonstrations, sculptures and photography exhibits, dance and music concerts. The base lodge is turned into a gallery, while the mountain makes an imposing backdrop for outside events.

From Stratton, wind northeast on a partially paved road, or go back to Route 30 and head east, until you come to Jamaica. White water slaloms are held in May.

South, on Route 100 (Vermont's famed "Skiers' Highway") lies West Dover, home of Mount Snow, the hulking four-season resort which has rebounded from bankruptcy in recent years under the guidance of the company which also owns Killington. In winter, Mount Snow guests can ski, ice skate, snowmobile, sleighride, and you-name-it. In the warm weather, there is the Mount Snow School of Golf plus indoor or outdoor tennis, horseback riding, hiking, biking, boating, fishing, learning to pilot a plane or, among other things, enjoying summer theater. Two smaller but still bustling ski areas nearby are Carinthia, which abuts Mount Snow, and Haystack, taken out of bankruptcy by new owners.

All along this stretch of Routes 100 and 30, food and lodging as well as nightclubs are plentiful.

Coming down to earth about 1,000 feet in elevation, you reach Wilmington. Once quiet, it has become a center for tourists and skiers in southern Vermont. Stores abound and anyone who desires to gaze through shops and buy useful or decorative items can spend hours here. Merchandise ranges from plants to health foods to Scottish woolens. The Quaigh Design Centre is one of the nicest in Wilmington. It has an array of Vermont-made crafts as well as imports. A loom, situated in one corner, is in constant use; you can watch new designs taking shape on its frame.

Turning west on Route 9 (which meets 100 in Wilmington), you will head toward the mountain town of Searsburg. When you reach Searsburg and the junction of Routes 8 and 9, turn south on Route 8 and travel this road until Routes 8 and 100 meet, taking 100 to Readsboro, Whitingham and Jacksonville, back north to Route 9. This is truly one of the most scenic Vermont rides. Here, in the southern section of the state, the mountain roads seem to carry you to the top of the world.

A monument commemorating Brigham Young stands in Whitingham, his birthplace. Head east to Jacksonville and the famous Stone Soldier Pottery. Pottery here is designed and hand thrown by the owner, Robert Burnell. Firsts and seconds of Stone Soldier Pottery, and the crafts of other area artists, are displayed for sale. Stone Soldier Pottery has a devoted following of collectors who consider it among the finest pottery being made. One of the more unusual sights—and sites—in Vermont is back up the road a piece: an 11-hole golf course in Stamford.

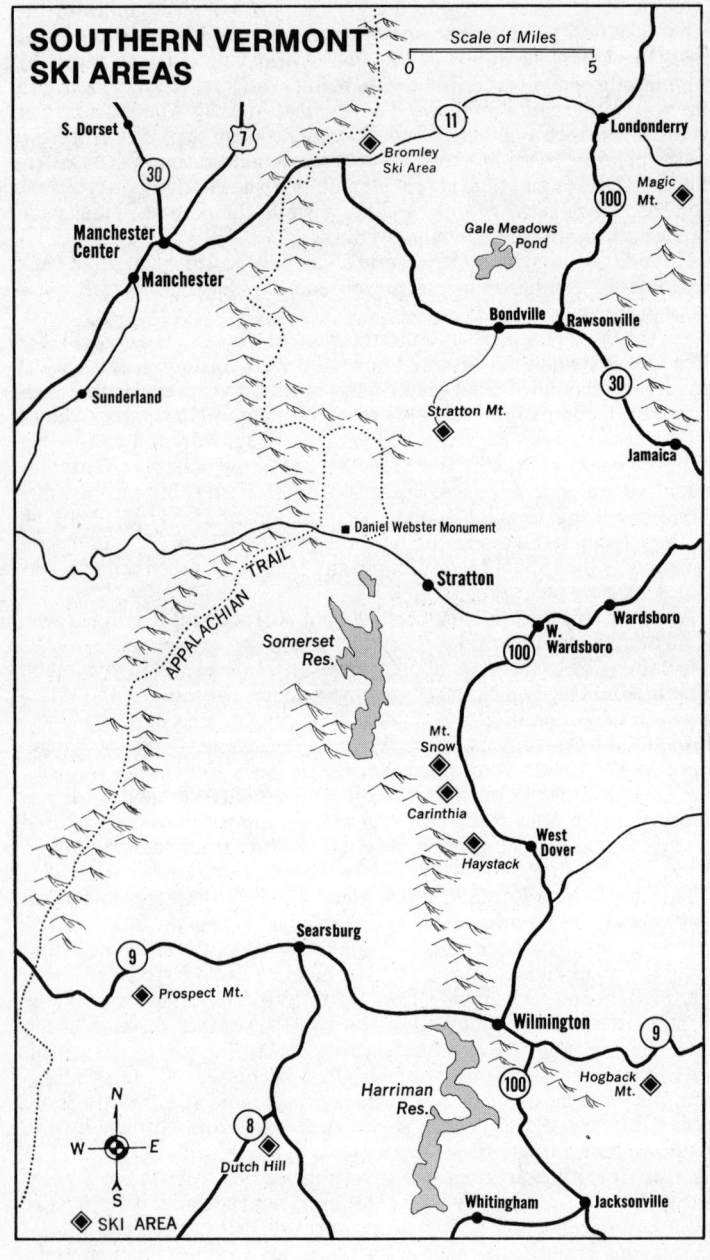

SOUTHERN VERMONT SKI AREAS

Scale of Miles
0   5

S. Dorset

30

7

Bromley Ski Area

11

Londonderry

100

Magic Mt.

Manchester Center

Manchester

Gale Meadows Pond

Bondville

Rawsonville

30

Sunderland

Stratton Mt.

Jamaica

Daniel Webster Monument

APPALACHIAN TRAIL

Stratton

W. Wardsboro

Wardsboro

100

Somerset Res.

Mt. Snow

Carinthia

West Dover

Haystack

Searsburg

9

Prospect Mt.

Wilmington

9

100

Hogback Mt.

Harriman Res.

N
W — E
S

8

Dutch Hill

Whitingham

Jacksonville

◆ SKI AREA

Southern Vermont: On to Brattleboro

When you come back to Route 9, you may head either east or west. West will bring you back to Bennington; along the way is Woodford State Park, where camping, boating, and fishing are enjoyed in a cozy atmosphere. On the northern side of Route 9, not far from Woodford State Park, is the Red Mill Brook Recreation Area. Tent and trailer sites are available here, and Red Mill Pond has fishing.

Further east on Route 9, at the junction of Routes 9 and 100, is the Coombs Beaver Brook Sugar House, where you can watch maple syrup being made. Adjacent to Coombs is a Vermont Information Center. Farther on is Hogback Mountain with its renowned 100-mile view of mountain ranges in New Hampshire and Massachusetts as well as the Green Mountains. Perched atop a ridge is a restaurant; you can enjoy the panorama while dining. The Luman Nelson Museum of New England Wildlife, located at Hogback, displays more than 500 specimens of regional flora and fauna.

Continue on to Marlboro, where, during July and August, the world-renowned Marlboro Music Festival presents summer weekend concerts under the directorship of Rudolf Serkin. The Brattleboro Music Center also gives concerts on the Marlboro campus.

Continuing east on 9, you'll reach Brattleboro, which is at the crossroads of routes 9, I–91, and U.S. 5. Although little farming is done in Brattleboro, the town is headquarters of the dairy farmers' Holstein-Friesian Association.

During the 19th century, Estey and Minshall organs were manufactured here. Today the town is the home of the Brattleboro Music Center, known for its excellent performances of Bach as well as contemporary music.

A collection of old Estey and Minshall organs is displayed at the Brattleboro Museum and Art Center, a recycled ex-train depot. If you are taking a train to Vermont, this town is Amtrak's first Vermont.

In Brattleboro, follow Route 30 north to Dummerston. Here, in 1892, Rudyard Kipling built "Naulahka," a home for his bride. During his stay in Dummerston, he wrote *Captains Courageous, Just So Stories* and the two *Jungle Books*. In West Dummerston you can see an unusually long, latticed, covered bridge.

Continue north on 30 to Newfane, which has two of the state's most famous restaurants, the Newfane Inn and the Four Columns Inn. A Greek revival courthouse stands at the center of the lovely village green. Around the greensward are well-restored white Vermont homes and the two impressive restaurants, one a Colonial structure, the other Victorian. Teddy Roosevelt was a visitor to this town; now it's the summer home of celebrated economist John Kenneth Galbraith; the late career diplomat Ellsworth Bunker and his wife used to live in Dummerston. You can visit the Windham County Historic Society Museum on Route 30, displaying items related to the county.

At Townshend, farther north on Route 30, you will enjoy the Townshend Dam Recreation Area. Hiking and camping are available in the Townshend State Forest. Spanning the West River here is the longest covered bridge within the state, the Scott Covered Bridge. Clarissa Nichols, an early reformer and leader in the women's movement, was born here. The town is home to the famed Townshend Furniture Company, and the excellent quality Mary Meyer stuffed toys are made and sold at reduced prices in an outlet store during summer and foliage season. (There also is a Mary Meyer outlet in the Outlet Center, Exit 1 off Route I–91 in Brattleboro.)

Take Route 35 north from Townshend to Grafton, one of Vermont's prettiest villages. Grafton has been restored to Colonial finery; one of its most impressive buildings is the Old Tavern, visited at one time or another by figures as diverse as Henry David Thoreau, Daniel Webster, Teddy Roosevelt, and Mr. and Mrs. Paul Newman (Joanne Woodward). The dining and lodgings are excellent. Covered Bridge Cheese is made here, almost around the corner from the tavern. The Grafton Historical Society displays many items of interest. West of Grafton, the area is untouched, lovely forest land.

From Grafton, follow Route 121 east to Saxton River, then head north on a paved secondary road to Rockingham. Make a short stop here to visit one of the state's oldest meetinghouses, now maintained as a museum and house of worship. The churchyard is notable for its very old gravestones.

To the River: Falls, Fish, Farms

Heading south on 103, you reach Bellows Falls which lost its sole tourist attraction in 1983 when Steamtown USA, the world's largest private collection of steam engines, rode the rails to Scranton, Pennsylvania. Officials there created a new "home" and promised heavy promotion. Work on the first canal in America began here in 1792 and work was completed by the mid 1980s on a fish ladder designed to entice the Atlantic salmon into coming back up the river to spawn farther north; the first fish returning was seen in the summer of 1985.

Continuing south on U.S. 5, you will go through Putney, where the internationally known Putney School is located. Many innovative programs are connected with this school, including the Antioch-Putney Graduate School. In February, Putney School is the starting point for the George Washington's Birthday Cross Country Ski race. Putney also was home to 1982 World Cup cross-country ski champion Bill Koch and four-time Olympian Tim Caldwell, two Putney School grads.

Putney has a fine old country store in the Vermont tradition. Also in Putney is Harlow's Sugar House, which in addition to maple products and orchards has strawberry fields, where customers pick their own berries.

To the west and north of Putney, in Brookline, is the only round schoolhouse in the country.

U.S. 5 will bring you back to Brattleboro; now you have come full circle in your tour of Vermont's two southern counties.

Route 7: Heading North to Rutland, Killington

North of Manchester on U.S. 7 and north of Pawlet on Route 30 lies Rutland County. Rutland is the state's second largest city and the area is famous for its marble. Such landmarks as the John F. Kennedy Memorial in Washington, D.C., the U.S. Supreme Court Building, and the New York Public Library are constructed of marble quarried in this section of Vermont.

A scenic entry to Rutland County is from Route 30. North of Pawlet is Poultney, where the lovely campus of Green Mountain College, a two-year women's college, is located. It was in East Poultney that Horace Greeley started his publishing career as a printer's devil. While here, visit the East Poultney Historical Society Museum, built in the 18th century. It was once a blacksmith shop and later a melodeon factory.

Danby illustrates Vermont's talent for the quietly unexpected. Pleasantly scenic, the area is covered with ferns that are grown for shipment to florists all over the country. For many years it was the home of Pearl S. Buck (1892–1973), author of *The Good Earth* (1931) and third American to win the Nobel Prize in Literature (1938). It was here that from 1932 to 1951 Helen and Scott Nearing conducted the experiment in independent subsistence farming that has made their book *Living the Good Life* one of the bibles of the counter-culture and of today's intermediate technology movement. (Disgusted by the effects upon the valley of large-scale ski-resort development, the Nearings moved to Maine in 1953.) And finally, Danby once had the state's only producer of alcoholic beverages, Vermont Wineries, Inc., founded in 1971. The winery burned down in 1978.

From Poultney take Route 140 east to Middletown Springs. This is a quiet valley town which has enjoyed periodic prosperity. A century ago elegant people came here to take the "healing waters." The mineral springs have once again been uncovered and a replica of a Victorian springhouse sits over the bubbling waters. The Community Church dates from 1796, making it one of Vermont's three oldest.

Heading north once more, you reach Lake Bomoseen, largest body of water entirely within Vermont. It has two lakefront towns, Hubbardton and Castleton. Hubbardton was the scene of the lone Revolutionary War battle fought in Vermont, a half-hour skirmish between the "rebels" and General Burgoyne. It was in Castleton that the Green Mountain Boys planned their attack on Fort Ticonderoga. Castleton is interesting for its architecture, the grand design of architect Thomas Royal Dake. Many of the structures are styled in Greek Revival. Ionic columns, Corinthian porticoes, and Palladian motifs are blended together in his frequently photographed houses, which are open to the public when Castleton celebrates Colonial Day in midsummer. Castleton is also the home of Castleton State College.

Bomoseen State Park has tent and trailer sites, picnic tables, boat rentals, fishing, and swimming. Four other, smaller, lakes nearby also have recreational facilities.

Farther north on Route 30 is Hubbardton, the site of the only Revolutionary battle fought on Vermont soil, July 7, 1777. There is disagreement as to whether the American side got a defeat, a standstill, or a moral victory, but General Burgoyne's forces turned back to Fort Ticonderoga before they headed southward to the battles of Bennington and Saratoga. The Hubbardton Battlefield Museum has an audiovisual display reenacting the battle. There is also a visitor's reception center.

From the Battle Monument, head east to U.S. 4, toward Rutland. On the way, turn north on Route 3 to Proctor, a town based on the marble industry. Even the bridge spanning Otter Creek is built of marble. The Vermont Marble Company has an exhibit hall with elaborate displays of marble and marble sculptures.

In Proctor Village watch for West Proctor Road and signs for Wilson Castle. Once the private residence of the late Colonel Herbert Wilson, this 115-acre estate has 16 buildings, including the 32-room, century-old, red brick castle. The castle and outbuildings are well worth visiting for their intriguing furnishings, 84 stained glass windows, 13 fireplaces (you can't see all the windows or fireplaces), antique armor and weapons. Open mid-May to late October.

Now enter Rutland, an industrial city and Vermont's second largest, lined with trees and curtained by the Taconic Mountain Range to the west and the Green Mountains to the east. In September, the annual week-long State Fair draws large numbers of visitors and exhibitors; and during the summer there are open-air band concerts on Sunday evenings. While here, visit the Chaffee Art Center in one of Rutland's many old mansions, on U.S. 7. The Tuttle Publishing Company of Tokyo, Japan, and Rutland, is located here and has a splendid bookshop. The city has a number of fine old houses which may be viewed in the walking tour of the Main Street laid out by the Rutland Historical Society.

North of Rutland on U.S. 7 is Pittsford, the home of Nicholas M. Powers, Vermont's master builder of covered bridges. In Pittsford, covered-bridge enthusiasts may see four of the special spans. Zigzagging east of Pittsford, a paved secondary road will take you to Chittenden Reservoir. The reservoir is used for sailing in summer and iceboating in winter. Mountain Top Inn overlooks the reservoir, offers a superb cross-country ski system and a growing roster of warmweather activities.

Returning to U.S. 7, continue to Brandon, hometown of Stephen Douglas, who campaigned against Abe Lincoln for the presidency. His home was near Brandon Inn, a well-preserved Colonial inn with good fishing nearby.

Traveling east on Route 73 through Brandon Gap, an awesome mountain pass, you descend into Rochester, where Appaloosas are raised. Turn south on Route 100. It is through this section of 100 that the White River rushes in springtime, offering excellent whitewater races.

Following south to Sherburne Center, you arrive at the base of Killington Ski Area, a major four-season resort area. In winter, Killington provides some of the most challenging ski trails in the state and annually has the longest season (mid-October to mid-June) of any eastern ski area, thanks to more than 40 miles of snowmaking equipment (40 mi. of equipment, not snow). In summer, Killington becomes a warm-weather resort, offering a seven-mile round trip ride on the world's longest gondola ski lift. It ends at the summit of Killington Peak, 4,241 feet up! There are also: a shorter chairlift ride; mountaintop dining; a professional summer theater group, the Killington Playhouse; a school for tennis; horseback riding; boating; fishing; and hiking. In 1763, the Reverend Samuel Peters ascended Killington Peak on horseback and christened the land *Verd Mont*. Now, Long Trail and Appalachian hikers make the same ascent on foot. The Appalachian Trail turns east toward New Hampshire and the White Mountains at Sherburne Pass. Pico Ski Area is on the Western Slope of the Pass.

Woodstock, Quechee, Plymouth, Weston

Driving south on Route 100, you will pass into Windsor County. At West Bridgewater, 100 meets U.S. 4. If you take 4 east, you will reach Woodstock; 100 south will take you to Plymouth and Weston.

Graceful and beautiful Woodstock is a year-round attraction to visitors from all over the world. The town escaped the post–Civil War industrialization that marred much of the country, and its beauty has attracted a large number of wealthy people who have helped to protect it from change. Its restoration program has had impressive results. Galleries, antique shops, and boutiques occupy 18th- and 19th-century houses. Power lines are buried out of sight, courtesy of a generous grant from Laurance Rockefeller, who owns an estate in town (as well as the Woodstock Inn and Resort). The Norman Williams Public Library, built in 1885 in a Romanesque style, has one of the most impressive collections of books and newspapers, old and new, in Vermont, as well as a good collection of Japanese art. The building is constructed of various Vermont granites and marbles, and has a Gothic wooden ceiling inside. The Dana House (Woodstock Historical Society) exhibits early documents, dolls, costumes, furniture, silver, and old Woodstock photos and has a lovely landscaped garden in back. Four of Vermont's eight Paul Revere bells are housed in Woodstock's three churches and the Masonic Temple. The best way to enjoy Woodstock is a walking tour of the Church Street, Elm Street, and Green area; a map showing the town's historic houses is provided by the Chamber of Commerce.

Woodstock Resort includes the colonial-style inn on the Green, Suicide Six alpine ski area, and Woodstock Ski Touring Center. South Woodstock is where the Green Mountain Horse Association has its summer-long equestrian events. Here, too, is a lovely old tavern and inn, Kedron Valley Inn, whose guests may use the hundreds of miles of horse trails that wind through the area.

East of Woodstock is the self-styled (and misleading) "Grand Canyon of New England," Quechee Gorge, 163 feet deep. The deep cut was formed by the Ottauquechee River flowing through the gorge. The Quechee Recreation Area is nearby.

North of Quechee and Woodstock are Pomfret and Barnard. Pomfret, one of the state's most beautiful regions, has the Skyline Trail for hikers, ski tourers, and horseback riders. Near Barnard is Silver Lake State Park and the Sonnenberg Resort.

Traveling south on 100, you will come to Plymouth Union. Turn north on 100A to visit Calvin Coolidge's Homestead, Plymouth Notch, open to tourists mid-May to mid-October. In the predawn hours of August 3, 1923, he took the oath of office of President, on the death of Harding. Also on the grounds are his mother's house, the Wilder House (now a coffee shop), a cheese factory, and the Wilder Barn, which houses the Vermont Agricultural Museum.

South of Plymouth on Route 100 three public fishing areas—Echo and Amherst lakes, and Lake Rescue—lead into Ludlow. North of town, just off State 103 in Healdville, you may watch cheese being made at Crowley's, Vermont's oldest cheese factory; it's open Monday through Friday and the retail shop is open Saturdays.

Ludlow is a fairly typical old mill town which is making the change to tourism. Okemo Mountain Ski Area was started as a local ski hill but has become a growing four-season operation. Heading south out of town on Route 100, you go over "Terrible Mountain," a seven-mile humpback in the road that leads to Weston, a village founded in 1799 which retains an early Victorian charm. Here is the well known Vermont Country Store and its restaurant. The Farrar-Mansur House, on the Village Green, is a 1797 tavern which has been turned into a memorial to the town's earliest settlers. The town is filled with interesting shops of all kinds, from children's toys and clothing to the Weston Bowl Mill, first opened in the 1890s. Also on the Green, the Weston Playhouse is Vermont's oldest professional summer theater. The first weekend in October, Weston has a three-day Antiques Show and Sale. North of town (a short right at the foot of Terrible Mountain) is the beautifully situated Weston Priory, a Benedictine Abbey. Open to visitors, the Abbey sells items produced by the monks, including eggs, honey, cider, craft objects, and records of the plainchant music for which this order is famous.

From Weston, a secondary road east will take you to Andover, home of the East Hill School and Summer Camp, the Swedish Ski Club, and public riding facilities. This road meets Route 11, which leads to Chester, where American Quarterhorses are bred at Butternut Farm.

Following Route 11 east you reach Springfield, "cradle" of the machine tool industry. Continuing east on 11, you see Eureka School House, Vermont's oldest school, built in 1790. Here, too, is the Springfield Art and Historical Society, where 19th-century toys and dolls are displayed.

Just north of Springfield are Ascutney State Park and Stoughton Pond Recreation Area, with boating, canoeing, fishing, and swimming.

The Windsor Area

In Springfield, take either I–91 or U.S. 5 to Windsor. It is here that on July 8, 1777 delegates adopted the Constitution of the "free and independent State of Vermont." The republic lasted until 1791; the Old Constitution House, originally a tavern, built around 1772, is open to visitors. Every room contains historical documents and relics. Windsor has a large number of very fine old houses; most of them are privately owned, but they may be viewed from the outside on a walking tour from the Constitution House along North Main and Main past Windsor House, which contains a state crafts center, and on to the American Precision Museum, which displays inventions, hand and machine tools from the Industrial Revolution to the present. Built in 1846, it was an Armory and produced 50,000 rifles during the Civil War. It has been designated as a National Historic Site.

The Cornish–Windsor Covered Bridge across the Connecticut River to New Hampshire is the longest covered bridge in the U.S. Built in 1866, it is 460 feet long and a National Historic Landmark.

Head north to White River Junction on I–91. Here you can join I–89 and go northward to Sharon, where the Joseph Smith Memorial, museum, library, and church are located in the hills of the town. Joseph Smith was the founder of Mormonism. A secondary road, north to Strafford, leads to the birthplace of Justin Smith Morrill, longtime U.S. Senator and author of the Morrill Act establishing America's land-grant colleges and universities.

From Strafford travel to Tunbridge. In mid-September, thousands of people gather for the century-old Tunbridge World's Fair.

At Brookfield, north on Route 14, the famous Floating Bridge connects the three villages of Brookfield township. The Historical Society Museum, in the 1835 Marvin Newton House, displays furniture, clothing, tools, books, etc.

Barre, Montpelier, Stowe, and Sugarbush Valley

Farther north on 14 is granite country. At the junction of 14 and U.S. 302 is Barre, where you can visit the world's largest granite quarry, Rock of Ages. The quarries are several hundred feet deep and have been worked since the Civil War. There are free guided tours, a Tourist Center, a Craftsmen's Center and a picnic area. At Graniteville, there are guided tours and a popular quarry train ride. The Vermont Farm Show is held here in February and the two-day Heritage Festival in July.

Montpelier, with its 8,250 residents, is set in a valley of the Winooski River. It is dominated by the green hills on each side, against which the gold dome of the State House stands out in sharp and elegant relief. There is something very appropriate to Vermont in this simple structure, modeled after the Temple of Theseus; the style is conservative and understated, yet dignified and grand enough for its function, while the scale is modest and eminently human. The interior decor is a mixture of Victorian and Rococo, with a number of interesting details, such as the chandelier in the House of Representatives. The State House was built in 1859, and cost less than $160,000.

Next to it stands the Pavilion Office Building, originally built in 1876 as a hotel to accommodate the legislators. It was bought in 1965 by the state, and after a four-year battle between conservationists and demolitionists was rebuilt in its present hybrid form, the brick state office building attached to the rear of the historic-looking hotel, as the legislative and state office building. It also has the Vermont Historical Society Museum and its sizeable collection of Vermontiana.

Many of the city's fine old houses are located north of the business district along State, Elm, and Main streets, and contain state offices. Other points of interest are the Washington County Courthouse, and Athenwood, a splendid example of wooden Gothic architecture now containing an art gallery.

Montpelier is alive with activities most of the year. During the summer, there are concerts in the Pavilion; a square dance festival is held and a statewide crafts fair offers handicraft demonstrations and wares for sale. During the legislative session, January to April, both chambers are open to visitors.

From Montpelier, follow U.S. 2 east to Plainfield, where the campus of Goddard College is located; drive on to Marshfield, where several Groton State Forest campgrounds are located and full recreational facilities are available. Farther north, on a secondary road, is Cabot, where tourists can visit the Cabot Cooperative Dairy to see several types of Vermont cheese being made. In the fall, this area is one of the six towns which host the annual Northeast Kingdom Fall Foliage Festival. Tours of homes, churches, and farms can be taken during this October event.

From here take Rte. 15 north and west to Morrisville, where 15 meets 100. Heading south, you'll reach Stowe, where there are six skiing mountains, including three at Smugglers' Notch, two at Stowe and one at Bolton Valley. There are also hundreds of miles of cross country ski trails, including one which links Bolton Valley with Trapp Family Lodge at Stowe.

This is another area where enjoyment is not limited to those times of the year when the mountains are covered by snow. The Long Trail passes through here on its arduous way to Canada, and at this point hikers must challenge the state's highest peak, Mount Mansfield (4,393 feet).

Stowe bills itself as the ski capital of the East; however, it was a popular resort long before skiing took over in the 1920s. Smugglers' Notch was used as a passageway between Canada and the states, during the War of 1812, for cattle, slaves, and general contraband.

Of some 60 member lodges (members of the Stowe Area Association), most are open to guests during the summer. Tennis, swimming, golf, horseback riding, fishing, antiquing and, among others, hiking, are all things to do while staying here. Take a ride on the Alpine Slide at Spruce Peak or the Mt. Mansfield gondola lift, or enjoy a drive up the scenic toll road to the ridge for a view of the White Mountains and Lake Champlain.

Boutiques, a gallery, general store, blacksmith shop, Stowe Pottery, Stoware (wooden products), and a summer theater all operate during warm weather, in addition to the summer-long string of special events, such as a tennis tournament, fine arts series, and antique auto rally.

By going south on Route 100 to Duxbury, one can reach several hiking trails that are part of the Long Trail. This region is dominated by another of the state's tallest peaks, Camel's Hump, which has been declared a natural area landmark.

Farther south is Waitsfield, where there are weekend polo matches in the summer and fall. Here, too, is an unusual round barn and the Bundy Museum, a modern structure exhibiting contemporary art and sculpture indoors and out.

The Waitsfield-Warren-Fayston area is alternately known as either Mad River Valley (for the river) or Sugarbush Valley (because of the growing resort). Sugarbush bought Glen Ellen in 1978, renamed it Sugarbush North Ski Area, and has put in high-elevation snowmaking to provide snow cover for skiing from October to mid-May. The resort also has seen explosive mountainside condo growth. In summer, the John Gardner Tennis Camp at Sugarbush Inn and the Robert Trent Jones golf course are especially busy. There are fishing, tennis, and hiking to enjoy, and some of the hotels offer saunas.

The Sugarbush-Warren Airport is the site of glider soaring during the summer; it is closed in winter.

Way down below is Lincoln Gap, or Pass, considered by some the most scenic spot in the state. Here is the grandeur of Vermont, with dense green mountains towering to the sky.

Champlain Valley, Vermont's West Side

Following 100 south again, you enter Addison County, dominated by beautiful Middlebury College, its Summer Language Schools, and the Bread Loaf School of English at its mountain campus in Ripton.

Sites of interest in Middlebury are the college campus, the historic Middlebury Inn, the Congregational Church (built in 1806, and among the finest in the state), the timeless "look" of pintsize downtown Middlebury, Frog Hollow Crafts Center, and the Sheldon Museum. The museum is a three-story brick building which displays early American furniture, glass, china, utensils, documents, firearms, and authentically reconstructed rooms.

East of town is Ripton, poet Robert Frost's last permanent residence. His farm here has been registered a national historic landmark. In 1921, Frost started the Bread Loaf Writers Conference. The Bread Loaf School and the Conference meet at the old Bread Loaf Inn, once owned by the eccentric, dictatorial but generous Joseph Battell. Battell left thousands of acres to Middlebury College. His farm was one of the first centers for the development of the purebred Morgan horse. The Bread Loaf campus is the starting point early each February of the 60-kilometer American Ski Marathon.

Middlebury is surrounded by recreation spots, such as Lake Dunmore and Moosalamoo Recreation Area. From Middlebury, travel north to Weybridge, where the University of Vermont Morgan Horse Farm is located. This land was also bequeathed by Joseph Battell. Visitors are welcome and may see descendants of the bay stallion, Justin Morgan, the first breed of horse developed in America.

From Weybridge, travel north to Addison to visit the General John Strong Mansion, built in 1796. It is a beautiful Georgian house, interesting for both its construction and its furnishings. Nearby is the D.A.R. State Park, with swimming, boating, and picnicking. Close to the park is the Dead Creek Waterfowl Refuge.

Beyond Addison is Chimney Point, where historians say Samuel de Champlain stood in July, 1609, and named the huge lake that lay before him.

On Route 22A, north of Addison, is Vergennes, which lays claim to the dubious title of "Smallest City in the U.S.A." The Bixby Library Museum has a collection of cups, plates, stamps, covers, shells and Indian artifacts. There is also an annual art exhibit in summer.

At Vergennes, 22A meets U.S. 7. On your way north to Burlington, Vermont's largest city, don't miss the Shelburne Museum in Shelburne. The museum was established in 1947 by Electra Havemeyer Webb and J. Watson Webb, her husband. Visiting this museum is no hurry-up deal; do it right and take your time (even if it means a second day) in prowling through the 35 buildings on 45 acres of land. It is ideally located on a bluff above the magnificent Lake Champlain. Most of the authentic buildings have been transported here from other parts of the state; all evince the spare, functional quality characteristic of the pioneers' structures. There is a covered bridge at the entrance to the grounds and the buildings are filled with colorful displays of toys, tools, quilts, cigar-store Indians, figureheads, old carriages, maps, books, drawings, china, glass, pewter, and clothing. The 220-foot sidewheel steamer *Ticonderoga* and the *Old 220,* Central Vermont Railroad's last ten-wheel steam locomotive, are part of the transportation exhibit. (A special package vacation is offered by the Shelburne Inn in conjunction with the Museum.)

Not far from Shelburne is Charlotte, where a ferry may be taken across Lake Champlain to Essex, N.Y., an entire town which has been designated an historic district. Neighboring Mount Philo State Park has tent sites and fishing.

In Ferrisburg, visit Rokeby, an underground railroad link during the Civil War.

To the north is Burlington, an industrial city but lovely nonetheless. The Robert Hull Fleming Museum of the University of Vermont has a fine collection of early American primitive, ancient, Oriental, and contemporary art. From August through October, the city is home to the Champlain Shakespeare Festival. Throughout the city the visitor will notice Historic Site markers, among them the General Ethan Allen Burial Place on Colchester Avenue. Burlington raised many Green Mountain Boys back in the 1700s, and more recently it was the hometown of John Dewey, philosopher and educator.

During the year, the Ira Allen Chapel (named after a founder of the University of Vermont) has concerts and the century-old Billings Center possesses many rare manuscripts.

Along the shores of Lake Champlain are many dairy farms, some of which are open to visitors.

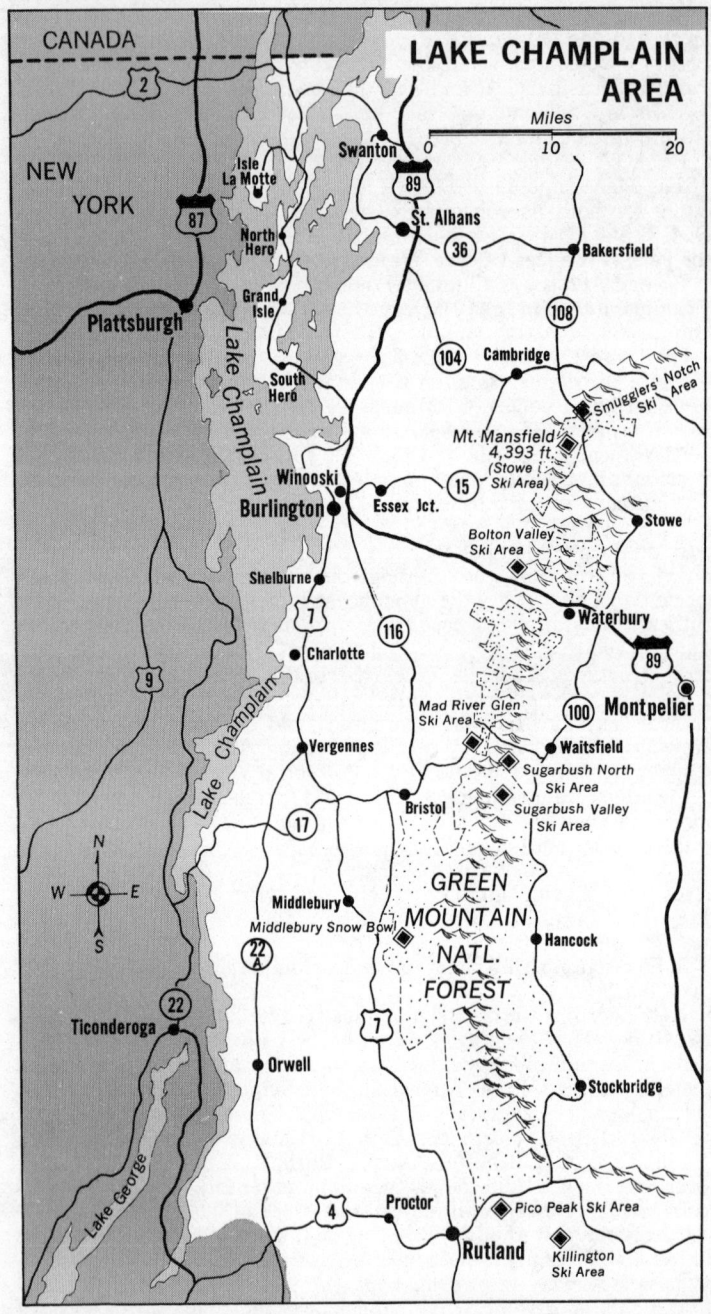

LAKE CHAMPLAIN AREA

CANADA

NEW YORK

Miles

0   10   20

Swanton

Isle La Motte

St. Albans

Bakersfield

North Hero

Grand Isle

Cambridge

Smugglers' Notch Ski Area

South Hero

Plattsburgh

Lake Champlain

Mt. Mansfield 4,393 ft. (Stowe Ski Area)

Winooski

Essex Jct.

Stowe

Burlington

Bolton Valley Ski Area

Shelburne

Waterbury

Charlotte

Montpelier

Mad River Glen Ski Area

Vergennes

Waitsfield

Sugarbush North Ski Area

Bristol

Sugarbush Valley Ski Area

GREEN MOUNTAIN NATL. FOREST

Middlebury

Middlebury Snow Bowl

Hancock

N
W   E
S

Ticonderoga

Orwell

Stockbridge

Lake George

Proctor

Pico Peak Ski Area

Rutland

Killington Ski Area

East of Burlington on U.S. 2 is Richmond, site of the Round Church Meetinghouse, a unique 16-sided structure with an octagonal belfry. The original Harrington's Smoke House is located here (others are in Manchester, Stowe, and Shelburne); you can buy meat smoked not with hickory but over corn cobs and maple wood. Guests are welcome for a view of the smoking and curing process.

Continue north on U.S. 7 from Burlington to Route 2. Here you will cross a small section of Lake Champlain to Grand Isle. North of South Hero is the Hyde Log Cabin, Americas oldest original log cabin, still in excellent condition. The cabin was built in 1783 by Jedediah Hyde, Jr., a soldier of the Revolution and a surveyor in this area.

North along U.S. 2, the Roman Catholic Shrine of St. Anne is located to the west on Isle La Motte. The shrine is on the site of Fort St. Anne, Vermont's oldest settlement (1666), where the first mass in Vermont was celebrated and from whence raids against the Iroquois were launched. Opposite the shrine is a granite statue of Samuel de Champlain.

Northward is Alburg, a promontory linking Vermont to Canada. Alburg was once a home of the Abnaki Indians. The area abounds with apple orchards, and is a good place for fishing enthusiasts.

Route 78 crosses east back to the mainland, running through the Missisquoi National Wildlife Refuge.

Approximately thirty miles east of this region is Jay Peak, Vermont's northernmost ski and four-season resort area.

Southward is St. Albans, where the Franklin County Maple Festival is held annually during the first part of April. Fiddling concerts and dancing are part of the festivities and tours are conducted to some of the county's maple farmers. From St. Albans, drive east on Route 36 to Fairfield, President Chester A. Arthur's birthplace, where a replica of the house in which he was born has been constructed and is partly furnished.

St. Johnsbury and the Northeast Kingdom

East of here are the three counties of Vermont's Northeast Kingdom: Orleans, Essex, and Caledonia.

In the county of Orleans is Jay Village, reached by Route 242, or a secondary road off 100. On the western side of the Village are the four peaks: North Jay Peak, 3,406 feet; Jay Peak, 3,861 feet; Big Jay, 3,780 feet; and Little Jay, 3,180 feet. At Jay Peak, summer and fall tourists can take Vermont's only aerial tram to the summit. Tennis and other warm-weather activities are available here. In winter, of course, there is some of the state's finest skiing.

This area yields soapstone, used for griddles and as a warming element. The Vermont Soapstone Company is located in Perkinsville, far south of here near Springfield.

Head south from Jay on Route 14 to Craftsbury and Craftsbury Common. In 1962, some musicians held a fiddling contest in Craftsbury Common. From that grew the Northeast Old Time Fiddlers Association, which holds contests around New England; however, local concern over the growing size of crowds attending Craftsbury events a couple of years ago led them to cancel future contests on the Common.

East Craftsbury's public library has a fine private collection of paintings and some Rodin sculptures.

Traveling south to Route 15 and St. Johnsbury you'll pass through Danville, site of what is called the country's biggest crossroads bank, Caledonia National Bank, open since 1825. Danville is also headquarters of the American Society of Dowsers (water searchers), which holds its annual convention in mid-September in Danville, bringing several hundred folks to town just before foliage season to discuss the various aspects of dowsing, which has expanded far beyond just searching for water. The event includes lectures, demonstrations, contests, and church suppers and is open to the public.

St. Johnsbury is located at the intersection of U.S. 2, U.S. 5, and I–91. Three rivers meet here, too: the Passumpsic, Moose, and Sleeper's. Like many river valley towns, it is terraced, and several fine Victorian houses, the Fairbanks Museum and Planetarium and the Athenaeum are located on its highest streets. The town is well known as the scale-manufacturing center of the world. Thaddeus Fairbanks, a prominent resident of St. Johnsbury, invented the platform scale in 1830.

The Fairbanks Museum and Planetarium has exhibits of birds, mammals, primitive arts, a Hall of Physical Science, as well as celestrial exhibits. It is open year round. The Athenaeum Art Gallery and Library houses over 34,000 books and exhibits paintings by European and American painters (particularly, the Hudson River School).

During the year, the Lyndon State College Chamber Music Society offers concerts in St. Johnsbury. All-season recreation is available near the city and in the surrounding mountain areas.

A major attraction in St. Johnsbury is the Maple Grove Museum and Sugar House, east of town on U.S. 2. This is the largest maple sugar plant in the United States and it operates tours all year long.

Southwest lies Peacham, which, with six other villages (including Barnet and Cabot), participates in the Northeast Kingdom Fall Foliage Festival in early October. Peacham region is one of the most photographed areas of the state. The Historical Society Museum has exhibits of local history.

Your travels will take you south on U.S. 5, past one of Vermont's most magnificent waterfalls, McIndoe Falls. U.S. 5 follows the Connecticut River; the farmland along the river unfolds pleasing pastoral scenes. Newbury, which captures the image of old New England, hosts a summer Cracker Barrel Bazaar.

Fairlee, also on U.S. 5, is the site of the Walker Museum and Lake Morey. The Museum has an Americana collection, as well as a Japanese bedroom and a model of a Persian bazaar! It also has revolving art exhibits. Lake Morey is a popular resort area, where the Vermont State Golf Championship is held each June. The lake was named for Samuel Morey, who launched the world's first steamship down the Connecticut River some fourteen years before Robert Fulton's *Clermont* embarked.

From here the Connecticut River winds down to Thetford. Just west of U.S. 5 is Thetford Hill, where celebrated pioneer woman Mrs. Richard Wallace once lived. She worked and maintained a farm alone while her husband was fighting in the Revolution. He was one of two soldiers who swam across Lake Champlain through the British fleet to deliver important dispatches.

Thetford Hill is another fine, quiet Vermont village, frequently photographed. Its Old Congregational Church, built in 1787, is the oldest church in Vermont to remain in continuous use.

This brings you to the southern limit of Orange County, and completes your tour of all of Vermont's counties. You can leave the state most directly by heading east into New Hampshire or south down I–91 to Massachusetts. Or, if you feel your trip has been all too short, you can head back on Route 9 toward Bennington, where there are a number of exit routes. This way, you can traverse once more the beauties of Vermont.

 **SIGHTSEEING CHECKLIST.** If you've only got a short time in Vermont, and you're wondering about some of the must-see or must-do things in the state, perhaps the following will serve as a starting point for your explorations.

Covered Bridges. There are more than 100 covered bridges in Vermont, including a half-dozen in and around Montgomery up near the Canadian border. The Windsor-Cornish Bridge, a 460-foot span across the Connecticut River, went up in 1866 and is the nation's longest covered bridge. State highway maps indicate bridges, or the Vermont Travel Division (Montpelier 05602) can provide information.

Bennington. In the southwest corner of the state, it has a surprising number of interesting points to see: the Bennington Battle Monument, the Bennington Museum, (with its Grandma Moses collection), the Park-McCullough House. Robert Frost is buried under a huge maple tree behind the photogenic Old First Church; his burial stone proclaims he had "a lover's quarrel with life."

The Alpine Slide at Bromley Ski Area. The first Slide in North America, and the world's longest, when the twin-track ride opened in July 1976, the installation now has three tracks, including a 4,600-foot hummer. There are other Slides at Pico, just east of Rutland, and farther north in Stowe, but Bromley offers the longest rides. It's not dangerous at all; you control your descent by using the dip stick which juts up between your knees as you sit in the specially engineered sleds with wheels.

The Coolidge Homestead. Calvin Coolidge was born in Vermont, sworn-in by his father as president here—a pre-dawn ceremony back in 1923 when Warren Harding died—and was buried in Plymouth Notch in 1933, in a simple hillside plot alongside generations of his family. The Homestead buildings welcome visitors during the warm weather and you can poke about on your own in the off-season, i.e., once the foliage season passes. Maps are available to explain the site.

Quechee Gorge. Just east of Plymouth Notch, you pass through the postcard-cute village of Woodstock, notable for its buried utility lines around the Town Green, and push on to Quechee Gorge. Route 4, which runs along what used to be the old Woodstock Railroad track bed, crosses the gorge and provides an obvious observation point. You also may hike your way down the sloping terrain on either side, but be careful because it's easy enough to lose your footing.

Granville Gulf and Moss Glen Falls. The gulf, which straddles Route 100 in the upper central part of the state near the Sugarbush Valley area, was given to the state to be "wilderness forever." The two-lane roadway is the only sign of progress in this nine-mile stretch of streams and ponds, tall trees and otherwise unspoiled landscape. Moss Glen Falls, which is a mile or so north of the southern edge of the gulf, is an impressive if small waterfall. The stream running out of the woods splashes over a couple of huge boulders, creating a refreshing, restful setting.

Morgan Horse Farm in Weybridge. A National Historic Site, the farm is located just west of the center of Middlebury and is just a big playpen for more than 50 Morgans, the rugged horse which proved so valuable—because of strength and stamina—in the early days of the United States. There are guided tours and other educational activities at the farm.

Lake Champlain. Okay, so it's a lake, but it's a beauty and when you're landlocked like Vermont—the only Northeastern state without a coastline—such a body of water takes on added significance, emotional and otherwise. The lake runs into Canada and separates the state from New York; ferries cross it at three points. One impressive view is from the top of the gondola at Sugarbush Valley Ski Area, but perhaps the finest is from the top of Main Street in Burlington, just as you clear the University of Vermont campus and start down the hill to the lake; the view runs across to the Adirondacks of New York, a vista that seems to look into the middle of next week.

Windjamming. Visions of acres of sails are conjured when someone mentions "windjammer." Long John Silver, pieces of eight and the Spanish Main. Well, it's not quite the same, but the 76-foot schooner *Homer W. Dixon* sails each week from Burlington. You can take part in as much—or as little—as you want, helping to swab the decks or just catching some sun while you read a book.

The Shelburne Museum. It's incredible to think that almost everything in this dandy of a museum, spread over 35 buildings and 45 acres, was collected by one woman, Electra Havemeyer Webb. It's almost as if she went to London or Rome or Athens and said, "Yes, put the city in a box for me." Statues and duck decoys, primitive art, a spectacular collection of circus memorabilia, and much more, including a former lighthouse and sidewheeler. The Museum is on Route 7, just south of Burlington, and is open daily in summer, on a reduced schedule during winter. For details, contact the museum (802–985–3344).

Isle La Motte. When Samuel de Champlain sailed through the region back in 1609 he became the first white man to look upon what has become the State of Vermont, and he was standing on the Isle La Motte at the northern end of Lake Champlain when he first enjoyed that view. A fort, built for defense against the Mohawks, was erected in 1666, and the shrine on the island commemorates the construction.

Rock of Ages Quarry. The cynic, or tired traveler, probably would kiss-off this quarry as just a big hole in the ground. But, the quarry has been worked since before the Civil War and they're still chiseling away for granite. There are free guided tours several times a day in summer. The counterpart to this in the marble industry is in Proctor, just west of Rutland. However, although there is an exhibit center in Proctor, you can't view the actual work since that takes place below ground. A 20-minute film outlines the story of getting marble to market, which goes back 400-million years.

The Northeast Kingdom. Media hyperbole often refers to the counties of Orleans, Orange and Essex—the Northeast Kingdom—as "unspoiled." Not quite true, although they are far less developed than anywhere else in Vermont and the uncluttered, undeveloped, unhurried pace is a perfect counterpoint to the spectacular scenery, especially during fall foliage.

That's a hasty sampler of Vermont, trying to put some of the highlights of the state in a nutshell. It doesn't include other attractions such as the two state craft centers (in Windsor and Middlebury), the Fairbanks Museum & Planetarium in St. Johnsbury, the scenic "gaps" which take you up and over the spine of the Green Mountains—Appalachian Gap near Waitsfield, and Lincoln, Brandon and Middlebury gaps, or Old Constitution House in Windsor where delegates drew up Vermont's constitution in 1777. But these, all or in part, can be saved for another time.

PRACTICAL INFORMATION FOR VERMONT

Note: Large sections in Practical Information have been organized by touring areas for your convenience.

VERMONT FACTS & FIGURES. Vermont's name is derived from the French for "green mountain": *vert mont,* said to have been bestowed upon it by the Rev. Samuel Peters atop 4,241-foot Killington Peak in 1763. Its nickname is the Green Mountain State. Red clover is the state flower; sugar maple, the state tree; the hermit thrush, the state bird; and the Morgan horse, the state animal. In 1978, the Legislature, in a burst of creativity, designated the trout as the State Cold Water Fish, the walleyed pike as the State Warm Water

Fish, and the honeybee as the State Insect. The State Motto is "Freedom and Unity"; the State song is "Hail Vermont" by Josephine Hovey Perry.

Somewhat wedge-shaped, Vermont is 151.5 miles from north to south, and from 40 to 90 miles wide. The total area is 9,609 square miles, slightly larger than neighboring New Hampshire, and 43rd among the 50 states. Montpelier is the capital, but Burlington, with about 40,000 people, is the largest city. Population of the state in the 1980 census was 511,456, ranking 48th nationally. The major towns and cities, in order of size, are Burlington, Rutland, Bennington, Brattleboro, Essex, Barre, Springfield, South Burlington, Colchester, and Montpelier. There are 14 counties. Vermont was the 14th state to enter the Union, on March 4, 1791.

Vermont is the only New England state to be wholly without the influence of the sea; it has neither coast nor shoreline, though freshwater Lake Champlain forms about half of its western border.

Much of the state is mountainous and the mountains are the source of a major portion of the state's revenue. Thousands of visitors flock to Vermont's 20-plus alpine and 60-plus cross country ski centers. In the summer, several of these areas provide a complete range of recreation. The mountains are also the source for timber, asbestos, granite and marble. Machine tools and electrical equipment are important industrially, but about 85% of the state's larger companies are absentee-owned by large outside conglomerates.

The rocky soil makes farming difficult, but resourceful Vermont farmers manage to make a living out of dairy products, hay, apples, Christmas trees, lumber and maple syrup. Vermont's winters are cold and snowy, although the recent tendency has been toward warmer weather. Summers are comfortably warm; hot, humid days are rare. Specifically, year-round average conditions are as follows:

	Jan.	Feb.	Mar.	Apr.	May	Jun.
Average Temperature (F)	16	18	27	41	54	64
Average Temperature (C)	−9	−8	−3	5	12	18
Days of Rain or Snow	13	12	13	12	13	11

	Jul.	Aug.	Sept.	Oct.	Nov.	Dec.
Average Temperature (F)	70	66	64	48	36	21
Average Temperature (C)	21	19	18	9	2	−6
Days of Rain or Snow	12	12	11	11	14	14

HOW TO GET THERE. By air: Major airfields in Vermont are in Burlington, Montpelier, Rutland, and Springfield, plus White River–Lebanon, just across the river in New Hampshire. The southern part of the state is also readily accessible from Albany Airport and from Hartford's Bradley Field.

Air North, Command Airways, Precision Airlines, PeoplExpress, USAir, and *United Airlines* serve the state. *United* flies to Burlington from Chicago; the others serve Boston and/or New York or Newark.

By train: *Amtrak* has two trains a day, one heading from Washington for Montreal (and going through Vermont at about dawn) and one heading back to Washington, via New York City, late at night. For further information contact any Amtrak office. In Vermont Amtrak has ticket agents at: Essex Junction (Burlington), St. Albans, White River Junction, Waterbury, and Montpelier Junction; additional stops at Bellows Falls and Brattleboro. Another line between New York and Montreal passes through Albany, Glens Falls, Port Kent and Plattsburgh.

By bus: *Vermont Transit Lines,* 135 St. Paul St., Burlington 05401 (864–6811) and its connecting lines service Vermont from all major points in New England and from New York City, Albany, Glens Falls, Montreal, Sherbrooke, and Quebec City. Connections are through Greyhound.

By car: From New York take the Thruway to Exit 24 to Rte. 7. Out of Troy, Rte. 7 will take you to the Vermont border, at which point it becomes Rte. 9

to Bennington and Brattleboro, across the southern end of the state. I–91 will take you from New Haven, Connecticut, through Massachusetts to the southeastern corner of Vermont, and from there up the eastern edge of the state to the Northeast Kingdom and on to Quebec. Vermont's other interstate is I–89, which comes down from Canada to Burlington, then cuts diagonally southeast across the entire state, into New Hampshire at White River Junction, then on south toward Concord, Manchester, and Boston.

By boat: There are scenic ferry rides across Lake Champlain between Burlington, VT, and Port Kent NY (mid-May to mid-Oct.); Grand Isle, VT, and Plattsburgh NY (Apr. through Nov.); Charlotte VT, and Essex NY (late May to late Nov.); *The Lake Champlain Transportation Co.,* King St. Dock, Burlington (864–9804) runs ferries at Burlington, Charlotte and Grand Isle. Larrabees Point VT, and Ticonderoga NY *Shorewell Ferry* at Larrabee's Point (897–7999) runs the ferry at Larrabee Point.

 **TELEPHONES.** The area code for all of Vermont is 802. Although the state is served by both New England Telephone Co. and a handful of smaller, independent phone companies, they are all interconnected and you will not experience any difficulty or difference in service. Information (known as directory assistance) is 1–555–1212 for all calls, regardless of whether local or non-local in Vermont. When direct-dialing a long distance number, you must dial "1" (one) *before* you dial the area code and the number. An operator will assist you on all person-to-person, credit card and collect calls if you dial "O" (zero) first. Pay telephones are usually 20 cents.

 **HOTELS AND MOTELS.** Generally speaking, the accommodations in Vermont are excellent, with many of the establishments gearing their entire range of services to the winter sportsman and the summer loafer. Recreation facilities, broad vistas of lakes and mountains, and strategically sited locations make these hotels, lodges, and motels perfect bases for vacation activities. The rise of tourism and first-class resorts has meant a similar increase in quality hotels, inns, and restaurants in Vermont. You're as likely to find color cable TV, computer games, and luxury service as the traditional, home-style inn. Unless otherwise indicated, properties are open year round. Special package rates are pretty much the order of business for properties near major resorts, for both summer and winter. Prices are based on double occupancy, European plan (room only), unless indicated. *Deluxe:* $75 and up, *Expensive:* $50–$75; *Moderate:* $30–$50; *Inexpensive:* $30 and under.

SOUTHERN REGION

ARLINGTON. Arlington Inn. *Moderate-Expensive.* Jct. U.S. 7 and Rte. 313 (375–6427). Greek Revival mansion (1847) converted to comfy country inn. Fresh vegetables from the inn's garden. Continental breakfast on lawn.

West Mountain Inn. *Moderate.* Rte. 313 (375–6516). Seven-gabled, hilltop inn surrounded by 150 acres of trees, trails, pastures and ponds. Swimming in rock quarry, cross-country ski trails. Excellent dining rm, lounge.

Cut Leaf Maples. *Inexpensive.* U.S. 7, south of village (375–2725). Rooms in main building or motel addition. Dining room, lounge with fireplace. Pets. Free cribs. TV.

Hill's Farm Inn. *Inexpensive.* Sunderland Rd., off U.S. 7 (375–2269). Inn and cabins; inn open year round, cabins May to Oct. Kids' rates (under 10).

Valhalla Motel. *Inexpensive.* U.S. 7 (375–2212). Pool, picnic and games area. TV.

BELLOWS FALLS. Highlands Motel. *Moderate.* Jct. U.S. 5 and Rte. 103, Exit 6 off I–91 (463–9840). Restaurant, lounge. TV.

BENNINGTON. Best Western New Englander. *Moderate-Expensive.* 220 Northside Dr., U.S. 7, 2 miles north of town (528–1234). Small dining room features Vermont-fresh produce; in-room coffee. Heated pool, play area, some steam bath rooms. Color TV (cable). Country club privileges.

Bulrushes Motor Court. *Moderate.* Rte. 9 (442–6222). Motel and cottages on pleasant grounds. Small, quiet, restful. Pool, play area. Pets. Open late June to Oct. 31.

Catamount Motel. *Moderate.* U.S. 7 (442–5977). Pool. In-room coffee. Pleasant rooms. Color TV (cable).

Fife 'n Drum Motel. *Moderate.* U.S. 7 (442–4074). Early American decor, of course. In-room coffee, picnic area with grills. Heated pool, spa, lawn games. Pets. Color TV (cable).

Kirkside Motor Lodge. *Moderate.* 250 W. Main St. (Rte. 9) (447–7596). Each room individually decorated. In-room coffee. Color TV (cable).

Knotty Pine Motel. *Moderate.* 130 Northside Dr. (442–5487). In-room coffee. Pool, play area. Kitchenettes available. Color TV (cable).

Mid-town Motel. *Moderate.* Rte. 9 (447–0189). Restaurant next door, free coffee. Solar-heated pool, picnic area, play area. Color TV (cable).

Paradise Motor Inn. *Moderate.* Rte. 9 (442–8351). Heated pool, saunas, tennis. Color TV.

South Gate Motel. *Moderate.* U.S. 7 (447–7525). In-room coffee. Heated pool. Color TV (cable).

Darling Kelly's Motel. *Inexpensive.* U.S. 7 (442–2322). Pool, lawn games. Color TV (cable).

Harwood Hill Motel. *Inexpensive.* U.S. 7–A (442–6278). Sweeping grounds with fine views. TV (Color or B&W).

BRATTLEBORO. Quality Inn. *Moderate-Expensive.* U.S. 5 (254–8701). Italian restaurant, lounge. Pool. Pets. Color TV.

Colonial Motel & Tavern. *Moderate.* U.S. 5, Exit 3 off I–91 (257–7733). Restaurant, lounge, patio dining in warm weather. Pool. Color TV.

Dalem's Chalet. *Moderate.* 16 South St., Exit 2 off I–91 (254–4323). Dining room. Indoor and outdoor pools, 2 ponds, play area, sauna.

Red Coach Motor Inn. *Moderate.* U.S. 5 (254–4583). Fine dining, lounge. Pool.

Susse Chalet Motor Lodge. *Inexpensive.* U.S. 5 (254–6007). Large motel, clean rooms. Restaurant, bar. Pool. Laundry. TV.

DORSET. Barrows House. *Deluxe.* (MAP or AP). Rte. 30 (867–4455). One of New England's finest country inns; 27 rms with 24½ baths and 2 kitchens in a rambling 200-yr.-old house and 6 smaller buildings; 6 acres of lawns, gardens, woods. First-rate dining room with nice balance between meat and fish dishes; excellent seafood. Pool, sauna, tennis, paddle tennis, bicycles, skiing, tobogganing, nearby golf privileges and trout fishing. Library, bar. Lawn games. Superb.

Dorset Inn. *Inexpensive-Moderate.* Rte. 30 (867–5500). Vermont's oldest inn (1800). Sunday buffets, Wed. cookouts. Pool, horseback riding, boating.

GRAFTON. The Old Tavern. *Expensive.* Rte. 121 (843–2231). An 1801 stagecoach inn with many antiques; 3 pleasant dining rooms with varied entrees, unusual soups, pleasing service. Jacket, please, at dinner. Natural pond swimming pool, tennis, lawn games, bikes, hiking and fishing. Closed Apr. and Christmas Day.

LONDONDERRY-SOUTH LONDONDERRY. Blue Gentian Lodge. *Moderate.* Rte. 11 (824–5908). Pond-studded grounds and large rooms, dining room, fine homemade soups, desserts. Pool, play area. Color TV (cable).

Dostal's Motor Lodge. *Moderate-Expensive.* At Magic Mtn. Ski Area (824–6700). Indoor and outdoor pools, whirlpools, game room. Color TV (cable).

Highland House. *Moderate-Expensive.* Rte. 100 (824–3019). Quiet, comfy inn in 1842 structure. Expecially fine dining (closed Mon.–Tues.). Pool.

Londonderry Inn. *Moderate.* Rte. 100, South Londonderry (824–5226). Another old homestead (1826) converted to an inn; charming hillside perch overlooking West River. Fine dining, tavern. Pool.

Post Horn Inn. *Moderate.* Rte. 11 (824–3131). Excellent dining, lounge. Fireplace, game room. Color TV (cable).

Swiss Inn. *Moderate.* Rte. 11 (824–3442). Full breakfast included; candlelight dining, Swiss cuisine a specialty. Pool, tennis.

Magic View Motel. *Inexpensive-Moderate.* Rte. 11 (824–3793). Breakfast room, game room. TV.

MANCHESTER (See also Peru). **The Equinox.** *Deluxe.* Rte. 7 (362–4700). Luxurious restoration of what was a 1769 tavern. Modern meeting facilities to go with century-old motif in guest rooms. Fine dining and Viennese desserts from its own bakery; heated pool, tennis. Free transportation to ski resorts.

Wilburton Inn. *Deluxe.* River Rd. (362–2500). Luxurious Georgian former estate with 30 rooms, 5 housekeeping units. Dining room, bar. Putting green, pitch 'n putt. Open mid-May to mid-Oct.

Kandahar Lodge. *Expensive.* Jct. Rtes. 11 and 30. Excellent restaurant, outdoor barbecues, fireside lounge. Heated pool, sauna, rec room. Stocked trout pond, skating, tobogganing, cross-country skiing in winter.

Palmer House Motel. *Expensive.* U.S. 7 (362–3600). 20 chock-full acres. Small refrigerators, in-room coffee. Heated pool, sauna, whirlpool, shuffleboard, putting green, tennis. Color TV (cable).

Reluctant Panther Inn. *Expensive.* West Rd., just off U.S. 7 (362–2568). Small inn, almost equally notable for delicious French-Continental cuisine and its purple decor. In any case, try the crepe Rangoon. Elegant service. Bar.

Four Winds Motor Inn. *Moderate-Expensive.* U.S. 7 (362–1105). Colonial motif, tastefully decorated rooms in 1853 country inn. Dining room. Golf and tennis privileges next door at Manchester CC.

Aspen Motel. *Moderate.* U.S. 7 (362–2450). Just north of the village, in-room coffee. Nice grounds, pool. Color TV (cable).

Avalanche Motor Lodge. *Moderate.* Rte. 11, on the way to Bromley (362–2622). Restaurant, lounge. Pool, sauna, game room. Golf privileges.

Barnstead Motel. *Moderate.* Rte. 30 (362–1619). Recycled 1830 hay barn, exposed beams. Cows never had it so good. In-room coffee. Heated pool, game room. Golf and tennis privileges. Color TV (cable).

Chalet Motel. *Moderate.* Rte. 11 (362–1622). Refrigerator and in-room coffee. Heated pool, hot tubs, game room, lawn games. golf and tennis privileges. Color TV (cable).

The Inn at Manchester. *Moderate.* U.S. 7 (362–1793). Tenderly restored mansion. Great breakfasts; try the cheese omelette. Pool plus golf and tennis privileges.

Red Sled Motel. *Moderate.* Rte. 11 (362–2161). Restaurant across the road; in-room coffee, refrigerators. Heated pool. Golf and tennis privileges. No pets. Color TV (cable).

Toll Road Motor Inn. *Moderate.* Rte. 11 (362–1711). In-room coffee, refrigerators. Pool. Golf and tennis privileges. Color TV (cable).

Weathervane Motel. *Moderate.* U.S. 7 (362–2444). Original oil paintings featured in large rooms. In-room coffee, continental breakfast. Pool and golf privileges.

Worthy Inn. *Moderate.* U.S. 7 (362–1792). Throwback to the old wide-porch inns. Restaurant, bar. Pool, tennis. Golf and tennis privileges.

Skylight Lodge. *Inexpensive-Moderate.* Rte. 11 (362–2566). Last of the original lodge owners from "back when." Family atmosphere, dorm-style bunks or modest, cozy rooms. Family-style meals, too. BYOB in cellar, along with piano and fieldstone fireplace.

MARLBORO. Whetstone Inn. *Moderate.* Rte. 9 (254–2500). Small, 190-yr.-old country inn. Pleasant rooms, some with shared baths. Kitchenettes.

Longwood Farms. *Inexpensive-Moderate.* Rte. 9 (257–1545). An inn set in a 200-yr.-old farmhouse. Candlelit dining room, excellent preparation.

Marlboro Inn. *Inexpensive.* On Hogback Mtn. (464–5494). Small house and cabins at 2,350 ft. with superb view of Hogback Mt. Walking distance to ski area and famed Skyline Restaurant.

MOUNT SNOW. The Hermitage. *Deluxe* (MAP). Coldbrook Rd., off Rte. 105, Wilmington (464–3511). Splendiferous. 16 guest rooms, 4 dining rooms and 30,000 bottles of wine. Lunch on the terrace in summer, cross-country ski out the back door in winter. Sauna, trout pond, game bird farm.

Inn at Sawmill Farm. *Deluxe* (MAP). Rte. 100, W. Dover (464–8131). Still more elegance: superb meals, wide selection of wines and tasteful furnishings in the luxurious rms. Restored group of farm buildings. Trout pond. Swimming, tennis, fishing. Closed mid-Nov. to early Dec.

Snow Lake Lodge. *Deluxe* (MAP). Mtn. Rd., off Rte. 100, Mt. Snow (464–3333). Centerpiece of the Mt. Snow complex, across Snow Lake from the ski area's base facilities. Heated pool, Japanese "leisure" pools. Lakeside dining, bar. Golf privileges.

The White House. *Deluxe* (MAP). Rte. 9, Wilmington (464–2135). Marvelous knolltop site for this handsome former mansion. More elegance and fine dining. Sauna, whirlpool, steam room. Cross-country skiing.

Chalet Waldwinkel. *Expensive.* Rte. 100, Mt. Snow (464–5281). Pool, 2 rec rooms, table tennis, billiards. Full breakfast.

Ironstone. *Moderate-Expensive.* (MAP). Rte. 100, Mt. Snow (464–3796). Fine dining, bar, fireplace. Sauna, game room. Color TV (cable).

Alp-Hof Lodge. *Moderate.* Handle Rd., Mt. Snow (464–3344). Tyrolean lodge 400 yds. from base area. Heated pool, whirlpool, sauna. Game rooms with TV.

Andirons Motor Lodge. *Moderate.* Rte. 100, West Dover (464–2114). Dining room, 2 lounges, 3 fireplaces. Indoor pool, sauna, whirlpool. Game room, in-room movies. Color TV (cable).

Mountaineer Lodge. *Moderate.* Handle Rd., Mt. Snow (464–5404). Modern-rustic design; antiques and contemporary furniture. Dining room, BYOB bar. Tennis, play area.

Nutmeg Inn. *Moderate.* Rte. 9, Wilmington (464–3351). Early American farmhouse converted into 9-room inn. Delicious homecooking; bar; fireplace. Library.

Red Cricket Inn. *Moderate.* Rte. 100, West Dover (464–8817). Only thing warmer than the homecooking are the 2 fieldstone fireplaces. BYOB bar. Sauna. Color TV (cable).

Snow Den Inn. *Moderate.* Rte. 100, West Dover (464–9355). Excellent cuisine at this small inn (9 rooms); however, no lunch in winter, no dinner in summer. BYOB bar. TV room.

Tamarack at Mt. Snow. *Moderate.* Rte. 100, Mt. Snow (464–8850). Attractive, well-appointed rooms, restaurant. Close to base area. Cable TV in lounge.

NEWFANE. The Four Columns Inn. *Expensive.* 230 West St (365–7713). Lovingly restored 1830 mansion with 10 rooms, 2 suites. Chef-owned, so you know the meals are excellent. French cuisine. Closed Tues., Apr. & Nov. Pool.

The Old Newfane Inn. *Expensive.* Rte. 30 (365–4427). The other "book end" in this pintsize town with two great inns. This one is 1787 inn with antiques-drenched rooms. Beamed dining room, Swiss–French cuisine. Closed April to mid-May and Nov. 15 to Dec. 15.

PERU (See also Manchester). Bromley Sun Lodge. *Moderate-Expensive.* Rte. 11 (824–6941). Right at the foot of Bromley slopes for skiing in winter, Alpine Slide in warm weather. Restaurant, lounge. Indoor pool.

Johnny Seesaw's. *Moderate-Expensive.* Rte. 11 (824–5533). Rustic inn, a half-mile from Bromley with accommodations from bunk rooms to cottages with fireplaces; it's a converted roadhouse and speakeasy. Pool, tennis, game room. Pets "selectively welcome." TV room.

Nordic Inn. *Moderate.* Rte. 9, over the line in Landgrove (824–6444). Relaxing site, back in the trees, yet a solarium dining room. Fine Scandinavian cuisine, marvelous cellar pub. Hiking in summer, miles of cross-country skiing in winter.

Wiley Foxx Inn. *Moderate.* Rte. 11 (824–6600). Meandering, 200-yr.-old inn. Hearty fare (chef-owned). Fireplaces, game room, pool, lawn games.

POWNAL. Ladd Brook Motor Inn. *Moderate.* Rte. 7 (823–7341). Well-appointed motel peering out over the valley, not far from Green Mtn. Race Track. Coffee shop. Pool. TV.

PUTNEY. Hickory Ridge House. *Moderate-Expensive.* Hickory Ridge Rd. (call for directions; 387-5709). Former estate house (1808); peaceful setting and good jump-off spot for hiking or biking, or maybe cross-country skiing in winter. Continental breakfast.

Putney Motor Inn. *Moderate.* Exit 4 off I–91 (387–5517). Dining room, friendly bar. Color TV (cable).

SAXTONS RIVER. Saxtons River Inn. *Moderate.* Main St. (869–2110). Turn-o'-century decor. Tiffany chandeliers, each room individually decorated. Dining room, lounge.

STRATTON MOUNTAIN. Liftline Lodge. *Deluxe* (MAP). Stratton base area, off Rte. 30 (297–2600). Closest inn to the ski lifts; some apt. units. Fine dining, lounge, fireplaces. Pool, tennis. Sauna, whirlpool, massage.

Stratton Mountain Inn. *Deluxe* (MAP). Stratton base area, off Rte. 30 (297–2500). Dining room, lounge, weekend entertainment. Pool, tennis, golf, horseback riding. Color TV (cable).

Stratton Mountain Condos. *Expensive-Deluxe.* Base area and walking distance (297–2200). Central lodging bureau handles reservations for growing pool of village condominiums.

Birkenhaus. *Moderate-Expensive.* Stratton base area, off Rte. 30 (297–2000). Austrian lodge with regular double rooms or bunk rooms. Superb cuisine; reservations needed. Pool.

WEST DOVER-WILMINGTON (See Mount Snow).

WESTON. Colonial House Inn & Motel. *Moderate.* Rte. 100 (824–6286). Rooms in inn or motel. Homemade breads and pies. A player piano spices up leisure time. TV. Cross-country skiing.

The Inn at Weston. *Moderate.* Rte. 100 (824–5804). Delightful dining with daily menu changes. Pub with fireplace, game room. TV.

CENTRAL VERMONT

BETHEL. Greenhurst Inn. *Moderate.* Rte. 12 (234–9474). Turreted Victorian inn with 9 rooms. Continental breakfast. Tennis. Old book shop on site.

BRANDON. Brandon Inn. *Expensive* (MAP). U.S. 7 (247–5766). Closing in on the end of its second century (1786), inn in National Register of Historic Sites. Excellent dining, lounge. Pool, shuffleboard, play area.

BROWNSVILLE. Ascutney Resort Hotel. *Moderate-Expensive.* Rte. 44 at Ascutney Mtn. Resort (484-7711). Tastefully designed, in keeping with village style. Restaurant, bar with health club nearby. Ski-in, ski-out.

CHITTENDEN. Mountain Top Inn. *Deluxe* (MAP). 6 mi off U.S. 4 (483–2311). Lovely mini-resort on 500 mountaintop acres peering into Chittenden Reservoir and across to gorgeous long-range vistas. Notable dining; try the seafood. Heated pool, sauna, whirlpool. Tennis, horseback riding, pitch 'n putt golf, fishing, hiking, canoeing. In winter, sleigh rides, skating, cross-country skiing on nearly 70 miles of trails, partly protected by snowmaking.

Tulip Tree Inn. *Deluxe* (MAP). Chittenden Dam Rd., off U.S. 4 (483–6213). Small inn beside trout stream and the Long Trail. Stick-to-ribs breakfasts, fine dining. Swimming, hiking, fishing, canoeing, cross-country skiing.

GASSETS. Old Town Farm Lodge. *Inexpensive-Moderate.* Rte. 13 (875–2346). Family-style lodge. Functional, not fancy.

GOSHEN. Blueberry Hill Inn. *Moderate.* Off Rte. 73, follow the signs (247–6735). Only 8 rooms; extremely popular with cross-country skiers. Fireplace, greenhouse off the kitchen, exposed beams. Comfy, cozy and fine food served family-style.

KILLINGTON-PICO. Killington Lodging Bureau (422–3711) is a central reservation office that—in one call—will make reservations for you, or you can write directly to the inn or condo of your choice. Or Pico Holidays can handle reservations in winter (775–1927) or tollfree (800–451–4321).

Cascades Lodge. *Deluxe.* Killington Rd. (the access road) off U.S. 4 (422–3731). Candlelight dining. Lounge w. fireplace and kingsize TV. Indoor pool, sauna, whirlpool, exercise room, game room. Color TV (cable).

Cortina Inn. *Deluxe* (MAP). U.S. 4 (773–3331). Vestpocket resort, a little of everything. Superb dining; fireplaces in some rooms. Indoor and outdoor pools, sauna, whirlpool, exercise, game room and plenty of tennis. Shuttle bus to ski areas, cross-country skiing. Color TV (cable).

Little Buckhorn Lodge. *Deluxe* (MAP). Killington Rd. (422–3314). Family-style meals, homecooking, fireside lounge. No dinner Fri. or Sun. nights. Sauna, game room, pool table. TV room.

The Mountain Inn. *Deluxe* (MAP). Killington Rd. (422–3595). Another new inn. Fine cuisine; fireside lounge with nightly entertainment in winter. Sauna, game room. Color TV (cable).

Summit Lodge. *Deluxe* (MAP). Killington Rd. (422–3535). Great hilltop site, excellent facilities and dining. 5 fireplaces. Heated pool, sauna, whirlpool, racquetball, and tennis, game room. Color TV (cable).

Mountain Meadows Lodge. *Expensive* (MAP). U.S. 4 (775–1010). Family-style lodge with dorm or inn rooms. Pool, hiking. Closed in May.

Vermont Inn. *Moderate-Expensive* U.S. 4, Mendon (773–9847). Converted 19th-century farmhouse with rustic bar, candlelight dining. Pool or stream swimming. Tennis, sauna. Cross-country skiing.

Edelweiss Motel & Chalets. *Moderate.* U.S. 4 (775–5577). Apts., chalets and motel rooms. Restaurant next door. Heated pool, game room, play area, picnic area. In-room coffee. Color TV (cable).

Friendship Inn-Tyrol Motel. *Moderate.* U.S. 4 (773–7485). Coffee shop and in-room coffee. Heated pool, lawn games, playground, picnic area (BBQ avail.). Color TV (cable).

Grey Bonnet Inn. *Moderate.* Rte. 100 (775–2537). Continental cuisine, candlelight dinners, lounge. Heated pool, tennis, hiking. Color TV (cable).

The Inn at Long Trail. *Moderate.* U.S. 4 at the crest of Sherburne Pass (775–7181). Rustic motif, accentuated by gargantuan boulder *inside* the building. Rooms are cozy, 2-room suites have their own fireplace. Hearty meals. Closed April 15 to June 15 and late Oct. to Thanksgiving.

Pico Bavarian Haus. *Moderate.* U.S. 4 next to Pico Ski Area (773–6331). Dining room, lounge, large fireplace. Pool, hiking, game room. Color TV (cable).

Sherburne-Killington Motel. *Moderate.* U.S. 4 (773–9535). Continental breakfast. Large rooms.

Skol Haus Motor Lodge. *Moderate.* Killington Rd. (422–3305). Light breakfast available. Fireside lounge with BYOB bar. TV.

Val Roc Motel. *Moderate.* U.S. 4 (422–3881). Some kitchenettes, in-room coffee. Pool, tennis. Color TV (cable).

Turn of River Lodge. *Inexpensive-Moderate.* U.S. 4 (422–3766). Rustic, several dorm-style rooms. Big stone fireplace and setup bar. Continental breakfast. Game room. TV room.

LAKE BOMOSEEN. Prospect House. *Moderate.* Rte. 30 (468–5581). Lakefront motel and 9-hole golf course. Restaurant. Beach, boating, fishing. Open May to Oct.

LAKE ST. CATHERINE. Lake St. Catherine Inn. *Moderate.* Rte. 30 (287–9347). Picturesque inn on lake of same name. American-Jewish cuisine. Marina. Open mid-May to Labor Day.

LUDLOW (Okemo Mtn.). **Combes Family Inn.** *Moderate.* Off Rte. 100 (228–8799). Secluded setting away from the main flow. Main building or motel units. Family-style meals, heaps of chow. Ponds handy, hiking, cross-country skiing.
Country Pleasant Inn. *Moderate.* Rte. 100 (228–8926). Pool, picnic area. Color TV room.
Governor's Inn. *Moderate.* Rte. 103 on The Green (228–8830). Small inn (8 rooms), candlelight dinners, will pack a lunch for you.
Inn Towne Motel. *Moderate.* Rte. 103 (228–8884). In the middle of town; kitchenettes. Pool. Color TV (cable).
Okemo Inn. *Moderate.* Rte. 100 (228–2031). Restored 1810 inn. Hefty helping in dining room; hearthside lounge. Pool, sauna, hiking. TV room.
The Winchester. *Moderate.* Rte. 103 (228–3841). Cozy rooms in 1813 inn or motel annex. Superb cuisine—try the filet mignon—and cozy bar. Tennis.
Okemo Lodging Bureau (228–4041). Can help make reservations for slopeside condos or surrounding lodging facilities.

MIDDLEBURY. Middlebury Inn. *Moderate-Expensive.* U.S. 7 on The Green (388–4961). Rooms in 1827 inn, motel annex. Fine dining, buffets in summer nightly, lounge. Relaxing parlor.
Blue Spruce Motel. *Moderate.* U.S. 7 (388–7512). Small motel, nice furnishings. Homey. Color TV (cable).
Greystone Motel. *Moderate.* U.S. 7 (388–4935). Another nice, small place, clean and home-like. Pets. Color TV (cable).
Sugarhouse Motor Inn. *Moderate.* U.S. (388–7773). Name tells the tale: like living in a sugarhouse; sugaring artifacts everywhere. Immense meals, great desserts. Coffee shop. Color TV (cable).
Waybury Inn. *Moderate.* Rte. 125 (388–4015). Colonial (1810), fireplaces. Excellent dining, lounge. Hiking, fishing. Serves as model for Stratford Inn in "Newhart" TV series.

NORWICH. Norwich Inn. *Expensive.* 225 Main St. (649–1143). Another inn *cum* motel annex. 1797 inn with fine dining, Early American decor, lounge. Color TV (cable).

PLYMOUTH. Echo Lake Inn. *Moderate-Expensive.* Rte. 100, Tyson (228-8602). Modernized century-old inn with condos in annex. Top-quality dining, excellent Sunday brunch; try the crab fondue.
Farmbrook Motel. *Inexpensive-Moderate.* Rte. 100-A (672–3621). Small motel, set off road, in-room coffee. Lawn games, picnic area. TV.

PROCTORSVILLE. Golden Stage Inn. *Moderate.* Off Rte. 103 (226–7744). Onetime stage stop. Excellent dining, fireplace.
Okemo Lantern Lodge. *Inexpensive-Moderate.* Rte. 131 nr. 103 (226–7770). One of the undiscovered pearls among New England country inns; only 7 rooms (22 guests capacity) in a tidy home (1850). Family-style food; piano; TV room.

QUECHEE. Inn at Marshland Farm. *Expensive.* River Rd. (295–3133). Former home of Vermont's first lieutenant governor. Folksy, warm, squeaky clean and always something happening. Farm-style luxury: crops in summer, grazing horses, pleasant grounds. In winter, you can cross-country ski out the front or back door down to Quechee Gorge or play hockey on the frozen pond. Superb dining in hushed, candlelight setting. Reservations recommended.

Quechee Motel. *Moderate.* Rte. 4 (295-7600). Set in among the tall pines. Restaurant. Color TV (cable).

ROCHESTER. Rochester Inn. *Moderate.* Rte. 100 (767–4711). Dining room, tavern.

RUTLAND. Hogge Penny Motor Inn. *Moderate-Expensive.* U.S. 4 (773–3200). Condomotel with luxury suites or motel rooms. Restaurant, lounge. Pool, tennis.

Holiday Inn. *Moderate-Expensive.* U.S. 7 (775–1911). Your basic Holiday Inn—functional, not flashy. Restaurant, bar, in-room coffee. Meeting rms., sauna, whirlpool, exercise room to go with pitch 'n' putt golf layout and shuffleboard. Color TV (cable).

Green Mont Motel. *Moderate.* U.S. 7 (775–2575). In-room coffee. Color TV (cable).

Royal Motel. *Moderate.* U.S. 4 (773–9176). Coffee shop. Heated pool, steam baths. Color TV (cable).

Rutland Motel. *Moderate.* U.S. 4 (775–4348). Coffee shop. Kitchenettes. Heated pool. Color TV (cable).

Woodstock East Motel. *Moderate.* U.S. 4 (773–2442). Kitchenettes, free coffee. Outdoor pool. Color TV (cable).

Country Squire. *Inexpensive.* Jct. U.S. 7-B and Rte. 103, North Clarendon (773–3805). Small motel, free Continental breakfast. Play area. Pets. TV.

SHREWSBURY. Shrewsbury Inn. *Moderate.* Rte. 103 (492–3355). Renovated inn with half-dozen rooms. Restaurant with extensive—not expensive—wine list.

SPRINGFIELD. Howard Johnson's Motor Lodge. *Moderate-Expensive.* Exit 7 at I–91 (885–4516). 24-hour restaurant, live entertainment in lounge. Indoor pool, sauna, game room. Color TV (cable).

Abby Lynn Motel. *Moderate.* Rtes. 106 and 10 (886–2223). Attractive motel. Continental breakfast. Heated pool, pitch 'n' putt golf, lawn games, grill and picnic area.

Hartness House. *Moderate.* 30 Orchard St. (885–2115). Former residence of a governor, now a tastefully decorated inn with modern motel units. Unusual underground lounge. Restaurant, bar. Heated pool, tennis, play area.

Pa-Lo-Mar Motel. *Inexpensive.* Rte. 11 (885–4142). Small motel, some kitchenettes. Coffee shop. Heated pool, picnic area. Color TV (cable).

WAITSFIELD-WARREN (Sugarbush Valley). **The Bridges.** *Deluxe.* Mountain Rd. (583–2922). Luxurious condos. Indoor-outdoor tennis, heated pool, sauna, lounge, game room. Color TV (cable).

Sugarbush Inn. *Deluxe.* Mountain Rd., off Rte. 100 (583–2301). Colonial-style decor with chalets for families, 14 kitchenettes. Lush condos, too. Superb dining, outdoor lunch in summer. Heated pool, 11 tennis courts, Robert Trent Jones golf course, cross-country skiing (40 miles of trails).

Tucker Hill Lodge. *Deluxe* (MAP). Rte. 17, Waitsfield (496–3983). Comfy rms with puffy quilts and fresh flowers. Superb dining, French cuisine. Pool, tennis, hiking, cross-country skiing.

White Horse Inn. *Deluxe* (MAP). German Flats Rd., Waitsfield (496–2476). At entrance to Sugarbush North. Fine meals, fireside bar.

The Valley Inn. *Expensive* (MAP). Rte. 100, Waitsfield (496–3450). Quilts on the beds, antiques all around. Hearty eats, bar. Sauna, game room.

Mountain View Inn. *Moderate-Expensive.* Rte. 17, Waitsfield (496–2646). Only holds a dozen guests; farmhouse turned inn, plenty of antiques and quilts. Hearty meals dished up family style.

Sugartree Inn. *Moderate-Expensive.* Sugarbush Access Rd. (583–3211). Handy to slopes or sports center, golf course or tennis. Friendly. Early American decor.

Waitsfield Inn. *Moderate-Expensive.* Rte. 100, Waitsfield (496–3979). Aging country inn (1825) given new life with renovation. Excellent meals, lounge.

Carpenter Farm. *Moderate.* Meadow Rd., Moretown (496–3433). Family rooms, family meals. Excellent homecooking.

Madbush Chalet. *Moderate.* Rte. 100, Waitsfield (496–3966). Some kitchenettes. Breakfast avail. Swimming pond, tennis, shuffleboard, saunas.

Mad River Barn. *Moderate.* Rte. 17, Waitsfield (496–3310). Fine homecooking. Heated pool, hiking, cross-country skiing, game room.

Christmas Tree Inn. *Moderate.* Mountain Rd. to Sugarbush (583–4800). Inn and condos. Dining room, small bar. TV room.

Knoll Farm Country Inn. *Inexpensive.* Bragg Hill, Waitsfield (496–3939). Modernized, century-old farmhouse and the whole farm scene. Family meals. Swimming in pond, boating, fishing, hiking, skating, cross-country skiing.

WEATHERSFIELD. Inn at Weathersfield. *Moderate.* Rte. 106 (263–9217). Another former stage stop carefully restored; exposed beams. Just 9 rooms, some with fireplaces. Dinner only, extensive wine cellar.

WHITE RIVER JUNCTION. Holiday Inn. *Moderate-Expensive.* Holiday Inn Dr., off U.S. 5 (295–7537). 2 restaurants, 2 bars. Indoor and outdoor pools, sauna, whirlpool. Color TV (cable).

Howard Johnson's Motor Lodge. *Moderate.* U.S. 5 near Jct. I–89 and I–91 (295–3015). Restaurant, lounge. Indoor pool, sauna, coin laundry. Spa next door for racquetball. Pets. Color TV (cable).

WINDSOR. Wolpert's Mountain Inn. *Inexpensive.* U.S. 5, north of town (674–5565). Bed and breakfast spot overlooking the Connecticut River.

WOODSTOCK. Woodstock Inn and Resort. *Deluxe.* U.S. 4 on The Green (457–1100). Luxurious Colonial style inn, handsome quilts on beds. Fine dining by candlelight. Inn is centerpiece for resort which includes pool, 10 tennis courts, 2 paddleball courts, Robert Trent Jones golf course, nature walks. In summer, Stanley Steamer rides at night; in winter, nighttime sleigh rides. Also alpine (Suicide Six) and cross-country skiing (45 miles of trails).

Kedron Valley Inn. *Moderate-Expensive.* Rte. 106, South Woodstock (457–1473). Rooms dispersed among 1828 inn, 1824 tavern, or log cabin motel annex. Very fine meals. Acre-plus pond provides swimming; riding stables.

Charleston House. *Moderate.* 21 Pleasant St., U.S. 4 (457–3843). Across from the Civil War statue, it's a little more than your basic B 'n ' B. Tasty eats, lovely building, postcard town.

Pond Ridge Motel. *Moderate.* U.S. 4 (457–1667). Nice roadside motel, 2 kitchenettes. Tennis, swimming n the river, picnic area, lawn games.

Village Inn at Woodstock. *Moderate.* U.S. 4 (457–9804). Restored, turreted Victorian inn, once part of an estate. Varied menu is surprise throw-in for tidy 9-room package. Third floor rooms can be hot in summer.

NORTHERN VERMONT

BARRE. Heiress Motel. *Moderate.* 573 N. Main on U.S. 302 (476–4109). In-room coffee. Heated pool. Pets. Color TV (cable).

Hollow Motel. *Moderate.* 278 S. Main on U.S. 302 (479–9313). Continental breakfast. Pool, sauna. Color TV (cable).

Arnholm's Motel. *Inexpensive-Moderate.* U.S. 302 (476–5921). Small but neat rooms; antique furnishings. Play area. Open May to Oct.

BOLTON (BOLTON VALLEY). Bolton Valley Resort. *Expensive-Deluxe.* Off U.S. 2 and I–89 (434–2131). Complete four-season resort in 6,000-acre, mountaintop setting. Condos or hotel rooms. Dining room and Italian café, bar and light meals saloon. New million–dollar sports center includes indoor and outdoor pools, indoor and outdoor tennis. Also, night skiing, alpine, & cross-country skiing, kids' programs, game room, saunas. TV.

The Black Bear. *Moderate.* Bolton Valley Rd. (434-2126). Modern inn with magnificent view and flower-filled balconies (in summer). Homecooked meals; bar. Heated pool, rec room, hiking, tennis privileges at BV. Color TV.

BURLINGTON (See also Shelburne). **Radisson Burlington.** *Expensive.* Burlington Sq., downtown. Largest hotel in Vermont. 2 restaurants, lounge. Indoor pool, whirlpool. Color TV (cable).

Holiday Inn. *Moderate-Expensive.* 1068 Williston Rd., U.S. 2 and I–89 (863–6363). First-rate dining, lounge. Heated pool. Color TV (cable).

Ramada Inn. *Moderate-Expensive.* 1117 Williston Rd., U.S. 2 near I–89 (658–0250). Restaurant, lounge, coffee shop. Pool. Color TV (cable).

Sheraton-Burlington Inn. *Moderate-Expensive.* Jct. U.S. 2 and I–89 (862–6576). Restaurant (try the fish), lounge. Pool, play area. Color TV (cable).

Anchorage Motor Inn. *Moderate.* 108 Dorset St. (658–3351). Heated pool, whirlpool. Color TV (cable).

Best Western Redwood. *Moderate.* 1016 Shelburne Rd. U.S. 7 near jct. Rte. 7 and I–89. Penthouse and suite, some kitchenettes, in-room steam baths. Heated pool. Fine dining, lounge. Color TV (cable).

Colonial Motor Inn. *Moderate.* 462 Shelburne Rd. (U.S. 7) (862–5754). Coffee shop. Pool. Color TV (cable).

Ethan Allen Motel. *Moderate.* 1611 Williston Rd., U.S. 2 (863-4573). Pool. Color TV (cable).

Handy's Town House Motel. *Moderate.* 2330 Shelburne Rd., U.S. 7 (862–9608). In-room coffee, pool (heated). Color TV (Cable).

Ho-hum Motel(s). *Moderate.* 2 motels: 1200 Shelburne Rd. (U.S. 7) and 1660 Williston Rd. (Rte. 2). In-room coffee. Pool. Color TV (cable).

Town & Country Motel. *Moderate.* 490 Shelburne Rd., U.S. 7 (862-5786). Free in-room coffee. Color TV (cable).

Harbor Sunset Motel. *Inexpensive.* 1700 Shelburne Rd. (U.S. 7) (864–5080). Lake view and in-room coffee. Pets. Color TV (cable).

CRAFTSBURY COMMON. The Inn on the Common. *Moderate.* Rte. 14 (586–9619). Small, unstuffy inn in charming Colonial village. Excellent menu.

FAIRLEE. Lake Morey Inn & Club. *Expensive-Deluxe.* Off Rte. 5 and I–91 (333–4311). Resort on 350-plus acres. Restaurant, lounge. Golf, riding. Open early June to mid-Oct.

HIGHGATE SPRINGS. The Tyler Place. *Deluxe* (AP). 868–3301 Potpourri of buildings: inn, apts., and 27 cottages on 165 wooded acres overlooking Lake Champlain. All water sports, tennis, riding, and golf privileges.

ISLE LA MOTTE. Ruthcliffe Lodge & Motel Resort. *Moderate.* On Lake Champlain (928–3200). Swimming, boating, fishing. Dining room, lounge.

JEFFERSONVILLE. Village at Smugglers' Notch. *Expensive.* Rte. 108 (644–8851). Self-contained resort village with condos and nice restaurants, indoor pool, organized trips. Alpine, cross-country skiing; tennis, hiking, fishing.

Windridge Inn. *Inexpensive-Moderate.* Rte. 15 (644–8281). Comfortable inn, from patchwork quilts to handmade braided rugs. Tennis inside and out on clay courts. Continental dining, excellent homemade breads.

LYNDONVILLE. Anchor Way Motel. *Moderate.* U.S. 5, Lyndon (626–5832). In-room coffee, pool. Color TV (cable).

Lynburke Motel. *Moderate.* Jct. U.S. 5 and Rte. 114 (626–3346). Restaurant next door. Pool. Color TV.

MALLETS BAY. Marble Island Club. *Moderate.* On Lake Champlain (864–4546). Yachting and golf resort on the lake. Luxurious accommodations. Fine dining, fireside lounge. Heated pool, tennis, 200-ft beach, marina.
Bay Shore Cottages. *Moderate.* Porters' Pt. Rd., Colchester (863–4631). Bayfront units, secluded, kitchenettes.

MONTPELIER. Brown Derby Motel. *Moderate.* 101 Northfield St. (Rte. 12) (223–5258). Traditional Northeastern fare in restaurant; lounge. Color TV (cable).
Lague Inns. *Moderate.* Airport Road (229-5766). Good commercial trade. Restaurant. Color TV (cable).
Terrace Motel. *Inexpensive.* 57 River St., U.S. 2 (223–6465). One mile from downtown. Color TV (Cable).

NORTH HERO. North Hero House. *Moderate-Expensive.* U.S. 2 (372–8237). Renovated 22-room inn on the water. Dining room, lounge. Homegrown vegetables. All water sports, sauna, tennis, biking. Open mid-June to Labor Day.
Holiday Harbor Motel. *Moderate.* U.S. 2 (372–4077). Lakefront, some kitchenettes. Boating, fishing, shuffleboard, lawn games, picnics and barbecues. Open May 1 to Nov. 1.
Shore Acres Resort Motel. *Moderate.* U.S. 2 (372–8722). Dining room, lounge. Half-mile shoreline, boating, fishing. Open mid-May to mid-Oct.

ST. ALBANS. Cadillac Motel. *Moderate.* U.S. 7 (524–2191). Color TV.
Champlain Inn & Motel. *Moderate.* U.S. 7 (524–5956). Restaurant, lounge, in-room coffee. Pool. Color TV (cable).

ST. JOHNSBURY. Aime's Motel. *Moderate.* U.S. 2 and Rte. 18 (748–3194). Family-owned for 4 decades. Dining room specializes in home baking and seafood; lounge. Color TV (cable).
Echo Ledge Farm. *Moderate.* U.S. 2, E. St. Johnsbury (748–4750). Family-style meals in redecorated farmhouse.
Maple Center Motel. *Moderate.* 20 Hastings St. (U.S. 5) (748–2393). Restaurant next door, lounge. Color TV (cable).
Yankee Traveler Motel. *Moderate.* 65 Portland St. (U.S. 2) (748–3156). Early American decor. Color TV (cable).

SHELBURNE (See also Burlington). **Shelburne Inn.** *Moderate-Expensive.* U.S. 7 opp. Shelburne Museum (985–3305). Remodeled old inn with newer motel units. Fine dining, especially the desserts.
Driftwood Motel. *Moderate.* U.S. 7 (985–3334). Pool, pond, picnics. Fishing, Color TV (cable).
Yankee Doodle Motel. *Moderate.* U.S. 7 (985–3374). Spacious grounds, in-room coffee. Pool. Color TV (cable).
Cedar Ridge Motel. *Inexpensive-Moderate.* U.S. 7 (985–2151). Small motel with some kitchenettes. Color TV (cable).
T-Bird Motel. *Inexpensive-Moderate.* U.S. 7 (985–3663). Pool. Color TV (cable).

STOWE. The Inn at the Mountain. *Deluxe* (MAP). Rte. 108 (253–7311). Condo complex a mile from the alpine ski slopes. Pool plus golf and tennis privileges.
Topnotch at Stowe. *Deluxe* (AP or MAP). Rte. 108 (253–8585). They don't make too many places nicer than Topnotch. Each room individually decorated; hushed elegance throughout the resort. Superb dining experience. Heated pool, sauna, whirlpool. 10 outdoor tennis courts, 4 indoors, health spa, riding stables. Vermont's finest resort property—unless you think you must have some place to tie-up your yacht.
Stowehof. *Deluxe.* Edson Hill Rd., off the Mountain Rd. (Rte. 108) (253–9722). Don't let the "different" architecture fool you; inside this ship's prow-

styled building is a truly first-rate inn. European cuisine, lounge. Game room, library, sauna.

Butternut Inn & Chalets. *Deluxe-Moderate.* Rte. 108 (253–4277). Inn has cozy, pine-paneled rooms; it gets expensive in the chalets. Full breakfast. Pool, golf privileges. Color TV (cable).

Golden Eagle Motor Inn. *Expensive-Deluxe.* Rte. 108 (253–4811). Large motel on tastefully landscaped grounds; rooms equally well-done (and big), many with fireplace and balcony. Kitchenettes avail. Coffee shop (no dinners) with restaurant, the Partridge Inn, across the road. Heated pool, tennis, sauna, whirlpool, exercise room. Play area. Color TV.

Ten Acres Lodge. *Expensive.* Barrows Rd., off Moutain Rd. (253–7638 or 253–9576). Renowned for quality dining and gracious service. Despite the name, it's on a 40-acre spread. Game room.

Alpine Motor Lodge. *Moderate-Expensive.* Rte. 108 (253–7700). Small lodge, breakfast-only, set-up bar. Heated pool, putting green, golf privileges. Game room. Color TV.

Edson Hill Manor. *Moderate-Expensive.* Off Rte. 108 (253–7371). Elegant country inn with fireplaces and pine paneling. Excellent dining, fireside lunches and lounge. Pool, trout pond, riding. Scene of winter segment in Alan Alda's *The Four Seasons.*

Trapp Family Lodge. *Moderate-Expensive.* Luce Hill Rd., off Rte. 108 (253–8511). Regrouping after 1980 fire leveled photogenic main lodge. Rustic time-sharing cottages and modern lodge go with the motel annex, which survived the fire. Austrian Tea Room is off-limits to anyone on a diet. Heated pool. In winter, sweet, sweet cross-country skiing starts here.

Buccaneer Motel & Lodge. *Moderate.* Rte. 108 (253–4772). Full breakfast, in-room coffee, pine-paneling in rooms. Heated pool, lawn games. Fireside lounge. Childhood home of Olympic medalist and world champion skier Billy Kidd.

Country Squire Motor Lodge. *Moderate.* Rte. 100, south of village (253–4207). Alpine architecture, great view of Mt. Mansfield. In-room coffee, steam baths. Color TV (cable).

Grey Fox Inn. *Moderate.* Rte. 108 (253–8921). Pool, sauna. Home baked breads and desserts, fine dining. Color TV (cable).

Salzburg Motor Inn. *Moderate.* Rte. 108 (253–8541). Right next door to Innsbruck, another piece of Austria. Also fine dining; lounge. Indoor and outdoor pools, sauna, lawn games, game room. Color TV (cable)

Mountaineer Motor Inn. *Moderate.* Rte. 108 (253–7525). Dining room, fireside lounge. Indoor pool, picnic area, trout tream. Color TV (cable)

Spruce Pond Inn & Motel. *Moderate.* Rte. 100 south of village (253–4828). Excellent cuisine, deep wine cellar, lounge. Pond swimming, fishing, hiking. In winter, skating, cross-country skiing. Color TV (cable).

Ski Inn. *Moderate.* Rte. 108 (253–4050). Last stop before the company-owned stuff near the mtn., a 10-room, no-meals inn.

Yodler Motor Inn. *Moderate.* Rte. 108 (253–4836). Some kitchenettes. Homecooked meals. Heated pool. Tennis.

Golden Kitz Lodge. *Inexpensive-Moderate.* Rte. 108 (253–4217). Like a European pension; relax and enjoy. But BYOB.

Innsbruck Motor Inn. *Inexpensive-Moderate.* Rte. 108 (253–8582). As the name indicates, a slice of Austria, right down to crepes for breakfast. Dining room, bar. Sauna. Cross-country skiing.

VERGENNES. Basin Harbor Club. *Deluxe* (MAP). Off Rte. 22-A (475–2311). Distinguished resort on 700 acres fronting Lake Champlain. Heated pool, golf, tennis, boating, kids' programs in July and August. Private airstrip.

WATERBURY CENTER. Acorn Lodge. *Moderate.* Gregg Hill (244–5543). Small, unheralded, friendly spot. Double fireplace in dining room; reservations preferred. Pond swimming (and skating in winter). Closed Nov. and May.

Holiday Inn. *Moderate.* Rte. 100, Exit 10 off I–89 (244–7822). Pretty hillside perch; dining room, lounge. Heated pool, sauna, steam baths. Tennis, nature walks, hiking. Color TV (cable).

BED AND BREAKFAST. Vermont has not only joined the bed & breakfast phenomenon moving across the U.S. from Europe, it even has its own company. *American Bed & Breakfast* is based in the Green Mountain State, at Box 983F, St. Albans VT 05478.

There are several dozen families which have signed on with various B&B organizations or simply hung out their own sign. It's a simple concept: you get breakfast the next morning in addition to your room, all covered in the room rate.

In addition to American B&B, two other possible sources for information about B&B in Vermont: *New England B&B,* 1045 Center St., Newton Center MA 02159 (617–498–9819) and *Pineapple Hospitality,* 384 Rodney French Blvd., New Bedford MA 02744 (617–997–9952).

Among homes offering B&B in Vermont:

Bethel. *Poplar Manor* (802–234–5426). Early American (1810) home filled with antiques. Accommodations for singles, couples or families.

Reading. *Peeping Cow Inn* (802–484–5036). Remodeled farmhouse in small (pop. 672), rural community near Woodstock. French spoken. One twin-bedded room with bath.

St. Albans. *The Woodens* (802–524–6035). Victorian home on quiet street. One double room with bath.

YOUTH HOSTELS. Compact, scenic, rural, Vermont is ideal for cycling, biking, and hosteling. There is occasional turnover in hostel management, but Vermont has had these low-cost places since after World War II. Technically, you have to be a member of the American Youth Hostels, but some hostels let you stay as a guest while others sell memberships. In Vermont, you may stay at: Calais (229–4570); Colchester (878–8222); Craftsbury Common (586–2514); Montpelier (223–2104); Rochester (767–9384); Stowe (253–4010 or 253–4014); Underhill Center (899–2375); and Woodford (442–2547).

For more information, call tollfree to AYH headquarters (800–424–9426). Or write AYH, Box 37613, Washington, DC 20013–7613.

FARM VACATIONS. There is a group of farms which features vacation accommodations. There are 15 participating farms listed by the State Department of Agriculture or the *Vermont Travel Division,* Montpelier 05602. Most are dairy farms offering farmhouse meals and lodging. Some have cottages, camping facilities, and trailer hookups.

HOW TO GET AROUND. By air: There are a couple of intra-state flights, but Vermont is so compact (and the flights so infrequent) that it probably would be just as quick to drive along the interstates, unless you're in an incredible hurry.

There are general aviation facilities at Bennington, Morrisville (Stowe), Mt. Snow, Basin Harbor-Champlain, Middlebury, Springfield, Lyndonville, Newport and Highgate Springs. Air taxi service for charter air passengers is available at airfields in Barre-Montpelier, Bennington, Springfield, Rutland, Middlebury, and Burlington. There is jet charter service from Burlington; the other air fields offer twin-engine charters. Car rentals and courtesy cars are available at various air fields.

By bus: *Vermont Transit Lines,* 135 St. Paul St., Burlington (864–6811), has extensive bus routes throughout the state, connecting with *Greyhound* buses in other states.

By car: I–89 and I–91 allow a fast flow of traffic through much of the state. Part of I–91 follows the Connecticut River and the Passumpsic River. It enters Vermont in the southeasternmost corner and exits to Canada at Derby VT. I–89 picks up at White River Junction (where it connects to I–91) and proceeds northwest, through Randolph, Montpelier, Burlington, and St. Albans, entering

Canada at Highgate Springs, Vt. Both highways are very scenic. For information on highway conditions, phone the Vermont Agency of Transportation, Montpelier VT 05602 (862–2475).

Car rental: Major car rental firms have desks at the major airports and in cities throughout Vermont. Check the local Yellow Pages.

By bicycle: Vermont is made for bicycling. It is neither too flat nor too hilly, the distances are short and the scenery varied, there is an extensive network of secondary roads that are relatively free of cars and which bring you into close contact with the nature and people of the state, and there is a good infrastructure of experience, information, hostels and organizations available. Certain areas—around Lake Champlain, the valley of the Connecticut River—are less demanding, but the entire state can be traversed quite handily from north to south in a week, or less. The *North American Bicycle Atlas* and the *Youth Hostel Handbook,* both available from American Youth Hostels, Inc., are your best planning aids for a trip of this kind; and the Vermont Dept. of Forests, Parks and Recreation in Montpelier has a booklet entitled *Bicycle Touring in Vermont* that suggests a number of itineraries. Group tours are offered by *American Youth Hostels,* Rochester VT 05767; *Bike Vermont,* Box 75, Grafton VT 01546; *Green Mtn. Holidays,* Box 207, Rutland VT 05701; *Vermont Bicycle Touring,* Box 711, Bristol VT 05443; *Vermont Country Cyclers,* Box 146, Waterbury Center VT 05677. Recommended: *20 Bicycle Tours in Vermont* (N.H. Publishing, Box 70, Somersworth, N.H. 03878).

On foot: The *Long Trail* is a 263-mile hiking path extending from Williamstown, MA (just south of Vermont), to Canada. Part of the way, the *Appalachian Trail* follows the Long Trail. At Mendon (Rte. 4), or the *Sherburne Pass,* the Appalachian Trail goes east and crosses into Hanover, NH, about 30 miles later. The Long Trail passes over the highest of the three parallel Green Mountain Ranges. In some places it dips down to valley streams and passes ponds, but for the most part the trail is ruggedly elevated, crossing Vermont's four highest peaks: Killington, Mt. Ellen, Camel's Hump and Mt. Mansfield. Along the trail are some secondary hiking paths, which provide a good day's hike and are suggested for novices before they attempt any prolonged adventure. The Trail is protected, maintained, and supervised by the Green Mountain Club (P.O. Box 889, 43 State St., Montpelier VT 05602), which publishes two helpful works: The *Guidebook of the Long Trail* for that route, and, for shorter hiking elsewhere, *Day Hiking in Vermont.* Also recommended: *Fifty Hikes in Vermont* (available from N.H. Publishing, Somersworth, NH 03878). These should be carefully studied before you set out. Plan to travel in a small group to protect the ground; an at-large membership in the Club will aid its work.

 **TOURIST INFORMATION SERVICES.** The most important source of information on Vermont is the *Vermont Travel Division,* 134 State St., Montpelier VT 05602, (828–3236). Three times a year it publishes a calendar of seasonal events listing hundreds of functions, from sophisticated music festivals to local auctions and church suppers. The *Vermont Council on the Arts,* 136 State Street, Montpelier VT 05602, publishes its own seasonal calendar, *The Arts in Vermont,* which includes crafts, performing arts, museums, and literary events. Before you ever get to Vermont there are: 1) the *New England Vacation Center,* 630 Fifth Ave., New York City (212–307–5780); and, 2) the *Vermont Information Center,* 2051 Peel St., Montreal (514–845–9840). As you enter the state there are Welcome Centers on Interstate 91 at Guilford on the Massachusetts border, on Interstate 89 at Highgate Springs on the Canadian border, I-93 at Waterford and on Rte. 4 in Fair Haven. Ask for the *Vermont Vacation Guide, The Traveler's Guidebook,* and the *Official State Map.* Area chambers of commerce or lodging bureaus also can provide assistance:

Vermont State Ch. of Commerce, Box 37, Montpelier 05602 (223–3443);
Barton Ch. of Commerce, Box 280, Barton 05822;
Bellows Falls Ch. of Commerce, 55 Village Sq., Bellows Falls 05101 (463–4280);
Greater Bennington Ch. of Commerce, Rte. 7, Bennington 05201 (442–5900);
Brandon Ch. of Commerce, Box 28, Brandon 05733;

Brattleboro Area Ch. of Commerce, 180 Main St., Brattleboro 05301 (254–4565);

Central Vermont Ch. of Commerce, Box 336, Barre 05641 (229–4619);

Fair Haven Ch. of Commerce, Fair Haven 05743 (265–8144);

Greater Jay Area Ch. of Commerce, Jay 05859;

Smugglers' Notch Area Ch. of Commerce, Box 3264, Jeffersonville 05464 (644–5440);

Killington–Pico Area Assn., Box 114, Killington 05751 (775–7070);

Lakes Region, Box 77, Bomoseen 05732 (represents lakes west of Rutland);

Lake Champlain Reg'l Ch. of Commerce, 209 Battery St., Box 453, Burlington 05401 (863–3489);

Ludlow Area Ch. of Commerce, Box 174, Ludlow 05149;

Lyndonville Ch. of Commerce, Box 886, Lyndonville 05851;

Manchester & the Mtns Ch. of Commerce, Manchester Center 05255 (362–2100);

Addison County Ch. of Commerce, 35 Court St., Middlebury 05753 (388–7579);

Mt. Snow Region Ch. of Commerce, Box 3005, Wilmington 05363 (474–8092);

Greater Newport Ch. of Commerce, Causeway, Newport 05855 (334–7782);

Quechee Ch. of Commerce, Box 757, Quechee 05059 (295–7900);

Rutland Region Ch. of Commerce, Box 67, Rutland 05701 (773–2747);

St. Albans Ch. of Commerce, Box 327, St. Albans 05478 (524–2444);

St. Johnsbury Ch. of Commerce, 33 Main St., St. Johnsbury 05819 (748–3678);

Springfield Ch. of Commerce, Springfield 05156 (885–2779);

Stowe Area Assn., Box 1230, Stowe 05672 (253–7321);

Valley Area Assn., Box 173, Waitsfield 05673 (496–3409);

Windsor Area Ch. of Commerce, Box 5, Windsor 05089 (674–5910);

Woodstock Area Ch. of Commerce, Woodstock 05091 (457–3951);

 **RECOMMENDED READING.** *Let Me Show You Vermont,* by Charles Edward Crane; *Vermont Tradition,* by Dorothy Canfield Fisher; *A Guide to the Green Mountain State,* by Ray Bearse; *The New England States, People, Power and Politics,* by Neal R. Pierce (Norton, 1976), and issues of the quarterly *Vermont Life,* published at 61 Elm Street, Montpelier VT 05602. *Vermont—A Guide to the Green Mountain State* (Houghton Mifflin, 1968), in the American Guide Series, contains a thorough description of the state and its history, as does *The Big Green Book* (Crown, 1976). *The Shaping of Vermont,* (Vermont Heritage Press, 1983) was compiled by a University of Vermont historian and gives a good profile of the state's first century.

 **SEASONAL EVENTS.** This rural state is no sleepy backwater. One 3-month edition of the Travel Division's pamphlet *Special Events* lists 55 year-round attractions, 110 continuing attractions, and well over 300 events for the summer months alone. Here we can only indicate the main types of seasonal events and specify a few of the most important ones: auctions, antique shows, bazaars and flea markets, church suppers, music festivals, summer theater, horse shows, crafts shows, historical festivals and pageants, town and regional fairs, sugaring and foliage festivals, summer and winter sports and carnivals.

During the winter months, skiing is the most popular pursuit. Until recently, alpine skiing was the heavy favorite; however, cross-country skiing, or ski touring, is fast catching up. The ski season usually begins in October for Killington and Sugarbush, by Thanksgiving for other major areas. It continues into April for everyone, and into May for the biggest areas. Middlebury College and the University of Vermont hold winter carnivals, as do groups in Brattleboro, Stowe, Ludlow, Woodstock, Springfield and the Burke-Lyndonville area. The state and various localities have set aside clearly marked areas for snowmobiling.

The *Vermont Philharmonic,* P.O. Box 826, Montpelier 05602, gives four main concerts and various special ones during the year. The *Vermont Symphony Orchestra,* 77 College St., Burlington 05401, founded in 1935, was the first state symphony orchestra in the country. It tours the state during the winter, and again in July, with a series of eight summer concerts. The *Vermont Farm Show* is held in Barre in February.

In the spring, the major event is sugaring. The production of maple products is observable at countless sugarhouses, including a couple of commercial places, throughout the state—just look for the smoking sugarhouses.

Summer brings antiques, art and craft shows and demonstrations around the state. Participating artists are both native and out-of-state people. Summer stock is presented at several theaters, notably the *Dorset Playhouse* and the *Weston Playhouse*. *Aquatic competitions* are held during the summer on Lake Champlain and on many of the state's 400 lakes.

Fall harvest and the turning of the leaves inspire festivals in all parts of Vermont. Some fairs are held in August before vacationers leave the state. Others are held in September and October to celebrate the bountiful harvest. Community programs are planned around the brilliant foliage displays, and bus tours around the state visit these.

Some other seasonal events you may want to try to catch are:

April. St. Albans celebrates the flow of syrup with the *Franklin County Maple Syrup Festival* in early or mid–April.

May. Outing and canoe clubs sponsor *slalom championships* on West River, Jamaica.

June. Burlington holds a month-long *"Discovery" festival* on the shores of Lake Champlain; Quechee's annual *hot air balloon festival* in late June.

July. Barre holds a two-day *Ethnic Festival* at mid month and Newbury's *Cracker Barrel Bazaar* (with fiddlin' contest at night) is in late July. Norwich hosts a weekend *quilt festival* in mid-July. Castleton celebrates *Colonial Day* and has open house in midsummer. The Fleming Art Museum and the Southern Vermont Art Center, in Burlington and Manchester respectively, host impressive exhibits. One of the most exciting events is the series of concerts given by the *Marlboro Music Festival* at Marlboro College during July and August.

August. Stratton Mtn. hosts top pros in the *Volvo International Tennis Tournament* in early August. Stowe has a unique *antique car rally* in August. The *Champlain Shakespeare Festival,* staged by professionals, begins in August and runs through October in the University of Vermont's Royall Tyler Theatre, Burlington. A favorite equestrian event staged by the Green Mountain Horse Association of South Woodstock is the *100-Mile Trail Ride,* which originates at South Woodstock during the last weekend in August. The *Addison County Field Days* are held in New Haven and feature horse shows and cattle judging.

September. The month-long *Stratton Arts Festival* at Stratton Mountain begins in mid-September. Bennington has an *antique car rally.* A week-long *State Fair* is held in Rutland. At Tunbridge, a 4-day *World's Fair* is held in mid-September. Danville holds its annual *Dowsing Convention* in September.

October. Montpelier has a *Square Dance Festival* in October and a statewide crafts fair on Columbus Day weekend. An outstanding regional festival is the *Fall Foliage Festival* of Northeast Kingdom, involving the villages of Walden, Cabot, Marshfield, Peacham, Barnet Center, and Groton, held in early October.

FALL FOLIAGE. Mother Nature's pyrotechnics every fall draw hundreds of thousands of tourists to Vermont to catch the changing colors of the leaves. It is a spectacular (and frantic) time. Two bits of advice: make certain you make lodging reservations ahead of time—don't just figure you'll "find a spot along the way" because you probably won't; the state gets mobbed—and, if possible, travel midweek because the weekends are especially hectic. The same phenomenon that creates maple sugar "runs" in March causes the changing colors, i.e., cool nights and warm days that trigger internal combustion in the trees; because Vermont is so blessed with maple trees, its foliage usually is exceedingly colorful. However, poor weather can mute the colors. Nonetheless, tourists will flock to the state because they've made plans and they're coming ahead anyway, so get those reservations in advance. Some roads, such as Rte. 4 from White River Junction to Rutland or Rte. 7 from Bennington almost all the way to Burlington, become especially crowded, so you may want to stick to the interstates—I–91 is particularly gorgeous in the Northeast Kingdom in and around St. Johnsbury—or head for the other secondary roads, away from the primary routes such as Rtes. 2, 4, 5, 7 and 9. One special route is Rte. 125 between Hancock and Middlebury, up and over Middlebury Gap. The foliage is at its peak up north in mid-September, moving down the state to explode in the Woodstock-Rutland belt by the first week of October, in southern Vermont around Columbus Day.

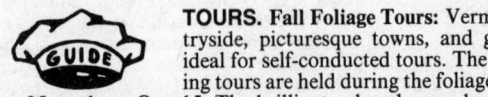

TOURS. Fall Foliage Tours: Vermont's beautiful countryside, picturesque towns, and green forestlands are ideal for self-conducted tours. The most popular motoring tours are held during the foliage period, usually from Sept. 25 to about Oct. 15. The brilliant color changes begin by the third week of September in the upper reaches of the Green Mountains and radiate southward to the Massachusetts line. The variations in color depend greatly on climatic conditions.

We would suggest the following tours: *Burlington to Swanton* via Rtes. 2 and 78; *Swanton to Stowe* via Rtes. 78, 36 and 108; *Stowe to Burlington* via Rtes. 100, 2 and 7 (approx. 180 mi.). *Rutland to Middlebury* via Rtes. 4A, 30, 73, 74 and 30; *Middlebury to Brandon* via Rtes. 7, 100 and 73; *Brandon to Rutland* via Rtes. 7 and 3 (approx. 130 mi.); *Montpelier to Lyme* via Rtes. 302, 110, 113, 113A; *Lyme to Woodstock* via Rtes. 10 and 4; *Woodstock to Montpelier* via Rte. 12 (approx. 150 mi.). *Bennington to Newfane* via Rtes. 9, 8, 100 and 30; *Newfane to Ludlow* via Rtes. 30, 35, 121 and 103; *Ludlow to Bennington* via Rtes. 100, 30, 11 and 7 (approx. 150 mi.).

The *Vermont Travel Division* publishes a brochure with 13 proposed scenic tours which take the motorist along marked paved roads lined with flaming colors in fall. Adequate housing accommodations are available in these areas.

SPECIAL-INTEREST TOURS. Agriculture: A number of farms and farm-product establishments sponsor the *Red Clover Trail.* These places welcome visitors; you can observe dairying, maple syrup and honey production, cattle and sheep raising, horse breeding, and cheese manufacture. Participants display a red clover to identify themselves as members of this program to bring agriculture closer to those who do not ordinarily have the chance to see life on a farm. Some of the Red Clover members will accept overnight guests.

Mountain Rides in Summer Months: The traditional scenic rides at ski areas include gondola rides at *Mount Snow, Killington,* and *Stowe* plus the tram ride at *Jay Peak.* There also are the Alpine Slide rides in summer at *Bromley* (three tracks, including the world's longest—4,600 feet), *Stowe's Spruce Peak* (two tracks), and *Pico* near Rutland (two tracks).

Covered Bridges: Vermont may have had between 500 and 1,000 covered bridges; 114 survive. They are marked on the highway map and on a special covered-bridge map available from the *Vermont Agency of Transportation.* Montpelier VT 05602. The largest grouping is in Lamoille County, east of Burlington, which has 16. The town of Montgomery has six. The *Pulp Mill Bridge* in Middlebury, a rare two-way span, is the oldest (1820). The longest is the *Scott Covered Bridge* in Townshend. The *Wolcott Covered Railroad Bridge* at Wolcott is the last railroad covered bridge in the U.S. still in use.

Horse Farm: The *University of Vermont Morgan Horse Farm,* Weybridge, welcomes visitors year round. Guided tours May through Oct. The last Sat. in May there is a 4-H Field Day and horse show: *Pond Hill Ranch* in Castleton has rodeos every Sat. night.

NATIONAL FORESTS. The *Green Mountain National Forest* in central and southern Vermont follows the main ranges of the Green Mountains. Established in 1928, the forest comprises 294,522 acres, flanked or traversed by U.S. 4, U.S. 7, and Rtes. 11 and 100. For maps and information write to: Forest Supervisor, Green Mountain National Forest, Box 519, 151 West Street, Rutland VT 05701. There are Ranger offices in Manchester Center, Middlebury, Rochester, and across the state line in Montou Falls NY.

Winter resorts predominate at the well-developed private facilities within the forest; there are six alpine areas (*Bromley, Carinthia, Haystack, Prospect, Mount Snow,* and *Sugarbush*) and five nordic centers (*Blueberry Hill Inn, Churchill House Inn, Mountain Top Inn, Wild Wings,* and *Nordic Inn*) which have trails within the forest.

Summer camping is featured at *Hapgood Pond, Greendale, Red Mill Brook, North Hartland Dam, Chittenden Brook,* and *Moosalamoo.* These areas, built and operated by the Forest Service, are on a first-come, first-served basis. No reservations are accepted and a daily camping fee of $4 or $5 is charged. A fourteen-day stay per family is maximum in summer. Fishing and hunting licenses may be obtained at the town clerk's offices. Adirondack shelters for overnight lodging are at 6-mile intervals along the 263-mile *Long Trail,* the well-known and well-traversed hiking route of which 130 miles are within the forest system. Good roads wind through opulent scenic areas. Trout are stocked in 23 lakes and ponds and 250 miles of streams. Forest officers are stationed in Middlebury, Rochester and Manchester Center.

Golden Age Passports, which provide a 50 percent discount on family camping and swimming fees, are available free of charge at the *U.S. Forest Service* offices in Rutland, Middlebury, Rochester and Manchester Center. These passports are issued to persons showing proof of being 62 years of age or older.

STATE PARKS AND FORESTS. Vermont has about 210,000 acres of public land in 45 state parks, 34 state forests and 2 recreation areas. This land is open to general recreational use except for motorized vehicles. The recreation areas of the parks and forests open to the public the Fri. preceding Memorial Day and close the Tues. after Columbus Day. The chief source of information on the locations, facilities, and regulations for the use of these lands is the Agency of Environmental Conservation, Montpelier. The Agency's Department of Forests, Parks and Recreation publishes a *Vermont Guide to State Parks and Forest Recreation Areas;* its Fish & Game Department issues a *Guide to Hunting* and a *Guide to Fishing.*

There's much variety offered at these areas to those who enjoy being outdoors. Aside from the winter sports, there are fair-weather activities to enjoy, such as swimming, fishing, boating, camping, and hiking in the state parks. *Mt. Mansfield State Forest* (33,840 acres) is a challenge to hiker and skier alike. Mt. Mansfield is the state's highest peak (4,393 ft.). *Allis State Park,* a recreation paradise, is reached via Rte. 14 over the *Brookfield Floating Bridge. D.A.R. State Park,* at Lake Champlain (Rte. 17), contains an historic area dating from before the Revolutionary War. Now it is used for picnic and shelter purposes. *Monroe State Park,* at the eastern base of Camel's Hump (in the Green Mountains), is maintained partly as a bird sanctuary and a botanical and game preserve. A beautiful sandy beach sparkles at *Branbury State Park* along the eastern shore of Lake Dunmore, between Middlebury and Brandon. The *Killington Ski Resort* is a focal point of the *Calvin Coolidge State Forest,* which also preserves the Calvin Coolidge Farm, where Coolidge was born, sworn in as president upon the 1923 death of Warren Harding and is buried beside his wife. *Emerald Lake State Park,* in Dorset off U.S. 7, is a beautiful area and a "complete park" with woodland picnic areas, campsites, foot trails and an emerald-green lake for swimming and boating.

CAMPING. The Department of Forests, Parks and Recreation operates 35 campgrounds with 2,200 campsites. Trailer sites are available at many of the campgrounds. The campgrounds open officially the Fri. preceding Memorial Day and close the Tues. after Columbus Day. Dates are subject to change and campers should always check with the individual campground or the *Department of Forests, Parks and Recreation,* Montpelier VT 05602, if they intend to camp early or late in the season. Camping reservations may be made with the Department of Forests, Parks and Recreation, Montpelier, for not less than six nights and not more than three weeks. Requests should be sent from January 1 to May 1. Apply directly to the individual park after May 1. No reservations are needed after Labor Day. Nominal fees are asked for camping and lean-to shelter reservations, and they must be paid in advance. A fee of 50 or 75 cents is charged daily to every person entering a park or forest.

The Department has opened three areas for youth-group camping. Groups must consist of youths under 18 years and be supervised by at least one adult. The groups must have an affiliation with an organization such as a church, Scout troop, school, 4-H club, etc. Youth Group areas are available year round except during the rifle deer-hunting season in November. One of the youth areas is *Kettle Pond,* located in the *Groton Forest,* 25 miles east of Montpelier, approached by U.S. 2 or U.S. 302. For information and reservations write *Park Manager, Groton State Forest,* Marshfield VT 05658. The others are *Underhill,* in the *Mt. Mansfield State Forest* 17 miles east of Essex Junction, and *Shaftsbury State Park,* 10 miles north of Bennington.

The Department has also designated certain areas in the *Groton* and *Coolidge State Forests* as rustic or primitive campsites. These can be reached only by foot.

Vermont has about 90 private campgrounds. Reservations are made directly with each individual campground. Write to the *Vermont Association of Private Campground Owners and Operators,* c/o Brattleboro North KOA, RD 2, Box 110, Putney VT 05346, for a free brochure.

SUMMER SPORTS. Golf: There are 41 public golf courses in Vermont, 8 in the south, 10 in the central part, 19 in the northwest, and 4 in the northeast. The following are among the best in Vermont: *Mount Snow G.C.,* West Dover. A rolling course at 2,000 ft. *Haystack,* Wilmington. New *Desmond Muirhead* course with spectacular mountain scenery. *Lake Morey Inn & C.,* Fairlee. Lakeside, rolling. Site of annual *Vermont Open. Crown Point C.C.,* Springfield. Flat, pretty. *Equinox Hotel & C.C.,* Manchester. Superbly groomed, rolling course. *Manchester C.C.* Attractive layout. *Stratton Mountain C.C.,* Stratton Mt. Designed by Geoffrey Cornish. *Sugarbush G.C.,* Warren. Robert Trent Jones course. *Stowe C.C.,* also Cornish-designed with large, well-trapped green. Open to guests of Stowe member lodges. *Woodstock C.C.,* Woodstock. Robert Trent Jones course in beautiful valley with brook. *Basin Harbor C.,* Vergennes. Bordered by woodland and Lake Champlain. In addition, there are 11 18-hole courses and 26 9-hole courses, some of which are open only to guests of certain hotels and lodges. Inquire locally. There's also an 11-hole course in Stamford. *The Stratton Mountain Golf Academy* is located at Stratton Mountain resort near Manchester and the *Mount Snow Golf School* is at that southern Vermont resort.

Tennis: Many resorts, such as Killington, Bolton Valley and Stratton Mountain, offer weekend or midweek programs with meals, lodging, instruction and social activities. Your best information on public outdoor courts will come from local municipal offices and parks departments, schools, and colleges. In summer there is a major tennis layout at Bolton Valley resort; Stowe (Topnotch, Inn at the Mtn., Stowehof); Jeffersonville (Smugglers' Notch resort & Windridge Tennis Camp); Warren (Sugarbush Inn & the Sugarbush Sports Center at Sugarbush Village); Cortina Inn near Rutland; Killington (Summit Lodge & the resort's School for Tennis); Stratton Mtn resort; Jay Peak; and Woodstock. There are indoor courts at Stowe, Rutland, South Burlington, the Sugarbush Sports Center in Warren, Bolton Valley, Woodstock and Smugglers' Notch. Top tennis pros play at Stratton Mtn. in early Aug. in the Volvo International.

Riding: From late May to late Sept., there are more than 30 riding events that occur in Vermont. Arlington, Brookfield, Proctorsville, Woodstock, Killington, and Windsor are just some of the villages in which riding events take place and where stables are located. Most of the stables offer trail rides, instruction, and boarding. During the last weekend in Aug., the *Green Mt. Horse Association of South Woodstock* has a 100-mile trail ride. For a listing of rental areas write: the *Vermont Travel Division.* Montpelier, VT 05602.

Boating: Canoe, sailboat, rowboat, and motorboat rentals are available throughout the state. In most state parks, rowboats and canoes are for rent. Canoeing is best in the spring, when the waters are high.

Lake Champlain is a favorite area for summer boating; other good spots are: St. Catherine, Seymour, Bomoseen, Memphremagog, Dunmore, Fairlee, Caspian. For a listing of rental areas write the *Vermont Travel Division.*

Hunting and fishing: The hunting season begins in Oct. and ends in Nov. Fishing starts in the early part of Apr. and extends through Oct., though some fishing can be done almost year round. All licenses are available from local town or city clerks. Nonresidents may apply by mail; but they must hold licenses in their own states, have held licenses in Vermont, or prove that they have passed a course in hunting safety. For full information contact the *Vermont Fish & Game Dept.,* Montpelier VT 05602; ask for its special booklets, *Guide to Hunting* and *Guide to Fishing.*

Hiking and Backpacking: Several organizations offer conducted hiking, backpacking, camping and rock climbing expeditions. *Killington Adventure,* Killington VT 05751 operates one-week outings that begin with 2 days of training, then 5 days in the mountains. *Dakin's Vermont Mountain Shop,* 227 Main St., Burlington VT 05401, takes small (3–5) groups of people for 1- and 2-day climbs. *Hike-Skitour Vermont,* RFD 1-A, Chester VT 05143 offers week-end backpacking trips and 1- and 2-week trips that include hiking, canoeing, horseback riding and cycling.

 **WINTER SPORTS.** Alpine and cross-country skiing, skating, snowshoeing, ice fishing, snowmobiling are things to do during the winter.

Alpine: Novice-Expert runs are at: *Killington,* Sherburne, with the world's longest gondola lift and 40-plus miles of machinemade snow covering a 3,060-ft. vertical drop; *Sugarbush Valley* resort—*Sugarbush* in Warren with a 2,400-ft. drop and *Sugarbush North* in Fayston with a 2,600-ft. drop; *Stowe,* with a gondola and a 2,150-ft. drop; *Okemo,* Ludlow, with a 2,150-ft. drop; *Jay Peak,* Jay, with a tramway, a 2,100-ft. drop; *Smugglers' Notch,* Jeffersonville, with a 2,610-ft. drop spread over three peaks; *Mad River Glen,* Waitsfield, with a 2,000-ft. drop; *Pico,* Sherburne, with a 1,967-ft. drop; *Stratton Mt.,* Stratton, with a 1,900-ft. drop; *Mt. Snow.,* W. Dover, with 2 gondolas and a 1,900-ft. drop; *Burke Mt.,* E. Burke, with a 2,000-ft drop; *Magic Mt.,* Londonderry, with a 1,500-ft. drop; *Ascutney,* Windsor, with a 1,530-ft. drop; *Bromley,* Peru, with a 1,385-ft. drop; *Bolton Valley,* Bolton, with a 1,100-ft. drop; *Middlebury Snow Bowl,* Middlebury, with a 1,100-ft. drop. Others, less challenging: *Maple Valley,* W. Dummerston, with an 850-ft. drop; *Prospect,* Bennington, with a 650-ft. drop; *Suicide Six,* S. Pomfret, with a 600-ft. drop; *Snow Valley,* Manchester, with a 575-ft. drop; *Timber Ridge,* Windham, with an 800-ft. drop; *Sonnenburg,* Barnard, with a 500-ft. drop; *Hogback,* Marlboro, with a 500-ft. drop; *Haystack,* Wilmington, with 1,400-ft. drop.

Cross-country skiing may be enjoyed at more than 60 touring centers; among the best: *Woodstock; Blueberry Hill* in Goshen; *Craftsbury Common; Stratton Mt.; Living Memorial Park* in Brattleboro; *Tater Hill* in Chester; *Trapp Family Lodge* in Stowe; *Sugarbush Inn* in Warren; *Mountain Meadows* in Killington; *Tucker Hill Lodge* in Waitsfield; and *Mountain Top Inn* in Chittenden. A 60-km. race is held in early Feb. from Ripton to Brandon.

Snowmobiling: Snowmobiling is forbidden on public highways, except to cross, and on privately owned land or water except with written consent of the owner. On public lands snowmobiles are forbidden except in six areas designated by the Agency of Environmental Conservation, which publishes maps of them. Privately, it is allowed at *Bread Loaf, Bridgewater, Castleton, Chittenden, Cornwall, E. Thetford, Hardwich, Landgrove, Ludlow, Lunenburg-Wilderness Farms Skimobile Resort, Manchester, Middleton Springs, Montpelier, Newport, Orleans, Plymouth, Ripton, Rochester, St. Johnsbury, Shrewsbury, Springfield, Stowe, Townshend, Victory-Henderson's in the Hills, Waitfield, Waterbury, Oxbow Mountain in West Bolton,* and *W. Dover.*

Ice skating: There are rinks at *Killington, Middlebury Snow Bowl, Mt. Snow, Oxbow Mountain,* and *Sugarbush Valley* ski areas and countless ponds or lakes statewide.

CHILDREN'S ACTIVITIES. A certain number of farms in Vermont, designated by a Red Clover emblem, allow tourists to visit their barns; your child can see a real cow (see above, *Special Interest Tours*). *Santa's Land, U.S.A.*, north of Putney, a Christmas fairyland in summertime, includes Santa's Alpine Railroad. The *Shelburne Museum* (Rte. 7), south of Burlington, comprises 35 early American buildings on 45 acres. *The Springfield Library,* 43 Main St., has a special reading, activity room for children. *Dana House,* Woodstock, has a children's room with doll exhibit and doll houses. When children reach the age of interest in things mechanical, the *American Precision Museum* in Windsor is a good bet. *The Discovery Museum* (51 Park St., 878-8687) in Essex Junction combines hands-on fun with exploration and education. Other sites likely to appeal to children are: the *Fairbanks Museum of Natural Science and Planetarium,* in St. Johnsbury; the *Fleming Museum,* in Burlington; the *Vermont Historical Society,* in Montpelier; the *Hyde Log Cabin,* in Grand Isle; the *Old School Museum,* in East Burke; and the *Eureka School House,* in Springfield. Also riding on the various Lake Champlain ferries and visiting maple sugar houses. *Frog Hollow,* the state Crafts center in Middlebury, sponsors a frog-jumping contest each July. For detailed information on the above, also see the *Museums and Galleries* and *Historic Sites and Homes* sections.

HISTORIC SITES AND HOMES. In 1961, the Vermont Board of Historic Sites was established by people eager to preserve the state's heritage. For a complete guide to Vermont's historical sites, write to Vermont Division for Historic Preservation, Montpelier 05602.

SOUTHERN REGION

BENNINGTON. *Bennington Battle Monument,* Rte. 9, Old Bennington. The 306-ft. stone monolith was built in 1891 to commemorate an attack by America's General John Stark on General Burgoyne's troops during the Revolutionary War. The battle occurred on August 16, 1777. Open daily, Apr. 1 to Oct. 31.

Old First Church. Rte. 9, Old Bennington. Photogenic clapboard church with box pews, high pulpit; graveyard contains remains of Revolutionary War soldiers and poet Robert Frost. Open daily spring through fall.

Park-McCullough Mansion, Off Rte. 67A, North Bennington (442–2747). 35-room Victorian mansion (1865) built by lawyer and rail tycoon. Period furniture, elegant surroundings. Guided tours July 1 to mid-Oct.; off-season tours by appointment.

BROOKLINE. *Round schoolhouse,* off Rte. 30. Built in 1822; still used for some town functions but hasn't been used as a school since 1928.

DUMMERSTON. *Naulahka,* Kipling Rd. Built in early 1890s, former estate of Rudyard Kipling and normally not open to the public.

GRAFTON. *Old Tavern,* Rte. 35 (843–2375). Handsomely restored inn (1801) spread over three buildings; 34 rooms, some with four-posters and canopies. Guests: U.S. Grant, Teddy Roosevelt, Woodrow Wilson, Kipling, Paul Newman and Joanne Woodward.

WHITINGHAM. *Brigham Young Monument,* east of Sadawga Pond, off Rte. 100. Mormon leader was born in this southern Vermont hamlet and the monument says so.

CENTRAL REGION

HUBBARDTON. *Hubbardton Battlefield and Museum,* 7 mi. off Rte. 4 (273–2282). Site of a brief Revolutionary War battle on July 7, 1777—the lone Revolutionary scrap staged in Vermont. Visitor's reception center and museum. Open late May to mid Oct., daily except Mon. and Tues.

PLYMOUTH UNION. *Calvin Coolidge Homestead,* Rte. 100A (672–3773). Birthplace of the former president. 7 restored buildings include homestead, birthplace, church and store. Coolidge is buried nearby in family plot. Visitors center with museum. Open late May to mid-Oct., daily.

PROCTOR. *Vermont Marble Company* exhibit hall, off Rte. 3 (459–3311). Production center for marble company, 20-minute movie of the story of marble, chance to watch artisans at work. Open daily mid-May to late-Oct., 9 to 5:30 P.M.

SHARON. *Joseph Smith Memorial,* off Rte. 14. 38-foot granite obelisk marks birthplace of Mormon founder; landscaped site on 360-acre tract.

STRAFFORD. *Justin Smith Morrill Homestead,* south of the village common. Onetime home of the man who authored the Land Grants Act which paved the way for many colleges to be opened. Open daily except Mon., mid-May to Columbus Day.

SPRINGFIELD. *Eureka Schoolhouse* and covered bridge, on Rte. 11 between Springfield and Exit 7 off I–91. Oldest (1785) schoolhouse in Vermont. Open late May to mid-Oct.

WINDSOR. *Old Constitution House,* on Rte. 5 (674–6628). Former tavern where the Republic of Vermont was declared in July 1777. Open daily except Mon., late May to mid-Oct.
Windsor House, Main St. (Rte. 5) in heart of downtown (674–6729). One of state's two crafts centers located on first floor.
Cornish-Windsor Covered Bridge, Union St., just off Rte. 5. Built in 1866 and, at 460 feet, the nation's longest covered bridge.

WOODSTOCK. *Dana House,* 26 Elm St. (457–1822). Built in 1807, this is headquarters for Woodstock Historical Society. Open late May to Oct. 31.
DAR House & Museum, Prospect St. Another 1807 gem. Revolutionary-era furnishings, memorabilia from Woodstock R.R. Summer only.

NORTHERN REGION

ADDISON. *General Strong Mansion,* Rte. 17. 1795 historic house furnished in period. Collections of china and glass. Open May 15 to Oct. 15, 10 to 5P.M. Closed Tues.

FAIRFIELD. *President Chester A. Arthur's Birthplace,* off Rte. 36 or 108. Reproduction of original house in a 35-acre park. Open mid-June to Sept., daily except Mon. and Tues.

MONTPELIER. *State House,* on State St. Your basic golden-domed State House, made of granite and set on a knoll with a broad, sloping lawn. Public invited to watch legislature in session. Revolutionary War cannon captured at Battle of Bennington and military flags among artifacts on display.

RIPTON. *Robert Frost's Cabin,* Rte. 125. Home to the late poet in the last years of his life; open by advance appointment through Middlebury College (388–3711).

GRAND ISLE. *Hyde Log Cabin,* U.S. 2. Built in 1783, it is the oldest log cabin in the U.S. Open July 4 through Labor Day, daily 10:30 to 5 P.M.

 MUSEUMS AND GALLERIES. Vermont's historic, cultural and artistic memorabilia are preserved in several of the state's museums and galleries. There are historical societies and museums in many of the towns throughout the state and if you have the time, they're worth a visit.

SOUTHERN REGION

BENNINGTON. *The Bennington Museum,* Rte. 9 (442–2180). Houses one of the best collections of early Americana including American glass and Bennington Pottery. The *Grandma Moses Schoolhouse* and paintings are part of the museum. Open Mar. 1 to Nov. 30, 9 to 5 P.M.

BRATTLEBORO. *Brattleboro Museum and Art Center,* Old Railroad Station, Vernon St. (257–0124). Contains Estey Organs and changing art and historical exhibits. Open May 1 to Dec. 1, Tues. through Sun., 1 to 4 P.M.

GRAFTON. *Grafton Historical Museum,* Main St. Open Memorial Day weekend to Columbus Day. Sat. in June; weekends and holidays July and Aug; Sat. and holiday weekends Sept. and Oct. until closing. 2:30 to 4:30 P.M. Exhibits local memorabilia.

MANCHESTER. *Southern Vermont Art Center,* off West Rd. (362–1405). Paintings, sculptures, prints, photography. Open daily except Mon. June to mid Oct. 10 to 5 P.M. Sun. Noon to 5 P.M.
Museum of American Fly Fishing, Rte. 7 at Orvis Co. showroom (362–3300). Open daily, free. A to Z on fly fishing at the home of renowned equipment manufacturer.

MARLBORO. *Luman Nelson Museum of New England Wildlife,* Rte. 9, Hogback Mt. (464–5494). Open daily (except Thanksgiving and Christmas), 9 to 5 P.M. Name says it all: stuffed exhibits of species found in New England.

NEWFANE. *Windham County Historical Museum,* Rte. 30. Open May to Nov. Sun 2:30 to 5P.M. Local memorabilia on display.

ROCKINGHAM. *Old Meetinghouse Museum,* Rte. 103. One of Vermont's oldest churches (1787), handsome in its white, clapboard, two-story simplicity.

SHAFTSBURY. *Peter Matteson Tavern* (Topping Tavern Museum), East Rd. off Rte. 7 (442–5225). Restored 18th-century public house. Furniture, antique tools and early breeds of farm animals. Open daily except Mon., May 1 to Nov. 1, 9–6P.M.

CENTRAL REGION

BROOKFIELD. *Marvin Newton House,* Ridge Rd. Historical society museum featuring Vermont memorabilia. Open July and Aug. Sun. 2 to 5 P.M.

DANBY. *Peel Gallery,* Rte. 7 (293–5230). Open daily except Tues. from 10 to 5 P.M. Ex-foreign service officer and his wife have graciously remodeled old barn and silo into rustic yet refined gallery. Heavy on regional artists.

EAST POULTNEY. *East Poultney Historical Society Museum,* Rte. 140, across from East Poultney Baptist Church. Open daily in summer, weekends otherwise. Local memorabilia and artifacts in two buildings.

LUDLOW. *Black River Academy Museum,* High St. Calvin Coolidge was an 1890 graduate. Displays Vermont and other local artifacts. Open May 26 to Oct. 13, 9 to 5P.M.

MIDDLEBURY. *The Sheldon Museum,* Park St. (388–2117). Open June 1 to Oct 15, daily 10 to 5 P.M. except Sun. and holidays; winter by appointment only. Tours on hour. "Window" on life in 19th century; three-story home serves as museum with displays ranging from blacksmith shop to tavern to formal parlor.

PLYMOUTH. *Vermont Agricultural Museum,* at the Coolidge Homestead (672–3773). Part of the Coolidge Historic Site, it's a modest museum in a century-old barn. More an oversized collection of tools, buggies and other farm gear than a true museum. Open mid-May to late-Oct., 9:30 to 5:30P.M.

PROCTOR. *Wilson Castle,* West Proctor Rd., off Rte 4 (773–3284). 19th-century architectural masterpiece containing European and East Asian furnishings. Guided tours. Open daily 8 to 6P.M.

RUTLAND. *Chaffee Art Gallery,* Rte. 7 (775–0356). Changing exhibits and special events. Open Mon. through Fri., 10 to 5P.M.; Sun. 11 to 4 P.M.
   Norman Rockwell Museum, Rte. 4, east of Rutland (773–6095). Open daily. Museum in a garage; extensive collection of Rockwell prints.

SPRINGFIELD. *Springfield Art & Historical Society,* 9 Elm Hill (885–2415). Features Bennington pottery, Richard Lee pewter, primitive portraits, dolls, carriages and changing art exhibits. Open May to Dec. Mon. through Fri., Noon to 4:30 P.M.

WAITSFIELD. *Millhouse/Bundy Performing and Fine Arts Center,* Rte. 100, south of village (496–3713). Art gallery, music, drama, dance. Open daily 10 to 4P.M.

WESTON. *Farrar-Mansur House,* on Green. 1797 Tavern, guided tours. Open on weekends from Memorial Day to July 4 and Labor Day through mid-Oct., Tues. through Sat., 1 to 5P.M.; Sun. 2 to 5 P.M. July 4 to Labor Day.

WINDSOR. *American Precision Museum,* 196 Main St. (Rte. 5)(674–5781). Hand and machine tools, precision machinery from the Industrial Revolution. Open May 26 to Nov. 1, 9 to 5 P.M.

WOODSTOCK. *Billings Farm Museum,* Rte. 12 at River Rd. (457–2355). Century-old farm recycled to spotlight life on a Vermont farm circa 1890. Rockefeller-funded, first-class production. Open May 15–Oct. 31.
   Charles Fenton Gallery., Woodstock East off Rte. 4 (457–3022). Works by regional artists. Mon. through Fri. 9 to 5P.M.; Sat. 11 to 4P.M. year round.
   Gallery 2, 65 Central St. (457–1171). Fine arts gallery specializing in Vermont artists. Sculpture garden in summer. Open daily except Sun. 10 to 5P.M.

NORTHERN REGION

BARRE. *Barre Historical Society Museum,* Washington St., 2nd floor of Aldrich Public Library (479–0450). Focus on the granite industry and ethnic heritage of the city. Hours vary, so call for details. Free.

BURLINGTON. *Robert Hull Museum,* Univ. of Vermont, Colchester Ave. (656–2090). Open year round, 9 to 5 P.M. Mon. through Fri.; 1 to 5 P.M. Sat. and Sun. Closed holidays. Free. Series of permanent and changing exhibits, from pre-Columbian art to textile displays.

CALAIS. *Kent Tavern Museum* at the (unpaved) crossroads in Kents Corners (828–2291). 1837 stage stop attached to country store. Miniature rooms, spinning and weaving rooms, herb garden. Open July to Labor Day and during Fall foliage season from noon to 5 P.M., Tues. through Sun.

FAIRLEE. *Walker Museum,* Rte. 5 (333–9572). Former two-story schoolhouse converted to museum several years ago. Americans as well as art exhibits. Open mid-June to Labor Day.

FERRISBURG. *Rokeby Museum,* Rte. 7 (877–3406). Home of Rowland E. Robinson, Vermont writer. Contains 18th- and 19th-century antiques and decorative arts. Also was a stop on the Underground Railroad. Open May 15 to Oct. 15, Mon. through Sat., 9:30 to 5 P.M.; Sun. 11:30 to 5 P.M. Closed Tues.

MONTPELIER. *Vermont Museum,* Pavilion Bldg., 109 State St. (828–2291). Open Mon. through Fri., 8 to 4:30 P.M.; Sat. and Sun. 10 to 5 P.M. July, Aug. and foliage season. Vermont in a nutshell. Period rooms, exhibits; first printing press in colonies.
Wood Art Gallery, 135 Main St. (229–0036). Over 250 originals and prints of Thomas Waterman Wood paintings and works by other American artists of the 1920s and '30s. Changing monthly exhibits. Open Tues. through Sat., noon to 4 P.M.; June through Sept. Sat. 9 to 1 P.M.

MORRISVILLE. *The Noyes House,* Rte. 100. Houses the historical society museum. Open June through Sept. daily except Mon 2 to 5 P.M. or by appointment.

SHELBURNE. *Shelburne Museum,* Rte. 9 (442–2180). 100 acres of Americana in 35 early American buildings. Features include the sidewheeler steamer, *Ticonderoga,* former lighthouse, one-cell jail, primitive American art, covered bridge. Open mid-May to mid-Oct., daily and Sundays in winter, 9 to 5 P.M.

ST. ALBANS. *Franklin County Museum,* Old Church St. School. Features Vermont memorabilia. Open July and Aug., Tues. through Sat., 2 to 5 P.M.

ST. JOHNSBURY. *Fairbanks Museum and Planetarium,* 83 Main St. (748–2372). Exhibits on New England natural environment, history. Some "hands-on" exhibits. Planetarium and astronomy exhibits. Cornucopia in easy-to-digest displays. Outdoor exhibits. Open year round, June 20 to Sept. 8, Mon. through Sat. 9 to 9 P.M.; Sun. 1 to 5 P.M.; Planetarium open daily 2:30 P.M. and until 8 P.M. Mon. through Sat.; Sun. 1 to 5 P.M.; closed major holidays.
Maple Grove Maple Museum, Rte. 2, east of downtown (748–5141). World's largest maple candy factory. Museum, theater, gift shop. Guided tours. Open daily 8 to 4:30 P.M.
St. Johnsbury Athenaeum Art Gallery, 30 Main St. (748–8291). Combination library and art gallery. Exhibit of 19th-century Hudson River School artists. Open Mon. and Fri., 9:30 to 8 P.M. Tues. through Thurs. and Sat., 9:30 to 5 P.M.

VERGENNES. *Bixby Library Museum,* 258 Main St. (877–2211). Local historical and Indian artifacts. Open afternoons daily except Sat., Sun. and holidays.

MUSIC. Vermont's most famous musical event, the *Marlboro Music Festival* (254–8163) is held on the Marlboro College Campus, approximately 8 mi. west of Brattleboro on Rte. 9 in July and Aug. Musical styles range from baroque through classical and contemporary. Concerts are Sat. evenings, Sun. afternoons, some Fri. evenings. If tickets for the auditorium are sold out, seating is available on the lawn. For tickets, write to: Marlboro Music Festival, 135 South 18 St., Philadelphia PA 19103; after June 10, to: Marlboro Festival, Marlboro VT 05344.

Founded in 1935, the 70-piece *Vermont Symphony Orchestra* (867–5741) is the oldest state orchestra in the country. It gives from 10 to 15 regular concerts and, during July, a series of eight summer concerts, all over the state each year, in addition to chamber recitals and special school programs, and hundreds of taped radio broadcasts.

In southern Vermont the *Bennington Choral Society and Orchestra* (442–8772) performs major works year round. The *Brattleboro Music Center* (R.F.D. 4, West Brattleboro VT 05301; 257–4523) gives a Bach Festival every fall, other programs in winter and spring. The *Stratton Arts Festival* (297–2200), in Sept. and Oct., devotes several days to music, from fiddling to rock, with sprinklings of classical. The *Oktoberfest* at Stowe offers lively music, yodeling, and dance during the fourth weekend in Sept. The *Southern Vermont Art Center & Music Pavilion* (362–1405 or call Bennington College Music Department 442–5401) in Manchester presents concerts in July and Aug. Chamber concerts are given at *Bennington College* in Aug. The *Sage City Symphony* (call Bennington College Music Department for information, 442–5401), North Bennington, gives five concerts a year featuring new works commissioned by the orchestra.

In central Vermont, concerts are given at the restored 650-seat *Chandler Music Hall* 728–9878 in Randolph, and at the chapel and theater of Middlebury College.

In the northwestern part of the state musical activities center on the *University of Vermont* (656–3480, or call the Music Dept. 656–3040), in Burlington, *Johnson State College* (635–2356) at Johnson, with chamber music and a touring opera company, and the *Vermont Philharmonic* (728–9136) in Montpelier. In the Northeast Kingdom, *Lyndon State College* (626–3335) in Lyndonville is the base for chamber groups, a chorus, and a summer youth orchestra.

There is a major fiddlers' contest at Barre in early Oct. Concerts are given in St. Johnsbury by the *Lyndon State College Chamber Music Society* (626–3335) during the year. From July to mid-Aug. on Sat. and Sun. evenings concerts are given at the *Kinghaven Music Center* (824–9592), Weston. In Middlebury there are concerts at *Mead Chapel* at Middlebury College (388–2663), Sun. evening, July to mid-Aug. Summer evening open-air band concerts are still held in Burlington (Sun.; 863–3489), Bristol (Wed.; 453–3491), Lyndonville (Wed.; 626–9696), South Royalton (Fri.; 763–7305), and Rutland (Sun.; 773–2747).

STAGE AND REVUES. There are a number of summer theaters in Vermont, and the season opens in July. In Middlebury, plays are produced at *Bread Loaf Little Theater,* at the *College Playhouse,* and at the foreign language schools. Dorset, Killington and Weston all have famous *Playhouses.* In Burlington, the *Champlain Shakespeare Festival* offers the Bard's finest at the *Royall Tyler Theatre* in the Military Science Building on the University of Vermont campus, late July and Aug., except Sun. *Park-McCullough Mansion,* in N. Bennington, and *St. Joseph's College* in Old Bennington, are increasingly being used for plays throughout the year. There are also summer theaters at West Dover, Bradford, Brattleboro, Essex Jct., Fairlee, Castleton, East Burke, Glover, Hyde Park, Johnson, Lyndonville, Marlboro, Norwich, Plainfield, Stowe, Warren, Windham, and Winooski.

SHOPPING. Although Vermont is limited in large shopping centers, there are many unique and interesting shops featuring pottery, leather and other crafts designed and made by local artists. Among the best known shops are:

Southern Vermont. In Putney, *Carol Brown,* for fabrics, especially Irish wool and linen. In Bennington, *the Ed Levin Workshop,* featuring hand-wrought silver and gold jewelry; *Bennington Gallery,* fine array of art; *Potters Yard,* contemporary stoneware (and a nifty restaurant, too, with patio lunches under the trees). In Arlington, *Griffin's* for Early American furniture; and in East Arlington, *the Candle Mill* for candles made in Colonial molds by the dripping methods. In Manchester and Putney, *Basketville,* bursting with baskets and wicker items. In Manchester, *the Enchanted Doll House,* dolls, authentic old doll houses, stuffed animals, toys; *Gooseberry* sells quality cookware accoutrements; *the Tree House* has Lilly Pulitzer fabrics; and *the Jelly Mill* has a clutch of shops (and another fine luncheon spot). In Wilmington, *Quaigh Design Centre,* local crafts and imports. In Jacksonville, *Stone Soldier Pottery.* In Weston, *Vermont Country Store* (and restaurant), everything from calico to coffee to churns; the *Weston Toy Works,* handcrafted, long-lasting toys; *Weston Priory,* sculptures, books, cards, musical recordings produced by the Benedictine monks. In Dorset, *J.K. Adams Co.,* wooden items—from tape measures to furniture.

Central Vermont. In Woodstock, *the Looking Glass* for children's wear and items; *The Whippletree* for yarns and patterns. In Quechee, *Simon Pearce,* for exquisite glassware made at the site; *Scotland by the Yard* for—what else?—Scottish imports. In Rutland, *Lamb's Yarn Shop* for native Vermont wool. In Bridgewater, *the Junction Country Store* has a wide selection of things from candy to candles to kitchenware. In Middlebury, the *Ski Haus,* Austrian clothing. In Waitsfield, the *Toy Store,* Vermont-made toys; the *Blue Building,* a half-dozen shops (antiques, dollhouse-size replicas, crafts, etc.). In Bethel, the *Silk Purse & Sow's Ear,* rafts of crafts, furniture restoring.

Northern Vermont. In Burlington, the *Cheese Outlet* with—you guessed it—all sorts of cheese, both Vermont cheddar as well as imported varieties; *Ebenezer Allen,* copper and brassware; *Sundance,* crafts of every type: leather, silver, pottery, iron work. In Shelburne, *Harrington's* (one of four outlets in the state; the others are in Stowe, Manchester Center and Richmond) for Vermont goods such as cob-smoked ham, cheese and maple syrup. In Stowe, *Stowe Woolens* for 100% woolen sweaters and other knitted goods; *Shaw's General Store,* a traditional emporium of potpourri from hiking gear to ski rentals, sportswear to maple syrup. In Vergennes, *Kennedy Brothers,* fine wooden products. In Waterbury, *Cold Hollow Cider Press,* for more Vermont crafts and products plus a chance to watch cider being made. In St. Johnsbury, the *Farmer's Daughter Gift Barn,* a unique mix of gifts and antiques; *Maple Grove Maple Museum,* an educational spin through the maple world.

Other shopping ideas include:

Antiquing: Antique shops are common along Vermont's roads and highways. Some specialize in bottles, others in picture frames or tools. About a hundred antique dealers belong to an association in Vermont. For a listing of their names and addresses, write for the *Vermont Antiques Dealers' Association Inc. Directory,* c/o Barbara Mills, RR 1, Box 76, Hartland, VT 05048.

Auctions are hard to resist. Dates and places are published in Vermont newspapers, beginning in the middle of the week.

Factory outlets: You save by cutting out the middleman when you buy directly from the factory. A directory of such opportunities is the *Factory Outlet Shopping Guide, New England States,* by Jean Bird, available from P.O. Box 256 N. Oradell NJ 07649. Multiple-outlet complexes have opened at two sites: the Outlet Center (Exit 1 off I-91) in Brattleboro and South Burlington Factory Outlet Center (Rte. 7). Each has more than a half-dozen outlets.

VERMONT 463

DINING OUT. Restaurants in Vermont take pride in several local specialties, such as roast turkey, clam chowder, griddle cakes with maple syrup, maple-cured ham, maple butternut pie, rum pie, and country-style sausage. The growth of the state's resort business has drawn other urban refugees to Vermont who have opened new, classy restaurants. The flow is not over by a long shot, and newer and spiffier eateries will continue to enable visitors to find lobster thermidor, quiche Lorraine, Peking duck and teppan yaki in the most unexpected places. Price ranges are based on a full dinner, but many restaurants serve à la carte meals, which will bring your tab up. Listings are based on the following price ranges; *Deluxe,* $30 and up; *Expensive,* $20–$30; *Moderate,* $10–$20; *Inexpensive,* under $10.

SOUTHERN VERMONT

ARLINGTON. West Mountain Inn. *Inexpensive.* Off Rte. 313 (375–6516). Homey inn with home baking, especially their own vegetables. Roast beef, steak are specialties. Bar. Children's portions. Reservations suggested.

BENNINGTON. Four Chimneys. *Expensive.* Rte. 9 (442–5257). Converted mansion, French and Continental cuisine. Lounge, wine cellar.
  Brasserie. *Moderate-Expensive.* 324 County St. (in Potter's Yard) (447–7922). French tavern-style restaurant with varied continental repertoire; seating inside or on the patio in summer. Own baking.
  Four Squires Restaurant. *Moderate.* 421 E. Main St. (Rte.9) (442–9251). Chophouse with some fish dishes.
  Heritage House. *Moderate.* Rte. 7-A (442–9586). Beef and seafood. Lounge.
  The Normandy. *Moderate.* 209 Northside Dr. (442–8974). French and American cuisine. Chef-owned. Closed Mon.
  Publyk House. *Moderate.* Harwood Hill on Rte. 7-A (442–8301). Remodeled barn, sensational view of Mt. Anthony and battle monument. Steak and seafood. Own baking. Children's portions.
  Geannelis' Restaurant. *Inexpensive.* 520 E. Main St. (Rte. 9) (442–9778). Good sandwiches, fine breakfasts.

BRATTLEBORO. Taft's. *Expensive.* 142 Elliot St. (257–2222). More gourmet dining. Suggested: pepper chicken, shrimp curry.
  Autumn Winds. *Moderate-Expensive.* 181–183 Main St. (257–7887). Riverside gourmet dining. At lunch, try the Reuben; at dinner, Coquilles St. Jacques.
  Common Ground Restaurant. *Moderate.* 25 Elliot St. (257–0855). Gourmet natural foods menu. International vegetarian meals on the terrace in good weather. Closed Tues. nights.
  Country Kitchen. *Moderate.* Rte. 9, west of I–89 (257–0338). Very popular locally. New England dishes, steaks, seafood. Children's portions.
  Jolly Butcher. *Moderate.* Rte. 9, west of I–89 (254–6043). Wide range of beef and seafood. Recommended: chicken teriyaki and Vermont cheesecake.
  Mole's Eye Restaurant. *Moderate.* 14 High St. (257–0771). Lunch and dinner, limited menu. Excellent soups, fine sandwiches.

DORSET. Barrows House. *Expensive.* Rte. 30 (867–4455). Built in 1776, it's been an inn since 1900. They specialize in—plain and simple—great food. Filet of beef Barrows, shrimp almondine, veal scallops, not to mention sauteed zucchini with pepper and onions. Reservations needed Nov. to June. Patio dining in warm weather.
  Chanticleer. *Moderate-Expensive.* Rte. 7, East Dorset (362–1616). Onetime dairy farm, decor is cross between French country look and sturdy, American barn. Candlelight dining. Beef and seafood but duckling L'Orange is a specialty. Homemade pastries.
  Village Auberge. *Moderate-Expensive.* Rte. 30 (867–5715). Restored, redecorated inn. Quiet luxury in the rooms, sheer heaven at the dinner table. Superb French cuisine. Where the locals go when they want something special.

GRAFTON. The Old Tavern. *Expensive.* Rte. 121 (842–2231). Delightful old country inn in beautifully restored 1801 homestead. New England beef and chicken specialties. Reservations required for dinner; jackets preferred for men.

LONDONDERRY-SOUTH LONDONDERRY (See also Stratton Mountain). **Londonderry Inn.** *Moderate-Expensive.* Rte. 100, S. Londonderry (824–5226). Comfortable dining room, tavern. Closed Tues.
    Nordic Inn. *Moderate-Expensive.* Rte. 11, Landgrove (824–6444). Solarium dining area. Light suppers, fireside lounge.
    Three Clock Inn. *Moderate-Expensive.* Just off Rte.100, behind the church in S. Londonderry (824–6327). 2 cozy dining rooms, only 4 guest rooms, and, like those old American dreams, the inn is surrounded by a white picket fence. Not your standard fare of beef and fish; the tournedos are superb but the veal scallopini piccata comes highly recommended, too. Desserts are sinful. Closed Mon.
    Country Villager. *Moderate.* Rte. 100 (824-6142). Hearty meals, morning to night. For dinner, try the chicken country village style (on rice with peppers, mushrooms, onions).

MANCHESTER. Reluctant Panther. *Expensive.* W. Rd., just off Rte. 7 (362–2568). Chef-owned. Dine & drink in 3 elegant rooms with romantic atmosphere. Superb food, good drinks and fine wines. Specialties: Crepes Rangoon, beef Wellington, rainbow trout à la mer or veal cordon bleu. Dinners only; reservations strongly advised. Closed Easter to May and Nov. through Dec.
    Sirloin Saloon. *Mderate-Expensive.* Rte. 11 (362–3600). It's far more than just a steakhouse, despite the name. They also do a fine job with chicken, lobster, crab. Fine desserts, too. Children's portions. Victorian decor. Bar.
    The Buttery. *Moderate.* Rte. 7, in the Jelly Mill (362–3544). Super luncheon spot. Excellent sandwiches but strongest with crepes and quiches. Good soups, too.
    Harvest Inn. *Moderate.* Rte. 7, Manchester Village (362–2125). Continental meals; own baking.
    The Sandtrap. *Moderate.* Rte. 30, just west of Rte. 7 (362–9822). Another good luncheon stop. Hefty, tasty sandwiches in a golf clubhouse atmosphere.
    Ye Olde Tavern. *Moderate.* Rte. 7 (362–3770). Fascinating decor (Early American); check the authentic stenciling on the walls. Then find a seat in this restored 1790 tavern and enjoy a marvelous meal, perhaps the lamb.
    Garlic John's. *Inexpensive.* Rte. 11 (362–9843). Italian menu, semi-à-la-carte. Children's portions. Chef-owned.

MARLBORO. Skyline Restaurant. *Moderate.* Rte. 9 (464–5535). The view upgrades the chow. Up on the "back" of Hogback Mt., it's a sensational view; 100 miles, they claim. Standard fare, but, oh, that view!

MOUNT SNOW AREA. The Hermitage. *Expensive.* Coldbrook Rd., off Rte. 100, Wilmington (464–3759). Dining area split into 4 rooms, creating intimate feel. Splendid meals, and if you just came to drink, the boss has a wine cellar with 30,000 bottles in it, so take off your coat. No credit cards.
    Inn at Sawmill Farm. *Expensive.* Rte. 100, W. Dover (464–8131). Dine in a converted sawmill with a Colonial decor. Chef-owned; Continental-French cuisine. Peppered shrimp, lobster Savannah, braised sweatbreads, rack of lamb garni, backfin crabmeat all worth a mention. Own desserts, too, of course. Bar.
    On the Rocks Lodge. *Expensive.* Smith Rd., off Rte. 100, W. Dover (464–8364). There are a couple of different soups daily, 3–4 desserts . . . and excellent preparation.
    Snow Lake Lodge. *Expensive.* Mtn. Rd., off Rte. 100 (464–3333). Lakeside dining, looking back at Mt. Pisgah, the mountain where Mt. Snow is located. Candlelight dining, impressive wine list. Stick with the beef.
    The White House. *Expensive.* Rte. 9, Wilmington (464–2135). Onetime mansion, now a country inn. International menu. Reservations suggested.

Poncho's Wreck. *Moderate.* S. Main St., Wilmington (464–9320). Wide assortment of entrees: Mexican, seafood, fowl, ribs, steak.

NEWFANE. Four Columns Inn. *Expensive.* 230 West St., on the Green (365–7713). Restored 1830 inn; dine on the terrace, if possible. Continental cuisine. Choose your own trout from their pond. Bar. Closed Apr., Nov. and Tues. Chef-owned, reservations recommended, jackets for dinner.

Old Newfane Inn. *Expensive.* Rte. 30 (365–4427). Distinguished 1787 inn with superb Continental cuisine. Fireside dining. Veal and lobster first-rate, but for a change, try the frogs legs. Also chef-owned. Reservations suggested.

STRATTON MOUNTAIN. Birkenhaus. Windham Hill Inn. *Deluxe.* West Townshend (874–4080). Elegant, antique-filled and furnished inn—and the dining is just as elegant. Recommended: poached baby sole mornay. *Moderate-Expensive.* At Stratton's base area, off Rte. 100 (297–2000). Reservations-only for dinner. Intimate. Continental cuisine. Excellent veal.

Liftline Lodge. *Moderate-Expensive.* At the Stratton base area (297–2600). Wild game specialties to go with Austrian cuisine. Fine spot for lunch, especially on sunny days.

Popover's. *Moderate-Expensive.* Jct. of Rtes. 30 and 100, Rawsonville (297–1146). Terrific appetizers set the stage for ample entrees. Start with veal ravioli.

Brookside Steak House. *Moderate.* Rte. 30, Jamaica (874–4271). Nothing fancy, just good steaks.

Tumbledown's at Winhall River Yacht Club. *Moderate.* Rte. 30 Bondville (297–1234). Apart from the fact there is no Winhall River Yacht Club . . . decor is nautical, atmosphere is fun, eats are fine. Go for the steak.

WEST DOVER-WILMINGTON (See Mount Snow).

WESTON. The Inn at Weston. *Moderate.* Rte. 100 (824–5804). Small inn but big visions of how to prepare good food. Everything fresh, homemade. Reservations recommended.

CENTRAL VERMONT

BARNARD. Barnard Inn. *Deluxe.* Rte. 12 (234–9961). Swiss-born and trained owner-chef turns out what may be the most expensive menu in Vermont —but it's worth it. Reservations recommended. From the curried mussels for appetizers past the entrees such as Chateaubriand or Tournedo Adriano and on to dessert from a dessert trolley. Closed Apr.

BRANDON. Brandon Inn. *Moderate-Expensive.* Rte. 7 (247–5766). Formal charm. Specialties are roast beef and compote of hot fruit. Bar.

The Adams. *Moderate.* Rte. 7 (247–6644). This restaurant in the picturesque Otter Valley serves a varied menu with its own pastries. Bar.

CHITTENDEN. Mountain Top Dining Room. *Expensive.* 6 miles off Rte. 4 (483–2311). Charming dining area in Colonial decor. Prime ribs featured. Bar.

FAIR HAVEN. Fair Haven Inn. *Moderate.* 5 Adams St. (265-4907). A Greek twist to continental meals.

KILLINGTON-PICO (See also Rutland). **Hemingway's.** *Expensive.* Rte. 4 (422–3886). A special experience with its French atmosphere (flowers, crystal, silver) and a menu that includes pheasant, rabbit, varied cheeses plus more than 100 wine labels. Magnifique!

Cortina Inn. *Moderate-Expensive.* Rte. 4 (773–3331). Fine dining in quiet comfort. Lively bar.

Back Behind Saloon. *Moderate.* Jct. Rtes. 4 and 100, W. Bridgewater (422–9907). Terrific burgers, fine steaks and seafood. Grab a beer, too, up in the caboose, which forms one wing of this rustic joint.

Charity's. *Moderate.* Mtn. Rd. off Rte. 4 (422–3800). Fine for lunch or dinner in rustic, Victorian decor. Good burgers at lunch, beef for dinner.

Pasta Pot. *Inexpensive.* Rte. 4 (422–3004). Cheap, cheap, cheap. Pasta, pizza, penny-pincher's paradise.

LUDLOW. The Winchester. *Moderate-Expensive.* Rte. 103 (228–3841). Candlelight dining in 170-yr.-old country inn. Good variety on menu with veal or steak first-rate. Hefty wine list, too. Bar.

The Hatchery. *Moderate;* Rte. 103 (228–8654). Perfect spot to make the day's plans over a king-size omelette for breakfast.

Nikki's Restaurant. *Moderate.* Rte. 100 (228–7797). Heavy on homemade soups, quiches for lunch. At dinner, try the seafood. Bar. Closed Tues.

Pot Belly Pub. *Inexpensive.* Rte. 103 (228–9813). Excellent luncheon stop with oversized sandwiches.

MIDDLEBURY. Dog Team Tavern. *Moderate.* 4 miles off Rte. 7 (388–7651). Charming country inn atmosphere. Very popular with locals. Home baking and New England cooking. Children's portions. Bar. Closed Mon.

Fire & Ice Restaurant. *Moderate.* 26 Seymour St. (388–9436). Another popular local hangout. Great sandwiches for lunch.

Middlebury Inn. *Moderate.* Rte. 7 (388–4961). On the Green, this Colonial inn has long been a favorite with Middlebury College families. Summer dining on the porch. Bar. Kids' portions.

Bakery Lane Soup Bowl. *Inexpensive-Moderate.* 5 Bakery Lane, alongside Otter Creek (388–2142). Home-baked breads, tasty soups, quiches.

NORWICH. Carpenter St. Restaurant. *Moderate.* Carpenter St. (649–2922). Fine cuisine, quietly elegant. Reservations suggested.

PLYMOUTH. Echo Lake Inn. *Moderate-Expensive.* Rte. 100, Tyson (228–8602). They call it "creative cuisine"; it's just good! Pork medallions breaded with hazelnuts tell the tale. Relaxing, enjoyable Sunday brunch.

QUECHEE. Inn at Marshland Farm. *Expensive.* River Rd. (295–3133). Reservations are a must; exceptional dining. Candlelight dinners. A hint of the palate-pleasers on the menu: Mermaid's Blessing, five wafer-thin layers of filo strudel dough around a steaming mix of king crabmeat, cheddar cheese, blanched cauliflower and a dollop of sour cream plus herbs and spices.

The Parker House. *Expensive.* River Rd. (295–6077). Great site by the Ottauquechee River. Lunches and dinners. European and American dishes.

Dana's by the Gorge. *Moderate.* Rte. 4 at the Gorge (295–6066). Good luncheons. Hearty soups, hefty burgers oromelettes.

RANDOLPH. Victoria's. *Moderate.* Park and Main Sts. (728–9777). Queen Victoria scowls down from several pictures on the walls, probably wondering what she's doing in a recycled gas station that drips with hanging greens. Menu pretty well balanced between beef and seafood. A good bet: filet mignon.

RUTLAND. Countryman's Pleasure. *Moderate-Expensive.* Just off Rte. 4 in Mendon, halfway between Killington and Rutland (773–7141). Chef-owned. European touch. Don't see too many snails in mushroom caps, mussels and steamers, sauerbraten, but they've got all that and more. Different specialty every night. Chef has a heavy hand—but light touch—with the sauces.

Royal's Hearthside. *Moderate-Expensive.* Rte. 7 (775–0856). Premiere restaurant in Rutland area and undeniably one of the best in Vermont. Specialties are lobster, charcoal-broiled steak, baked stuffed shrimp, roast prime ribs and chowders. Functional decor with emphasis on the food. Kids' portions. Bar. Gourmet shop next door open seven days a week, too. Dinner only Sun.

Sirloin Saloon. *Moderate-Expensive.* Rte. 7 (773–7900). Just as much emphasis on "sirloin" as on "saloon." Pleasant hangout for the evening: good steaks or seafood, combined with heavy-handed bartenders.

Vermont Inn. *Moderate-Expensive.* Rte. 4, Mendon (773–9847). Charming farm house with cozy fireplaces. Homemade Northeastern and continental cuisine features baked stuffed jumbo shrimp and veal piccata. Bar. Children's portions.

Governor's Table. *Moderate-Expensive.* Rte. 7 (775-7277). Varied menu in pleasant atmosphere. Fine chicken tarragon.

SPRINGFIELD. The Paddock. *Moderate.* Rte. 11 (885–2720). Oversized, family-style servings with a you-want-it, you-got-it attitude from the chef. Tables and booths are part of remodeled horse barn, hence the name. Desserts are even more varied than the entrees. Home baking at its best. Closed Mon. and Jan.

Penelope's Restaurant/McKinley's. *Moderate.* On the Square (885–9186). Penelope's upstairs, McKinley's (limited menu, live entertainment) down. Homemade breads, soups and desserts. Immense luncheon sandwiches and generous dinner portions, too.

STRAFFORD. Stone Soup. *Moderate.* On the Green, off Rte. 132. Five-star selection of soups, entrées. Try medieval chocolate cake for dessert.

WARREN-WAITSFIELD (Sugarbush Valley). **China Barn.** *Moderate-Expensive.* Rte. 17, Waitsfield (496–3579). Superb Mandarin and Szechuan cuisine. Cantonese, too. Closed Tues.

The Common Man. *Moderate-Expensive.* German Flats Rd. (583–2800). European dishes in an elegantly converted 100-yr.-old hay barn. Crystal chandeliers, huge fireplace and classic music. A favorite: Gruyere cheese melted over pork chops. Home baking. Closed Mon. Chef-owned.

The Waitsfield Inn. *Moderate-Expensive.* Rte. 100 (496-3979). Continental dining in early American decor. Save a spot for amaretto cheesecake.

Chez Henri. *Moderate.* Sugarbush Village (583–2600). Good for quick lunches between ski runs, great for candlelight dinners in the atmosphere of a French bistro. Dinner reservations suggested.

Edison's Studio. *Moderate.* Rte. 100, Waitsfield (496–2336). Great for light meals, plus a chance to catch a flick at night. Unique concept.

Phoenix. *Moderate.* Sugarbush Village (583–2777). Excellent international cuisine, antique decor, hanging plants. Desserts stop everyone cold.

Sam Rupert's. *Moderate.* Mtn. Rd., off Rte. 100 (583–2421). Like eating in a greenhouse with all the plants. Menu offers pleasant emphasis on lamb and veal (plus some fish and steak dishes) and fine salads.

Odyssey. *Inexpensive.* Sugarbush Village (583–2001). Italian menu, beer and wine. Generally pleasant and unpretentious. Takeouts, too.

WINDSOR. Ascutney Harvest Inn. *Moderate-Expensive.* Ascutney Mountain Resort, Rte. 44, Brownsville (484–7711). Pretty fancy for li'l ol' Brownsville but in keeping with "new look" at the resort. Luncheon specials and bell-ringer dinners; if you don't care for the roast duck, maybe the veal Wellington will appeal.

Windsor Station. *Moderate-Expensive.* Off Main St. (674–9907). Recycled train depot. Menu leans toward steaks and seafood. Good chops.

WOODSTOCK. Bentley's. *Moderate-Expensive.* 7 Elm St. (457–3232). Hanging plants, polished woods—hardly the dry goods or floor covering place that was there a few years ago. Sumptuous meals, great desserts.

Kedron Valley Inn. *Moderate-Expensive.* Rte. 106, S. Woodstock (457–1473). Traditional Vermont, Northeastern dishes, e.g. Vermont Tom turkey. Superb Sat. night buffet. Great perch for drinks on the porch in summer.

Prince & Pauper. *Moderate-Expensive.* 24 Elm St. (457–1818). Intimate feel, candlelight dining. French, Continental cuisine and lengthy wine list. Reservations preferred.

Rumble Seat Rathskeller. *Moderate-Expensive.* Woodstock East mall (457–3609). Best known for luncheons; excellent sandwiches. Quiet at night.

Spooner's. *Moderate-Expensive.* Rte. 4 (457-4022). they've got steak & seafood like most places, but their stir-fried (i.e.; wok) dishes stand alone.

Woodstock Inn. *Moderate-Expensive.* On the Green (457–1100). Music accentuated peaceful tone of meals at the inn, and candlelight emphasizes the point at dinner. All baking done on premises. Fresh fish is a favorite as is the Sat. night buffet. Jackets preferred for men.

Enes' Table. *Moderate.* Rte. 12 at Valley View Motel (457–2512). Italian cuisine with *primo clasa* lasagne. Dinner only. Closed Tues.

NORTHERN VERMONT

BARRE. Country House Restaurant. *Moderate.* 276 N. Main St. (476–4282). Italian fare plus Maine lobster, prime ribs. Closed Sun., major holidays.

Jack's Backyard. *Inexpensive.* 9 Maple Ave. (479–9134). A little different, such as alternating Italian and Chinese luncheon specials. Fine quiches.

BERLIN. Philuria's. *Moderate.* US 302 (479-0892). Victorian motif to go with good fish, extensive wine list.

BOLTON. Fireside Restaurant. *Moderate-Expensive.* At Bolton Valley resort, off U.S. 2 (434–2131). Top restaurant at the resort; fireside meals. Continental cuisine at night, hefty breakfasts. Kids' dining, entertainment program. Italian café; pizza spot in basement.

BURLINGTON-SO. BURLINGTON-SHELBURNE. Black Angus. *Moderate.* 1710 Shelburne Rd. (U.S. 7) (862–0244). Name tells it all: your basic steakhouse (with sprinkling of fish and chops). Luncheons in summer. Bar.

Ice House Restaurant. *Moderate-Expensive.* 171 Battery St. (863–9330). Recycled ice house, near Perkins Pier. Lakeside dining in superb eatery. Seafood, obviously, is the specialty. Oyster bar. Reservations recommended.

Pierre. *Moderate-Expensive.* U.S. 7, Colchester (878–3377). Elegant decor, classical music. French cuisine; fish, veal and desserts noteworthy. Excellent wine list. Bar. Children's portions. Reservations.

Sirloin Saloon. *Moderate-Expensive.* U.S. 7, Shelburne (985–3226). Just like Rutland and Manchester, a lively steakhouse with pretty fair seafood, too.

Boye's Restaurant. *Moderate.* 68 Pearl St. (864–6651). Close your eyes and you're eating in Italy.

Potting Shed. *Moderate.* U.S. 7, Shelburne (985–3279). Steak, seafood, own baking. Children's portions. Chef-owned.

Windjammer. *Moderate.* 1076 Williston Rd. (U.S. 2) (862–6585). Good chowders and plenty of shrimp or crab, but also fine ribs and steaks.

Carbur's. *Inexpensive-Moderate.* 119 St. Paul St. (862–4106). Mod-Victorian decor, young crowd, dazzling array of sandwiches and other goodies; 26-page menu proposes 100 items.

Deja Vu Café. *Inexpensive-Moderate.* 185 Pearl St. (864–7919). Cerebral cuisine, easy elegance. French and Provincial specialties, a menu nicely laced with crepes plus fowl, fish, filet. Fantastic.

Ben & Jerry's Homemade. *Inexpensive.* Cherry St. and Winooski Ave. (862–9620). Well-known for ice cream but they should take a bow for crepes and homemade soups, too. Desserts aren't too shabby, either.

Tower Restaurant. *Inexpensive.* 1234 Williston Rd (U.S. 2) (864–9817). Country-style breakfasts and then Italian fastfood (pizza, subs, etc.). Other locations: Barre, Essex Junction.

DERBY LINE. Michael's. *Moderate-Expensive.* Between the U.S. and Canadian border stations. Victorian atmosphere and continental dinners.

FAIRLEE (Lake Morey). **Lake Morey Inn.** *Moderate-Expensive.* Off U.S. 5 (333–4311). Northeastern fare with Continental flourishes. Sun. night buffet.
Rutledge Inn. *Moderate.* Lake Morey Dr., off I–91 (333–9722). Colonial decor. Own baking and desserts. Open mid-June to Labor Day.

ISLAND POND. Buck & Doe Restaurant. *Inexpensive-Moderate.* 135 Main St. (723–4712). Renowned for its "Mile-high pie."

JEFFERSONVILLE. Smugglers' Notch. *Moderate-Expensive.* Rte. 108 (644 –8851). *Crown & Anchor* restaurant is an olde English pub.
Windridge Inn. *Moderate.* Rte. 15 (644–8281). Continental cuisine and home-made breads.

MONTGOMERY CENTER. Zack's on the Rocks. *Expensive.* Hazen's Notch Rd. (326–4500). Out-of-the-way, built on rocks overhanging the valley. An organ instead of piano bar. Reservations are highly recommended.

MONTPELIER. Tubbs. *Moderate–Expensive.* 22 Elm St. at Jailhouse Common (229–9202). Part of N.E. Culinary Institute system; *nouvelle cuisine* with master chef supervising gourmet dining. Get a terrace seat in summer. Closed Sun. Also, try **Elm Street Cafe,** 38 Elm St. (223-3188), another NECI project but more relaxed atmosphere.
The Stockyard. *Moderate.* 3 Bailey Ave. Extension (223–7811). As the name implies, go for the beef.
Brown Derby. *Inexpensive-Moderate.* 101 Northfield St. (Rte. 12) (223–5258). Beef, seafood. Children's portions.
The Thrush. *Inexpensive.* 107 State St. (223–2030). Just a step up from a political hangout; luncheons are fast and hefty, dinners are filling. Great fries.

NEWPORT. The Landing. *Moderate.* On Lake Memphremagog (334–6278). Only restaurant on the lake. Popular lunchtime and dinner. Understandably heavy with fish and seafood, but you can get a fine steak, too. Outdoor luncheons in warm weather are unbeatable. Bar.

ST. ALBANS. China Palace. *Moderate.* 6 N. Main St. (524–6608). The usual heaps of Chinese cuisine. Closed Tues.

ST. JOHNSBURY. Rabbit Hill Motor Inn. *Moderate-Expensive.* Rte. 18, Lower Waterford, 10½ mi. from St. Johnsbury (748–9766). Restored 20-room country inn with perch above the Connecticut River, White Mtns. in the distance. Menu features stuffed sole, baked stuffed shrimp, Vermont cob-smoked ham, even clambakes. Homemade pastries. Bar. Children's portions. Reservations suggested, definitely in winter.

STOWE. Isle de France. *Expensive.* Rte. 108 (253–7751). Chef-owned. Fancy wine list and fancier foods, or vice-versa. Tasteful atmosphere. Try the pheasant.
Ten Acres Lodge. *Expensive.* Barrows, Rd., off Mountain Rd. (253–7638 or 253–9576). One of the nicest inns in the East. Venison steak or rainbow trout, or maybe some pheasant? For dessert, apple spice cake with maple frosting.
Topnotch Resort. *Expensive.* Rte. 108 (253–8585). Hard to figure where to start with this menu, it's a peach. Place oozes quality and professionalism. Appetizers lean toward seafood, entrees nicely balanced: Rock Cornish game hen, London broil with Bordelaise sauce, escalope of veal cordon bleu, roast duckling or filet of sole Veronique.
Austrian Tea Room. *Moderate-Expensive.* At Trapp Family Lodge, off Rte. 108 (253–8511). Excellent European cuisine—try the cucumber stuffed with

smoked salmon, just to get you started—and all of it topped off with sinfully sensational pastries for dessert. Tortes and strudels from heaven.

Fox Fire. *Moderate.* Rte. 100 (253-4887). Excellent Italian cuisine..

Green Mountain Inn. *Moderate.* Rte. 100 (253–7301). Colonial inn (1833) with menu that features crabmeat au gratin, homemade pastries. Bar. Children's portions.

The Salzburg Inn. *Moderate.* Rte. 108 (253–8541). Austrian cuisine, of course, so look for the wiener schnitzel. And don't miss dessert.

Spruce Pond Inn. *Moderate.* "Born again" farmhouse. Specializes in brook trout, probably caught out the back door. Filet mignon stuffed with oysters, homemade soups, pastries all rate mention. Bar. Children's portions.

Three Green Doors. *Moderate.* Rte. 108 (253–8979). Wide assortment of entrees, from burgers to seafood, or a pizza to travel.

The Shed. *Inexpensive-Moderate.* Rte. 108 (253–4364). Dining room in one of the buildings, a gin mill and sandwich section in the other. Standard tasty fare in the dining section, or hulking sandwiches to go with a beer or take with you on a daylong hike or drive.

VERGENNES. Basin Harbor Club. *Expensive.* On Lake Champlain, off Rte. 22-A (475–2311). Wide range of dishes served in resort's spacious dining room and cocktail area. Jackets and ties, please, for dinner. Closed mid-Oct. to mid-June.

WATERBURY. Golden Horn East. *Moderate-Expensive.* Kneeland Flat Rd. (244-7855). Continental dining in a converted barn. Pastries from their own bakery up the road.

NIGHTLIFE AND BARS. No one ever will confuse Vermont nightlife with the pulsating beat of a New York or Paris, Waikiki or Rome. It simply is not in the make-up of most Vermonters to boogie 'til dawn; disco is as foreign to the Green Mountains as palm trees. However, that doesn't mean locals don't enjoy some libation after dark; maybe it's just sitting in a darkened, barnboard-paneled saloon and discussing the latest Red Sox tailspin or hydro proposal or maybe it's listening to some group cut loose with country & western or rock 'n roll. In any event, be sure there is an emporium of nocturnal merriment in just about every corner of the state. Predictably, some of the top watering holes are near the state's major ski areas; most places have live entertainment on weekends, sometimes during midweek. Keep one thing in mind: what's "hot" or "in" one month can be stone cold the next; popularity may not ebb and flow like the ocean, but nothing is set in concrete and favored saloons come and go. Some of the obvious and not-so-obvious night spots and bars: **Southern Vermont**—Brattleboro: *Flat Street,* 17 Flat St., 254–8257 (youthful, mostly rock or C&W); *Red Coach Motor Inn,* Rte. 5, 254–4583 (moderate, relaxing); Manchester: *Alfie's,* Rte. 11, 362–2637 (not quite a disco, not quite a saloon); *Kandahar,* junction of Rtes. 11 & 30 near Bromley, 824–5531 (no live entertainment but terrific atmosphere); *The Mill Steakhouse,* Rte. 100, Londonderry, 824–3247 (roadhouse atmosphere, fun time). **Mount Snow area:** *Deacon's Den,* Rte. 100, West Dover, 464–9361 (rock 'n roll); *Mount Snow Lodge,* Mount Snow, 464–3333 (relaxing, low-key). **Central Vermont**—Ludlow-Okemo area: *The Chopping Block,* Rte. 103 in Proctorsville, 226–7794 (rustic, raucous rock 'n roll); **Killington-Rutland area:** *The Wobbly Barn,* Killington Access Road, 422–3392 (loud, louder, loudest); *The Pickle Barrel,* Killington Access Road, 422–3035 (Wobbly Barn clone); *Cortina Inn,* Rte. 4, 773–3331 (soft, sane and dancing, too); Middlebury: *Fire and Ice,* Seymour St., 388–9436 (occasional entertainment, eternal fun). **Sugarbush-Warren-Waitsfield area:** *Blue Tooth,* Sugarbush Access Road, Warren, 583–2736 (action central); *Back Room* at Chez Henri, Sugarbush Village, 583–2600 (late-night starts); *Moose Lips,* Rtes. 100 & 17, Waitsfield, 496–3937 (r 'n r). **Northern Vermont**—Montpelier-Barre: *Murphy's Law,* 310 North Main St., Barre, 479–1404 (C&W plus some rock); *Brown Derby,* Rte. 12, Montpelier, 223–5258 (up-tempo); Burlington: *Great Escape,* 125 Pearl St., 863–9295 (lively); Stowe: *Rusty Nail,* Rte. 108, 253–9444 (rock 'n rowdy); *B.K. Clark's,* Rte. 108, 253–9300 (jazz, soft rock, mellow); *Sister Kate's,* Rte. 108, 253–8987 (diverse with bluegrass, rock, piano sing-a-long, or singing waiters and waitresses); *Baggy Knees,* Rte. 108, 253–8983 (traditional rock spot with occasional special headliners); Newport: *The Creamery,* Coventry Rd., 334–7752 (country & western parlor).

DRINKING LAWS. Bars are illegal in Vermont except in restaurants and hotels. Most are open until 2 A.M. weeknights, and 1 A.M. Sat. night. No sale of alcoholic liquors is allowed between 1 A.M. and 12 noon on Sun. Consumption of alcoholic beverages allowed until 2:30 A.M. weeknights and until 1:30 A.M. on Sat. night. Hours of operation are the same with or without entertainment. The minimum drinking age is 21. (This does not apply to those who obtained the age of 18 by June 30, 1986.)

Bottled beer and light wine to take out are sold at stores with second class licenses. Bottled liquor is sold at state liquor stores and agencies. Local option forbids the sale of liquor in some Vermont towns. However, it is all right to bring in your own liquor and buy setups.

Speak a foreign language in seconds.

Now an amazing space age device makes it possible to speak a foreign language *without* having to learn a foreign language.

Speak French, German, or Spanish.
With the incredible Translator 8000—world's first pocket-size electronic translation machines —you're never at a loss for words in France, Germany, or Spain.

8,000-word brain.
Just punch in the foreign word or phrase, and English appears on the LED display. Or punch in English, and read the foreign equivalent instantly.

Only 4¾″ x 2¾″, it possesses a fluent 8,000-word vocabulary (4,000 English, 4,000 foreign). A memory key stores up to 16 words; a practice key randomly calls up words for study, self-testing, or game use. And it's also a full-function calculator.

150,000 sold in 18 months.
Manufactured for Langenscheidt by Sharp/Japan, the Translator 8000 comes with a 6-month warranty. It's a valuable aid for business and pleasure travelers, and students. It comes in a handsome leatherette case, and makes a super gift.

Order now with the information below.

INDEX

(The letters H and R indicate hotel and restaurant listings.)

MASSACHUSETTS

Practical Information

Geographical

NEW HAMPSHIRE
Practical Information

RHODE ISLAND
Practical Information

Geographical

VERMONT

Practical Information

Geographical